America's
TEST KITCHEN

ADDITIONAL COOKBOOKS AND DVD SETS
AVAILABLE FROM
THE PUBLISHER OF COOK'S COUNTRY INCLUDE:

The *America's Test Kitchen* Family Cookbook
America's Best Lost Recipes
The Best of *America's Test Kitchen* 2008
The Best of *America's Test Kitchen* 2007
Cook's Country 2006 Annual Edition
Cook's Country 2005 Annual Edition

THE BEST RECIPE SERIES
The Best International Recipe
The Best 30-Minute Recipe
The Best Light Recipe
The *Cook's Illustrated* Guide to Grilling and Barbecue
Best American Side Dishes
Cover & Bake
The New Best Recipe
Steaks, Chops, Roasts, and Ribs
Baking Illustrated
Restaurant Favorites at Home
Perfect Vegetables
The Quick Recipe
Italian Classics
The Best American Classics
The Best Soups & Stews

THE AMERICA'S TEST KITCHEN SERIES
(companion cookbooks and DVD sets
to our hit public television series)

Behind the Scenes with *America's Test Kitchen*: 2008 season companion cookbook
Test Kitchen Favorites: 2007 season companion cookbook
Cooking at Home with *America's Test Kitchen*: 2006 season companion cookbook
America's Test Kitchen Live! 2005 season companion cookbook
Inside *America's Test Kitchen*: 2004 season companion cookbook
Here in *America's Test Kitchen*: 2003 season companion cookbook
The *America's Test Kitchen* Cookbook: 2002 season companion cookbook
The *America's Test Kitchen* 2007 season 4-DVD boxed set
The *America's Test Kitchen* 2006 season 4-DVD boxed set
The *America's Test Kitchen* 2005 season 4-DVD boxed set
The *America's Test Kitchen* 2004 season 4-DVD boxed set
The *America's Test Kitchen* 2003 season 4-DVD boxed set
The *America's Test Kitchen* 2002 season 4-DVD boxed set
The *America's Test Kitchen* 2001 season 2-DVD boxed set

ADDITIONAL BOOKS FROM
THE EDITORS OF COOK'S ILLUSTRATED MAGAZINE INCLUDE:

The Cook's Bible
The *Cook's Illustrated* Complete Book of Pasta and Noodles
The Kitchen Detective
834 Kitchen Quick Tips
1993–2007 *Cook's Illustrated* Master Index
Cook's Illustrated Annual Editions from each year of publication (1993–2007)

To order any of our cookbooks listed above, give us a call at 800-611-0759 inside the U.S.,
or at 515-246-6911 if calling from outside the U.S.
You can order subscriptions, gift subscriptions, and any of our books
by visiting our online store at www.cookscountry.com

$35.00

Published by America's Test Kitchen, 17 Station Street, Brookline, MA 02445
ISBN-13: 978-1-933615-13-4   ISSN: 1552-1990

To get home delivery of *Cook's Country*, call 800-526-8447 inside the U.S., or 515-247-7571 if calling from outside the U.S., or subscribe online at www.cookscountry.com.

2007 Recipe Index

C

Cook's Country

FEBRUARY/MARCH 2007

Crunchy Potato Wedges
Crispy Secrets Revealed

Hot Fudge Pudding Cake
2-in-1 Chocolate Dessert

Maryland Fried Chicken
With Authentic Pepper Gravy

STICKY RIBS
Sweet and Spicy Oven Recipe

ITALIAN POT ROAST
Bold Flavors, Tender Meat

FROZEN PIZZA TASTE TEST
Which Brand Is Best?

ORANGE BUNDT CAKE
Building Big Citrus Flavor

CHICKEN POT PIE
Easy Freeze Method

FAMILY-STYLE SCAMPI
Saucy Shrimp for a Crowd

MEATY LASAGNA
Gets Healthy Makeover

RATING STOCKPOTS
A Cheap Pan Does It All

SPICY BEEF NACHOS
Ultimate Game-Day Recipe

$4.95 U.S./$6.95 CANADA

03>

0 74470 05251 7

Our $1,000 Contest Winner!
Mary Ann Lee of Clifton Park, N.Y., won first place in our chicken soup contest with a hearty recipe that relies on an unlikely ingredient—boxed corn muffin mix. See page 4 for her **Chicken and Corn Chowder with Sweet Potatoes.**

Cook's Country

Dear Country Cook,

Sugaring is the "spring break" of Vermont (and anywhere else they boil sap). The roads are muddy, the weather is raw, the days are gray, and everyone is plenty sick of winter. Spending a couple of weeks stoking up the "arch" (an evaporator) with neighbors is more eagerly anticipated than Christmas. I fire up the arch first thing in the morning; in just minutes, the steam pours out of the stacks and the sap bubbles hard, and in an hour or two, we start pulling off hot, sweet syrup.

Like most kids in Vermont, I grew up sugaring. Charlie Bentley had a small sap house up by his farm, on the road to the gravel pit, and I remember Fred Woodcock checking the syrup by letting it drip off the end of his scoop. He didn't need a fancy hydrometer. He could tell if it was ready just by how the hot syrup beaded on the edge and dripped back into the pan. I can still feel that small, dark room: hot, humid, and faintly sweet. After a long winter, the sap house was a place where life was born again. It was a precursor to spring, time to start checking the fields for planting and changing the oil in the tractor.

Last fall, I went over to see if Charlie's sap house was still standing. It was there, all right, but it had sunk down into the weeds. But I hadn't forgotten what happened inside all those years ago. It was dark magic. We turned water into syrup, and that simple shack was transformed into a place of worship. Fred is up in the cemetery now, the one above the Methodist Church. I went to visit him recently. I just wanted to thank him for the memories.

[signature]

Christopher Kimball
Founder and Editor, Cook's Country Magazine

Maple Syrup, January 1943: A maple tree grove in New Hampshire, where buckets catch the trees' sweet sap as it oozes from a waist-high incision. The sap is later reduced to syrup before being evaporated again to produce sugar. (Photo by Keystone/Getty Images)

FEBRUARY/MARCH 2007

Cook's Country

19
17
20

departments

Founder and Editor Christopher Kimball
Editorial Director Jack Bishop
Senior Editors Scott Kathan
Bridget Lancaster
Test Kitchen Director Erin McMurrer
Associate Editor Jeremy Sauer
Test Cooks Stephanie Alleyne
Katie Henderson
Cali Rich
Diane Unger
Assistant Test Cook Meredith Butcher
Web Managing Editor Katherine Bell
Web Editor Kate Mason
Copy Editor Will Gordon
Market Research Manager Melissa Baldino
Editorial Assistant Meredith Smith
Kitchen Assistant Nadia Domeq
Contributing Editor Eva Katz
Contributor Keri Fisher

Design Director Amy Klee
Senior Designer, Magazines Julie Bozzo
Designers Jay Layman
Christine Vo
Staff Photographer Daniel J. van Ackere

Production Director Guy Rochford
Traffic and Projects Manager Alice Cummiskey
Production Assistant Lauren Pettapiece
Color and Imaging Specialist Andrew Mannone
Internet Technology Director Aaron Shuman
Systems Administrator S. Paddi McHugh

Chief Financial Officer Sharyn Chabot
Human Resources Manager Adele Shapiro
Controller Mandy Shito
Office Manager Saudiyah Abdul-Rahim
Receptionist Henrietta Murray
Publicity Deborah Broide

Vice President Marketing David Mack
Circulation Director Bill Tine
Fulfillment Manager Carrie Horan
Circulation Assistant Elizabeth Dayton
Direct Mail Director Adam Perry
Products Director Steven Browall
E-Commerce Marketing Manager Hugh Buchan
Marketing Copywriter David Goldberg
Junior Developer Doug Sisko
Customer Service Manager Jacqueline Valerio
Customer Service Representatives Julie Gardner
Jillian Nannicelli

Vice President Sales Demee Gambulos
Retail Sales Director Jason Geller
Retail Sales Associate Anthony King
Corporate Marketing Manager Emily Logan
Partnership Account Manager Allie Brawley
Marketing Assistant Connie Forbes

features

10 Maryland Fried Chicken
This fried chicken is heavy on the seasoning, light on the coating, and sauced with a peppery cream gravy.

11 Corn Dodgers
Looking for an alternative to ho-hum corn bread? Try these old-fashioned cornmeal cakes with the funny name.

12 Family-Style Shrimp Scampi
Our recipe delivers a big bowlful of saucy shrimp.

13 Ultimate Spicy Beef Nachos
For nachos that are never bland or soggy, our recipe uses five kinds of "heat" and some creative assembly work.

14 Crunchy Potato Wedges
Skip the drive-through and make them at home.

17 Hot Fudge Pudding Cake
Can a recipe for moist, rich chocolate cake enhanced with pockets of gooey chocolate pudding really be this easy?

18 Cincinnati Chili
This Cincinnati classic relies on cinnamon, an unusual cooking method, and a host of garnishes—including spaghetti!

19 Freezer Chicken Pot Pies
These individual pot pies are ready when you are.

20 Better Citrus Salads
Freshen up winter salads with oranges and grapefruit.

22 Chinese Sticky Ribs
These oven-baked ribs boast tender meat and a sweet glaze.

24 Lemon Chicken
What sounds like a complicated restaurant dish is, with a few tricks, an easy homemade meal.

25 Italian Pot Roast
Our new take on pot roast is brimming with the flavors of garlic, tomatoes, mushrooms, and red wine.

26 Orange Bundt Cake
We take a three-pronged route to building big orange flavor.

in every issue

On the cover: PHOTOGRAPHY: StockFood/Loftus ILLUSTRATION: John Burgoyne.
In this issue: COLOR FOOD PHOTOGRAPHY: Keller + Keller. STYLING: Mary Jane Sawyer, Marie Piraino, Monica Mariano. ILLUSTRATION: Lisa Perrett.

Editorial Office: 17 Station Street, Brookline, MA 02445; 617-232-1000; fax 617-232-1572
Subscription Inquiries: Cook's Country, P.O. Box 8382, Red Oak, IA 51591-1382; 800-526-8447

Cook's Country magazine (ISSN 1552-1990) (number 13) is published bimonthly by Boston Common Press Limited Partnership, 17 Station Street, Brookline, MA 02445. Copyright 2006 Boston Common Press Limited Partnership. Periodicals postage paid at Boston, Mass., and at additional mailing offices, USPS 023453. POSTMASTER: Send address changes to Cook's Country, P.O. Box 8382, Red Oak, IA 51591-1382. For subscription and gift subscription orders, subscription inquiries, or change-of-address notices, call 800-526-8447 in the U.S. or 515-247-7571 from outside the U.S., or write us at Cook's Country, P.O. Box 8382, Red Oak, IA 51591-1382. PRINTED IN THE USA

Visit us at CooksCountry.com!
Go online for hundreds of recipes, food tastings, and up-to-date equipment reviews. You can get a behind-the-scenes look at our test kitchen, talk to our cooks and editors, enter recipe contests, and share recipes and cooking tips with the *Cook's Country* community.

Kitchen Shortcuts

READERS SHARE CLEVER TIPS FOR EVERYDAY COOKING CHALLENGES

Simultaneous Seasoning

When preparing chicken for a hot skillet, I use this method to evenly season the meat while drying off any excess moisture that might cause the oil to splatter. I take two layers of paper towels and lay them flat on a cutting board. I sprinkle salt, pepper, and any other seasonings right onto the paper towels. I lay the chicken pieces on the paper towels and season the side facing up. When the skillet is nice and hot and ready to go, I take the chicken pieces with tongs and place them on the skillet. Both sides are evenly seasoned, and the excess moisture is gone!

Judy Lee Burbank, Calif.

Super-Thin Sliced Apples

When making a dish that calls for pared, cored, and sliced apples, here is what I do: I peel my apples, then take my V-slicer (the "large slice" side of a box grater works well, too) and run the apple

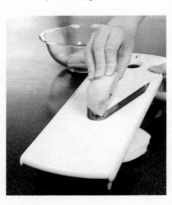

over the blade until I get down to the core. Then I rotate the apple and run it through the slicer again. I continue this until only the core is left. The slices come out uniform in size—without all the knife work—and are great for pies or any other recipe that calls for thinly sliced apples.

Marie Walsh Lincoln, Calif.

A "Grate" Way to Soften Butter

My mother-in-law just taught me a great trick. If a recipe calls for softened butter and all you have is chilled, use a cheese grater! Grate up the amount of butter needed on the large holes of the box grater. The thin pieces of butter will soften up in no time!

Sara Platt Alexandria, Va.

No-Slip Grip!

YOGA FOR COOKS

As the designated "cook" in my extended family, I'm usually the one assigned to bring the dessert, the party trays, the potato salad. But transporting all those bowls, platters, and casseroles by car can be a tricky—and sometimes messy—business. Luckily, I found that a yoga "sticky" mat unrolled in the cargo area of my vehicle grips plates and containers firmly and keeps them from sliding or overturning, even during sudden traffic stops. Now I have two yoga mats: one for inner peace and one for peace of mind.

Pat Sommers Elverson, Pa.

CRUSHING CANDY

Here's a tip for crushing hard candy such as candy canes, peppermint disks, or toffee to use as toppings for ice cream or in recipes. Take two plastic lids from Cool Whip–style containers and place one upside down on the counter. Place the candy on it in a single layer and cover it with the other lid top side up. Carefully hold the lids together and tap the top one with a hammer. No plastic bags to break, and the candy doesn't fly all over the kitchen!

Marcia Klimes
George, Iowa

BOIL YOUR MESS AWAY

If you've got a stuck-on mess in your skillet or Dutch oven, don't spend all day scrubbing—just fill the pot about halfway with water and simmer it on the stovetop for a couple minutes. By the time the rest of the dishes are put away, your stuck-on mess will be easy to remove.

Marissa Taylor
Portland, Conn.

CHEESE MILL

I find that the best tool for shredding fresh mozzarella (for pizza, pasta, or sandwiches) is a food mill. Mine has interchangeable disks, so I can shred the cheese really fine or nice and rough, depending on my mood.

Robert Duff
Iowa City, Iowa

EASY MICROWAVE LIDS

When cooking or defrosting in the microwave, containers often need to be covered. I recently discovered that using a paper towel works best to absorb the steam. However, the paper towel would catch along the sides of the microwave as the container rotated, causing it to fall off the container. I found that misting the edges of the paper towel with water (once it is on the dish) caused it to conform to the shape of the dish and hang down around the sides, fitting even the most oddly shaped containers. After the water evaporates, the paper towel holds its shape as if it were a lid.

Vic Amburgey
Manhattan, Kan.

MAKESHIFT LAZY SUSAN

It is always an adventure for me when I try to dig out spices, honey, or olive oil from my cabinets. To ease the juggling act, I have placed everything in a baking tin (an edged cookie sheet) in the cabinet. I then use the baking tin as a drawer and simply slide it out whenever I need something. This makes it much easier to reach the items in the back.

Emily Hess
Ashland, Ohio

BREADBOX ALTERNATIVE

What to do with fresh-baked bread (or whole loaves from the bakery) once you've cut the pieces you want? Storing in plastic bags or Tupperware containers can cause moisture to collect and turn the bread soggy. A breadbox is ideal, but it takes up counter space and not everyone has one. I think the best way is to store my already-cut loaves in the toaster oven. It's already on my counter, it looks like a breadbox, and it can serve the same function. Just remember to take the bread out before you preheat!

Daniel Boucher
Ithaca, N.Y.

BETTER BUTTER FOR TOAST

I hate trying to butter my toast with cold butter—the toast always tears, while the butter stays put in big hunks. So I recently decided to do something about it. Now, while my toast is cooking, I put a tablespoon or two of butter in a ramekin on top of my toaster oven. The heat from the toaster melts the butter ever so slightly, so when my toast is golden brown, my butter is perfectly softened.

Edith McKeown
Bohemia, N.Y.

CANDY GLOVES

Making candy can be tough on the hands. Shards of hardened caramel can easily cut you, while the shells of nuts have a tendency to get right under your fingernails. Now when I make my soda cracker candy, I have a pair of yellow latex gloves I use just for breaking up the candy. They make it easy to grip the candy, and they are thick enough to prevent any cut fingers. Once I'm done, they go back in their special box marked "candy gloves."

Cindy Gannon
Seal Beach, Calif.

ROLL YOUR OWN

I've got five kids, so I always keep tortillas on hand for quick "cheesy melt" snacks. Since I usually buy a couple of packages of tortillas at a time, I keep most of them in the freezer. To quickly make them ready to use, I microwave the whole package for one minute, then roll it like a roll of paper towels. This loosens the tortillas, so they don't tear apart when you separate them. They are then ready to fill for enchiladas or microwave with cheese for cheesy melts.

Amiee House
Kensington, Md.

SPINACH SPINNER

When I make a large bowl of my famous spinach dip for a party, instead of squeezing batch after batch of frozen spinach to release the liquid, I use a new technique. Once the spinach is thawed, I put it in my salad spinner and give it a whirl. Within seconds, almost all of the water is whisked away!

Nanci York
Hamilton, Ohio

NO MORE SOGGY SANDWICHES

To avoid soggy sandwiches (especially if you are preparing them the night before for work or school), place the condiments (mayo or mustard) and any extras such as tomatoes, pickles, or olives between the cold cuts and cheeses and not touching the bread. As for the lettuce, place it between the meat and bread. This trick will keep your sandwich as fresh as if it were made minutes before.

Sharon Sawdaye
Montreal, Quebec

BAKE THE RUST AWAY

I've had a problem with rust on my metal bakeware. All the nooks and crannies collect water and are nearly impossible to dry—especially on things with "folded" corners, like Chicago Metallic pans, or the seams on muffin pans. I've been able to solve this problem by washing the pans immediately, then popping them right back into the oven. Usually just the residual heat left from my baking is enough to dry them in all the places I could never reach with a dish towel.

Dana Thompson
Gresham, Ore.

KEEP TORTILLAS WARM

Keep large amounts of flour tortillas warm by lining the bottom of a large disposable aluminum pan with wet paper towels, then loosely covering the towels with a layer of foil to prevent sticking. Then place the tortillas on the foil (up to 10 large packages of flour tortillas), wrap the pan in another layer of foil, and place them in the oven to steam. This method keeps them moist, warm, and pliable for hours!

Fran Ferlazzo
Pleasanton, Calif.

CLEAN UP IN THE FREEZER

I have found that the easiest way to clean pasta machine disks, rotary cheese graters, and even candle holders is to place them in the freezer for a few hours or even overnight. A few taps on the counter and the stuck ingredients, including candle wax, usually pop right out!

Stephanie M. Zorie
Santa Fe, N.M.

A CLEAN SWEEP

For dry messes on the counter (spilled flour, sugar, bread crumbs, etc.), I keep a small dustpan and broom at hand. I can easily sweep the crumbs right off the counter and into the dustpan. It's neater and easier than using a damp cloth, and they're cheap to boot— I purchased mine at a dollar store!

Mica Storer
Roslyn, Pa.

Pie Transport

Last week I needed to take a quiche to brunch an hour away by car. I didn't have any passengers to hold the quiche for me, so I had to get creative. I noticed I had an empty Priority Mail box (size: 14 by 12 by 3 inches) in the kitchen. I taped up the open side and traced the outline of the rim of an empty pie plate onto the box. Then I cut a hole 1/2 inch inside my line. I set the pie plate in the opening in the box. Aha! No damage to the crust! What a great way to combine my passion for cooking with my passion for shopping online!

Allison Anthony Pottersville, N.J.

Herding Veggies

NEAT TRICK

I don't have the greatest knife skills, so chopping vegetables or herbs used to take me what seemed like hours. Then I discovered this shortcut. Since some pro-

duce comes in bunches that are kept together with a thick rubber band (asparagus and scallions, for example), I use it to my advantage. The rubber band keeps the veggies from rolling all over the cutting board, so I can cut them all at once into even-sized pieces.

Camillia Jacobs
Bethesda, Md.

Save Packing Labels

Whether it's chicken breasts or ground beef, I usually buy more than I need and freeze whatever I don't use. But instead of writing the contents and date on the outside of the freezer bag, I just cut the pack-age label off the grocery

store container and stick it face-up inside the freezer bag. It clearly describes the cut of meat and its packing date without the worry of illegible handwriting.

Derek Blaylock Seattle, Wash.

Double Duty!

MAGNETIC ATTRACTION

Whenever I open an aluminum can with my handheld can opener, the lid falls back into the can and I have to find some way to fish it out without cutting myself. Yesterday, I spied a free refrigerator magnet and held it above the can lid. To my delight, the can lid immediately stuck to the magnet and was easily retrieved from the thick contents of the can without risk to my fingers or prying with another kitchen utensil. This trick also came in handy when I had set the lid on the counter and needed to pick it up later as I cleaned up. No more lacerated fingers!

Holly Walstead Gig Harbor, Wash.

Take Your Pick

I have never had success splitting an English muffin with a fork. Instead I use a clean Ace hair pick that I keep in my kitchen drawer. Two cross swipes into the muffin and it's open!

Nancy Andren
Saint Charles, Mo.

Recipe Contest CHICKEN SOUPS

An Unlikely Ingredient Transforms Chicken Soup into Hearty Chowder

Our $1,000 Grand-Prize Winner!

Mary Ann Lee Clifton Park, N.Y.

Our chicken soup contest brought in hundreds of recipes inspired by the great cuisines of the world. Our runners-up reflect the influences of New Orleans, Italy, Mexico, and Thailand. Our grand-prize winner, however, relied on a creative technique, rather than exotic ingredients. Chunks of sweet potato and frozen corn kernels begin the process of transforming a basic chicken soup into hearty chowder. But it's the corn muffin mix (yes, dry muffin mix!) that makes Mary Ann Lee's recipe unique. The corn muffin mix is dissolved in milk and then stirred into the soup for a thickened, creamy consistency and extra corn flavor. As Mary Ann told us: "The hearty chowder-like base combined with sweet potatoes, chicken, and corn really sticks to your ribs." We agree. This soup is definitely a meal in a bowl.

CHICKEN AND CORN CHOWDER WITH SWEET POTATOES SERVES 8 TO 10

Although any yellow corn muffin mix will work in this recipe, Jiffy is the test kitchen's top-rated brand.

- 3 cups whole milk
- 1 cup yellow corn muffin mix (see note)
- 2 tablespoons unsalted butter
- 1 onion, chopped fine
- 2 garlic cloves, minced
- 1/2 teaspoon ground cumin
- 1/2 teaspoon dried oregano
- 2 quarts low-sodium chicken broth*
- 1 1/2 pounds boneless, skinless chicken breasts, cut into 1/2-inch cubes
- 2 sweet potatoes (about 1 1/2 pounds), peeled and cut into 1/2-inch pieces
- 1 cup shredded Monterey Jack cheese
- 3 cups frozen corn (not thawed)
- 1/2 cup chopped fresh parsley
  Salt and pepper

1. Mix milk and muffin mix in bowl until well combined. Meanwhile, heat butter in large Dutch oven over medium heat until foaming. Add onion and cook until softened, about 8 minutes. Stir in garlic, cumin, and oregano and cook until fragrant, about 30 seconds. Add broth, chicken, and sweet potatoes. Bring to boil, reduce heat, and simmer until sweet potatoes are just tender, about 8 minutes.

2. Stir in milk and muffin mixture and simmer until soup thickens, about 10 minutes. Add cheese and corn and cook until cheese begins to melt, about 2 minutes. Stir in parsley and season with salt and pepper. Serve. (Soup can be refrigerated in airtight container for up to 3 days.)

*See page 31 for information on the test kitchen's top-rated brand of chicken broth.

Simple supermarket ingredients come together to create a warm, earthy, and unique soup.

Virginia Syrylo
DuBois, Pa.

Heather Ricciarelli
Weymouth, Mass.

Judith Mack
Anchorage, Alaska

Jo Ann Willis
San Francisco, Calif.

CHICKEN AND SPINACH TORTELLINI SOUP SERVES 8 TO 10

Virginia writes: "Using a few store-bought products makes this impressive-looking soup deceptively easy. My guests always think I've spent hours making it." Poaching the chicken in the store-bought broth improves the flavor of both components. This soup doesn't hold well and should be served as soon as it's ready.

- 6 slices bacon, cut into ¹/₂-inch pieces
- 1 onion, chopped fine
- 2 garlic cloves, minced
- 1 teaspoon red pepper flakes
- 3 quarts low-sodium chicken broth*
- 1¹/₂ pounds boneless, skinless chicken breasts
- 1 (10-ounce) package frozen chopped spinach, thawed and drained
- 2 (9-ounce) packages fresh spinach tortellini
  Salt and pepper
  Grated Parmesan cheese (for serving)

1. Cook bacon in large Dutch oven over medium heat until crisp, about 7 minutes. With slotted spoon, transfer bacon to paper towel–lined plate.

2. Stir onion into bacon fat in now-empty Dutch oven and cook until browned, about 8 minutes. Stir in garlic and red pepper flakes and cook until fragrant, about 30 seconds.

3. Add broth and chicken, bring to boil, reduce heat, and simmer until chicken is cooked through, about 20 minutes. Turn off heat. With slotted spoon, remove chicken; cool slightly and shred into small pieces.

4. Return soup to simmer. Add drained spinach and tortellini and simmer until tortellini are tender, about 3 minutes. Add shredded chicken and salt and pepper to taste. Ladle soup into bowls and garnish with bacon and cheese, passing more cheese at the table.

NEW ORLEANS CHICKEN AND SAUSAGE SOUP
SERVES 8 TO 10

Heather writes: "I love jambalaya, but I make chicken soup more often. I combined the two, creating a New Orleans–inspired soup."

- 1 tablespoon vegetable oil
- 1 pound smoked sausage, such as andouille or kielbasa, cut into ¹/₄-inch pieces
- 2 medium onions, chopped fine
- 1 red bell pepper, seeded and chopped fine
- 1 celery rib, chopped fine
- 6 medium garlic cloves, minced
- 1 teaspoon dried thyme
- ¹/₂ teaspoon cayenne pepper
- ¹/₄ cup all-purpose flour
- 2 quarts low-sodium chicken broth*
- 1¹/₂ pounds boneless, skinless chicken breasts, cut into ¹/₂-inch cubes
- 1 cup long-grain rice
  Salt and pepper

1. Heat oil in large Dutch oven over medium-high heat. Add sausage and cook until lightly browned, about 8 minutes. With slotted spoon, transfer sausage to paper towel–lined plate.

2. Add onions, pepper, and celery to fat in now-empty Dutch oven and cook over medium heat, stirring frequently, until softened, about 8 minutes. Stir in garlic, thyme, and cayenne and cook until fragrant, about 30 seconds. Add flour and stir constantly with wooden spoon until mixture is golden brown, about 10 minutes.

3. Whisk in chicken broth and 2 cups water; bring to boil. Add chicken and rice and simmer until rice is tender and chicken is cooked through, about 10 minutes. Add reserved sausage and simmer until soup is slightly thickened, about 5 minutes. Season with salt and pepper. Serve. (Soup can be refrigerated in airtight container for up to 3 days.)

THAI CHICKEN SOUP
SERVES 8 TO 10

Judith writes: "My family loves Thai flavors, so it was easy to become inspired to create this soup." Use the side of a chef's knife to smash the ginger and garlic. Serve with lime wedges.

- 3 quarts low-sodium chicken broth*
- 1¹/₂ pounds boneless, skinless chicken breasts
- 1 tablespoon grated zest plus 1 tablespoon juice from 1 lime
- 1 (3-inch) piece fresh ginger, peeled, sliced thick, and smashed
- 6 large garlic cloves, unpeeled and smashed
- 5 jalapeño chiles, halved lengthwise and seeded
  Salt
- ¹/₂ pound rice noodles (width of angel hair pasta)
- 3 tablespoons minced fresh cilantro
- 3 tablespoons minced fresh basil
- 5 medium scallions, sliced thin
  Pepper
  Lime wedges (for serving)

1. Simmer broth in large Dutch oven. Add chicken, zest, ginger, garlic, chiles, and 1 teaspoon salt; reduce heat, cover, and simmer until broth is flavorful and chicken is cooked through, about 20 minutes. Remove chicken; cool and shred into small pieces. Discard ginger, garlic, and chiles.

2. Return broth to simmer and add rice noodles. Reduce heat and simmer until noodles are tender, about 8 minutes. Stir in shredded chicken, lime juice, cilantro, basil, scallions, and salt and pepper to taste. Serve with lime wedges.

CHICKEN TORTILLA SOUP
SERVES 8 TO 10

Jo Ann writes: "The condiments allow you to make the soup in your own unique way. I like to add hot sauce to make it spicier!" Serve with tortilla chips, avocado, and shredded Monterey Jack cheese.

- 1 tablespoon vegetable oil
- 1 onion, chopped fine
- 1 red bell pepper, seeded and chopped fine
- 1 jalapeño chile, seeded and chopped fine
- 1 tablespoon chili powder
- 2 garlic cloves, minced
- 2 quarts low-sodium chicken broth*
- 1¹/₂ pounds boneless, skinless chicken breasts
- 1 (14.5-ounce) can diced tomatoes, drained
- 1 tablespoon chopped fresh cilantro
- 2 tablespoons lime juice
  Salt and pepper

1. Heat oil in large Dutch oven over medium heat. Add onion, bell pepper, and jalapeño and cook, stirring frequently, until softened, about 8 minutes. Stir in chili powder and garlic and cook until fragrant, about 30 seconds.

2. Add broth and chicken and bring to boil. Reduce heat and simmer until chicken is cooked through, about 20 minutes. With slotted spoon, remove chicken; cool and shred into small pieces.

3. Return shredded chicken to pot along with tomatoes, cilantro, and lime juice. Season with salt and pepper. Serve with recommended garnishes. (Soup can be refrigerated in airtight container for up to 3 days or frozen for up to 1 month.)

We are looking for holiday side dish recipes for an upcoming contest.
Please submit entries by March 31, 2007. E-mail us by visiting **CooksCountry.com/recipecontests** or write to us at Recipe Contest, Cook's Country, P.O. Box 470739, Brookline, MA 02447. Include your name, address, and daytime phone number and tell us what makes your recipe special. The grand-prize winner will receive $1,000. All entries become the property of *Cook's Country*. Visit our website at **CooksCountry.com** for more information on this and other contests.

Ask Cook's Country

WE'LL ANSWER ANY QUESTION YOU THROW AT US!

FLAVOR WITHOUT THE FAT?

I've noticed several brands of milk in the supermarket that promise a richer taste with less fat; 1-percent milk, for instance, that tastes like whole milk. Do these milks really deliver and, if so, how?

Scott Smith Cambridge, Mass.

New England dairies Garelick Farms and Hood both market skim and 1-percent milks that, they claim, taste like 2-percent milk and whole milk, respectively. These products are made by fortifying low-fat milks with large amounts of calcium and other nutrients, which are supposed to add body and creaminess to the milk. But do they?

Ten *Cook's Country* staffers compared Garelick Farms' Over the Moon Skim Milk and Hood's Simply Smart 1% Fat Milk with whole milk and, for the most part, were pleasantly surprised by the results. A few keen tasters tagged both new products as "suspiciously sweet" and slightly "watery," but most tasters admitted that they couldn't tell much difference. We had similar results when we cooked with the milks. Pitting the newer milks against both whole and 2-percent versions from their parent brands, we made sweet-milk scones and double-chocolate pudding; while the higher-fat milks garnered the most praise, several tasters favored the Simply Smart 1% and Over the Moon 1% in both the scones and the pudding, and others found little disparity.

BUTTERMILK PRIMER

I see a lot of recipes that call for buttermilk, but I'm not sure I even know what it is. And why is the expiration date on the carton so much longer than on a carton of milk?

Sue Gagne Dover, N.H.

How long will buttermilk hold?

Old-fashioned buttermilk (which is almost never found outside of working dairies) is the liquid left over after churning cream into butter. The cultured buttermilk sold in supermarkets today, however, is something else entirely: ordinary skim or low-fat milk that is heat-fermented and then dosed with cultures until it's thick, tangy, and smooth.

The appeal of buttermilk in cooking is that it adds tangy richness (similar to sour cream) not found in other liquid dairy products. We use buttermilk in pancakes, biscuits, coleslaw, corn bread, and marinades for chicken, among other applications.

Buttermilk has a long life in your refrigerator, because much of the harmful bacteria that can cause spoilage in milk are killed in the heat-fermenting process. Another reason for buttermilk's longevity is the presence of lactic acid, which, aside from giving buttermilk its characteristic tang, further retards bacterial growth. As buttermilk ages toward and beyond its "sell by" date, the levels of lactic acid increase, eventually turning the buttermilk sour and causing it to curdle (definite signs that it's time to throw it out).

THE STATE OF NUTMEG

I've heard that freshly grated nutmeg is worlds better than the ground supermarket kind. But all of my recipes call for such a small amount—can you really tell a difference?

Dan Petrella Cromwell, Conn.

Most chefs sing the praises of freshly grated nutmeg, claiming that its full, complex aroma will make a big difference in your cooking. To see whether freshly grated nutmeg was truly superior, we pitted it against preground nutmeg in a creamed spinach recipe (which called for a pinch) and a nutmeg donut recipe (which called for 1½ teaspoons). To our surprise, in both applications tasters preferred the versions made using preground nutmeg to those with the freshly grated variety, citing the more assertive flavor of the preground. Since this flew in the face of expectation, we wondered about the cause.

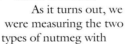

Fresh nutmeg really is better than preground.

As it turns out, we were measuring the two types of nutmeg with a spoon, when we should have been weighing the samples. Because our favorite tool for grating whole nutmeg, a Microplane grater, produced fluffy wisps of the spice, we found that an equal volume of the finely milled preground nutmeg weighed nearly three times as much as the fresh. When we repeated our tests using an equal weight of each type of spice, although preground was deemed acceptable, the freshly grated nutmeg was roundly preferred for its "light peppery" flavor and "warm, woodsy" aroma. We determined that when substituting freshly grated nutmeg for the preground variety, you will need to use roughly twice the volume.

BENT OUT OF SHAPE

I've recently seen dented canned goods for sale at a discounted price, but I thought denting was a warning sign for botulism. Are these canned goods safe to use?

Sarah Johnson Atlanta, Ga.

Although botulism, an illness caused by the bacteria *Clostridium botulinum*, is definitely something to be aware of, there are, on average, only 25 cases reported in the United States each year, most of which are related to home canning, not commercial cans. Since the Food and Drug Administration has very strict regulations on canning, botulism in commercially canned goods is only a concern if the can has been damaged. Because the bacteria responsible for botulism need oxygen to grow, the greatest risk comes when a can's airtight seal has been compromised. Although any dent can put pressure on a can's seal, shallow denting should not cause alarm. On the other hand, if you notice sharp denting (particularly along the top or side seams), swelling, bulging, leaking, or any rust, the can should be discarded. Finally, as with any potentially spoiled food product, it is always best to err on the side of caution. If the canned food has an abnormal color, texture, or odor, do not "taste test" the contents; just reach for another can.

FINDING FLAT IRON

I've had "flat iron" steak in restaurants and loved it, but I can't find it in my supermarket. Is there another name for it, or is it just a restaurant cut?

Michael Tucker Anchorage, Alaska

According to a recent study, flat iron steak is second to only filet mignon in tenderness. Cut from the top blade, near the shoulder, flat iron steaks are not only tender—they also have great beefy flavor and, best of all, a modest price tag (typically between $4.99 and $8.99 per pound).

Unfortunately, true flat iron steaks can be difficult to find in the grocery store. The most similar readily available cut is the "top blade" or "blade" steak, which, although every bit as tasty and tender as the flat iron, is plagued by a thick line of gristle that makes it more suitable for slicing or cubing than serving whole (flat iron and blade steaks are cut differently from the same muscle group). Since restaurants purchase flat iron steaks directly from meat companies, your best option for procuring one is to special order it from your local butcher shop or grocery store (most supermarkets we contacted were happy to accommodate us with only a few days' notice).

SISTER STEAKS: FLAT IRON AND BLADE
Both flat iron (left) and blade steaks (right) are flavorful, tender, and inexpensive. The blade steak has a line of gristle that must be removed, so it's best cut up before cooking. A flat iron steak has very little gristle, making it the perfect choice for grilling.

To ask us a cooking question via e-mail, visit **CooksCountry.com/askcookscountry**. To use postal mail, write to Ask Cook's Country, P.O. Box 470739, Brookline, MA 02447. See if you can stump us!

Recipe Makeover MEATY LASAGNA

A "meaty" lasagna made with ground turkey will be low in fat—and flavor. We set out to create a lasagna with big flavor from lean ingredients.

There are two basic types of meaty lasagna recipes. The more familiar recipe alternates layers of noodles, beefy tomato sauce, and loads of gooey cheese. The other (and my favorite) is lasagna Bolognese, which lives up to its fancy name with two sauces—a rich meat sauce simmered for hours with milk or cream as well as a creamy white sauce (called béchamel)—and plenty of Parmesan cheese. Could I lighten this elegant lasagna?

Many low-fat recipes for this dish omit the beef, pork, veal, and bacon in favor of ground turkey. The recipes I made with just turkey, however, tasted "light" and lacked depth of flavor. Having recently seen another test cook develop a recipe for vegetarian mushroom lasagna, I wondered if I might be able to harness that "meaty" flavor and texture in my recipe. It turned out that a pound of finely chopped mushrooms, sautéed with onion, carrot, and garlic, worked like a charm. Not only did the mushrooms add bulk to the sauce (meaning I could cut back on ground turkey), but they lived up to their "meaty" reputation.

Classic lasagna Bolognese recipes call for simmering the meat in wine as well as milk or cream. The wine adds flavor and the dairy tenderizes the meat. To save calories, I omitted the wine—the mushroom mixture was flavorful without it. But I found the dairy to be essential—without any, the ground turkey turned tough and grainy. Fortunately, 2-percent milk tenderized the meat and enriched the sauce nicely.

Béchamel is a classic white sauce made with milk, butter, and flour. Many low-fat recipes use skim milk and replace the butter with low-fat cream cheese, but my tasters groaned about the gummy texture and artificial flavors in these sauces. After many failures, I finally found success by making a white sauce with 2-percent milk and chicken broth thickened with flour. Parmesan added directly to the sauce helped thicken it further.

To build the lasagna, I assumed I would alternate meat sauce, white sauce, and noodles. But the resulting lasagna was disappointing; the white sauce was lost in the middle of the dish, its cheesy flavor muscled out by the meat sauce. It turned out that saving the white sauce for the top of the lasagna made its flavor more pronounced, and I didn't need as much of it. I could finally tuck into a hefty plate of low-fat lasagna Bolognese that didn't look, feel, or taste "light."

–Diane Unger

LOW-FAT MEATY LASAGNA
SERVES 8
For bolder flavor, add ¼ teaspoon red pepper flakes to the meat sauce and a pinch of nutmeg to the white sauce. If you don't have a food processor, finely chop the vegetables by hand.

- 1 small carrot, cut into chunks
- 1 pound cremini or white mushrooms
- 6 garlic cloves, peeled
- 2 (28-ounce) cans whole tomatoes with juice
- 2 teaspoons extra-virgin olive oil
- 1 medium onion, minced
  Salt and pepper
- 3 tablespoons tomato paste
- 1¼ pounds 93% lean ground turkey
- 2 cups 2% milk
- 2 cups low-sodium chicken broth
- 1 bay leaf
- ½ cup minced fresh basil
- 5 tablespoons all-purpose flour
- 1 cup grated Parmesan cheese
- 12 no-boil lasagna noodles

1. Pulse carrot, mushrooms, and garlic in food processor until finely chopped; transfer to bowl. Process tomatoes in food processor until almost smooth. Combine 1 teaspoon oil, onion, ½ teaspoon salt, and ¼ teaspoon pepper in Dutch oven. Cover and cook over medium-low heat until onion is softened, 3 to 4 minutes. Add carrot, mushrooms, and garlic and cook, uncovered, until mushrooms release their liquid, 5 to 7 minutes. Increase heat to medium-high and cook until liquid has evaporated, 3 to 5 minutes.

2. Add tomato paste and cook until paste begins to brown, about 2 minutes. Stir in turkey and 1 cup milk, using wooden spoon to break up any large chunks, and cook until most of milk has evaporated, 5 to 7 minutes. Stir in tomatoes, 1 cup broth, and bay leaf; bring to simmer and cook until sauce has thickened and most of liquid has evaporated, 45 to 60 minutes. Off heat, remove bay leaf, stir in basil, and season with salt and pepper.

3. Meanwhile, whisk remaining 1 cup milk, remaining 1 cup broth, and flour together in medium saucepan until smooth. Bring mixture to simmer over medium-high heat and cook, stirring constantly, until thickened, about 2 minutes. Off heat, stir in remaining 1 teaspoon oil and cheese. Season with salt and pepper.

4. Adjust oven rack to upper-middle position and heat oven to 425 degrees. Spread 2 cups meat sauce in 13 by 9-inch baking pan. Lay 3 noodles over sauce, leaving space between them. Repeat with 3 more layers sauce and noodles. Spread white sauce evenly over top layer of noodles, leaving 1-inch border around edge. Bake until lasagna is bubbling around edges and top begins to brown, 25 to 30 minutes. Cool on rack 20 minutes. Serve.

Make Ahead: You can make both the meat sauce and the white sauce up to 2 days in advance and refrigerate them until ready to use. Gently reheat the sauces separately before proceeding with step 4.

And the Numbers...
All nutritional information is for one serving.

TRADITIONAL
Meaty Lasagna
CALORIES: **600**
FAT: **30g**
SATURATED FAT: **16g**

COOK'S COUNTRY
Low-Fat Meaty Lasagna
CALORIES: **360**
FAT: **11g**
SATURATED FAT: **3.5g**

Meaty Mushrooms
Sliced mushrooms had the wrong texture for our lasagna. Finely chopping the mushrooms in the food processor gave them a meaty texture similar to that of the ground turkey.

SLICED

FINELY CHOPPED

With a full two cups of meat sauce between each layer of noodles, this lasagna is rich and hearty.

Cooking with Guinness can leave a bad taste in your mouth. For beer flavor minus the bitterness, the secret's in the sauce.

Our recipe adds Guinness in two stages—and tempers it with chocolate—to create a stew any Irish pub would be proud to serve.

Slow cookers and beef stews are a match made in heaven—their shared mantra of "slow and low" produces succulent meat, fork-tender vegetables, and a rich, beefy broth. But add Guinness to the mix and things quickly go wrong. Instead of imparting its complex, malted aroma to an already satisfying stew, the stout's assertiveness is intensified, leaving the dish bitter and harsh.

After making a few preliminary (and disastrous) recipes for Guinness beef stew, I decided to scrap them all and start from scratch. When it comes to braising, the test kitchen has always been partial to the chuck cut, from the shoulder of the cow; it's well marbled and has great beefy flavor. I found that searing the meat before adding it to the slow cooker helped balance the strong taste of the stout. To keep with the Irish theme, I included carrots, parsnips, and potatoes (waxy, red skin potatoes hold their shape nicely as they cook) as my vegetables of choice, making sure to cut them into large, rustic pieces so they would absorb lots of flavor without falling apart during the long cooking.

When it came to the liquid, tasters preferred the neutral meatiness of chicken broth to stale, slightly metallic beef broth. As for the beer, some recipes

called for the better part of a six-pack, but I found these versions so harsh and bitter that they were nearly inedible. Starting with two bottles, I gradually reduced the amount of beer in each test. But by the time the bitterness was subdued, so was most of the beer flavor. Adding the Guinness in two stages (at the beginning for a base flavor and at the end for a fresh kick) helped, but it wasn't until I used a little culinary trickery that I made real progress.

Since stout drinkers often extol the beer's complex coffee/chocolate aroma, I wondered if enhancing these flavors might bolster the perceived stout character of the stew without adding any harshness. I first tested coffee (both instant and fresh-brewed) in the stew, but tasters instantly rejected its distinctive taste. For my next test, I added cocoa to the slow cooker, and tasters raved about the improved stout flavor and lack of bitterness.

The only downside to the cocoa was its slightly acidic nature, but a quick switch to bittersweet chocolate left me with a beefy stew that was long on flavor and short on bitterness. Chocolate in beef stew—who would have guessed? It must have been the luck of the Irish.

—Jeremy Sauer

GUINNESS BEEF STEW
SERVES 6 TO 8

Make sure to buy large chunks of stew meat. Trim meat of excess fat, as necessary, and cut into 1½-inch pieces. Be gentle when stirring in the flour in step 3—the fork-tender beef will fall apart if stirred too aggressively.

    4   pounds boneless beef chuck stew
        meat (see note)
        Salt and pepper
    2   tablespoons vegetable oil
    2   onions, chopped
    4   cups low-sodium chicken broth
 1½   cups Guinness Draught (see box)
    1   tablespoon light brown sugar
    1   teaspoon dried thyme
    1   ounce bittersweet chocolate, chopped
    2   bay leaves
    5   carrots, peeled and cut into 1-inch
        chunks
    1   pound parsnips, peeled and cut into
        1-inch chunks
 1½   pounds baby red potatoes, scrubbed
  ¼   cup all-purpose flour
    2   tablespoons minced fresh parsley

1. Pat beef dry with paper towels and sprinkle with salt and pepper. Heat 2 teaspoons oil in large skillet over medium-high heat until just smoking. Cook half of beef until browned on all sides, about 8 minutes. Transfer to slow cooker insert and repeat with additional 2 teaspoons oil and remaining beef.

2. Add remaining 2 teaspoons oil, onions, and ¼ teaspoon salt to skillet and cook until onions are lightly browned, about 5 minutes. Add broth, 1¼ cups stout, sugar, thyme, chocolate, and bay leaves and bring to boil, using wooden spoon to scrape up browned bits. Transfer to slow cooker insert.

3. Add carrots, parsnips, and potatoes to slow cooker insert. Cover and cook on low until meat is tender, 9 to 10 hours (or cook on high for 6 to 7 hours). Set slow cooker to high. Whisk flour and remaining ¼ cup beer until smooth, then stir mixture into slow cooker. Cook, covered, until sauce thickens, about 15 minutes. Stir in parsley, season with salt and pepper, and discard bay leaf. Serve.

Make Ahead: You can prepare the recipe through step 2 the night before the ingredients go into the slow cooker. Refrigerate the browned beef and the onion mixture in separate containers. In the morning, transfer the beef and the onion mixture to the slow cooker and proceed with step 3.

Chocolate to the Rescue

We found that chocolate emphasized the rich flavor in Guinness without adding any bitterness. But not all chocolate worked in our recipe. Unsweetened chocolate was much too astringent and imparted chalkiness to the stew. Semisweet chocolate was too sweet, making the stew taste like a "meaty candy bar." Bittersweet chocolate was the perfect compromise.

A BITTERSWEET SOLUTION
Bittersweet chocolate enhances the flavor of the beer without adding any harsh notes.

Choosing the Right Beer

While shopping for our Guinness Beef Stew recipe, we were surprised to find two options in the beer aisle: Guinness Extra Stout and Guinness Draught. Straight from the bottle, both beers have their merits. But after nine hours in the slow cooker, Guinness Draught was the clear winner. Tasters noticed the "clean, toasted taste" of the stew made with Guinness Draught, while the stew made with Guinness Extra Stout, although still acceptable, was noted for having a slightly "tannic, bitter" aftertaste.

SHOP CAREFULLY
When cooking, choose the mellower Guinness Draught (right) rather than Guinness Extra Stout.

Lost Recipes JOE FROGGERS

This Massachusetts spice cookie dates back 200 years and was originally made with seawater and rum.

I know my way around the cookie jar, but that doesn't mean I can't still be taken by surprise. A few years ago, I ran across a "new" cookie that actually dates back to the late 1700s. I was in a bakery in Marblehead, Mass., when I spied several dark spice cookies in the display case. They were as big as my face and as flat as a pancake. I bit into one. It was incredibly moist from molasses, tasted strongly of clove (which numbed my tongue), and was heavy with rum (which I loved) and just a little salty. "What am I eating?" I asked. "Joe frogger—it's a Marblehead cookie," the clerk said. That bakery is now closed, so I recently began my search for an authentic recipe.

I got several recipes from websites, cookbooks, and magazines, but they baked up hard, with no warm and salty rum flavor. I e-mailed the Marblehead Museum and Historical Society, and they recommended I consult *The Spirit of '76 Lives Here*, by Virginia Gamage and Priscilla Lord (Chilton Book Company, 1971). The authors tell the story of Joseph Brown, a freed slave and Revolutionary War veteran who lived in Marblehead more than 200 years ago.

Brown (known as "Old Black Joe") and his wife, Lucretia (affectionately known as Auntie Cresse), opened up Black Joe's Tavern in a part of Marblehead called Gingerbread Hill. Besides serving drinks (mostly rum), Joe and Auntie Cresse baked cookies: large, moist molasses and rum cookies made salty by the addition of Marblehead seawater. These cookies were popular sustenance on long fishing voyages, as they had no dairy to spoil and the combination of rum, molasses, and seawater kept them chewy for weeks.

According to Samuel Roads Jr.'s *History and Traditions of Marblehead*, published in 1879, the funny name for these cookies referred to the lily pads (similar in size and shape to the cookies) and large croaking frogs that would fill the pond behind Joe's Tavern. Thus the cookies became known as Joe froggers.

At Marblehead's Abbot Public Library, the librarians produced recipes from local news journals and town cookbooks, such as the *Marblehead, Massachusetts, Baptist Women's Fellowship* (1965). These recipes first stirred molasses together with baking soda. The reaction between the two made the mixture bubble and froth, leaving the soda with little leavening power. That, combined with the absence of egg, explained why the cookies are so flat. (The soda does contribute a deep, dark color.)

Thinking back to the bracing Joe froggers I tasted in the bakery, I doubled the rum and halved the water. I wasn't going to call for seawater (although we did test it), but dissolving 1½ teaspoons of salt into the rum and water worked fine. Some recipes called for shortening (Auntie Cresse most likely used lard), but butter tasted better.

My version of this old-fashioned American cookie won't stay fresh for weeks at sea like the original, but they are so salty, spicy, sweet, and chewy I'm not sure that matters. **–Bridget Lancaster**

JOE FROGGERS
MAKES 2 DOZEN COOKIES
Place only 6 cookies on each baking sheet—they will spread. If you don't own a 3½-inch cookie cutter, use a drinking glass. Use regular (not robust) molasses. Make sure to chill the dough for a full 8 hours or it will be too hard to roll out.

- ⅓ cup dark rum (such as Myers's)
- 1 tablespoon water
- 1½ teaspoons salt
- 3 cups all-purpose flour, plus extra for rolling out dough
- ¾ teaspoon ground ginger
- ½ teaspoon ground allspice
- ¼ teaspoon ground nutmeg
- ⅛ teaspoon ground cloves
- 1 cup molasses (see note)
- 1 teaspoon baking soda
- 8 tablespoons (1 stick) unsalted butter, softened but still cool
- 1 cup sugar

1. Stir rum, water, and salt in small bowl until salt dissolves. Whisk flour, ginger, allspice, nutmeg, and cloves in medium bowl. Stir molasses and baking soda in large measuring cup (mixture will begin to bubble) and let sit until doubled in volume, about 15 minutes.

2. With electric mixer, beat butter and sugar on medium-high speed until fluffy, about 2 minutes. Reduce speed to medium-low and gradually beat in rum mixture. Add one-third of flour mixture, beating on medium-low until just incorporated, followed by half of molasses mixture, scraping down sides of bowl as needed. Add half of remaining flour mixture, followed by remaining molasses mixture, and finally remaining flour mixture. Using rubber spatula, give dough final stir (dough will be extremely sticky). Cover bowl containing dough with plastic wrap and refrigerate until stiff, at least 8 hours or up to 3 days.

3. Adjust oven racks to upper-middle and lower-middle positions and heat oven to 375 degrees. Line 2 baking sheets with parchment paper. Working with half of dough at a time on a heavily floured work surface, roll out to ¼-inch thickness. Using 3½-inch cookie cutter, cut out 12 cookies. Transfer 6 cookies to each baking sheet, spacing cookies about 1½ inches apart. Bake until cookies are set and just beginning to crack, about 8 minutes, rotating rack position and direction of baking sheets halfway through baking time. Cool cookies on sheets 10 minutes, then transfer cookies to rack to cool completely. Repeat with remaining dough. (Cookies may be stored in airtight container for up to 1 week.)

Good Reaction
Molasses on its own is thick and sticky (top), but after baking soda is added it becomes light and frothy. This mixture gives the cookies a rich color and flavor.

MOLASSES

MOLASSES WITH BAKING SODA

These oversized cookies were originally developed for long journeys at sea, but they're delicious on land, too.

Maryland Fried Chicken
with Cream Gravy

In Maryland, fried chicken should be deeply seasoned and boast a thin, crisp crust. Creating a foolproof coating was straightforward, but the seasonings and traditional cream gravy were trickier.

Whether it's dark meat or light, extra-crispy or original, Americans are very particular when it comes to fried chicken. This is especially true in Maryland, where both raising and frying chicken are ways of life. While other regions of the country rely on a thick buttermilk batter and a deep-fat fryer to deliver a crusty crunch, in Maryland the chicken parts are simply seasoned, floured, and shallow-fried. This old-fashioned cooking method results in crisp, mahogany chicken that, with a gentle tug, sheets off the bone with its deliciously brittle skin still intact. But what really sets Maryland fried chicken apart is the creamy, black pepper–spiked pan gravy that's equally fit for drumstick dunking or mopping up with a biscuit.

To stay true to the Maryland style, I wanted to stick with the flour-dredged, shallow-fried cooking technique. But even though this method produces perfectly browned chicken, my first try resulted in one bland bird. Tasters loved the idea of adding Old Bay seasoning (a ubiquitous blend in the Chesapeake region) to the flour dredge, but it had a scorched flavor coming out of the hot oil. Instead, I added salt, dry mustard, and garlic powder (time-tested fried chicken seasonings) to the flour for a base flavor, then sprinkled the chicken with Old Bay once it came out of the pan. Now the seasoned flour and Old Bay made for a tasty crust, but the chicken itself was barely seasoned.

As it turned out, sprinkling the salt, mustard, and garlic powder directly on the chicken pieces before dredging them in flour was key: It assured that the seasonings were hitting the meat and not being sloughed off in the excess flour. Resting the seasoned and floured chicken in the fridge for 30 minutes improved it even further, allowing the seasonings and flour to take hold for an extra-tasty, extra-crispy coating.

I turned my attention to the defining element of Maryland fried chicken, the cream gravy. To thicken the gravy, most recipes start with a roux made from pan drippings and flour, and I wasn't about to argue with that. As for the liquid base of the gravy, tasters found that milk alone made the gravy too sweet. Cutting it with chicken broth added a savory element but also made the gravy pale and soupy—not the rich and creamy sauce I had imagined. Since adding more flour made the gravy sludgy, I tried keeping the broth but switching the dairy. Half-and-half was a step in the right direction, but cream was a giant leap, providing a silky texture and honest dairy taste. With a good hit of pepper in the gravy, my Maryland fried chicken could stake its claim as a great American recipe. **–Jeremy Sauer**

MARYLAND FRIED CHICKEN SERVES 4 TO 6

To ensure even cooking, breasts should be halved crosswise and leg quarters separated into thighs and drumsticks.

Fried Chicken
- 4 pounds bone-in, skin-on chicken pieces (see note above)
- 1 tablespoon dry mustard
- 1 tablespoon garlic powder
- 1 teaspoon salt
- 2 cups all-purpose flour
- 1 teaspoon baking powder
- 3 cups peanut oil or vegetable shortening (see box on page 11) Old Bay seasoning

Cream Gravy
- 1/4 cup pan drippings (from frying chicken)
- 1/4 cup all-purpose flour
- 2 cups low-sodium chicken broth
- 1 cup heavy cream
- 1 teaspoon pepper Salt

1. For the chicken: Pat chicken dry with paper towels. Combine mustard, garlic powder, and salt in small bowl and sprinkle evenly over chicken. Combine flour and baking powder in shallow dish and, working one piece at a time, dredge chicken parts until well coated, shaking off excess. Refrigerate on plate for 30 minutes (or up to 2 hours).

2. Adjust oven rack to middle position and heat oven to 200 degrees. Heat oil in large Dutch oven over medium-high heat to 375 degrees. Arrange half of chicken in pot, skin side down, cover, and cook until well browned, about 5 minutes

This simple, traditional fried chicken is dressed up with a peppery cream gravy.

side. Lower temperature to
lium, adjusting burner as neces-
· to maintain oil temperature
veen 300 and 325 degrees.
ɔk uncovered, turning chicken
ecessary, until cooked through,
ut 5 minutes. (Internal tempera-
: should register 160 degrees
white meat and 175 degrees for
k meat.) Transfer chicken to wire
: set over baking sheet, season
ı Old Bay, and transfer to oven.
ıg oil back to 375 degrees and
:at with remaining chicken.
3. For the gravy: Pour off all
¼ cup oil in pot. Stir in flour
cook until golden, about 2
utes. Slowly whisk in broth,
m, and pepper. Simmer until
kened, about 5 minutes. Season
ı salt and serve with chicken.

rying without Fear

/hile developing our recipe for
ˀaryland Fried Chicken, batch
fter batch of the chicken was
ıarred by an odd "fishy" flavor.
ɔ find the culprit, we tried
djusting every variable in the
ecipe, but nothing worked. As
last resort, we switched from
egetable oil (our usual frying
ıedium) to peanut oil (another
ommonly used frying oil), and
ıe problem was solved. As it
ırns out, after a total frying
me of roughly 30 minutes,
ıe vegetable oil was begin-
ng to break down and impart
spoiled, fishy flavor to the
ıicken. Peanut oil (which has
higher smoke point) fared
etter and didn't break down,
esulting in no off-flavors in the
ıicken. We also tried safflower
l, canola oil, and vegetable
ıortening. The peanut oil was
ill best, but the vegetable
shortening was
the runner-up,
winning praise
for its "clean"
flavor.

NO FISHY FLAVOR
Refined peanut oil, such as Planters, and vegetable shortening, such as Crisco, withstood prolonged frying better than other oils we tested and didn't impart any off-flavors.

FOOD QUOTE: *"The universal food of the people of Texas, both rich and poor, seems to be corn-dodger and fried bacon."*
Frederick Law Olmsted, A Journey through Texas *(1856)*

Corn Dodgers

A Civil War corn bread gets a 21st-century update.

Abraham Lincoln was raised on them, George Washington Carver took them to school, and John Wayne used them for target practice in the movie *True Grit*. They're corn dodgers, little cornmeal cakes with a strange oval shape, a historic pedigree, and a funny name. Dating back to the 1800s, the first corn dodgers were made from "hot water corn bread," a mixture of cornmeal, pork fat, salt, and boiling water that was formed into small oblong loaves and baked. Corn dodgers were a cheap staple for Civil War troops and traveling pioneers.

Unfortunately, most corn dodger recipes have changed little during the past 150 years. Those I tried were dense, gritty, and hard as a brick (not surprising: They're called "dodgers" because a person should move quickly if one is thrown his way). A few recipe writers have made changes over the years, adding milk or cream, leaveners, eggs, or sugar. Even these small embellishments improved the flavor and texture, giving me some optimism for my testing.

Flavor was up first, so starting with the base recipe of cornmeal, salt, butter (or a little rendered bacon fat, if I had it on hand), and hot water, I added a bit of sugar (just 1½ tablespoons) to bring out the cornmeal's sweet side. Replacing some of the water with buttermilk gave my dodgers a tangy flavor that tasters loved. Baking soda (which reacts with the buttermilk) and baking powder helped to lighten my dodgers considerably, and a single egg provided richness to the lean batter and gave the dodgers a creamy interior.

All was well except for the cornmeal, which stayed hard and gritty even when mixed with hot water. Some recipes required resting the dough overnight to soften the cornmeal. But, being impatient, I tried simmering the cornmeal in hot water and buttermilk. Cooled, shaped, and baked, these corn dodgers were crisp on the outside and creamy on the inside. Hot from the oven and with a good smear of honey butter, they were worthy of a president—or a Duke. **–Bridget Lancaster**

These easy-to-make cornmeal cakes were popular with Civil War soldiers and pioneers heading West.

CORN DODGERS

MAKES 24

Corn dodgers go great with fried chicken, catfish, chili, or barbecue. The honey butter is an optional (but great) final touch. Maple butter and maple syrup are other traditional accompaniments.

Corn Dodgers

- **1 tablespoon corn or vegetable oil**
- **2 cups yellow cornmeal**
- **1½ tablespoons sugar**
- **½ teaspoon baking soda**
- **½ teaspoon salt**
- **2 cups water, plus extra for forming dodgers**
- **1 cup buttermilk**
- **1 tablespoon unsalted butter**
- **2 teaspoons baking powder**
- **1 large egg**

Honey Butter

- **8 tablespoons (1 stick) unsalted butter, softened**
- **¼ cup honey**
- **⅛ teaspoon salt**

1. For the corn dodgers: Adjust oven rack to middle position and heat oven to 400 degrees. Spread oil on rimmed baking sheet.

2. Whisk cornmeal, sugar, baking soda, and salt in medium bowl. Heat water, buttermilk, and butter in large saucepan over medium-high heat until just simmering. In slow, steady stream, whisk cornmeal mixture into liquid. Reduce heat to medium-low and cook until mixture begins to bubble, about 6 minutes. Remove from heat and cool until warm, about 10 minutes.

3. Whisk baking powder and egg in small bowl, then stir into cornmeal mixture. Fill medium bowl with tap water. Scoop out ¼ cup mixture and, using wet hands, form into 4 by 1½-inch loaf shape. Place on prepared baking sheet and repeat with remaining mixture, spacing dodgers about ½ inch apart. Bake until deep brown on bottom and golden brown on top, rotating pan halfway through baking, 25 to 30 minutes. Transfer corn dodgers to rack to cool.

4. For the honey butter: Meanwhile, mix all ingredients in medium bowl until smooth. Serve corn dodgers, split open, with honey butter. (Corn dodgers can be refrigerated for up to 2 days; reheat on baking sheet in 350-degree oven.)

A Dodger by Any Other Name

Starting with the same recipe, quick cornmeal cakes were given different names depending on how the dough was shaped and cooked. Here are the differences:

Corn pone: Same oblong shape as dodgers, but cakes were pan-fried in lots of oil.
Johnnycake: Dough was flattened into a small pancake, then griddle-fried.
Ashcake: Rounds of dough were wrapped with cabbage leaves, then placed in the ashes of the campfire to cook.
Hoecake: Dough was formed into a small pancake, then placed on the flat side of a garden hoe (really) and cooked over the campfire.

Family-Style Shrimp Scampi

How do you prepare this restaurant classic for a crowd at home?

Our recipe turns down the heat—and the stress—to produce a big bowlful of shrimp in a richly flavored sauce.

Shrimp scampi is a straightforward preparation: The shrimp are seared over high heat in garlicky butter, a dash of wine is added to the skillet, and the sauce is finished with lemon juice and parsley.

While this formula works in a restaurant when you're cooking a handful of shrimp for just one diner, I quickly found out that it yields rubbery shrimp and a watery sauce when you super-size this recipe to a feed a family. I set out to create a big platter of tender shrimp in a rich sauce that would actually cling to the shrimp.

Right away, I could see that two pounds of shrimp weren't going to fit in my skillet. Turning to the bigger Dutch oven, I started by sautéing four cloves of garlic in half a stick of butter, adding the shrimp and wine, and covering the pot. As I had hoped, the lid trapped steam in the big pot and helped cook the shrimp gently and evenly.

Unfortunately, by the time the sauce was thickened to the proper consistency, the shrimp were very tough.

For my next test, I tried removing the shrimp from the pot when they were partially cooked and simmering the butter and wine (with the lid off) to a saucy consistency. I then added the shrimp back to warm up and finish cooking. This time the shrimp were plump and juicy, but the sauce was still too thin and the reduced wine tasted harsh. Adding bottled clam juice cut the intensity of the wine and created a briny, bright sauce with real depth. Too bad most of the sauce was still resting on the bottom of the platter.

Since many restaurant sauces are thickened by adding butter at the end of cooking, I thought I'd give this method a try. I cooked the garlic in just a tablespoon of olive oil before adding the shrimp, wine, and clam juice and covering the pot. Minutes later, I removed the tender shrimp, reduced the sauce to intensify flavors, and began whisking in butter a little at a time. As long as the butter was chilled, it thickened the sauce to a glossy consistency that coated the shrimp nicely. A splash of lemon juice and a generous handful of parsley, and my scampi was perfect. –Katie Henderson

FAMILY-STYLE SHRIMP SCAMPI SERVES 4 TO 6

Buy extra-large shrimp (21 to 25 per pound) for this recipe, which makes enough to dress one pound of dried pasta (optional).

- 1 tablespoon olive oil
- 4 garlic cloves, minced
- 1/4 cup dry white wine
- 1/4 cup clam juice
  Salt and pepper
- 2 pounds extra-large shrimp, peeled
- 4 tablespoons cold unsalted butter, cut into 4 pieces
- 2 tablespoons lemon juice
- 2 tablespoons chopped fresh parsley
  Lemon wedges for serving

1. Heat oil in Dutch oven over medium-high heat until shimmering. Add garlic and cook until fragrant, about 30 seconds. Add wine, clam juice, 1/4 teaspoon salt, and 1/8 teaspoon pepper; bring to boil. Add shrimp, cover, and cook until shrimp are slightly translucent, about 2 minutes. Reduce heat to medium, stir, cover, and cook until shrimp are just cooked through, about 2 minutes.

2. Using slotted spoon, transfer shrimp to medium bowl. Bring sauce to boil over medium-high heat and cook until reduced by half, about 1 minute. Whisk butter, 1 piece at a time, into sauce; stir in lemon juice and parsley. Season to taste and pour mixture over shrimp in serving bowl. Serve with lemon wedges.

Easier Than You Think: One-Minute Salsa

Could we create a fresh salsa that's almost as easy as opening a jar?

A jarred salsa might be quick, but it's never very good. That is, unless you like watery, bland salsa. Could I create a fresh salsa with not much more effort?

Instead of coring, seeding, and dicing fresh tomatoes, I found that canned diced tomatoes work great in salsa, as long as you drain them first. Canned pickled jalapeños add heat and a vinegary kick—and I didn't have to wear rubber gloves (as I do when working with fresh jalapeños) when I opened the can.

To boost the flavor and color of this salsa, I augmented these canned products with fresh red onion (for color, sweetness, and bite), cilantro, lime juice, and garlic. To save on chopping, I turned to my food processor. A final quick drain of the finished salsa got rid of excess moisture.

–Cali Rich

ONE-MINUTE SALSA
MAKES ABOUT 1 CUP

The salsa will keep for 2 days in the refrigerator. Reseason to taste before serving. Make sure to drain both the tomatoes and the jalapeños before processing.

- 1/2 small red onion
- 1/4 cup fresh cilantro leaves
- 1 tablespoon lime juice
- 1 garlic clove, peeled
- 2 tablespoons canned pickled jalapeños, drained
- 1/4 teaspoon salt
- 1 (14.5-ounce) can diced tomatoes, drained

Pulse onion, cilantro, lime juice, garlic, jalapeños, and salt in food processor until roughly chopped, about five 1-second pulses. Add tomatoes and pulse until chopped, about two 1-second pulses. Transfer mixture to fine-mesh strainer and drain briefly. Serve.

Canned tomatoes and fresh produce work together to create a lively, bright salsa that comes together in no time.

Ultimate Spicy Beef Nachos

Why are most nachos soggy, bland, and greasy, when they should be crisp, flavorful, and fresh?

Most of the "ultimate nachos" I've ordered in restaurants come to the table loaded down with bland, greasy beef, dry beans, and cold strings of unmelted cheese smothering tough, soggy chips. They might be an "ultimate" kitchen disaster but are otherwise unremarkable. That's a shame, because great nachos shouldn't be that hard to prepare. My ideal nachos would cover hot, crisp chips with spicy beef, creamy refried beans, gooey melted cheese, and plenty of jalapeños.

To boldly season the beef, I tested a slew of spices before settling on a smoky mixture of chili powder, cumin, and oregano. Tomato paste, brown sugar, and canned chipotle chiles added a sweet richness and touch of heat, while fresh lime juice brightened it all up. To take care of the grease problem, I used 90-percent lean ground beef and drained the cooked meat on paper towels, pressing with more towels to blot up excess fat.

My tasters preferred refried beans to plain beans, but when used straight out of the can, their stodgy flavor and chalky texture were a turnoff. Processing the beans with pickled jalapeños and cheese produced a lively, spreadable puree. As for the cheese, it turns out that cheddar (the choice in many recipes) doesn't melt nearly as well as Monterey Jack. My tasters preferred the kick of pepper Jack, but plain Jack is fine, too.

Early in my testing, I had been dumping a bag of tortilla chips on a platter, piling them with the toppings, and baking them until the cheese melted. After much trial and error, I learned two tricks about assem-bly that make for better nachos. First, the order of ingredients is important. The beans should be added first, so you can spread them evenly; the beef comes next, so it can adhere to the beans and not roll off the chips; then the cheese goes on, to blanket everything. Second, to prevent all the toppings from being eaten with the top layer of chips, I found it necessary to make two layers of chips and toppings.

A quick addition of sliced fresh jalapeños turned up the heat and brought the pepper count to five: chili powder, chipotle chile, pepper Jack cheese, pickled jalapeños, and fresh jalapeños. There's no way anyone will think these nachos are bland or boring. –Cali Rich

ULTIMATE SPICY BEEF NACHOS SERVES 8

Top with our One-Minute Salsa (page 12), sour cream, chopped cilantro, and diced avocado.

Refried Beans
- 1/2 cup canned refried beans
- 3 tablespoons shredded pepper Jack cheese
- 1 tablespoon chopped canned pickled jalapeños

Spicy Beef
- 2 teaspoons vegetable oil
- 1 small onion, chopped fine
- 3 garlic cloves, minced
- 1 tablespoon chili powder
- 1 teaspoon ground cumin
- 1/2 teaspoon dried oregano
- 1 teaspoon salt
- 1 pound 90-percent lean ground beef
- 2 tablespoons tomato paste
- 1 teaspoon brown sugar
- 1 medium canned chipotle chile, chopped, plus
- 1 teaspoon adobo sauce
- 1/2 cup water
- 2 teaspoons lime juice

Assembly
- 1 (9 1/2-ounce) bag tortilla chips (see page 30)
- 4 cups shredded pepper Jack cheese
- 2 jalapeño chiles, sliced into thin rings

1. Adjust oven rack to middle position and heat oven to 400 degrees.

2. For the beans: Pulse ingredients in food processor until smooth. Transfer to bowl and cover with plastic wrap.

3. For the beef: Heat oil in large skillet over medium heat until shimmering. Cook onion until softened, about 4 minutes. Add garlic, chili powder, cumin, oregano, and salt and cook until fragrant, about 1 minute. Add beef and cook, breaking meat into small bits with wooden spoon and scraping pan bottom to prevent scorching, until no longer pink, about 5 minutes. Add tomato paste, sugar, chile, and adobo sauce and cook until paste begins to darken, about 1 minute. Add water, bring to simmer, and cook over medium-low until mixture is nearly dry, 5 to 7 minutes. Stir in lime juice and transfer mixture to plate lined with several layers of paper towels. Use more paper towels to blot up excess grease (see photos at right).

4. To assemble: Spread half of chips on large serving platter or 13 by 9-inch baking dish. Dollop half of bean mixture over chips, then spread evenly. Scatter half of beef mixture over beans, top with 2 cups cheese and half of jalapeños. Repeat with remaining chips, beans, beef, cheese, and jalapeños. Bake until cheese is melted and just beginning to brown, 12 to 14 minutes. Serve with salsa and other suggested garnishes.

Using the right ingredients is important, but the real secret to perfect nachos lies in the assembly.

Kitchen Know-How
GREASE BE GONE

1. Transfer the cooked beef mixture to a plate lined with paper towels, then place several more paper towels on top of beef.

2. Using your hands, press the paper towels in order to extract as much extra grease as possible from the beef.

Crunchy Potato Wedges

A secret recipe delivers fast food–style potato wedges at home.

The fried chicken at KFC is pretty good, but I find myself in line at the drive-through at least once a week just to order the fried potato wedges. The spicy, light, and crunchy coating contrasts perfectly with the fluffy interior. These potatoes taste so much like their fried chicken counterpart that I assume they are made using the same coating. I wanted to duplicate these wedges at home, so I could enjoy them somewhere other than the front seat of my car.

To obtain a perfectly cooked interior and a nicely crisped exterior, I knew I'd have to precook my potato wedges before they were fried—otherwise the outside would burn by the time they were cooked through. Taking a cue from the test kitchen's recipe for steak fries, I placed the cut spuds in a bowl with a little vegetable oil, covered them with plastic, and microwaved them until they were just shy of being done. Since the potatoes were tightly covered, they didn't lose any moisture, which made them fry up especially fluffy inside. Now I could concentrate on the crunch and flavor of the coating.

I started with a traditional fried chicken method, dipping my potato wedges in flour, then buttermilk, then back into the flour before frying. The coating was too heavy and tough. Some fried chicken recipes add baking powder or baking soda to either the flour or buttermilk. After a few tests, I found that mixing baking soda right into the buttermilk did the trick. You could see the soda reacting with the buttermilk, making it foam and bubble. Potatoes coated with this mixture were especially crunchy and deep golden brown. To lighten things even further, I tried replacing some of the flour with cornstarch. Sure enough, this coating was incredibly crisp and light. Even better, the cornstarch kept the fries from sogging out even after they'd sat around for a few minutes. During one round of tests, I chomped down on a fry that had been sitting on the plate for 30 minutes. Although it was cold, the coating was still crunchy.

Next I moved on to the seasonings. After trying countless combinations of herbs and spices, I settled on just six: salt, pepper, onion powder, garlic powder, cayenne, and oregano. Together these seasonings approximated KFC's secret blend, but just adding my seasoning mixture to the flour left the wedges somehow lacking. I found that tossing the wedges in the seasoning as they came out of the oil worked better, but the centers of the potatoes were still bland.

Since I season potatoes with salt when I boil them, it only seemed right to season my wedges as they precooked in the microwave. Now the spice flavor permeated the potatoes all the way from their fluffy interiors to their crunchy exteriors. Sorry, Colonel, but from now on I'm frying my wedges at home. **–Katie Henderson**

CRUNCHY POTATO WEDGES SERVES 6

If you don't have buttermilk, substitute 1 cup milk mixed with 1 tablespoon lemon juice. Let the mixture sit 15 minutes before using. See page 30 for dipping sauce recipes.

- 4 teaspoons kosher salt
- 1/2 teaspoon pepper
- 2 teaspoons onion powder
- 1 teaspoon garlic powder
- 3/4 teaspoon cayenne pepper
- 1 teaspoon dried oregano
- 3 large russet potatoes (about 1 3/4 pounds), scrubbed and cut into 1/4-inch wedges
- 1/4 cup vegetable or peanut oil, plus 3 quarts for frying
- 1 1/2 cups all-purpose flour
- 1/2 cup cornstarch
- 1 cup buttermilk (see note)
- 1/2 teaspoon baking soda

1. Combine salt, pepper, onion and garlic powders, cayenne, and oregano in small bowl.

2. Toss potato wedges with 4 teaspoons spice mixture and

We season our wedges with our "secret" spice blend while they're precooking in the microwave, which results in potatoes that are flavored from the inside out.

¼ cup oil in large microwave-safe bowl; cover tightly with plastic wrap. Microwave on high until potatoes are tender but not falling apart, 7 to 9 minutes, shaking bowl (without removing plastic) to redistribute potatoes halfway through cooking. Slowly remove plastic wrap from bowl (be careful of steam) and drain potatoes. Arrange potatoes on rimmed baking sheet and cool until potatoes firm up, about 10 minutes. (Potatoes can be held at room temperature for up to 2 hours.)

3. Heat remaining 3 quarts oil in large Dutch oven over high heat to 340 degrees. Meanwhile, combine flour and cornstarch in medium bowl and whisk buttermilk and baking soda in large bowl. Working in 2 batches, dredge potato wedges in flour mixture, shaking off excess. Dip in buttermilk mixture, allowing excess to drip back into bowl, then coat again in flour mixture. Shake off excess and place on wire rack. (Potatoes can be coated up to 30 minutes in advance.)

4. When oil is ready, add half the coated wedges and fry until deep golden brown, 4 to 6 minutes. Transfer wedges to large bowl and toss with 1 teaspoon spice mixture. Drain wedges on baking sheet lined with paper towels. Return oil to 340 degrees and repeat with second batch of wedges. Serve with extra seasoning on side.

Make Ahead: Our Crunchy Potato Wedges freeze very well. Follow steps 1 through 4, frying each batch of wedges until they are light golden brown, 2 to 3 minutes. Do not toss with seasoning, and drain and cool potatoes completely on baking sheet lined with paper towels. Freeze wedges on baking sheet until completely frozen, about 2 hours, then transfer potatoes to zipper-lock storage bag for up to 2 months. When ready to eat, heat 3 quarts oil to 340 degrees and cook in 2 batches until deep golden brown, about 3 minutes. Toss with seasonings, drain, and serve.

Regional Favorites:
Iowa Skinnies

This sandwich showcases tender pork pounded thin, battered, and pan-fried to a crunchy golden brown.

In the Midwest, pork is king. That's because the heartland of America, sometimes called the Hog Belt, produces most of the pork we eat in this country. But Iowa stands out not only for its pork production but also for its preparation.

Iowa is home to the "skinny," a fried pork sandwich that's as good and as simple as it gets. It starts with a chunk of pork tenderloin that is pounded to platter size before being lightly breaded and fried. A skinny is served on a soft bun with lettuce, tomato, and a slather of mayo.

While nearly every recipe agrees on the meat (pork tenderloin) and the method (pounded extra-thin and shallow-fried), there is little consensus regarding the coating. To get the requisite golden brown, crunchy coating, we tried a number of batters and breadings before settling on a basic flour, egg, and bread crumb approach. Although we found fresh bread crumbs preferable to the sandy store-bought variety, they cooked up bland and boring. Adding crushed saltines (an ingredient I had come across in a few recipes) to the bread crumbs provided a welcome saltiness and even more crispness, but the flavor was still too mild.

Since these sandwiches are served with mayonnaise, I wondered if switching mayo for the egg might add some flavor. It did, but the layer of mayonnaise made the crumbs greasy. A combination of eggs and mayo fared better, adding a nice richness and sweet tang that enhanced the flavor of the pork without weighing down the crust.

Speaking of the pork, I found that one tenderloin was the perfect amount for four sandwiches. Once cut into four pieces and pounded to a ¼-inch thickness (any thicker and the coating burned before the pork was cooked through), a quick spin in the skillet was all that stood between me and an authentic Iowa skinny. **–Jeremy Sauer**

Don't let the name "skinny" fool you—this is one hefty sandwich.

CRISPY IOWA SKINNY
SERVES 4

- 1 pork tenderloin (about 1 pound), prepared according to photos (right)
  Salt and pepper
- ½ cup all-purpose flour
- 2 large eggs
- ¼ cup mayonnaise, plus extra for serving
- 3 slices hearty white sandwich bread, torn into rough pieces
- 16 saltines
- 1 cup vegetable oil
- 4 soft hamburger buns
- ¼ head iceberg lettuce, shredded
- 1 medium tomato, sliced

1. Adjust oven rack to middle position and heat oven to 200 degrees. Pat pork cutlets dry with paper towels and season with salt and pepper.

2. Place flour in shallow dish. Beat eggs and ¼ cup mayonnaise in second shallow dish. Combine bread and saltines in food processor and pulse to fine crumbs; transfer to third shallow dish.

3. Coat cutlets in flour, shaking off excess. Dip both sides of cutlets in egg mixture, then dredge in crumbs, pressing on crumbs to adhere. Place cutlets on wire rack set over baking sheet and let dry 5 minutes (or refrigerate up to 1 hour).

4. Heat ½ cup oil in large nonstick skillet over medium heat until shimmering. Lay 2 cutlets in skillet and fry until crisp and deep golden, about 2 minutes per side. Transfer to large paper towel–lined plate and place in warm oven. Discard oil, wipe out skillet, and repeat with remaining oil and cutlets. Place 1 cutlet on each bun and top with lettuce, tomato, and mayonnaise. Serve.

How to MAKE PORK CUTLETS

①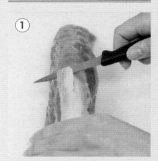

②

③

1. Use a paring knife to remove any silver skin or extraneous fat from the tenderloin.
2. Cut the tenderloin into 4 equal pieces.
3. Arrange pieces of tenderloin cut side up on cutting board. Cover with plastic wrap and pound into ¼-inch-thick cutlets.

I'm Looking for a Recipe

READERS HELP READERS FIND RECIPES

We've Got Mail

Several readers sent us recipes in response to the request for pumpkin coffee can bread in our June/July 2006 issue. We really liked the recipe sent by Priscilla Potter (right). Go to CooksCountry.com and click **Looking for a Recipe** to find dozens more recipes submitted by readers who responded to other recipe requests in previous issues of *Cook's Country*.

PUMPKIN COFFEE CAN BREAD Priscilla Potter, Westfield, Maine

MAKES THREE 5 BY 3-INCH LOAVES

My mom got this recipe from her sister-in-law, and since it was a hit at a Halloween-themed party, it has been referred to as Witch's Nut Cake in our family. Folger's coffee cans were her can of choice, as others sometimes have a "lip" around the top that makes it hard to remove the cakes.

Amount	Ingredient	Instructions
3	eggs	**INSTRUCTIONS:** Beat together eggs, pumpkin, oil, and water in large bowl. Whisk flour, sugar, baking soda, salt, nutmeg, and cinnamon in medium bowl. Whisk dry ingredients into egg mixture in 3 additions. Stir in raisins and walnuts and pour batter into 3 buttered and floured coffee cans. Bake at 350 degrees until skewer or witch's broom inserted in bread comes out clean, about 1 hour and 15 minutes. Cool and frost with cream cheese icing.
1	15-ounce can pumpkin puree	
3/4	cup vegetable oil	
1/2	cup water	
2 1/2	cups all-purpose flour	
2 1/4	cups sugar	
1 1/2	teaspoons baking soda	
1 1/4	teaspoons salt	
3/4	teaspoon nutmeg	
3/4	teaspoon cinnamon	
1	cup golden raisins	
1/2	cup chopped walnuts	

Chicken Wellington

Recently, I was in Las Vegas at the Bellagio Hotel buffet, and they served the most delicious thing I have ever tasted: Chicken Wellington. It was chicken with a bunch of gooey heaven inside of a pastry crust. After many attempts to contact the hotel for the recipe with no success, I am hoping someone out there can get it or knows of a similar one.

Dixie Wise
Idaho Falls, Idaho

Butterscotch Meringue Cookies

My grandmother used to make my all-time favorite cookie. It was layered and had a cake-like cookie bottom; the middle contained chocolate chips and walnut bits; and it was topped with a butterscotch meringue. My grandmother has passed, and no one in my family can locate this recipe. I would love the recipe to carry on in my family.

Michele Tenore
Gladstone, N.J.

Johnson's Bakery Almond Cake

When I was a teenager growing up in Glendale, Calif., in the 1960s, my mother used to order this almond cake in a full sheet cake size for special occasions. It was a moist yellow cake with almond flavor, and it was topped with toasted sliced almonds and powdered sugar. I believe it needed to be refrigerated, as it may also have had a lemon filling in it. I have never seen a recipe that even comes close, and I cannot find a listing for the bakery. If anyone has a recipe for this type of cake, I would appreciate it.

Linda Everett
Rindge, N.H.

Banana Bars

Several years back, a neighbor gave me a recipe for a very decadent banana bar. The pat-in-pan crust was divided and served double duty as a crumbled topping. I believe it may have contained oatmeal, brown sugar, and butter. The filling was a rich, cooked banana pudding containing sweetened condensed milk and bananas. The recipe was lost when we moved, and I haven't been able to find a recipe like it anywhere.

Jill Comeau
Pittsburg, Kan.

Jellied Chicken Loaf

In the 1940s, when I was growing up on the northwest side of Chicago, my mother shopped in a store on the 5900 block of West Irving Park Road called Fred's Meat Market. Fred's wife made a jellied chicken loaf that was sold from the refrigerated meat case. It consisted of only cooked, diced chicken meat floating in a flavorful, vinegary-tasting jelly that was firm enough to cut for sandwiches, and it was always molded in a meat loaf–sized pan. Over the years, I have never forgotten its unique flavor or found a recipe that comes close in taste. My family still talks about it, and I'd love to make it for them.

Nancy Andren
Saint Charles, Mo.

Sherry Bars

A distant relative of mine won't give me the recipe for her sherry bars. I have tried to re-create this recipe many times, but nothing comes close. I know that the bars have sherry, nuts, and a confectioners' sugar icing that also has sherry in it. I love these bars. Please help.

B. Elery
via e-mail

English Drop Cookies

For as long as I can remember, the Woodward & Lothrop Department Store (Woodies) in Washington, D.C., had a bakery and did all of their baking on the premises. They made everything from breads and rolls to cakes, cupcakes, and cookies. Among their best were their English Drop Cookies. They were loaded with raisins and spices and were more the consistency of a chewy and soft chocolate chip cookie than a cake-like Hermit. When Woodies closed in 1995, those cookies were gone forever, unless someone out there knows their recipe!

Tawana Gormley
Mitchellville, Md.

Gumfuddie

My grandmother talked about a recipe she enjoyed as a child called gumfuddie. She said it had eggs and cream and was like a pudding. The recipe has since been lost, and I would love to surprise her with a bowl of it.

Dawn Eckelberry
Peyton, Colo.

European Baked Cheesecake

Years ago, in the Wieboldt's department stores in Illinois, you could get a Baked European Cheesecake that was like no other cheesecake in the U.S. They have since gone out of business, and the last time I tasted something like it was in Austria. Does anyone have this recipe?

Margiaret Porteous
Round Lake, Ill.

Dutch Loaf

I am looking for a bread recipe that is called Dutch Loaf. My grandparents used to buy it every time we visited them. It was made at Ed's Bakery on Chestnut Street in Lynn, Mass., in the 1950s and 1960s. It was a very moist white bread made in a round tube. Any information would be great!

NHquilt
via e-mail

Chocolate Cottage Cheese Drop Cookies

Years ago, I had a recipe for moist chocolate drop cookies that used cottage cheese. They stayed nice and soft and had a cake-like texture. I would love to find this recipe again.

Karen Brantis
Marietta, N.Y.

Lime Fluff

My husband brags about his great-aunt's Lime Fluff. He hasn't had it for 20 years but can still recall this refreshing pie. I have tried several recipes, but he always says, "It's just not it." He can only remember a few things: It was made in an Oreo pie crust, and it did not have any marshmallows or fruit.

Jennifer Cochran
Alpine, Calif.

Caramel Ice Cream

The Chocolate Shop in Kalamazoo, Mich., made the most wonderful caramel ice cream. I have tried every printed recipe, and nothing has the same flavor. Mr. Al Heilman was the last owner, and I heard a large ice cream company got the recipe from him. I would really like to taste this ice cream again before I leave this earth.

Carl Schuett
South Bend, Ind.

Are you looking for a special recipe? Or do you have a recipe a fellow *Cook's Country* reader is seeking? Post your requests and recipes by visiting **CooksCountry.com** and clicking on **Looking for a Recipe**. We'll share recipe requests and found recipes on CooksCountry.com and print as many as we can in the magazine. You may also write to us at Looking for a Recipe, Cook's Country, P.O. Box 470739, Brookline, MA 02447.

Find the Rooster!

A tiny version of this rooster has been hidden somewhere in the pages of this issue. If you find it, write to us with its location (plus your name and address) and you will be entered into a random drawing. The winning entry will receive the All-Clad stainless 12-quart stock pot (our test winner—see page 29), and the next five correct entries drawn will each receive a complimentary one-year subscription to *Cook's Country*. To enter the contest, visit us at **CooksCountry.com/emailus**, or write to us at Rooster, Cook's Country, P.O. Box 470739, Brookline, MA 02447. Entries are due by March 31, 2007.

Did you find the rooster in the October/November 2006 issue? It was hidden on page 24 in the bowl of stuffing. Geraldine M. Hughes of Council Bluffs, Iowa, spotted it and won a set of Forschner knives and a one-year subscription to *Cook's Country*.

BALSAMIC GLAZED CHICKEN

**TEXAS-SIZED BBQ CHICKEN
AND CHEDDAR SANDWICHES**

BAKED FOUR-CHEESE PASTA

**BROILED RIB-EYE STEAKS
WITH FRESH HERB BUTTER**

TEXAS-SIZED BBQ CHICKEN AND CHEDDAR SANDWICHES SERVES 4

Texas Best barbecue sauce is the favorite brand here in the test kitchen.

- 4 slices bacon, halved crosswise
- 4 boneless, skinless chicken breasts (about 1½ pounds)
  Salt and pepper
- 1 cup barbecue sauce (see note)
- 1 canned chipotle chile in adobo sauce, minced
- ¼ cup water
- 4 large onion rolls, split in half
- 1½ cups shredded cheddar cheese

1. Adjust oven rack to upper-middle position and heat oven to 400 degrees. Fry bacon in large nonstick skillet over medium-high heat until crisp, about 4 minutes. Transfer to large plate lined with paper towels and pour off all but 1 tablespoon fat.

2. Pat chicken dry with paper towels and season with salt and pepper. Cook chicken in bacon fat until browned on one side, about 4 minutes. Flip chicken and add barbecue sauce, chipotle, and water. Cover, reduce heat to medium, and simmer until chicken is cooked through and sauce is slightly thickened, about 8 minutes. Remove chicken from skillet and slice crosswise into ¼-inch pieces.

3. Arrange rolls cut side up on baking sheet. Divide chicken among bottom halves of rolls and top with sauce, cheese, and bacon. Bake open-faced sandwiches in oven until cheese melts and rolls are golden brown, about 4 minutes. Top each sandwich with toasted roll top. Serve.

BALSAMIC GLAZED CHICKEN SERVES 4

To save time, simmer the balsamic vinegar mixture while the chicken is in the oven.

- 2 tablespoons unsalted butter, softened
- 3 garlic cloves, minced
- ½ teaspoon minced fresh rosemary
  Salt and pepper
- 4 bone-in, skin-on split chicken breasts (about 3 pounds)
- ¼ cup balsamic vinegar
- 2 tablespoons dark brown sugar

1. Adjust bottom oven rack to lowest position (rack should be 13 inches from broiler element) and top rack to highest position (rack should be 5 inches from broiler element) and heat broiler. Line bottom of broiler pan with foil and fit with slotted broiler-pan top.

2. Combine butter, garlic, rosemary, ¼ teaspoon salt, and ¼ teaspoon pepper in bowl. Pat chicken dry with paper towels and, using fingers, carefully loosen skin from meat. Spoon butter mixture under skin of each breast, then work butter evenly under skin. Season with salt and pepper and arrange chicken skin side down on broiler-pan top.

3. Broil on lower rack until just beginning to brown, 10 to 15 minutes. Turn chicken skin side up and continue to broil until skin is slightly crisp and chicken registers 160 degrees, 10 to 15 minutes. Move pan to upper rack and broil until skin is spotty brown and crisp, about 1 minute.

4. While chicken is cooking, simmer vinegar and sugar in small saucepan set over medium heat until slightly thickened, about 3 minutes. Brush vinegar glaze over cooked chicken. Serve.

BROILED RIB-EYE STEAKS WITH FRESH HERB BUTTER
SERVES 4 TO 6

Because the strength of broilers can vary significantly, don't wander from the kitchen while the steaks are cooking. This recipe calls for large steaks (each 12 to 16 ounces), so it can easily feed six people.

- 4 tablespoons unsalted butter, softened
- 2 tablespoons minced fresh parsley
- 2 teaspoons minced fresh thyme
- 1 garlic clove, minced
- 4 boneless rib-eye steaks, 1 to 1½ inches thick
- ¼ cup Worcestershire sauce
  Salt and pepper
- 2 teaspoons dark brown sugar

1. Adjust oven rack to upper position (rack should be 5 inches from broiler element) and heat oven to broil. Combine butter, parsley, thyme, and garlic in bowl.

2. Marinate steaks in Worcestershire sauce for 10 minutes. Pat steaks dry with paper towels and season with salt and pepper.

3. Line bottom of broiler pan with foil and fit with slotted broiler-pan top. Arrange steaks on pan and broil until beginning to brown, about 2 minutes. Flip steaks, sprinkle with sugar, and continue to broil until well browned and cooked to desired doneness, about 5 minutes for rare, up to 12 minutes for well done. Transfer to platter. Top steaks with herb butter, tent with foil, and rest 10 minutes. Serve.

BAKED FOUR-CHEESE PASTA SERVES 4

Any of the commercially available preshredded Italian cheese blends, from 3 cheese to 7 cheese, can be used here.

- 4 slices bacon, chopped fine
- 1 small onion, chopped fine
- 2 garlic cloves, minced
- 3 cups low-sodium chicken broth
- 1 cup heavy cream
- ¾ pound penne or ziti (about 4 cups)
  Salt
- ½ cup grated Parmesan cheese
- 1 cup frozen peas
  Pepper
- 1 cup shredded Italian 4-cheese blend (see note)

1. Adjust oven rack to upper-middle position and heat oven to 500 degrees. Cook bacon, onion, and garlic in large nonstick skillet over medium-high heat until onion is softened, about 5 minutes. Add broth, cream, pasta, and ½ teaspoon salt, cover, and bring to boil. Once boiling, reduce heat to medium-low and simmer, stirring frequently, until pasta is tender, about 15 minutes.

2. Off heat, stir in Parmesan and peas and season with salt and pepper. Transfer to 2-quart casserole dish and sprinkle with shredded cheese. Bake until cheese is melted and spotty brown, about 5 minutes. Serve.

POACHED SALMON WITH DILL-YOGURT SAUCE

SOUTHERN HAM AND BEAN SOUP

SESAME CHICKEN FINGERS
WITH SPICY PEANUT SAUCE

SEARED PORK CHOPS WITH MUSHROOM GRAVY

SOUTHERN HAM AND BEAN SOUP SERVES 4 TO 6

The ham steak is very salty, so you probably won't need any additional salt.

- 3 tablespoons unsalted butter
- 1 onion, chopped fine
- 2 celery ribs, chopped fine
- 3 garlic cloves, minced
- 1 pound ham steak, chopped fine
- 2 tablespoons dark brown sugar
- 3/4 teaspoon dried thyme
- 2 (16-ounce) cans white beans, drained and rinsed
- 4 cups low-sodium chicken broth
- 2 cups frozen chopped green beans

1. Melt butter in Dutch oven over medium-high heat. Cook onion, celery, garlic, ham, sugar, thyme, and half of white beans, covered, until vegetables are soft, about 8 minutes.

2. Using potato masher, mash beans and vegetables to rough paste. Stir in remaining white beans and broth. Simmer, covered, until slightly thickened, about 10 minutes. Add green beans and cook until heated through, about 2 minutes. Serve.

POACHED SALMON WITH DILL-YOGURT SAUCE SERVES 4

Do not remove the skin before poaching or the fish may fall apart during cooking. The vegetables in the pot can be served alongside the fish or discarded.

- 2 carrots, chopped
- 1 small onion, chopped
- 1 1/2 cups white wine
- 4 sprigs fresh dill, plus 1 tablespoon chopped
- 1 lemon, sliced
  Salt
- 6 cups water
- 1/2 cup plain yogurt
- 1 tablespoon drained capers, chopped
- 1 tablespoon lemon juice
  Pepper
- 4 skin-on salmon fillets (about 1 1/2 pounds)

1. Bring carrots, onion, wine, dill sprigs, lemon slices, 2 teaspoons salt, and water to boil in Dutch oven over high heat. Reduce heat to low and simmer, covered, for 15 minutes.

2. Meanwhile, combine yogurt, capers, lemon juice, chopped dill, and salt and pepper to taste in bowl.

3. Add salmon to pot, cover, and simmer gently until fish is opaque and flakes easily at thickest point, 8 to 10 minutes. Using slotted spatula, carefully transfer salmon to serving platter. Serve with dill-yogurt sauce.

SEARED PORK CHOPS WITH MUSHROOM GRAVY
SERVES 4

To save time, look for sliced mushrooms in the produce section.

- 4 bone-in rib or center-cut pork chops, 3/4 to 1 inch thick
  Salt and pepper
- 2 teaspoons vegetable oil
- 3 tablespoons unsalted butter
- 1 pound white mushrooms, sliced (see note)
- 1 small onion, chopped fine
- 3 tablespoons all-purpose flour
- 2 cups low-sodium chicken broth
- 2 teaspoons minced fresh thyme
- 1 tablespoon Dijon mustard

1. Pat chops dry with paper towels and season with salt and pepper. Heat oil in large skillet over medium-high heat until just smoking. Cook chops until well browned and meat registers 145 degrees, about 5 minutes per side. Transfer to plate and tent with foil.

2. In now-empty skillet, cook butter, mushrooms, onion, and 1/4 teaspoon salt, covered, until softened, about 5 minutes. Remove lid and cook until moisture has evaporated, about 5 minutes. Sprinkle flour over mushrooms and stir to coat. Slowly stir in broth, thyme, and any accumulated pork juices and simmer until gravy has thickened, about 3 minutes. Off heat, stir in mustard and season with salt and pepper. Serve.

SESAME CHICKEN FINGERS WITH SPICY PEANUT SAUCE
SERVES 4

If your grocery store doesn't carry chicken tenderloins, make your own by slicing boneless, skinless breasts lengthwise into 3/4-inch strips.

- 6 tablespoons warm water
- 1/4 cup creamy peanut butter
- 1/4 cup hoisin sauce
- 1 garlic clove, minced
- 1 teaspoon red pepper flakes
- 1/4 cup chopped fresh cilantro
- 3/4 cup sesame seeds
- 1 1/2 pounds chicken tenderloins (see note)
  Salt and pepper
- 6 tablespoons vegetable oil

1. Whisk water, peanut butter, hoisin, garlic, pepper flakes, and cilantro in bowl. Place sesame seeds in shallow dish. Season chicken with salt and pepper and roll in sesame seeds, pressing to adhere.

2. Heat 3 tablespoons oil in large nonstick skillet over medium-high heat until just smoking. Cook half of chicken until golden brown and cooked through, about 3 minutes per side. Transfer to large plate lined with paper towels, wipe out skillet, and repeat with remaining oil and chicken. Serve with dipping sauce.

Hot Fudge Pudding Cake

We make a rich chocolate sauce for this cake by . . . pouring boiling water over the raw batter?

An unexpected technique turns regular pantry ingredients into a gooey, double-chocolate delight.

Most recipes for hot fudge pudding cake read like recipes for disaster. You mix flour, sugar, cocoa powder, baking powder, milk, and oil by hand—much like a brownie batter. Once the batter is scraped into the pan, the fun starts. A mixture of cocoa powder and sugar is sprinkled over the top, and then boiling water is poured into the pan. The "batter" goes into the oven—no stirring allowed—looking like a mess.

But as it bakes, the water, cocoa, and sugar bubble and brew and—as if by magic—form a chocolate sauce while the cake rises to the top. The result is a chewy, brownie-like cake saturated with pockets of pudding-style chocolate sauce. It's scooped out of the dish (not sliced like a regular cake) and usually gilded with a dollop of whipped cream or a scoop of ice cream that melts into the hot pudding.

Although this might sound like chocolate heaven (chocolate cake and chocolate sauce!), this recipe isn't without problems. What looks deceptively rich and fudgy often has little chocolate flavor, and the cake layer can be hit or miss—it can easily get too dry or too wet in the center. My goal was to develop a hot fudge pudding cake with the texture and flavor of a brownie and plenty of spoon-clinging pudding sauce dotted throughout.

For fuller, rounder chocolate flavor, I switched from the natural cocoa powder used in most old-fashioned recipes to Dutch-processed cocoa, the European-style cocoa now available in American supermarkets. I also doubled the amount of cocoa in the batter. A big handful of semisweet chocolate chips added another layer of chocolate flavor and ensured plenty of gooey pockets in the baked cake. Trading flavorless vegetable oil for melted butter was another big improvement. For a more brownie-like texture, I added an egg yolk.

I found that the success of the sauce depends on using the right ratio of boiling water, sugar, and cocoa. Too much water (a common problem in the recipes I tested) and the sauce turned out thin and watery. I found that 1 cup of boiling water poured over ½ cup of sugar and ¼ cup of cocoa created a thick sauce with solid chocolate flavor.

My recipe still seems pretty unlikely, but now it has big chocolate flavor to match its gooey, fudgy appearance.

–Stephanie Alleyne

HOT FUDGE PUDDING CAKE SERVES 6 TO 8

Do not overbake this cake or the pudding sauce will burn in the pan and the cake will be dry, not fudgy. Store leftovers, covered with plastic, in the refrigerator. Reheat individual servings in a microwave on high power until hot (about 1 minute).

- 1 cup sugar
- ½ cup Dutch-processed cocoa powder
- 1 cup all-purpose flour
- 2 teaspoons baking powder
- ¼ teaspoon salt
- ½ cup milk
- 4 tablespoons (½ stick) unsalted butter, melted
- 1 large egg yolk
- 2 teaspoons vanilla extract
- ½ cup semisweet chocolate chips
- 1 cup boiling water
  Vanilla ice cream or whipped cream

1. Adjust oven rack to middle position and heat oven to 350 degrees. Spray 8-inch square glass or metal cake pan with cooking spray. Whisk ½ cup sugar with ¼ cup cocoa in small bowl.

2. Whisk flour, remaining ½ cup sugar, remaining ¼ cup cocoa, baking powder, and salt in large bowl. Whisk milk, butter, egg yolk, and vanilla in medium bowl until smooth. Stir milk mixture into flour mixture until just combined. Fold in chocolate chips (batter will be stiff).

3. Using rubber spatula, scrape batter into prepared pan and spread into corners. Sprinkle reserved cocoa mixture evenly over top. Gently pour boiling water over cocoa. Do not stir.

4. Bake until top of cake looks cracked, sauce is bubbling, and toothpick inserted into cakey area comes out with moist crumbs attached (see photos), about 25 minutes. Cool on rack for at least 10 minutes. To serve, scoop warm cake into individual serving bowls and top with vanilla ice cream or whipped cream.

BABY CAKES

Put a fancy spin on this homey recipe by baking up individual pudding cakes. Spray eight 6-ounce ovenproof ramekins or coffee cups with cooking spray. Fill each with 2 tablespoons batter. Top each with 1½ tablespoons cocoa mixture, followed by 2 tablespoons boiling water. Arrange cups on rimmed baking sheet and bake until tops are just cracked, 20 to 25 minutes.

Kitchen Know-How
IS IT DONE YET?

This highly unconventional cake breaks most of the usual rules, including how to judge when it's ready to come out of the oven.

1. When the top is crackled like a brownie and the sauce is bubbling up from the bottom, it's time to start testing for doneness. For the most accurate test, insert the toothpick close to the edge, where the cake is firmest. (Don't insert the toothpick in the center, where the cake should be gooey.)

2. The toothpick should have large, moist crumbs—but no gooey batter—attached. Check at least 2 spots to be certain that what's sticking to the toothpick isn't just a melted chocolate chip.

Cincinnati Chili

Warm spices and a host of garnishes lend this regional chili its unique character.

We set out on the road to discover the secrets to this chili that's heavily spiced but never spicy.

Road Trip: A Taste of Cincinnati

Where do the citizens of Cincinnati go for their chili? There are hundreds of choices, from mega-chains like Skyline and Gold Star to small independents like Camp Washington and U.S. Chili. After visiting a half-dozen chili parlors in one day (yes, I ate a lot of chili), I favored Empress Chili, the birthplace of Cincinnati chili.

Empress Chili was opened by two Greek immigrants, Tom and John Kiradjieff, in 1922. What was originally a hot dog cart set up outside a burlesque club has become a chain with 10 franchises. I ate at the Vine Street location, where the ambiance is Greek diner meets high school cafeteria. The food is served on thick white plates and cafeteria-style trays that you slide down the counter to the cashier. Each tiny table is stocked with hot sauce, paper napkins, and oyster crackers to crumble over the chili.

On my first visit, the franchise owner, Edie, called out from behind the counter to check on me before turning to her next customer. And if I wasn't charmed enough by the friendly Midwestern atmosphere, as I sat down to eat I watched a police officer walk behind the counter to pour himself a root beer before heading out on patrol. –J.S.

I had traveled to Cincinnati for the sole purpose of tasting the city's famous chili, but I was still surprised when it was placed on my tray. It was brown, thin, and served over a mound of spaghetti—it was nothing like the thick, red stew I've called "chili" my entire life. I quickly learned that this chili is almost never served by itself; it is either spooned atop hot dogs (called Coneys) or ladled over spaghetti. What's more, Cincinnati residents top their chili with beans, onions, oyster crackers, and a high pile of shredded cheese. As for the flavor, Cincinnati chili is packed with warm spices, such as cinnamon, allspice, and cloves, that taste more like Morocco than Tex-Mex. Although it looked a bit odd, I was immediately impressed by this strange concoction.

On my first day back in the test kitchen, I pulled together every recipe I could find in hopes of re-creating that chili. Unfortunately, what I discovered was a list of ingredients that read like a veritable census of spices. In addition to the warm spices I had detected on my trip, many recipes included nutmeg, mace, ginger, mustard, thyme, and even chocolate to round out the flavor. Through several tests, I cut the ingredients down to a manageable list. Cinnamon, allspice, chili powder, and oregano made the cut. Chocolate (despite whisperings that it's a secret ingredient in some of the city's chili parlors) didn't—whether I used cocoa powder or bar chocolate, my tasters didn't like it. With a bit of tomato paste for color and richness, and dark brown sugar to add a molasses tang, I had authentic Cincinnati flavor with a minimum of spice jars.

But Cincinnati chili isn't defined by spices alone—another hallmark is the saucy, ultra-tender texture of the ground beef. From my time in Cincinnati, I knew that most chili parlors boil the raw meat in water, drain it, and then add it to the spiced liquid. Boiling helps keep the beef extremely tender during the cooking process, which takes just minutes, not hours like most chili recipes. Instead of boiling the beef in a separate pot (a procedure that makes sense in a big restaurant kitchen but not at home), I hoped to simmer the raw meat directly in my spices and liquid; this way, I could get the correct texture while also infusing the meat with flavor (and saving on dishes).

For my simmering medium, I sautéed some onion and garlic with the dry spices and then added chicken broth (beef broth deadened the flavors) and tomato sauce (for its smooth texture). After simmering the ground beef for about 15 minutes, the chili was flavorful and the meat very tender. I boiled up some spaghetti, spooned my chili on top, and added cheese, onion, beans, and oyster crackers. After just one bite, I felt like I was back in Cincinnati. –Jeremy Sauer

CINCINNATI CHILI
SERVES 6 TO 8

Use canned tomato sauce for this recipe—do not use jarred spaghetti sauce. For the 5 ways to serve Cincinnati Chili, see page 31.

- 1 tablespoon vegetable oil
- 2 onions, chopped fine
- 1 garlic clove, minced
- 2 tablespoons tomato paste
- 2 tablespoons chili powder
- 1 tablespoon dried oregano
- 1½ teaspoons cinnamon
  Salt
- ¾ teaspoon pepper
- ¼ teaspoon allspice
- 2 cups low-sodium chicken broth
- 2 cups canned tomato sauce
- 2 tablespoons cider vinegar
- 2 teaspoons dark brown sugar
- 1½ pounds 85-percent lean ground beef

1. Heat oil in Dutch oven over medium-high heat until shimmering. Cook onions until soft and browned around edges, about 8 minutes. Add garlic, tomato paste, chili powder, oregano, cinnamon, 1 teaspoon salt, pepper, and allspice and cook until fragrant, about 1 minute. Stir in chicken broth, tomato sauce, vinegar, and sugar.

2. Add beef and stir to break up meat. Bring to boil, reduce heat to medium-low, and simmer until chili is deep brown and slightly thickened, 15 to 20 minutes. Season with salt and serve. (Chili can be refrigerated in airtight container for up to 3 days or frozen for up to 2 months.)

Freezer Chicken Pot Pies

How to Make
INDIVIDUAL POT PIES

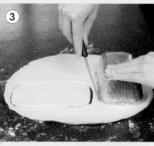

1. Brush pie crust with beaten egg.
2. Place a second crust over egg-washed dough.
3. Use a disposable aluminum pan turned upside down to cut out 3 pastry toppings from double-thick pie dough. Repeat with 2 more pie crusts.
4. Place 1 piece of pastry over the filling in each pan and use a fork to seal the edges.

What's the secret to frozen pot pies that are creamy, not dry?

Chicken pot pie is comfort food, so when I really feel like eating it, I definitely don't feel like making it. Could I streamline chicken pot pie and make it into something I could pull out of the freezer and bake whenever I needed some TLC?

Most recipes call for sautéing vegetables and making a creamy sauce in the same pan. I was willing to do this work, but I didn't want to poach or roast a whole chicken—the usual protocol in classic recipes. Could I use boneless breasts to simplify the process? Simmering the breasts in chicken broth yielded bland results, but browning them first made the chicken taste better.

Homemade pie crust seemed like too much labor, but store-bought refrigerator pie crusts didn't work as I had hoped—they were about half the ideal thickness. Inspiration struck: Why not "glue" two pieces of dough together with a beaten egg to make a double-thick crust? Sure enough, this easy trick worked.

My recipe was progressing, but how would it do coming out of the freezer? I divided the filling into disposable individual loaf pans (to make thawing and cooking faster) and froze them for a few days. Then I heated the frozen pot pies in the oven. Although the flavor was great, the filling was mysteriously dry and the pastry was charred.

I discovered that the crust was absorbing sauce on either side of the freezer. The solution was to add what looked to be too much sauce to each pie: By the time they were frozen and then baked, the consistency was just right. And to make sure the crust browned more slowly (thus giving the filling time to heat up), I covered the pot pies for about half of their baking time. I now had freezer-friendly chicken pot pies to enjoy whenever the mood strikes.

–Katie Henderson

FREEZER CHICKEN POT PIES SERVES 6

To preserve their color, don't thaw the peas before using. Each box of pie dough contains 2 crusts; you will use all 4 crusts for this recipe.

- 1½ **pounds boneless, skinless chicken breasts**
  Salt and pepper
- 2 **tablespoons vegetable oil**
- 5½ **cups low-sodium chicken broth**
- 2 **tablespoons unsalted butter**
- 1 **medium onion, chopped fine**
- 3 **medium carrots, peeled and chopped**
- 1 **celery rib, chopped fine**
- ½ **cup all-purpose flour**
- ¼ **cup milk**
- 2 **teaspoons minced fresh thyme**
- 2 **tablespoons lemon juice**
- 2 **(15-ounce) boxes Pillsbury Ready to Roll Pie Crust (see note)**
- 1 **large egg, beaten, plus 1 large egg, beaten, for baking**
- 1½ **cups frozen peas**

1. To make ahead: Pat chicken dry with paper towels and season with salt and pepper. Heat 1 tablespoon oil in large Dutch oven over high heat until just smoking. Cook chicken until well browned, about 2½ minutes per side. Add broth and bring to boil. Cover and simmer over low heat until chicken is cooked through, 6 to 8 minutes. Transfer chicken to large plate and strain broth into bowl.

2. Melt butter with remaining 1 tablespoon oil in now-empty Dutch oven over medium-high heat. Cook onion, carrots, celery, and ¼ teaspoon salt until lightly browned and softened, 8 to 10 minutes. Reduce heat to medium, add flour, and cook 1 minute. Whisk in reserved broth, milk, and thyme and simmer until sauce thickens, about 10 minutes.

3. Meanwhile, using 2 forks, shred chicken into bite-sized pieces. Off heat, add chicken and lemon juice to sauce and season with salt and pepper. Transfer filling to medium bowl and cool until just warm. Cover with plastic wrap and refrigerate until well chilled, about 1 hour.

4. Unwrap and unroll pie crusts onto lightly floured counter. Following photos at left, glue 2 crusts together using 1 beaten egg. Repeat with remaining 2 crusts. Cut out 6 pastry toppings. Stir frozen peas into cold filling and divide mixture among six 2-cup disposable aluminum loaf pans. Top with pastry and use fork to seal edges. Using paring knife, make 3 steam vents in each crust.

Tightly wrap each loaf pan in 2 layers of plastic wrap and 1 layer of aluminum foil. Freeze for up to 2 months.

5. When ready to serve: Adjust oven rack to middle position and heat oven to 400 degrees. Unwrap frozen pot pies and arrange on rimmed baking sheet. Brush crusts with egg, cover with foil, and bake 40 minutes. Uncover and bake until crusts are golden brown, about 35 minutes. Let pot pies rest 10 minutes before serving.

A Freezer-Worthy Filling

When we tried freezing standard chicken pot pie recipes, the filling baked up too dry. Our solution was to make the filling extra saucy—but this only works if you freeze the pot pies.

FROZEN THEN BAKED
Our saucy filling can withstand freezing and emerges rich and creamy from the oven.

BAKED WITHOUT FREEZING
If baked right away, our saucy filling creates a soupy mess.

A saucy filling and double-thick crust are the secrets to a pot pie that can be successfully frozen before baking.

Better Citrus Salads

With the help of carefully chosen supporting ingredients—and an easy but essential technique—citrus can bring new life to winter salads.

Fresh orange and grapefruit can add spark to savory green salads—especially in the middle of winter, when citrus fruit is the most appealing thing in the produce aisle. But in most of the recipes we tried for this kind of salad, the fruit tended to get lost in the mix.

For maximum impact, get to the heart of citrus fruit by removing not only the peel but also the bitter pith and fibers. Some simple knife work produces perfect segments of grapefruit or orange flesh. To really play up the citrus component in these salads, we also built the dressings from the juice of citrus fruits. You don't need a blender or a whisk for these dressings, as everything can be shaken together in a jar.

–Stephanie Alleyne

> **Visit us online**
> For a Citrus Blue Cheese Salad recipe, visit **CooksCountry.com** and look for Cook's Country Extras.

Packaged greens help these sweet-tart salads come together quickly.

ORANGE GINGER SALAD
SERVES 4

You can find sliced glazed nuts in the party-nut aisle of your supermarket (see page 31).

- 1 cup segments plus 2 tablespoons juice from 3 large navel oranges (see photos)
- 2 cups packaged shredded cabbage or coleslaw mix
- 4 scallions, sliced thin
- 1 teaspoon soy sauce
- 1 teaspoon honey
- 1 teaspoon grated fresh ginger
- 1/4 teaspoon pepper
- 3 tablespoons extra-virgin olive oil
- 1 (5-ounce) bag arugula
- 1/2 cup sliced glazed almonds (see note)

Roughly chop orange segments and toss with cabbage and scallions in medium bowl. Combine orange juice, soy sauce, honey, ginger, pepper, and oil in small jar. Seal tightly with lid and shake dressing to combine. Toss cabbage mixture with 1 tablespoon dressing. Toss arugula with remaining dressing in large bowl and divide among 4 plates. Top arugula with cabbage mixture and sprinkle with almonds. Serve.

MEXI-CALI SALAD
SERVES 4

Oranges, black beans, and avocado get a kick from tangy lime.

- 1 cup segments from 3 large navel oranges (see photos)
- 3/4 cup canned black beans, rinsed and drained
- 1 ripe avocado, pitted, peeled, and cut into 1/4-inch chunks
- 2 tablespoons lime juice
- 1/2 garlic clove, minced
- 1/8 teaspoon dried oregano
- 1/8 teaspoon chili powder
- 1/4 teaspoon salt
- 3 tablespoons extra-virgin olive oil
- 1 (6-ounce) bag baby spinach

Roughly chop orange segments and toss with beans and avocado in medium bowl. Combine lime juice, garlic, oregano, chili powder, salt, and oil in small jar. Seal tightly with lid and shake dressing to combine. Toss bean mixture with 1 tablespoon dressing. Toss spinach with remaining dressing in large bowl and divide among 4 plates. Top spinach with bean mixture. Serve.

GOAT CHEESE AND DOUBLE CITRUS SALAD
SERVES 4

Spring lettuce mix is also sold as mesclun mix, baby greens mix, or mixed field greens.

- 1/3 cup segments plus 1 tablespoon juice from 1 large navel orange (see photos)
- 1/2 cup segments plus 1 tablespoon juice from 1 Ruby Red grapefruit (see photos)
- 1 teaspoon minced shallot
- 1/4 teaspoon salt
- 1/4 teaspoon pepper
- 3 tablespoons extra-virgin olive oil
- 1 (5-ounce) bag spring lettuce mix
- 1 cup crumbled goat cheese
- 3/4 cup glazed pecans (see page 31)

Roughly chop orange and grapefruit segments. Combine juices, shallot, salt, pepper, and oil in small jar. Seal tightly with lid and shake dressing to combine. Toss citrus with 1 tablespoon dressing in medium bowl. Toss lettuce mix with remaining dressing in large bowl and divide among 4 plates. Top lettuce with citrus, cheese, and pecans. Serve.

Kitchen Know-How SEGMENTING CITRUS

Cutting perfect, jewel-like segments from citrus is much easier than you think—especially if you use a sharp paring knife or small serrated knife. Work over a bowl to catch the juices.

1. Cut the ends from the fruit. Following the natural curve of the fruit, trim the peel away, down just beyond the white pith, to expose the flesh of the fruit.

2. Insert the blade between the membrane and pulp of each segment and cut toward the center, separating the fruit from the membrane.

3. After releasing the segment, wiggle the blade away from you. The segment should pop right out.

Getting to Know Citrus Fruits

Sweet, tart, and high in vitamin C, citrus fruits are favorites across the globe. We picked, peeled, and ate 16 varieties, some common, some obscure. Listed below are our tasting notes.

Orange
COLORFUL AND FRAGRANT

The name of this fruit does not refer to its color—the word *orange* comes from the ancient Tamil word *naru*, which means "fragrant." The most common supermarket variety is the Valencia, a type of navel orange. Its flesh is "juicy and smooth," with a "mild, tangy acidity."

White Grapefruit
PUCKER UP

These large tropical fruits are grown primarily in the southern U.S. and are so named because they grow in tight clusters, much like grapes. Their "dense" flesh holds an abundance of "bracingly sharp" juice that has hints of "raw sugar cane" sweetness.

Blood Orange
ITALIAN CONNECTION

These thin-skinned oranges are sometimes called Moro oranges. Originally cultivated in Italy, they have a red blush on their skin and magenta to blood-red flesh. Their flavor is "winy and complex," with a "fresh berry" character.

Lime
MARGARITAS AND MORE

The common Persian lime is just as likely to garnish a tall glass of cola as it is to season a spicy salsa. Limes have a "clean, bright" flavor with "herbal" and "floral" overtones and juice with slightly "less bite than a lemon."

Key Lime
TART AND TINY

Although named for the Florida Keys, these golf ball–sized limes are native to Southeast Asia. Key limes have a complex "earthy-floral" aroma and "sharp" juice. You'll need at least four Key limes to equal the juice of one Persian lime.

Clementine
SEEDLESS SWEETIES

Clementines are typically imported from Spain or North Africa. Their thin skin peels easily to reveal plump, seedless segments. Clementines have a "perfumed, floral aroma" and a "honey-sweet" flavor.

Tangelo
BRIGHT AS THE SUN

An orange and grapefruit hybrid, the tangelo is slightly larger than an orange, with a small, tapered neck. Neon orange in color, its flesh has a "silky, fine-grained" quality and a "bright acidity" that is reminiscent of the fruit drink Sunny Delight.

Cara Cara Orange
PRETTY IN PINK

Originally cultivated in Venezuela, this medium-sized variety of navel orange is notable for its "salmon-colored" flesh. Its flesh is "light, sweet," and relatively "low in acidity," with a "flowery" aroma and "subtle strawberry finish."

Lemon
SAVORY AND SWEET

The common lemon is a variety called Eureka. Its juice has a mouth-puckering "white wine vinegar" tartness, with a hint of "Granny Smith apple."

Ruby Red Grapefruit
SWEET AND SOUR

This sweet variety of grapefruit, with its blushing orange rind and meaty, brilliant-pink flesh, is most commonly associated with Texas. Its flavor is "slightly sour," with "hints of honey and lime" and a "pleasantly bitter" finish.

Tangerine
HOLIDAY SPECIAL

Tangerines belong to the mandarin family of oranges, which have thin, loose skins. They are easily peeled, but they can also be "very seedy." They are "full of juice" and "low in acid," with a sweet flavor that reminded some tasters of "baby aspirin."

Kumquat
SWEET-SKINNED

This olive-sized fruit from China has sweet skin and sour flesh. The entire fruit, from seeds to skin, can be eaten, making kumquats excellent candidates for preserves and pickling. They're "crunchy" and "bittersweet," with a "complex, anise" aroma. Eat whole or slice and cook.

Pummelo
BIG DADDY

The largest citrus fruit, a pummelo can measure 12 inches across and weigh upward of 15 pounds. They have light yellow skin and "sweet-sour" flesh. Although their flavor is "light and almost nutty," an abundance of "chewy" membranes can leave a "bitter aftertaste."

Seville Orange
LADY MARMALADE

This sour orange has very tart flesh and high pectin content, making it ideal for use in marmalades. Its aromatic zest is used to flavor a number of products, from liqueurs to perfumes. Its "dry" texture and "bitter" flavor make it more suitable for cooking than eating out of hand.

Ugli Fruit
HOMELY BUT TASTY

With its wrinkled, haggard appearance, this fruit certainly lives up to its name. Relatively large in size, the ugli fruit is related to the tangerine, grapefruit, and sour orange. Its thick, greenish skin drapes "candy-sweet, fibrous" flesh that tastes like "an orange with a hint of banana."

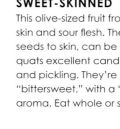

Meyer Lemon
HYBRIDIZED LEMON

Some botanists believe this fruit is a cross between a lemon and an orange (the exact origin is unkown). The Meyer's skin is smooth and deep yellowish-orange, and its juice is sweeter than other types of lemon. It has a "green grapey" taste that is "aromatic" but still "assertively acidic."

Chinese Sticky Ribs

When done right, these ribs are tender, meaty, and sweet. But, just as often, they turn out tough, greasy, and saccharine.

These sticky ribs are spicy, sweet, and tender.

When I was a kid, Friday nights meant a visit to our local Chinese restaurant. My favorite thing to order—besides a Shirley Temple—was the sticky barbecued ribs appetizer. The ribs were exotically spicy, moist, and tender, and they were so sticky that Dad always had to flag down the waiter for extra napkins.

Since then I've ordered ribs from many Chinese restaurants, and what I usually get is a carton of red bones with a minuscule amount of dry, jerky-like meat. They are more greasy than sticky, and their neon-red color is a sad attempt at camouflaging their leathery exterior. If I wanted ribs as good as the ones I remembered, I'd have to make them at home.

I found recipes for sticky ribs that used five different cooking methods, then headed into the test kitchen to try all five. Ribs that were boiled, broiled, steamed, and baked on a rack (or some combination of these methods) were all tough, fatty, and flavorless, but one technique showed promise: oven-braising. Slowly cooked in a flavorful sauce, these ribs were tender, most of the fat had rendered out, and the Asian flavors in the braising liquid permeated the meat. Although they still needed work, I decided to pursue this method.

I set two racks of spareribs in my roasting pan and then turned to flavoring components from the first round of recipes. Ginger, garlic, cilantro, scallion, and orange peel went into the pan. To get the barbecue and sweet components, I added hoisin sauce (a flavorful Chinese barbecue sauce), sugar, and sherry. The ribs started out steaming in the hoisin/sherry mixture. As moisture came out of the pork and the liquid level rose, the ribs braised to a falling-off-the-bone texture. They were juicy and meaty, but the cooking liquid wasn't the sticky glaze I had hoped for.

I tried skimming the fat off the braising liquid and reducing it to a thicker consistency. This mixture was getting stickier but still wasn't syrupy enough to brush on like a coat of paint. Looking for a sticky ingredient to add, I first tried honey, but the resulting glaze was sickly sweet. I had better luck adding spicy red pepper jelly. After a few minutes under the broiler and several coats of glaze, the ribs were a rich mahogany color and as sticky as a lollipop—but not too sweet. I sliced the ribs between the bones and glazed them one last time. I may have graduated from Shirley Temples, but I'll never outgrow sticky ribs.

—Diane Unger

CHINESE STICKY RIBS
SERVES 6

Regular full-size spareribs will not work in this recipe; they are too large and fatty. Hoisin sauce can be found in the international aisle of your supermarket. Use a vegetable peeler to remove wide strips of orange peel. For tips on removing the membrane from the ribs as directed in step 1, see page 31.

Ribs

- 2 racks pork ribs (2½ to 3½ pounds each), preferably St. Louis cut or baby back ribs
- 1 cup hoisin sauce
- 1 cup sugar
- ½ cup soy sauce
- ½ cup dry sherry
- 1 (6-inch) piece ginger, peeled and sliced into rounds
- 6 garlic cloves, smashed
  Strips of peel from 1 orange
- 1½ teaspoons cayenne pepper
- 30 sprigs fresh cilantro, stems chopped coarse (reserve leaves for glaze)
- 8 scallions, white parts cut into 1-inch pieces (reserve green parts for garnish)

Glaze

- 1 (10-ounce) jar hot red pepper jelly (see box at left)
- ½ cup cider vinegar
- ¼ cup minced fresh cilantro leaves
- ¼ teaspoon cayenne pepper
  Minced scallion greens

1. For the ribs: Adjust oven rack to middle position and heat oven to 350 degrees. With tip of paring knife, loosen membrane on underside of each rack of ribs. Grab membrane with paper towel and pull it off slowly in single piece. Combine remaining ingredients in large roasting pan. Add spareribs to pan, turning to coat both sides, and arrange meaty side down. Cover pan tightly with foil and cook until just tender, 2½ to 3 hours. Transfer ribs to large plate.

2. For the glaze: Strain 3 cups cooking liquid from roasting pan into large nonstick skillet (do not wash roasting pan) and discard solids and remaining liquid. Using wide spoon, skim fat from liquid. Stir in jelly and vinegar. Bring to simmer over medium-high heat and cook until syrupy and reduced to 2 cups, 15 to 20 minutes. Off heat, stir in cilantro and cayenne.

3. Heat broiler (do not raise oven rack). Pour enough water into roasting pan to cover bottom and fit pan with flat roasting rack. Reserve ½ cup glaze for serving. Arrange ribs on rack meaty side down and brush with glaze. Place roasting pan back on middle rack in oven and broil until beginning to brown, 2 to 4 minutes. Flip ribs over, brush with more glaze, then broil, brushing ribs with glaze every 2 to 4 minutes, until ribs are deep mahogany color, 9 to 12 minutes (watch broiler carefully). Transfer ribs to cutting board, tent with foil, and let rest 10 minutes. Slice between bones, transfer ribs to platter, and brush with reserved glaze. Sprinkle with scallions. Serve.

Make Ahead: The ribs and glaze can be prepared through step 2 up to 2 days in advance. Wrap the ribs tightly in foil and refrigerate. Transfer glaze to microwave-safe bowl, cover, and refrigerate. Before serving, allow ribs to stand at room temperature for 1 hour. Heat glaze in microwave on high power until warm, about 1 minute. Proceed with step 3 as directed.

What to Do with Leftovers: Pork Fried Rice

Made at home, fried rice can be light and fresh—and fast.

Fried rice is a great way to use up leftover meat from our Chinese Sticky Ribs. Recipes for fried rice typically call for cold (leftover) white rice, so if you served white rice with the sticky ribs, you can certainly use any leftovers for this recipe. But if you don't have leftover rice, Uncle Ben's Ready Rice works especially well. This rice is precooked, so all you have to do is warm it in the skillet. I also found that packaged coleslaw mix made a great stand-in for the usual shredded cabbage and required no prep.

–Diane Unger

PORK FRIED RICE SERVES 4

Be sure to avoid "seasoned" rice vinegar, which contains sugar and will make the fried rice too sweet. Feel free to use 4 cups of leftover rice instead of the Uncle Ben's Ready Rice. This recipe works with any leftover roast pork or ham.

- 3 tablespoons soy sauce
- 2 tablespoons rice vinegar or cider vinegar
- 1 tablespoon hot sauce
- 2 tablespoons vegetable oil
- 4 large eggs, beaten lightly
- 8 ounces white button mushrooms, sliced
- 2 cups packaged coleslaw mix
- 8 scallions, white parts sliced thin, green parts cut into 1/2-inch pieces
- 2 (8.8-ounce) packages Uncle Ben's Original Long Grain Ready Rice
- 1–2 cups shredded leftover meat from Chinese Sticky Ribs
- 1 cup bean sprouts, chopped coarse

1. Combine soy sauce, vinegar, and hot sauce in small bowl. Heat 2 teaspoons oil in large nonstick skillet over medium-high heat until just smoking. Cook eggs, scrambling and breaking into small pieces, until cooked through, about 1 1/2 minutes. Transfer to separate small bowl.

2. Return skillet to medium-high and heat 2 teaspoons oil until just smoking. Cook mushrooms until lightly browned, about 5 minutes. Transfer to medium bowl. Heat remaining 2 teaspoons oil in skillet until just smoking. Cook coleslaw mix and scallion whites until just softened, about 1 minute. Add rice, soy sauce mixture, rib meat, bean sprouts, egg, and scallion greens and cook, stirring constantly, until heated through, 1 to 2 minutes. Serve.

On the Side: Stir-Fried Sesame Broccoli

Sesame seeds and sesame oil create a sauce with bold—but not greasy—flavor.

A lot can go wrong with this deceptively simple Asian stir-fry. What should be bright, tender-crisp broccoli dressed with the toasty flavor of sesame is usually overcooked, army-issue trees drowned in a pool of greasy sesame oil. The right stir-fry method (see page 30) takes care of the broccoli. As for the sauce, I ramped up the flavor with toasted sesame seeds. Along with just a tablespoon of sesame oil, the seeds gave my sauce big, bold flavor without the usual oil slick.

To round out the sauce, I settled on a trio of salty, sweet, and tart ingredients (soy sauce, brown sugar, and orange juice), along with ginger, garlic, and hot red pepper flakes. Cornstarch gave the sauce plenty of glossy sheen and helped it cling to the broccoli. **–Bridget Lancaster**

SESAME BROCCOLI SERVES 4

Use a chef's knife to trim away the fibrous outer peel on the broccoli stems.

- 1/4 cup orange juice
- 2 tablespoons soy sauce
- 1 tablespoon toasted sesame oil
- 1 1/2 teaspoons brown sugar
- 1/4 teaspoon red pepper flakes
- 1 1/2 teaspoons cornstarch
- 3 garlic cloves, minced
- 2 teaspoons minced fresh ginger
- 2 teaspoons sesame seeds
- 2 teaspoons vegetable oil
- 2 1/2 pounds broccoli, florets cut into 1-inch pieces; stems trimmed, peeled (see note), and sliced into 1/4-inch rounds

1. Whisk orange juice, soy sauce, 2 teaspoons sesame oil, brown sugar, pepper flakes, and cornstarch in medium bowl. Combine garlic, ginger, and remaining 1 teaspoon sesame oil in small bowl.

2. Toast sesame seeds in large nonstick skillet over medium heat until golden, about 8 minutes, shaking pan frequently. Transfer sesame seeds to plate.

3. Heat vegetable oil in now-empty skillet over medium-high heat until just smoking. Add broccoli and stir-fry for 30 seconds. Add 1/2 cup water, cover, and cook over medium heat until broccoli is tender-crisp, 2 to 4 minutes. Transfer to serving bowl and tent with foil. Add garlic mixture to empty skillet and cook over medium-high heat until fragrant, about 30 seconds. Add orange juice mixture and cook until sauce thickens and coats back of spoon, about 1 minute. Pour sauce over broccoli and sprinkle with sesame seeds. Serve.

Lemon Chicken

Lemons should be able to transform plain old chicken into something exciting. Then why do most lemon chicken recipes have so little flavor?

This dish's bright lemon flavor comes from adding lemon twice and using ingredients—like honey and sour cream—that enhance its flavor.

Chicken and lemon is a classic paring, but infusing the meat with bright lemon flavor can be difficult. Roasting, sautéing, and broiling chicken with lemon showed me just how fleeting lemon can be. Simmering browned chicken breasts in a lemon sauce (a process called braising) seemed more promising—in part because the chicken was literally bathed in lemon. As a bonus, I could then reduce the braising liquid into a sauce for another hit of lemon flavor.

Using bone-in, skin-on chicken breasts proved to be immeasurably beneficial in this recipe; by first browning the skin I was able to create a flavorful base of chicken flavor that only intensified as I continued cooking. The bones added flavor to the braising liquid and protected the meat from the direct heat of the pan.

To bulk up the dish, I played around with different vegetables, trying various combinations of carrots, celery, bell pepper, and onion, among others. I was surprised that my tasters overwhelmingly preferred whole—not minced—shallots paired with the bold taste of lemon in this recipe. I added a head of peeled whole garlic cloves, treating them, like the shallots, more as a vegetable than a seasoning. Blooming additional minced garlic in the oil added another layer of flavor to the dish.

It was time to refine the lemon flavor. Many recipes call for braising the chicken in white wine and lemon, but my tasters found the combination of the wine and lemon juice too acidic. I had much better luck using chicken broth, which provided richness and chicken flavor without overpowering the lemon. A little honey kept the lemon from tasting sour.

After about 25 minutes, the chicken was moist and lemony. I set the cooked chicken aside and cranked up the heat to reduce the braising liquid into a sauce. My key discovery was that adding a few lemon slices to the sauce as it simmered down provided fresh lemon flavor and brought the whole dish back to life. A tablespoon of fresh thyme added a welcome herbal note, and sour cream thickened the sauce and enhanced the tang of the lemon. In just over a half-hour, I had created an easy, rustic recipe that was bursting with lemon flavor. –**Stephanie Alleyne**

LEMON CHICKEN
SERVES 4

Adding the sour cream to the sauce off heat will prevent the sauce from curdling. Shallots are used as a vegetable here, but if you prefer you can add one medium red onion, minced, with the whole garlic cloves instead.

- 4 bone-in, skin-on split chicken breasts (about 3 pounds), ribs removed (see below)
  Salt and pepper
- 2 tablespoons olive oil
- 12 shallots, peeled and halved lengthwise if large
- 16 garlic cloves, peeled, 12 cloves left whole, 4 cloves minced
- 1 tablespoon chopped fresh thyme
- 1½ cups low-sodium chicken broth
- 3 tablespoons juice plus 4 thin slices from 2 lemons
- 1 tablespoon honey
- ¼ cup sour cream
- 1 tablespoon chopped fresh parsley

1. Pat chicken dry with paper towels and season with salt and pepper. Heat oil in large skillet over medium-high heat until just smoking. Cook chicken skin side down until well browned, about 4 to 6 minutes. Transfer chicken to large plate.

2. Reduce heat to medium and add shallots, whole garlic cloves, and ½ teaspoon salt to empty pan. Cook until vegetables begin to soften and turn spotty brown, about 5 minutes. Add minced garlic and thyme and cook until fragrant, about 30 seconds. Stir in broth, lemon juice, and honey. Return chicken (skin side up) and accumulated juices to skillet. Bring to boil, cover, and reduce heat to medium-low. Simmer until thickest part of chicken registers 160 degrees, 20 to 25 minutes.

3. Transfer chicken to serving platter and tent with foil. Add lemon slices to pan, increase heat to high, and boil until sauce is slightly thickened, about 7 minutes. Off heat, whisk in sour cream and parsley and season with salt and pepper. Pour sauce over chicken. Serve.

Kitchen Know-How RIB REMOVAL

Most skin-on, bone-in chicken breasts are sold with a portion of the ribs still attached, but the ribs don't contain much meat and are awkward to eat around. Here's how we remove them.

1. Place the chicken breasts skin side down on a cutting board and pull the rib cage taut, away from the meat. Cut in a straight line between the ribs and breast meat to remove the ribs.

2. Turn the chicken breasts skin side up and snip away stray bits of fat and sinew. Chicken fat is butter yellow, in contrast to the skin, which is pinkish-white.

Italian Pot Roast

How do you use tomatoes, red wine, garlic to complement—but not overpower—pot roast?

Italian pot roast replaces the potatoes, carrots, and thin gravy of its American cousin with mushrooms, onions, and a thick sauce based on tomatoes, red wine, garlic, and herbs. Changing the vegetables was as easy as it sounds, but getting the sauce just right was not.

Many early recipes that I tried tasted like meat boiled in bad spaghetti sauce. The tomatoes, wine, garlic, and herbs competed with each other and tasted harsh, not complex. I decided to start at the beginning to create my version of this Italian classic.

Traditional pot roasts use fatty cuts of meat suited to long, slow cooking. With its beefy flavor and sufficient fat, the chuck-eye roast is the test kitchen's favorite cut for American pot roast, and I found no reason to change course.

After trying every likely tomato product—and in various combinations—I found that a mixture of canned diced tomatoes, tomato sauce, and tomato paste produced a rich, thick sauce that perfectly complemented the meat. The diced tomatoes added a fresh tomato flavor missing in recipes that called for just tomato sauce, while the tomato paste added intensity and helped give the finished sauce body.

Too much red wine added at the outset overpowered the other flavors in the pot. A modest ½ cup of wine boosted the flavor and deepened the color of the sauce. But after three hours in the oven, the brightness had cooked out of the wine. I found that refreshing the sauce with another ½ cup of wine at the end of cooking brought the brightness back.

My tasters thought the flavor of minced garlic (the traditional choice) was spent after three hours in the pot, no matter how much I used. I had better luck cutting a whole head of garlic in half and dropping it right into the pot, where it gently perfumed the meat and sauce. Another bonus: I could now squeeze some of the softened, mellowed garlic cloves right back into the pot for even more garlic flavor.

After testing a handful of different herbs, tasters preferred rosemary (added at the end of cooking so it didn't overpower everything) along with woodsy thyme (mellow enough to add at the start).

–Meredith Butcher

ITALIAN POT ROAST
SERVES 4 TO 6

Every piece of meat cooks differently, so start checking the roast after 2 hours. If there is a little resistance when prodded with a fork, it's done. Light, sweeter red wines, such as a Merlot or Beaujolais, work especially well with this recipe.

- 1 boneless chuck-eye roast (3½ to 4 pounds), tied (see photo, below right)
  Salt and pepper
- 2 tablespoons vegetable oil
- 1 medium onion, chopped
- 1 large celery rib, chopped
- 1 pound cremini or white mushrooms, quartered
- 2 tablespoons tomato paste
- 1 (14.5-ounce) can diced tomatoes
- ½ cup canned tomato sauce
- 2 teaspoons sugar
- ½ cup water
- 1 cup red wine (see note)
- 1 large garlic head, outer papery skins removed, then halved (photo 1, at right)
- 1 large sprig fresh thyme
- 1 sprig fresh rosemary

1. Adjust oven rack to middle position and heat oven to 300 degrees. Pat roast dry with paper towels and season with salt and pepper.

2. Heat oil in Dutch oven over medium-high heat until just smoking. Brown roast on all sides, 8 to 12 minutes. Transfer roast to large plate. Reduce heat to medium and cook onion, celery, mushrooms, and tomato paste until vegetables begin to soften, about 8 minutes. Add diced tomatoes, tomato sauce, sugar, water, ½ cup wine, garlic, and thyme. Return roast and accumulated juices to pot and bring to simmer over medium-high heat. Place piece of foil over pot (see page 31), cover with lid, and transfer pot to oven.

3. Cook until roast is just fork-tender, 2½ to 3½ hours, flipping roast after 1 hour. Uncover pot and let roast rest in juices for 30 minutes, skimming surface fat after 20 minutes. Transfer roast to carving board and tent with foil. Remove and reserve garlic head and skim remaining fat from pot. Add remaining ½ cup wine to pot, bring to boil over medium-high heat, and cook until sauce begins to thicken, about 12 minutes. Meanwhile, carefully squeeze garlic from halves and mash into paste. Add rosemary to pot and simmer until fragrant, about 2 minutes. Remove and discard rosemary and thyme sprigs, stir in mashed garlic, and season sauce with salt and pepper.

4. Remove twine from roast and cut meat against grain into ½-inch-thick slices, or pull apart into large pieces. Transfer meat to serving platter and pour ¾ cup sauce over meat. Serve with remaining sauce.

To ensure even cooking, simmer pot roast in the oven rather than the stovetop, where the sauce can scorch.

Kitchen Know-How
GETTING THE GARLIC RIGHT

Here's how we infuse our Italian Pot Roast with mellow garlic flavor.

1. Slice a whole head of garlic in half and add it to the pot.
2. Once the roast is done, squeeze the garlic cloves from their skins and mash the garlic with a fork.
3. Stir the mashed garlic back into the sauce.

To Tie or Not to Tie?

A tied roast will cook evenly and won't fall apart during the long cooking time. If your supermarket hasn't already done so, tie pieces of kitchen twine around the roast every inch or so.

FIT TO BE TIED
Make sure to use food-safe cotton twine (often sold as butcher's twine) when tying the roast.

1. Brushing the just-baked cake with a thin glaze produces a moist and flavorful crust.
2. When the cake is partially cooled, slowly pour the thicker second glaze over the cake.
3. Sprinkle the orange sugar over the glazed cake.

Can Do

A few tablespoons of thawed frozen orange juice concentrate gives our glaze a potent orange flavor without compromising its texture.

BIG FLAVOR
Orange juice concentrate (along with lemon juice and orange zest) adds zip to our potent orange glaze.

Orange Bundt Cake

Oranges don't pack the wallop of lemons—especially in baked goods. Could we coax big flavor out of this subtle citrus?

An orange Bundt cake should be moist, rich, and tender. While the correct texture is relatively easy to achieve, developing assertive orange flavor is more of a challenge. All citrus dulls when baked, but while a lemon is tart and bright—thanks to its high acidity—the mild flavor of an orange is especially fleeting. I armed myself with a crate of Florida's finest and headed to the test kitchen to create an orange Bundt cake that tasted like it was straight from the grove.

Since most lemon cakes are flavored with lemon zest, I used a favorite lemon Bundt cake recipe, swapping the lemon zest for orange zest. The recipe called for a mere teaspoon of zest, but tasters demanded 2 tablespoons, which yielded the most orange flavor without tasting medicinal.

The zest did produce a fair amount of orange flavor, but it was one-dimensional and flat. I wondered if any other orange ingredients might help. I baked cakes with powdered Tang, orange juice concentrate, orange extract, and orange oil. The cakes made with Tang and juice concentrate were sickeningly sweet, with weak orange flavor, while the cakes made with extract and oil tasted like furniture polish. I returned my attention to fresh oranges—but this time, to their juice.

Bundt cake recipes typically call for about a cup of dairy, usually milk or buttermilk. I wondered if I could replace the dairy with fresh orange juice. I made a cake with each of the three liquids. It was clear that the juice lent a mellow orange background flavor to the more astringent and perfumed zest, whereas the cakes made with milk and buttermilk seemed bland.

For more orange flavor, I made a thin confectioners' sugar glaze that easily absorbed into the hot cake, then added more confectioners' sugar to the mixture to thicken it for an eye-catching glaze. I had been using a mixture of orange juice, lemon juice (for brightness), and confectioners' sugar in the glaze, but replacing the juice with undiluted orange juice concentrate provided an extra punch of flavor.

A dusting of granulated sugar flavored with orange zest lent a final burst of flavor and delicate crunch to my cake. With three layers of orange flavor—zest, fresh juice, and concentrate—my cake now tasted as bright as the Florida sun. –Cali Rich

ORANGE BUNDT CAKE

SERVES 12
When grating orange zest, remove just the outer orange part of the peel—the inner white part is very bitter.

Cake
- 18 tablespoons unsalted butter (2¼ sticks), softened but still cool, plus extra for greasing pan
- 2½ cups all-purpose flour, plus extra for dusting pan
- 4 large eggs, room temperature
- 2 tablespoons grated orange zest, chopped, plus ¾ cup juice from 2–3 oranges
- 1 teaspoon vanilla extract
- 2 cups granulated sugar
- 1 teaspoon baking powder
- ½ teaspoon baking soda
- 1 teaspoon salt

Glaze and Orange Sugar
- 2 cups confectioners' sugar
- ½ cup frozen orange juice concentrate, thawed
- 4 teaspoons lemon juice
  Pinch salt
- 1½ teaspoons grated orange zest
- 3 tablespoons granulated sugar

A double hit of tangy orange glaze and a sprinkling of orange sugar provide a flavorful and attractive addition to this cake.

1. For the cake: Adjust oven rack to middle position and heat oven to 350 degrees. Butter 12-cup nonstick Bundt pan; dust pan with flour, then tap out excess. Whisk eggs, zest, juice, and vanilla in medium bowl.

2. With electric mixer, combine flour, sugar, baking powder, baking soda, and salt on lowest setting in large bowl. Add butter, 1 tablespoon at a time, and beat at medium-low speed until mixture is crumbly with pea-sized pieces, about 30 seconds after last tablespoon of butter is added. Add egg mixture in steady stream. Scrape down sides of bowl, increase speed to medium-high, and beat until batter is light and fluffy, about 2 minutes. Use rubber spatula to give batter final stir. (It's fine if batter looks slightly broken.)

3. Scrape batter into prepared pan and smooth out surface. Bake until skewer inserted into middle of cake comes out clean, 45 to 55 minutes.

4. For the glaze and orange sugar: While cake bakes, whisk 1½ cups confectioners' sugar, juice concentrate, lemon juice, and salt in small bowl until smooth. Cool cake in pan on cooling rack for 20 minutes, then turn out onto rack placed over rimmed baking sheet. Brush still-warm cake with ¼ cup glaze (see photo 1) and let stand until just warm, about 1 hour. Whisk remaining ½ cup confectioners' sugar into remaining glaze and pour evenly over top of cake (see photo 2). Using fork, mix zest and granulated sugar together in small bowl and sprinkle over glaze (see photo 3). Cool cake completely, about 2 hours. (Cake can be stored, tightly wrapped, at room temperature for up to 3 days.) Serve.

Easier Than You Think: Hot Cocoa Mix

Several unlikely ingredients create an instant cocoa mix that's rich and chocolaty—and ready in less than five minutes.

When I was a kid, a steaming mug of hot cocoa could turn a snowstorm into sunshine. Now that I'm older, watery hot cocoa and dehydrated mini marshmallows just don't have the same effect. I decided to see if I could make my own "instant" mix. I'd make a big batch to keep in the cupboard, ready whenever a craving for hot cocoa hit.

I started with the main ingredient. Tasters preferred the mild but honest chocolate flavor of Dutch-processed cocoa (cocoa powder that has been treated with an alkali to neutralize some of its natural acidity) to the slightly bitter regular cocoa. To add sweetness, granulated sugar was fine, but confectioners' sugar was better. It dissolved easily, and the cornstarch (which is added to prevent clumping) thickened the hot cocoa, giving it a rich, smooth texture. Nonfat dry milk added a sweet dairy flavor, especially when I reconstituted my mix with hot milk rather than hot water.

Although my mix was good, tasters wanted more chocolate flavor. I tried unsweetened, milk, and semisweet chocolates (grinding them with the other ingredients to help them melt quickly), but my tasters were not

impressed. Almost on a whim, I turned to white chocolate, and I knew right away that this was my secret ingredient. In addition to providing a soft, creamy texture, the white chocolate married perfectly with the cocoa powder, pushing the chocolate flavor to new heights (see page 31 for details). Finally, I had a cocoa mix that was worthy of my childhood memories.

–Jeremy Sauer

BEST-EVER HOT COCOA MIX
MAKES ABOUT 20 SERVINGS

3	cups nonfat dry milk
2	cups confectioners' sugar
1½	cups Dutch-processed cocoa powder
1½	cups white chocolate chips
¼	teaspoon salt

Combine ingredients in large bowl. Working in two batches, pulse ingredients in food processor until chocolate is finely ground. Store in airtight container for up to 3 months. To make hot cocoa, stir ⅓ cup of this mix into 1 cup of hot milk. Top with whipped cream or mini marshmallows.

RASPBERRY HOT COCOA MIX
Add 1 (3-ounce) box raspberry gelatin and reduce confectioners' sugar to 1½ cups.

PEANUT BUTTER HOT COCOA MIX
Substitute 1½ cups peanut butter chips for white chocolate chips.

BUTTERSCOTCH-MOCHA HOT COCOA MIX
Substitute 1½ cups butterscotch chips for white chocolate chips and add ½ cup instant coffee to mix.

Bake-Sale Favorite: Seven-Layer Bars

We keep the kitchen-sink approach but refine the ingredient list to improve this classic bar cookie.

With layers of chocolate chips, coconut, and nuts piled high over a buttery graham cracker crust, seven-layer bars sound appealing. There's no batter or dough to make—just layer pantry staples into a baking dish and wait for the oven to transform a jumble of ingredients into a chewy, crispy, sweet bar cookie. But after testing the original recipe (first published on a can of Eagle brand sweetened condensed milk), I wasn't very impressed. Yes, the recipe was easy, but the crust was bland and soggy, the coconut and nuts tasted raw, and the bars were dry. I decided to give this 1950s classic a makeover.

I started with the crust. Prebaking produced the crisp texture I was looking for. I experimented with ingredients to boost flavor in the crust and finally hit upon the solution: toffee bits. Their buttery, salty flavor gave the crust real personality.

To improve their flavor and texture, I pretoasted the coconut and nuts. Rice Krispies (not part of the original recipe) lent welcome crunch and lightness. To emphasize the chocolate flavor, I added a layer of milk chocolate, melted right over the hot crust, in addition to the usual chocolate chips.

For me, the best part of this recipe is the rich butterscotch flavor and chewy texture added by the sweetened condensed milk. To remedy the sandy, dry texture of the original recipe, why not use more than one can? I found that two full cans created a rich, moist, candylike bar cookie with plenty of chew and great caramel flavor. –Diane Unger

SEVEN-LAYER BARS MAKES 45 BARS
Toast the coconut and pecans separately on a baking sheet in a 350-degree oven until golden—5 minutes for the coconut and 8 minutes for the pecans.

1	cup toffee bits (such as Heath)
12	whole graham crackers
8	tablespoons (1 stick) unsalted butter, melted
8	ounces milk chocolate, chopped coarse
1	cup Rice Krispies
1	cup pecans, toasted and chopped coarse
1	cup semisweet chocolate chips
1	cup sweetened flaked coconut, toasted
2	(14-ounce) cans sweetened condensed milk
1	tablespoon vanilla extract

1. Adjust oven rack to middle position and heat oven to 350 degrees. Line 13 by 9-inch baking pan with foil, allowing excess to overhang pan edges. Generously coat foil with cooking spray. Process toffee bits in food processor to fine powder. Add graham crackers and process to fine crumbs. Transfer mixture to bowl and stir in butter. Press mixture firmly into prepared baking pan. Bake until beginning to brown, about 10 minutes.

2. Remove pan from oven, sprinkle crust with milk chocolate, and allow chocolate to soften, about 2 minutes. Using spatula, smooth chocolate into even layer. Scatter Rice Krispies over chocolate, pressing to adhere. Add layers of pecans, chocolate chips, and coconut, in that order, pressing each layer to adhere. Combine condensed milk and vanilla in small bowl and pour over coconut.

3. Bake until golden brown, 25 to 30 minutes. Cool on wire rack, about 2 hours. Using foil overhang, lift from pan and cut into 45 squares. (The bars can be stored in airtight container for up to 3 days.)

Food Shopping

FROZEN PIZZA: What's the Cost for Convenience?

It's been said that pizza is like your first kiss: Even when it's bad, it's still pretty good. But what about frozen pizza? Americans spent more than $2.6 billion on frozen pizza last year. To find out how good today's frozen pizzas are, we rounded up nine national brands and fired up the test kitchen ovens.

Wanting no distractions, we selected plain cheese pizzas with thin or "regular" crusts and no fancy ingredients. We prepared each pizza according to the instructions on the box and served hot slices to our tasters. Our tasting panel rated the crust, sauce, cheese, and overall quality of each sample.

So what did we find out? Frozen pizza is not going to fool anybody into thinking it's fresh. That said, our winning pizza, California Pizza Kitchen Margherita, tastes very good, and several tasters said they'd be happy to have it in their home freezers. In fact, our panel recommends the top four pizzas listed below. As for the remaining pies, they ranged from imperfect (with muted flavors and soggy crusts) to inedible.

What separates the good from the bad? The top-scoring pizzas all tasted fresh (not freezer burnt) and lacked offensive or off flavors—in other words, they didn't taste mass-produced. Most of our winning pizzas had shorter, simpler ingredient lists (Tombstone lists 13 ingredients total), whereas the pies with lots of ingredients—including preservatives that are supposed to retain freshness—tasted old and tired (Celeste has 13 ingredients in its imitation cheese alone and another 13 in its crust). The pizzas are listed in order of preference. –Scott Kathan

Recommended

1. **California Pizza Kitchen Crispy Thin Crust Margherita** 12.8 ounces, $5.99
   This sauceless pizza had "nice" chunks of fresh tomato that tasters praised for their ability to make it "seem less like frozen pizza." Most tasters agreed that this pizza had a "nice overall combination of flavors."

2. **Freschetta Ultra Thin Golden Baked Crispy 5-Cheese Pizza** 12.8 ounces, $6.29
   This pizza scored especially well for its "thin and flaky," "crispy" crust and "complex" cheese flavor that "actually tastes like real cheese." With a better sauce (this one was "dusty and oregano-y"), this might have been the winner.

3. **Tombstone Extra Cheese Original** 20.5 ounces, $5.19
   Tasters found this pizza met expectations, noting that it "tastes like frozen pizza, in the best possible way." It scored well for its "very good" cheese and "nice and crunchy" crust.

4. **Amy's Cheese Pizza** 13 ounces, $3.99
   This organic product had a distinctive whole-grain crust that one taster said was "full of flavor, like real bread." The sauce was praised for being "tomatoey, with good herb flavor." The cheese was called "just okay."

Recommended with Reservations

5. **Tony's Original Crust Cheese Pizza** 15.1 ounces, $3.99
   Tasters were split on their reactions to the sweet sauce: "Sweet sauce, which I like," said one, while another countered that it "takes me back to my high school cafeteria." The crust lost points for being "flabby."

6. **Red Baron Thin Crust 5-Cheese Pizza** 19 ounces, $6.49
   Ingredients include vinegar, molasses, soy sauce solids, and smoke flavor. One taster called the sauce "too spicy, with strange flavors," while another called it "smoky and strangely sweet." "Plasticky" cheese.

7. **DiGiorno Thin Crispy Crust Four Cheese Pizza** 23 ounces, $6.29
   "Like the frozen pizza from my childhood—sauce is too sweet, and the cheese tastes processed," said one taster. "Cheese is chewy, fake, and bland—what's it made of?" asked another. Another taster simply stated, "Decent."

Not Recommended

8. **Mr. P's Crispy Thin Crust Cheese Pizza** 6.5 ounces, $1.00
   "Pizza candy—way too sweet," said one taster. With a crust "like a wet cracker" and "chewy, rubbery" cheese, one taster asked, "Is it prison pizza?"

9. **Celeste Original Pizza for One** 5.58 ounces, $1.69
   "Rancid" and "a sad specimen," said the panel. "Typical bad frozen pizza," said one taster. "You eat it and then ask yourself, 'Why did I just eat that?'"

Taste Test Dried Herbs

We use plenty of dried herbs in the test kitchen, but we don't use every dried herb. That's because delicate leafy herbs, such as basil, parsley, chives, mint, and cilantro, become musty and stale-tasting when dried. But heartier herbs, such as oregano, sage, and thyme, dry well and are good substitutes for fresh in most recipes—especially those in which the herbs will cook in liquid (such as stews and sauces). We've found that two herbs, tarragon and dill, fall into a middle category: They do add flavor in their dried form, but that flavor is more muted than that provided by other dried herbs.

A few general rules: Use only half as much dried herbs as fresh, and add them at the same time as you would add fresh. Dried herbs lose their potency six to 12 months after opening; you can test dried herbs for freshness by rubbing them between your fingers—if they don't smell bright, throw them away and buy a new jar. Here are the dried herbs we use in the test kitchen and our favorite uses for each. –Scott Kathan

Oregano
Great in tomato sauces, chili, Mexican and Latin dishes, and sprinkled on pizza. Dried oregano does not have the same sharp bite as fresh, but it does have a distinct and recognizable floral element.

Thyme
Good for long-cooked soups and stews and with roasted meats and poultry; pairs especially well with the flavors of mustard and lemon.

Sage
We prefer rubbed (or finely crumbled) sage to the ground or chopped kinds. Use with poultry, stuffings, pork, and full-flavored vegetables (like squash), and in butter sauces.

Marjoram
This pungent herb is especially good with beans, lamb, and other red meats.

Rosemary
Works well in long-cooked dishes (especially those with Italian flavors) like soups, stews, and braises. Too much dried rosemary can turn a dish bitter, so use sparingly.

Equipment Roundup

STOCKPOTS: Do You Have to Spend Big Money for a Big Pot?

Here in the test kitchen, we have 15 stockpots of varying sizes, and we use them often. Most home kitchens, however, have room for a single stockpot, so it must handle a variety of big jobs—from steaming lobsters and cooking bushels of corn to canning and making huge batches of chili or homemade stock.

So what size is best? After substantial pretesting, we determined that a 12-quart stockpot is the most useful size—it's the "smallest" big pot, meaning it can handle most big jobs yet is small enough to store with your other pots and pans. So how much do you have to spend to get a good 12-quart stockpot? We bought nine basic stockpots (no fancy steaming or boiling inserts), ranging in price from $25 to $325, and headed into the test kitchen to find out.

We boiled water, cooked mounds of pasta (two pounds of pasta and eight quarts of water at a time), prepared two dozen ears of corn, and made double batches of beef chili in each pot. To evaluate the pots, our testers used digital scales, thermometers, stopwatches, gas and electric burners, and plenty of elbow grease. They handled each stockpot extensively to get a sense of its overall feel (both empty and full) and handle design. We washed the pots repeatedly and practiced stowing them away. What did we find out?

SHAPE-SHIFTING: The best stockpot we tested, the $325 All-Clad, impressed us more for what it didn't do—scorch on the bottom or feel awkward or flimsy—than for what it did do; after all, how sexy can a stockpot be, even when it's performing flawlessly? That said, our testers preferred wide stockpots (such as the All-Clad) to tall and narrow ones (such as the Vollrath), as greater width allows you to see and manipulate food better and makes for easier cleaning and storage.

A WEIGHTY ISSUE: The heavier pots (all weighed without lids) outperformed the lighter models. The four heaviest pots in our testing were all made of stainless steel with an aluminum core. Aluminum conducts heat very well and ensures more even cooking and fewer hot spots. The aluminum core also makes the bottom of the pot thicker, which reduces scorching. The lighter pots (including those without aluminum cores) did a fine job cooking corn and pasta—in fact, they heat up faster than the more even-heating pots with aluminum cores. But for cooking applications where sticking and scorching are risks (such as chili), a heavier pot is a must.

GET A GRIP: Handles matter—a lot. We found that the best handles extend from the pot at least 1¾ inches and are either flat or thick and round, for easy gripping. The All-Clad, Cuisinart, Lincoln, and Arcosteel pots had the best handles—they were easy to grip, even with potholders and a pot full of steaming chili. Pots made by Vollrath and Farberware performed well in cooking tests but were severely downgraded because testers found their thin handles to be awkward and poorly designed.

SUMMING UP: You can buy a solid, aluminum-core 12-quart stockpot (like the Cuisinart) for $65—or you can drop $325 on the beautiful All-Clad pot, which didn't have a single flaw. If you use a stockpot primarily to boil corn or pasta, it makes sense to buy the Cuisinart model and use the savings to upgrade something else in your kitchen. Whatever your price range, opt for a pot that feels heavy for its size. And when shopping, give the handles a test-run by picking up pots with potholders. The pots (which are all available from Cooking.com) are listed at right, with comments, in order of preference. **–Scott Kathan**

Highly Recommended
All-Clad Stainless 12-Quart Stock Pot
Price: $324.95
Material: stainless steel with aluminum core
Weight: 5.5 lb.
Comments: This pot was lauded for being "nice and heavy," with "easy-to-grip" handles that "didn't get too hot" (although we still needed potholders). The aluminum core runs up the side of the pot—other pots have aluminum cores only in the bottom, if anywhere—which ensures more even heating than most of us will ever need.

Recommended
Cuisinart Chef's Classic Stainless 12-Quart Stock Pot
Price: $64.95
Material: stainless steel with aluminum core
Weight: 4.35 lb.

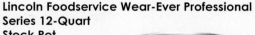
Best Buy!

Comments: Very similar to the All-Clad pot, the Cuisinart comes with handles that are "easily grippable" and "sit well in your hand." The upward tilt of the handles made it especially easy to pour out the contents. This pot was also praised for being "plenty heavy," and the bottom was pristine after cooking the chili.

Lincoln Foodservice Wear-Ever Professional Series 12-Quart Stock Pot
Price: $59.90 (with lid, which must be purchased separately)
Material: aluminum
Weight: 3.85 lb.
Comments: This all-aluminum pot fared well in the test kitchen. Testers loved its "light weight," "solid feel," and "sturdy raised handles," which made handling and pouring easy. Aluminum is not as durable as stainless steel, which may lead to problems down the road.

Recommended with Reservations
Arcosteel 12-Quart Stock Pot
Price: $49.95
Material: stainless steel with aluminum core, tempered glass lid, silicone handle covers
Weight: 3.7 lb.
Comments: This pot heated relatively evenly—there was only a tiny patch of chili stuck after 2½ hours of cooking. The handles are "sturdy" and offer "good control," but this pot was downgraded for dangerous bare spots (no silicone) on the handles.

Farberware Classic Series Stainless Steel 12-Quart Stock Pot
Price: $70.95
Material: stainless steel with aluminum core
Weight: 4.5 lb.
Comments: With better handles (these were deemed "uncomfortable" and "slippery"), this heavy aluminum-core pot would have been in the "recommended" category. It heated very evenly, and testers liked how the lip of the lid "caught a lot of condensation."

Vollrath Stainless Intrigue Professional Cookware 12-Quart Stock Pot
Price: $88.48 (with lid, which must be purchased separately)
Material: stainless steel with aluminum core
Weight: 6.35 lb.
Comments: This tall and narrow pot "felt tippy" and "cumbersome" and was "harder to pour" and clean than squatter pots. It did, however, cook with very even heat and was the heaviest of all the pots we tested.

Endurance R.S.V.P. Stainless Steel 12-Quart Stock Pot
Price: $37.95
Material: stainless steel with aluminum core, tempered glass lid
Weight: 3.25 lb.
Comments: "Shallow," "thin," and "narrow" handles made it hard for testers to grip this pot. This pan heated fairly evenly (thanks to its aluminum core), and there was very little sticking during the chili test.

Not Recommended
Metro 12-Quart Stock Pot
Price: $24.95
Material: stainless steel with tempered glass lid
Weight: 2.3 lb.
Comments: There was serious burning/sticking at the bottom of this very light pot during the chili test. The handles taper into a point, making it "hard to get your hand in to grip it."

Metro Set of 3 Nested Stock Pots with lids: 8-, 12-, and 16-quart
Price: $49.99
Material: stainless steel
Weight: 1.8 lbs
Comments: Testers said this pot, the lightest of the lot, "felt like a toy and would dent too easily." With handles that rose above the top of the pot, it was very awkward to pour because "the leverage is all wrong." There was major sticking and burnt matter on the bottom of the pot after the chili test.

Notes from Our Test Kitchen

TIPS, TECHNIQUES, AND TOOLS FOR BETTER COOKING

Kitchen Creations
Quick and Creamy Dipping Sauces

Our **Crunchy Potato Wedges** (page 14) are great on their own, but they're even better with our easy mayo-based dipping sauces. Each sauce will keep in the refrigerator for up to two weeks.

CREAMY BBQ SAUCE

Combine ³/₄ cup mayonnaise, ¹/₄ cup barbecue sauce, 1 minced garlic clove, 3 tablespoons cider vinegar, ¹/₄ teaspoon pepper, and ¹/₈ teaspoon salt.

CURRIED CHUTNEY SAUCE

Combine ³/₄ cup mayonnaise, ¹/₄ cup yogurt, ¹/₄ cup minced fresh cilantro, 3 tablespoons mango chutney, 2 teaspoons curry powder, ¹/₄ teaspoon pepper, and ¹/₈ teaspoon salt.

HONEY DIJON SAUCE

Combine ³/₄ cup mayonnaise, ¹/₄ cup Dijon mustard, 1 minced garlic clove, 3 tablespoons honey, ¹/₄ teaspoon pepper, and ¹/₈ teaspoon salt.

BUFFALO BLUE CHEESE SAUCE

Combine ³/₄ cup mayonnaise, ¹/₄ cup blue cheese salad dressing, 1 minced garlic clove, 3 tablespoons hot sauce, ¹/₄ teaspoon pepper, and ¹/₈ teaspoon celery salt.

Stir-Frying Tip

When stir-frying green vegetables such as broccoli (as in our recipe for **Sesame Broccoli**, page 23), green beans, or asparagus, we like the work to be as streamlined as possible. While many recipes call for the vegetables to be preboiled before sautéing (which requires two pots), we prefer to sauté the vegetables in hot oil before adding liquid to the pan and putting the lid on; this lets the vegetables steam to the perfect crisp-tender texture without dirtying another pot.

Picking the Perfect Chip

A sturdy chip is a must when making our **Ultimate Spicy Beef Nachos** (page 13). Tostitos was the top-rated brand in a kitchen taste test, but not all varieties are suitable for nachos.

TOSTITOS RESTAURANT STYLE CHIPS
These thin chips are a test kitchen favorite with salsa or guacamole but are too thin for nachos.

TOSTITOS NATURAL CHIPS
These hearty chips will support plenty of toppings and are our top choice for nachos.

Inside the Test Kitchen Whole Lot of Shakin' Going On

Instead of coating Maryland Fried Chicken (page 10) by hand, save yourself some mess by using a brown paper grocery bag. But don't add the seasonings and flour at the same time. Jeremy Sauer found that shaking the chicken with the seasonings first results in much better flavor. You may need to double up if the bags are flimsy.

1. Pat the chicken dry with paper towels, then place it in the bag. **2.** After shaking the chicken with seasonings, add the flour to the bag. **3.** Tightly close the bag and shake until all the chicken pieces are well coated with flour.

Chili Out

While touring Cincinnati's chili parlors, I had occasion to visit a couple of dry cleaners, too. Whether it's a spaghetti-strewn five way (spaghetti with chili, cheese, beans, and onions) or a heaping cheese Coney (a chili-cheese hot dog), Cincinnati chili can be tough to keep off of your shirt. Luckily, Edie Mathews, owner of Empress Chili, taught me a quick and effective way to avoid big dry-cleaning bills. Her instructions were simple: Rub liquid dish-washing detergent into the fresh stain, let the soap dry, and throw the shirt in the wash when you get home. I was rewarded with a perfectly clean shirt—and a new solution for taking care of stains while staying on the go. Thanks, Edie! –Jeremy Sauer

Shred It and Forget It

One of the hallmarks of **Cincinnati Chili** (page 18) is the wisp-thin tangle of shredded cheese that graces the top of the chili or cheese Coney. To produce cheese with this perfect airy texture, chili restaurants use industrial-strength cheese shredders, but where does that leave the home cook? We found that the best way to re-create these gossamer strands of cheddar, provided the cheese is well chilled, is to use the fine holes of a box grater. To get the longest, thinnest strands possible, grasp the refrigerated cheese and run it down the length of the box grater in a slight arcing motion; this way the shreds will run the entire length of the block of cheese.

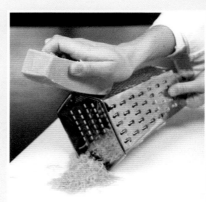

Long, light strands of cheese are essential for authentic Cincinnati chili.

Shopping with the Test Kitchen Glazed Nuts

Glazed nuts add the perfect sweet and crunchy accent to some of the salads on page 20. We tried making our own glazed nuts but found that it took too much time—especially when tasty ready-made versions are now available at supermarkets. Sunkist Almond Accents ($3.69 for a 7-ounce bag) and Emerald of California Glazed Walnuts ($3.99 for a 7-ounce bag) and Glazed Pecans ($3.99 for a 5-ounce bag) were the test kitchen favorites.

Salt Watch

When testing the **Chicken Soup** recipes for this issue's recipe contest (page 4), we were reminded of just how important it is to use low-sodium chicken broth. On the one day that we accidentally used a "full salt" version, the soups were unpalatably salty. In the test kitchen, we use Swanson Natural Goodness 33% Less Sodium Chicken Broth, which won our recent taste test of low-sodium broths.

Less salt, more flavor.

A Little Rosemary Goes A Long Way

Rosemary can quickly go from pleasantly piney to bitter and medicinal if it cooks for too long (and especially if it's allowed to boil). In our recipe for **Italian Pot Roast** (page 25), we found that simmering a whole sprig of rosemary in the last two minutes of cooking was the perfect way to add flavor without the rosemary becoming too harsh. Using a whole sprig is easier than stripping and chopping leaves, and it also makes it easy to remove the rosemary once the sauce is done. **–Meredith Butcher**

Put a Lid on It

Cooking the chuck-eye roast in our **Italian Pot Roast** (page 25) with the cover on wasn't enough to prevent moisture loss—we also had to make a second lid out of aluminum foil. Here's how we did it: After you add the meat back into the Dutch oven, loosely tent a sheet of foil over the roast and cover the pot with the lid. When it's time to flip the roast, carefully remove the aluminum foil, give the roast a flip, and tent again. The foil keeps the moisture in proximity to the meat, which ensures a moist and tender roast. **–Meredith Butcher**

How Do You Juice a Clam?

Clam juice is water that has been flavored by the cooking of clams; it is sold in glass jars near the canned tuna in your supermarket. Here in the test kitchen, we use clam juice as a quick replacement for any number of seafood stocks, including clam (for quick clam chowder) and shrimp (as in our recipe for **Family-Style Shrimp Scampi**, page 12). A word of caution, though: Many brands of clam juice are very salty, so wait to season your dish until after you've added the clam juice.

–Katie Henderson

A quick substitute for seafood stocks.

White Chocolate Chips

White chocolate chips are the key to our **Hot Cocoa Mix** (page 27), giving it intense chocolate flavor. Since white chocolate doesn't have much chocolate flavor on its own, we were more than a little surprised by this test kitchen discovery.

It turns out that cocoa powder (the main ingredient in any hot cocoa mix) is almost entirely cocoa solids (the stuff that gives chocolate its flavor), but it does not contain much fat. When we added white chocolate to our cocoa mix, we were really adding fat, which carries flavors and makes the cocoa powder taste better. Think of the difference between chocolate pudding made with skim milk (bland) and chocolate pudding made with whole milk (rich and chocolaty).

We had one more surprise. It doesn't matter whether you use real white chocolate (made with cocoa butter) or white "baking" chips (made with palm kernel oil or another source of fat). In this case, it's the amount of fat, not the type, that counts.

–Jeremy Sauer

White chocolate adds fat, which is essential for full chocolate flavor.

Five Ways to Cincinnati

Those in the know can order their chili without a second thought, but for the uninitiated, here's a quick guide to the five ways of Cincinnati chili. The chili is almost never served on its own (one-way). Just don't forget the oyster crackers!

TWO-WAY CHILI
Served over spaghetti.

THREE-WAY CHILI
Served over spaghetti and topped with cheese.

FOUR-WAY CHILI
Served over spaghetti and topped with onions and cheese.

FIVE-WAY CHILI
Served over spaghetti and topped with onions, beans, and cheese.

Kitchen Technique REMOVING THE MEMBRANE

To make our recipe for **Chinese Sticky Ribs** (page 22), you must remove the tough membrane from the underside of each rack of St. Louis–cut spareribs. Here's how we do it.

1. At one end of the rack, loosen the membrane with the tip of a paring knife.

2. Grab the membrane with a paper towel to keep it from slipping. Pull slowly—it should come off in 1 piece.

When Things Go Wrong in the Kitchen

READERS SHARE FUNNY STORIES ABOUT COOKING MISHAPS

A VERY VALIANT BIRD

A few months after our wedding, my husband left to fight in Vietnam. When he returned a year later, we finally unpacked the wedding gifts that had been stored for the first year of our marriage. I was thrilled when my cousin came for a visit and I could finally entertain as a married woman. I decided to cook a chicken on our new grill and rotisserie. My husband brought the nicely browned chicken in from the patio and began to carve it. To my utter dismay, the first cut of the knife showed that the interior of the chicken was still raw, and red juices covered the platter. I was in tears because my first attempt at entertaining was a disaster. However, my gallant military husband dashed into the bedroom and returned with his Purple Heart medal to pin on the chicken! After we finished a good laugh, we popped the "wounded" chicken into the oven and eventually enjoyed a nice meal.

Kathleen Graler Corvallis, Mont.

SECRET INGREDIENT

When my husband and I settled into our honeymoon apartment, my parents called to say they were coming for a visit. I knew that my dad loved freshly perked coffee for dessert, so I decided to make a pot with our new percolator. I remembered my cooking teacher adding a pinch of salt for flavor, so I figured if a pinch is good, then a couple of tablespoons would probably make it even better!

I watched in anticipation as Dad took his first sip. His sweet smile turned into a pained expression. As tears streamed down his cheeks, Dad said, "Linda, what did you do to this coffee? I've never tasted anything like it in my whole life!" They almost fell off their chairs laughing when I told them about my special ingredient. Needless to say, Dad always checks before he drinks any of my coffee!

Linda Breschini Cleveland, Ohio

AN EXTREMELY RARE MISTAKE

When I got married, I was a very inexperienced cook. As a surprise for my new husband, I decided to cook a London broil for dinner. I turned on the broiler and placed the meat in the bottom drawer. After an hour I was convinced that it must be done, even though it was only a little warm to the touch. My husband sliced into the meat with eager anticipation, which quickly turned to shock when he saw the bluish tint to the meat. My husband politely said that the meat wasn't cooked and went to examine the oven to make sure it was working properly. At that point, he began to laugh hysterically, realizing that I had tried to cook the meat in the warming drawer in the bottom of the oven!

Ginger Meagher Brick, N.J.

THE YEAST WITHIN

After a power outage, I had to throw away four 3-packs of frozen bread dough that had gone bad. A few days later, my husband wanted to know what happened to our garbage can. I had no idea what he was talking about, so I went outside to look for myself. I couldn't believe my eyes when I saw a huge ball of bread dough expanding inside the can. To this day, I have to smile when I think of the bread dough that rose to the occasion.

Linda Schiller Waubun, Minn.

LANGUAGE BARRIER

When studying in China in the late 1980s, my American classmates and I decided to prepare a traditional Thanksgiving meal for our Chinese classmates. As one of the only cooks in the group, I was put in charge of the feast. I asked one of my classmates to go to the local market to buy some chickens and ducks (turkeys were unavailable). Later that day, I looked across the compound toward my classmate's apartment, where, through his window, I could see him flailing around frantically. I ran over to see what was happening, only to find him trying to corral several live chickens into the corner of his room. Apparently with his limited Chinese skills he did not know how to specify that he didn't want live birds. Neither of us could bring ourselves to kill the birds, but luckily a Chinese instructor didn't share our squeamishness, and he came over to dispatch the birds and prepare them for our Thanksgiving table. My classmate and I could only stomach the side dishes that night.

James Glucksman Fairfax, Va.

DISHWATER PUNCH

Many years ago, while giving my first bridal shower for a friend, I decided to serve fruit punch. The recipe called for orange, lime, lemon, or raspberry sherbet for flavor and color. While I was in the grocery store, I came up with the idea that if I used rainbow sherbet the punch would be a fun rainbow color. To my horror, the rainbow sherbet turned the punch the color of dirty dishwater! With my guests arriving I had no choice but to serve the brown punch. My friends coined my concoction Dottie's Dishwater Punch.

Dottie Hendricks Hayward, Wis.

CARAMEL CASSEROLE

My friend Alexandra, recently married to her high school sweetheart, invited a few of us over to dinner in their new apartment. Alexandra was creating one of her staples, a satisfying pan of macaroni and cheese. The ingredients flew together with speed, and the casserole was in the oven in no time. Unfortunately, instead of using evaporated milk, she accidentally used sweetened condensed milk, which caramelized in the oven and resulted in a sweet, cheesy, salty mess. We ordered Chinese that evening.

Matthew Nathan San Francisco, Calif.

Send us your funniest kitchen disaster stories. E-mail us by visiting **CooksCountry.com/kitchendisasters**. Or write to us at Kitchen Disasters, Cook's Country, P.O. Box 470739, Brookline, MA 02447. If we publish your story, you'll receive a complimentary one-year subscription to *Cook's Country*.

COFFEE SMILES

When I graduated from college, my mom tried to teach me how to cook. After a few weeks, I thought I was getting good and offered to help my mom by cooking a simple but elegant dinner for my father's boss. I had decided to serve a chocolate mousse for dessert, and I referenced a recipe that called for coffee. I served the mousse with flourish, each in its own crystal bowl. As I served the last guest, I noticed that my mom had something in her teeth. I bent over to whisper in her ear, and she looked at me and said sweetly, "Honey, did you put coffee grounds in this?" At that moment I realized my mistake of not brewing the coffee first, and I looked up at the rest of the table. Everyone burst out laughing with coffee grounds all over their teeth and lips. They finished the dessert, I think out of pity for me, and stayed up way past their bedtimes. Every year on my birthday, I get a pound of coffee from my dad's boss. What a great way to be remembered.

Julie Denton Lawrenceville, Ga.

The Great American Cake

Cherry Chocolate Chip Cake

A homespun cake that tastes like chocolate-covered cherries is the perfect way to celebrate Valentine's Day or Presidents' Day. Most recipes add mini chocolate chips and maraschino cherries to the batter. However, we found that the cherries in canned pie filling taste better than pretty maraschino cherries, which we dipped in melted chocolate and reserved for garnishing the cake.

To make this cake you'll need:

- 1 (21-ounce) can cherry pie filling
- 2 cups mini chocolate chips
- 1 recipe white cake batter*
- 1 tablespoon vegetable shortening
- 1 (10-ounce) jar maraschino cherries with stems, drained and wiped dry
  Red food coloring
- 4 cups vanilla buttercream*
- 1/2 cup heavy cream, whipped

For the cake: Drain and rinse cherry pie filling under running water. Press cherries between sev-eral layers of paper towels until very dry. Chop cherries fine and reserve 1/2 cup (discard remaining cherries). Gently fold cherries and 1/2 cup chips into cake batter. Grease and flour three 8-inch cake pans and divide batter among pans. Bake on middle rack in 350-degree oven until toothpick inserted in middle comes out clean, 20 to 25 minutes. Cool cakes in pans 10 minutes, then turn out onto rack to cool completely.

For the cherries: Melt remaining 1 1/2 cups chips and shortening in bowl. Holding stems, partially dip maraschino cherries into chocolate and place on parchment-lined plate. Refrigerate until hardened, at least 10 minutes.

For the frosting: Beat 5 drops red food coloring into buttercream; add more coloring as desired.

To assemble: Spread 3/4 cup buttercream on bottom cake layer. Repeat with 3/4 cup more buttercream and second cake layer. Top with final cake layer and frost top and sides with remaining buttercream. Decorate with whipped cream and cherries.

* Go to **CooksCountry.com** for cake and frosting recipes or use your own.

Recipe Index

RC = Recipe Card

Cook's Country

APRIL/MAY 2007

A Better Way to Grill Chicken
Start with Scissors and Lemons

Potluck Mac and Cheese
Creamy Southern Recipe

Tropical Carrot Cake
With Pineapple and Coconut

MAKE-AHEAD EASTER MENU
Test Kitchen Favorites

KING RANCH CHICKEN
The Best Casserole in Texas

TESTING COFFEE MAKERS
Top Drip Machines under $50

BLACK-BOTTOM CUPCAKES
Chocolate Meets Cheesecake!

HERB SALAD DRESSINGS
Two Steps to Unlock Flavor

SUPER-STUFFED POTATOES
Creamy, Cheesy, Crispy

MAKEOVER MOUSSE
Less Fat, More Chocolate Flavor

ITALIAN SUNDAY GRAVY
Best Slow-Cooker Recipe

HOT DOG TASTE TEST
We Pick the Top Dog

$4.95 U.S./$6.95 CANADA

0 74470 05251 7

0 5>

Our $10,000 Lost Recipes Contest Winner!

Lois Schlademan of Stow, Ohio, beat out nearly 3,000 other home cooks to claim first place in our heirloom recipe contest. Her recipe for **Peach Puzzle** deserves a place alongside crisp and cobbler in the pantheon of simple American fruit desserts.

Cook's Country

Dear Country Cook,

An egg-rolling contest may seem old-fashioned, even archaic, but in the country, the line between past and present is thankfully faint. Every summer, our family still attends the Washington County Fair, where I check over the blue-ribboned glass bottles of silage, the summer squash monsters, the cake and pie exhibits, and all the rest: pole climbing, log hauling, rock throwing, baby crawling, and hog calling. And trying to dunk the dope (our son actually sat in as the dope last summer) is always worth a couple dollars' worth of softballs.

So when folks say that traditions have been lost to the past, well, they just don't know where to look. In the kitchen, the story is the same. Our recent lost recipe contest turned up nearly 3,000 heirloom recipes (see page 6 for the top five winners), and I can assure you that the past tasted more than pretty good. It was a real pleasure to taste-test recipes such as Peach Puzzle, Tennessee Stack Cake, and Naked Ladies with Their Legs Crossed.

It's easy to look at the past and think of it as quaint or somehow separated from the present. Sure, I grew up with neighbors who still baked cookies, biscuits, and bread in a wood cookstove and who remember to this day how to use a side hill plough and are apt to say that they prefer horses to tractors, since "You always know that a horse is going to start on a cold morning."

But around the dinner table, there are no modernists. Green Bean Casserole is still the most requested recipe in America. New or old, recipes just have to taste good. That's about it.

So for those of us who still love to cook—and I mean really love the cooking, not just the eating—it's nice to know that some things never change.

Christopher Kimball
Christopher Kimball
Founder and Editor, Cook's Country Magazine

Youngsters during Egg-Rolling Contest, Palisades Park, New Jersey, April 20, 1946
These kids are tense as they wait for the starting signal in an egg-rolling contest—just another example of how food is woven into many of our childhood rituals. The winner gained bragging rights, but there was a consolation prize for each contestant. The eggs were hard-boiled, and the kids ate them after the race.
© Bettmann/CORBIS

APRIL/MAY 2007

Cook's Country

departments

features

in every issue

Founder and Editor Christopher Kimball
Editorial Director Jack Bishop
Deputy Editor Bridget Lancaster
Senior Editors Scott Kathan
Jeremy Sauer
Test Kitchen Director Erin McMurrer
Test Cooks Stephanie Alleyne
Kelley Baker
Meredith Butcher
Greg Case
Cali Rich
Diane Unger
Assistant Test Cook Lynn Clark
Web Managing Editor Katherine Bell
Web Editor Kate Mason
Copy Editor Will Gordon
Market Research Manager Melissa Baldino
Editorial Assistant Meredith Smith
Kitchen Assistant Nadia Domeq
Contributing Editor Eva Katz
Contributor Keri Fisher

Design Director Amy Klee
Senior Designer, Magazines Julie Bozzo
Designers Jay Layman
Christine Vo
Staff Photographer Daniel J. van Ackere

Production Director Guy Rochford
Traffic and Projects Manager Alice Cummiskey
Production Assistant Lauren Pettapiece
Color and Imaging Specialist Andrew Mannone
Technology & Operations Director Aaron Shuman
Systems Administrator S. Paddi McHugh

Chief Financial Officer Sharyn Chabot
Human Resources Manager Adele Shapiro
Controller Mandy Shito
Office Manager Elizabeth Pohm
Receptionist Henrietta Murray
Publicity Deborah Broide

Vice President Marketing David Mack
Circulation Director Bill Tine
Fulfillment Manager Carrie Horan
Circulation Assistant Elizabeth Dayton
Direct Mail Director Adam Perry
Products Director Steven Browall
E-Commerce Marketing Manager Hugh Buchan
Marketing Copywriter David Goldberg
Junior Developer Doug Sisko
Customer Service Manager Jacqueline Valerio
Customer Service Representatives Julie Gardner
Jillian Nannicelli

Vice President Sales Demee Gambulos
Retail Sales Associate Anthony King
Corporate Marketing Manager Emily Logan
Partnership Account Manager Allie Brawley
Marketing Assistant Connie Forbes

On the cover: PHOTOGRAPHY: Ellen Silverman/StockFood. ILLUSTRATION: John Burgoyne.
In this issue: COLOR FOOD PHOTOGRAPHY: Keller + Keller. STYLING: Mary Jane Sawyer, Marie Piraino. ILLUSTRATION: Lisa Perrett.

Editorial Office: 17 Station Street, Brookline, MA 02445; 617-232-1000; fax 617-232-1572
Subscription Inquiries: Cook's Country, P.O. Box 8382, Red Oak, IA 51591-1382; 800-526-8447

Cook's Country magazine (ISSN 1552-1990), number 14, is published bimonthly by Boston Common Press Limited Partnership, 17 Station Street, Brookline, MA 02445. Copyright 2007 Boston Common Press Limited Partnership. Periodicals postage paid at Boston, Mass., and at additional mailing offices, USPS #023453. POSTMASTER: Send address changes to Cook's Country, P.O. Box 8382, Red Oak, IA 51591-1382. For subscription and gift subscription orders, subscription inquiries, or change-of-address notices, call 800-526-8447 in the U.S. or 515-247-7571 from outside the U.S., or write us at Cook's Country, P.O. Box 8382, Red Oak, IA 51591-1382.
PRINTED IN THE USA

Visit us at CooksCountry.com!
Go online for hundreds of recipes, food tastings, and up-to-date equipment reviews. You can get a behind-the-scenes look at our test kitchen, talk to our cooks and editors, enter recipe contests, and share recipes and cooking tips with the *Cook's Country* community.

Kitchen Shortcuts

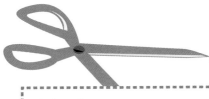

Scrap Bag

When chopping vegetables, I often place a plastic bag from the grocery store right under the edge of the cutting board so that I can brush vegetable scraps and other debris directly into the bag as I go along. Saves lots of time!

Meena Thayu
Philadelphia, Pa.

Tray Cool

For inexpensive cutting boards, I go to the local restaurant supply store and pay $2 each for the trays commonly used at fast food restaurants and cafeterias. They stack nicely in the pantry, and the small edge is great for catching juices when carving meat, keeping chopped carrots from

escaping, and preventing eggs from rolling off the counter. They are very durable and cheap to replace. I've gotten many raised eyebrows when I pull one out to carve a roast, but the naysayers are always converted when they see how great these trays work!

Victoria Jensen
Via e-mail

Picture This

To keep your recipe cards in good shape, put them in a clear acrylic picture frame before you start cooking. The cards slide easily in and out and stay clean no matter how much splattering or spilling goes on in the kitchen. The frames can hold large or small recipe cards, and they're dishwasher-safe!

Kathleen Harbin
Alpharetta, Ga.

Freshen Up!

MINTY FRESH

Having an abundance of spearmint plants in my garden, I found that if I grind some of the leaves in my disposal, it gets rid of any unpleasant smells. It leaves my sink and disposal smelling minty fresh!

Barbara Perrin Wheat Ridge, Colo.

2 JOBS, 1 TOOL

I often use one of those splatter screens to keep my stovetop cleanup to a minimum. So instead of dirtying a colander as well, when something such as ground beef needs to be drained, I use the splatter screen as my "strainer." I hold it tight to the top of the pan and turn the pan over the sink to drain off the grease.

Patricia Ingalls
West Paterson, N.J.

AVOID ICY ICE CREAM

After scooping myself some ice cream, I always place a sheet of plastic wrap directly on the surface of the ice cream before replacing the lid and putting the container back in the freezer. The plastic wrap helps prevent icy ice cream, and it also keeps it tasting fresh for much longer!

Jacqueline Hisrich
Canton, Ohio

TAMING ELECTRICAL CORDS

I can't stand having loose electrical cords tangled up on my countertop, so now I use an empty toilet tissue roll to contain the power cords of my kitchen appliances. Just fold the cord back and forth to create a bundle and push one end of the bundle through the tube. No more crazy cords!

Elise Newman
Bellaire, Texas

WHEN LIFE GIVES YOU LEMONS . . .

My daughters hate it when melted ice cubes dilute their lemonade. So now whenever I make a batch of lemonade, I pour some into ice cube trays and use those in their glasses instead of ice. No more watered-down lemonade! You can also freeze coffee for iced coffee or tea for iced tea.

Rose Brooks
Ellensburg, Wash.

IT'S IN THE BAG!

Instead of buying an expensive cover to protect my standing mixer from dust and debris, I discovered that a Reynolds Oven Bag (turkey size) fits perfectly over the top. Even better, it is clear plastic, so I can still show off my mixer on the countertop.

Eloise C. Keefe
Columbus, Ohio

BROWN BAG IT

When I'm cooking chicken or pork cutlets, I like to drain them on top of a brown paper bag. Once they have drained, I put the cutlets on a plate and slip it inside the bag to keep them warm until they're ready to serve.

Janet Chino
Temecula, Calif.

PLAN AHEAD

Whenever I am cooking chicken breasts, I always cook extra to freeze for later use. I usually cube or shred the chicken before I freeze it; once it's frozen, I divide it into 1-cup portions. They are perfect for adding to a casserole or soup— it saves so much prep time.

Kristina Tolman
Gilbert, Ariz.

STACK 'EM UP

To protect my older plates and bowls, I line each plate with a coffee filter. Now I don't have to worry about chipping or scratching my favorite dishes.

Caroline Tesiorowski
Santa Barbara, Calif.

SKILLET CORN ON THE COB

I love fresh corn on the cob, but boiling a huge pot of water for only a few ears of corn seems silly. Instead, I place the corn in my skillet, along with an inch or two of water, and bring it all to a simmer. I then cover the skillet and let it steam, off heat, for a few minutes. Prepared this way, the corn is fully cooked before a large pot of water would even begin to simmer.

Mary Louder
San Anselmo, Calif.

If you'd like to submit a tip, please e-mail us by visiting **CooksCountry.com/ emailus**. Or send a letter to Kitchen Shortcuts, Cook's Country, P.O. Box 470739, Brookline, MA 02447. Include your name, address, and phone number. If we publish your tip, you will receive a free one-year subscription to Cook's Country.

SPIN CYCLE

When I need to clean a lot of mushrooms, I don't wipe them by hand. I put them in the strainer part of a salad spinner and rinse off the dirt with water from my kitchen sink. After pouring off the excess water, I give them a quick spin. The mushrooms come out clean as a whistle!

Michael Paulini
Elmhurst, Ill.

CORN BREAD WAFFLES

During the summer months, I hate to heat up the oven for a small pan of corn bread. Instead, I use a trick that I learned from my grandmother. I "bake" the corn bread batter in a hinged waffle pan. Coat both surfaces of the pan with cooking spray and preheat it over medium-low to medium heat. Just spoon the batter in and cook until nicely browned, about 10 minutes or so.

Glenna Anderson Muse
Springfield, Mo.

SODA YOU CAN SHAKE

My favorite kitchen cleanser is plain baking soda because it is inexpensive and food-safe. I keep it in a mesh-topped shaker for sprinkling over messes on my countertop. I always leave it sitting by the sink so that it's on hand whenever disaster strikes. The stainless steel container isn't bad looking, either!

Dana Thompson
Gresham, Ore.

INSTANT THINKING

I always keep a box of instant mashed potatoes in the cupboard, just in case I accidentally add too much milk to my mashed potatoes. It is a quick fix that doesn't require cooking more potatoes. You can't even tell that I have used instant potatoes as a thickener.

Maggie Sebastian
Denver, Colo.

PUT A CORK IN IT

To give your dirty food processor bowl a good soak, put a wine or champagne cork in the center hole. Now you can fill the bowl all the way to the top with hot water.

Carol Canfield
St. Paul, Minn.

CHECK THE OIL

I used to have a hard time knowing when my oil was hot enough to start frying. Now I just hold the tip of a carrot in the oil. If it's bubbling rapidly, I know the oil is ready for frying.

Lara Cooper
Cincinnati, Ohio

DISHWASHER DUTY

Lightweight plastic containers and cups often turn over in the dishwasher and fill with water. To prevent this, I arrange them on the top shelf and lay a cooling rack on top. The weight of the rack keeps them in place during the rinse cycle.

Joan Jensen
Coulee Dam, Wash.

RECIPE REMEMBERED

When traveling, I like to buy a few postcards of the area I'm visiting. If I find a recipe on the trip (and I usually do), I write it on the back of the postcard. On my return home, I place the postcard in my recipe box, so I always have a visual memory of the places where I find my favorite recipes.

Carol Jemison
Chico, Calif.

SWEETER SURFACE

When I make sugar cookies, I always use confectioners' sugar instead of flour to dust the surface before rolling. It makes the cookies taste even better and gives them a crispy golden color. It also eliminates any unpleasant residual taste of flour.

Linda Bibbo
Chagrin Falls, Ohio

ANOTHER WAY TO BAKE

I don't have a tube pan, so whenever I want to make an angel food cake, I use a springform pan with an empty can of soup placed in the middle. I spray the can and pour the batter around it. When the cake is done, simply remove the can and slide a plate underneath the bottom of the cake. The cake will come out perfect, without any cracks or crumbs from lifting.

Cathy Zipp
Gambier, Ohio

Safe Skewer Disposal

Whether it's beef kebabs, shrimp skewers, or chicken satay, I love any meat that's grilled on a wooden stick. Unfortunately, when the skewers are discarded, they often pierce the garbage bag and cause it to tear open. To avoid this messy situation, I keep a lidded container in the kitchen—an empty coffee can, peanut jar, or a soda bottle—for collecting the used skewers, bending or breaking them in half if necessary to fit. Once the container is filled, I just throw it in the garbage. No more torn trash bags!

Tim Greening Shreveport, La.

Quick Cross

Traditionally, individual peanut butter cookies are scored with a fork to form a crisscross pattern. To speed up the process, I spray a crosshatched cooling rack with vegetable oil spray and press the rack onto a baking sheet full of preshaped cookie dough. This way, I can do all the cookies at once.

Bob Langston
Fort Smith, Ark.

Cupcake Protector

To make transporting cupcakes easy, just buy two disposable muffin tins. Use one to bake and frost the cupcakes and use the other as a cover. Use tape to keep them together and you'll never have a cupcake disaster again!

Suzanne Burns
Bend, Ore.

A Safe Temperature

Whenever I make candy, I'm always hesitant to hold my thermometer too close to the scorching-hot pot. To save my fingers, I now stick my candy thermometer through the holes of my potato masher and lower it into the pot. This way I can read the temperature without the risk of getting burned!

Cindy Chartier
Lumberton, N.J.

Not Just for Teeth!

A RAINBOW OF CHOICES

I use toothbrushes to clean various pieces of equipment in my kitchen, but I don't like to use the same toothbrush for everything, because they retain odors. Instead, I use different color toothbrushes depending on the piece of equipment. I use a yellow toothbrush for my lemon zester, orange for my cheese grater, and clear for my garlic press. This way I never get confused.

Marion Marcinek Palm Bay, Fla.

Everyone has a different take on this Italian favorite. Ours happens in a slow cooker—no nonna required.

Italian gravy is a hearty, slow-simmered tomato sauce enriched with three kinds of meat.

My friend Pam's Italian grand-mother wakes up early every Sunday and begins the arduous process of making the meaty tomato sauce her family calls "gravy." This involves making meatballs, stuffing and rolling up a flank steak to make braci-ole, and adding whole pork chops and sausage to a vat of simmering sauce. With incredible patience and stamina, she stirs and tends to her sauce until you can smell the rich flavors all the way down the street (so it's a good thing she makes enough to feed the entire block). Since this dish is all about long, slow cooking, I wondered if I could use a slow cooker to streamline its preparation.

Stovetop recipes call for a large stock-pot, so the quantity and variety of meat doesn't really matter. In my 6-quart slow cooker, I had to be more selec-tive. The meatballs disintegrated when I added them at the outset, and I didn't want to come home just to add them at the halfway mark, so they failed to make the cut. Braciole tasted great, but it was too unwieldy for a slow cooker, so it, too, was omitted.

But without the meatballs and braci-ole, my sauce lacked depth. To replace their beefy flavor, I tried other cuts of beef that work well in long-cooked recipes. My tasters preferred flank

steak to brisket and chuck roast (both of which made the sauce too greasy). Moving on to the pork, regular chops were tough and chewy, and baby back ribs didn't add enough flavor. But country-style spareribs provided flavor-ful meat that fell off the bone after eight hours in the slow cooker. In fact, both the steak and the spareribs were tender enough to shred and stir back into the sauce. Sweet and hot Italian sausage, both sliced in half, added kick to the sauce while staying juicy.

I thought the tomatoes would be the easy part, but many of my early tests were too watery. There wasn't much evaporation as the sauce cooked, so I needed to use something thicker than canned diced tomatoes, the test kitch-en's first choice for most tomato sauces. Further testing and tasting revealed that a combination of drained diced toma-toes, canned tomato sauce, and tomato paste had the best balance of flavor and texture. As for other flavors, I found that cooking onions, lots of garlic (a whop-ping 12 cloves), wine, and oregano in the sausage drippings at the onset built a rich flavor base that carried through to the end of cooking. And to brighten the finished sauce, I added fresh basil. I now had my own version of Italian Sunday Gravy, and it was worthy of any Italian grandmother's praise. **–Meredith Butcher**

ITALIAN SUNDAY GRAVY
SERVES 8 TO 10
Most sausage has enough seasoning to make extra salt unnecessary. The hearty sauce makes a meal when paired with 2 pounds of rigatoni, ziti, or penne.

  1 **tablespoon vegetable oil**
  1 **pound sweet Italian sausage**
  1 **pound hot Italian sausage**
  2 **onions, chopped medium**
 12 **garlic cloves, minced**
  2 **teaspoons dried oregano**
  1 **(6-ounce) can tomato paste**
 ½ **cup dry red wine**
  1 **(28-ounce) can diced tomatoes, drained**
  1 **(28-ounce) can tomato sauce**
  2 **pounds bone-in country-style spareribs, trimmed of excess fat**
1½ **pounds flank steak**
  3 **tablespoons chopped fresh basil Pepper**

1. Heat oil in Dutch oven over medium-high heat until just smoking. Add sweet sausage and cook until well browned and fat begins to render, about 8 minutes. Using slotted spoon, transfer sausage to paper towel–lined plate to drain, then place in slow-cooker insert. Repeat with hot sausage.

2. Cook onions in sausage fat over medium heat until well browned, about 6 minutes. Stir in garlic and oregano and cook until fragrant, about 1 minute. Add tomato paste and cook until paste begins to brown, about 5 minutes. Stir in wine and simmer, scraping browned bits from pan bottom with wooden spoon, until wine is reduced, about 3 minutes. Transfer to slow-cooker insert and stir in diced tomatoes and tomato sauce.

3. Submerge spareribs and flank steak in sauce in slow-cooker insert. Set slow cooker on low, cover, and cook until meat is tender, 8 to 10 hours. (Alternatively, cook on high for 4 to 5 hours.)

4. About 30 minutes before serving, transfer sausages, ribs, and flank steak to baking sheet and set aside until cool enough to handle. Shred ribs and flank steak into small pieces, discarding excess fat and bones; slice sausages in half crosswise. Use wide spoon to skim fat off surface, then stir sausages and shred-

ded meat back into sauce. Stir in basil and season with pepper. Serve. (Leftover gravy can be stored in airtight container in refrigerator for up to 3 days.)

Make Ahead: The recipe can be prepared through step 2 up to 2 days in advance. After reducing the wine in step 2, add the diced tomatoes, tomato sauce, and browned sausages to the Dutch oven and simmer over medium-low heat until the sausages are cooked through, about 12 minutes. Refrigerate the sausage and sauce mixture in an air-tight container until ready to use. When ready to cook the gravy, warm the sauce and the sausages together over medium heat until heated through and transfer to slow-cooker insert. Proceed with step 3.

The Meat Matters
Ask a hundred Italian grandmothers what meat they use for Sunday gravy and you'll get a hundred different answers—everything from meatballs to pork chops. For our easy slow-cooker version, we prefer the taste, texture, and convenience of the fol-lowing combination.

ITALIAN SAUSAGES
Browning the sausage in advance helps build deep flavor.

FLANK STEAK
This lean cut adds beefy flavor without too much grease.

COUNTRY-STYLE SPARERIBS
These meaty ribs become fall-apart tender in a slow cooker.

Recipe Makeover CHOCOLATE MOUSSE

How do you make a low-fat version of a dessert whose two main ingredients are whipped cream and chocolate?

When presented with the challenge of developing a low-fat chocolate mousse recipe, I admit I was daunted. After all, traditional chocolate mousse—essentially melted chocolate, cocoa, beaten egg whites, and whipped cream—is mostly fat. Besides preserving the rich chocolate flavor, I wanted to keep that irresistible silky, fluffy texture. How was I going to pull this off?

Since this dish is as much about texture as flavor, I was hoping to find an alternative to the whipped cream. It didn't take me long to find a stack of "healthy" mousse recipes that relied on various low-fat dairy products. Even when I pureed them first, part-skim ricotta cheese and extra-firm tofu made mousses with unpleasant granular textures; mousse made with low-fat yogurt was runny and sour; and light cream cheese yielded a dense and gummy texture.

Leaving low-fat dairy behind, I tested unflavored gelatin, but tasters rejected its bouncy, "set" quality. Marshmallow crème (Fluff) gave mousse a light, lofty texture without any fat, but the Fluff lent a distinct marshmallow flavor that wasn't right for chocolate mousse. The Fluff did, however, remind me of seven-minute frosting, an old-fashioned icing made by beating egg whites with sugar over heat for seven minutes. I tried this

and finally had some hope; there was no marshmallow flavor, but the airy frosting made the mousse too light. Staying with cooked egg whites, I made an Italian meringue by beating egg whites in a mixer until fluffy, then "cooking" them by adding a hot sugar syrup. This fat-free mixture (which is denser than the seven-minute frosting) became suitably voluminous and gave the mousse the creamy texture I was looking for—without a drop of heavy cream.

Using this Italian meringue as my base, I folded in melted chocolate (for richness) and cocoa powder (for intensity) and chilled my mousse. The texture was perfectly creamy and light. Now my tasters' only complaint was about the flavor—it was harsh, one-dimensional, and actually too chocolaty.

I tried scaling back the amount of chocolate, but I was just reducing the chocolate flavor, not the harshness. I played around with every amount and combination of semisweet, bittersweet, milk, and unsweetened chocolate, all to no avail. And then it hit me that there was one chocolate I hadn't tried: white chocolate.

In the end, just ⅓ cup of white chocolate chips took the edge off the other chocolate and cocoa—and tacked on only 10 extra calories per serving. Why did it work? White chocolate isn't actually chocolate—it's mostly fat and sugar.

It turns out that chocolate and cocoa need fat to temper their harshness and bring out their full, well-balanced flavor. Without any cream in my mousse, the chocolate and cocoa were too harsh. A little white chocolate added just enough fat to keep them in check.

–Stephanie Alleyne

LOW-FAT CHOCOLATE MOUSSE
SERVES 6
The meringue and chocolate mixture are combined in two stages so the meringue doesn't collapse. For the best texture, chill the mousse overnight.

- 4 ounces semisweet chocolate, broken into pieces
- ⅓ cup white chocolate chips
- 2 tablespoons Dutch-processed cocoa powder
- 6 tablespoons plus ½ cup water
- 1 teaspoon vanilla extract
- ½ cup sugar
- 3 large egg whites
- ¼ teaspoon cream of tartar

1. Melt semisweet chocolate, white chocolate, cocoa powder, 6 tablespoons water, and vanilla in medium bowl set over pot of barely simmering water until smooth. Set aside to cool slightly.

2. Bring ½ cup water and sugar to vigorous boil in small saucepan over high heat. Boil until slightly thickened and large bubbles rise to top, about 4 minutes. Remove from heat while beating egg whites.

3. With electric mixer on medium-low speed, beat egg whites in large bowl until frothy, about 1 minute. Add cream of tartar and beat, gradually increasing speed to medium-high, until whites hold soft peaks, about 2 minutes. With mixer running, slowly pour hot syrup into whites (avoid pouring syrup onto beaters or it will splash). Increase speed to high and beat until meringue has cooled to just warm and becomes very thick and shiny, 2 to 3 minutes.

4. Whisk one-third of meringue into chocolate mixture until combined, then whisk in remaining meringue. Spoon mousse into six 6-ounce ramekins or pudding cups. Cover tightly with plastic wrap. Chill overnight. (Mousse can be refrigerated for up to 4 days.)

White chocolate is the secret ingredient in our velvety mousse; it can also be used as a garnish.

And the Numbers...
All nutritional information is for a single 6-ounce serving of chocolate mousse.

TRADITIONAL CHOCOLATE MOUSSE
CALORIES: **380**
FAT: **32g**
SATURATED FAT: **19g**

COOK'S COUNTRY LOW-FAT CHOCOLATE MOUSSE
CALORIES: **230**
FAT: **10g**
SATURATED FAT: **5g**

Three Chocolates Are Better than One

SEMISWEET CHOCOLATE
Adds rich chocolate flavor and creaminess.

DUTCH-PROCESSED COCOA
Adds intense chocolate flavor.

WHITE CHOCOLATE CHIPS
Tempers the harshness of the chocolate and cocoa.

Fluffiness without the Fat

Instead of whipped cream, our recipe relies on the soft, billowy texture of a fat-free Italian meringue made by beating hot sugar syrup into whipped egg whites.

Heirloom Recipe Preservation Project

Thousands of home cooks helped our test kitchen rescue "lost" recipes too good to forget.

When we announced our Heirloom Recipe Preservation Project last summer, we didn't know what to expect. We knew that our culinary heritage was in danger of disappearing, but we wondered if it was already too late. Were Grandma's handwritten recipe cards even relevant in this age of food websites and computers? And how many heirloom recipes are really worth saving? After all, there's a good reason many old-fashioned recipes are no longer made!

The only way to find out was to take action. Just as farmers are trying to maintain our agricultural heritage through seed preservation, the editors of *Cook's Country* decided to put our test kitchen's expertise to work, doing what we do best—creating recipes that work. But we needed to collect ideas.

To get home cooks to check their recipe boxes, some prize money was in order. We hoped that $10,000 would encourage a few hundred cooks to write down recipes and send them to us. Well, it turns out there were nearly 3,000 cooks across the country who were interested in recipe preservation. Your letters crammed our e-mail inboxes and letters piled up on our desks.

And what did we find? Two editors read every single letter and were amazed at the simplicity and ingenuity displayed in your recipes. Our five prize winners represent the best of the best, but we discovered hundreds of exciting recipes.

At least half of your recipes were desserts. Cakes and cookies were well represented, but so were old-fashioned puddings, candies, and breads. Cabbage and potatoes topped the list of most popular vegetables. Recipe yields were huge (families used to be larger), and there were plenty of recipes with funny names (Lazy Day Cobbler and Orange Kiss Me Cake sure sound good). We received a surprising number of what we called "nostalgia" recipes, which rely on popular twentieth-century convenience foods—everything from Mile-High Bologna Pie to Chocolate Marlow, a mousse made with marshmallows and evaporated milk. We also received several family recipes dating back to the Revolutionary War.

All five recipes presented here offer an intriguing bite of our culinary history. We are confident a new generation of cooks will delight in discovering them.

$10,000 GRAND-PRIZE WINNER

Peach Puzzle
WINNING COOK: **Lois Schlademan** Stow, Ohio
Peach Puzzle relies on an inventive technique to elevate the simple combination of flaky biscuit dough, sweet peaches, and brown sugar syrup.

Meet Our Winners

$10,000 Grand-Prize Winner
Peach Puzzle
Lois Schlademan
Stow, Ohio

$1,000 Prize Winner
Runsas
Pam Patterson
Leon, Kan.

$1,000 Prize Winner
Tennessee Stack Cake
Andrea Hall
Puyallup, Wash.

$1,000 Prize Winner
Hungarian Sweet Rolls
Erin Glaspy
Camano Island, Wash.

$1,000 Prize Winner
Naked Ladies with Their Legs Crossed
Shirley Sieradzki
Mishawaka, Ind.

COMING SOON:
America's Best Lost Recipes Cookbook

We were so overwhelmed by the response to our request for heirloom recipes that we are working on a book to include more of your submissions. *America's Best Lost Recipes* will be published in the fall. Here's a sampling of recipes in the book.

Cold-Oven Pound Cake: Starting the batter in a cold oven yields an extra-crisp, souffléed crust.

Corn Rivel Soup: This Pennsylvania Dutch specialty is made with hearty flour dumplings called rivels.

Pioneer Bread: This sweet whole-wheat bread was favored by pioneers moving west in the nineteenth-century.

If you have an old family recipe you want to share and preserve, visit us at CooksCountry.com. We'd love to hear from you. On our website, you'll also find more heirloom recipes from cooks across the country.

Peach Puzzle

WHY THIS RECIPE WON: Our grand prize–winning recipe has all the abracadabra of a magic trick as well as beautiful presentation and all-around good taste. It deserves a place alongside cobbler and crisp in the pantheon of simple American fruit desserts.

RECIPE HISTORY: One-of-a-kind family recipe created by Lois's mother in the 1940s.

UNIQUE TECHNIQUE: This unlikely recipe begins by placing a custard cup upside down in the center of a pie plate. Peeled peaches are arranged around the cup and then drizzled with a mixture of brown sugar, butter, and vanilla. Buttery biscuit dough is domed over the peaches, and then this puzzling dessert goes into the oven. Once cooled, the pie plate is flipped over to reveal tender peaches nestled into the flaky biscuit. So where's the butterscotch-like syrup? It's all in the cup!

WHAT OUR WINNER SAYS: "When you pour a spoonful of syrup over the warm peach and it soaks into the biscuit crust, you will think you died and went to heaven—where, when greeting my mom, she would be pleased that it was her recipe that made you come visit!"

PEACH PUZZLE SERVES 7
Choose peaches that are neither very ripe nor rock-hard. They should give a little when squeezed. Be sure to invert the pie plate quickly to avoid losing any of the syrup. Serve with vanilla ice cream or sweetened whipped cream.

Peaches and Syrup
- 7 medium peaches, peeled (see note)
- 3/4 cup packed light brown sugar
- 6 tablespoons water
- 2 tablespoons unsalted butter
- 1/2 teaspoon vanilla extract
- 1/8 teaspoon salt

Dough
- 1 1/4 cups all-purpose flour
- 2 tablespoons granulated sugar

ASSEMBLING PEACH PUZZLE

 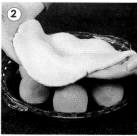 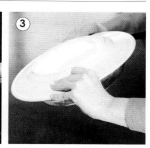

1. Place a custard cup or ramekin upside down in the center of a 9-inch pie plate. Arrange the peeled peaches around the cup. **2.** Fit the dough snuggly around the peaches without attaching the dough to the pie plate. Bake as directed. **3.** Once cooled, quickly and carefully invert the puzzle onto a rimmed serving plate.

1   tablespoon baking powder
1/4 teaspoon salt
5   tablespoons unsalted butter, cut into
     1/4-inch pieces and chilled
6   tablespoons milk

1. For the peaches and syrup: Adjust oven rack to middle position and heat oven to 400 degrees. Place 6-ounce custard cup or ramekin upside down in center of 9-inch pie plate and arrange peaches around ramekin (photo 1). Combine brown sugar, water, butter, vanilla, and salt in medium saucepan and stir over medium heat until sugar dissolves and butter melts, about 5 minutes. Pour syrup over peaches.

2. For the dough: Pulse flour, sugar, baking powder, and salt in food processor until blended. Add butter and pulse until flour mixture is pale yellow and resembles coarse cornmeal, five to six 1-second pulses. Turn mixture into medium bowl. (To make dough by hand: Use large holes on box grater to grate frozen butter into bowl with flour mixture, then rub flour-coated pieces between your fingers until flour mixture turns pale yellow and coarse.)

3. Using rubber spatula, fold milk into flour mixture, pressing mixture against sides of bowl to form dough. Squeeze dough together and flatten into disk. On lightly floured work surface, roll dough into 9-inch circle. Lay dough directly over peaches and press dough so that it fits snuggly around peaches (photo 2). The dough will stretch as you fit it around peaches, but do not attach dough to pie plate. Bake until top is golden brown, 25 to 30 minutes. Cool on rack for 30 minutes.

4. Place large rimmed serving plate over top of pie plate and quickly invert Puzzle onto plate (photo 3). Cut into wedges around each peach and serve, pouring syrup over each portion.

Runsas

WHY THIS RECIPE WON: The combination of soft, sweet yeast dough surrounding a quick filling made with ground beef, browned cabbage, and cheese is both simple and addictive.

RECIPE HISTORY: Square-shaped beef and cabbage buns brought to the United States by Russian-German farmers who immigrated to the Midwest a century ago. Pam's sister, Jeanne, created this recipe in the 1960s and was inspired by a local fast-food restaurant in Lincoln, Neb., where the sisters grew up. Pam now lives in Kansas, where these buns are round (a shape she prefers) and called bierocks.

SECRET INGREDIENT: Sweetened condensed milk in the dough.

WHAT OUR WINNER SAYS: "My contribution to this family recipe is the sliced American cheese in the filling. How else do you get kids to eat something with cabbage?"

RUNSAS (Beef and Cabbage Buns with Cheese) SERVES 8

Don't overcook the cabbage—you want it to provide some crunch when you bite into these sandwiches.

Dough

3/4 cup warm water (110 degrees)
1/2 cup sweetened condensed milk
1/4 cup vegetable oil
2   tablespoons sugar
1   large egg
3 1/2 cups all-purpose flour, plus extra for rolling out dough
2   packages instant or rapid-rise yeast
1   teaspoon salt

Filling

3   tablespoons unsalted butter, 2 tablespoons melted
1 1/2 pounds 90-percent lean ground beef

Runsas
WINNING COOK: **Pam Patterson** Leon, Kan.
Runsas give solid Midwestern Germanic fare an original—and unexpected—twist.

1   large onion, chopped fine
1/2 small head cabbage, chopped (about 3 cups)
     Salt and pepper
8   slices deli American cheese

1. For the dough: Lightly grease large bowl with cooking spray. Mix water, sweetened condensed milk, oil, sugar, and egg in large measuring cup. Mix flour, yeast, and salt in bowl of standing mixer fitted with dough hook. With mixer on low, add water mixture. After dough comes together, increase speed to medium and mix until shiny and smooth, 4 to 6 minutes. Turn dough out onto heavily floured work surface, shape into ball, and place in greased bowl. (To make dough by hand: Combine dry ingredients in large bowl, make well in center of dry ingredients, add wet ingredients, and mix with wooden spoon until shaggy dough forms. Turn dough out onto heavily floured work surface and knead until shiny and smooth, about 10 minutes.) Cover bowl with plastic wrap and let rest in warm place until doubled in size, about 1 hour.

2. For the filling: Melt 1 tablespoon butter in large skillet over medium-high heat. Add beef and cook until just beginning to brown, about 6 minutes, breaking up any large clumps. Using slotted spoon, transfer beef to paper towel–lined plate.

3. Pour off all but 2 tablespoons fat from pan. Add onion and cook until softened, about 3 minutes. Add cabbage and toss until just beginning to wilt, 2 to 4 minutes. Return beef to pan and season with salt and pepper.

4. To assemble and bake: Adjust oven racks to the upper-middle and lower-middle positions and heat oven to 350 degrees. Coat 2 baking sheets with cooking spray. Divide dough into 8 equal pieces. Working on lightly floured work surface, roll each piece of dough into 7-inch circle. Place one dough round in deep cereal bowl and top with one slice of cheese. Spoon 3/4 cup filling over cheese and pinch edges of dough together to form bun. Transfer bun, seam side down, to prepared baking sheet. Repeat with remaining dough, cheese, and filling, placing 4 buns on each baking sheet. Cover buns with plastic wrap and let rise until puffed, about 20 minutes.

5. Bake buns until golden brown, about 20 minutes, switching and rotating position of baking sheets halfway through baking time. Brush buns with melted butter and serve.

$1,000 PRIZE WINNER

Tennessee Stack Cake
WINNING COOK: **Andrea Hall** Puyallup, Wash.
Tennessee Stack Cake looks impressive, but the roots of this regional recipe are really quite humble.

Tennessee Stack Cake

WHY THIS RECIPE WON: Good things come to patient cooks, as this cake must sit for an entire day before being served. During that time, the oversized sugar cookies soak up moisture from the apple butter and become tender and cake-like.
RECIPE HISTORY: Appalachian specialty known by various names, including apple stack cake, pioneer stack cake, and washday stack cake.
SECRET INGREDIENT: Homemade apple butter.
WHAT OUR WINNER SAYS: "My grandmother (Mom-Mom) was born in 1917 into, a family of ten in Lone Mountain, Tenn. Baking day was Saturday, and dried apple rings were brought down from the attic, where they had been hung every fall, reserved mainly for use in this special cake. The baked cake was placed on the dining room table to cool, then covered with a clean tablecloth to keep the flies off. Mom-Mom remembers how she loved to go downstairs on Sunday morning and see the large hump under the cloth where the stack cake lay. The anticipation was heightened by the fact that the cake could not be eaten until after Sunday dinner, and all day the scent of spiced apples and baked sugar cookies filled the house."

TENNESSEE STACK CAKE
SERVES 10 TO 12
Be sure to let the cake set at least 24 hours, as the moisture from the filling transforms the texture of the cookie-like layers into a tender apple-flavored cake.

Filling
- 3 (6-ounce) bags dried apples
- 1 cup packed light brown sugar
- 1½ teaspoons ground cinnamon
- ½ teaspoon ground cloves
- ½ teaspoon ground allspice

Layers
- 6 cups all-purpose flour
- 1 tablespoon baking powder
- 1 teaspoon baking soda
- ¼ teaspoon salt
- ½ cup buttermilk
- 2 large eggs
- 1 teaspoon vanilla extract
- 16 tablespoons (2 sticks) unsalted butter, softened
- 2 cups granulated sugar
  Confectioners' sugar for dusting

1. For the filling: Bring apples and water to cover to boil in medium saucepan. Reduce heat and simmer until apples are completely softened, about 10 minutes. Drain apples and let cool until just warm, about 15 minutes. Puree apples in food processor until smooth. Transfer to bowl and stir in sugar, cinnamon, cloves, and allspice. (Filling can be refrigerated for up to 2 days.)

2. For the layers: Adjust oven racks to the upper-middle and lower-middle positions and heat oven to 350 degrees. Coat 2 baking sheets with cooking spray. Whisk flour, baking powder, baking soda, and salt in medium bowl. Whisk buttermilk, eggs, and vanilla in large measuring cup.

3. With electric mixer at medium-high speed, beat butter and granulated sugar in large bowl until fluffy, about 2 minutes, scraping down bowl as necessary. Add one-third of flour mixture and beat on medium-low speed until just incorporated, about 30 seconds. Add half of buttermilk mixture and beat on low speed until combined, about 30 seconds. Scrape down bowl as necessary and repeat with half of remaining flour mixture, remaining buttermilk mixture, and remaining flour mixture. Give bowl a final scrape. (Dough will be thick.)

4. Divide dough into 8 equal portions. Working with 2 portions at a time, roll each out into 10-inch circle about ¼ inch thick. Using 9-inch cake pan as template, trim away excess dough to form two perfectly round 9-inch disks. Transfer disks to prepared baking sheets and bake until golden brown, 10 to 12 minutes, rotating and switching baking sheets halfway through baking time. Transfer disks to rack and cool completely, at least 1 hour. Repeat with remaining dough. (Layers can be wrapped tightly in plastic and stored at room temperature for up to 2 days.)

5. Place 1 layer on serving plate and spread with 1 cup filling. Repeat 6 times. Top with final layer, wrap tightly in plastic, and refrigerate until layers soften, at least 24 hours or up to 2 days. Dust with confectioners' sugar and serve.

Hungarian Sweet Rolls

WHY THIS RECIPE WON: With a flaky crust and sweet meringue center, these delicate rolls nearly melt in your mouth.
RECIPE HISTORY: Erin credits this family favorite to her grandmother and great-aunt Lois. Erin's grandfather and great-grandfather were Lutheran pastors in Chicago, and this recipe was printed in a church cookbook back in the 1930s.
SECRET INGREDIENT: Walnut meringue spread over pastry dough.
WHAT OUR WINNER SAYS: "To know that my ancestors smelled the same warm scents that fill the house as these rolls bake creates a unique kinship with the past. And I know that someday my future children will taste their great-grandmother's rolls and experience the same euphoria that I did as a child."

HUNGARIAN SWEET ROLLS
MAKES 24 ROLLS
Use plenty of confectioners' sugar to roll out the dough, which is quite sticky.

Dough
- 4 cups all-purpose flour
- 1 package rapid-rise or instant yeast
- ½ teaspoon salt
- 24 tablespoons (3 sticks) unsalted butter, cut into ½-inch pieces and chilled
- 3 large egg yolks (save whites for filling)
- 1 cup sour cream
- 1 teaspoon vanilla extract

Filling
- 3 large egg whites
- 1 cup sugar
- ¼ teaspoon vanilla extract
- ½ cup walnuts, chopped fine
  Confectioners' sugar, for rolling dough

1. For the dough: Pulse flour, yeast, and salt in food processor until blended. Add butter and pulse until flour is pale

FORMING HUNGARIAN SWEET ROLLS

1. On a work surface sprinkled heavily with confectioners' sugar, roll one piece of dough out into 16-inch circle about ⅛ inch thick. Spread the filling over the dough. **2.** Using a knife, cut the dough into 12 equal wedges. **3.** Starting at the wider end of each wedge, gently roll up the dough, ending with the pointed end on the bottom.

SHAPING THE "LADIES"

1. Cut the 18 by 14-inch rectangle of dough in half lengthwise, then cut each half crosswise into 1½-inch-wide strips. **2.** Cut each strip lengthwise, three-quarters of the way to the top, to make a pair of "legs." **3.** Twist the legs around each other twice.

yellow and resembles coarse cornmeal, ten to fifteen 1-second pulses. Turn mixture into large bowl. (To do this by hand: Use large holes on box grater to grate frozen butter into bowl with flour mixture, then rub flour-coated pieces between your fingers until flour mixture turns pale yellow and coarse.)

2. Beat egg yolks, sour cream, and vanilla in bowl. Using rubber spatula, fold yolk mixture into flour mixture, pressing mixture against sides of bowl to form sticky dough. Divide dough into 2 pieces and flatten each into 4-inch disk. Wrap disks in plastic and refrigerate until well chilled, at least 4 hours or up to 24 hours.

3. For the filling: Adjust oven racks to upper-middle and lower-middle positions and heat oven to 400 degrees.

Line 2 baking sheets with parchment paper. With electric mixer at medium-low speed, beat egg whites in large bowl until frothy, about 1 minute. Increase speed to medium and gradually add sugar until incorporated, about 1 minute. Add vanilla, increase speed to high, and beat until whites hold soft peaks, about 2 minutes. Using rubber spatula, fold in walnuts.

4. Heavily sprinkle work surface with confectioners' sugar. Working with one piece of dough at a time, form rolls according to photos. Arrange 12 rolls on each baking sheet, spacing them about 2 inches apart. Bake until tops are golden brown and puffed, 15 to 18 minutes, rotating and switching baking sheets halfway through baking time. Serve warm or at room temperature.

Naked Ladies with Their Legs Crossed

WHY THIS RECIPE WON: The recipe title caught our eye, but the addition of mashed potatoes to the dough gives these crullers a crisp crust and soft, chewy interior that makes this fried dough a winner.
RECIPE HISTORY: Created by Shirley's grandmother nearly a century ago. Shirley credits her grandmother's German ancestry with the recipe's secret ingredient.
SECRET INGREDIENT: Mashed potatoes.
WHAT OUR WINNER SAYS: "When my granddaughter was in the fourth or fifth grade, her teacher asked her what she did that weekend. Can you picture the look on the teacher's face when my granddaughter said, 'We made Naked Ladies with Their Legs Crossed'? Eventually, all was explained, and I treated the teacher and her class to a plate of donuts."

NAKED LADIES WITH THEIR LEGS CROSSED
(Spiced Crullers) MAKES 24

Don't be tempted to use leftover mashed potatoes. We tried this shortcut but found that leftover mashed potatoes invariably contain butter, which makes the dough too sticky.

1	russet potato, peeled and cut into 1-inch chunks
1	large egg
2	tablespoons milk
1¼	cups sugar
½	teaspoon vanilla extract
1½	cups all-purpose flour, plus extra for rolling out dough
1½	teaspoons baking powder
½	teaspoon salt
½	teaspoon ground cinnamon
⅛	teaspoon ground nutmeg
2	quarts vegetable or peanut oil

1. Bring potato and water to cover to boil in small saucepan. Reduce heat and simmer until potato is tender, about 15 minutes. Drain potato, then mash until smooth. Let cool completely, at least 30 minutes.

2. Transfer ½ cup mashed potato to medium bowl (discard remaining potato) and beat in egg, milk, ½ cup sugar, and vanilla until combined. Whisk flour, baking powder, salt, cinnamon, and nutmeg in large bowl. Make well in center of flour mixture and add potato mixture. Stir to form moist and sticky dough.

3. On heavily floured work surface, roll dough into 18 by 14-inch rectangle about ¼ inch thick. Cut dough into strips, make slit in each strip, and twist to shape dough to resemble crossed legs (see photos). Transfer crullers to floured baking sheet and refrigerate until ready to fry. (Crullers may be covered with plastic wrap and refrigerated for up to 24 hours.)

4. Heat oil in large Dutch oven over medium heat until temperature reaches 350 degrees. Carefully lower 6 crullers into hot oil and fry, maintaining temperature between 325 and 350 degrees, until crisp and deep brown on both sides, 4 or 5 minutes. Using slotted spoon, transfer crullers to paper towel–lined plate and drain for 3 minutes. Toss crullers in bowl with remaining ¾ cup sugar and transfer to serving plate. Repeat with remaining crullers, regulating oil temperature as necessary. Serve.

FOOD FACT: *The highest price ever fetched for a hog in the United States was at the Houston Livestock Show in 1998, where a group of Houston businessmen paid $105,000 for the Grand Champion barrow exhibited by Brittany Muery.*

Grilled Stuffed Pork Chops

Kitchen Know-How
STUFFING PORK CHOPS

The key to tidy stuffing is to create a large pocket with a small opening. Here's how we do it.

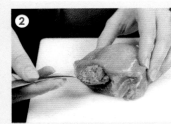

1. Insert a small sharp knife through the side of the chop until the tip almost reaches the opposite edge. Swing the knife through the meat, creating a large pocket.
2. Use your finger to widen the pocket almost to the edge of the chop. Spoon a small amount of filling into the chop.
3. Thread a toothpick through the side of the chop to seal in the filling.

Visit us online!
For Sausage Pizza and Southwestern stuffing variations for these pork chops, visit CooksCountry.com and click on Cook's Country Extra.

Can the right stuffing boost flavor and rescue lean chops from their usual leathery end?

Americans are very fickle about pork. We insist on the leanest meat possible, but then we complain when our pork tastes and chews like shoe leather. Soaking pork chops in a saltwater brine is a good way to combat dryness and deeply season the meat, but this trick takes an hour. Could I accomplish the same thing by stuffing pork chops with moist, flavorful ingredients while the grill was heating up?

After trying all the chops at my supermarket, I realized that thick loin chops have the largest expanse of meat, making them ideal for stuffing. Bones were awkward to navigate around, so I chose boneless chops for my working recipe. With a quick swipe with a paring knife, I had cut a stuffing-ready pocket in each chop. As long as I kept the size of the opening to an inch or so, I could easily seal each stuffed chop with a toothpick.

Because pork chops are so lean and mild, I wanted a filling that would add moisture as well as a big hit of flavor. I didn't have much room inside each chop, so I needed something potent. My first thought was to start with barbecue sauce. Instead of slapping sauce on the exterior of the meat, what if I spooned the sauce inside each chop?

Tasters said I was off to a good start, but the filling needed some bulk. I tried everything from sautéed mushrooms (too mild) to relishes and chutneys (too overpowering) before settling on the sweet flavor of caramelized onions. The barbecue sauce and onion filling tasted good,

but it was too runny. Cubes of bread—a constant in stuffed pork chop recipes—added heft to my filling, but no flavor. Fortunately, inspiration struck. Wouldn't cheese melt and hold the filling together? Sure enough, the gooey cheese turned the barbecue sauce and onions into a stable, hearty filling and added a lot of flavor. Tasters especially like smoked gouda and smoked cheddar.

Simply grilling the stuffed chops over high heat caused the outside to burn before the inside was even warm. Instead, I built a two-level fire, banking all the coals in one half of the grill. I seared the chops on the hot side of the grill, then transferred them to the cooler side and covered them (creating an oven-like effect) to finish cooking. I had finally created a formula for juicy, tender chops with big flavor and little advance work. **–Keri Fisher**

GRILLED STUFFED PORK CHOPS SERVES 4
See page 30 for information about buying pork chops.

- 1 tablespoon olive oil
- 1 large onion, halved and sliced thin
- 1/4 cup barbecue sauce
- 1 cup shredded smoked gouda or cheddar cheese
- 4 boneless loin chops, about 1 1/2 inches thick (about 8 ounces each)
- Salt and pepper

1. Heat oil in large skillet over medium heat until shimmering. Cook onion until soft and deeply browned, 15 to 20 minutes. Transfer to bowl and stir in barbecue sauce and cheese.
2. Using sharp paring knife,

We add moisture and flavor by packing these chops full of cheese and other savory ingredients.

cut 1-inch opening into side of each chop, then cut pocket for stuffing (photo 1). Place one-quarter of stuffing in pocket of each chop (photo 2). Seal chops with toothpicks (photo 3) and season with salt and pepper. (Chops can be stuffed and refrigerated up to 1 day in advance.)
3. Light large chimney starter filled with charcoal briquettes (about 100 coals) and burn until coals are covered with fine gray ash. Pour coals into pile on one side of grill. Set cooking grate in place, cover, and let heat for 5 minutes. Scrape cooking grate clean.
4. Grill chops directly over coals until browned on both sides, about 2½ minutes per side. Transfer chops to cooler side of grill, cover with disposable aluminum foil pan, and

cook until internal temperature reaches 140 degrees, 6 to 8 minutes longer. Transfer chops to platter, cover with foil pan, and let rest for 5 minutes. (Internal temperature should rise to 145 degrees.) Serve.

GRILLED STUFFED PORK CHOPS FOR GAS GRILL
Prepare recipe for Grilled Stuffed Pork Chops through step 2. Heat all burners on high for 15 minutes. Scrape cooking grate clean. Grill pork chops, with lid down, until browned on both sides, about 2½ minutes per side. Leave primary burner on high and turn all other burners to low. Move chops to cool side of grill and cook, with lid down, until internal temperature reaches 140 degrees, 6 to 8 minutes. Let chops rest as directed.

Best Potluck Macaroni and Cheese

This sturdy, casserole-style mac and cheese should sit up straight on the plate. So why do so many recipes slump into a runny mess?

A crisp bread crumb topping adds textural contrast to this thick and creamy mac and cheese.

Casserole-style macaroni and cheese can be found at every BBQ joint, fish fry, and covered-dish supper in my home state of North Carolina. Why? Because it feeds a crowd and can go straight from the oven to the buffet table. Unlike ultracreamy stovetop versions that puddle on the plate, this baked mac and cheese absorbs the cheesy sauce as it bubbles away in the oven, evolving into a dense mixture that sets up in hearty scoops. I always make sure my serving contains a blanket of the buttery bread crumbs that develop a toasty crunch during baking.

Although I've eaten this kind of macaroni and cheese my entire life, I didn't have a good recipe. My research turned up plenty of recipes for baked mac and cheese, but I quickly realized that the majority of them were misnamed—they weren't baked at all. Most of the real cooking (making an egg-based custard or a white sauce) was done on top of the stove, and the casseroles were then finished under the broiler for a few minutes. Impostors!

After making a handful of recipes that were actually baked, I saw why so many had abandoned the oven. Time after time, the custard-based recipes came out of the oven broken and curdled. These recipes were failing because they contain eggs, milk, and half-and-half, all ingredients that will separate and clump when baked. Recipes based on a white sauce—called béchamel, it's made by cooking butter, flour, and milk—also separated when baked (even when I increased the amount of flour) but were more promising, because at least they didn't contain eggs.

To prevent béchamel sauces from breaking, other casseroles replace the milk with canned condensed soup, but I wasn't about to go that route. But I did try another canned product, evaporated milk, which contains stabilizers that prevent it from breaking when heated. When I used evaporated milk in my béchamel, the casserole baked up satiny smooth.

Up until this point I had been adding Monterey Jack, a creamy but very mild cheese. Tasters loved the full flavor of extra-sharp cheddar, but its relatively dry texture meant it didn't melt as well, and it became greasy and separated when baked. A batch made with equal parts cheddar and Monterey Jack was better but still not right.

Since the stabilizers in the condensed milk had helped with the sauce, I wondered if I could rely on a cheese that contained similar stabilizers to fix the separating cheese. I made a batch with American cheese (for stability), Monterey Jack (for creaminess), and cheddar (for flavor) and had great results. Homemade bread crumbs, enriched with melted butter and Parmesan cheese, created a flavorful, crunchy topping that provided a nice contrast to the soft casserole.

I finally had a baked mac and cheese that was creamy, sturdy, and rich. I'm ready for the next potluck supper. –Cali Rich

BEST POTLUCK MACARONI AND CHEESE

SERVES 8 TO 10

Block American cheese from the deli counter is best here, as pre-wrapped singles result in a drier mac and cheese.

- 3–4 slices hearty white sandwich bread, torn into large pieces
- 8 tablespoons (1 stick) unsalted butter, 4 tablespoons melted
- 1/4 cup grated Parmesan cheese
  Salt
- 1 pound elbow macaroni
- 5 tablespoons all-purpose flour
- 3 (12-ounce) cans evaporated milk
- 2 teaspoons hot sauce
- 1/8 teaspoon ground nutmeg
- 1 teaspoon dry mustard
- 2 cups shredded extra-sharp cheddar cheese
- 1 1/4 cups shredded American cheese (about 5 ounces)
- 3/4 cup shredded Monterey Jack cheese

1. Adjust oven rack to middle position and heat oven to 350 degrees. Pulse bread, melted butter, and Parmesan in food processor until ground to coarse crumbs. Transfer to bowl.

2. Bring 4 quarts water to boil in large pot. Add 1 tablespoon salt and macaroni to boiling water and cook until al dente, about 6 minutes. Reserve 1/2 cup macaroni cooking water, then drain and rinse macaroni in colander under cold running water. Set aside.

3. Melt remaining 4 tablespoons butter in now-empty pot over medium-high heat until foaming. Stir in flour and cook, stirring constantly, until mixture turns light brown, about 1 minute. Slowly whisk in evaporated milk, hot sauce, nutmeg, mustard, and 2 teaspoons salt and cook until mixture begins to simmer and is slightly thickened, about 4 minutes. Off heat, whisk in cheeses and reserved cooking water until cheese melts. Stir in macaroni until completely coated.

4. Transfer mixture to 13 by 9-inch baking dish and top evenly with bread crumb mixture. Bake until cheese is bubbling around edges and top is golden brown, 20 to 25 minutes. Let sit for 5 to 10 minutes before serving.

Make Ahead: The macaroni and cheese can be made in advance through step 3; since the pasta continues to absorb moisture, adjustments must be made to avoid dryness. To do so, increase amount of reserved pasta cooking water to 1 cup. Pour macaroni mixture into 13 by 9-inch baking dish, lay plastic wrap directly on surface of pasta, and refrigerate for up to 1 day. The bread crumb mixture may be refrigerated in airtight container for up to 2 days. When ready to bake, remove plastic wrap, cover macaroni mixture with foil, and bake for 30 minutes. Uncover, sprinkle bread crumbs over top, and bake until topping is golden brown, about 20 minutes longer.

Stable Condition

Using already stabilized ingredients like American cheese and evaporated milk ensures that this cheesy sauce doesn't break in the oven.

AMERICAN CHEESE   EVAPORATED MILK

On the Side: Super-Stuffed Baked Potatoes

We set out to make an overstuffed potato with big garlic flavor.

Years ago at a steakhouse in California, I had a potato epiphany. Along with my steak, I was served a stuffed baked potato flavored with garlic, herbs, and creamy cheese packed into a perfectly crisped potato-skin shell. I've been searching for that potato ever since, and having never found it, I decided to develop the recipe myself.

I started by precooking the potatoes in the microwave. The flesh wasn't as fluffy as when I baked the potatoes in the oven, but the microwave shaved an hour off the cooking time and the differences disappeared once I added the cheese and butter.

Most recipes for stuffed baked potatoes call for cutting the potatoes in half, but the end results looked like floppy potato skins. I prefer to lop off just the top quarter of the potato and then hollow it out. Once dried in the oven, these crispy shells hold more filling.

I tried fillings based on cream cheese, sour cream, heavy cream, and evaporated milk, but my tasters preferred Boursin cheese. This creamy cheese gave my filling garlic and herb flavor and a smooth texture. I boosted the flavor even more by cooking minced garlic in butter and adding that to the cheese mixture.

After hollowing out the potatoes, there was enough filling for each, but not enough to mound on top. More cheese just weighed down the potato. A simple solution was to cook an extra potato just for its flesh (discarding the shell). I now had enough filling to mound into each potato shell. I sprinkled more cheese over the top for a final burst of flavor.

–Meredith Butcher

SUPER-STUFFED BAKED POTATOES SERVES 6
This recipe calls for 7 potatoes, but only 6 of them make it to the table. The remaining potato is used for its flesh; you should have 5 cups of scooped potato flesh in step 2.

- 7 large russet potatoes (about 12 ounces each), scrubbed
- 6 tablespoons unsalted butter, 3 tablespoons melted
- 3/4 teaspoon salt
- 1 (5.2-ounce) package Boursin cheese, crumbled
- 1/2 cup half-and-half
- 2 garlic cloves, minced
- 1/4 cup chopped fresh chives
- 1 teaspoon pepper

1. Adjust oven rack to middle position and heat oven to 475 degrees. Set wire rack inside rimmed baking sheet. Prick potatoes all over with fork, place on paper towel, and microwave on high until tender, 20 to 25 minutes, turning potatoes over after 10 minutes.

2. Slice and remove top quarter of each potato, let cool 5 minutes, then scoop out flesh, leaving 1/4-inch layer of potato on inside (see photos on page 30). Discard 1 potato shell. Brush remaining shells inside and out with melted butter and sprinkle interiors with 1/4 teaspoon salt. Transfer potatoes scooped side up to baking sheet fitted with wire rack and bake until skins begin to crisp, about 15 minutes.

3. Meanwhile, mix half of Boursin and half-and-half in bowl until blended. Cook remaining butter with garlic in saucepan over medium-low heat until garlic is straw-colored, 3 to 5 minutes. Stir in Boursin mixture until combined.

4. Set ricer or food mill over medium bowl and press or mill potatoes into bowl. Gently fold in warm Boursin mixture, 3 tablespoons chives, remaining salt, and pepper until well incorporated. Remove potato shells from oven and fill with potato-cheese mixture. Top with remaining crumbled Boursin and bake until tops of potatoes are golden brown, about 15 minutes. Sprinkle with remaining chives. Serve.

On the Side: Italian Spinach with Raisins and Pine Nuts

The big key to this simple side dish is avoiding soggy spinach.

The combination of sautéed spinach, fruity olive oil, sweet raisins, and toasted pine nuts is a Mediterranean classic. But most recipes I made left me with a puddle of watery greens pocked with shriveled raisins and bland pine nuts.

To avoid soggy spinach, most recipes either cook it over high heat until the residual liquid has evaporated or wring out the sautéed spinach like laundry. Since the former yielded tough, overcooked greens and the latter dry, stringy leaves, I decided to keep it simple. Starting with curly leaf spinach (its water content is lower than flat leaf or baby spinach), I sautéed handfuls until it was glossy and evenly wilted. I then put the spinach into a colander to drain, pressing it a few times with a wooden spoon to help coax the water out. This left me with tender greens with just enough moisture.

Most recipes call for garlic to add a background flavor, but tasters preferred the milder taste of sliced shallots. Straight out of the box, raisins were too chewy, so I plumped them in hot water. Balsamic vinegar and a touch of brown sugar lent a sweet-sour element. The pine nuts were at their crunchy best when toasted to golden brown at the outset and then sprinkled over the dish right before serving. **–Jeremy Sauer**

ITALIAN SPINACH WITH RAISINS AND PINE NUTS SERVES 4
One small red onion can be substituted for the shallots. Using a Dutch oven (rather than a skillet) makes wilting the spinach easier and faster.

- 1/4 cup golden raisins
- 1/4 cup hot water
- 2 tablespoons pine nuts
- 3 tablespoons extra-virgin olive oil
- 3 (10-ounce) bags curly-leaf spinach, stemmed and torn into bite-sized pieces
- 3 shallots, sliced thin
- 1/4 cup balsamic vinegar
- 1 teaspoon light brown sugar
  Salt

1. Plump raisins in bowl of hot water, about 5 minutes. Toast nuts in Dutch oven over medium heat, stirring often, until golden, about 5 minutes. Transfer to plate.

2. Heat 1 tablespoon oil in now-empty Dutch oven over high heat until shimmering. Add spinach in handfuls, stirring to allow each batch to wilt slightly before adding next. Continue to cook until spinach is uniformly wilted and glossy, about 1 minute. Transfer spinach to colander set over bowl and press with wooden spoon to release extra liquid.

3. Wipe out Dutch oven, add remaining oil, and set over medium heat until shimmering. Cook shallots until softened, about 3 minutes. Drain raisins and add to shallots. Stir in vinegar and sugar and cook until syrupy, about 2 minutes. Add spinach and toss to coat. Season with salt and sprinkle with nuts. Serve.

Grilled Butterflied Lemon Chicken

Opening up a whole chicken with a pair of scissors promises crisper skin and the opportunity to put bold seasonings in direct contact with the meat.

Butterflying a chicken may sound intimidating, but with a pair of scissors and practice, it's no harder than chopping an onion. But why do it? The advantages of butterflying—cutting out the backbone and opening up the chicken like a book—are many, but the three most important are these: You create a flat surface that makes for easy grilling; you can easily rub seasonings directly under the skin to flavor the meat; and the skin becomes especially crisp.

I gathered up some recipes for butterflied lemon chicken and headed outside. I should have taken the fire extinguisher with me. Recipes that cooked the chicken directly over hot coals had too many flare-ups (from the fat dripping into the hot coals), which caused the skin to burn. The recipes that used bricks (one even called for a can of tomatoes) to weigh down the birds invariably resulted in scorched skin and leathery meat. Many recipes put the chicken through a tumbling routine of flips and rotations on the grill, which just seemed to prolong the cooking time. I had a long way to go.

In these early tests, I had the best luck with an indirect, moderate fire, a technique called grill-roasting. Banking all the coals on one side of the grill, placing the chicken opposite the coals, and setting the lid on the grill allowed the fat under the chicken's skin to render slowly without flare-ups, and the relatively gentle heat

resulted in a moister bird.

After much trial and error, I discovered that placing the chickens on the grill skin side down reduced cooking time and allowed the most fat to render. Simply positioning the legs, which are dark meat, closest to the coals enabled the white and dark meat to come up to temperature (160 degrees for white and 175 degrees for dark) at the same time without rotating or flipping. A final sear directly over the dying coals at the end of cooking crisped and browned the skin nicely—without the risk of flare-ups.

Now I needed to introduce big lemon flavor. Butterflying a chicken allows easy access to the meat. I tried slipping various combinations of lemon zest and seasonings under the skin; raw garlic was too strong, fresh herbs offered little flavor, and dried herbs tasted too

dusty. I settled on a simple mixture of lemon zest, salt, and pepper.

The rub was okay, but my tasters wanted more lemon flavor, so I made a vinaigrette with fresh lemon juice and olive oil and poured it over the cooked chickens; the lemon flavor was still muted. Gradually increasing the lemon juice worked to a point, but by the time we could taste the lemon, the vinaigrette was too sour.

Since I already had the grill going, it occurred to me that I might try grilling the lemons. Although my colleagues were skeptical, this trick worked perfectly. Quickly caramelizing lemon halves over the hot part of the grill concentrated their flavor and tempered their acidity, resulting in a bright, smoky juice that infused the vinaigrette—and the chicken—with lemon flavor. **–Cali Rich**

To finish these butterflied chickens with intense lemon flavor, we grill lemon halves and make a sauce from their juice.

GRILLED BUTTERFLIED LEMON CHICKEN SERVES 8

You may not need to squeeze all the grilled lemons in step 5 to obtain 1/3 cup of lemon juice. Cut any unsqueezed lemons into wedges for serving.

Chicken and Rub

- 2 teaspoons grated lemon zest from 1 lemon (reserve lemon for vinaigrette)
- 2 teaspoons salt
- 1 teaspoon pepper
- 2 (3 1/2- to 4-pound) whole chickens, prepared according to photos 1 through 3
- Vegetable oil for grill grate

Vinaigrette

- 4 lemons, halved; plus halved, zested lemon from rub
- 1 garlic clove, minced
- 1/2 teaspoon salt
- 2 teaspoons Dijon mustard
- 1 teaspoon sugar
- 1/2 teaspoon pepper
- 2 tablespoons minced fresh parsley
- 2/3 cup extra-virgin olive oil

1. For the chicken and rub: Combine lemon zest, salt, and pepper in bowl. Rub zest mixture under chicken skin and tuck wings according to photo 4. Transfer chickens to rack set over rimmed baking sheet and refrigerate, uncovered, for 30 minutes. (Chickens may be prepared up to this point 24 hours in advance; allow chickens to sit at room temperature 30 minutes before grilling.)

2. Open bottom grill vents completely. Light large chimney starter filled with charcoal briquettes (about 100) and burn until charcoal is covered with fine gray ash. Place 13 by 9-inch disposable aluminum roasting pan on one side of grill and pour hot coals into pile on opposite side. Evenly scatter 20 unlit coals on top of hot coals and set cooking grate in place. Cover, with lid vents positioned over cooler side of grill and opened fully. Let grill heat up 5 minutes. Scrape grate clean.

3. Dip wad of paper towels
continued on page 14

BUTTERFLY A CHICKEN

With a few scissor snips and a little leveling from a meat pounder, whole chickens can be quickly flattened to promote even cooking on the grill.

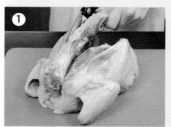

1. Cut through the bones on either side of the backbone and trim any excess fat or skin at the neck.

2. Flip the chicken over and use the heel of your hand to flatten the breastbone.

3. Cover the chicken with plastic wrap. Using a meat pounder or rubber mallet, pound the breast to the same thickness as the leg and thigh meat.

4. Slip your hand between the skin and meat to loosen the skin. Rub salt mixture under skin and into breast and leg meat.

Grilled Butterflied Lemon Chicken

continued from page 13

in oil and oil grate, holding paper towels with long-handled tongs. Place lemon halves cut side down over hot side of grill. Place chickens skin side down over cooler side of grill, with legs positioned closest to the coals. Cover, with opened vents in lid over chicken.

4. Grill lemons until deep brown and caramelized, 5 to 8 minutes. Transfer to bowl. Grill chickens until skin is well browned and breast meat registers 160 degrees, 45 to 55 minutes. Move chickens to hot side of grill and sear, uncovered, until deep brown, 2 to 4 minutes longer.

5. For the vinaigrette: While chickens are grilling, squeeze ⅓ cup juice from grilled lemons into bowl. Using flat side of knife, mash garlic and salt into paste and add to bowl with lemon juice. Stir in mustard, sugar, pepper, and parsley, then slowly whisk in olive oil until emulsified.

6. Transfer chickens to cutting board and let rest 10 to 15 minutes. Carve, transfer to serving platter, and pour ⅓ cup vinaigrette over chicken. Serve, passing remaining vinaigrette at table.

GRILLED BUTTERFLIED LEMON CHICKEN ON A GAS GRILL

Prepare recipe for Grilled Butterflied Lemon Chicken through step 1. Heat all burners on high, covered, for 15 minutes. Scrape cooking grate clean and oil cooking grate. Leave primary burner on high and turn all other burners to low. Place lemons over primary burner; place chickens skin side down over cooler part of grill, with legs positioned closest to heat; cover and proceed with recipe from step 4, adjusting primary burner as necessary to maintain temperature of 350 to 375 degrees. When chickens are cooked, transfer to hot part of grill and sear, uncovered, until deep brown, 2 to 4 minutes. Proceed with recipe from step 5.

King Ranch Casserole

This cheesy chicken and tortilla casserole is comfort food in Texas. We keep its mildly spicy flavor but rework the recipe without the usual canned soup.

We oven-toast fresh corn tortillas to keep this layered casserole from becoming soggy and leaden.

King Ranch just might be the most famous casserole in Texas. Layers of tender chicken, corn tortillas, and spicy tomatoes are bound together in a rich, cheesy sauce. Favored by home cooks and Junior Leaguers, this subtly spicy casserole dates back to the 1950s. Although owners of the King Ranch, the state's largest cattle operation, deny any hand in its creation, this dish became popular for its mildly spicy Southwestern flavors as well as its convenience (most recipes start with one can each of cream of chicken and cream of mushroom soup).

After a disappointing round of tests, I wondered if my Texan friends had been telling me tall tales about this dish. The tortillas were soggy, the chicken was overcooked, and the sauce was made gloppy and bland by the undiluted canned soup. Given the outsized reputation of this dish, I had to do better. I found a few modern recipes that called for a freshly poached chicken and homemade cheese sauce, but their instructions seemed overly fussy for a casserole. Could I find a middle road that lost the canned soup but kept the work reasonable?

Starting with the sauce, I cooked onions and chiles in butter, then added ground cumin and Ro-Tel tomatoes, the Texas brand of spicy canned tomatoes that are the hallmark of this recipe (for more information on Ro-Tel tomatoes, see box below). Instead of draining the tomatoes and discarding the flavorful juice (as most recipes instructed), I reduced the liquid to intensify the tomato flavor. Then I stirred in flour for thickening, cream for richness, and chicken broth for flavor. Twenty minutes of kitchen work yielded a silky, flavorful sauce that put canned soup to shame.

To assemble the casserole, I layered the sauce with corn tortillas and cooked chicken, then topped it with cheese before baking. It smelled fantastic coming out of the oven, but the chicken was leathery and the tortillas had disintegrated into corn mush. To solve the chicken problem, I tried layering raw chicken in between the tortillas, but it failed to cook through. The solution was to partially poach the chicken in the sauce before assembling the casserole, which guaranteed perfectly cooked, well-seasoned meat.

I tried replacing the soggy tortillas with store-bought tortilla chips, but my tasters complained about the extra grease in the middle of the casserole. Crisping the tortillas in the oven (in effect, making homemade chips) kept them from turning to mush in the casserole and cut out the greasiness.

All my casserole needed now was a crisp topping. Having abandoned store-bought tortilla chips inside my casserole, I decided to give them a shot as a crushed-up crunchy topping. The flavor and texture were fine, and after trying different brands to find the perfect fit, I finally hit on one that everyone loved: Fritos corn chips. They crowned this Texas classic with just the right amount of saltiness, corn flavor, and crunch. **–Diane Unger**

KING RANCH CASSEROLE SERVES 6 TO 8

If you can't find Ro-Tel tomatoes, substitute one 14.5-ounce can diced tomatoes and one 4-ounce can chopped green chiles. Cojack is a creamy blend of Colby and Monterey Jack cheeses. Jack cheese can be used in its place.

- 12 (6-inch) corn tortillas
- 1 tablespoon unsalted butter
- 2 medium onions, chopped fine
- 2 jalapeño chiles, minced
- 2 teaspoons ground cumin
- 2 (10-ounce) cans Ro-Tel tomatoes (see note)
- 5 tablespoons all-purpose flour
- 1 cup heavy cream
- 3 cups low-sodium chicken broth
- 1½ pounds boneless, skinless chicken breasts, halved lengthwise and cut crosswise into ½-inch slices
- 2 tablespoons minced fresh cilantro
- 4 cups shredded Cojack cheese (see note)
- Salt and pepper
- 2¼ cups Fritos corn chips, crushed

A Taste of Texas

Carl Roettele opened a small canning plant in Elsa, Texas, in the early 1940s. By the 1950s, his blend of tomatoes, green chiles, and spices had become popular throughout the state and beyond. His spicy, tangy tomatoes are used in countless local recipes, including King Ranch casserole and a mixture of Velveeta and Ro-Tel tomatoes known locally as Ro-Tel dip (chili con queso, to the rest of the country).

RO-TEL TOMATOES

On the Side: Southwestern Caesar Salad

A Casserole Fit for a President

Lady Bird Johnson (shown here with LBJ) frequently served King Ranch Casserole at the Johnson ranch in Stonewall, Texas.

1. Adjust oven rack to upper-middle and lower-middle positions and heat oven to 450 degrees. Lay tortillas on two baking sheets, lightly coat both sides with cooking spray, and bake until slightly crisp and browned, about 12 minutes. Cool slightly, then break into bite-sized pieces. Using potholders, adjust top oven rack to middle position.

2. Heat butter in Dutch oven over medium-high heat. Cook onions, chiles, and cumin until lightly browned, about 8 minutes. Add tomatoes and cook until most of liquid has evaporated, about 10 minutes. Stir in flour and cook 1 minute. Add cream and broth, bring to simmer, and cook until thickened, 2 to 3 minutes. Stir in chicken and cook until no longer pink, about 4 minutes. Off heat, add cilantro and cheese and stir until cheese is melted. Season with salt and pepper.

3. Scatter half of tortilla pieces in 13 by 9-inch baking dish set over rimmed baking sheet. Spoon half of filling evenly over tortillas. Scatter remaining tortillas over filling, then top with remaining filling.

4. Bake until filling is bubbling, about 15 minutes. Sprinkle Fritos evenly over top and bake until Fritos are lightly browned, about 10 minutes. Cool casserole 10 minutes. Serve.

Make Ahead: The casserole can be assembled through step 3 and refrigerated for up to 1 day. When ready to serve, cover casserole with foil and bake until filling is bubbling, about 30 minutes. Remove foil, top with Fritos, and proceed with rest of step 4 as directed.

What's the best way to spice up this classic salad?

Everyone knows Caesar salad—the classic combination of romaine lettuce drizzled with a creamy dressing flavored with garlic, anchovy, Worcestershire, lemon, and Parmesan cheese and topped with seasoned croutons. What most people don't know is that Caesar salad was invented in Mexico, not Italy (see below).

For a twist that would bring this salad closer to its geographic roots, I tried adding canned chipotle chiles (smoked jalapeños packed in a vinegary tomato sauce called adobo) to the test kitchen's favorite Caesar dressing. The chiles seemed like a perfect way to balance the richness of the creamy dressing. While everyone liked the smoky chile flavor, it completely clashed with the anchovy and lemon juice. I took out the anchovy and replaced the lemon juice with lime; the flavors were in closer harmony, but the dressing was a bit harsh.

Traditional recipes use raw (or barely cooked) eggs for richness and thickening power. Searching the kitchen for a rich, thick ingredient that worked well with Southwestern flavors, I thought of sour cream. Stirring some into the dressing tamed the chile punch and added the requisite creamy consistency. I had also neatly avoided the raw egg issue.

It's a shame that so many people use mediocre boxed croutons, because it's so easy to make great ones at home. I tossed cubed white bread with garlic and olive oil. To carry the Southwest flavors further, I added adobo sauce from the can of chipotles. Toasted in the oven until golden brown and crunchy, these smoky, garlicky croutons paired perfectly with the bright flavors in the salad dressing. **–Diane Unger**

SOUTHWESTERN CAESAR SALAD

SERVES 6 TO 8

Mild olive oil (not extra-virgin) works best here. Chipotle chiles are smoked jalapeños; look for them canned and packed in adobo sauce.

- 1 cup olive oil
- 2 teaspoons minced canned chipotle chile, plus 1 tablespoon adobo sauce
- 4 garlic cloves, minced
- 6 slices hearty white sandwich bread, cut into 1/2-inch cubes (about 4 cups)
- 1 cup grated Parmesan cheese
- 1/2 cup sour cream
- 3 tablespoons lime juice
- 2 teaspoons Worcestershire sauce
- 2 teaspoons Dijon mustard
- 3 romaine hearts, torn into bite-sized pieces (about 12 cups)

1. Adjust oven rack to middle position and heat oven to 350 degrees. Whisk 1/4 cup oil, adobo sauce, and half of garlic in large bowl. Toss in bread cubes and season with salt and pepper. Spread bread cubes on rimmed baking sheet and bake, shaking pan occasionally, until golden brown, 20 to 25 minutes. Cool completely.

2. Whisk 1/4 cup Parmesan, sour cream, lime juice, Worcestershire, mustard, and chile in bowl until smooth. Whisk in remaining oil in steady stream and season with salt and pepper.

3. Toss romaine, remaining Parmesan, and dressing in large bowl. Toss in croutons and serve.

Make Ahead: The croutons and dressing can be made up to 2 days in advance. Store the croutons at room temperature; the dressing should be refrigerated.

FOOD HISTORY: The First Caesar

Most sources credit Caesar Cardini with the invention of this famous salad. An Italian immigrant living in San Diego, Cardini created this salad over the Fourth of July weekend in 1924, when his Tijuana restaurant ran low on food and he needed to improvise.

Our favorite description of the original Caesar salad comes from Julia Child. In 1970, she wrote in *From Julia Child's Kitchen*: "One of my early remembrances of restaurant life was going to Tijuana in 1925 or 1926 with my parents, who were wildly excited that they should finally lunch at Caesar's restaurant. . . . My parents, of course, ordered the salad. Caesar himself rolled the big cart up to the table, tossed the romaine in a great wooden bowl, and I wish I could say I remember his every move, but I don't. The only thing I see again clearly is the eggs. I can see him break two eggs over that romaine and roll them in, the greens going all creamy as the eggs flowed over them. Two eggs in a salad? Two one-minute coddled eggs? And garlic-flavored croutons, and grated Parmesan cheese? It was a sensation of a salad from coast to coast, and there were even rumblings of its success in Europe."

I'm Looking for a Recipe

We've Got Mail

Several readers sent us recipes in response to the request for Shrewsbury Biscuits in our August/September 2006 issue. We really liked the recipe sent by Laura Peterson (right). Go to **CooksCountry.com** and click **Looking for a Recipe** to find hundreds of recipes submitted by readers who responded to other recipe requests in previous issues of *Cook's Country*.

Quaker Bonnet Buffalo Chips

I had the most delicious chocolate-dipped coconut macaroon cookies, called Buffalo Chips, at the Quaker Bonnet restaurant in Buffalo, N.Y. I have tried to reproduce this cookie, but I cannot achieve the same dense and chewy consistency. Does anyone have this recipe?

Karen Brantis
Marietta, N.Y.

C&H Peanut Butter Cookies

When I was younger, I remember making peanut butter cookies from a recipe that was on the package of C&H Brown Sugar. It was on every box, so we never wrote it down. Does anyone have this recipe?

Joann Kondo
Palo Alto, Calif.

German Sweet Rolls

My German grandmother used to make these wonderful crescent-shaped sweet rolls. They were very tender and iced with a powdered sugar glaze (maybe with almond flavoring). Unfortunately, no one ever got the recipe from her. These rolls were so special that her grandchildren often requested them as birthday presents. Any help would be appreciated.

Jan Ackerly
Lawrence, Kan.

Croce's Minestrone

In the late 1970s and early 1980s, my family used to eat at a restaurant in Lodi, Calif., called Croce's. Their minestrone soup was so good that we would fill up on it and not be able to eat our entrees until later. The soup was bean-based, but it had very few vegetables or pasta. All of the food at Croce's was delicious, but that soup was incredible!

Carla Sanders
Topsham, Maine

Crunchy Topping and Cake

In the 1970s, there was a bakery on Harding Way in Stockton, Calif., named Ruhl's Bakery. One of my favorite childhood memories was eating the crunchy topping that graced one of their cakes. Although I can't remember the name of the cake, the topping was bits of crunchy, caramelized sugar, and it was buttery and aerated, almost like a malted milk ball. I would really love to have the recipe for this topping. Does anyone remember having this cake, too? I would also love to know the name of the cake.

Aileen Mah
Elk Grove, Calif.

Koloc

I am looking for a recipe for koloc, a Polish sweet bread with raisins and baked cheese on the top. Thirty-five years ago, I lived in Chicago, and on Fridays I would go to this little bakery in Logan Square near Central Park and get this round bread while it was still warm. They used to make the best Polish pastries, as well. I have tried and tried to find a recipe for this, and no one seems to know what I am talking about. Please help!

Nancy Nelson
Apache Junction, Ariz.

Pagachi

When I was a little girl in the 1950s, a neighbor of ours who was from Slovenia used to make us a delicious baked treat that she called pagachi. It was a bread dough that was spread out like pizza dough and filled with mashed potatoes and cheese. She cut it into squares and sprinkled it with sugar, and we ate it hot out of the oven. Does anyone know how to make this?

Mary Scherer
Brockway, Pa.

Baked Banana Pudding

My mother used to make a banana pudding that was baked, not like the ones today that are no-bake. I cannot remember how she did it, and she passed in 1974. I am now a new bride and my husband loves banana pudding made the old-fashioned way. Can anyone help me find a recipe for baked banana pudding?

Carolyn Campbell
via e-mail

Egg Pancakes

I am looking for a recipe for something that my grandmother used to make called egg pancakes. They were made like a pancake but were less floury and dry. I seem to remember them being thinner than normal pancakes, with more oil and eggs. She often served them with butter and powdered sugar. She never wrote the recipe down, and, unfortunately, she passed away many years ago and no one in my family got the recipe from her. Now that I'm grown, I would love to be able to make them for my family and bring back some good memories from my childhood.

Mirandy Fuhrmann
via e-mail

Johnny Mazetti Macaroni Casserole

In 1949, I was 7 years old and we lived in a three-flat in Chicago. My aunt used to surprise us with a casserole called Johnny Mazetti, and I loved it! To the best of my memory, it had elbow macaroni, tomatoes, ground beef, green peppers, and onions, and it was topped with American cheese. If anyone can find this recipe, I'll eat my hat!

Sherri Felt
via e-mail

Square Cupcakes

Back in the 1960s, there was a bakery in Los Angeles called Grace's Pastries. The bakers were Japanese (raised in Hawaii), and they sold Asian pastries as well as the standard cakes, cookies, and pies. What I am looking for are these delicious square cupcakes that they used to sell. The cupcakes had a light glaze that was possibly maple flavored, and the cake had the coloring of a spice cake, but it wasn't a spice cake—it had a very rich, buttery taste. Can anyone help me find this recipe?

Joyce Baba
Huntington Beach, Calif.

Jack-o'-Lantern Meat Pie

When I was in second or third grade, as a Halloween cooking project, our class made a meat pie shaped like a jack-o'-lantern. The only ingredients I remember are refrigerator biscuits, ground beef, and yellow mustard. The meat was precooked, mixed with mustard and some other ingredients, and then tucked between two rolled-out refrigerator biscuits. The top biscuit had a face cut out to make it look like a jack-o'-lantern. The biscuits were sealed together and baked. I remember thinking these were delicious! I now have a young daughter, and these would be an easy and fun project for us to do together, if only I knew the recipe!

Jenny Hamon
Red Lodge, Mont.

Are you looking for a special recipe? Or do you have a recipe a fellow *Cook's Country* reader is seeking? Post your requests and recipes by visiting **CooksCountry.com** and clicking on **Looking for a Recipe**. We'll share recipe requests and found recipes on CooksCountry.com and print as many as we can in the magazine. You may also write to us at Looking for a Recipe, Cook's Country, P.O. Box 470739, Brookline, MA 02447.

SHREWSBURY BISCUITS Laura S. Peterson, Homosassa, Fla.

Laura says: "My mother used to take care of our neighbor Shani's daughter a few days a week. Shani was from India but had lived in England (where she found this recipe) before coming to the U.S. My mother would never take money for baby-sitting, so Shani would make these wonderful biscuits for us."
If you don't have superfine sugar, grind granulated sugar in a food processor for 30 seconds.

MAKES 20 BISCUITS

8	tablespoons unsalted butter, softened but cool
3/4	cup superfine sugar
1	teaspoon grated lemon zest
2	large egg yolks
1 3/4	cups all-purpose flour

INSTRUCTIONS:

1. Adjust oven rack to middle position and heat oven to 350 degrees.

2. Cream butter, sugar, and zest with electric mixer on medium-high speed until pale and fluffy, about 2 minutes. Add egg yolks and beat until incorporated. Reduce speed to low and add flour in 3 additions, mixing until nearly combined after each. (Mixture should appear slightly dry and crumbly.)

3. Lightly knead dough on floured surface. Roll out dough to 1/4-inch thickness, then cut into 2 1/2-inch rounds and transfer rounds to parchment-lined baking sheet. Bake until lightly brown and firm to the touch, 10 to 12 minutes. Cool biscuits on baking sheet for 5 minutes, then transfer to rack to cool completely.

Find the Rooster!

A tiny version of this rooster has been hidden somewhere in the pages of this issue. If you find it, write to us with its location (plus your name and address) and you will be entered into a random drawing. The first winning entry will receive the Black & Decker SmartBrew coffee maker (our test winner—see page 29), and the next five winners will each receive a complimentary one-year subscription to *Cook's Country*. To enter the contest, visit us at **CooksCountry.com** or write to us at Rooster, Cook's Country, P.O. Box 470739, Brookline, MA 02447. Entries are due by May 31, 2007.
Did you find the rooster in the December/January 2007 issue? It was hidden in the Monte Cristo photo on page 11. Norine Enz of Lake Odessa, Mich., spotted it and won a Calphalon Contemporary Stainless Steel Roasting Pan.

STEAK, MUSHROOM, AND BLUE CHEESE SALAD

CRAB CAKES WITH IMPERIAL SAUCE

SKILLET MACARONI AND BEEF

QUICK CHICKEN PAD THAI

CRAB CAKES WITH IMPERIAL SAUCE SERVES 4

You'll need 1 sleeve of saltines here; crush them until most have turned to dust, leaving a few pieces no bigger than a pebble.

- 1¼ cups mayonnaise
- ¼ cup juice from 2 lemons
- 1 tablespoon Worcestershire sauce
- 2 teaspoons hot sauce
- ½ teaspoon Old Bay seasoning
- 1½ pounds crabmeat, picked over for shells
- 1¼ cups crushed saltines (see note)
- 4 scallions, minced
- 4 tablespoons vegetable oil

1. Combine mayonnaise, lemon juice, Worcestershire, hot sauce, and Old Bay in large bowl. Reserve ½ cup sauce for serving.

2. Fold crabmeat, saltines, and scallions into remaining sauce until combined. Form crabmeat mixture into eight 1-inch-thick patties.

3. Heat 2 tablespoons oil in large nonstick skillet over medium-high heat until just smoking. Add 4 crab cakes and cook until golden brown, 2½ to 3 minutes per side. Transfer to platter and tent with foil. Repeat with remaining oil and crab cakes. Serve with reserved sauce.

STEAK, MUSHROOM, AND BLUE CHEESE SALAD SERVES 4

Cooking the mushrooms in a few tablespoons of vinaigrette (rather than the usual oil) gives them a tangy flavor.

- 2 strip steaks (10 to 12 ounces each), about 1 inch thick
  Salt and pepper
- ½ cup extra-virgin olive oil
- ¼ cup red wine vinegar
- 1 shallot, minced
- 1 tablespoon Dijon mustard
- 10 ounces white mushrooms, sliced thin
- 6 cups baby spinach
- 2 tablespoons capers, minced
- 1 cup crumbled blue cheese

1. Pat steaks dry with paper towels and season with salt and pepper. Heat 2 teaspoons oil in large skillet over medium-high heat until just smoking. Cook steaks until well browned, 3 to 5 minutes per side. Transfer to plate and tent with foil. Pour off fat but do not wipe out pan.

2. Meanwhile, whisk vinegar, shallot, mustard, and remaining oil in bowl. Season with salt and pepper.

3. Return skillet to medium-high heat. Add mushrooms and 3 tablespoons vinaigrette and cook until mushrooms are golden, 6 to 8 minutes. Set aside and allow mushrooms to cool for 5 minutes.

4. Toss spinach, capers, mushrooms, and remaining vinaigrette in large serving bowl. Slice steak thinly and arrange over salad. Sprinkle with blue cheese. Serve.

QUICK CHICKEN PAD THAI SERVES 4

If you can't find fish sauce, substitute a combination of 4 minced anchovy fillets and ¼ cup soy sauce. Rice stick noodles can be found in the Asian section of most supermarkets. If desired, top Pad Thai with chopped peanuts and scallions.

- 8 ounces dried rice stick noodles, about ⅛ inch wide
- ¾ cup warm water
- ¼ cup fish sauce (see note)
- ¼ cup juice from 2 limes
- ¼ cup packed dark brown sugar
- 1 tablespoon vegetable oil
- 1 rotisserie chicken, skin discarded, meat shredded into bite-sized pieces (about 3 cups)
- 4 garlic cloves, minced
- ¼ cup bean sprouts
- ¼ cup chopped fresh cilantro

1. Cover rice sticks with hot tap water in large bowl and soak until softened but not fully tender, about 20 minutes. Drain noodles. Meanwhile, whisk ¾ cup warm water, fish sauce, lime juice, and sugar in bowl until sugar is dissolved.

2. Heat oil in large nonstick skillet over high heat until just smoking. Add chicken and garlic and cook until lightly browned and fragrant, about 2 minutes. Add noodles and fish sauce mixture and cook until noodles are coated with sauce, about 3 minutes. Scatter bean sprouts and cilantro over noodles and continue to cook, tossing constantly, until noodles are fully tender, about 3 minutes. Serve.

SKILLET MACARONI AND BEEF SERVES 4

Serve with hot sauce and sour cream if desired.

- 1½ pounds 85-percent-lean ground beef
- 1 large onion, chopped fine
- 1 red bell pepper, chopped fine
- 6 garlic cloves, minced
- 2 cups elbow macaroni
- 1 (29-ounce) can tomato sauce
- 2 cups low-sodium chicken broth
- 1½ teaspoons dried oregano
  Salt and pepper
- 1 cup shredded cheddar cheese

1. Cook beef in large nonstick skillet over medium-high heat until no longer pink, about 7 minutes. Drain beef, leaving 2 tablespoons fat in skillet, and reserve. Add onion, red pepper, and garlic to fat in skillet and cook, covered, until softened, about 3 minutes.

2. Add macaroni, tomato sauce, broth, oregano, and reserved beef to skillet and bring to boil. Cover, reduce heat to low, and simmer, stirring occasionally, until pasta is tender, 8 to 10 minutes. Season with salt and pepper. Sprinkle with cheese. Serve.

**SAUTÉED CHICKEN
WITH PESTO-MUSHROOM CREAM SAUCE**

INDOOR BBQ CHICKEN SKEWERS

PLUM-GLAZED GRILLED PORK TENDERLOIN

GREEK PITA PIZZAS

INDOOR BBQ CHICKEN SKEWERS SERVES 4

Texas Best and Bull's-Eye barbecue sauces are the test kitchen's favorite brands. You will need four 12-inch metal skewers for this recipe.

- 3 tablespoons brown sugar
- 1 tablespoon paprika
- 1/2 teaspoon ground cumin
- 1/2 teaspoon cayenne pepper
- 1/4 teaspoon salt
- 4 boneless, skinless chicken breasts (about 1 1/2 pounds), cut into 1-inch chunks
- 1 cup barbecue sauce (see note)
- 1/4 cup cider vinegar
- 1/2 cup sour cream
- 2 tablespoons minced fresh cilantro

1. Adjust oven rack to highest position (about 5 inches from broiler element) and heat broiler. Set wire rack over rimmed baking sheet. Combine sugar, paprika, cumin, cayenne, and salt in large bowl. Add chicken and toss to coat. Thread seasoned chicken onto four 12-inch metal skewers.

2. Whisk 3/4 cup barbecue sauce and 2 tablespoons vinegar in small bowl. In second bowl, combine sour cream, cilantro, remaining barbecue sauce, and remaining vinegar; set aside for serving.

3. Brush each kebab with barbecue sauce–vinegar mixture. Broil until lightly browned, 5 to 7 minutes. Flip kebabs, brush with remaining sauce, and continue to broil until chicken is lightly charred and cooked through, 5 to 7 minutes. Serve with sour cream sauce.

SAUTÉED CHICKEN WITH PESTO-MUSHROOM CREAM SAUCE SERVES 4

Be sure to use fresh or refrigerated pesto rather than the jarred variety in this recipe.

- 4 boneless, skinless chicken breasts (about 1 1/2 pounds)
  Salt and pepper
- 3 tablespoons vegetable oil
- 10 ounces white mushrooms, sliced thin
- 6 garlic cloves, minced
- 1 cup heavy cream
- 1/2 cup low-sodium chicken broth
- 1/4 cup basil pesto (see note)
- 2 tablespoons lemon juice

1. Pat chicken dry with paper towels and season with salt and pepper. Heat 1 tablespoon oil in large skillet over medium-high heat until just smoking. Cook chicken until golden brown, about 3 minutes per side. Transfer to plate and tent with foil.

2. Add remaining oil to skillet and cook mushrooms until browned, about 5 minutes. Stir in garlic and cook until fragrant, about 30 seconds. Add cream, broth, and chicken to skillet and bring to boil. Reduce heat to low, cover, and simmer until chicken is cooked through, about 15 minutes.

3. Transfer chicken to serving platter and tent with foil. Return skillet to high heat and simmer until sauce is thickened, about 5 minutes. Off heat, stir in pesto and lemon juice and season with salt and pepper. Pour sauce over chicken. Serve.

GREEK PITA PIZZAS SERVES 4

Packaged hummus is available in many flavor varieties; red pepper hummus works very well here.

- 4 tablespoons extra-virgin olive oil
- 4 (8-inch) pita breads
- 2 tablespoons red wine vinegar
  Salt and pepper
- 1 small red onion, sliced thin
- 1/2 cup pitted kalamata olives, chopped
- 1/2 cup hummus (see note)
- 1 cup shredded Italian cheese blend
- 1 cup crumbled feta cheese
- 2 cups arugula

1. Adjust oven rack to middle position and heat oven to 475 degrees. Brush 2 tablespoons oil over top and bottom of pita breads. Transfer to baking sheet and bake until golden, about 5 minutes.

2. Meanwhile, combine remaining oil, vinegar, and salt and pepper to taste in bowl. Toss onion, olives, and 2 tablespoons vinaigrette together in separate bowl.

3. Spread 2 tablespoons hummus on each toasted pita round. Sprinkle cheeses evenly over hummus, then top with onion mixture. Bake until onions soften and cheese is melted, 6 to 8 minutes. Just before serving, toss arugula with remaining vinaigrette. Arrange arugula on top of pita pizzas. Serve.

PLUM-GLAZED GRILLED PORK TENDERLOIN SERVES 4

To prevent the tenderloins from burning, don't apply the sticky glaze until the meat is fully cooked. Plum jam or plum sauce can also be used here.

- 1/2 cup plum jelly (see note)
- 2 tablespoons lime juice
- 2 scallions, minced
- 2 garlic cloves, minced
- 1 teaspoon grated fresh ginger
- 2 pork tenderloins (1 1/2 to 2 pounds total)
- 2 tablespoons vegetable oil
  Salt and pepper

1. Combine plum jelly, lime juice, scallions, garlic, and ginger in bowl.

2. Rub tenderloins with oil and season with salt and pepper. Grill meat over hot fire until browned on all sides and internal temperature reaches 145 degrees, about 12 minutes. Brush with plum glaze and cook 1 minute longer. Transfer to platter, cover with foil, and let rest 5 minutes. Slice pork and serve with remaining glaze.

Cinnamon Swirl Bread

Soft, sweet bread enriched by a pretty swirl of cinnamon sugar sounds appealing—but the problems can spiral out of control.

Once sliced, this breakfast bread freezes beautifully—and you can defrost slices right in the toaster.

A sticky cinnamon bun is love at first sight. But with cinnamon swirl bread, the appreciation comes with time. Soft and sturdy, with a neat cinnamon swirl inside, a good loaf will last for days. That means I can stagger out of bed, pop a few slices into the toaster, and fill my kitchen with the aroma of hot cinnamon bread—all before 6:00 a.m.

But making a handful of recipes for this bread tempered some of my initial enthusiasm. The loaves turned out dense and chewy or dry and cottony—not a single one was nice and soft. As for the cinnamon, some loaves offered nothing of the spice while others gushed cinnamon-sugar goo all over the cutting board. But most annoying was that every single loaf of bread came apart at its swirly fault line and spiraled into a cinnamon Slinky. Could I produce a soft, sweet, and structurally sound cinnamon swirl bread that was worth getting out of bed for?

The recipes I uncovered were all based on sweet yeast doughs. Flour, sugar, salt, yeast, and milk were universal. Some loaves added a tablespoon or two of butter, but tasters deemed them too lean and tough, more sandwich bread

than morning sweet bread. Loaves with a stick of butter and half a dozen eggs were akin to rich babkas. I chose a middle path, something similar to challah bread. I quickly settled on 3 tablespoons of butter as the right amount for a single loaf, but the eggs proved more difficult to pin down. When I used fewer than two, the bread was too lean, but two or more made the bread bounce. Suspicious that the egg whites were the culprit, I tried using only three yolks and finally achieved a rich but not bouncy crumb.

For the cinnamon-sugar filling, tasters liked a combination of white and light brown sugars, with a hefty 5 teaspoons of cinnamon. One-half cup of the filling gave just the right amount of swirl without the wave of goo. To complement the swirl, tasters liked the bread even more when I added some of the cinnamon sugar directly to the dough and saved a little to sprinkle on top.

The separating spiral was all that stood between me and cinnamon swirl bread perfection. The spiral is formed by patting out the dough, moistening the surface, sprinkling it with the cinnamon-sugar mixture, and then rolling it up into a loaf; the spiral is sandwiched between layers of dough. Milk, corn syrup, beaten egg yolks, and melted butter all worked well to get the cinnamon-sugar mixture to stick to the moist side, but when I rolled it up, the mixture wasn't adhering to the dry top layer of dough. I was left with sloppy spirals.

I eventually found salvation in a spray bottle of water. A thin coat of water sprayed on the dough made the cinnamon mixture stick, and then a second light coat sprayed directly onto the mixture created a glue that adhered to the bread when it was rolled. I finally had a filling that stayed intact, in place, and in a perfect swirl. It was time to break out the toaster. **–Stephanie Alleyne**

CINNAMON SWIRL BREAD SERVES 8

You will need a spray bottle filled with water for this recipe. Whole milk is best in the dough, although low-fat milk will work; skim milk will make the bread too dry.

Cinnamon Sugar
- ¹/₂ cup granulated sugar
- ¹/₄ cup packed light brown sugar
- 5 teaspoons ground cinnamon

Bread
- 1¹/₂ cups milk, heated to 110 degrees
- 4 tablespoons unsalted butter, 3 tablespoons melted
- 3 large egg yolks
- 4¹/₄ cups all-purpose flour, plus more as needed
- 1 envelope (2¹/₄ teaspoons) rapid rise or instant yeast
- 1 tablespoon sugar
- 1¹/₂ teaspoons salt

1. For the cinnamon sugar: Combine ingredients in small bowl, breaking up clumps. Cover tightly with plastic wrap.

2. For the bread: Spray large bowl with cooking spray. Whisk milk, melted butter, and yolks in large liquid measuring cup. Mix ¹/₄ cup cinnamon sugar, flour, yeast, sugar, and salt in large bowl of standing mixer fitted with dough hook. Turn mixer to low and slowly add milk mixture. After dough comes together, increase speed to medium and mix until dough is smooth and comes away from sides of bowl, 5 to 6 minutes. (If dough seems too sticky, add up to ¹/₄ cup more flour during mixing.) Turn dough out onto unfloured counter and knead to form smooth, round ball. Transfer dough to greased bowl and turn to coat. Cover bowl with plastic wrap and let rise in warm place until doubled in size, about 1 hour. (Do not place in warm oven or sugar in dough will melt.)

3. Spray 9 by 5-inch loaf pan with cooking spray. On lightly floured surface, press dough

continued on page 18

We found that water—not milk, butter, or beaten eggs—was the trick to anchoring the cinnamon sugar to the dough. Once the dough has been rolled out, spray it with water, sprinkle with the cinnamon sugar, and then spray the cinnamon sugar until slightly damp. Once rolled up and baked, the swirl will remain attached to the bread, even when sliced thin for toasting.

Getting the Right Swirl

When testing other recipes, we uncovered two recurring problems: the swirl separating and the filling leaking out. Using a modest amount of cinnamon sugar and gluing the cinnamon sugar to the dough with water solved these common problems.

SWIRL SEPARATES AND FILLING OOZES OUT

Cinnamon Swirl Bread

continued from page 17

into 20 by 8-inch rectangle, with short side facing you. Using spray bottle, lightly and evenly spray dough with water. Sprinkle ½ cup cinnamon sugar over dough, leaving 2-inch border along top edge. Lightly spray cinnamon sugar with water until damp but not wet (see photo on page 17). Starting at edge nearest you, roll up dough, then pinch seam and ends closed. Place loaf seam side down in prepared pan, cover loosely with plastic wrap, and let rise at room temperature until 1 inch above rim of pan, 1 to 1½ hours.

4. Adjust oven rack to middle position and heat oven to 350 degrees. Melt remaining butter and brush over top of dough. Sprinkle with remaining cinnamon sugar and bake until top is deep brown and center of bread registers 185 to 190 degrees on instant-read thermometer, 45 to 60 minutes. Turn bread out onto rack and cool to room temperature, about 2 hours. Slice as desired. (Bread can be kept in airtight container at room temperature for up to 3 days.)

CINNAMON SWIRL RAISIN BREAD

Follow recipe for Cinnamon Swirl Bread. In step 2, after turning dough out onto counter, knead ½ cup raisins in by hand until evenly distributed. Proceed as directed.

Don't Have a Mixer?

In step 2, mix flour, cinnamon sugar, yeast, sugar, and salt in large bowl. Make well in flour, then add milk mixture to well. Stir until dough comes together. Turn out onto heavily floured work surface and knead until dough forms cohesive ball and is smooth, about 10 minutes. Proceed as directed.

Pittsburgh Wedding Soup

Tender meatballs, pasta, and greens are a great match, but could we divorce ourselves from most of the usual kitchen work?

Pittsburgh wedding soup (also called Italian wedding soup) has an interesting history that actually has nothing to do with matrimony. The recipe is based on a centuries-old southern Italian meat and vegetable soup called *minestra maritata*; the "marriage" (maritata) is of flavors and ingredients—in this case, meatballs and greens. Lovers of this Italian soup are passionate about it, but nowhere is it more popular than in Pittsburgh, where it appears on menus at high-end and fast food restaurants alike. You can even order wedding soup at the local McDonald's. And of course it's a staple at wedding receptions in the Pittsburgh area.

Wedding soup is traditionally made with a slow-simmered homemade chicken broth (*brodo*, in Italian). To streamline this recipe, my goal was to start with decent store-bought broth (the test kitchen's taste-test winner, Swanson) and make it taste better. Cooking garlic and red pepper flakes in olive oil before adding the broth was an obvious first step to building better flavor.

The meat varies from only ground beef to a combination of pork and beef. I tried them both, but what my tasters really loved was meatloaf mix (a mixture of ground beef, pork, and veal). Some recipes suggest cooking the meatballs separately and then adding them to the soup. However, I found that poaching the raw meatballs directly in the broth not only saved time but also added more flavor to the broth.

The greens proved to be a challenge. Most recipes call for stirring chopped spinach or escarole into the soup just before serving. But my tasters found these greens too bland

and too delicate (they dissolved into the soup). After testing several different types of hearty greens, I settled on chopped kale. It added great flavor and texture and was hearty enough to withstand the hot broth.

My pasta choices were small—literally. Most recipes used tiny ditalini, tubetti, or orzo. Of these, tasters preferred the slender pieces of orzo, which easily fit on the spoon.

A final garnish of grated Parmesan and a splash of fruity olive oil just before serving lent extra depth of flavor. The final test: I asked my colleagues in the test kitchen if they wanted another bowl of my soup, and they all answered with a hearty "I do." **–Stephanie Alleyne**

Poaching the meatballs in store-bought chicken broth adds depth of flavor to this quick soup.

PITTSBURGH WEDDING SOUP SERVES 6 TO 8

If meatloaf mix isn't available, substitute 1 pound of 85-percent lean ground beef. Serve with extra Parmesan cheese and a drizzle of extra-virgin olive oil.

Meatballs

- 2 slices hearty white sandwich bread, torn into pieces
- ½ cup milk
- 1 large egg yolk
- ½ cup grated Parmesan cheese
- 3 tablespoons chopped fresh parsley
- 3 garlic cloves, minced
- ¾ teaspoon salt
- ½ teaspoon pepper
- ½ teaspoon dried oregano
- 1 pound meatloaf mix

Soup

- 1 tablespoon extra-virgin olive oil
- 2 garlic cloves, minced
- ¼ teaspoon red pepper flakes
- 3 quarts low-sodium chicken broth
- 1 large head kale or Swiss chard, stemmed, leaves chopped
- 1 cup orzo
- 3 tablespoons chopped fresh parsley
- Salt and pepper

1. For the meatballs: Using potato masher, mash bread and milk in large bowl until smooth. Add remaining ingredients, except meatloaf mix, and mash to combine. Add meatloaf mix and knead by hand until well combined. Form mixture into 1-inch meatballs (you should have about 55 meatballs) and arrange on rimmed baking sheet. Cover with plastic wrap and refrigerate until firm, at least 30 minutes. (Meatballs can be made up to 24 hours in advance.)

2. For the soup: Heat oil in Dutch oven over medium-high heat until shimmering. Cook garlic and red pepper flakes until fragrant, about 30 seconds. Add broth and bring to boil. Stir in kale and simmer until softened, 10 to 15 minutes. Stir in meatballs and pasta, reduce heat to medium, and simmer until meatballs are cooked through and pasta is tender, about 10 minutes. Stir in parsley and salt and pepper to taste. Serve. (Leftover soup can be refrigerated for up to 3 days.)

Easy Mini Meatballs

We found that the large end of a melon baller guarantees uniform meatballs that will cook evenly. The melon baller also greatly speeds up the shaping process.

NOT JUST FOR MELONS

Authentic Beef Enchiladas

Traditional beef enchiladas simmer steak for hours. Bad convenience versions opt for hamburger and canned sauce. We stick with the steak but use a few shortcuts to cut the cooking time.

Serve these enchiladas with diced avocado, shredded lettuce, and lime wedges at the table.

Traditional beef enchiladas—corn tortillas stuffed with silky, slow-cooked meat and baked under a blanket of hearty chile sauce and cheese— are the ultimate in Mexican comfort food. Too bad they take so long to make. Common shortcuts include using ground beef instead of stew meat and opening canned enchilada sauce instead of making your own from dried chiles and tomato. But the recipes I made using these tricks were awful, with none of the richness of the original. Could I shorten the traditional process without shortchanging the flavor?

Starting with the sauce, I hoped that store-bought chili powder would work well as a base. (I didn't want to have to find, toast, and grind my own chiles.) When I tried adding chili powder to pureed tomatoes, however, its flavor was flat. But when I added the chili powder to sautéing onions and garlic before adding the tomatoes, its flavor opened up and bloomed. The sauce tasted even better when I spiked it with cumin, coriander, and a little sugar for balance.

One benefit of the tradi- tional stewing method is that it tenderizes inexpensive cuts of beef by submerging them in the flavorful sauce over low heat for hours, enriching both the meat and sauce. Cuts from the chuck (the shoulder) are particularly good here, but large pieces (such as a whole chuck roast) took too long to cook. Cubes of chuck sold as stew meat seemed like a natural choice, but tasters found the flavor to be a little shallow and the texture tender in some bites, chewy in others. I got the soft chew and beefy flavor I was looking for with another cut from the chuck, the inexpensive top blade, and I kept the stewing time to an hour and a half by cutting the steaks into small pieces.

Assembling and baking the enchiladas goes quickly and smoothly—if you use a few tricks. Authentic recipes fry the corn tortillas and then dip them in sauce to simultane- ously soften and season them. This was a lengthy, messy procedure, so I opted instead to microwave the tortillas to soften them before filling them with tender beef, rolling them up, and topping the enchiladas with sauce and cheese. After they spent just 30 minutes in the oven, I sat down to a plate of spicy beef enchiladas that only tasted like they took all day to make. –Adam Ried

BEEF ENCHILADAS

SERVES 4 TO 6

Cut back on the pickled jalape- ños if you like your enchiladas on the mild side. Our flavored sour creams (page 30) are a great finishing touch.

- 3   garlic cloves, minced
- 3   tablespoons chili powder
- 2   teaspoons ground coriander
- 2   teaspoons ground cumin
- 1   teaspoon sugar
-    Salt
- 1¼ pounds top blade steaks, trimmed according to photo at right
- 1   tablespoon vegetable oil
- 2   medium onions, chopped
- 1   (15-ounce) can tomato sauce
- ½ cup water
- 2   cups shredded Monterey Jack or mild cheddar cheese
- ⅓ cup chopped fresh cilantro
- ¼ cup chopped canned pickled jalapeños
- 12 (6-inch) corn tortillas

1. Combine garlic, chili powder, coriander, cumin, sugar, and 1 teaspoon salt in small bowl. Pat meat dry with paper towels and sprinkle with salt. Heat oil in Dutch oven over medium-high until shimmering. Cook meat until browned on both sides, about 6 minutes. Transfer meat to plate. Add onions to pot and cook over medium heat until golden, about 5 minutes. Stir in garlic mixture and cook until fragrant, about 1 minute. Add tomato sauce and water and bring to boil. Return meat and juices to pot, cover, reduce heat to low, and gently simmer until meat is tender and can be broken apart with wooden spoon, about 1½ hours.

2. Adjust oven rack to middle position and heat oven to 350 degrees. Strain beef mixture over medium bowl, breaking meat into small pieces; reserve sauce. Transfer meat to bowl and mix with 1 cup cheese, cilantro, and jalapeños.

3. Spread ¾ cup sauce in bottom of 13 by 9-inch baking dish. Microwave 6 tortillas on plate on high power until soft, about 1 minute. Spread ⅓ cup beef mixture down center of each tortilla, roll tortillas tightly, and set in baking dish seam side down. Repeat with remaining tortillas and beef mixture (you may have to fit 2 or more enchiladas down the sides of the baking dish). Pour remaining sauce over enchiladas and spread to coat evenly. Sprinkle remaining cheese evenly over enchiladas, wrap with aluminum foil, and bake until heated through, 20 to 25 minutes. Remove foil and continue baking until cheese browns slightly, 5 to 10 minutes. Serve.

Make Ahead: Although it's best to roll and bake the enchiladas right before serving, the beef filling and sauce can be prepared through step 2 and refrigerated in separate containers for up to 2 days.

Kitchen Know-How
TRIMMING BLADE STEAKS

After testing various beef cuts, we found that blade steaks (which are cut from the chuck) had enough marbling to produce silky, flavorful shredded beef for our enchiladas. The only trick is to cut away the center strip of gristle, which is very easy to do because the strip is in plain sight in the middle of each steak. Simply halve each steak lengthwise and then slice away the gristle, as shown here.

Test Kitchen's Easter Menu

A holiday celebration doesn't have to require endless trips to the market and several days in the kitchen. This streamlined menu puts an emphasis on make-ahead work, so the cook can enjoy the day, too.

CREAMY PEA SOUP SERVES 8

Fresh tarragon may be substituted for the mint garnish.

- 2 tablespoons unsalted butter
- 1 medium onion, chopped fine
  Salt
- 2 tablespoons all-purpose flour
- 4 cups low-sodium chicken broth
- 1½ pounds frozen peas, thawed
- ½ cup half-and-half
  Pepper
- 1 tablespoon minced fresh mint

1. Melt butter in Dutch oven over medium heat. When foaming subsides, cook onion and ½ teaspoon salt until softened, about 5 minutes. Stir in flour and cook for 1 minute. Slowly whisk in broth, bring to simmer, and cook until slightly thickened, about 5 minutes. Add peas and simmer until tender, 7 to 10 minutes. Puree soup in 2 batches in blender (or food processor) until smooth.

2. Return pureed soup to pot with half-and-half and warm over medium heat until just simmering. Season with salt and pepper. Ladle into individual bowls and garnish with mint. Serve.

Make Ahead: The soup can be made through step 1 and refrigerated for up to 3 days. When ready to serve, add half-and-half and proceed with step 2 as directed.

ROAST LEG OF LAMB WITH GARLIC-HERB CRUST

SERVES 8 TO 10

A semiboneless leg of lamb has had the hipbone removed to facilitate carving. This recipe makes enough bread crumbs to use for the Lemon Asparagus Casserole.

Roast Lamb

- 1 semiboneless leg of lamb (6 to 8 pounds)
- 4 garlic cloves, sliced thin
- 1 tablespoon fresh rosemary leaves
- 2 tablespoons extra-virgin olive oil
  Salt and pepper

Garlic-Herb Crust

- 6 slices hearty white sandwich bread
- 5 garlic cloves, minced
- ¼ cup extra-virgin olive oil
- ½ cup chopped fresh parsley
- 1 teaspoon minced fresh rosemary
- 2 tablespoons Dijon mustard

1. For the lamb: Adjust oven rack to lower-middle position and heat oven to 450 degrees. Using paring knife, cut 1-inch-deep slits all over lamb and poke garlic slivers and rosemary leaves inside slits. Rub lamb with oil and season with salt and pepper. Place leg meaty side down on wire rack set inside rimmed baking sheet. Roast lamb for 15 minutes, flip, and roast 15 minutes longer.

2. For the crust: Meanwhile, pulse bread, garlic, oil, and parsley in food processor until coarsely ground. Reserve 2 cups crumb mixture for Lemon Asparagus Casserole. Stir rosemary into remaining crumbs.

3. Lower oven temperature to 325 degrees. Remove lamb from oven and brush meaty side with mustard. Press bread crumb mixture into mustard and continue roasting until temperature registers 130 to 135 degrees for medium, 30 to 45 minutes. Transfer lamb to cutting board and tent loosely with foil. Let rest 15 to 20 minutes. Slice and serve.

Make Ahead: Make slits in lamb, fill with garlic slivers and rosemary, wrap tightly in plastic, and refrigerate for up to 2 days. The garlic-herb crust may be prepared as directed in step 2 and refrigerated for up to 1 day.

BOILED POTATOES WITH GARLIC, LEMON, AND FETA

SERVES 8

If you cannot find baby red potatoes, substitute larger red potatoes that have been quartered.

- ½ cup crumbled feta cheese
- ¼ cup chopped fresh parsley
- 2 garlic cloves, minced
- 2 teaspoons grated zest plus 2 tablespoons juice from 1 lemon
- 2 tablespoons extra-virgin olive oil
- 3 pounds baby red potatoes, scrubbed and dried, halved if large
  Salt and pepper

1. Combine ¼ cup feta, parsley, garlic, zest, juice, and oil in large bowl. Place potatoes in large Dutch oven and add water to cover. Bring to boil over medium-high heat. Add 1 tablespoon salt, reduce heat to medium, and simmer until potatoes are tender, 10 to 15 minutes.

2. Drain potatoes and add to bowl with cheese mixture. Toss to combine and season with salt and pepper. Sprinkle with remaining feta. Serve.

LEMON ASPARAGUS CASSEROLE SERVES 8

Some of the garlic-herb crumb topping from the lamb is combined with crushed canned fried onions to create the crisp topping for this casserole.

Topping

- 2 cups crumb mixture from Roast Leg of Lamb recipe
- 1½ cups canned fried onions, crushed

Asparagus

- Salt
- 3 pounds asparagus, trimmed and cut into 1-inch pieces
- 3 tablespoons unsalted butter
- 1 small red onion, minced
- 4 garlic cloves, minced
- 1 tablespoon grated lemon zest
- 3 tablespoons all-purpose flour
- 1½ cups low-sodium chicken broth
- 1 cup heavy cream
  Pepper

1. For the topping: Combine crumb mixture with onions.

2. For the asparagus: Adjust oven rack to middle position and heat oven to 425 degrees. Fill large bowl with ice water. Bring 4 quarts water to boil in Dutch oven over medium-high heat. Add 2 tablespoons salt and asparagus and cook until just tender, about 6 minutes. Transfer asparagus to ice water, cool, and drain on paper towels.

3. Melt butter in now-empty Dutch oven over medium-high heat. Cook onion until golden brown, about 5 minutes. Add garlic, zest, and flour and cook until fragrant, about 1 minute. Whisk in broth and cream and simmer over medium heat until thickened, about 10 minutes. Toss in asparagus and season with salt and pepper.

4. Transfer mixture to 13 by 9-inch baking dish. Top with crumbs and bake until golden brown, about 15 minutes. Serve.

Make Ahead: Topping, asparagus, and sauce can be refrigerated separately for up to 1 day. When ready to serve, heat sauce until hot and toss with asparagus. Proceed with step 4 as directed.

MAPLE-BALSAMIC ROASTED CARROTS SERVES 8

Don't be tempted to use pancake syrup for this recipe. Pure maple syrup is a key to the great flavor of these carrots.

- 1 teaspoon salt
- 2 pounds carrots, peeled and cut on bias into ½-inch slices
- 3 tablespoons unsalted butter
- 4 shallots, sliced thin
- 2 teaspoons minced fresh thyme
- ¼ teaspoon cayenne pepper
- ½ cup maple syrup
- ¼ cup low-sodium chicken broth
- ¼ cup plus 1 teaspoon balsamic vinegar

1. Bring 2 quarts water to boil in large pot over medium-high heat. Add salt and carrots and cook until just tender, about 8 minutes. Drain, then transfer to paper towel–lined plate.

2. Meanwhile, melt 1 tablespoon butter in large skillet over medium-high heat. When foaming subsides, cook shallots until lightly browned, about 2 minutes. Stir in thyme, cayenne, maple syrup, broth, and ¼ cup vinegar. Bring to simmer and cook until thick and syrupy, 5 to 7 minutes. Stir in carrots and simmer until carrots are well glazed and tender, 3 to 5 minutes. Off heat, stir in remaining butter and vinegar. Serve.

Make Ahead: The carrots can be cooked as directed in step 1, rinsed under cold water to stop cooking process, drained on paper towels, and refrigerated for up to 2 days. Proceed as directed in step 2.

These boldly flavored dressings are just as good drizzled over meats and steamed vegetables as they are on salads.

Herb Vinaigrettes

The secret to making a salad dressing with rich herb flavor isn't just using more fresh herbs—it's how you handle them.

Kitchen Know-How
SECRETS TO BIG HERB FLAVOR

1. Heating fresh herbs in oilve oil creates an herb-infused oil that offers a good foundation for our dressing.

2. Making the dressing in a blender (and adding more fresh herbs) extracts every bit of flavor from the herbs.

Homemade vinaigrettes are simple to make, good to have on hand, and a darn sight better than bottled salad dressings. The problem with most herb vinaigrettes is that the subtle herb flavor can get lost behind strong vinegars, pungent mustards, and assertive olive oils. I set out to create herb-packed dressings that would be great on delicate greens yet also flavorful enough to spoon onto roasted meat or steamed fish for an added boost.

I began by making basic herb vinaigrettes with vegetable, canola, olive, and extra-virgin olive oils. My tasters much preferred the dressing made with regular olive oil; it added some flavor (more than the canola or vegetable oils did) without overpowering the herb character (like the extra-virgin oil did).

As for the mixing method, I tried whisking the oil and vinegar together in a bowl, shaking them in a jar, and emulsifying them in a blender. My tasters preferred the bolder herb flavor of the dressing made in the blender, as the pulverizing extracted more flavor from the fresh herbs. Looking for even more flavor, I tried bumping up the amount of herbs and adding them at different times during the blending—all to no avail.

Then a colleague suggested making homemade herb oil. At first, this sounded like a tiresome project. But I found that gently heating some olive oil with a fresh herb created an infused oil that was loaded with flavor. And it took just two to three minutes. I turned off the heat, let the herbs steep for five minutes longer, and then proceeded to use this herb oil to make dressing. Tasters liked the addition of shallot, garlic, mustard, and more fresh herbs to create dressings with plenty of personality. **–Diane Unger**

OREGANO-BLACK OLIVE VINAIGRETTE

MAKES 1 CUP, ENOUGH TO DRESS 8 CUPS OF GREENS
Don't add the olives to the blender; they will turn the dressing black.

- 3/4 **cup olive oil**
- 2 **tablespoons minced fresh oregano**
- 1 **shallot, peeled**
- 1 **garlic clove, peeled**
- 1/4 **cup red wine vinegar**
- 1/2 **teaspoon salt**
- 1/4 **teaspoon pepper**
- 1 **tablespoon Dijon mustard**
- 1/4 **cup pitted kalamata olives, minced**

1. Heat ¼ cup oil with 1 tablespoon oregano in medium saucepan over medium heat until oregano turns bright green and small bubbles appear, 2 to 3 minutes. Turn off heat and steep 5 minutes.

2. Process shallot, garlic, vinegar, salt, pepper, mustard, and remaining oregano in blender until garlic and shallot are finely chopped, about 15 seconds. With blender running, slowly add remaining oil and steeped oregano oil and continue to process until dressing is smooth and emulsified, about 15 seconds. Transfer to bowl and stir in olives. (Dressing can be refrigerated in airtight container for up to 3 days.)

THYME-MUSTARD VINAIGRETTE

MAKES 1 CUP, ENOUGH TO DRESS 8 CUPS OF GREENS
Whole-grain mustard adds texture to this dressing, but you can use any mustard in its place.

- 3/4 **cup olive oil**
- 2 **tablespoons minced fresh thyme**
- 1 **shallot, peeled**
- 1 **garlic clove, peeled**
- 1/4 **cup cider vinegar**
- 1/2 **teaspoon salt**
- 1/4 **teaspoon pepper**
- 2 **tablespoons whole-grain mustard**

1. Heat ¼ cup oil with 1 tablespoon thyme in medium saucepan over medium heat until thyme turns bright green and small bubbles appear, 2 to 3 minutes. Turn off heat and steep 5 minutes.

2. Process shallot, garlic, vinegar, salt, pepper, mustard, and remaining thyme in blender until garlic and shallot are finely chopped, about 15 seconds. With blender running, slowly add remaining oil and steeped thyme oil and continue to process until dressing is smooth and emulsified, about 15 seconds. (Dressing can be refrigerated in airtight container for up to 3 days.)

FRESH BASIL VINAIGRETTE

MAKES 1½ CUPS, ENOUGH TO DRESS 8 CUPS OF GREENS
Basil is not as potent as other herbs, so you need to use an entire bunch.

- 3/4 **cup olive oil**
- 2 **cups chopped fresh basil**
- 1 **shallot, peeled**
- 1 **garlic clove, peeled**
- 1/4 **cup red wine vinegar**
- 1/4 **cup water**
- 1/2 **teaspoon salt**
- 1/4 **teaspoon pepper**
- 2 **teaspoons Dijon mustard**

1. Heat ¼ cup oil with 1 cup basil in medium saucepan over medium heat until basil turns bright green and small bubbles appear, 2 to 3 minutes. Turn off heat and steep 5 minutes.

2. Process shallot, garlic, vinegar, water, salt, pepper, and mustard in blender until garlic and shallot are finely chopped, about 15 seconds. With blender running, slowly add remaining oil and steeped basil oil and continue to process until dressing is smooth and emulsified, about 15 seconds. Pack remaining 1 cup basil into blender and process until dressing is smooth, about 15 seconds. (Dressing can be refrigerated in airtight container for up to 3 days.)

Visit us online!
For an Orange-Tarragon Vinaigrette variation, visit **CooksCountry.com** and click on **Cook's Country Extra.**

Getting to Know Fresh Herbs

Many supermarkets stock a half-dozen or more fresh herbs, and there are dozens more options for gardeners. Here are our tasters' notes on 12 popular fresh herbs, along with test kitchen tips for using each.

Basil
SWEET ITALIAN

Sometimes labeled Genoa basil, this "slightly acidic" herb balances "licorice" and "citrus" notes. Basil bruises and discolors easily, so shred or chop leaves just before using. Basil's delicate flavor is greatly muted when cooked; therefore, it's best as a finishing herb.

Cilantro
FAR-EAST FLAVOR

Also called Chinese parsley, cilantro's flavor is "soapy" and "aromatic," with a "refreshing, peppery finish." Cooking deadens its pungency, so it's best as a finishing herb. The stems can be minced along with the leaves. When dried, the seeds are known as coriander.

Curly-Leaf Parsley
GREAT FOR GARNISH

Curly-leaf parsley is "milder" than its flat-leafed cousin, with a "peppery, earthy," and "straightforward vegetal" taste. Uncooked, its texture is "plasticky," so curly-leaf parsley should be allowed time to cook when added to soups and sauces.

Dill
PICKLES AND MORE

Dill's feathery fronds are "slightly bitter," with a "refreshing, lemony" quality and an aroma akin to "caraway seeds." Dill matches perfectly with cucumbers (both pickled and raw); its "summery freshness" also works well with seafood, potatoes, and eggs. Best used as a finishing herb.

Flat-Leaf Parsley
CLEAN AND FLORAL

This popular herb possesses a "palate-cleansing astringency" that's balanced by a "hint of lemon pepper." Add whole leaves to salads or chop and use as a finishing herb in a variety of cooked dishes. Parsley stems have a lot of flavor and can be used to flavor soups and stocks.

Marjoram
FRENCH FAVORITE

A member of the mint family, fresh marjoram is often mistaken for oregano. Its flavor is "sweet, like juniper berries," with a "delicate, fleeting spiciness." Marjoram is often paired with poultry, lamb, or vegetables and is best used as a finishing herb.

Mint
REFRESHING BITE

Although there are over 2,000 varieties of mint, spearmint is the most common. The flavor of mint can be described as "smooth and bright," with a "eucalyptus quality." Mint is often bruised or muddled to release its flavor. Best used as a finishing herb.

Oregano
MUSTY AND FUZZY

This hearty perennial shrub has fuzzy, spade-shaped leaves and tough, viny stems. Another member of the mint family, its potent flavor can be described as "earthy" and "musty," with a "spicy-hot" bite. Discard the stems and add the chopped leaves at the outset of cooking.

Rosemary
PINE TIME

This evergreen-like herb has an "obvious pine aroma." In moderation, its taste is "clean, sweet, and floral," but if overused it can be "like Vicks VapoRub." Strip leaves off stems and mince or add whole sprigs during the last 30 minutes of cooking and remove before serving.

Sage
FURRY AND FUNKY

Perhaps best known as the main herb in poultry seasoning, sage flavors a range of foods from breakfast sausages to Thanksgiving stuffing. Its taste is "earthy and floral," with a "musky" bite. Because of its "cottony texture" when raw, sage should be cooked.

Tarragon
DRAGON'S TONGUE

In France, this slender-leafed herb is called "little dragon" because of its fiery quality. Its flavor is very assertive, with a "mouth-numbing, anesthetic quality" and a sweet "orange-anise" aroma. Tarragon can be used sparingly in fish, egg, and chicken dishes.

Thyme
DELICATE LEAVES

This low-lying bushy herb has woody stems and tiny greenish-gray leaves. Thyme has a distinct "menthol aroma" and a "deep, grassy" taste with a slight hint of "Lemon Pledge." It is usually added early in cooking. Strip the leaves off the stems or add whole sprigs to soups and stocks.

Chicken and Rice with Spring Vegetables

Can spring vegetables and a San Francisco secret take chicken and rice out of the fog?

We freshen up this often-stodgy dish by adding peas, asparagus, basil, and the earthy flavor of toasted orzo.

Toast of the Town

Orzo is a rice-shaped pasta that adds chewy texture to our Chicken and Rice with Spring Vegetables. To improve its flavor, we toasted the orzo before adding it to the pot. With just five minutes in a dry pan, the orzo took on a deep caramel color and a nutty flavor that worked wonders in this dish.

PALE & BLAND

TOASTED & TASTY

Chicken and rice should be a part of every cook's weeknight repertoire. After all, it's a hot, hearty, one-pot supper that can be on the table in well under an hour. But for all the convenience, most recipes are fraught with problems. All too often the rice is crunchy, the chicken is rubbery, the vegetables are shriveled, and everything is bland.

The key to properly cooked rice lies in the ratio of liquid to rice. I found that 2¼ cups of liquid to 1½ cups of rice produced perfectly plump grains. Since the rice cooks in 30 minutes, I learned it's best to avoid using dark meat (which is better suited to longer cooking). Bone-in, skin-on breasts added a lot of flavor, but their fatty skin left the rice slick and heavy. Boneless, skinless breasts solved the grease problem, but they dried out when cooked with the rice. Ultimately, I found that if I removed the boneless, skinless breasts from the pot (tenting them with foil to keep them warm) when the rice was halfway done, the chicken was fully cooked and still moist when added back in just before serving.

Tasters loved the combination of asparagus and peas. But while the peas were easy—I simply stirred frozen peas into the rice at the end—the asparagus wasn't. Adding asparagus at the outset left it overcooked and bitter, but adding raw spears any later messed up the timing of the rice. I decided to cook the asparagus first. Since blanching and steaming didn't add any flavor, I quickly seared the asparagus before the chicken went into the pan. This way, the perfectly cooked asparagus was nicely caramelized and could be added to the pot along with the peas.

The rice, chicken, and vegetables were properly cooked, but the dish was bland. To pump up the flavors, I took a key from rice pilaf and sautéed the rice (along with onion and garlic) before adding the liquid. This added a toasty aroma, but the rice still lacked depth. I tried different types of rice (long-grain was the favorite), bouillon cubes (too assertive and salty), even searing the chicken in butter rather than oil (the butter burned), but nothing worked.

Running out of options, I found my unlikely muse in the supermarket: Rice-A-Roni, which combines pasta with rice to lend a distinct texture and flavor to its boxed dinners. In hopeful desperation, I gave this concept a shot, adding my "roni" in the form of orzo (a rice-shaped pasta). To my surprise, the orzo (with an extra ¼ cup of liquid) cooked at exactly the same rate as the rice and added a welcome texture to the dish. To improve its flavor, I tried toasting the orzo along with the rice, but that didn't do much. However, toasting the orzo in a dry pan gave it a deep caramel color and an earthy taste that worked wonders.

For the finishing touch, tasters asked for a few flavorful stir-ins. The addition of fresh basil, raw garlic, and lemon zest transformed this humble dish into something worthy of a special occasion. **–Jeremy Sauer**

CHICKEN AND RICE WITH SPRING VEGETABLES SERVES 4

The rice will cook unevenly if the pot is uncovered for too long, so work quickly in step 3.

- ½ **cup orzo**
- 4 **tablespoons vegetable oil**
- 1 **pound asparagus, trimmed and cut into 1-inch pieces**
- 4 **boneless, skinless chicken breasts (about 1½ pounds) Salt and pepper**
- 1 **cup long-grain white rice**
- 1 **onion, chopped fine**
- 4 **garlic cloves, minced**
- 2¼ **cups low-sodium chicken broth**
- ¼ **cup white wine**
- 1 **cup frozen peas, thawed**
- 2 **tablespoons chopped fresh basil**
- ½ **teaspoon grated lemon zest**

1. Toast orzo in Dutch oven over medium-high heat until deep brown, about 5 minutes. Transfer to bowl. Heat 1 tablespoon oil in now-empty pot until shimmering. Cook asparagus until lightly browned and nearly tender, about 3 minutes. Transfer to plate.

2. Season chicken with salt and pepper. Heat remaining oil in now-empty pot until just smoking. Cook chicken until lightly browned, about 3 minutes per side. Transfer chicken to plate, leaving fat in pan. Add rice, onion, and ¾ teaspoon salt to pot and cook until rice is sizzling and toasted, about 3 minutes. Add three-quarters of garlic and cook until fragrant, about 30 seconds. Stir in toasted orzo, broth, and wine and bring to simmer. Nestle chicken into rice and pour in any juices accumulated on plate. Cover pot, reduce heat to low, and simmer until chicken is cooked through, about 12 minutes.

3. Working quickly, transfer chicken to plate and cover loosely with foil. Stir rice, replace cover, and continue cooking until rice is tender and liquid is absorbed, about 12 minutes. Off heat, gently fold in peas, basil, zest, remaining garlic, and reserved asparagus. Cover and let sit until heated through, about 2 minutes. Transfer to serving platter and top with chicken. Serve.

Skillet Supper: Beef Stroganoff

Could we remake this classic Russian dish as an easy, inexpensive one-pot meal?

Beef Stroganoff is a sneaky dish. It looks like a long-cooked stew of inexpensive beef, mushrooms, and gravy, but it's really a quick sauté made with the most tender and expensive cut on the steer, filet mignon. The beef is cooked with wine and stock, finished with cream, and served over egg noodles. But when I spend $25 on filet, I'm not going to smother it in gravy. I wanted a cheaper alternative that would make better sense for a weeknight dinner.

Since cheaper cuts of meat are generally tough, I knew I'd have to shift from a quick sauté to a longer braise. The moist heat breaks down the fibers and collagen in meat, making tough cuts tender. Sliced blade steaks shrank into unappetizing curls. Sirloin tips were tender, but they looked odd—with an accordion shape—at the end of cooking. I found that pounding the tips before cutting them into strips compressed the fibers in the meat and helped keep the strips neat and uniform as they cooked.

After trading out cooking time for a cheaper cut of meat, I hoped to steal back a few minutes by cooking the egg noodles right in the skillet with the saucy beef. Adding extra broth (and brandy, which tasters preferred to the usual red wine) allowed me to cook the entire dish in one pan. I finally had an easy meal that would make both my family and my wallet smile. **–Diane Unger**

SKILLET BEEF STROGANOFF SERVES 4

Brandy can ignite if added to a hot, empty skillet. Be sure to add the brandy to the skillet after stirring in the broth.

1 1/2	**pounds sirloin tips, pounded and cut according to photos on page 31**
	Salt and pepper
4	**tablespoons vegetable oil**
10	**ounces white mushrooms, sliced thin**
1	**onion, chopped fine**
2	**tablespoons all-purpose flour**
1 1/2	**cups low-sodium chicken broth**
1 1/2	**cups low-sodium beef broth**
1/3	**cup brandy**
1/3	**pound wide egg noodles (3 cups)**
2/3	**cup sour cream**
2	**teaspoons lemon juice**

1. Pat beef dry with paper towels and season with salt and pepper. Heat 1 tablespoon oil in large skillet over medium-high heat until just smoking. Cook half of beef until well browned, 3 to 4 minutes per side. Transfer to medium bowl and repeat with 1 tablespoon more oil and remaining beef.

2. Heat remaining oil in now-empty skillet until shimmering. Cook mushrooms, onion, and 1/2 teaspoon salt until liquid from mushrooms has evaporated, about 8 minutes. (If pan becomes too brown, pour accumulated beef juices into skillet.) Stir in flour and cook for 30 seconds. Gradually stir in broths, then brandy, and return beef and accumulated juices to pan. Bring to simmer, cover, and cook over low heat until beef is tender, 30 to 35 minutes.

3. Stir noodles into beef mixture, cover, and cook, stirring occasionally, until noodles are tender, 10 to 12 minutes. Off heat, stir in sour cream and lemon juice. Season with salt and pepper. Serve.

Recipe Revival: Creamy Broccoli and Cheddar Soup

Cheddar cheese adds plenty of flavor, but how do you make the broccoli more than just green filler?

Cheddar broccoli soup is old-fashioned comfort food. But for something so simple (basically broccoli, chicken broth, cream, and cheese), a lot can go wrong. Many recipes yield either a gloppy, glorified cheese sauce or a mealy mess of bland, gray vegetables. I wanted a creamy soup that tasted like fresh, bright-green broccoli.

Since this soup is almost always pureed, I wondered if I could include the fibrous stems for flavor. I made what amounted to a broccoli stock by sautéing broccoli stems with onion and garlic and then adding chicken broth and cooking the stock until the stems were soft. It was only then that I added the broccoli florets and cream; this ensured that the florets didn't overcook and retained their bright color and fresh flavor.

I kept increasing the amount of broccoli until I was using 1 1/2 pounds (twice as much as many recipes) for just six bowls of soup. The soup was so thick from the broccoli and cheddar (added at the end to keep it from separating and clumping) that I didn't need to thicken the soup with flour or cornstarch.

–Bridget Lancaster

CREAMY BROCCOLI AND CHEDDAR SOUP SERVES 6

Taste the soup before adding any salt; both the cheese and the chicken broth can be quite salty.

3	**tablespoons unsalted butter**
1	**large onion, chopped**
2	**garlic cloves, chopped**
1 1/2	**pounds broccoli, stems peeled and sliced into 1/2-inch pieces, florets chopped into 1/2-inch pieces**
4	**cups low-sodium chicken broth**
1	**cup heavy cream**
1/4	**teaspoon ground nutmeg**
3	**cups shredded mild cheddar cheese, plus extra for garnish**
	Salt and cayenne pepper

1. Melt butter in large pot over medium heat. Add onion and cook until soft, about 5 minutes. Add garlic and cook until fragrant, about 1 minute. Add broccoli stems and cook until bright green and just beginning to soften, about 5 minutes. Stir in broth, increase heat to medium-high, and simmer until stems are tender, about 5 minutes. Add florets, cream, and nutmeg and simmer until florets are tender, about 5 minutes.

2. Puree soup in 2 batches in blender until smooth, return to pot, and bring to simmer over medium heat. Stir in cheddar until melted and season with salt and cayenne pepper. Serve, garnished with extra cheese. (Soup can be refrigerated for up to 3 days. Reheat over medium heat until hot, but do not boil or cheese will separate.)

Tropical Carrot Cake

When you're feeling rundown, a trip to the tropics can rejuvenate you. We were hoping the same treatment would work for stodgy old carrot cake.

Making a homemade coconut sugar in the food processor is just one of the secrets to this cake's fresh tropical flavor.

Existing somewhere between health food and decadent dessert, carrot cake was the cake to make during the 1960s. And it wasn't long before cooks came up with variations like chocolate, banana, and my favorite, tropical carrot cake. Building on the warm flavors of traditional carrot cake, the tropical version adds coconut, pineapple, dried fruit (papaya, mango, or raisins), and macadamia nuts.

But in making several of these cakes, I found quite a few problems. The most obvious was the flavor—or lack thereof. Tasters were hard-pressed to identify anything tropical. The texture was even worse; while a regular carrot cake can be made soggy by the carrots and oil, tropical carrot cake compounds the problem by adding juicy pineapple. And the dried fruit and nuts made the cake too heavy, like bad fruitcake. My tasters told me they wanted coconut and pineapple to be the predominant flavors, so the nuts and dried fruit were out. I set out to make a light, moist cake with big hits of coconut and pineapple.

Starting with the coconut, I wanted to intensify its profile in the cake while eliminating its stringy texture. Toasting the coconut improved the flavor incrementally, but it made the stringy bits even tougher. Thinking about how some recipes use flavored sugars

(vanilla sugar being the most common), I wondered what would happen if I ground the coconut and sugar into a powder in the food processor. This worked great; the stringy texture was gone, and the grinding extracted maximum coconut flavor.

Moving on to the pineapple, I tried building flavor by substituting pureed canned pineapple for some of the oil in my recipe. Unfortunately, it added weak flavor and was too wet (even when drained before pureeing). Frozen pineapple chunks worked much better, adding fresher flavor—although not quite enough of it—and a drier texture.

Since I was looking for concentrated pineapple flavor, it made sense to try frozen pineapple juice concentrate; I mixed the concentrate with the pureed frozen pineapple and cooked

it down with a little cornstarch to evaporate excess moisture. I added this homemade pudding to the cake batter in place of much of the oil; I knew I was onto something when, after 20 minutes in the oven, the test kitchen was filled with the aromas of coconut and pineapple. Tasters lined up to help me try this fluffy cake, and then they came back for seconds.

A plain cream cheese frosting was good, but I wanted to add another layer of tropical flavors. Since I had some extra pudding mixture, I tried incorporating it into the cream cheese frosting; it worked like a charm. To

put this dessert over the top, I toasted coconut and pressed it into the sides and on top of the cake. Now my light, full-flavored carrot cake both looked and tasted like it was enjoying a nice vacation in the tropics. –Diane Unger

TROPICAL CARROT CAKE SERVES 12

You'll need one 14-ounce bag of sweetened shredded coconut for this recipe. To toast the coconut for the frosting, spread it on a rimmed baking sheet and bake in a 325-degree oven, stirring often, until golden brown, about 15 minutes.

Pineapple Pudding
- 1 pound frozen pineapple chunks, thawed
- 1/2 cup frozen pineapple juice concentrate, thawed
- 6 tablespoons cornstarch

Cake
- 2 1/2 cups all-purpose flour
- 1 tablespoon baking powder
- 4 teaspoons pumpkin pie spice
- 3/4 teaspoon ground ginger
- 1/2 teaspoon salt
- 3/4 pound carrots (about 6 medium), peeled and cut into 1-inch chunks
- 1 cup sweetened shredded coconut
- 1 1/4 cups granulated sugar
- 1/2 cup packed light brown sugar
- 4 large eggs
- 1 1/2 cups vegetable oil

Cream Cheese Frosting
- 12 tablespoons (1 1/2 sticks) unsalted butter, softened
- 3 cups confectioners' sugar
- 16 ounces cream cheese, cut in 8 pieces and softened
  Pinch salt
- 3 cups sweetened shredded coconut, toasted (see note)

1. For the pudding: Process pineapple chunks and concentrate in food processor until smooth. Transfer to medium

The Proof Is in the Pudding

To add great pineapple flavor to both the cake and the frosting, we made a pineapple pudding with frozen pineapple chunks and frozen pineapple juice concentrate, both thawed and thickened with cornstarch.

FROZEN PINEAPPLE CHUNKS

+

PINEAPPLE JUICE CONCENTRATE

+

CORNSTARCH

=

EASY PINEAPPLE PUDDING

saucepan and whisk in corn-starch until smooth. Bring to simmer over medium heat and cook, stirring constantly, until thickened, about 2 minutes. Transfer to bowl and refrigerate until cold, at least 1½ hours.

2. For the cake: Adjust oven rack to middle position and heat oven to 350 degrees. Spray two 9-inch cake pans with cooking spray. Line pans with parchment and spray parchment with cooking spray. Whisk flour, baking powder, pumpkin pie spice, ginger, and salt in large bowl.

3. Process carrots in food processor until finely ground. Transfer to large bowl and wipe processor bowl dry. Process coconut with granulated sugar until coconut is finely chopped. Add brown sugar and eggs and blend until mixture is smooth, about 1 minute. With machine running, slowly pour in oil and process until combined.

4. Transfer mixture to bowl with carrots. Add flour mixture and ¾ cup pudding mixture and stir until no streaks of flour remain. Pour into prepared pans and bake until toothpick inserted into center of cake comes out clean, 30 to 35 minutes, rotating pans halfway through baking time. Cool cakes in pans 10 minutes, then turn out onto rack, peel off parchment, and let cool completely, about 2 hours.

5. For the frosting: With electric mixer at medium-high speed, beat butter and sugar until fluffy, about 2 minutes. Add cream cheese, 1 piece at a time, and beat until incorporated. Beat in remaining 1 cup pineapple pudding and salt. Mixture will appear slightly grainy.) Refrigerate until ready to use.

6. When cakes are cooled, spread 2 cups frosting on 1 cake. Top with second cake and spread top and sides with remaining frosting. Refrigerate for 15 minutes. Sprinkle toasted coconut on top and press into sides of cake. Cover and refrigerate until ready to serve, up to 2 days.

Bake-Sale Favorites: Black-Bottom Cupcakes

With our tangy cheesecake filling, you can forget about frosting.

Every time I visit New York, I make a point to stop by my favorite bakery. As a chocolate lover, my standing order had always been the devil's food cupcake, but on my last visit the girl behind the counter suggested another treat that would "change my life": the black-bottom cupcake. The near-black cupcake was the most moist I've ever eaten, especially at the fudgy bottom. But the bonus was on the inside—a creamy center of tangy cheesecake studded with mini chocolate chips.

Back in Boston, I realized that the girl at the bakery was right—I couldn't get that cupcake out of my mind. Determined to make my own, I gathered a stack of printed recipes and headed to the kitchen with high hopes. But I soon wondered if a trip back to NYC would be easier than salvaging the sad display of cupcakes I'd just made. Most of them were greasy, slumped, and devoid of rich chocolate flavor. As for the cheesecake centers, they baked up dry, chalky, or completely separated from the cake in sunken craters. I was looking for a cake that had big chocolate flavor and was sturdy enough to support the cheesecake filling.

The cake portion of black-bottom cupcakes traditionally gets its dark color and chocolate flavor from cocoa. My tasters much preferred the rounded flavor of Dutch-processed cocoa to natural cocoa. Adding a little sour cream to the batter accentuated the chocolate and added richness. Although the cake was now tasting good, I was frustrated that the cheesecake center was still pulling away. It turns out the problem was with the cake, not the filling.

Black-bottom cupcakes are usually made with oil, which contributes to the soft, fudgy texture. But oil also makes the cake leaden and greasy—so greasy that the filling couldn't adhere to it. However, when I used butter (creaming it with the sugar) instead of oil, the aerated batter baked up too tender to support the filling. As a last resort, I tried melting the butter. The batter looked dense and sticky (just like the batter made with oil), but as the cupcakes cooled I saw a big difference. The butter had resolidified and the cake was no longer greasy. Best of all, it was sturdy enough to support the cheesecake filling.

But I still wasn't happy with the filling's

flavor. Most recipes consist of cream cheese, sugar, and a whole egg, but the yolk lent an unappealing yellow hue and mealy texture when baked. Using two whites added moisture and helped the filling look better, but it also dulled the tang of the cream cheese. Since I was already using sour cream in the cake batter, I added some to the cheesecake filling, and it restored a needed tang. The inclusion of mini chocolate chips made the filling complete. I finally had the cupcake I'd been dreaming about—and I didn't have to travel to New York to enjoy it.

—Cali Rich

BLACK-BOTTOM CUPCAKES
MAKES 24

Do not substitute regular chocolate chips for the miniature chips. Regular chips are much heavier and will sink to the bottom of the cupcakes.

- 16 ounces cream cheese, at room temperature
- 1¾ cups sugar
- ¾ teaspoon salt
- 2 large egg whites, at room temperature
- 2 tablespoons plus ¾ cup sour cream, at room temperature
- ⅓ cup miniature semisweet chocolate chips
- 1½ cups all-purpose flour
- ½ cup Dutch-processed cocoa powder
- 1¼ teaspoons baking soda
- 1⅓ cups water
- 8 tablespoons (1 stick) unsalted butter, melted and slightly cooled
- 1 teaspoon vanilla extract

1. Adjust oven rack to lower-middle position and heat oven to 400 degrees. Line 2 standard muffin tins with cupcake liners.

2. With electric mixer on medium speed, beat cream cheese, ½ cup sugar, and ¼ teaspoon salt in medium bowl until smooth, about 30 seconds. Beat in egg whites and 2 tablespoons sour cream until combined, about 1 minute. Stir in chocolate chips and set aside.

3. Whisk remaining sugar, remaining salt, flour, cocoa, and baking soda in large bowl. Make well in center, add remaining sour cream, water, butter, and vanilla and whisk until just combined. Divide batter evenly among 24 cupcake liners and top each batter with 1 rounded tablespoon cream cheese mixture. Bake until tops of cupcakes just begin to crack, 23 to 25 minutes. Cool cupcakes in tins for 10 minutes before transferring to wire rack to cool completely. (Cupcakes can be refrigerated in airtight container for up to 2 days.)

We add sour cream to both the chocolate and cheesecake components to bring out the best in each.

Food Shopping

HOT DOGS: Sweet Dogs Finish Last

Hot dogs inspire passion. Just try serving an Oscar Mayer dog to a Hebrew National devotee or handing a mustard-and-sauerkraut dog to someone who takes ketchup and onions, and you'll see what I mean. Passion begets consumption, and Americans spend over $1.5 billion on store-bought hot dogs each year. To determine which all-beef hot dog is best, we bought nine brands at our local supermarket and headed into the test kitchen to cook and taste them.

Much to the chagrin of our 20-person tasting panel, condiments and buns were off-limits—we wanted to taste the hot dogs and nothing but. All dogs were boiled for exactly 4 minutes in water to cover, then sliced into rounds and served warm. Tasters scored each sample on appearance, flavor, texture, and overall quality. Who was the top dog?

Not surprisingly, our panel preferred dogs with rich, beefy flavor and a good mixture of seasonings. We were surprised to find that sugar level tracked with our final rankings: Our top three dogs—Nathan's, Johnsonville, and Hebrew National—all list 0 grams of sugar, and all were praised for their meaty flavor. With 2 grams of sugar per dog, the Ball Park, Kahn's, and Healthy Choice franks all finished toward the bottom of our rankings and were criticized for their sweet, "unnatural" flavor.

Texture was also important. Testers wanted firm dogs that had some snap. Samples with a soft, "bologna-like" texture were downgraded. The hot dogs are listed below in order of preference. **–Scott Kathan**

Highly Recommended

1. NATHAN'S Famous Beef Franks 8 dogs, 1 pound, $4.99
Our tasters heralded Nathan's dogs for their "meaty," "hearty," "robust" flavor and "firm," "craggy" texture—all qualities that separate them from the overprocessed competition. "Juicy, crunchy, salty, yum," said one happy taster.

Recommended

2. JOHNSONVILLE Stadium Style Beef Franks 6 dogs, 14 ounces, $2.99
Tasters appreciated the girth and richness of these franks, which were the largest in our tasting. Their flavor was described as "big and meaty but not hot-doggy," with a "strong spice blend." Texture was deemed "good and firm."

3. HEBREW NATIONAL Beef Franks 7 dogs, 12 ounces, $4.69
These franks scored especially well for their "crunchy," "nice and juicy" texture and "garlicky," "spicy," "beefy," and "smoky" flavor. One gushing taster called them "almost perfect—well seasoned and juicy."

Recommended with Reservations

4. OSCAR MAYER Beef Franks 10 dogs, 1 pound, $3.99
While some tasters liked Oscar Mayer's "smoky, strong flavor," these franks lost points for being "ridiculously salty," "mushy," and tasting like "a mixed-meat hot dog, not an all-beef one."

5. KAYEM DELI Jumbo Beef Hot Dogs 8 dogs, 1 pound, $3.99
"Nothing fancy, like a hot dog should be," said one pleased taster. "A little greasy, but with good flavor," said another. Less glowing comments included "bland and sour," "rubbery filling," and several references to a "strange and sweet" aftertaste.

6. BALL PARK Beef Franks 8 dogs, 1 pound, $3.99
One taster called these dogs "classic but unremarkable." Negative remarks included "mushy," "strange sweetness," and a mention of unpleasant "chewy membranes."

Not Recommended

7. BOAR'S HEAD Skinless Beef Frankfurters 10 dogs, 1 pound, $4.29
Tasters found something amiss with these "rubbery," "artificial-looking (too red)" hot dogs. While the flavor was deemed "beefy," the "chewy" texture was a big turnoff. "Smells a little like wet socks," complained one member of our panel.

8. KAHN'S Bun Size Beef Franks 8 dogs, 1 pound, $3.99
The general consensus was that these dogs "taste like they have a lot of filler" and have a "very processed" texture. Most tasters complained about too much salt and "no meat flavor or texture." "Like sour, salty bologna," said one critic.

9. HEALTHY CHOICE Low Fat Beef Franks 8 dogs, 14 ounces, $3.49
Our tasters didn't think these franks looked ("strange dark color") or tasted ("livery undertones," "plasticky") like hot dogs. The "gummy-mushy-grainy" texture drew serious complaints.

Taste Test Rice

With so many types of rice available in supermarkets, how do you know which one to buy and how to prepare it? After much cooking and tasting, here's what we've learned about rice in the test kitchen. **–S.K.**

Brown Rice

Brown rice is whole-grain rice with the hull intact. It has a chewy texture and nutty flavor. To prevent scorching or sogginess, we rely on the gentle, even heat of the oven to cook brown rice. Combine brown rice, boiling water (1½ cups per cup of rice), and salt to taste in baking dish, cover with foil, and bake for about 1 hour. Let rice rest for 5 minutes, fluff with fork, and then serve.

White Rice

White rice has been refined to remove the brown hull. It comes in three basic sizes: long-grain, medium-grain, and short-grain. As a rule, the shorter the grain, the starchier the rice. For risotto and other dishes where stickiness is an asset, we use a medium-grain rice, such as Arborio. For most other uses, we rely on long-grain rice, which cooks up very fluffy, with separate, distinct grains. Cook each cup of long-grain white rice in 1½ cups of water (not the 2 cups many packages recommend). For added flavor, sauté the rice in a little butter or oil before adding the water.

Converted Rice

Converted rice (also called parboiled rice) is steam-treated before packaging. This process removes excess starch, helping the rice cook up with distinct, separate grains, which our tasters found too bouncy. This rice has a yellowish hue and assertive flavor that we don't like.

Fully Cooked Rice

This product, which is relatively new to supermarket shelves, comes sealed in a bag and only needs quick reheating before serving. This rice is surprisingly good—much better than other convenience options, such as boil-in-bag rice and instant or minute rice. We recommend fully cooked rice for dishes (like soups) where the rice isn't the star of the show.

Wild Rice

Authentic wild rice is harvested by hand from lakes and rivers in the upper Great Lakes region. We prefer not-so-wild wild rice—cultivated in man-made paddies in California—for its more resilient texture and lower price. Its strong flavor is earthy, woody, and complex and works best when mixed with white rice. Simmer wild rice separately (in chicken stock to mute its flavor) and then combine with cooked white rice for an interesting pilaf.

Equipment Roundup

DRIP COFFEE MAKERS: Does an Inexpensive Model Have to Feel Cheap?

Since Mr. Coffee introduced the first affordable, automatic drip coffee maker in 1972, they have become staple appliances in American kitchens—24 million of them are sold each year. Although you can spend a few hundred dollars on high-end models, we were more interested in the under-$50 machines. Do they brew coffee reliably well? Are they easy to use? To find out, we rounded up eight popular models and headed to the test kitchen.

HOW DOES THE COFFEE TASTE? Each of the machines made good (but not great) coffee that suffered somewhat because of low brewing temperature and slow brewing speed. To coax optimum flavor out of ground coffee, it should be brewed with water that is 195 to 200 degrees, and the brewing process for a full pot should take no longer than six minutes (lest overextraction—and the more bitter coffee it produces—occur). These inexpensive machines don't have the heating power to bring water to such high temperatures (only two machines, the Braun and Mr. Coffee, produced water hotter than 180 degrees), and they aren't designed to brew a full pot so quickly (the brew times ranged from 9:40 to 11:55).

STAYING POWER: Once coffee was brewed, we tasted it every 15 minutes for an hour, and the results were disappointing: The coffee was noticeably worse after only 15 minutes and progressively worse at each increment. Since coffee suffers with continued heating, we recommend immediately pouring the brewed coffee into a thermal carafe (see box) to retain freshness.

USER-FRIENDLY AT 6 A.M.? Since we didn't find much difference in coffee flavor, this category proved to be the most important. Testers were annoyed by machines with a small filling area, like the Proctor Silex model, which makes you pour the water into an opening just 1½ inches wide (by comparison, the Black & Decker well is 4½ inches wide at the pouring point). The accessibility and perceived solidity of the filter basket mechanism were also important, and the ratings for the Kenmore (flimsy feel) and Mr. Coffee (you have to manually push the hinged water-spout arm out of the way) machines suffered as a result. Testers also preferred coffee makers (Black & Decker, Braun, and DeLonghi) that offered easy one-handed access to the spent grounds.

THE CARAFE: The Kenmore carafe did not easily nestle back into the machine after being removed for pouring. The Braun, by contrast, felt solid and ergonomic, and clicked back into its nest on the first try.

SUMMING UP: Making coffee should be easy. The Black & Decker and Braun machines felt solid and were very user-friendly. They earned top marks from our testers. **–Scott Kathan**

Recommended

BLACK & DECKER SmartBrew 12-Cup Coffeemaker (model DCM2000)
Price: $34.95 at Cooking.com
Carafe Capacity: 64 ounces
Brew Time (for full pot): 11:21
Water Temperature: 175 degrees
Comments: Testers loved how easy it was to pour water into the wide tank of this model. All controls were intuitive and "dummy-proof." Very easy to clean and very accurate pouring.

BRAUN AromaDeluxe (KF 510)
Price: $49.95 at Cooking.com
Carafe Capacity: 48 ounces
Brew Time: 10:26
Water Temperature: 186 degrees
Comments: Felt very solid and well made, and testers praised the carafe's grip and handling. Accessing the grounds was easy. While some testers downgraded this machine for its lack of a program mode, most admitted they'd never use it.

MR. COFFEE 12-Cup Programmable (VBX23)
Price: $29.99 at Target.com
Carafe Capacity: 60 ounces
Brew Time: 11:30
Water Temperature: 186 degrees
Comments: "Everything is easy and straightforward," said one tester. The only complaint was a swinging arm inside the machine, which a few testers thought was "just another thing that could break." "A very big carafe."

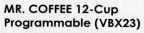

Rating Thermal Carafes

We tested a half-dozen thermal carafes, focusing on capacity, heat retention, ease of use and cleaning, and overall design. Our favorite was the Thermos Nissan Stainless Steel Carafe ($46 at baldmountaincoffee.com). Unlike many of its competitors, this large (51-ounce) carafe didn't leak or dent when knocked over, it poured cleanly and had a very stable base, and its lever opening action allowed for easy one-handed operation. It also kept coffee hot longer than the competition—a full 14 hours. Visit **CooksCountry.com** for the full results of this testing.

THERMOS NISSAN STAINLESS STEEL CARAFE
Durable, easy-to-use, and holds heat the longest

Recommended with Reservations

CUISINART Programmable Filter Brew 12-Cup Coffeemaker (DCC-1000)
Price: $49.95 at Cooking.com
Carafe Capacity: 52 ounces
Brew Time: 9:43
Water Temperature: 177 degrees
Comments: Some odd design quirks (no hinged carafe lid, no markings under 6 cups on the carafe, and excessive height), but overall a solid machine with ergonomic pouring and a good system for accessing the grounds.

DELONGHI Caffe Elite (DC76T)
Price: $49.99 at Cooking.com
Carafe Capacity: 60 ounces
Brew Time: 10:36
Water Temperature: 178 degrees
Comments: Testers liked the easy-to-read exterior water gauge and "good" feel of the carafe. Negatives include a narrow filling area and a filter-basket release button that swings the hot grounds open a little too fast for comfort.

PROCTOR SILEX 12-Cup Programmable (48574)
Price: $22.99 at Sears.com
Carafe Capacity: 54 ounces
Brew Time: 11:14
Water Temperature: 176 degrees
Comments: Testers didn't like the narrow filling area for water, but they did appreciate that the pot resettled back into the machine effortlessly. Coffee strength dial deemed superfluous. Functional but unremarkable.

Not Recommended

HAMILTON BEACH BrewStation Plus (47665)
Price: $49.95 at Cooking.com
Carafe Capacity: 66 ounces
Brew Time: 9:40
Water Temperature: 178 degrees
Comments: No carafe—the coffee is brewed into an internal insulated chamber. The "landing pad" below the dispenser is too small to rest a mug on, meaning that your mug must hover while being filled. Definitely not intuitive.

KENMORE 12-Cup Programmable Coffee Maker (69327)
Price: $34.99 at Sears.com
Carafe Capacity: 56 ounces
Brew Time: 11:55
Water Temperature: 175 degrees
Comments: Testers noted that the different components of the coffee maker didn't fit well together. Accessing the grounds was awkward, and the carafe felt dangerously unstable when full. Machine "just feels cheap."

Notes from Our Test Kitchen

TIPS, TECHNIQUES, AND TOOLS FOR BETTER COOKING

Kitchen Creations
Flavored Sour Creams

Since a dollop of plain sour cream does wonders for tacos, nachos, and our **Authentic Beef Enchiladas** (page 19), we figured that a doctored dollop might work even better. Here are three Southwestern-inspired sour creams that work well as toppings, dips, or simple sauces for grilled fish, chicken, or meats. Each yields about one cup and can be refrigerated, covered, for up to two days.

CILANTRO-LIME SOUR CREAM

Process 1 cup sour cream, 1/4 cup chopped fresh cilantro, 1 teaspoon grated lime zest, 1/4 teaspoon pepper, and 1/8 teaspoon salt in food processor until smooth.

AVOCADO-CHILE SOUR CREAM

Process 1 cup sour cream, 1/2 pitted avocado, 1 seeded and chopped jalapeño, 1 teaspoon lemon juice, 1/4 teaspoon pepper, and 1/8 teaspoon salt in food processor until smooth.

CHIPOTLE-SCALLION SOUR CREAM

Process 1 cup sour cream, 1 canned chipotle chile in adobo, 1 chopped scallion, 1/4 teaspoon pepper, and 1/8 teaspoon salt in food processor until smooth.

Vinaigrette 101

To squeeze every ounce of herb flavor into our **Herb Vinaigrettes** (page 22), we used the blender to pulverize the herbs and release all of their essential flavors. But you don't have to break out the blender to make a basic oil-and-vinegar salad dressing: Whisking the ingredients in a bowl works fine, as does shaking in a jar with a tight-fitting lid. We prefer a ratio of 4 parts oil to 1 part vinegar (plus salt, pepper, and any other seasonings you like). For one serving, you'll need 2 tablespoons of vinaigrette per 2 cups of greens. And remember to toss your greens and vinaigrette well to evenly distribute the dressing.

–Diane Unger

More Bang for Your Broccoli Buck

Broccoli stems have a lot of flavor, but they can also be tough—most home cooks opt to use just the florets. One of the secrets of our **Creamy Broccoli and Cheddar Soup** (page 25) is to use a large amount of chopped broccoli stems to give the soup body and deep vegetal flavor. The outside of the stems is the most fibrous part, so we always peel broccoli stems with a vegetable peeler before cooking. Also, broccoli stems take slightly longer to cook than florets, so if you're using both in a recipe, add the stems first.

Smooth Garlic

When developing our recipe for **Grilled Butterflied Lemon Chicken** (page 13), getting salt and an even layer of garlic under the chicken skin was a priority. To do this most efficiently, we employed a test kitchen trick and finely chopped the garlic, sprinkled it with salt (which softens the garlic), and then smeared the salted garlic with the flat of our chef's knife. This action breaks the garlic down into a paste that is easy to rub under the skin of the chicken. And because the garlic is so smooth, you don't get any strong hits of garlic from oversized chunks. –**Cali Rich**

Keeping Herbs Fresh

We use a lot of fresh herbs in the test kitchen, so we know firsthand that their shelf life is short. To get the most life out of your herbs, gently rinse and dry them (a salad spinner works perfectly) and then loosely roll them in a few sheets of paper towel. From here, seal the roll of herbs in a zipper-lock bag and place it in the crisper drawer of your refrigerator. Stored in this manner, your herbs will be fresh, washed, and ready to use for a week or longer. –Jeremy Sauer

Freezing Tortillas

Our recipe for **Authentic Beef Enchiladas** (page 19) uses corn—not flour—tortillas. Corn tortillas are smaller and richer in flavor than their flour cousins, and they are often sold in packages of 24 or more. To freeze corn tortillas, gently peel individual tortillas from the stack and place them between pieces of wax or parchment paper, then freeze up to 12 tortillas in a zipper-lock freezer bag. When you're ready to use them, defrost stacks of four to six tortillas in the microwave at 50-percent power until thawed, 10 to 20 seconds per stack. –Scott Kathan

Bigger, Better Stuffed Potatoes

During testing for our **Super-Stuffed Baked Potatoes** (page 12), I found that most recipes called for the baked potatoes to be cut right in half before being filled. But these skimpy spuds were far from the super-stuffed garlic potato I was looking for. Instead, I found the best way was to cut off only the top quarter of the potato—leaving a much more substantial spud to stuff. –**Meredith Butcher**

1. Slice the top quarter off the potato before scooping out its interior.

2. Use a spoon to scoop out the interior of the potato, being careful to leave a 1/4-inch layer of potato in the shell.

Fruit and Fire

Grilling the lemons for our **Grilled Butterflied Lemon Chicken** (page 13) enhanced their bright flavor and tempered their tartness. But lemons aren't the only fruit that does well on the grill. Grilling pineapple (first peeled and cut into rounds), peaches (halved, pits removed), and pears (halved and cored) over a medium-hot fire for about four minutes (or until slightly charred and softened) caramelized the sugars in the fruit and gave them a complex, smoky flavor that pairs well with other grilled meats and vegetables. But grilling isn't for every fruit. It's best to use firm-fleshed, even slightly underripe fruits rather than soft-fleshed varieties (such as melons or papaya), which may not hold up to the direct heat of the grill. –Jeremy Sauer

Shopping with the Test Kitchen   The Right Chop

Our recipe for **Grilled Stuffed Pork Chops** (page 10) comes out great every time—as long as you use the right chops. While both rib loin chops and center-cut loin chops had an unbroken eye of meat that was easy to stuff, we preferred the rib loin chop because they had more marbling and thus remained juicy after grilling. The center-cut chops were also good, but they came off the grill a little dry.

RIB LOIN CHOP
Fat—in the form of marbling—keeps rib loin chops moist.

CENTER-CUT LOIN CHOP
Lean center-cut loin chops have a tendency to dry out on the grill.

Shopping with the Test Kitchen The Best Lemon Curd

Our **Lemon Lover's Cake** (inside back cover) is crowned with a layer of tart lemon curd, a custard-style sauce made from eggs, sugar, butter, and, of course, lemon juice. We wondered if we could substitute a store-bought curd for homemade, so we tasted four jarred varieties both right out of the jar and spread on a piece of pound cake. The results were shocking. Two of the four were deemed nearly inedible because of their "waxy," "gelatinous" texture and cloying sweetness.

The Wilkin and Sons curd was the clear winner for its smooth and creamy texture and "real lemon flavor," but the $9 price tag raised eyebrows. Dickinson's, the distant runner-up, received lukewarm reviews for "gumdrop texture" and "sweet and sour lemon candy" flavor but costs about half as much as the Wilkin and Sons curd.

WILKIN AND SONS
Best flavor but expensive.

DICKINSON'S
Distant second . . . but a relative bargain.

Gremolata Adds Great Flavor

When it came time to spruce up our **Chicken and Rice with Spring Vegetables** (page 24), we took a cue from the old country. Many Italian recipes, particularly stews and other slow-cooked dishes, add a potent seasoning mixture called a gremolata (grated citrus zest, fresh herbs, and raw garlic) at the end of cooking to brighten up the dish. For our recipe, we relied on the freshness of sharp lemon zest and floral basil to pair with the heady garlic. These clean flavors cut through the richness of the rice and chicken and were also perfect complements to the fresh spring vegetables. **–Jeremy Sauer**

Boursin Bonus

Boursin is a soft, spreadable cheese that comes in several varieties available in every supermarket. The Garlic and Fine Herbs flavor was a key ingredient in our **Super-Stuffed Baked Potatoes** (page 12), as it added creamy texture, cheese flavor, and a big hit of aromatic garlic and herbs. This versatile cheese works well as a sandwich spread (try it with roast beef), as a stuffing for chicken breasts, spread on steaks, in mashed potatoes, on crackers, in dips, or as part of a cheese plate. **–Meredith Butcher**

SECRET INGREDIENT

Country-Style Ribs

In our slow-cooker recipe for **Italian Sunday Gravy** (page 4), we call for three different types of meat, including country-style pork ribs. Cut from the upper side of the rib cage, these pork ribs come from the blade end of the loin, closest to the shoulder. They are typically meatier than baby back or spareribs and have a little more fat, too, making them perfect candidates for the slow cooker. **–Meredith Butcher**

Stemming Greens

As we found when prepping the kale for our **Pittsburgh Wedding Soup** (page 18), stemming and cleaning greens can be tedious. To make quick work of a bunch of greens, stack four or five similarly sized leaves on top of each other on the cutting board and make a V-cut to remove the tough part of the stems. Then wash and dry the stemmed greens in a salad spinner, and the greens are ready to go. **–Jeremy Sauer**

Trim hearty greens with a V-cut to remove the fibrous stem.

Crab in a Can

In our recipe for **Crab Cakes with Imperial Sauce** (recipe card), nothing beats the sweet, briny flavor of freshly picked crabmeat. But if you live inland, fresh crabmeat can be difficult to find—and exorbitantly expensive—because it spoils so quickly. Pasteurized crabmeat, on the

other hand, is available nationwide.

To see if pasteurized crab could hold a candle to fresh, we gathered four widely available crab products—imitation crabmeat, canned pasteurized jumbo lump crabmeat, canned pasteurized lump crabmeat, and canned pasteurized shredded crabmeat—and lined them up for a side-by-side tasting with fresh picked lump crabmeat. While none of the pasteurized products were as good as fresh, canned pasteurized lump crabmeat was a reasonable alternative for crab cakes (pasteurized jumbo lump was overkill for this recipe—why pay for big chunks when

GOOD CRAB, BAD CRAB
Canned pasteurized lump crabmeat is a viable option, but imitation crabmeat isn't.

you'd just have to chop them?). At half the price of fresh crabmeat (which can run upward of $20 per pound), pasteurized lump was a great bargain, and it won praise for its "meaty" texture and "fresh, oceany" taste. On the flip side, avoid shredded and especially imitation crabmeat. Its "candy sweet" flavor and "Velveeta-esque" texture were nothing close to the real thing.

Kitchen Know-How
Turning Sirloin Tips into Stroganoff

When we were developing our recipe for **Skillet Beef Stroganoff** (page 25), we wanted to use a cut other than the traditional—and expensive—filet mignon. With a little work, we found that sirloin tips (also called flap meat) were a great alternative. Here's how we transformed them into tender, flavorful strips for this recipe.

1. Use a meat pounder to pound the meat to an even ½-inch thickness.

2. Cutting with the grain, slice the pounded meat into strips about 2 inches wide.

3. Slice each piece of meat against the grain into ½-inch strips.

Test Kitchen Tip Don't Throw Your Back(s) Out

Instead of throwing out the backbones from the butterflied chickens in our recipe for **Grilled Butterflied Lemon Chicken** (page 13), save them to build a flavorful stock. Cut the backbone in half and freeze it in a zipper-lock bag. When you have accumulated 4 pounds of backs (or necks, wings, wingtips, or other parts), thaw the chicken overnight in the refrigerator. Then simply season and brown half the parts over medium-high heat in 1 tablespoon oil, drain, and repeat with remaining parts. After discarding excess fat, sauté 1 chopped onion (with carrot and celery, if you like) until softened. Next, add browned chicken (skin removed), 3 quarts water, 2 bay leaves, and 1 tablespoon salt back to pot. Cover and simmer for 30 minutes, then strain; chicken stock freezes well and can be refrigerated in an airtight container for up to 3 days. **–Cali Rich**

When Things Go Wrong in the Kitchen

READERS SHARE FUNNY STORIES ABOUT COOKING MISHAPS

CATNAP

When a coworker asked me to make a cake for an upcoming work function, I decided to make my favorite apple cake, which bakes in a 13 by 9-inch pan. Once it was baked, I immediately placed it on the counter to cool. After covering it with a tea towel, I turned off the lights and retired for the night. But apparently I wasn't the only one ready for bed. My cat, Katie, looking for a warm place to sleep, cozied up on top of my freshly baked cake! The next morning there was a very distinct feline imprint that could only be covered with extra whipped cream. No one at work knew the difference, but I haven't been able to bake another apple cake since.

Amy Mori Sunnyvale, Calif.

TASTES LIKE CHICKEN!

I often buy meat in large quantities and freeze it in smaller packages for later use. One day I had a craving for old-fashioned chicken and pastry, so I rummaged through the freezer and found an unmarked package of chicken breasts just the right size. In a hurry, I popped the frozen meat into the boiling water. When I opened the pot to drop in the pastry strips, I was surprised to see strange-looking bones bubbling to the top. Turns out I had used a package of frozen frog legs from one of my son's hunting expeditions. With no time to rethink dinner, I proceeded with the pastry. My kids still ask when I'm going to make "frog leg pastry" again!

Laurie Hamilton Clinton, N.C.

HOT DOG SORBET

Once, when I was preparing a grapefruit sorbet for a dinner party, I realized my children needed their lunch. Setting the sugar syrup for my sorbet aside to cool, I boiled some hot dogs for the kids. With the kids fed and happy, I returned to preparing my sorbet, carefully pouring the syrup into the grapefruit juice. A few hours later, when I went to check on the sorbet, I found the pot of sugar syrup still sitting on the stove. I was perplexed until I realized I had poured the hot dog water into the grapefruit juice!

Donna R. Himelfarb Skaneateles, N.Y.

BLOOMING BREAKFAST

Soon after we married, my wife surprised me with breakfast in bed. She made my favorite, scrambled eggs with onions, but I noticed that the onion tasted a little strange and was light pink in color. I asked my wife where she had gotten this red onion. When she told me that she had found it on the shelf of the pantry door, I immediately jumped out of bed and ran to rinse out my mouth. My wife had cut up one of the hyacinth bulbs (which are poisonous) that I was planning to plant in our flower garden! Fortunately, no harm was done, and we still have breakfast in bed, though I am now the one who cooks.

Reggie Grosse Nunda, N.Y.

COCOA, JAPANESE STYLE

My parents met in postwar Japan, and my dad was intent on introducing American foods to his future wife and all of her friends. One cool evening, he thought that he would impress them with his hot cocoa. He bought cocoa powder, vanilla, sugar, and milk and mixed it carefully. He had recently found this amazing new food additive that seemed to make everything taste better. It was called *aji-no-moto* ("basis for taste" in English), and he decided to add it to his cocoa. He served his sweet-smelling cocoa to everyone as they all "oohed" and "aahed" at the concoction, but when they sipped it, they looked like they wanted to spit! My dad was puzzled: How could they not love hot cocoa? He then took a sip and gagged! Unbeknownst to him, aji-no-moto was MSG. It may help enhance some savory dishes, but definitely not hot cocoa!

Janette R. Smith Rockville, Md.

A LITTLE HAM

Since oven space is always at a premium on Thanksgiving Day, one year I decided to cook my ham (I cook a turkey, too) the night before. Since it was already late, I popped the ham into the oven, set both my alarm clock and oven timer, and went off to bed. A few hours later, when my alarm went off, I sleepily went to the kitchen and turned off the timer—but not the oven. When I got up the next morning, the house was filled with the delicious smell of baked ham. To my horror, the ham had shrunk to one-fourth its original size. When my in-laws came later that day, we had only enough edible ham for a few sandwiches!

Judith G. Smith Elliston, Va.

TIE-DYE DINNER

When I was a teenager, my parents sometimes went to our cottage and left us kids behind for the weekend. Our only responsibility was to put the Sunday roast in the oven, so we could all sit down to a family dinner that evening when they returned. One Sunday morning, my friend and I decided to tie-dye some T-shirts. That afternoon I dutifully prepared the chicken, carrots, and onions and stuck them in the oven. You can imagine my mother's horror when she got home on Sunday evening to find a bright green chicken in the oven. I guess I hadn't thoroughly washed the roasting pan I used to tie-dye the shirts!

Mary Greenley Ottawa, Ontario

TARTAR SAUCE COOKIES

My neighbor loved my chocolate chip meringue cookies, so I gladly shared my recipe with her. The next day, she phoned to see if I could come over, because something was terribly wrong with the cookies she had made. I immediately saw that the mixing bowl was filled with greenish globs. Confused by the smell and color of the batter, I had to laugh when she confessed she didn't have any cream of tartar, so she had substituted tartar sauce instead!

Ruth Cohen Huntington, N.Y.

Send us your funniest kitchen disaster stories. E-mail us by visiting **CooksCountry.com/emailus.** Or write to us at Kitchen Disasters, Cook's Country, P.O. Box 470739, Brookline, MA 02447. If we publish your story, you'll receive a complimentary one-year subscription to *Cook's Country.*

The Great American Cake
Lemon Lover's Cake

A lemon layer cake is an elegant way to greet spring. Like the season, lemon cake can resemble either a lion or a lamb. With potent citrus punches in the cake, frosting, lemon curd topping, and candied lemon garnish, our cake positively roars.

To make this recipe you'll need:

1   recipe yellow cake batter (enough to make two 9-inch layer cakes)*
2   tablespoons grated zest plus ¹/₄ cup juice from 2 lemons
3   cups vanilla buttercream frosting*
1   (4-ounce) chunk white chocolate
2   cups jarred or homemade lemon curd*
    Sugared lemon slices (optional)*

For the cake: Prepare the cake batter, then stir 1 tablespoon lemon zest into batter. Divide batter between 2 greased and floured 9-inch cake pans and bake as directed. Cool cakes in pans 10 minutes, then turn out onto rack to cool completely.

For the frosting: Stir 1 tablespoon lemon zest and juice into buttercream.

For the chocolate curls: Heat chocolate in microwave on lowest power until exterior just begins to feel sticky, 10 to 20 seconds. Run vegetable peeler along 1 side of chocolate to create curls. (Don't worry if some curls break—they'll still look attractive piled on the cake.)

To assemble the cake: Slice cake layers in half, creating 4 layers. Place 1 cake round on serving platter. Spread ¹/₂ cup frosting over cake. Repeat twice more with 2 cake rounds and ¹/₂ cup frosting per layer. Top with final cake round. Spread 1¹/₄ cups frosting on sides of cake, then spread remaining frosting in 2-inch band on top of cake, leaving center of cake bare. Spread lemon curd on center of cake, using spoon to bring curd to edge of frosting. Arrange chocolate curls in frosting on top of cake and press lemon slices around bottom edge of cake.

*Visit **CooksCountry.com** for our recipes for yellow cake, buttercream, lemon curd, and sugared lemon slices or use your own recipes.

Recipe Index

RC = Recipe Card

Cook's Country

JUNE/JULY 2007

BBQ Chicken
Perfectly Cooked Every Time

Spicy Grilled Shrimp
Tender, Juicy, and Smoky

High-Rise Herb Biscuits
With Big Cheese Flavor

CALIFORNIA GRILLED SIRLOIN
Smoky, Garlicky, and Tender

BIG CHOCOLATE SHAKE!
Ultra-Creamy and Chocolaty

SMOKED PORK CHOPS
Double-Thick, Double-Flavor

NEW CHICKEN SALADS
Bold Flavors, Quick Method

TUSCAN POTATO SALAD
Parmesan and Roasted Peppers

RATING SAUCEPANS
How to Save $160

ICEBOX KEY LIME PIE
No Eggs, No Cooking

GRILLED PORK LOIN
Triple-Mustard Glaze

TASTING STRAWBERRY JAM
Big Supermarket Brands Win

LOW-FAT DRESSINGS
Blue Cheese and Ranch

Our $1,000 Contest Winner!
Barb Schaecher of Kansas City, Mo., won first place in our bar cookie recipe contest with a chocolaty, crunchy bar that uses oatmeal as both a base and a topping. See page 4 for her **Oatmeal Fudge Bars.**

$4.95 U.S./$6.95 CANADA

07>

0 74470 05251 7

Cook's Country

Dear Country Cook,

A few years ago, we took the kids out to Montana and spent a week at a dude ranch. We rode up to 12,000 feet, where the fields were woven with Indian paintbrush, forget-me-nots, mule's ears, larkspur, elephant head, pussy toes, shooting stars, and lady-slippers. A mule was spooked and a wrangler was thrown from his horse. We saw elk and huge sandhill cranes, cooked lunch over a campfire, and then headed down a draw through Sage Valley to dinner, a cookout over a wagon wheel. Jim McGuiness, who heads up the dude operation, made beer-batter buttermilk biscuits in two large Dutch ovens heated over a fire, placed in a shallow pit, and then covered with coals. They were perfectly browned and fluffy, the best biscuits I have ever eaten. We saddled up and headed through the valley at a lope under a robin's-egg sky, down the trail toward camp. It was dusty and you could smell the sagebrush and sweat from the horses. I was sore and my knees ached from the long ride, but I could still taste those Dutch oven biscuits.

The area was once inhabited by the Crow, Shoshone, and Blackfeet, and the lodgepole pines, which they used for tepees, are still used for fence posts. Jim told me that he had been chased on horseback by a grizzly (I half believed him), he has a taste for Rocky Mountain oysters, and he grew up on a Norwegian diet of flat bread, potato dumplings, and meat—the foods of choice for the wranglers. (The guests prefer pasta and vegetables, a difference of opinion that causes a lot of grumbling among the hands.)

As soon as I saw this photo, it reminded me of that trip and of how much better food tastes when cooked and served out-of-doors. Freshly baked beer-batter biscuits and the sizzle of steaks over an open fire. Early morning June frost and the sharp smell of wood stoves and pine. Nothing beats simple country cooking.

Christopher Kimball

Christopher Kimball
Founder and Editor, Cook's Country Magazine

Texas cowboy cooking, May 1949. Biscuits bake to a golden brown inside a hot Dutch oven.
Photographer: Leonard McCombe, Time & Life Pictures/Getty Images

JUNE/JULY 2007

Cook's Country

departments

in every issue

features

Founder and Editor Christopher Kimball
Editorial Director Jack Bishop
Deputy Editor Bridget Lancaster
Senior Editors Scott Kathan
Jeremy Sauer
Test Kitchen Director Erin McMurrer
Test Cooks Kelley Baker
Meredith Butcher
Greg Case
Cali Rich
Diane Unger
Assistant Test Cook Lynn Clark
Web Managing Editor Katherine Bell
Web Editor Kate Mason
Copy Editor Will Gordon
Market Research Manager Melissa Baldino
Editorial Assistant Meredith Smith
Kitchen Assistant Nadia Domeq
Contributing Editor Eva Katz

Design Director Amy Klee
Senior Designer, Magazines Julie Bozzo
Designers Jay Layman
Christine Vo
Staff Photographer Daniel J. van Ackere

Production Director Guy Rochford
Traffic and Projects Manager Alice Cummiskey
Production Assistant Lauren Pettapiece
Color and Imaging Specialist Andrew Mannone

Vice President New Technology Craig Morrow
Systems Administrator S. Paddi McHugh
Web Developer Justin Greenough
Web Designer Lillian Chan

Chief Financial Officer Sharyn Chabot
Human Resources Manager Adele Shapiro
Controller Mandy Shito
Senior Accountant Aaron Goranson
Staff Accountant Connie Forbes
Office Manager Elizabeth Pohm
Receptionist Henrietta Murray

Vice President Marketing David Mack
Circulation Director Bill Tine
Circulation and Fulfillment Manager Carrie Horan
Circulation Assistant Elizabeth Dayton
Direct Mail Director Adam Perry
Direct Mail Analyst Jenny Leong
Products Director Steven Browall
Product Promotions Director David Sarlitto
E-Commerce Marketing Manager Hugh Buchan
Marketing Copywriter David Goldberg
Junior Developer Doug Sisko
Customer Service Manager Jacqueline Valerio
Customer Service Representatives Julie Gardner
Jillian Nannicelli

Vice President Sales Demee Gambulos
Corporate Marketing Manager Emily Logan
Retail Sales Associate Anthony King
Partnership Account Manager Allie Brawley
Publicity Deborah Broide

ON THE COVER: PHOTOGRAPHY: Michael Paul, StockFood Munich/StockFood America. ILLUSTRATION: John Burgoyne.
IN THIS ISSUE: COLOR FOOD PHOTOGRAPHY: Keller + Keller. STYLING: Mary Jane Sawyer, Marie Piraino. ILLUSTRATION: Lisa Perrett.

Cook's Country magazine (ISSN 1552-1990), number 15, is published bimonthly by Boston Common Press Limited Partnership, 17 Station Street, Brookline, MA 02445. Copyright 2007 Boston Common Press Limited Partnership. Periodicals postage paid at Boston, Mass., and at additional mailing offices, USPS #023453. POSTMASTER: Send address changes to Cook's Country, P.O. Box 8382, Red Oak, IA 51591-1382. For subscription and gift subscription orders, subscription inquiries, or change-of-address notices, call 800-526-8447 in the U.S. or 515-247-7571 from outside the U.S., or write us at Cook's Country, P.O. Box 8382, Red Oak, IA 51591-1382.
PRINTED IN THE USA

Visit us at CooksCountry.com!
Go online for hundreds of recipes, food tastings, and up-to-date equipment reviews. You can get a behind-the-scenes look at our test kitchen, talk to our cooks and editors, enter recipe contests, and share recipes and cooking tips with the Cook's Country community.

Kitchen Shortcuts

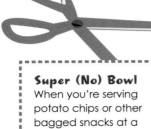

Super (No) Bowl

When you're serving potato chips or other bagged snacks at a casual party or picnic, forget the bowl! Just lay the unopened bag flat on the table and cut a large opening in the front. No more bags falling over and spilling their contents, and cleanup's a snap, too—just toss the empty bags into the trash.

Karen Bland Gove, Kan.

Seasoned Traveler

Whenever I go on a vacation where I will be doing some cooking, I prepare seasoning packets to go. I place the dried seasonings or herbs that I might need on sheets of aluminum foil, fold each one into a small envelope shape, and label the exterior with permanent marker. The little packages of herbs are light and compact, making them easy to fit into my luggage. Since I travel prepared, I don't have to waste money buying whole jars of spices once I arrive at my destination.

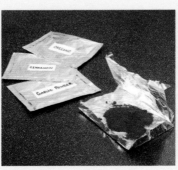

Janet Rego East Freetown, Mass.

No-Mess Popsicles

My kids love Popsicles, but I hate the drippy mess they make. For a no-mess version, I punch the Popsicle stick through a small paper cup (cut down in height) to catch the drips. It keeps my kids' hands from getting sticky and their shirts from getting stained.

Julie Hartin Dallas, Texas

KEEP IT CLEAN

Spicy Protection!

SQUIRRELS BEWARE

To keep squirrels and other pests from eating the herbs in your garden, sprinkle the leaves and soil lightly with cayenne pepper. The cayenne won't hurt your plants, and the squirrels won't come near them! Just make sure to rinse your herbs before using.

Brian McKeown Bohemia, N.Y.

RICING AHEAD

When I use my rice cooker, I make the full capacity even if I don't need all the rice for my meal that day. I freeze any leftover rice in plastic bags, so the next time I want to make a quick bowl of fried rice, my rice is at the ready!

Ana Torres Borrego Springs, Calif.

DAIRY-FRESH FINGERS

I love cooking with chile peppers, but sometimes the essential oils from the chiles can stay on my fingers for what seems like days. To counteract the heat of the chiles, I put a little whole milk, cream, or plain yogurt in my palm and scrub my hands for a few minutes. The dairy fat neutralizes the heat, so I won't burn my eyes if I touch them by accident.

JoAnn DeMartini Sarasota, Fla.

INSTANT ICED TEA

Sometimes I really want a glass of fresh iced tea but I don't want to wait to brew a large pot that will need to cool. A quick solution for small amounts: Put hot tap water, a tea bag, and sugar in a cocktail shaker, shake vigorously for a minute, and pour over ice. The resulting tea tastes great and is ready in no time at all!

Kelley Alison Smith Riverside, R.I.

STEAMED TO PERFECTION

Whenever I grill hamburgers, instead of warming the buns over the hot fire (I would inevitably burn two or three), I came up with this shortcut. I take the buns out of the bag, top them with the cooked burgers, and put the hot sandwiches back into the bag. Once the bag is twisted closed, the heat from the burgers steams the buns, making them nice and warm, with a perfect, soft texture. This works especially well if the buns have staled a little.

Jonathan Wilson Lake Norman, N.C.

BUTTER SPRITZER

I bake bread so often that I've developed a quick and easy way to "brush" the top of my dough with butter before baking. I put a stick of butter into a clean spray bottle, microwave it on low until the butter is melted, and then put the top on and spray away. I find that spraying the butter is much easier than brushing, and when I'm done, I just put the spray bottle (with any remaining butter) back into the fridge so that it's ready the next time I bake.

Karen Mizener North Huntingdon, Pa.

GRILLED FLAVOR BOOST

To add even more flavor to grilled foods, I soak handfuls of various woody herbs (such as rosemary, thyme, or lavender) in water before sprinkling them on top of the hot coals. The herbs will gently smoke and infuse fish, chicken, or beef with a subtle herb taste.

Suzanne McGrath San Diego, Calif.

KEEP COFFEE TASTING FRESH

To avoid a stale Thermos of coffee, I place six or seven whole coffee beans in the empty Thermos before adding the brewed coffee. The beans impart a fresh taste that seems to make the flavor last.

Joan Fortier Holden, Mass.

REACH THE UNREACHABLE

After a busy day of cooking, my kitchen can be quite a mess. To clean those hard-to-reach places like the crevises in the stove or underneath the fridge, I attach an empty paper towel roll to the end of my vacuum hose. It can be bent or flattened to squeeze through any narrow opening.

Amy LaPlume West Roxbury, Mass.

If you'd like to submit a tip, please e-mail us by visiting **CooksCountry. com/emailus** or send a letter to Kitchen Shortcuts, Cook's Country, P.O. Box 470739, Brookline, MA 02447. Include your name, address, and phone number. If we publish your tip, you will receive a free one-year subscription to *Cook's Country.*

DISTINGUISH YOUR KNIVES

Practically everything in my kitchen is dishwasher-safe, except my good knives. Unfortunately, this distinction is lost on my husband when he takes a stab at cleaning up the kitchen. So I now label my knife handles with "No DW" or "Handwash" using my label maker. The labels stay on forever, and it's a discreet way to keep my best cutlery safe from the dishwasher (and my husband).

Sam Mix
Streamwood, Ill.

DON'T FILL 'ER UP

Lightweight plastic storage containers and cups often turn over in the dishwasher and fill with water. To keep this from happening, I arrange all my plastic containers on the top shelf and lay a cooling rack on top of them. The weight of the rack keeps them in their place during the rinse cycle.

Joan Jensen
Coulee Dam, Wash.

SLIDE RIGHT UP

When preparing poached eggs for eggs Benedict, I used to remove the eggs from the poaching liquid and lay them on paper towels to dry off. When ready to assemble, I found it difficult to remove the eggs from the towel without them sticking and the yolks breaking. Now, I place the eggs on individual squares of nonstick aluminum foil. The excess water still drains off, but the eggs don't stick.

Bernard Cohn
Elmsford, N.Y.

COOLER KITCHEN

I was hosting a barbecue on a hot day in Tulsa and I was reluctant to cook beans on my stovetop, since my kitchen can really get warm and I wanted to be outside near the grill. So I put my beans in my trusty slow cooker and plugged it into the outside electrical outlet. My beans cooked outside, and I could watch them without returning to the kitchen.

Ruby Shupper
Tulsa, Okla.

QUICK CORN HUSKING

Love corn on the cob but hate to do all that shucking? Here's the fastest way to get it done. From the top of the cob, pull down approximately one inch of the husk (with its silk), leaving the pulled husk attached. From here, just snap off the stalk and remove the entire husk, silk and all, with just one tug!

Sandy Warner
Elk Grove, Calif.

SILPAT STORAGE

Anyone who uses Silpat mats knows that finding a way to store them can be very frustrating. The simple method I use is to roll one or several mats stacked on top of each other into a cylinder small enough to fit inside a poster tube. The poster tube then stores horizontally or vertically in my drawer or cupboard.

William Powell
Half Moon Bay, Calif.

SHORTCUT FOR SHORTCUTS

I love your Kitchen Shortcuts, but I always forget to use them. To remind me of the tips I've read over the years, I now jot the shortcuts down on index cards and place them in my recipe box at the beginning of the section that they relate to. Once I've done the shortcut for those recipes a couple of times, the trick is not forgotten.

Dianne Walterscheid
Muenster, Texas

MICROWAVE MAGIC

Instead of blanching a tomato in boiling water and then transferring it to an ice bath in order to loosen its skin, I simply score the bottom of the tomato with an X and microwave it for 30 to 60 seconds. The tomato skin loosens and can be easily removed by hand. If using more tomatoes, adjust time accordingly.

Charatphan Viravan
San Jose, Calif.

Neat Trick!
PRACTICAL PICNIC

When I go on a picnic, I don't want a bunch of condiment bottles taking up all the space in my picnic basket. Instead, I put the mustard, mayonnaise, etc., in zipper-lock sandwich baggies. When it's time to eat, I snip the corners and squeeze the condiments onto the sandwiches. When everyone is done, I just toss the bags. Without all those condiment bottles, I always have plenty of room in my picnic basket for dessert!

Shari Shintaku Elk Grove, Calif.

Flash Freeze

The best way to freeze fresh strawberries is to put them in ice cube trays. The stacked trays take up much less space in the freezer than a cookie sheet. Plus, the berries can't roll off onto the floor when I remove the trays. When the berries are frozen, I transfer them to freezer bags for storage. This method works great with other types of berries, too.

Sara Morey
Bellevue, Wash.

Customized Flavors

Want gourmet-style ice cream at half the cost? Just soften regular vanilla ice cream in a bowl at room temperature and add your favorite ingredients. It can be crushed cookies, candy, berries, liqueur, or anything else you can think of! Once mixed, put the ice cream back into its original container, label it, and enjoy your own custom-flavored gourmet ice cream.

Anastasia Simpson
Marina, Calif.

New Use for Tongs

Since they can be so expensive, I like to wash and reuse my freezer storage bags. But hand-drying the just-washed bags is a pain. Instead, I let them air dry by placing tongs in a heavy-bottomed drinking glass and draping the bag over the tongs.

Emily Lewis
Eustis, Fla.

Quick Reference

I have an extensive cookbook collection, so it's always a challenge to remember which book holds what recipe. To help catalog my recipes, I bought a small Rolodex file with tabbed index cards. Now I divide the recipes into categories—poultry, beef, pork, etc.—and write down the name of the cookbook and page number for all my favorites.

Rochelle Oberholser
Charlotte, N.C.

Oatmeal Fudge Bars Are Both Crunchy and Creamy

Our winning bar cookies are dense and fudgy, with a crunchy oatmeal topping. Barb created this recipe after sampling something similar at a Kansas City deli. Her secret ingredient is instant coffee, which deepens the chocolate flavor without calling attention to itself.

OATMEAL FUDGE BARS MAKES 36 BARS
Be sure to cool the crust before proceeding to step 2.

Crust and Topping
- 3/4 cup all-purpose flour
- 1 cup quick-cooking oats
- 1 cup packed light brown sugar
- 1/4 teaspoon baking powder
- 1/4 teaspoon baking soda
- 1/8 teaspoon salt
- 8 tablespoons (1 stick) unsalted butter, melted and cooled slightly

Filling
- 1/2 cup all-purpose flour
- 1/2 cup packed light brown sugar
- 1 tablespoon instant coffee granules or espresso powder
- 1/4 teaspoon salt
- 2 cups semisweet chocolate chips
- 4 tablespoons unsalted butter, chopped
- 3 large eggs

1. For the crust: Adjust oven rack to middle position and heat oven to 325 degrees. Prepare 9 by 9-inch baking pan (see note below). Whisk flour, oats, sugar, baking powder, baking soda, and salt in bowl. Stir in butter until combined. Set 1¼ cups oatmeal mixture aside. Press remaining oatmeal mixture firmly into prepared pan. Bake until light golden brown, about 8 minutes. Cool completely.

2. For the filling: Whisk flour, sugar, instant coffee, and salt in bowl. Melt chocolate chips and butter in large bowl; whisk in eggs, then stir in flour mixture. Pour filling over cooled crust and sprinkle with reserved oatmeal mixture.

3. Bake until toothpick inserted into center comes out with few crumbs attached, 35 to 40 minutes. Cool to room temperature, at least 1 hour. Cut into 1½-inch squares.

Note: For all bar cookies, spray baking pan with cooking spray and line with aluminum foil, allowing excess to overhang pan edges. Spray foil with cooking spray. Once bar cookies have been baked and cooled, use foil overhang to lift bars from pan. (All bar cookies can be refrigerated for up to 3 days.)

A chewy crust, dense filling, and crunchy topping give this bar a nice contrast of textures.

Robin Peterson
Peoria, Ariz.

Camilla Saulsbury
Nacogdoches, Texas

Cynthia Messenger
Mount Pleasant, S.C.

Trisha Kruse
Eagle, Idaho

SNICKERS BARS MAKES 36 BARS

Robin writes: "I created these bars because they are so easy to prepare, yet they are elegant enough to serve at a dinner party."

Crust

- 1 cup all-purpose flour
- 1/4 teaspoon baking soda
- 1/8 teaspoon salt
- 5 tablespoons unsalted butter, softened
- 1/2 cup packed light brown sugar

Filling

- 20 soft caramel candies
- 1/4 teaspoon salt
- 3 tablespoons water
- 5 (2.07-ounce) Snickers Bars, chopped
- 2 tablespoons milk
- 2 tablespoons unsalted butter
- 1/4 cup salted roasted peanuts, chopped

1. For the crust: Adjust oven rack to middle position and heat oven to 350 degrees. Prepare 9 by 9-inch baking pan (see note on page 4). Whisk flour, baking soda, and salt in medium bowl. With electric mixer on medium speed, beat butter and sugar in large bowl until fluffy, about 2 minutes. On low speed, beat in flour mixture until incorporated, about 1 minute. Press mixture firmly into prepared pan. Bake until golden brown, about 12 minutes. Cool slightly.

2. For the filling: Melt caramels, salt, and water in saucepan over medium-low heat, 3 to 4 minutes. Pour mixture over crust and refrigerate until set, about 30 minutes.

3. Meanwhile, heat Snickers Bars, milk, and butter in medium saucepan over medium heat, stirring constantly, until Snickers have melted, about 5 minutes. Pour over chilled caramel.

4. Bake until filling is set, about 12 minutes. Top with peanuts, cool to room temperature, and refrigerate until chilled, at least 4 hours. Cut into 1½-inch squares.

TEXAS PINK GRAPEFRUIT BARS MAKES 16 BARS

Camilla writes: "This recipe is similar to a lemon square, but with a Texas twist. The addition of cardamom in the crust enhances the citrus flavor even more."

Crust

- 1⅓ cups all-purpose flour
- 1/3 cup packed light brown sugar
- 1/8 teaspoon ground cardamom
- 1/8 teaspoon salt
- 8 tablespoons (1 stick) unsalted butter, cut into 8 pieces

Filling

- 4 large eggs
- 1¼ cups granulated sugar
- 2 teaspoons grated zest plus 2/3 cup juice from 1 large pink grapefruit
- 2 teaspoons grated zest plus 1 tablespoon juice from 1 lime
- 1/8 teaspoon salt
- 3 drops red food coloring (optional) Confectioners' sugar for dusting

1. For the crust: Adjust oven rack to middle position and heat oven to 350 degrees. Prepare 8 by 8-inch baking pan (see note on page 4). Combine flour, sugar, cardamom, and salt in food processor. Add butter and pulse until mixture resembles coarse meal. Press mixture firmly into prepared pan. Bake until golden brown, 30 to 35 minutes. Cool slightly.

2. For the filling: Meanwhile, cook all ingredients except confectioners' sugar in medium saucepan over medium-low heat, whisking constantly, until pudding-like consistency, 6 to 8 minutes. Strain over warm crust and spread into even layer.

3. Bake until filling is set, about 10 minutes. Cool to room temperature, then refrigerate until chilled, at least 4 hours. Cut into 2-inch squares. Dust with confectioners' sugar just before serving.

RASPBERRY-ALMOND CHEESECAKE BARS MAKES 24 BARS

Cynthia writes: "I first made these bars for a family dinner, but now I get requests to bring them to other functions."

Crust

- 1¾ cups all-purpose flour
- 1/4 cup granulated sugar
- 1/4 cup packed light brown sugar
- 1/4 cup sliced almonds
- 1/2 teaspoon salt
- 12 tablespoons (1½ sticks) unsalted butter, cut into 12 pieces

Filling

- 2 (8-ounce) packages cream cheese, softened
- 3/4 cup granulated sugar
- 1 large egg
- 1 teaspoon vanilla extract
- 1/4 teaspoon almond extract
- 3/4 cup seedless raspberry preserves

1. For the crust: Adjust oven rack to middle position and heat oven to 350 degrees. Prepare 13 by 9-inch baking pan (see note on page 4). Combine flour, sugars, almonds, and salt in food processor. Add butter and pulse until mixture resembles coarse meal. Press mixture firmly into prepared pan. Bake until light golden brown, about 15 minutes. Cool completely.

2. For the filling: With electric mixer on medium speed, beat cream cheese and sugar in large bowl until smooth, about 2 minutes. Beat in egg and extracts until incorporated, about 1 minute.

3. Spread preserves over cooled crust, leaving ½-inch border around edge. Dollop tablespoonfuls of cream cheese mixture over jam and spread into even layer.

4. Bake until slightly puffed, 30 to 35 minutes. Cool to room temperature, then refrigerate until chilled, at least 4 hours. Cut into 2-inch squares.

APPLE-PEAR-COFFEE STREUSEL BARS MAKES 24 BARS

Trisha writes: "The cinnamon and coffee flavors really complement each other."

Crust

- 2 cups all-purpose flour
- 1 cup packed light brown sugar
- 1 tablespoon instant coffee granules
- 1/2 teaspoon ground cinnamon
- 1/4 teaspoon salt
- 8 tablespoons (1 stick) unsalted butter, cut into 8 pieces

Filling

- 3 large eggs
- 1½ cups packed light brown sugar
- 2 teaspoons vanilla extract
- 1/2 teaspoon ground cinnamon
- 1/4 teaspoon salt
- 1 large Granny Smith apple, peeled, cored, and cut into 1/4-inch pieces
- 2 ripe Bosc pears, peeled, cored, and cut into 1/4-inch pieces
- 1 cup walnuts, toasted and chopped
- 1 cup granola cereal without dried fruit
- 4 tablespoons unsalted butter, melted

1. For the crust: Adjust oven rack to middle position and heat oven to 325 degrees. Prepare 13 by 9-inch baking pan (see note on page 4). Combine flour, sugar, coffee, cinnamon, and salt in food processor. Add butter and pulse until mixture resembles coarse meal. Press mixture firmly into prepared pan. Bake until golden brown, 15 to 20 minutes. Cool slightly.

2. For the filling: Whisk eggs, 1 cup sugar, vanilla, cinnamon, and salt in medium bowl. Stir in apple and pears and spread over cooled crust.

3. Bake until filling is bubbling, about 30 minutes. Toss walnuts, granola, remaining sugar, and butter in bowl. Sprinkle mixture over hot filling and bake until golden brown, 15 to 20 minutes. Cool to room temperature, at least 1½ hours. Cut into 2-inch squares.

Ask Cook's Country

WE'LL ANSWER ANY QUESTION YOU THROW AT US!

SOUR CREAM'S FRENCH COUSIN

I've seen recipes call for crème fraîche, but I can't find it at my grocery store. What is it, and is there anything I can substitute for it?

Sally Pearsall Laramie, Wyo.

Crème fraîche, contrary to its English translation as "fresh cream," is actually heavy cream that has been soured with a bacterial culture. Texturally, it is similar to sour cream, but with a lighter, more refined flavor. Because crème fraîche will not curdle when boiled, it is often stirred into savory soups or sauces to add a lush finish. If your

LIGHT AND LUSH
Crème fraîche adds creaminess, richness, and body—and unlike sour cream, it doesn't curdle when boiled.

supermarket doesn't carry crème fraîche (or if you aren't willing to pay the hefty price), it can be made at home. Simply stir one tablespoon of cultured buttermilk into one cup of heavy cream, cover, and let sit at room temperature until the mixture has thickened (at least eight hours or up to two days). Refrigerated in an airtight container, homemade crème fraîche will keep for about two weeks. If you're in a pinch, whisking 2 tablespoons of heavy cream into 1 cup of sour cream will give you the correct flavor and texture, but if you're adding the mixture to a soup, be aware that it will separate if boiled.

VANILLA, PURE BUT NOT SIMPLE

Can I use imitation vanilla when baking, or will it ruin my favorite cakes and cookies?

Mary Craig Tenille San Francisco, Calif.

Pure vanilla extract is made by soaking vanilla beans in a solution of water and alcohol and then aging the mixture in holding tanks—sometimes for a few months—prior to bottling. This lengthy production process contributes to the high cost of pure vanilla extract. The less expensive imitation extract, on the other hand, relies primarily on the synthetic compound vanillin to mimic the smell and taste of real vanilla.

We compared batches of chocolate chip cookies and pastry cream made with each extract. When it was baked into the cookies, most of the tasters actually preferred the artificial vanilla, claiming that its "mild, natural" flavor melded nicely with the buttery, chocolaty cookies. When tasted in the pastry cream (where the extracts were added after cooking), the opinions were more varied. Some tasters lauded the "clean, floral" aroma of the pure vanilla, but others found it to be "too strong" and "boozy."

Ultimately, since both extracts were deemed acceptable in both recipes, the choice comes down to cost and personal philosophy about using imitation products. Imitation vanilla certainly will not ruin your baked goods.

IT'S NOT EASY BEING GREEN

Are potatoes that have turned green on the outside safe to eat?

Ray Case Rochester, N.Y.

When potatoes are exposed to light for prolonged periods of time, they begin to produce chlorophyll in the form of a green ring under their skin. While the chlorophyll itself is tasteless and harmless, it does mark the potential presence of solanine, a toxin that can cause gastrointestinal distress. Since solanine develops on the skin of the potato (or just below), discarding the peel

GREEN BE GONE
Remove all green flesh with a peeler.

greatly reduces the risk of becoming ill from a slightly green spud. In the test kitchen, we've found that potatoes stored in a well-ventilated, dark, dry, cool place will stay solanine-free for up to a month, while potatoes that are left on the countertop will begin to exhibit signs of solanine in as little as a week.

SCALDED MILK: THEN AND NOW

Some of my bread recipes call for scalding milk. What does this do?

Connie Colburn Lexington, Ky.

To scald milk is to bring it to the verge of a boil (about 180 degrees), after which it must be skimmed of the thin skin that forms on top. In bread recipes, scalding has historically served two purposes: to kill harmful microbes in the milk and to break down the milk proteins that can otherwise thicken and hinder the rise of yeast. Since the advent of modern pasteurization, the risk of harmful microbes has been negated. But what about scalding's impact on yeast and rising?

To test whether scalded milk actually produces a higher rise in bread, we prepared two loaves of American-style sandwich bread, one made with scalded milk (heated to 180 degrees) and one made with milk warmed just enough to activate the yeast (to 110 degrees). The loaf made with scalded milk did have a slightly higher rise, but the loaf made with warmed milk was still very good. Since scalding introduces the possibility of killing the yeast if the baker doesn't let the hot milk cool down sufficiently (temperatures higher than 120 degrees will kill most yeast), we don't recommend this step; the small benefit isn't worth the risk.

STORING CITRUS

My wife says that it isn't necessary to refrigerate citrus, but I've always thought it is. Can you shed some light on this family disagreement?

Roger Littlejohn Bermuda Run, N.C.

Unlike bananas or peaches, which ripen at room temperature, citrus fruits stop ripening the moment they are picked, thus beginning a slow and steady decline in texture and flavor. To improve their shelf life, commercially grown citrus are buffed with a thin layer of food-safe wax that prevents moisture from escaping through the fruits' porous rind. To test how well the wax coating works, we bought lemons, limes, and oranges and stored half in the refrigerator and half at room temperature. The fruit that was refrigerated remained firm and juicy for about three weeks, while citrus that was left at room temperature began to discolor and dehydrate in as little as five days. Ultimately, the only downside to storing citrus in the fridge is that it's more difficult to squeeze juice from a cold citrus fruit. To make life easier, let your citrus sit at room temperature for about 15 minutes before juicing.

I CAN BELIEVE IT'S NOT BUTTER

Can I use Butter Flavor Crisco instead of regular Crisco to bake or fry?

Gail Shapiro Santa Monica, Calif.

The J.M. Smucker Co., the manufacturer of Crisco, claims that Butter Flavor Crisco can be used interchangeably with regular Crisco to add "a rich buttery flavor to foods." To judge for ourselves, we baked pie crusts and fried french fries with each of the short-

BUTTER FLAVOR CRISCO
Don't be fooled by this gimmicky hybrid.

enings. In the pie crust test, while both types of Crisco produced incredibly flaky crusts, most tasters found the "artificial, margarine" taste of the Butter Flavor Crisco to be too strong to overlook. In the french fry test, Butter Flavor Crisco fared even worse.

The "horrible chemical aroma" of the frying potatoes sent a handful of tasters out of the kitchen, and those who remained complained of the "movie theatre popcorn flavor" and "fake butter aftertaste." Based on these tests, we don't recommend buying Butter Flavor Crisco. Although it will produce a perfectly flaky pie crust, so will regular Crisco—without any lingering aftertaste. As for frying, we prefer to stick to a tasteless fat (like plain shortening or vegetable oil) that won't compete with the flavor of the food.

To ask us a cooking question, visit **CooksCountry.com/emailus**. Or write to Ask Cook's Country, P.O. Box 470739, Brookline, MA 02447. See if you can stump us!

Lost Recipe TICK TOCK ORANGE STICKY ROLLS

These sticky rolls were the star attraction at a now-shuttered Hollywood tea room for more than half a century. Could we bring these rolls back for an encore performance?

While the entertainment industry immortalizes its stars in celluloid and cement handprints, Hollywood residents fondly recall another local legend—the Tick Tock Tea Room. From 1930 through 1988, the Tick Tock served up countless platters of meatloaf, roast turkey, and fried chicken to its working-class clientele. The restaurant's defining touch was the complimentary basket of hot sticky rolls that preceded each meal. When the Tick Tock closed its doors almost 20 years ago, it also closed the book on those incredible orange rolls.

I found two recipes for these rolls, one from a 1977 *Los Angeles Times* article and one from a 1994 cookbook called *Hollywood du Jour*. The recipes are very similar: Packaged biscuit mix dough is rolled out, covered in cinnamon sugar and orange zest, and then rolled into a log. Individual pieces are cut, then set in a baking dish (spiral side up, like cinnamon rolls or sticky buns) atop a glaze made with orange juice concentrate, sugar, and butter. When the rolls come out of the oven, they are turned out with the gooey glaze on top. Unfortunately, both recipes produced sloppy, soggy rolls soaked through with glaze.

The fluffy boxed-mix biscuits had soaked up too much liquid. Homemade cream biscuits were sturdier but didn't have much flavor. Biscuits made with buttermilk and melted butter (instead of

cream) tasted great and stood up to the glaze better—especially when I defied convention and kneaded the dough before rolling and cutting. After five minutes of kneading, the biscuits were still plenty tender, but now they offered some resistance to the glaze.

The candy-sweet original orange glaze started with ¾ cup of orange juice concentrate. I tried fresh and store-bought orange juice, but neither packed enough orange flavor. To temper its sweetness, I reduced the concentrate by ¼ cup and cut the cloying granulated sugar with an equal amount of brown sugar. The glaze was still too thin and easily absorbed into the biscuits. For my next test, I simmered the ingredients in the saucepan until they formed a thick glaze.

A happy kitchen accident took this recipe home. I had made the glaze and then gotten distracted before I had a chance to start the dough; by the time the dough was ready, the glaze had hardened in the cake pan. I went ahead and threw the rolls in anyway. Starting with a hardened glaze kept the rolls from soaking up too much liquid, and the rolls now browned much better than when they'd been saturated with the orange syrup.

With their orange-cinnamon filling and caramely, sticky orange glaze, these Tick Tock Rolls quickly became legendary in these parts, too.

–Bridget Lancaster

Fluffy Tick Tock Rolls feature a lively orange glaze and rich cinnamon-sugar filling.

TICK TOCK ORANGE STICKY ROLLS SERVES 8

Don't let the buns sit in the pan for more than 5 minutes after baking. The glaze will begin to harden and the buns will stick.

Orange Glaze
- ½ cup frozen orange juice concentrate, thawed
- ¼ cup packed light brown sugar
- ¼ cup granulated sugar
- 3 tablespoons unsalted butter

Orange-Cinnamon Filling
- ½ cup packed light brown sugar
- ¼ cup granulated sugar
- 2 teaspoons ground cinnamon
- 1 teaspoon grated orange zest
- ⅛ teaspoon ground cloves
- ⅛ teaspoon salt
- 1 tablespoon unsalted butter, melted

Biscuit Dough
- 2¾ cups all-purpose flour, plus extra for work surface
- 2 tablespoons granulated sugar
- 2 teaspoons baking powder
- ½ teaspoon baking soda
- ½ teaspoon salt
- 1¼ cups buttermilk
- 6 tablespoons unsalted butter, melted

1. For the glaze: Grease 9-inch cake pan with cooking spray. Bring all ingredients to simmer in small saucepan over medium heat. Cook until mixture thickens and clings to back of spoon, about 5 minutes. Pour mixture into prepared pan. Cool until glaze hardens, at least 20 minutes.

2. For the filling: Adjust oven rack to lower-middle position and heat oven to 350 degrees. Combine all ingredients except butter in bowl. Using fork, stir in butter until mixture resembles wet sand.

3. For the dough: Whisk flour, sugar, baking powder, baking soda, and salt in bowl. Whisk buttermilk and butter in small bowl (mixture will clump), then stir into flour mixture until combined. Knead dough on lightly floured work surface until smooth, about 5 minutes.

4. Roll dough into 12 by 9-inch rectangle. Pat filling into dough, leaving ½-inch border around edges. Starting at one long end, roll dough into tight cylinder and pinch seam together. Cut log into 8 pieces and arrange cut side down on cooled glaze, placing 1 roll in center and remaining rolls around edge of pan.

5. Bake until rolls are golden and glaze is darkened and bubbling, 18 to 25 minutes. Cool in pan 5 minutes, then turn out onto platter. Let rolls sit 10 minutes before serving.

The American Table: A Time for Good Food

The Tick Tock Tea Room opened in 1930, when Norwegian immigrants Arthur and Helen Johnson bought a run-down home on North Cahuenga Boulevard and converted it into a restaurant. They hung their most prized possession, an antique clock, on the wall and the rest was history; soon there were 48 clocks decorating the restaurant.

For those without movie studio expense accounts, the Tick Tock Tea Room offered three courses of good, humble cooking at affordable prices. The Johnsons would serve more than 2,000 three-course meals on busy days. The Tick Tock was such a success, thanks in part to the sweet rolls that came with every meal, that the family opened up two more locations in the Los Angeles area. The last Tick Tock closed for good in 1988.

Most low-fat creamy salad dressings taste like the plastic they're bottled in. Could we develop a fresh-tasting alternative?

A salad might seem like a healthy meal option, but many creamy dressings have as much fat per serving as a fast-food cheeseburger. That's because most creamy dressings use mayonnaise, sour cream, or both as a base. Bottled low-fat creamy dressings are made with so much corn syrup and chemicals that their flavor is cloyingly sweet, thin, and artificial. I wanted to create creamy low-fat versions of blue cheese, Parmesan peppercorn, and ranch dressings that, unlike bottled low-fat versions, were rich and fresh-tasting.

Many of the recipes I found were very imaginative in their approach to replacing the mayo and sour cream. "Imitation mayo" (a mixture of cottage cheese and apple juice concentrate), tofu, mashed white beans, tapioca, and even flax seed oil were a few of the products I tested. But despite their ingenuity, these recipes were all lacking in flavor and texture.

Having exhausted inventive ingredients, I turned to more conventional options. Tasters rejected the non-fat mayonnaise and non-fat sour cream in my first attempt, but a dressing made with their reduced-fat counterparts

was an improvement. Better still was a version that replaced the reduced-fat sour cream (which a few tasters thought tasted "artificial") with low-fat plain yogurt. The yogurt was smooth and creamy—unlike other ingredients, such as cottage and cream cheeses, which had to be pureed—and thinning it with a little water brought it to just the right consistency.

Now that I had a creamy base, I could begin to add potent ingredients to build flavor. Using strong cheeses like Roquefort or Stilton and freshly grated Parmesan meant that I could use less of them. Fresh garlic lent pungency and depth to all three dressings. And for the ranch dressing, my secret was using three fresh herbs—dill, chives, and cilantro. These bright, fresh, creamy salad dressings have a quarter of the calories and a sliver of the fat of their full-fat predecessors.

–Cali Rich

Our full-flavored creamy dressings have about 90 percent less fat than their traditional counterparts.

And the Numbers...
All nutritional information is for a 2-tablespoon serving.

	Before	After
BLUE CHEESE DRESSING		
CALORIES:	130	35
FAT:	13g	2.5g
SATURATED FAT:	2.5g	1g
PARMESAN PEPPER-CORN DRESSING		
CALORIES:	140	30
FAT:	14g	1.5g
SATURATED FAT:	2.5g	0.5g
RANCH DRESSING		
CALORIES:	170	25
FAT:	18g	1g
SATURATED FAT:	3g	0g

LOW-FAT BLUE CHEESE DRESSING
MAKES ABOUT 1 CUP, ENOUGH FOR 8 SERVINGS
Each 2-tablespoon serving of these dressings should be tossed with 2 cups of sturdy, leafy greens. For the most flavor, use a pungent blue cheese like Roquefort or Stilton.

    ¹/₂ cup low-fat plain yogurt
    ¹/₄ cup reduced-fat mayonnaise
    ¹/₄ cup crumbled blue cheese (see note)
    2   tablespoons water
    2   teaspoons lemon juice
    1   garlic clove, grated (see box at right)
    ¹/₄ teaspoon salt
    ¹/₈ teaspoon pepper

Whisk all ingredients in medium bowl until smooth. Dressing can be refrigerated for up to 4 days.

LOW-FAT PARMESAN PEPPERCORN DRESSING
MAKES ABOUT 1 CUP, ENOUGH FOR 8 SERVINGS
Smooth Dijon mustard, not grainy, works best here.

    ¹/₂ cup low-fat plain yogurt
    ¹/₄ cup reduced-fat mayonnaise
    ¹/₄ cup finely grated Parmesan cheese
    1   garlic clove, grated (see box below)
    2   tablespoons water
    2   teaspoons lemon juice
    1   teaspoon Dijon mustard (see note)
    ¹/₂ teaspoon pepper
    ¹/₄ teaspoon salt

Whisk all ingredients in medium bowl until smooth. Dressing can be refrigerated for up to 4 days.

LOW-FAT RANCH DRESSING
MAKES ABOUT 1 CUP, ENOUGH FOR 8 SERVINGS
Buttermilk makes a nice substitute for the water here, and it adds only ¹/₂ gram of fat and virtually no calories.

    ¹/₂ cup low-fat plain yogurt
    ¹/₄ cup reduced-fat mayonnaise
    2   tablespoons water (see note)
    2   teaspoons white wine vinegar
    1   garlic clove, grated (see box below)
    1   tablespoon minced fresh chives
    1   tablespoon minced fresh cilantro
    1   teaspoon minced fresh dill
    ¹/₄ teaspoon salt
         Pinch cayenne pepper

Whisk all ingredients in medium bowl until smooth. Dressing can be refrigerated for up to 4 days.

Grating Garlic
Using grated garlic ensures a uniform consistency that will evenly incorporate into these dressings. While garlic presses and box graters are test kitchen workhorses, neither tool provides fine enough processing for this application. We prefer to use a rasp-style grater (our favorite is the Microplane); alternatively, you can mince the garlic on a cutting board, add the ¹/₄ teaspoon salt from the recipe, and mash it to a smooth paste with the side of a chef's knife.

BEST GRATER FOR GARLIC
A rasp grater ensures perfectly grated garlic every time.

A slow cooker can be tough on delicate chicken. What's the secret to producing bold flavors and tender meat?

One of my family's favorite dishes is the simple French braise called chicken *chasseur*, or hunter-style chicken. With the strong flavors of mushrooms, white wine, chicken stock, tomatoes, onions, and herbs, I thought this might be a good candidate for the convenience of my slow cooker.

I collected a half-dozen slow-cooker recipes for hunter-style chicken and got to work. After eight hours of tantalizing smells, my tasters sat down to sample each version. The dry and stringy meat, pieces of chicken bone floating in thin, greasy broth, and washed-out flavors failed to impress. If I was going to make this recipe work, I would have to perform a complete overhaul.

I replaced the traditional whole cut-up chicken with bone-in, skin-on chicken thighs, our preferred cut for braising (white meat doesn't have enough fat to withstand prolonged stewing). Using chicken broth as my liquid, I found that 4 to 5 hours on low produced fully cooked meat that wasn't too dried out. Browning the thighs on the stovetop to render fat and build flavor before adding them to the slow cooker did make for tastier sauce, but it also turned the meat tough and stringy. I decided to skip the browning; this meant I had to lose the skin, which was rubbery and greasy when not browned.

Because I'd lost the flavor from the chicken skin and the browned meat, I had to compensate with bold flavors in the sauce. I started by sautéing the mushrooms and onions in rich bacon fat, which lent a deep smokiness. Dried porcini mushrooms (which I rehydrated in wine) contributed a meaty complexity, and a mere tablespoon of soy sauce further enriched the sauce.

Wanting to keep my braising liquid concentrated and potent, I increased the white wine from ½ cup to 1½ cups and reduced it in the skillet to intensify its flavor. Tomato paste worked better than the juicy canned tomatoes called for in most recipes. A mere ⅔ cup of chicken broth, down from the typical 2 cups, combined with the reduced wine to provide ample liquid to cover the meat and vegetables.

We provide make-ahead instructions for most of our recipes, and my testing for this turned up an important finding. Refrigerating the cooked vegetables, wine, and tomato paste ahead of time actually improves the recipe, because the cold mixture slows the cooking time down to 6 hours. This allows the chicken to cook more gently, resulting in juicier, more tender meat. **–Eva Katz**

HUNTER-STYLE CHICKEN
SERVES 4 TO 6

Dried porcini mushrooms are available at most supermarkets and wholesale clubs. Be sure to refrigerate the mushroom mixture until it is thoroughly chilled. Serve with buttered egg noodles, mashed potatoes, or boiled potatoes.

- 1½ **cups dry white wine**
- 5 **tablespoons tomato paste**
- 1 **tablespoon minced fresh thyme**
- ¼ **ounce (about ⅓ cup) dried porcini mushrooms, rinsed and chopped fine**
- 8 **ounces bacon, chopped**
- 1¼ **pounds cremini or white mushrooms, cleaned and quartered**
- 1 **large red onion, chopped fine**
  Salt
- 4 **garlic cloves, minced**
- ½ **teaspoon red pepper flakes**
- 3 **pounds bone-in, skin-on chicken thighs, skin removed and fat trimmed**
  Pepper
- 1 **tablespoon soy sauce**
- ⅔ **cup low-sodium chicken broth**
- 2 **tablespoons chopped fresh tarragon**

1. Whisk wine, tomato paste, thyme, and porcini mushrooms in liquid measuring cup; set aside. Cook bacon in large skillet over medium-high heat until crisp, about 8 minutes. Using slotted spoon, transfer bacon to paper towel–lined plate.

2. Pour off all but 2 teaspoons fat from skillet. Add cremini mushrooms, onion, and ¼ teaspoon salt and cook over medium heat until mushrooms have released their moisture, about 5 minutes. Increase heat to medium-high and cook until mushrooms brown, about 5 minutes. Add garlic and red pepper and cook until fragrant, about 1 minute. Add porcini mixture and simmer until mixture has thickened, about 5 minutes. Transfer to medium bowl and stir in bacon. Cool slightly, cover with plastic wrap, and refrigerate until cold, at least 2 hours or up to 2 days.

3. Season chicken thighs with salt and pepper and place in single layer in slow-cooker insert. Spread cold mushroom mixture over chicken. Add soy sauce and chicken broth. Set slow cooker on low, cover, and cook until chicken is tender, about 6 hours. Stir in tarragon and let sit for 10 minutes before serving.

Kitchen Know-How
BUYING DRIED MUSHROOMS

Porcini mushrooms are sometimes referred to by their French name, *cèpes*. When shopping for porcini, look for mushroom pieces that are large, thick, and either tan or light brown—never black. Avoid packages with lots of dust and crumbled bits, which don't rehydrate well. Lastly, dried porcini should have an earthy (not musty or stale) aroma; mushrooms with no aroma are likely to have little flavor.

DRIED PORCINI

Chicken cooks quickly, making it a challenge for the slow cooker. We devised a way to slow things down enough to produce tender, juicy chicken in a rich, deeply flavored sauce.

Regional Favorites: *California Barbecued Beans*

This dish traditionally uses a bean variety and chili sauce that are rarely seen outside of California. Could we re-create this regional recipe with supermarket ingredients?

In Santa Maria, no plate of grilled sirloin is complete without a generous scoop of barbecued pinquito beans, which are native to the Santa Maria Valley. Rather than being sweet and molasses-y, like most versions of barbecued beans, they are draped in a piquant red chili sauce that's flecked with plenty of smoky-sweet pork. These beans are tangy, smoky, and a little spicy, but most of all, they're a perfect accompaniment to garlicky grilled tri-tip.

Unfortunately, outside of Santa Maria, pinquito beans and red chili sauce (a canned sauce consisting of pureed red chiles) aren't everyday fare. Pink kidney beans proved to be a good stand-in for the pinquitos. Most recipes call for jarred taco sauce (a pureed condiment that tastes like salsa) as a substitute for the red chili sauce, but I found its flavor and texture too thin. I built a substantial base of flavor by frying bacon and ham with onion and garlic, then tried enhancing the taco sauce/pork mixture with canned enchilada sauce and even Heinz chili sauce. Neither worked as well as a simple combination of tomato puree and brown sugar. Upping the dry mustard to a full tablespoon, more than twice the usual amount, helped recapture some of the chili sauce's bite.

With a foundation of savory pork, a spicy-sweet dose of tomato, and a finishing punch of cider vinegar and cilantro, I managed to re-create the clean, fresh flavor of the original in my California Barbecued Beans.

–Jeremy Sauer

CALIFORNIA BARBECUED BEANS
SERVES 4 TO 6

If you can find them, pinquito beans (a variety grown in the Santa Maria Valley) are traditional in this dish. Bottled taco sauce is available in the Mexican aisle of most grocery stores. Don't add the tomato puree, taco sauce, brown sugar, and salt before the beans have simmered for an hour; they will hinder the proper softening of the beans.

- 4 slices bacon, chopped fine
- 1/2 pound deli ham, chopped fine
- 1 onion, chopped fine
- 4 garlic cloves, minced
- 1 pound pink kidney beans (see note), soaked overnight and drained (see page 30)
- 6 cups water
- 1 cup canned tomato puree
- 1/2 cup bottled taco sauce
- 5 tablespoons packed light brown sugar
- 1 tablespoon dry mustard
  Salt
- 1/4 cup chopped fresh cilantro
- 2 tablespoons cider vinegar

1. Cook bacon and ham in Dutch oven over medium heat until fat renders and pork is lightly browned, 5 to 7 minutes. Add onion and cook until softened, about 5 minutes. Stir in garlic and cook until fragrant, about

30 seconds. Add beans and water and bring to simmer. Reduce heat to medium-low, cover, and cook until beans are just soft, about 1 hour.

2. Stir in tomato puree, taco sauce, sugar, mustard, and 2 teaspoons salt. Continue to simmer, uncovered, until beans are completely tender and sauce is thickened, about 1 hour. (If mixture becomes too thick, add water.) Stir in cilantro and vinegar and season with salt. Serve. (Beans can be refrigerated for up to 4 days.)

Regional Favorites: *Santa Maria Salsa*

Unexpected ingredients transform ordinary salsa into the perfect partner for barbecued tri-tip.

Most styles of barbecue are defined by their sauce—in North Carolina it's tart with vinegar, and in Kansas City it's sweet with molasses. In Santa Maria, the home of California barbecue, the preferred sauce is a simple, chunky salsa made with tomatoes, chiles, celery, dried oregano, and a dash of Worcestershire. At first glance, the ingredients may seem more suited to a bloody mary than to barbecue, but the crunchy texture of the celery and the complex, almost meaty flavor of the Worcestershire prove to be a natural match for the tender, smoky tri-tip.

Since most recipes for this salsa are similar, my kitchen work was pretty straightforward. I discovered that the tomatoes needed to be salted and drained to prevent the excess tomato liquid from drowning the salsa. And tasters preferred the moderate heat of jalapeños to the milder Anaheim and poblano chiles found in other recipes.

–Jeremy Sauer

SANTA MARIA SALSA
MAKES ABOUT 4 CUPS

The distinct texture of each ingredient is part of this salsa's identity and appeal, so we don't recommend using a food processor.

- 2 pounds ripe tomatoes, cored and chopped
- 2 teaspoons salt
- 2 jalapeño chiles, chopped fine
- 1 small red onion, chopped fine
- 1 celery rib, chopped fine
- 1 garlic clove, minced
- 1/4 cup juice from 2 limes
- 1/4 cup chopped fresh cilantro
- 1/8 teaspoon dried oregano
- 1/8 teaspoon Worcestershire sauce

1. Place tomatoes in strainer set over bowl and sprinkle with salt; drain for 30 minutes. Discard liquid. Meanwhile, combine remaining ingredients in large bowl.

2. Add drained tomatoes to jalapeño mixture and toss to combine. Cover with plastic wrap and let stand at room temperature for 1 hour before serving. (Salsa can be refrigerated for up to 2 days.)

California Barbecued Tri-Tip

What's the secret to the subtly smoky, garlicky flavor of California tri-tip?

Hidden in California's Santa Maria Valley lies a barbecue tradition all its own. There they grill tri-tip, a large, boomerang-shaped cut of beef from the bottom sirloin, over red oak embers until it's lightly charred on the outside and rosy on the interior. Unlike most other styles of barbecue, in which the meat is slathered with sauce, Santa Maria tri-tip is seasoned with only salt, pepper, garlic, and the sweet smoke of the grill. It's sliced thin and served with tangy barbecued beans, fresh salsa, and buttered French bread.

Most of the recipes I found for California tri-tip were loaded with problems. While other types of barbecue utilize indirect heat, long cooking times, and low temperatures, tri-tip recipes call for the meat to be grilled directly over high heat. But grilling a 2-pound, 3-inch-thick cut of meat over a hot fire consistently produced a charred exterior and a very rare center. In addition to the cooking issue, the recipes I tried all left me with overly smoky meat, with nary a hint of garlic flavor.

Tri-tip is usually referred to as a steak, but at this size, it needs to be cooked like a roast. Following the test kitchen's method for grilling large cuts, I pushed all the coals to one side of the grill to create a hot cooking zone and a cooler one. This way I could sear the tri-tip over the hot fire and then finish it slowly on the cooler side, leaving it with a flavorful char and a perfectly cooked interior.

For the smoke flavor, I knew from past experience that a handful of soaked wood chips would be plenty; what I didn't anticipate was that searing the tri-tip directly above the smoldering wood chips would leave it tasting like the inside of a chimney. To lessen the impact of the smoke, I held off on the wood chips until after I'd seared the meat and moved it to the cool part of the grill. This allowed the smoke to dissipate slightly before contacting the meat, perfuming—but not overpowering—the tri-tip with a subtle smoke flavor.

When it comes to seasoning, most recipes rely on garlic salt rather than fresh garlic. But if I added too much garlic salt, it scorched and turned bitter on the grill; if I cut back on the garlic salt, the meat was underseasoned. I wondered if a marinade with fresh garlic might help infuse the meat with garlic flavor. I made a paste with minced garlic, olive oil, and salt and rubbed it over the tri-tip,

Using oak chips best approximates the flavor of red oak embers, the traditional grilling fuel for tri-tip in Santa Maria.

leaving it to marinate for just an hour. From here, I wiped off the garlic and oil (the garlic burned if left on the meat), sprinkled the tri-tip with a bit of garlic salt and pepper, and set it on the grill. The double dose of garlic left the exterior of the meat richly seasoned, but the interior of this thick cut of meat was still slightly bland. I solved this problem by pricking the roast with a fork before I applied the marinade; this ensured that the salty garlic paste would penetrate deep into the interior to thoroughly season this hefty cut.

With its beefy, garlicky, and subtly smoky flavor, California barbecue is nothing like the barbecue I grew up eating— looks like I've got some catching up to do. **–Jeremy Sauer**

CALIFORNIA BARBECUED TRI-TIP SERVES 4 TO 6

If you can't find tri-tip, bottom round is an acceptable alternative (see page 30 for tips on preparing bottom round). The traditional accompaniments to tri-tip are Santa Maria Salsa and California Barbecued Beans (both page 10).

- 1 tri-tip roast (about 2 pounds), trimmed
- 6 garlic cloves, minced
- 2 tablespoons olive oil
- 3/4 teaspoon salt
- 2 cups wood chips, preferably oak
- 1 teaspoon pepper
- 3/4 teaspoon garlic salt

1. Pat roast dry with paper towels. Using fork, prick roast about 20 times on each side.

Combine garlic, oil, and salt and rub over roast. Cover with plastic wrap and refrigerate for 1 hour or up to 24 hours.

2. Soak wood chips in bowl of water to cover for 15 minutes. Open bottom vents on grill. Light large chimney starter filled with charcoal briquettes (about 100 coals) and burn until charcoal is covered with fine gray ash. Pour hot coals in even layer over one half of grill. Set cooking grate in place, cover, open lid vents completely, and let grill heat for 5 minutes. Scrape cooking grate clean.

3. Using paper towels, wipe garlic paste off roast. Rub pepper and garlic salt all over meat. Grill directly over coals until well browned, about 5 minutes per side. Carefully

continued on page 12

continued from page 11

remove roast and cooking grate from grill and scatter wood chips over coals. Replace cooking grate and arrange roast on cooler side of grill. Cover, positioning lid vents directly over meat, and cook until roast registers about 130 degrees (for medium-rare), about 20 minutes. Transfer meat to cutting board, tent loosely with foil, and let rest for 20 minutes. Slice thinly across the grain. Serve.

CALIFORNIA BARBECUED TRI-TIP ON A GAS GRILL

Prepare recipe for California Barbecued Tri-Tip through step 1. Soak wood chips in bowl of water to cover for 15 minutes, seal in foil packet (see page 31), and place over primary burner. Turn all burners to high and close lid, keeping grill covered until wood chips begin to smoke heavily, about 15 minutes. Scrape cooking grate clean. Wipe garlic paste off roast. Rub pepper and garlic salt all over meat. Place roast on side of grate opposite primary burner and grill, covered, until well browned, about 5 minutes per side. Leave primary burner on high and turn all other burners off; cook until roast registers about 130 degrees (for medium-rare), about 20 minutes. Rest and slice as directed.

What Is a Tri-Tip?

Also known as a "bottom sirloin roast," "bottom sirloin butt," or "triangle roast," tri-tip is cut from the bottom sirloin primal, an area near the rear leg of the cow, adjacent to the round and flank. Before being "discovered" as a steak (see "The American Table," page 11), this cut was thought to be tough and was typically ground into hamburger or cut into stew meat.

Tuscan Potato Salad

The bold flavors of garlic, rosemary, roasted red peppers, and Parmesan put an Italian spin on a classic summertime salad.

When it comes to potato salad, the creamy American version still reigns supreme. But we also like a lighter Italian-inspired preparation flavored with olive oil, wine vinegar, garlic, and herbs. Unfortunately, things tend to get lost in translation. Many American recipes for Tuscan potato salad start with bottled Italian salad dressing, which makes the salad taste bitter. Others begin with homemade dressing (better), but the results are oddly bland or greasy.

I started with the vinaigrette. Tasters preferred red wine vinegar above all others—especially when I cut it with a little water to temper its harshness, which was also balanced by the assertive flavor of extra-virgin olive oil. Garlic was a natural addition; two minced cloves proved to be just right. As for the herbs, tasters opted for a mere teaspoon of potent rosemary (its flavor intensified the longer the dressing sat) and a finishing hit of parsley. A little mustard tied everything together and helped emulsify the dressing.

Russets and Yukon Golds were too tender and mealy; the sturdy, waxy texture of small red potatoes was ideal. Slicing the potatoes rather than quartering them created more surface area for the vinaigrette to soak into (see photos at right).

When it came time to select the Italian-accented add-ins, I tried artichokes, anchovies, olives, sun-dried tomatoes, and capers, but their pungent flavors were too dominant. It was clear that a little touch of Tuscan restraint was key. Briny roasted red peppers added subtle smoky flavor, and Parmesan cheese offered a nutty richness that worked perfectly with the tart vinaigrette. –Kelley Baker

TUSCAN POTATO SALAD
SERVES 6

Shred the cheese on the big holes of a box grater. This potato salad can be refrigerated for up to 2 days.

- 2 pounds small red potatoes (about 2 inches in diameter), scrubbed and sliced 1/4 inch thick
  Salt and pepper
- 3 tablespoons red wine vinegar
- 2 tablespoons water
- 2 garlic cloves, minced
- 1 teaspoon minced fresh rosemary
- 2 teaspoons Dijon mustard
- 1/4 cup extra-virgin olive oil
- 2 tablespoons finely chopped fresh parsley
- 2 large jarred roasted red peppers, drained and sliced thin
- 1/2 cup shredded Parmesan cheese (see note)

1. Bring potatoes, 2 tablespoons salt, and enough water to cover potatoes by 1 inch to boil in large saucepan over high heat. Reduce heat to medium and simmer until potatoes are just tender, about 5 minutes.

2. Drain potatoes thoroughly in colander and spread in even layer on rimmed baking sheet. Drizzle half of vinegar mixture over hot potatoes and

Careful assembly and a little restraint with the ingredient list ensure that the bold flavors of this salad complement (and don't compete with) each other.

While potatoes simmer, whisk vinegar, water, garlic, rosemary, 1/2 teaspoon salt, and 1/4 teaspoon pepper in large bowl.

let stand until cool, about 20 minutes. Stir mustard into remaining vinegar mixture, then slowly whisk in oil.

3. Scatter parsley, peppers, and Parmesan evenly over potatoes. Transfer potato mixture to bowl with vinaigrette and toss gently until combined. Serve.

Kitchen Know-How DRESSED FOR SUCCESS

When we tossed hot potatoes with vinaigrette, we found that the oil coated the potatoes, preventing the dressing from penetrating and deeply seasoning them. In addition, rigorous tossing of the dressed potatoes and add-ins resulted in torn skins and broken spuds. We addressed these problems by spreading the hot potatoes on a baking sheet and sprinkling on the oil-free vinaigrette base. This step infused the potatoes with flavor while minimizing the need to toss them later on.

1. After arranging the hot potatoes in a single layer on a rimmed baking sheet, evenly drizzle on the vinegar mixture.

2. Once the potatoes are cooled, scatter the parsley, red pepper, and cheese evenly over the potatoes.

3. Transfer the potato mixture to a bowl with the vinaigrette and gently toss until evenly coated.

Grilled Mustard-Glazed Pork Loin

To fully infuse the pork loin with mustard flavor, we apply our spicy-sweet glaze before, during, and after grilling.

Two surefire ways to dress up a pork roast are to give it a flavorful, deeply caramelized crust on the grill and to serve it with a savory-sweet mustard glaze. So why not the best of both worlds: a grilled pork roast cloaked in a sharp and sweet mustard glaze?

Identifying the right roast was easy. Boneless pork loin roasts are large, tender, widely available, quick to cook, and easy to carve. This cut is very lean and can easily dry out if overcooked, so I'd have to be careful not to mishandle it. Loin roasts come with a thin layer of fat on the surface, and my tasters much preferred the added moisture and flavor that resulted from leaving it untrimmed, especially when I scored the fat (see photo at right).

The test kitchen's method for grilling large cuts is to use indirect heat, which allows the meat to cook through without the exterior burning. Indirect heat is easy to set up; simply isolate the fire on one side of the grill and place the meat on the cooler side, opposite the flame. I did find, however, that a better crust developed when I browned the roast directly over the flame before moving it to the cool side.

I turned my attention to the mustard glaze. I bought a dozen types of mustard, slathered them onto as many roasts, and gathered my tasters to evaluate. Aside from the awful dry mustard powder (one taster said he could understand why mustard gas was used in warfare), none were total failures. The clear winner, however, was grainy mustard, which tasters loved for its spicy crunch. After rejecting honey as too distinct and various jams and jellies as too chunky and sweet, I was relieved that my last test turned up the ideal base for the mustard glaze: Apple jelly was smooth and not too sweet, and its flavor married perfectly with the main attractions. A little brown sugar (for flavor and improved browning), garlic, and fresh thyme (preferred for its ability to draw flavors out of the other ingredients) added extra layers of flavor to the glaze.

Most recipes brush the glaze onto the roast in the last few moments of cooking, but this resulted in barely perceptible mustard flavor. I made some extra glaze and rubbed it into the meat prior to grilling, then brushed the roast with the remainder early and often once it hit the grill. The initial wet rub improved the crust, and frequent applications helped develop a thick, attractive, and flavorful shellac of glaze on the roast. For a final hit of mustard flavor, I reserved some glaze to drizzle on the slices of meat just before serving. –Adam Ried

GRILLED MUSTARD-GLAZED PORK LOIN
SERVES 6 TO 8
Dijon and yellow mustards also work well in the glaze, but make certain to use apple jelly, not apple butter. Look for a pork roast with about 1/4 inch of fat on top and tie the roast at 1-inch intervals to ensure an even shape.

1/2   **cup grainy mustard**
6   **tablespoons apple jelly**
2   **tablespoons dark brown sugar**
2   **tablespoons extra-virgin olive oil**
1   **large garlic clove, minced**
2   **teaspoons minced fresh thyme**
1/2   **teaspoon salt**
3/4   **teaspoon pepper**
1   **boneless pork loin roast (2 1/2 to 3 pounds), fat on top scored lightly (see photo at right) and tied (see note)**

1. Open bottom vent on grill. Light large chimney starter filled with charcoal briquettes (about 100 coals) and burn until covered with fine gray ash. Pour coals evenly over one half of grill. Set cooking grate in place, cover, open lid vent completely, and let grill heat for 5 minutes. Meanwhile, whisk mustard, jelly, sugar, oil, garlic, thyme, salt, and pepper in medium bowl. Reserve one-third of mustard mixture for serving. Coat meat completely with half of remaining mustard mixture.

2. Scrape and oil cooking grate. Grill pork directly over coals until well browned all over, 12 to 15 minutes. Place pork fat-side up on cooler side of grill and brush with about one-third of remaining mustard mixture. Cover, open lid vents completely, and cook, brushing with mustard mixture every 10 minutes, until meat registers 140 degrees, 25 to 40 minutes.

3. Transfer pork to cutting board, tent with foil, and let rest 15 minutes (temperature should rise to 150 degrees). Pour accumulated juices into reserved mustard mixture and whisk to combine. Cut roast into 1/4-inch slices, transfer to platter, and spoon mustard mixture over top. Serve.

GRILLED MUSTARD-GLAZED PORK LOIN ON A GAS GRILL
Heat all burners on high, covered, for 15 minutes. Meanwhile, prepare glaze as directed in step 1, reserving one-third of glaze for serving. Pour half of remaining mustard mixture over pork and rub into meat until completely covered. Scrape and oil cooking grate. Place roast opposite primary burner and grill until well browned all over, 15 to 20 minutes. Turn pork fat-side up, leave primary burner on high, and shut off other burners. Brush roast with one-third of remaining mustard mixture, cover, and cook, brushing with mustard mixture every 10 minutes, until meat registers 140 degrees, 35 to 50 minutes. Proceed with recipe from step 3.

We like to keep a spray bottle of water on hand to quell any flare-ups that occur when browning the pork.

Test Kitchen Know-How
THE BENEFITS OF SCORING

Scoring fat means using a sharp knife to cut a shallow cross-hatch pattern into the fat layer. Use gentle pressure and avoid cutting through the fat and into the meat, which will result in moisture loss. Scoring helps the fat to render (basting the meat and keeping it moist as it cooks) and creates an uneven surface that holds the glaze.

Bolder, Fresher Chicken Salads

Back off the mayo and bump up the seasonings for chicken salads with a creative spin.

Buffalo and Blue Cheese Chicken Salad

Thai Peanut Chicken Salad

Carolina Pimento Cheese Chicken Salad

Cobb Chicken Salad

Call me a heretic, but to me a jar of mayonnaise and some boiled chicken does not a chicken salad make. Sure, some recipes may throw in a rib of celery here or a hard-boiled egg there, but the end result is always the same: a sloppy, stodgy mess of mayo and underseasoned chicken masquerading as chicken salad.

Since bland chicken begets bland chicken salad, I ignored the fact that most recipes call for poached (or even steamed) chicken meat. Instead, I thought I'd develop flavor by starting with a whole bird, seasoning it with salt and pepper, and roasting it to a crisp, golden finish. Although tasters appreciated the rich flavor of the roasted chicken, they were turned off by the soft texture of the dark meat in the chicken salad, and I was turned off by the bird's lengthy cooking time.

Switching to white meat, I tried roasting whole chicken breasts, but this still took a good bit of time. Quickly cooking boneless, skinless chicken breasts on the stovetop proved to be a better option. Not only did they cook in mere minutes, but sautéed to a golden brown, they were every bit as tasty as the roasted chicken.

My goal was to create four distinctly flavored salad variations. Mayonnaise was important in all of them for a smooth and creamy texture, but too much mayo makes any chicken salad heavy and dull. I found that I could replace some of the mayo in each of my dressings with a more flavorful and equally creamy ingredient, such as blue cheese dressing, peanut butter, or sour cream. To lighten the texture of my dressings, I added a potent liquid, such as hot sauce, soy sauce, or lemon juice. My revamped dressings were tastier than plain mayo and also less thick, so they didn't weigh the chicken down.

With a sprinkling of fresh herbs, crumbled cheese, or chopped vegetables, these creamy, creatively flavored chicken salads are worlds better than their deli case counterparts. **–Jeremy Sauer**

SAUTÉED CHICKEN BREASTS FOR SALAD
MAKES 5 CUPS
The sautéed chicken breasts can also be sliced thin and tossed in green salads or pasta dishes.

- 4 boneless, skinless chicken breasts (about 1 1/2 pounds)
  Salt and pepper
- 2 tablespoons vegetable oil

Pat chicken dry with paper towels and season with salt and pepper. Heat oil in large nonstick skillet over medium heat until shimmering. Cook chicken until golden brown and cooked through, about 6 minutes per side. Transfer to plate and refrigerate until chilled, about 30 minutes. Cut into 1/2-inch chunks. Chicken can be refrigerated for up to 2 days.

BUFFALO AND BLUE CHEESE CHICKEN SALAD
MAKES ABOUT 6 CUPS, ENOUGH FOR 6 SANDWICHES
Serve this spicy chicken salad on soft onion rolls. Use a mild hot sauce (like Frank's) here.

- 1/2 cup mayonnaise
- 1/4 cup crumbled blue cheese
- 3 tablespoons hot sauce
- 2 tablespoons bottled blue cheese salad dressing
- 2 celery ribs, sliced thin
- 1 carrot, peeled and chopped fine
- 5 cups cooked chicken breast meat (see box at left)
  Salt and pepper

Combine mayonnaise, cheese, hot sauce, dressing, celery, and carrot in large bowl. Add chicken and toss until coated. Season with salt and pepper. Serve or cover and refrigerate for up to 2 days.

THAI PEANUT CHICKEN SALAD
MAKES ABOUT 6 CUPS, ENOUGH FOR 6 SANDWICHES
Serve wrapped in lavash bread or a tortilla. Use more or less jalapeño as desired.

- 1/2 cup mayonnaise
- 1/4 cup chopped fresh cilantro
- 2 tablespoons peanut butter
- 1 tablespoon soy sauce
- 1 tablespoon lime juice
- 2 teaspoons grated fresh ginger
- 1 red bell pepper, seeded and sliced thin
- 1–2 jalapeño chiles, seeded and minced
- 5 cups cooked chicken breast meat (see box at left)
  Salt and pepper

Combine mayonnaise, cilantro, peanut butter, soy sauce, lime juice, ginger, bell pepper, and jalapeño in large bowl. Add chicken and toss until coated. Season with salt and pepper. Serve or cover and refrigerate for up to 2 days.

CAROLINA PIMENTO CHEESE CHICKEN SALAD
MAKES ABOUT 6 CUPS, ENOUGH FOR 6 SANDWICHES
Serve on a croissant or a split buttermilk biscuit.

- 1 cup shredded cheddar cheese
- 1/2 cup mayonnaise
- 1/2 cup jarred chopped pimentos, drained
- 2 tablespoons sour cream
- 2 tablespoons lemon juice
- 1/8 teaspoon cayenne pepper
- 2 scallions, sliced thin
- 1 garlic clove, minced
- 5 cups cooked chicken breast meat (see box at left)
  Salt and pepper

Combine cheese, mayonnaise, pimentos, sour cream, lemon juice, cayenne, scallions, and garlic in large bowl. Add chicken and toss until coated. Season with salt and pepper. Serve or cover and refrigerate for up to 2 days.

COBB CHICKEN SALAD
MAKES ABOUT 6 CUPS, ENOUGH FOR 6 SANDWICHES
Serve on toasted white bread or a baguette. If making salad in advance, refrigerate bacon separately.

- 1/2 cup mayonnaise
- 1/2 cup crumbled blue cheese
- 2 tablespoons sour cream
- 2 tablespoons lemon juice
- 2 hard-boiled eggs, chopped fine
- 1 avocado, pitted, peeled, and diced
- 5 cups cooked chicken breast meat (see box at left)
  Salt and pepper
- 4 slices bacon, cooked and crumbled

Mix mayonnaise, cheese, sour cream, and lemon juice in large bowl until combined. Add eggs, avocado, and chicken, then toss gently until coated. Season with salt and pepper. Sprinkle with crumbled bacon. Serve or cover and refrigerate for up to 2 days.

High-Rise Herb Biscuits

Jazzing up simple cream biscuits with cheese and dill sounds easy, but the results are usually heavy, greasy, and bland. Could a mystery ingredient save these biscuits from their doorstop fate?

I make simple cream biscuits at least once a week. But having recently sampled a biscuit flavored with bright dill and savory cheese at a local bakery, I had to ask myself, "Why haven't I expanded my repertoire?" After rounding up and baking off several recipes for dill biscuits with cheese, the answer was clear: because all of these biscuits were awful. They were heavy and greasy, and the dill flavor was nonexistent. I set out to create a light biscuit with a perfect balance of herb and cheese flavors.

Starting with my favorite cream biscuit recipe, which contains only flour, cream, salt, sugar, and baking powder, I began by adding varying amounts of both fresh and dried dill. My tasters never warmed to dried dill, but they did like a mere tablespoon of fresh dill for 10 big biscuits.

The cheese proved to be much trickier. All of the recipes I found for cheesy dill biscuits rely on cheddar for bold flavor. But the biscuits I made with cheddar were greasy, because the cheddar separated during baking. Looking for cheeses that don't separate when melted, I tested both American and gouda, but neither added much flavor. Parmesan worked texturally but was too mild on its own, even in large amounts. That's when it hit me: Since these were dilly biscuits, why not try dill Havarti? In combination with the Parmesan, the moist dill Havarti tasted great, melted well, and added another layer of dill flavor.

My biscuits tasted great, but the extra cheese made them too heavy. I tried replacing the cream with milk but was disappointed. Then a taster commented that my biscuits reminded her of "casserole bread," a loaf bread made with cottage cheese and dill that was popular in the 1970s. I gave cottage cheese a shot and was mostly pleased with the results. It added a nice tang and lightened the overall texture of the biscuits. But no one liked risking an encounter with the odd mushy chunk of partially melted cottage cheese. A quick spin in the food processor solved this problem.

My herb biscuits were now lighter, but I wanted a still-fluffier texture. More baking powder gave the biscuits a chemical flavor, but adding baking soda (in combination with lemon juice to trigger its rise) made the biscuits rise up high. With this last change, I finally had well-shaped, light, and rich herb biscuits that were loaded with the flavors of dill and cheese, and I didn't have to go to the bakery to get them.

–Diane Unger

HIGH-RISE HERB BISCUITS

MAKES 10 LARGE BISCUITS

Use fresh, bright green dill for the best herb flavor.

- 2 cups all-purpose flour
- 1 tablespoon sugar
- 1 tablespoon baking powder
- 1 teaspoon baking soda
- 1/2 teaspoon salt
- 1/8 teaspoon cayenne pepper
- 6 tablespoons unsalted butter, 3 tablespoons chilled and cut into 1/2-inch pieces, 3 tablespoons melted
- 1/2 cup shredded dill Havarti cheese
- 1/2 cup grated Parmesan cheese
- 3/4 cup cottage cheese
- 1/2 cup whole milk
- 1 tablespoon chopped fresh dill
- 2 teaspoons lemon juice

We use two leaveners—and a careful cutting technique—to ensure tall, fluffy biscuits every time.

1. Adjust oven rack to upper-middle position and heat oven to 450 degrees. Line baking sheet with parchment paper.

2. Pulse flour, sugar, baking powder, baking soda, salt, cayenne, chilled butter, Havarti, and Parmesan in food processor until mixture resembles wet sand, about ten 1-second pulses. Transfer to large bowl. Process cottage cheese, milk, dill, and lemon juice in food processor until smooth. Stir cottage cheese mixture into flour mixture until combined.

3. On lightly floured countertop, knead dough until smooth, 8 to 10 kneads. Pat dough into 7-inch circle about 1 inch thick. Using 2-inch biscuit cutter dipped in flour, cut out rounds of dough and invert onto prepared baking sheet according to photos at right. Gather remaining dough and pat into 1-inch-thick circle and cut out remaining biscuits.

4. Bake until golden brown, 13 to 15 minutes. Remove from oven and brush tops with melted butter. Cool 5 minutes. Serve warm or hot. The biscuits will keep at room temperature for up to 1 day. (Reheat individual biscuits by microwaving them on highest power for 10 seconds.)

Kitchen Know-How
GUARANTEEING A MILE-HIGH RISE

1. When cutting out the biscuits, use even pressure on both sides of the cutter and don't twist the cutter. You want the circles of dough to have a consistent thickness.
2. Transfer the dough rounds to a parchment-lined baking sheet, inverting them in the process so the flat underside is now facing up. If you skip this step, the biscuits might tip over as they bake.

Secrets to Big Cheese Flavor

Our biscuits use three cheeses—dill havarti, cottage cheese, and Parmesan—to produce hearty cheese flavor.

DILL HAVARTI CHEESE
Another layer of dill flavor

COTTAGE CHEESE
Creamy texture and tang

PARMESAN
Deep nutty flavor

I'm Looking for a Recipe

READERS HELP READERS FIND RECIPES

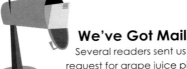

We've Got Mail

Several readers sent us recipes in response to the request for grape juice pie in our August/September 2006 issue. We really like the one submitted by Molly Vaughan (right). Go to **CooksCountry.com** and click **Looking for a Recipe** to find hundreds of recipes submitted by readers who responded to requests in previous issues of *Cook's Country*.

GRAPE JUICE PIE Molly Vaughan Ashtabula, Ohio

SERVES 8

Molly says: My mom and her sister have competed through the years as to who makes the best grape juice pie. My aunt actually bakes a fresh grape filling, but it's my mom's version (which I think she got from the back of a grape juice bottle) that wins with my kids every time. Maybe it's the creamy ice cream filling or that nostalgic flavor combo of peanuts and jelly. I hope you enjoy!

1	envelope plain gelatin
1/3	cup sugar
	Pinch salt
1 1/4	cups boiling grape juice
1/2	teaspoon chopped lemon zest
2	tablespoons lemon juice
2	cups vanilla ice cream
1	baked 9-inch pie crust
	Sweetened whipped cream
	Chopped salted peanuts

INSTRUCTIONS: Dissolve gelatin, sugar, and salt in hot grape juice. Stir in lemon zest and juice, then pour over ice cream. Stir until smooth. Pour into pie crust and chill until set. Pipe whipped cream around pie edges and sprinkle with peanuts.

Glossy Fudge Frosting

While visiting a friend in the South, I enjoyed a delicious slice of fudge cake blanketed with a smooth, glossy, almost translucent fudge frosting with good chocolate flavor. It came from a shop called the Buttercup Bakery, and I've had something similar on fudge cake purchased at Mike's Pastry in Boston. I would like to learn how to make frosting like this, but the recipes I've found for fudge frosting all produce a firm, often slightly grainy, opaque frosting that is much more like finished fudge. If anyone has a recipe for the glossy kind, I would love to be able to make it at home.

Rachel Billings
Holland, Mich.

Putsins

My mother's family used to make putsins around the holidays. They resembled large potato dumplings with salt pork in the center, and they were served in broth. My grandmother was Canadian, but these were completely different from the putsins I have seen in Canada, which are more like french fries covered in gravy and cheese. In my grandmother's recipe, all of the potato processing was done by hand. Does anyone have this recipe?

Matt Foderado
Via e-mail

Patience Fudge

I have vivid memories of my mother and my grandmother standing over a pot, stirring for ages while they made what they called patience fudge. I have searched for burnt-sugar fudge and burnt-butter fudge but have had no luck finding a similar recipe. Does anyone have a recipe for this caramel-flavored candy?

J. Klinsky
Watsonville, Calif.

York Steak House Honey-Roasted Chicken

In the 1980s, there was a chain restaurant called the York Steak House. This cafeteria-type restaurant always featured a honey-roasted chicken. I would appreciate it if anyone could send me this recipe.

Bonnie Traverse
Madison, Wis.

OK Café's Squash Casserole

I am looking for the recipe for squash casserole from a restaurant in Atlanta called OK Café. They serve wonderful Southern comfort food in a fun, diner-like atmosphere. It is so rich and creamy and truly delicious. I was told it has mayonnaise in it!

Alison Huie
Denver, Colo.

Mary McBride's Chocolate Cream Pie

There was a chocolate cream pie recipe in one of the books of Mary Margaret McBride's 12-volume *Encyclopedia of Cooking*. My mother used to make this, and it was awesome. Can anyone help me find this recipe?

Russ Freeman
Antioch, Ill.

Cookies from Calabria

I am looking for the recipe for a cookie that I ate many years ago. My grandmother would bring them back from Calabria, Italy, in the 1950s. I believe that they were made with honey and almonds. Some recipes I have found online have stated that grape juice was used as a sweetener. These cookies were not too soft, and they had a nice taste. They were brown in color and had a fish shape. Please help me in finding this recipe.

Ralph DeMasi
Mount Vernon, N.Y.

DeFusco's Pagoda Cake

I have searched and searched and asked all around. Has someone else besides me heard of a pagoda cake? It is a flaky concoction featuring several different fillings located all around the "pagoda" sections (chocolate pudding, different fruit fillings, custard, etc.). Basically, each slice brings a different taste. From what I understand, it is sometimes referred to as a good-luck cake and given as a housewarming gift. Can anyone out there help me with this? I had this delectable delight while in Cranston, R.I., from a bakery called DeFusco's, but they aren't talking!

Rose-Marie Vieira
Leicester, N.C.

Cranberry Mold from Lansing

In the early 1970s, the Lansing, Mich., Board of Water and Light held an open house, and they passed out a recipe booklet that I have since lost. It contained a recipe for a cranberry mold that used canned cranberries, walnuts, cream cheese, and some type of gelatin, as well as some other ingredients. I would love to have this recipe again. It was heavenly, and I always made it for Thanksgiving and Christmas.

Jennifer Roop
Via e-mail

Gooey Butter Cake

I grew up in St. Louis, and my grandmother used to buy square coffeecakes called gooey butter cakes. I've come across a few recipes for this delicious treat, but I am always disappointed.

Andrea Powell
Via e-mail

Pear Honey

When I was living in Georgia, I came across a wonderful recipe for pear honey in an Atlanta newspaper. Besides pears, one of the other ingredients was vinegar. I hope someone can help me find this recipe or one that is similar.

Maryann Hering
Hamilton, Ohio

Sneakers' Subs

I grew up in Portage, Mich., close to Long Lake. There was a little takeout place there called Sneakers. It was a great place to get subs, pizza, and ice cream. My family and I loved their sub sandwiches. They marinated their veggies in what I would call their special sub sauce. They closed about 17 years ago. If anyone has the recipe, please let me know. I have spent years trying to copy it, and our family went into mourning when they closed.

Kristen M. Thompson
Portage, Mich.

Grandma's Fruitcake

When I was younger, my grandmother, who was from North Carolina, made this great fruitcake. It was full of pecans and dried fruit, and it was very moist. She would wrap it in aluminum foil and keep it in the fridge for several weeks before serving it for Christmas. She would take it out every single day and sprinkle something over it; I thought it was rum, but my mom disagrees. No one in our family has the recipe, and I have tried numerous others, but I just can't get that rich and dark flavor. Does this sound familiar to anyone? I sure would like to revive that holiday tradition!

Debbie Brown
Coarsegold, Calif.

Are you looking for a special recipe? Or do you have a recipe a fellow *Cook's Country* reader is seeking? Post your requests and recipes by visiting **CooksCountry.com** and clicking on **Looking for a Recipe**. We'll share recipe requests and found recipes on **CooksCountry.com** and print as many as we can in the magazine. You may also write to us at Looking for a Recipe, Cook's Country, P.O. Box 470739, Brookline, MA 02447.

Find the Rooster!

A tiny version of this rooster has been hidden somewhere in the pages of this issue. If you find it, write to us with its location (plus your name and address) and you will be entered into a random drawing. The first correct entry drawn will receive the All-Clad Stainless 4-Quart Sauce Pan (our test winner—see page 29), and the next five will each receive a complimentary one-year subscription to *Cook's Country*. To enter the contest, visit **CooksCountry.com/emailus** or write to us at Rooster, Cook's Country, P.O. Box 470739, Brookline, MA 02447. Entries are due by July 31, 2007.

Did you find the rooster in the February/March 2007 issue? It was hidden in the Crunchy Potato Wedges photo on page 14. Emily Smith of South Bend, Ind., spotted it and won an All-Clad Stainless 12-Quart Stock Pot.

GRILLED PORK TENDERLOIN WITH CORN SALAD

PORK CHOPS WITH ORANGE-GINGER GLAZE

PENNE WITH SUN-DRIED TOMATO CREAM SAUCE

**GARLIC CHICKEN
WITH SWEET ROASTED PEPPER SAUCE**

PORK CHOPS WITH ORANGE-GINGER GLAZE
SERVES 4

Use a vegetable peeler to obtain wide strips of orange zest. Frank's is our favorite brand of hot sauce. If using a hotter brand, such as Tabasco, reduce the amount to 1 teaspoon.

- 4 bone-in center-cut pork chops, about 1 inch thick
  Salt and pepper
- 2 tablespoons vegetable oil
- 1/2 small onion, chopped fine
- 1/2 teaspoon ground ginger
- 1 cup juice plus 2 strips zest from 3 to 4 oranges (see note)
- 1/2 cup low-sodium chicken broth
- 1/4 cup packed dark brown sugar
- 1 tablespoon hot sauce (see note)
- 1 tablespoon unsalted butter

1. Pat chops dry with paper towels and season with salt and pepper. Heat 1 tablespoon oil in large skillet over medium-high heat until just smoking. Add chops and cook until well browned, about 4 minutes per side. Transfer to plate.

2. Add remaining oil and onion to skillet and cook until lightly browned, about 3 minutes. Stir in ginger and cook until fragrant, about 30 seconds. Stir in juice, zest, broth, sugar, and hot sauce, scraping up any browned bits from bottom of pan. Cook until sauce thickens slightly, about 3 minutes.

3. Return chops and any accumulated juices to skillet. Simmer, turning once or twice, until sauce glazes chops and meat registers 145 degrees, 3 to 5 minutes. Transfer chops to platter. Off heat, whisk butter into glaze and season with salt and pepper. Spoon glaze over chops. Serve.

GRILLED PORK TENDERLOIN WITH CORN SALAD
SERVES 4

Frozen Shoepeg, a sweet white corn, works well here.

- 6 tablespoons extra-virgin olive oil
- 5 tablespoons red wine vinegar
- 2 garlic cloves, minced
- 1 teaspoon ground cumin
  Salt and pepper
- 1 (9-ounce) package frozen corn, thawed (see note)
- 1 (15.5-ounce) can pinto beans, drained
- 1/4 cup chopped fresh cilantro
- 4 scallions, sliced thin
- 2 pork tenderloins (1 1/2 to 2 pounds total)

1. Whisk oil, vinegar, garlic, and cumin in large bowl and season with salt and pepper. Reserve 1/4 cup vinaigrette. Stir corn, beans, cilantro, and scallions together with remaining vinaigrette. Cover and let sit while grilling pork.

2. Season pork with salt and pepper and grill over hot fire until browned on all sides and internal temperature reaches 145 degrees, about 12 minutes. Transfer to cutting board, tent with foil, and let rest 5 minutes. Slice pork into 1-inch pieces and drizzle with reserved vinaigrette. Spoon corn salad onto individual plates and top with pork. Serve.

GARLIC CHICKEN WITH SWEET ROASTED PEPPER SAUCE
SERVES 4

Divinia brand jarred roasted peppers were the winners of a test kitchen taste test.

- 4 boneless, skinless chicken breasts (about 1 1/2 pounds)
  Salt and pepper
- 2 tablespoons vegetable oil
- 1 small onion, sliced thin
- 6 garlic cloves, sliced thin
- 1 (12-ounce) jar roasted peppers, drained and chopped (see note)
- 2 teaspoons sugar
- 1 1/2 cups low-sodium chicken broth
- 1/4 cup chopped fresh basil
- 2 tablespoons unsalted butter

1. Pat chicken dry with paper towels and season with salt and pepper. Heat oil in large skillet over medium-high heat until just smoking. Cook chicken until golden brown, about 5 minutes per side. Transfer to plate.

2. Add onion to fat in skillet and cook until lightly browned, about 3 minutes. Stir in garlic and cook until fragrant, about 1 minute. Add peppers, sugar, broth, and browned chicken along with any accumulated juices and bring to boil. Reduce heat to medium and simmer until chicken is cooked through, about 5 minutes.

3. Transfer chicken to serving platter and tent with foil. Return skillet to high heat and simmer until sauce is slightly thickened, about 5 minutes. Off heat, whisk in basil and butter. Season with salt and pepper. Pour sauce over chicken. Serve.

PENNE WITH SUN-DRIED TOMATO CREAM SAUCE
SERVES 4

If desired, sprinkle with grated Parmesan before serving.

- 2 tablespoons unsalted butter
- 1 small onion, chopped fine
- 2 garlic cloves, minced
- 1/2 cup sun-dried tomatoes packed in oil, rinsed, patted dry, and minced
- 1 (14.5-ounce) can diced tomatoes
- 1 cup heavy cream
  Salt
- 1 pound penne or ziti
- 1/4 cup chopped fresh basil
  Ground black pepper

1. Bring 4 quarts water to boil in large pot. Meanwhile, melt butter in large skillet over medium heat. Cook onion until soft and lightly browned, about 5 minutes. Stir in garlic and cook until fragrant, about 30 seconds. Stir in sun-dried tomatoes, diced tomatoes, and cream. Increase heat to medium-high and simmer until slightly thickened, about 5 minutes.

2. Add 1 tablespoon salt and pasta to boiling water and cook until al dente. Reserve 1/4 cup cooking water, drain pasta, and return to pot. Add sauce and basil to pot and toss to combine, adding reserved pasta water as needed. Season with salt and pepper. Serve.

TUSCAN GRILLED CHICKEN SALAD

THREE-MEAT CALZONE

BEER-STEAMED SHRIMP WITH GARLIC BUTTER

SWEET-AND-SOUR STIR-FRIED CHICKEN

THREE-MEAT CALZONE
SERVES 4
Serve this overstuffed calzone with your favorite tomato sauce if desired.

- 6 ounces thinly sliced deli salami
- 2 ounces thinly sliced deli pepperoni
- 1 cup ricotta cheese
- 1/2 cup grated Parmesan cheese
- 1/2 cup chopped fresh basil
- 2 tablespoons extra-virgin olive oil
  Flour for dusting
- 1 (1-pound) ball ready-made pizza dough
- 4 ounces thinly sliced deli capiccola
- 8 ounces thinly sliced deli mozzarella cheese

1. Adjust oven rack to upper-middle position and heat oven to 450 degrees. Arrange salami and pepperoni on microwave-safe plate lined with paper towels. Cover with 2 more paper towels and microwave on high until fat begins to render, 1 minute. Combine ricotta, Parmesan, and basil in bowl.

2. Brush 1 tablespoon oil over rimmed baking sheet. On lightly floured work surface, roll dough into 14-inch round about 1/4 inch thick. Layer half of salami, pepperoni, capiccola, and mozzarella on one half of dough round, leaving 1-inch border around edges. Spoon ricotta mixture over mozzarella and layer with remaining salami, pepperoni, capiccola, and mozzarella. Brush edges of dough with water, fold over filling, and crimp edges to seal.

3. Transfer to oiled baking sheet and cut four 1-inch slits on top of calzone. Brush with remaining oil and bake until golden brown, about 15 minutes. Transfer to wire rack and let cool for 5 minutes. Cut into 4 wedges. Serve.

TUSCAN GRILLED CHICKEN SALAD
SERVES 4
If you can find them, tiny balls of fresh mozzarella (sometimes labeled "bocconcini") make a nice presentation here instead of the chunks of mozzarella.

- 3/4 cup extra-virgin olive oil
- 1/4 cup red wine vinegar
- 3 small garlic cloves, minced
  Salt and pepper
- 8 ounces fresh mozzarella, cut into 1/2-inch chunks (see note)
- 1 pint cherry tomatoes, halved
- 1/2 cup pitted kalamata olives, chopped
- 4 boneless, skinless chicken breasts (about 1 1/2 pounds)
- 4 (1-inch-thick) slices crusty Italian bread
- 1 (8-ounce) bag baby arugula (about 8 cups)

1. Whisk oil, vinegar, and garlic in small bowl and season with salt and pepper. Toss mozzarella, tomatoes, olives, and 2 tablespoons vinaigrette in large bowl.

2. Season chicken with salt and pepper. Grill over hot fire until cooked through, about 5 minutes per side. Brush bread slices with 2 tablespoons vinaigrette and grill over hot fire until golden brown on both sides, about 1 minute per side.

3. Add arugula and remaining dressing to bowl with mozzarella mixture and toss until combined. Transfer to individual plates. Slice chicken and place on top of salad. Serve with grilled bread.

SWEET-AND-SOUR STIR-FRIED CHICKEN
SERVES 4
We like a mixture of broccoli, snow peas, peppers, red onion, and baby corn from the supermarket salad bar. Serve over steamed rice, with soy sauce or hot sauce, if desired.

- 6 tablespoons red wine vinegar
- 1 (20-ounce) can pineapple chunks in juice, drained, 6 tablespoons juice reserved
- 6 tablespoons sugar
- 3 tablespoons ketchup
- 1 tablespoon cornstarch
- 3 tablespoons vegetable oil
- 4 boneless, skinless chicken breasts (about 1 1/2 pounds), cut crosswise into 1/2-inch-thick slices
- 1 pound salad bar vegetables, cut into bite-sized pieces (see note)
- 3 garlic cloves, minced
- 1 tablespoon grated fresh ginger

1. Whisk vinegar, reserved pineapple juice, sugar, ketchup, and cornstarch in bowl. Heat 1 tablespoon oil in large nonstick skillet over medium-high heat until just smoking. Add half of chicken and cook, stirring often, until no longer pink, about 3 minutes. Transfer to plate and repeat with additional 1 tablespoon oil and remaining chicken.

2. Add remaining oil and vegetables to now-empty skillet and cook until softened, 4 to 6 minutes. Add pineapple chunks, garlic, and ginger and cook until fragrant, about 1 minute. Add vinegar mixture and chicken along with any accumulated juices to skillet and simmer until sauce is thickened, about 2 minutes. Serve.

BEER-STEAMED SHRIMP WITH GARLIC BUTTER
SERVES 4
If you can find them, use E-Z Peel shrimp; the shells on these shrimp have already been slit open, which makes peeling the cooked shrimp at the table easier. Either way, this dish makes for messy eating, so serve with plenty of napkins.

- 6 tablespoons unsalted butter
- 4 garlic cloves, minced
- 1 tablespoon lemon juice
- 1 teaspoon hot sauce
- 1 (12-ounce) can beer
- 4 teaspoons Old Bay seasoning
- 2 pounds extra-large shell-on shrimp (see note)

1. Heat butter and garlic in Dutch oven over medium heat until sizzling and fragrant, about 4 minutes. Pour garlic butter into serving bowl and stir in lemon juice and hot sauce. Cover and keep warm.

2. Fit Dutch oven with steamer basket, add beer, and bring to boil over medium-high heat. Sprinkle Old Bay evenly over shrimp and transfer to steamer basket. Cover and steam until shrimp are cooked through, 4 to 6 minutes. Transfer to serving platter. Serve with warm garlic butter for dipping.

Ultimate Chocolate Milkshake

It takes more than ice cream, chocolate syrup, and milk to create a chocolate shake worthy of the "ultimate" title.

Our creamy, deeply chocolaty shakes are thicker and richer than anything you can order at the ice cream shop.

The first thing my husband, Woody, does when we eat at a new restaurant is scan the menu for a chocolate shake, claiming he's "out to find the best in Boston." Since most of his orders arrive with the overflow in a frosty metal cup, I long ago assumed ownership of this second serving and have joined him in his search. It has been a long and disappointing journey. Time after time, the shakes arrive thin and soupy and melt into chocolate milk before the final slurp. And the flavor is just as bad—the chocolate always seems like an afterthought, most likely supplied by a meager squeeze of syrup. Tired of waiting for the perfect shake to come to me, I dusted off my blender and set out to create my own thick, creamy, and super-chocolaty milkshake.

Finding the perfect texture was a matter of determining the right ratio of ice cream to milk. Most of the recipes I found called for 2 to 3 cups of ice cream and ½ cup of milk for four servings; my tasters, however, thought that ratio made skimpy shakes. After testing various amounts, they settled on a whopping 5 cups of ice cream to pair with ½ cup of whole milk. (Leaving no stone unturned, I did test half-and-half, heavy cream, skim milk, and even melted ice cream as replacements for whole milk: None were improvements.) My shake was now just thin enough to be enjoyed with a straw but thick enough to keep its chill while drinking.

It was time to incorporate "ultimate" chocolate flavor. Chocolate shakes are usually made by adding chocolate syrup to vanilla ice cream, but I wondered if I could get more chocolate flavor by using chocolate ice cream. The chocolate ice cream did give the shakes more chocolate flavor, but it wasn't better: My tasters rejected these shakes as "sour," even when I used high-priced gourmet ice cream. Using a mixture of chocolate and vanilla ice creams eliminated the sourness, but now my shakes weren't chocolaty enough.

I had another idea—chocolate sorbet, which packs more intense chocolate flavor than chocolate ice cream. As I'd suspected, shakes made with just the sorbet were granular and slushy. But when I cut the sorbet with twice as much vanilla ice cream, my shakes were thick, creamy, and definitely chocolaty.

But I didn't want "chocolaty"; I wanted ultimate chocolate flavor. The chocolate syrup was still part of my working recipe, but frankly didn't seem to be doing much—it was more sweet than chocolaty. Trying to think creatively, I gathered a lengthy lineup of chocolate products to try in my shakes: hot cocoa mix, pudding cups, pudding mix, chocolate Yoo-Hoo, chocolate milk, and even hot fudge. But everything was either too sweet or whirled up with a whimper—until I tried the hot fudge. The deep, almost bittersweet flavor of the hot fudge was worlds better than the syrup.

And for the final taste test, I headed home and whipped up my new concoction for Woody. Silence, and then, with a crooked smile, he said, "Looks like the search is over." That's good enough for me. **–Cali Rich**

ULTIMATE CHOCOLATE MILKSHAKE SERVES 4

Soften the ice cream and sorbet at room temperature for 5 minutes before scooping. If your hot fudge sauce is refrigerated, microwave 2 tablespoons in a small dish for 5 seconds. This recipe is easily halved.

- **3 cups vanilla ice cream, cut into large chunks**
- **1½ cups chocolate sorbet, cut into large chunks**
- **½ cup whole milk**
- **2 tablespoons hot fudge sauce, at room temperature**

Combine all ingredients in food processor or blender and puree until smooth, scraping down sides as needed. Pour into chilled glasses. Serve.

Shake Up Your Shake

If you're craving a little something extra in your shake, these add-ins should hit the spot.

COOKIES

Oreos, Nutter Butters, and Keebler's Fudge Shoppe Grasshoppers are our favorites. Before adding ice cream and sorbet to food processor or blender, pulse ¾ cup milk, hot fudge sauce, and 8 cookies until finely ground. Add ice cream and sorbet and continue to blend until smooth.

CANDY

We like to use 1 Snickers or Milky Way Bar, 4 Reese's Peanut Butter Cups, or ½ cup Whoppers. Before adding ice cream and sorbet to food processor or blender, pulse ½ cup milk, hot fudge sauce, and candy until finely ground. Add ice cream and sorbet and continue to blend until smooth.

Building the Best Chocolate Flavor

While most shake recipes rely solely on chocolate syrup, we got a super-jolt of chocolate flavor by using a couple of unusual suspects. Chocolate sorbet (paired with vanilla ice cream) gave our shake a potent—but not too sweet—chocolate punch, while using hot fudge topping (see page 30 for our taste test results) instead of the syrup made our chocolate shake downright fudgy.

HOT FUDGE

CHOCOLATE SORBET

Smoked Double-Thick Pork Chops

I do okay with most items on the grill, but not with double-thick pork chops. If I reduce the heat too much in order to maintain juiciness, they are gray and pale. Can the home cook get great taste, good color, and tenderness on the grill out of today's pork? –Glenn R. Baker, Decatur, Ill.

In the heart of grilling season, supermarket butchers tag all cuts of meat with stickers promising "Always Juicy" and "Great on the Grill!" Recently a package of huge, double-thick pork chops—adorned with a "Great on the Grill!" sticker—caught my eye. They were a good 2 inches thick, with a giant rib bone that could barely be contained by the plastic wrapping. Wanting to see if these mammoths of the meat case would live up to their promise, I bought some and headed to the grill.

These chops were so big that they felt more like mini-roasts, so I knew that grilling them over a hot fire, as I do with regular pork chops, was out of the question because the exterior would burn before the inside was done. Brining, a common test kitchen technique of soaking meat in a salt-water solution to promote even seasoning and cooking, would be redundant here because my chops, like most pork sold today, were already "enhanced," or injected with a solution to keep the meat from drying out (hence the "Always Juicy" stickers). My goal was evenly cooked meat with more flavor than just the salt added during the "enhancement" process.

Tackling the even cooking problem first, I decided to try the authentic barbecue method of "low and slow," whereby meat is cooked, covered and with indirect heat, for a long time on the cooler side of the grill. This technique gives meat plenty of time to cook through evenly at a relatively gentle temperature. I started with a full chimney of coals, hefted my chops onto the grill opposite the coals, and waited patiently for them to cook. When I pulled the lid off an hour later, the good news was that the meat was tender and juicy throughout; the bad news was that it tasted steamed and the exterior was pale.

Normal-sized pork chops are not on the grill long enough to merit smoking. But because these huge chops were spending about an hour on the covered grill, adding wood smoke seemed like a good way to increase the flavor. As it turned out, there's a fine line between subtle flavor and suffocating smoke. After testing wood amounts ranging from ½ to 3 cups, I settled on 2 cups of hickory chips, presoaked and wrapped in a foil packet, which provides steady smoke throughout the cooking time by slowing the rate at which the wood burns (see page 31). My chops were finally moist and tender and had a nice level of smoke flavor, but they were still missing something.

I recalled what I liked most about thinner, quicker-grilling chops: the crisp texture and smoky flavor of a seared crust. To create the most flavorful crust possible, I started by coating the raw chops with a spice rub; after a lot of testing, my tasters settled on a combination of brown sugar, fennel, cumin, coriander, paprika, salt, and pepper. Then, when the chops were almost done, I uncovered the grill and moved them to the hot side of the grate. The coals still had enough life left in them to toast the spices on the surface of the meat, giving the chops richer flavor, and the brown sugar in the rub caramelized to a gorgeous mahogany color. With a method that combined elements of barbecue and quick grilling, I'd finally figured out how to make these behemoth chops truly "Great on the Grill!"

–Diane Unger

SMOKED DOUBLE-THICK PORK CHOPS SERVES 6 TO 8

We prefer blade chops, which have more fat to prevent drying out on the grill, but leaner loin chops will also work. These chops are huge and are best sliced off the bone before serving.

- ¼ cup packed dark brown sugar
- 1 tablespoon ground fennel
- 1 tablespoon ground cumin
- 1 tablespoon ground coriander
- 1 tablespoon paprika
- 1 teaspoon salt
- 1 teaspoon pepper
- 4 (20- to 24-ounce) bone-in blade-cut pork chops, about 2 inches thick (see note)
- 2 cups wood chips, preferably hickory (see page 30)

1. Combine sugar, fennel, cumin, coriander, paprika, salt, and pepper and rub mixture all over pork chops. Cover with plastic wrap and refrigerate for at least 1 hour or up to 24 hours.

2. Soak wood chips in bowl of water to cover for 15 minutes. Prepare chips in foil packet as directed on page 31. Open bottom vent on grill. Light large chimney starter filled with charcoal briquettes (about 100) and burn until charcoal is covered with fine gray ash. Pour hot coals into pile on one side of grill and lay foil packet over coals. Set cooking grate in place, cover, open lid vent halfway, and let grill heat for 5 minutes. Scrape cooking grate clean.

3. Arrange chops, bone side toward fire, on cooler side of grill. Cover, positioning lid vents directly over meat, and cook until chops register 145 degrees, 50 to 60 minutes (if your chops are less than 2 inches thick, start checking them for temperature after 30 minutes). Slide chops directly over fire and cook, uncovered, until well browned, about 2 minutes per side. Transfer to platter and let rest 20 minutes. Serve.

SMOKED DOUBLE-THICK PORK CHOPS ON A GAS GRILL

Prepare recipe for Smoked Double-Thick Pork Chops through step 1. Soak wood chips in bowl of water to cover for 15 minutes, seal in foil packet (cutting vent holes in top), and place over primary burner. Turn all burners to high and close lid, keeping grill covered until wood chips begin to smoke heavily, about 15 minutes. Scrape cooking grate clean. Turn primary burner to medium and turn all other burners off, adjusting temperature of primary burner as needed to maintain average temperature of 275 degrees. Proceed with step 3 as directed.

Deep smoke flavor and a lively spice rub work together to boldly season the ultimate grilled chop.

Spicy Grilled Shrimp

When grilling shrimp, I never know whether to marinate them or brush a sauce on when they are cooking. Which method provides the most flavor? And how do you keep them from overcooking?

–Karen Saracina, North Berwick, Maine

Jolts of grill flavor and spicy heat can enhance the delicately sweet and briny flavor of shrimp, but it's easy to overdo it. Most recipes overcook the shrimp and finish them in a bath of mouth-numbing sauce; I wanted to find a way to produce tender, juicy, perfectly cooked shrimp with a smoky, charred crust and chile flavor that was more than just superficial.

Lean, quick-cooking shrimp can easily become tough and dry, especially when seared over the high heat of the grill. Following the test kitchen's recommended method, I packed peeled shrimp very tightly onto skewers so they would cook more slowly, sprinkled one side of the shrimp with sugar to promote browning, and grilled the sugared side over high heat for a few minutes. When a nice crust had developed, I flipped the skewers and turned off the burners, allowing the second side to finish cooking by gentle residual heat. (A good sear on one side provides plenty of flavor, and searing the second side results only in over-cooking.) This worked like a charm, allowing the interior to stay moist and tender while the exterior developed a flavorful char. This method is easily modified for a charcoal grill by positioning all the coals on one side of the grill to create hot and cool zones.

Now I could concentrate on spicy kick. Starting with the assertive but not incendiary heat of puréed jalapeños and working with flavors that go well with chiles, I added olive oil, lime juice and zest, garlic, cumin, and cayenne and brushed the mixture on my shrimp as they came off the grill. They tasted OK, but the flavor of the sauce wasn't permeating the shrimp. My tasters were more pleased by my next batch, in which I used some of the flavor mixture as a 30-minute marinade and reserved the rest to employ as a finishing sauce.

I was clearly on to something, but I still wanted to get more flavor inside the shrimp. Adding more spice to the marinade overwhelmed the delicate shrimp flavor, and marinating for more than an hour made the shrimp mushy. Looking to get the marinade in more physical contact with the shrimp, it occurred to me to try butterflying them, which would open up more shrimp flesh for the marinade and finishing sauce to flavor. Sure enough, the butterflying worked perfectly and produced the most flavorful shrimp yet.

–Cali Rich

Our grilling technique builds flavor while ensuring that the delicate shrimp don't overcook.

How to SKEWER SHRIMP

Butterflying the shrimp helps the marinade to penetrate and exposes more surface area to which the finishing sauce can cling. Packing the shrimp head-to-tail on the skewers makes a more compact mass, which allows the shrimp to stay on the grill longer without drying out, giving more time for a good sear to develop.

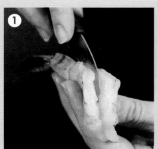

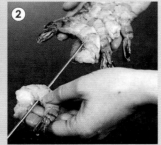

1. Using a paring knife, make a shallow cut down the outside curve of the shrimp to open up the flesh.

2. Alternating the direction of each shrimp as you pack them tightly on the skewer allows about a dozen shrimp to snuggly fit on each skewer.

SPICY GRILLED JALAPEÑO AND LIME SHRIMP SKEWERS
SERVES 4

Buy extra-large shrimp (21 to 25 per pound) for this recipe. Make the marinade with one chile, taste it, and add more to taste if desired. We prefer flat metal skewers (see page 31) that are at least 14 inches long.

Marinade

- 1 jalapeño chile, seeded and chopped (see note)
- 3 tablespoons olive oil
- 1 teaspoon grated lime zest plus 5 tablespoons juice from 3 limes
- 6 garlic cloves, minced
- 1/2 teaspoon ground cumin
- 1/4 teaspoon cayenne pepper
- 1/2 teaspoon salt

Shrimp

- 1 1/2 pounds extra-large shrimp, peeled and deveined
- 1/2 teaspoon sugar
- 1 tablespoon minced fresh cilantro

1. For the marinade: Process all ingredients in food processor until smooth. Reserve 2 tablespoons marinade; transfer remaining marinade to medium bowl.

2. For the shrimp: Pat shrimp dry with paper towels and butterfly according to photo 1 (at left). Add to bowl with marinade and toss to coat. Cover and refrigerate for at least 30 minutes or up to 1 hour.

3. Heat all burners on high for 15 minutes. Scrape cooking grate clean. Meanwhile, thread marinated shrimp on skewers according to photo 2 (at left). Sprinkle one side of shrimp with sugar. Grill shrimp, sugared side down, with lid down, until lightly charred, 3 to 4 minutes. Turn all burners off, flip skewers, close lid, and cook until other side of shrimp is no longer translucent, 1 to 2 minutes. Using tongs, slide shrimp into medium bowl and toss with reserved marinade. Sprinkle with cilantro and serve.

SPICY GRILLED JALAPEÑO AND LIME SHRIMP SKEWERS FOR CHARCOAL GRILL

Prepare recipe for Spicy Grilled Jalapeño and Lime Shrimp Skewers through step 2. Light large chimney starter filled with charcoal briquettes (about 100 coals) and burn until coals are continued on page 20

covered with fine gray ash. Meanwhile, thread marinated shrimp on skewers and sprinkle one side of shrimp with sugar. Pour coals into pile on one side of grill. Set cooking grate in place, cover, and let heat for 5 minutes. Scrape grill grate clean. Grill shrimp sugared side down over the hot part of the grill until lightly charred, 3 to 4 minutes. Flip skewers and move them to cool side of grill. Close lid and let rest until other side of shrimp is no longer translucent, 1 to 2 minutes. Finish shrimp as directed.

SPICY GRILLED RED CHILE AND GINGER SHRIMP SKEWERS

Prepare recipe for Spicy Grilled Jalapeño and Lime Shrimp Skewers, replacing marinade with 1 to 3 seeded and chopped small red chiles (or jalapeños), 2 tablespoons soy sauce, 1 tablespoon toasted sesame oil, 3 tablespoons rice vinegar, 1 minced garlic clove, 1 tablespoon grated fresh ginger, 2 teaspoons sugar, and 1 minced scallion. Prepare and grill shrimp as directed. Replace cilantro with 1 thinly sliced scallion and serve with lime wedges.

SPICY GRILLED CARIBBEAN SHRIMP SKEWERS

Prepare recipe for Spicy Grilled Jalapeño and Lime Shrimp Skewers, replacing marinade with 1 to 2 seeded and chopped habanero or serrano chiles, ¼ cup pineapple juice, 2 tablespoons olive oil, 1 tablespoon white wine vinegar, 3 minced garlic cloves, 1 teaspoon grated fresh ginger, 1 teaspoon brown sugar, 1 teaspoon dried thyme, ¼ teaspoon ground allspice, and ½ teaspoon salt. Prepare and grill shrimp as directed. Replace cilantro with 1 tablespoon minced fresh parsley.

Classic Barbecued Chicken

I love barbecued chicken with a tomato-based sauce "painted" on. My problem is knowing when to add the sauce. Too soon and the chicken is burned outside, too late and the sauce doesn't have time to flavor the meat.

–Sandy Olson, Northwood, Iowa

Smoky grilled chicken smothered in a thick barbecue sauce is one of America's favorite summer meals. But despite its popularity, this recipe causes backyard grillers plenty of headaches. Who hasn't served barbecued chicken that was nearly blackened on the outside yet bloody near the bone? Chicken is hard enough to grill, because the skin races ahead of the meat. Adding barbecue sauce just makes the problem worse. My goal in developing a foolproof recipe for barbecued chicken was to produce perfectly cooked meat that boasted intense flavor from both the grill and a liberal application of tangy-sweet barbecue sauce.

I decided to start with the cooking technique and get to the sauce later. Most recipes call for searing the chicken quickly over high heat to render the fat in the skin and then finishing it over lower heat to gently cook the interior. But we've found that placing raw chicken over a hot (or even medium-hot) fire causes too many flare-ups, resulting in burnt skin. The test kitchen has had much better luck starting chicken over lower heat to slowly and completely render the fat without the danger of flare-ups. Following this method, I spread the coals in an even layer on one side of the grill, added the chicken skin side down to the other side, and covered the grill. We call this method grill-roasting. Thirty minutes later, I had tender chicken that was almost

cooked throughout. But it didn't have much flavor.

I've always been told to never, ever add barbecue sauce to anything until just before it was ready to be pulled off the grill—otherwise the sugar in the sauce will burn. But since my grill-roasted parts weren't cooked directly over a flame, I wondered if I could sauce them at the outset. I couldn't: The sauce turned black and bitter. How could I get deep layers of barbecue flavor without saucing earlier? Seasoning the chicken with a mixture of salt, pepper, and cayenne before it went on the grill added some flavor, but not enough. Then it occurred to me that if I wanted layers of flavor, I needed to have layers of barbecue sauce.

When the chicken was mostly cooked through over the indirect heat, I moved the pieces to the center of the grill (near the coals, but not over them) and introduced sauce in several applications. Constant turning

Our "baste and turn" method builds layers of complex, rich barbecue flavor.

Kitchen Know-How BARBECUED CHICKEN, SLOW AND LOW

First grill-roasting, then basting over moderate heat, and finally finishing with more basting over higher heat ensures rendered, saucy, perfectly cooked chicken. Here's how we do it.

1. Cook the chicken skin side down on the cool side of the grill for about 30 minutes.

2. Move the chicken into a single line near the coals. Begin basting and turning the pieces.

3. When nicely glazed, move the pieces directly over the coals to caramelize the sauce.

and moderate heat allowed me to continually sauce the chicken for about 20 minutes while it finished cooking. This worked great, because just as one layer of sauce was drying, I was adding another coat on top of it, creating a thick, complex, multilayered "skin" of barbecue flavor.

Wanting to finish this chicken with a bang, I moved the pieces directly over the coals, which were fading but still relatively hot, and continued to flip them and slather them with sauce for the final five minutes of cooking. This created a robust, crusty char that my tasters loved. I finally had perfectly cooked chicken with intense barbecue flavor—summer never tasted so sweet. **–Meredith Butcher**

CLASSIC BARBECUED CHICKEN SERVES 4 TO 6
You can use a mix of chicken breasts, thighs, and drumsticks, making sure they add up to about 10 pieces. Any more than that and you won't be able to line them up on the grill. Although our jazzed-up barbecue sauce is best, this recipe also works with plain store-bought sauce; our favorite brand is Bull's-Eye.

Quick BBQ Sauce
    3   cups bottled barbecue sauce
    ¹/₂ cup molasses
    ¹/₂ cup ketchup
    ¹/₄ cup cider vinegar
    3   tablespoons brown mustard
    2   teaspoons onion powder
    1   teaspoon garlic powder

Chicken
    1   teaspoon salt
    1   teaspoon pepper
    ¹/₄ teaspoon cayenne pepper
    3   pounds bone-in, skin-on chicken pieces (breasts, whole legs, thighs, and/or drumsticks), trimmed and breasts halved (see page 30)

1. For the sauce: Whisk all ingredients in medium saucepan and bring to boil over medium-high heat. Reduce heat to medium and cook until

sauce is thick and reduced to 3 cups, about 20 minutes. (Sauce can be refrigerated in airtight container for up to 1 week.)

2. For the chicken: Mix salt, pepper, and cayenne in small bowl. Pat chicken dry with paper towels and rub spice mixture all over chicken pieces.

3. Open bottom vent on grill. Light large chimney starter filled with charcoal briquettes (about 100 coals) and burn until charcoal is covered with fine gray ash. Place 13 by 9-inch disposable aluminum roasting pan on one side of grill and pour coals in even layer over other side of grill. Set cooking grate in place, cover, open lid vents completely, and let grill heat for 5 minutes. Scrape cooking grate clean.

4. Oil grate and place chicken skin side down on cooler side of grill. Cover, with half-opened lid vents over chicken, and cook until chicken begins to brown, 30 to 35 minutes. Move chicken into single line close to coals. Begin flipping chicken and brushing with 2 cups sauce every 5 minutes until sticky, about 20 minutes. Slide chicken pieces over coals and continue to brush chicken until sauce on chicken becomes crusted and internal temperature of breast meat registers 165 degrees and legs, thighs, and drumsticks register 175 degrees, about 5 minutes. Transfer chicken to platter, tent with foil, and let rest 10 minutes. Remove foil and serve, passing remaining sauce at table.

CLASSIC BARBECUED CHICKEN ON A GAS GRILL
Prepare recipe for Classic Barbecued Chicken through step 2. Turn all burners to high, close lid, and heat grill for 15 minutes. Scrape cooking grate clean and oil grate. Leave primary burner on high and turn all other burners off. Position chicken over cooler side of grill, cover, and proceed as directed.

Summer Suppers: Antipasto Pasta Salad

An appetizer platter can shake up a bland and boring pasta salad, but only if you keep the fat in check.

An antipasto platter includes a variety of cured meats, cheeses, and pickled vegetables. As a whole, it's full-flavored and hearty—perfect attributes for a main-course pasta salad. But the recipes I tried for this type of salad were greasy and heavy, with lackluster dressing and not enough flavor in the pasta itself.

My tasters liked pepperoni and sopresatta (a spicy, cured Italian sausage) for the meat component, particularly after I quickly microwaved them to remove excess grease. Strong aged provolone was preferred over milder cheeses, especially when I grated it into the salad for even distribution. For vegetables, my tasters loved roasted red peppers for sweetness, pepperoncini for heat, and homemade marinated mushrooms for earthy flavor. (See page 31 for information on making these in minutes.)

Pasta salads typically use a 2-to-1 ratio of oil to vinegar, but since the meats and cheese were so rich, I found I had to nearly reverse this ratio. Some vinegary brine from the pepperoncini further sharpened the dressing, while a bit of mayonnaise added body and promoted cling.

Most pasta salad recipes call for rinsing the cooked noodles, but this method left me with bloated pasta that didn't absorb any flavor from the dressing. Tossing the hot pasta with the dressing and extra vinegar made the pasta an equal partner in this salad, which is anything but boring.
–Diane Unger

ANTIPASTO PASTA SALAD
SERVES 6 TO 8
We also liked the addition of 1 cup chopped, pitted kalamata olives or 1 cup jarred artichokes, drained and quartered. Use any curly-shaped pasta for this recipe.

    8   ounces sliced pepperoni, cut into ¹/₄-inch strips
    8   ounces thick-sliced sopresatta or salami, halved and cut into ¹/₄-inch strips
    10 tablespoons red wine vinegar
    6   tablespoons extra-virgin olive oil
    3   tablespoons mayonnaise
    1   (12-ounce) jar pepperoncini, drained (2 tablespoons juice reserved), stemmed, and chopped coarse
    4   garlic cloves, minced
    ¹/₄ teaspoon red pepper flakes
        Salt and pepper
    1   pound fusilli or campanelle (see note)
    1   pound white mushrooms, quartered
    1   cup shredded aged provolone
    1   (12-ounce) jar roasted red peppers, drained, patted dry, and chopped coarse
    1   cup finely chopped fresh basil

Quickly cooking the meats in the microwave helps keep this salad from becoming greasy.

1. Place one paper towel on microwave-safe plate. Arrange pepperoni in single layer on paper towel. Cover with another paper towel and layer sopresatta on towel. Top with another paper towel and microwave on highest power until meat begins to render fat, about 1 minute. Set meat aside.

2. Whisk 5 tablespoons vinegar, olive oil, mayonnaise, pepperoncini juice, garlic, red pepper flakes, ¹/₂ teaspoon salt, and ¹/₂ teaspoon pepper in medium bowl.

3. Bring 4 quarts water to boil in large pot. Add 1 tablespoon salt and pasta and cook until al dente. Drain pasta, return to pot, and toss with ¹/₂ cup dressing and remaining vinegar. Adjust seasonings, spread dressed pasta on rimmed baking sheet, and refrigerate until chilled, about 30 minutes.

4. Meanwhile, bring remaining dressing to simmer in large skillet over medium-high heat. Add mushrooms and cook until they release their juices and are lightly browned, about 8 minutes. Transfer to large bowl and cool.

5. Add meat, provolone, roasted red peppers, basil, and cooled pasta to mushrooms and toss well. Season with salt and pepper. Serve at room temperature. Salad can be refrigerated for up to 3 days.

Best Blueberry Streusel Muffins

No matter what I've tried, the streusel either melts into the muffins or stays as a dry layer that falls off when you try to eat it. I want to make a blueberry streusel muffin as good as those from coffeehouses. –Michele Greiman, Mason City, Iowa

When Good Muffins Go Bad

There are plenty of things that can go wrong with blueberry muffin recipes. Here are two of the worst problems we encountered.

GREEN WITH ENVY
Baking soda may have its merits for lift and browning, but it reacts with blueberries to create an unappealing green hue.

SOGGY BOTTOM
Think more blueberries make better muffins? Think again. When more than 1 1/2 cups of berries are used, the extra moisture creates muffins with fruit-soaked bottoms.

You'd think it would be easy to find plenty of great recipes for something as popular as blueberry muffins. But most recipes I've found bake up either dry or spongy, with an ugly blue (or even green!) color and weak blueberry flavor. A streusel topping usually adds to the trouble by being tough, sandy, or so heavy it sinks. I wanted to create a tender, cakey muffin bursting with berries and crowned with chewy nuggets of butter and sugar.

The first step was to create a tender muffin sturdy enough to support the streusel. The test kitchen's blueberry muffin recipe is great, but the use of sour cream makes them too soft and delicate to support streusel. I tried replacing the sour cream with heavy cream, yogurt, milk, and buttermilk and found that buttermilk created muffins with a sturdy-but-light texture.

My initial testing proved that dealing with the blueberries wasn't as easy as it might seem. Fresh berries are often bland and usually pretty large and juicy, which made my muffins soggy. Frozen berries are smaller and more flavorful, but they weren't perfect, either. When allowed to thaw—which happened quickly—they stained the batter an unappealing blue. Keeping the berries frozen until the last second helped, and tossing them with flour before adding them to the batter prevented the berries from sinking to the bottom of the muffins.

Although streusel toppings can include oats, nuts, or dried fruit, tasters felt these additions were distracting and preferred a simple mixture of flour, butter, dark brown sugar (for butterscotch flavor), granulated sugar, and cinnamon. Unlike an ultra-tender crumb topping, streusel should have a slight chew. Since streusel can be made with cold, room temperature, or melted butter, I made a batch using each. The streusels made with cold and room temperature butter baked into dry, powdery crumbs. The streusel made with melted butter was moist enough to clump in my hands, which allowed me to break it into perfect nuggets that provided a nice contrast to the muffins. –Cali Rich

BLUEBERRY STREUSEL MUFFINS MAKES 12

To prevent a streaky batter, leave the blueberries in the freezer until the last possible moment. Wyman's brand frozen wild blueberries are our first choice, but an equal amount of fresh blueberries may be substituted.

Streusel
- 1 1/4 cups all-purpose flour
- 1/3 cup packed dark brown sugar
- 1/3 cup granulated sugar
- 1/2 teaspoon ground cinnamon
  Pinch salt
- 7 tablespoons unsalted butter, melted

Muffins
- 4 tablespoons unsalted butter, melted and cooled slightly, plus extra for preparing muffin tin
- 2 cups all-purpose flour, plus extra for preparing muffin tin
- 1 large egg
- 1 teaspoon vanilla extract
- 1 cup granulated sugar
- 1 teaspoon grated lemon zest
- 1/2 cup buttermilk
- 1 tablespoon baking powder
- 1/2 teaspoon salt
- 1 1/2 cups frozen blueberries (see note)

1. For the streusel: Combine flour, sugars, cinnamon, and salt in bowl. Drizzle with melted butter and toss with fork until evenly moistened and mixture forms large chunks with some pea-sized pieces throughout.

2. For the muffins: Adjust oven rack to middle position and heat oven to 375 degrees. Grease and flour 12-cup muffin tin. Whisk egg in medium bowl until pale and evenly combined, about 30 seconds. Add vanilla, sugar, and zest and whisk vigorously until thick, about 30 seconds. Slowly whisk in melted butter; add buttermilk and whisk until combined.

3. Reserve 1 tablespoon flour. Whisk remaining flour, baking powder, and salt in large bowl. Fold in egg mixture until nearly combined. Toss blueberries with reserved flour and fold into batter until just combined.

4. Divide batter in muffin tin and top with streusel. Bake until light golden brown and toothpick inserted into center of muffin comes out with few dry crumbs attached, 23 to 27 minutes. Cool muffins in tin for 20 minutes, then carefully transfer muffins to rack to cool completely. (Muffins can be stored in airtight container at room temperature for 3 days.)

The sweet streusel topping adds substantial chew to these tender, berry-filled mu

Getting to Know Melons

Melons come in nearly every shape, size, and color. What lies beneath the thick rinds of these fruits? To find out, we sampled 12 varieties that range from everyday to heirloom. Below are our tasting notes.

Watermelon
BIG AND JUICY

The most consumed melons in the U.S., watermelons often surpass 20 pounds. They have green-striped skin and red, "porous" flesh that is heavily seeded, "sticky-sweet," and "refreshing." Aside from the flesh, the rind (usually pickled) and seeds (roasted and salted) are edible.

Cantaloupe
AMERICAN BEAUTY

Named for the Italian town Cantalupo, the common North American variety of this melon boasts a netted, greenish-tan rind and fragrant orange flesh. Sometimes referred to as "muskmelons," cantaloupes are at once "sugary and savory," with a distinct "peppery, musky overtone."

Sun Jewel
MILD AND CRUNCHY

These oblong, yellowish-white melons hail from Asia. Their "mild" flesh is "crisp" and "almost savory." Tasters found the flavor to be "more vegetal than fruity" and pegged it as a "perfect addition to a green salad."

Honeydew
GREEN SWEETIE

Slightly oval, with smooth, pale yellowish-green skin, the honeydew melon has been a favorite in Africa and the Middle East for thousands of years. The pastel green flesh of this medium-sized melon is "velvety smooth" and "super-sweet," with a bare hint of "honeysuckle."

Golden Midget
CRISP AND BRIGHT

This petite heirloom watermelon is recognizable for its golden rind and salmon-pink flesh. Its texture is more "finely grained and crisp" than that of the common watermelon. The flavor is "bright and acidic," with an "understated sweetness" and "cucumber" overtones.

Casaba
THICK-SKINNED

This wrinkly-skinned melon is named for Kasaba, Turkey, the city that first exported the fruits. The silky flesh of the Casaba is "watery and mild," with a "papaya-like" flavor. Since their rind is so thick, the melons are rarely fragrant; to best gauge their ripeness, look for deep-yellow, evenly colored fruits.

Charentais
FRENCH CANTALOUPE

A European cantaloupe that is available in specialty markets in the U.S., this melon is smaller than the North American variety and has a thin, smooth, khaki-colored rind. Not as sweet as the common cantaloupe, it has a "tannic acidity" and a "spicy and lemony" complexity.

Sharlyne
TROPICAL-TASTING

Although the netted skin of this melon is similar to that of a cantaloupe, its ivory-colored flesh is a stark contrast. This flesh is "juicy and smooth," with a "tropical flavor" tinged with a distinct "root beer" taste. Sharlyne melons tend to spoil quickly and should be eaten within a few days of purchase.

Canary
LITTLE JOHN

Sometimes called "Juan Canary," these oblong melons have waxy, bright-yellow skin and cream-colored flesh. Their flavor is "luscious and rich," but some tasters found the notes of "cotton candy" and "brown sugar" to be "over-the-top sweet." Texturally, canary melons are "velvety smooth" and "very juicy."

Kiwano
JELLY BELLY

Also called "horned melon," this New Zealand fruit is recognizable for its leathery, bright-orange, spike-covered skin. The interior of the kiwano is filled with an emerald green "jelly-like pulp" that has a texture similar to pomegranate seeds. Its "sweet-sour" flavor recalls "banana, lime, and watermelon."

Pepino
GOLDEN GOOSE

This egg-shaped Peruvian fruit can vary widely in size from just a few inches to almost a foot in length. The flesh underneath its light golden, purple-streaked skin has an "earthy" flavor and a "sweet honey aftertaste." The tough skin, though edible, can be easily removed with a vegetable peeler if desired.

Crenshaw
SPICY AND SMOOTH

This large, slightly elongated melon has bright, creamy yellow skin and pinkish-orange flesh. A cousin of the Casaba melon, this extremely fragrant variety has a strong "peppery-floral" aroma, a "balanced, slightly musty" acidity, and "dense, smooth" flesh.

Ultimate Seven-Layer Dip

I struggle with the consistency of the layers in this dip. Spreading one soft layer over another just makes a mess. And if the bean layer is stiff enough to support the next layer, it breaks the chips. Can you help?

–Jessica Davis, Saint Albans, W.Va.

The key to this dip is infusing each layer with enough fresh flavor and structure to prevent separate components from becoming muddled.

With its bold Tex-Mex flavors and contrasting textures, seven-layer dip sounds like a hit. The ingredient list—refried beans, sour cream, shredded cheese, guacamole, diced tomatoes, scallions, and black olives—is certainly appealing. But most versions of this party classic seem to assume that guests won't notice that the layers are messy and the flavors are tired.

I figured fixing the messy layers would be pretty easy. I'd start with the heavier layers first and try to "stiffen" each for neater spreading. Getting each layer to taste good seemed more challenging, especially after I prepared a number of published recipes. Most of these relied entirely on canned or processed ingredients—and they tasted like it. Even salty chips and cold beers failed to get my tasters excited about these dips.

I began my overhaul of this recipe at the bottom, with the beans. Straight from the can, refried beans taste stale, and their pasty consistency shattered chips on contact. Knowing that making my own refried beans would take too much time, I wondered if I could use canned black beans instead of refried. To approximate the texture of refried beans, I mashed the drained black beans (breaking with test kitchen protocol by not rinsing them, which left them silker and more dipable) and seasoned them with fresh garlic, chili powder, and lime juice. Five minutes of extra work yielded a big improvement in flavor. One layer down, six to go.

Sour cream is a must for its cool flavor, but it can turn into a runny mess; I needed a way to give it more structure. Since I was going to layer cheese over it anyway, I tried pulsing the cheese (my tasters preferred the creamy kick of pepper jack) and sour cream together in the food processor to make one unified layer. This worked great, especially when I doubled up on the cheese by adding it again as its own distinct layer.

I tried using store-bought guacamole, but every brand I tested was stale and some were rancid-tasting. Fresh guacamole (see page 25) is a must here. Next up was the tomato layer. My tasters gave an emphatic thumbs down to both canned tomatoes and jarred salsa, complaining that they just didn't taste fresh. But when I tried diced fresh tomatoes, my tasters thought they lacked punch. I found my solution in the form of a homemade pico de gallo, a chunky, dry salsa that I made by combining chopped tomatoes, jalapeños, cilantro, and scallions with lime juice and salt and then letting the mixture drain before adding it to the dip. Pico de gallo can also be made in the food processor (see box at right), but its texture will not be as uniform.

A layer of sliced scallions added bite and color. I was almost in the end zone, but I couldn't figure out the final layer of canned sliced black olives. Rinsing helped mitigate the metallic flavor, but the olives were still bland. After several frustrating rounds of testing, I decided to punt and eliminate the olives. Yes, my recipe has just six layers, but each is so distinct and fresh-tasting that no one will complain. **–Kelley Baker**

ULTIMATE SEVEN-LAYER DIP SERVES 8 TO 10

This recipe is usually served in a clear dish so you can see the layers. For a crowd, double the recipe and serve in a 13 by 9-inch glass baking dish. If you don't have time to make fresh guacamole as called for, simply mash 3 avocados with 3 tablespoons lime juice and 1/2 teaspoon salt.

- 4 large tomatoes, cored, seeded, and chopped fine
- 2 jalapeño chiles, seeded and minced
- 3 tablespoons finely chopped fresh cilantro
- 6 scallions, 2 minced and 4 with green parts sliced thin (white parts discarded)
- 2 tablespoons plus 2 teaspoons juice from 2 limes
- 1/4 teaspoon salt
- 1 (16-ounce) can black beans, drained but not rinsed
- 2 garlic cloves, minced
- 3/4 teaspoon chili powder
- 1 1/2 cups sour cream
- 4 cups shredded pepper jack cheese
- 3 cups Chunky Guacamole (see page 25)
  Tortilla chips for serving

1. Combine tomatoes, jalapeños, cilantro, minced scallions, and 2 tablespoons lime juice in medium bowl. Stir in 1/8 teaspoon salt and let stand until tomatoes begin to soften, about 30 minutes. Strain mixture into bowl and discard liquid.

2. Pulse black beans, garlic, remaining lime juice, chili powder, and remaining salt in food processor until mixture resembles chunky paste. Transfer to bowl and wipe out food processor. Pulse sour cream and 2 1/2 cups cheese until smooth. Transfer to separate bowl.

3. Spread bean mixture evenly over bottom of 8-inch-square glass baking dish or 1-quart glass bowl. Spread sour cream mixture evenly over bean layer, and sprinkle evenly with remaining cheese. Spread guacamole over cheese and top with tomato mixture. Sprinkle with sliced scallions and serve with tortilla chips. (Dip can be refrigerated for up to 24 hours. Let dip stand at room temperature 1 hour before serving.)

ULTIMATE SMOKY SEVEN-LAYER DIP

Pulse 1 to 3 teaspoons minced canned chipotle chiles in adobo sauce with the black beans in step 2. Along with scallions, garnish dip with 4 slices cooked and crumbled bacon.

Processing Your Pico

Although the pico de gallo topping in our Ultimate Seven-Layer Dip adds a ton of fresh flavor, chopping all the ingredients by hand takes some work. We found that a food processor gets the job done, but the texture won't be as perfectly uniform as pico made by hand. To make pico de gallo in the food processor, start by pulsing jalapeños with cilantro until finely chopped. Then add quartered, cored, and seeded tomatoes and pulse in 1-second bursts until the tomatoes are evenly chopped. Add minced scallions and lime juice. Drain as instructed.

For Your Convenience:
Chicken and Cheese Quesadillas

With a few kitchen tricks, we transform supermarket convenience items into a stack of piping hot quesadillas that never touch a skillet.

Quesadillas are Tex-Mex cuisine's answer to the grilled cheese sandwich. But the simplicity of cheese and tortillas becomes complicated when chicken and other fillings are added. There's cooking the chicken, keeping the salsa from making everything soggy, and the laborious one-at-a-time skillet method. Could I find a faster, easier way?

Thanks to the rotisserie birds available in most supermarkets, the chicken was easy—all I had to do was shred it. Another supermarket convenience item, shredded Mexican-blend cheese, was also a hit.

Salsa is a must for flavor, but jarred stuff made the filling messy. Straining the salsa allowed me to use it twice. The flavorful liquid was quickly absorbed by the chicken and cheese mixture, and I saved the chunks for a final topping. Pickled jalapeños and a teaspoon of taco seasoning spiced up the filling even more.

Standing by a skillet for 20 minutes to cook the quesadillas one at a time seemed silly for such a simple recipe. Turning to the oven, I placed four prepared quesadillas on a baking sheet brushed with vegetable oil (cooking spray made the tortillas leathery). Just 10 minutes on each side cooked the tortillas to a crispy golden brown.

–**Meredith Butcher**

CHICKEN AND CHEESE QUESADILLAS
SERVES 4 TO 6
Kraft Natural Shredded Four Cheese Blend is our favorite Mexican cheese blend.

- 1 (16-ounce) jar prepared salsa
  Vegetable oil
- 1 rotisserie chicken, skin discarded, meat shredded into medium bite-sized pieces (about 3 cups)
- 1 teaspoon taco seasoning
- 1/4 cup canned pickled jalapeños, drained and minced
- 1 1/2 cups packaged Mexican cheese blend (see note)
- 4 (12-inch) flour tortillas
  Sour cream for serving

1. Drain salsa in mesh strainer over bowl. Reserve strained salsa and 1/3 cup juice separately. Meanwhile, adjust oven rack to middle position and heat oven to 450 degrees. Brush rimmed baking sheet with 2 tablespoons oil.

2. Combine chicken, taco seasoning, jalapeños, cheese, and salsa juice in bowl. Spread 1 cup filling over half of each tortilla, leaving 1/2-inch border around edge. Brush plain half of tortillas with oil, fold over filling, and press down firmly. Transfer to prepared baking sheet and brush top of each tortilla with 1/2 teaspoon oil.

3. Bake until tops of quesadillas begin to brown, about 10 minutes. Flip quesadillas over, press with spatula, and bake until crisp and golden brown on second side, 8 to 10 minutes. Cool quesadillas on wire rack for 10 minutes before slicing. Cut each quesadilla into 4 wedges and serve with reserved salsa and sour cream.

On the Side: Chunky Guacamole

The best guacamole stars ripe avocados—but if you're not careful, the other ingredients can overwhelm their delicate flavor.

For great guacamole, it goes without saying that ripe avocados are a must, but so is a light hand. Many recipes ruin the guacamole by mashing the avocados to death, leaving a puree that's better served with a baby spoon than a crispy chip. To provide a little textural contrast, I found that mashing two-thirds of the avocado and roughly chopping the rest was the key to a silky-yet-chunky dip.

As for the flavor, almost all basic guacamole recipes rely on the same ingredients: garlic and onion for bite, jalapeño for kick, cilantro for a refreshing herbal element, and a splash of lime juice to brighten it all up. My tasters were happy with everything except the raw onion, which they felt was harsh and overpowered the avocados. In an attempt to temper the onions, I experimented with yellow, red, and white varieties and even shallots, but a mere tablespoon still proved to be too much for tasters. Scallions worked better, adding a nice depth to the guacamole, but even they were slightly harsh.

To mellow the scallions' flavor, I steeped the more assertive white parts, along with the garlic and jalapeño, in lime juice for a few minutes before combining them with the avocados. The acidity of the juice mellowed the onion flavor. With a pinch or two of salt (don't use too much if you are serving the guacamole with salty tortilla chips), I had a recipe that wouldn't disappoint.

–**Jeremy Sauer**

CHUNKY GUACAMOLE
MAKES ABOUT 3 CUPS
Preparing guacamole ahead of time helps the flavors marry, but it should not be prepared more than 1 day in advance. To prevent the dip from turning brown, press a sheet of plastic wrap directly onto the surface and refrigerate until ready to use. We prefer pebbly Hass avocados to the smoother Fuerte variety.

- 2 scallions, sliced thin, green and white parts separated
- 1 jalapeño chile, minced
- 1 small garlic clove, minced
- 1/4 teaspoon finely grated zest plus 2 tablespoons juice from 1 lime
- 3 avocados, pitted, peeled, and chopped
- 3 tablespoons chopped fresh cilantro
  Salt

1. Combine white parts of scallions, jalapeño, garlic, and lime juice in large bowl. Let sit for 30 minutes.

2. Add two-thirds of the avocado to bowl with jalapeño mixture and mash with potato masher until smooth. Gently fold remaining avocado into mashed avocado mixture. Gently stir in lime zest, green parts of scallions, and cilantro. Season with salt. Serve.

Strawberry Poke Cake

My mother used to make a funny-looking cake streaked with red Jell-O. I'd love to create this cake for my kids but haven't had much luck with the recipes I've tried. –Sally Arthur, Red Oak, Ill.

Kitchen Know-How
PERFECTING THE POKE

Finding the right poking device wasn't as simple as you might think. Toothpicks were too small, while straws, handles of wooden spoons, pencils, and fingers were too big. A wooden skewer finally did the trick. But just poking didn't create a large enough hole for the liquid to seep into. In order to create deep lines of red color against the white crumb, we had to poke and then twist the skewer to really separate the crumb.

1. Using a skewer, poke about 50 deep holes all over the top of the cake, but be careful not to poke all the way through to the bottom. Twist the skewer to make the holes slightly bigger, which will allow more liquid to sink into each hole.

2. Slowly pour the cooled gelatin mixture evenly over the entire surface of the cake.

Bright-red streaks of strawberry gelatin—and a layer of our homemade topping—give this cake moist texture, big strawberry flavor, and a novel appearance.

Strawberry poke cake, a tender white cake streaked with strawberry gelatin, was invented by Kraft Kitchens in 1969 as a vehicle to increase strawberry Jell-O sales. Most corporate recipes are quickly forgotten, but strawberry poke cake became extremely popular thanks to its festive look and ease of assembly. The original recipe has only three ingredients: strawberry Jell-O, white cake mix, and whipped cream. Strawberries, cake, and cream sounded pretty good to me.

But when I made this cake, my optimism quickly faded. The boxed-mix cake was so tender and fine that the hot gelatin made it soggy, especially around the edges, where the domed shape of the cake had channeled most of the liquid. And the strawberry gelatin was bright in color but dim in flavor. I headed into the test kitchen to see if I could make a sturdier, flatter cake with big strawberry flavor.

All boxed cake mixes contain extra leavener, which ensures tender texture and a nice dome every time. I would have to make my sturdy, flatter white cake from scratch. The test kitchen's recipe for white cake worked perfectly, giving me a sturdy crumb and little doming, which meant the gelatin mixture didn't pool around the edges of the pan.

Using strawberry gelatin as the streaking agent gave the cake beautiful red stripes. I now needed some berry flavor. Strawberry soda and syrup both tasted artificial, while strawberry jams and jellies looked and tasted washed-out. Pureed fresh strawberries produced inconsistent results, as sometimes the berries were soft and

sweet and other times they were hard and sour. I turned to frozen strawberries, which are reliably sweet. Blending and straining the frozen berries gave me the best flavor, but the texture was too thick.

A colleague suggested cooking the frozen strawberries with orange juice and sugar. This released strawberry juice, which, when strained out of the solids and mixed with the strawberry gelatin, was thin enough to pour and potent with rich strawberry flavor. My cake now tasted as good as it looked.

I made a homemade "jam" from the leftover berry solids and spread the mixture on top of the cake for an extra layer of flavor. When it was topped with sweetened whipped cream and served cold, I could finally see—and taste—why strawberry poke cake has remained so popular. –Meredith Butcher

STRAWBERRY POKE CAKE SERVES 12

The top of the cake will look slightly overbaked—this keeps the crumb from becoming too soggy after the gelatin is poured on top.

Cake
- 12 **tablespoons (1¹/₂ sticks) unsalted butter, softened, plus extra for preparing pan**
- 2¹/₄ **cups all-purpose flour, plus extra for preparing pan**
- 4 **teaspoons baking powder**
- 1 **teaspoon salt**
- 1 **cup whole milk**
- 2 **teaspoons vanilla extract**
- 6 **large egg whites**
- 1³/₄ **cups sugar**

Syrup and Topping
- 4 **cups frozen strawberries**
- 6 **tablespoons sugar**
- 2 **tablespoons orange juice**
- ¹/₂ **cup water**
- 2 **tablespoons strawberry-flavored gelatin**
- 2 **cups heavy cream**

1. For the cake: Adjust oven rack to middle position and heat oven to 350 degrees. Grease and flour 13 by 9-inch baking pan. Whisk flour, baking powder, and salt in bowl. Whisk milk, vanilla, and egg whites in large measuring cup.

2. With electric mixer on medium-high speed, beat butter and sugar until fluffy, about 2 minutes, scraping down bowl as necessary. Add flour mixture and milk mixture alternately, in two batches, beating after each addition until combined, about 30 seconds each time. Using rubber spatula, give batter final stir. Scrape into prepared pan and bake until toothpick inserted in center comes out clean, about 35 minutes. Cool cake completely in pan, at least 1 hour. Once cool, cake can be wrapped in plastic and kept at room temperature for up to 2 days.

3. For the syrup and topping: Heat 3 cups strawberries, 2 tablespoons sugar, juice, and water in medium saucepan over medium-low heat. Cover and cook until strawberries are softened, about 10 minutes. Strain liquid into bowl, reserving solids, then whisk gelatin into liquid. Let cool to room temperature, at least 20 minutes.

4. Meanwhile, poke 50 holes all over top of cake (see photo at left). Evenly pour cooled liquid over top of cake. Wrap with plastic wrap and refrigerate until gelatin is set, at least 3 hours or up to 2 days.

5. Pulse reserved strained strawberries, 2 tablespoons sugar, and remaining strawberries in food processor until mixture resembles strawberry jam. Spread mixture evenly over cake. With electric mixer on medium-high speed, beat cream with remaining sugar to soft peaks. Spread cream over strawberries. Serve. (Cake will keep, refrigerated, for up to 2 days.)

Icebox Key Lime Pie

Authentic Key lime pie used to be a simple, no-cook dessert—but it contained raw eggs, a no-no in modern times. Could we develop an eggless refrigerator recipe as bright and custardy as the original?

A trio of no-cook thickeners—instant pudding, cream cheese, and gelatin—makes this recipe easy and reliable.

Key lime pie was invented in the Florida Keys more than 100 years ago. The original recipe was considered an icebox pie because the filling of sweetened condensed milk, egg yolks, and lime juice wasn't cooked. Everything was simply stirred together and poured into a prebaked graham cracker crust. The pie was then placed in the refrigerator for several hours, where the lime's acid "cooked" the protein in the milk and yolks, creating a custardy, firm filling bursting with lively lime flavor.

Due to concerns about eating raw eggs, today's Key lime pies fall into two distinct camps: uncooked pies that replace the eggs with whipped cream or gelatin and those whose egg-based filling is cooked on the stovetop. I tried a handful of uncooked pies and was consistently disappointed. Their texture was never custardy; the pies were either too fluffy from whipped cream or too rubbery from gelatin. The cooked custard pies had the velvety texture right, but at the expense of time and effort at the stovetop. I set my goal high: to create a Key lime pie as easy and custardy as the original without having to cook the filling.

I started with the lime juice. Most recipes don't use enough, and the resulting pie is too timid. I found that I needed a full cup of fresh lime juice (bottled lime juice tasted artificial) to produce a pie with bracing lime flavor. Lime zest added another layer of flavor, and processing the zest with a little sugar offset

its sourness and eliminated the annoying chewy bits.

To the juice and zest, I added a can of sweetened condensed milk. I now needed something other than egg yolks to thicken this soupy mixture. Potato starch, non-fat dry milk, Egg Beaters, and store-bought lime curd failed miserably, producing weepy pies I could have eaten with a straw. Cream cheese had the opposite problem; it made the filling too dense—more cheesecake than custard pie. Then I tried instant pudding mix—not the cook-and-serve kind, but the stuff you just mix with milk, chill, and serve. While I wasn't crazy about the flavor (tasters rejected lemon and lime varieties, but vanilla was deemed acceptable), the texture was almost custard-like. The filling was still a little too thin, but it gave me a glimmer of hope.

Going back to the drawing board, I decided to try the instant vanilla pudding mix in combination with small amounts of gelatin and cream cheese—two ingredients that showed promise but had each caused textural problems when used as the sole thickener. After several days of trial and error, I finally hit on the right ratios to thicken my pie filling into custardy perfection. A block of cream cheese, ⅓ cup of instant vanilla pudding mix, and a stingy 1¼ teaspoons of gelatin did the trick. After squeezing and scraping 250 limes into 29 pies, I'd discovered the secrets to a custardy no-cook, no-egg Key lime pie.

–Diane Unger

ICEBOX KEY LIME PIE
SERVES 8 TO 10
Use instant pudding that requires no stovetop cooking for this recipe. Do not be tempted to use bottled lime juice, which lacks depth of flavor.

Crust
- **8 whole graham crackers, broken into small pieces**
- **2 tablespoons sugar**
- **5 tablespoons unsalted butter, melted**

Filling
- **¼ cup sugar**
- **1 tablespoon grated lime zest**
- **8 ounces cream cheese, softened**
- **1 (14-ounce) can sweetened condensed milk**
- **⅓ cup instant vanilla pudding mix**
- **1¼ teaspoons unflavored gelatin**
- **1 cup fresh juice from 6 to 8 limes (see page 31)**
- **1 teaspoon vanilla extract**

1. For the crust: Adjust oven rack to middle position and heat oven to 350 degrees. Pulse crackers and sugar in food processor until finely ground. Add melted butter

in steady stream while pulsing until crumbs resemble damp sand. Using bottom of dry measuring cup, press crumbs firmly into bottom and sides of 9-inch pie plate. Bake until fragrant and browned around edges, 12 to 14 minutes. Cool completely.

2. For the filling: Process sugar and zest in food processor until sugar turns bright green, about 30 seconds. Add cream cheese and process until combined, about 30 seconds. Add condensed milk and pudding mix and process until smooth, about 30 seconds. Scrape down sides of bowl. Stir gelatin and 2 tablespoons lime juice in small bowl. Heat in microwave for 15 seconds; stir until dissolved. With machine running, pour gelatin mixture, remaining lime juice, and vanilla through feed tube and mix until thoroughly combined, about 30 seconds.

3. Pour filling into cooled crust, cover with plastic, and refrigerate at least 3 hours or up to 2 days. To serve, let pie sit at room temperature for 10 minutes before slicing.

A Mystery of Pie History
Before Gail Borden invented sweetened condensed milk in 1856, drinking milk was a health risk, as there was no pasteurization or refrigeration for fresh milk. The shelf-stability and safety of sweetened condensed milk made it especially popular in areas like the Florida Keys, where the hot climate promoted rapid spoilage of anything perishable. Like many of our iconic foods, no one knows for sure when or by whom the first Key lime pie was made, but with canned milk in every pantry by the 1870s and an abundance of tiny Key limes throughout the area, it was only a matter of time. Most food historians trace the history of this pie back to the 1890s, but there are those—especially in the Keys—who claim the recipe is decades older.

FLORIDA'S MOST FAMOUS PIE

Food Shopping

STRAWBERRY PRESERVES: Balancing Sweet and Tart Is Key

Trailing only grape jelly, strawberry preserves are America's second-favorite spreadable fruit. We rounded up eight nationally available brands of strawberry preserves and headed into the tasting lab to see which one we liked best.

Two familiar names, Welch's and Smucker's, were our big winners. Our tasters preferred these brands because they didn't taste too sweet, and they packed big, distinct strawberry flavor. Interestingly, Welch's and Smucker's preserves contain more total sugar (from the fruit as well as sugar and/or corn syrup) per serving than most other brands, and yet they weren't perceived as too sweet. Why?

First, not all sugars are equally sweet. Bonne Maman and Welch's both contain 13 grams of sugars per tablespoon, but Bonne Maman's primary sweetener is sugar, which tastes sweeter than the corn syrup listed first on the Welch's label. Second, the amount of acid (citric acid or lemon juice concentrate) added to balance the sugar had a big impact on overall flavor. We measured the pH (the acidity or alkalinity) of each sample and found that the brands tasters had called too sweet (like Bonne Maman and Cascadian Farm) had the highest pH readings, indicating that they were least acidic. Lower pH readings—signifying more added acid—generally translated into better, more-rounded strawberry flavor.

Our lowest-scoring brands, Polaner and Cascadian Farm, were judged to have the weakest strawberry flavor—no surprise considering neither brand uses strawberries as its primary ingredient.

Testers weren't too concerned about texture. As long as there was a noticeable combination of "jellied" matter and fruit chunks, they were pretty happy. The preserves are listed below in order of preference. **–Scott Kathan**

Recommended

1. Welch's Strawberry Preserves $3.49 for 16 ounces
Comments: Tasters praised this brand for its "great" and "natural-tasting" strawberry flavor, a result of being perceived as "not too sweet," with a "perfect sugar level." These preserves won top scores for their "thick" and "spreadable" texture.

2. Smucker's Strawberry Preserves $3.59 for 18 ounces
Comments: "Ripe berry flavor" and "sweet with a slight tartness" were the rallying cries for Smucker's, which scored very well for its "straightforward" strawberry flavor. Tasters also appreciated its "thick and chunky texture."

3. Smucker's Simply Fruit Strawberry Spreadable Fruit $2.69 for 10 ounces
Comments: With about a third less sugar than the top two brands, Smucker's Simply Fruit was lauded for being "very fruity" and "very strawberry-y" but "without too much sweetness." A few tasters would have appreciated a chunkier texture.

Recommended with Reservations

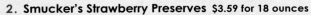

4. Smucker's Strawberry Low Sugar Preserves $3.69 for 15.5 ounces
Comments: With the least sugar of any brand, this sample was liked for its "mellow strawberry flavor." It was disliked for its "unnatural" color (it has red color added).

5. Dickinson's Pure Pacific Mountain Strawberry Preserves $4.79 for 10 ounces
Comments: Tasters liked the "appealing," "chunky" texture, but not the "Jolly Rancher–like flavor" that was deemed much too sweet.

6. Bonne Maman Strawberry Preserves $4.19 for 13 ounces
Comments: Tasters likened this sample to strawberry "lollipops" and "syrup" because of its "sickly-sweetness." Many thought the texture was "too runny" and "not well-mixed."

7. Polaner All Fruit Strawberry Fruit Spread $3.49 for 15.25 ounces
Comments: The "weird brown color" and "generic, non strawberry fruit flavor" (pear and grape juice concentrates are the first two ingredients) were big turnoffs.

Not Recommended

8. Cascadian Farm Organic Strawberry Fruit Spread $3.19 for 10 ounces
Comments: "All sugar syrup and no strawberry flavor" and "so sweet it made my teeth hurt," said our tasters. Comments like "slimy" and "gloppy" are never good signs.

Taste Test Cooking Oils

In the test kitchen, we use different cooking oils to suit the flavor and cooking temperature requirements of the recipe at hand. Here are the oils we commonly use in the test kitchen.

Canola and Vegetable Oils

These oils both have high smoke points and almost no flavor, so we use them interchangeably in the kitchen. Vegetable oil is usually made from soybeans and canola oil from rapeseed. These oils are fine for quick deep-frying but will begin to break down and create unpleasant flavors after about 15 minutes. We also use these oils for shallow-frying, sautéing, and stir-frying, as well as in dressings with strong flavors.

Olive Oil

Also called "pure" olive oil, this product adds some—but not too much—fruity flavor to foods. We especially like to use olive oil for dishes with Mediterranean flavors. We use it to brown meats, to start soups and stews, and in sauces and dressings with strong flavors.

Extra-Virgin Olive Oil

Although many cooks never use extra-virgin olive oil for cooking (because its flavors dissipate when exposed to high heat), we like its strong flavor in dishes that are cooked quickly. We also use extra-virgin olive oil to dress blanched or steamed vegetables and to drizzle over soups and grilled foods; additionally, it's our first choice in most vinaigrettes.

Toasted Sesame Oil

The potent flavor of toasted sesame oil (sometimes labeled Asian sesame oil) fades quickly when exposed to heat, so we like to add this oil to Asian-inspired dishes in the final moments of cooking. We also use toasted sesame oil in dressings, sauces, and marinades. This oil is highly perishable, so store it in the refrigerator.

Peanut Oil

Refined peanut oil, such as Planters, has a neutral flavor and high smoke point, making it our first choice for deep-frying chicken, fish, and potatoes. Best of all, it doesn't break down and impart off flavors, even with prolonged heat—a problem we've had with other oils. Unrefined peanut oil, which has a nutty flavor that we like in stir-fries, is sold in small bottles for a hefty price, making it inappropriate for frying. **–S.K.**

Equipment Roundup

LARGE SAUCEPANS: Can a $20 Pan Outperform One That Costs Nearly $200?

In the test kitchen, we use our large saucepans for making rice and oatmeal; blanching vegetables; and cooking small amounts of pasta, soup, stew, and all manner of sauces. The test kitchen's favorite large saucepan is the $184 All-Clad 4-Quart Sauce Pan. But can you get away with something less pricey at home?

We rounded up 8 large saucepans (ranging in capacity from 3.3 to 4 quarts, all with traditional finishes) priced from $20 to $100 and pitted them against the All-Clad in a battery of tests. We had several testers cook onions, marinara sauce, and chocolate pudding in each saucepan. Testers whisked, stirred, poured, and handled the pans extensively. What did we find out?

SLOW AND STEADY: To determine the relative cooking speed of each saucepan, we sautéed onions over medium heat for 10 minutes, and purposely burned marinara sauce (not stirring for 45 minutes) in each pan. The best pans were the ones that cooked slowly and steadily, resulting in perfectly golden onions and less-burnt sauce. The worst pans cooked too fast and produced burnt, inedible onions and sauce over the same time and heat. Using a pan with slow sauté speed means you can leave the stove to answer the phone while you're cooking, and dinner won't be ruined. In short, a slower saucepan is a better saucepan.

All the stainless-steel pans in our testing have aluminum in their bases to evenly disperse the heat, but there were huge differences in their cooking speeds. The slowest pans—the All-Clad, Berndes, Cuisinart, and Pinzon Stainless Steel—were either very heavy (All-Clad and Berndes, both of which feature a full aluminum core) or had relatively thick bottoms (Cuisinart and Pinzon). As for the fast pans, the Anolon had the thinnest bottom and the Farberware was the lightest in our lineup.

DESIGN MATTERS: The design of a saucepan impacts how user-friendly it is. The Anolon and Farberware models feature two small handles instead of the one long handle commonly found on saucepans. Our testers found these small handles awkward, and because they are so close to the pans' sides, they get very hot. Also, saucepan applications often require the user to hold the pan with one hand and scrape out the contents with a utensil in the other, and the small handles made it very difficult to do this.

SUMMING UP: The most important quality for a saucepan is even and slow heating; our testing found the heavy All-Clad and Berndes and the lighter (but thick-bottomed) Cuisinart and Pinzon Stainless Steel to be the best at this task. Some testers did find the virtually indestructible All-Clad and Berndes pans to be quite heavy when full; if weight is a concern, you may want to trade out a little performance for a lighter pan like the Pinzon Stainless or Cuisinart. The $20 Pinzon costs just a fraction as much as the All-Clad and is a true best buy. **–Scott Kathan**

Highly Recommended

All-Clad Stainless 4-Quart Sauce Pan
Price: $183.99 at Cooking.com
Weight: 3.3 lb. (pans were weighed without lid)
Materials: Stainless steel with full aluminum core
Sauté Speed: Slow
Comments: The only pan to pass every test with flying colors. Testers like the "solid," "restaurant-quality" feel and "perfectly proportioned" shape. Two minor points that don't affect cooking performance: The "helper" handle gets very hot, and the pan doesn't have a pouring lip.

Recommended

Pinzon 3.5-Quart Stainless Steel Sauce Pan
Price: $19.99 at Amazon.com
Weight: 2.6 lb.
Materials: Stainless steel with aluminum disk in base
Sauté Speed: Slow
Comments: With its "sleek" lines and "nimble" performance, a few testers likened this pan to a sports car. The comfortable "squared" handle and internal measurement markings were big hits. Even though this pan is relatively light, a thicker-than-usual bottom ensured slow sauté speed.

Best Buy!

Berndes Tricion 3.5-Quart Stainless Steel Sauce Pan
Price: $99 at Cooking.com
Weight: 2.75 lb.
Materials: Stainless steel with full aluminum core
Sauté Speed: Slow
Comments: The full aluminum core (which extends throughout the pan) promoted even cooking that helped this pan score well in our tests. This pan was slightly downgraded for being "awkwardly weighted" and having a handle that was "too short."

Cuisinart Chef's Classic Stainless 4-Quart Sauce Pan
Price: $54.95 at Cooking.com
Weight: 2.45 lb.
Materials: Stainless steel with aluminum disk in base
Sauté Speed: Slow
Comments: This solid-feeling (yet quite light) pan "handles well," has a "good feel," and, most important, sautés slowly. A few testers thought its high sides impaired sightlines and ease of stirring.

Recommended with Reservations

Emerilware Stainless 4-Quart Covered Saucepan
Price: $69.95 at Amazon.com
Weight: 3.85 lb.
Materials: Stainless steel with aluminum disk (and copper center) in base
Sauté Speed: Medium
Comments: Testers thought this pan was "heavy but well-weighted" and "very solid feeling." The "helper" handle gets very hot.

Martha Stewart Everyday 3.3-Quart Stainless Steel Saucepan
Price: $29.99 at Kmart.com
Weight: 2.55 lb.
Materials: Stainless steel with aluminum disk in base; silicone handle covers
Sauté Speed: Medium
Comments: The rounded shape provided great access. But this pan sautéed a bit fast, and its squat shape led to faster evaporation and more scorching.

Pinzon 3.5-Quart Hard Anodized Sauce Pan
Price: $27.63 at Amazon.com
Weight: 2.25 lb.
Material: Hard-anodized aluminum
Sauté Speed: Medium
Comments: Our testers disliked the dark surface of this pan because "you can't see what you're doing." This pan handled pretty well but had only average performance.

Not Recommended

Farberware Classic Series Stainless 4-Quart Sauce Pan
Price: $39.95 at Cooking.com
Weight: 2.15 lb.
Materials: Stainless steel with aluminum disk in base; plastic handles
Sauté Speed: Fast
Comments: The double handles were deemed "awkward when pouring" and became very hot. As the lightest pan in the field, it heated too quickly.

Anolon Advanced Clad 4-Quart Covered Saucepot
Price: $88.99 at Amazon.com
Weight: 2.7 lb.
Materials: Stainless steel with aluminum disk in base; silicone handle covers
Sauté Speed: Fast
Comments: Testers hated the two handles, and this pot scored the lowest on each cooking test. It has the thinnest bottom of any pan in our testing.

Notes from Our Test Kitchen

TIPS, TECHNIQUES, AND TOOLS FOR BETTER COOKING

Kitchen Creations
Crispy Homemade Tortilla Chips

Our **Ultimate Seven-Layer Dip** (page 24) and **Chunky Guacamole** (page 25) are great with regular tortilla chips, but for a special snack, we prefer to make our own. To make these easy and tasty chips, spray four large flour tortillas on both sides with cooking spray and cut each into eight wedges. Using one of the variations below, season the chips and arrange in a single layer on two baking sheets. Bake in a 350-degree oven until they are golden and crisp, about 10 to 15 minutes. Once cooled, the chips can be stored at room temperature in an airtight container for up to four days.

HOT RANCH CHIPS
Sprinkle tortillas evenly with 1 tablespoon powdered ranch salad dressing mix and 1/4 teaspoon cayenne pepper.

SESAME-CURRY CHIPS
Sprinkle tortillas evenly with 1 1/2 teaspoons each of curry powder, and sesame seeds, and 1/8 teaspoon cayenne pepper.

BBQ CHIPS
Sprinkle tortillas evenly with 2 teaspoons chili powder, 1 teaspoon ground cumin, and 1/4 teaspoon salt.

PIZZA CHIPS
Sprinkle tortillas evenly with 1 teaspoon Italian seasoning, 1 teaspoon paprika, 1 teaspoon garlic powder, and 1/4 teaspoon salt.

Inside the Test Kitchen How to Slice Bottom Round

Since the tri-tip for our California Barbecued Tri-Tip (page 11) can be hard to find in some parts of the country, we looked for a widely available substitute steak. We tried flank steak (too thin), shoulder steak (too tough), and strip steak (too pricey) before we arrived at bottom round steak. Aside from being similar to tri-tip in thickness and weight (and therefore cooking time and yield), bottom round also has the big, beefy flavor of tri-tip at a modest price. Unfortunately, the long muscle fibers of this cut can make it extremely tough. We found that thinly slicing the steak straight down on a 45-degree angle shortened the muscle fibers and dramatically reduced the chewiness.

What's a Pepperoncini?

Since the typical antipasto platter can have a dozen or more options, our tasters were faced with some tough decisions when it came to paring down the ingredient list in our **Antipasto Pasta Salad** (page 21). The one ingredient that we couldn't live without was the pepperoncini. Sometimes referred to as Tuscan peppers, in a nod to their region of origin, pepperoncini are most commonly found pickled and packed in a vinegary brine. More tangy than spicy, these little green peppers have a salty, slightly bitter flavor that is great for pizza, sandwiches, salads—or just eating out of the jar. **–Diane Unger**

Pepperoncini pack big briny flavor

Smoke Signals

Sprinkling some soaked wood chips (or scattering a few wood chunks) over a pile of hot coals adds a great smoky flavor to grilled foods. While developing our **California Barbecued Tri-Tip** (page 11) and **Smoked Double-Thick Pork Chops** (page 18) recipes, we found that the type of wood used can make a huge difference in the finished

product. Wood from fruit trees, such as apple, cherry, and peach, produces a slightly sweet smoke with a hint of fruitiness. Hickory and pecan woods both produce a hearty smoke that cuts through even the spiciest rubs. Maple, the traditional choice for ham, produces a mellow, sweet smoke, while oak lends a faint acidic note that many people enjoy. Ultimately, the only wood that left tasters a bit wary was mesquite. Although the heavy, assertive flavor of mesquite smoke was enjoyable in quickly cooked meats, it had a tendency to turn bitter over long periods of cooking. **–Jeremy Sauer**

Speeding Up Dried Beans

In our recipe for **California Barbecued Beans** (page 10), we soak the beans in water overnight to ensure they cook evenly. But there is a faster way.

Kitchen Technique
PREPARING CHICKEN PIECES FOR THE GRILL

In developing our recipe for **Classic Barbecued Chicken** (page 20), we found that trimming the excess skin from the fatty thighs helped minimize flare-ups. To ensure even cooking, we found it necessary to remove the ribs and halve the breasts. This way, the thick breasts would cook at the same rate as the smaller thighs and legs.

–Meredith Butcher

1. Using scissors, trim the skin on each thigh so there isn't any overhang.
2. Cut the ribs off each breast and split each breast in half to reduce cooking time.

Simply cover the beans with water in a Dutch oven, bring them to a boil over high heat, and let them boil for 5 minutes. Remove the beans from the heat and allow them to sit, covered, in the hot water for 1 hour. Drain the beans and proceed with the recipe as directed. The quick-soaked beans taste just as good as beans that are soaked overnight.

Shopping with the Test Kitchen
Hot Fudge

Move over, chocolate syrup. Tasters loved the thick, rich, chocolaty flavor hot fudge lent to our **Ultimate Chocolate Milkshake** (page 17). In search of the finest fudge, we tasted five national brands blended into our shakes as well as straight from the jar. While they were all good in our shakes, Hershey's won top billing for its "buttery" texture and "true fudge flavor" when tasted plain. **–Cali Rich**

BEST HOT FUDGE

Bigger Limes = Less Work

When developing our recipe for **Icebox Key Lime Pie** (page 27), we found the flavor of Key limes and regular supermarket limes (called Persian limes) to be almost identical in our pie recipe. But there was a big difference in squeezing time.

KEY LIMES
We had to squeeze 40 Key limes to yield 1 cup of juice.

PERSIAN LIMES
Just 6 to 8 Persian limes gave us all the juice we needed.

Better Marinated Mushrooms

In the course of developing our recipe for **Antipasto Pasta Salad** (page 21), our tasters wanted mushroom flavor in the salad, but not the mushy texture of jarred marinated mushrooms. Marinating our own mushrooms was too time-consuming. Fortunately, we found that if we sautéed quartered mushrooms in a vinaigrette, rather than in plain oil or butter, they developed a deep, tangy flavor while maintaining their firm texture. And they're ready in just eight minutes. Our quick and easy homemade marinated mushrooms add bright, earthy flavor to salads, pizzas, sandwiches, and, of course, antipasto platters.

When Is an Avocado Ripe?

Our **Chunky Guacamole** (page 25) starts with perfectly ripe Hass avocados, but finding them at the ideal level of ripeness can be difficult. When these avocados are at their creamy best, they are purple-black (not green) and yield slightly when gently squeezed. Avoid avocados that are overly mushy or bruised or flat in spots or whose skin seems loose—these are well past their prime. If you can't find perfectly ripe avocados, buy the fruit while it's still hard and be patient. Even though we tried all the tricks—from burying the avocados in rice to enclosing them in a paper bag (with or without another piece of fruit)—we found that nothing sped the ripening process except for time. Left on the countertop, even the hardest of avocados will ripen to perfection in two to five days.

—Jeremy Sauer

Wrapping Wood Chips

If wood chips aren't soaked and wrapped in foil, they combust quickly and produce an immediate cloud of smoke that doesn't penetrate the chops. Here's how we prepare the chips to ensure they burn slowly and still infuse our **Smoked Double-Thick Pork Chops** (page 18) with flavor.

Gadgets & Gear Skewers

While developing our recipe for **Spicy Grilled Shrimp** (page 19), we learned a lot about which skewers were best—and worst—for grilling. We had the worst experience with wooden skewers; no matter how long we soaked them (even for a few days!), they would burn and break over high heat. Turning to metal skewers, we were frustrated by how the shrimp would continually spin and flop around on the round variety. Our favorite skewers were the flat metal kind, which never burn, last forever, and hold the food in place.

FLAT'S WHERE IT'S AT
The test kitchen prefers flat metal skewers for grilling.

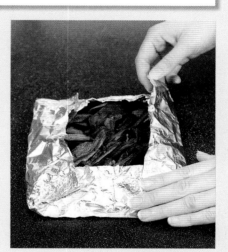

Spread the soaked, drained wood chips in the center of 15 by 12-inch piece of heavy-duty aluminum foil. Fold the edges of the foil toward the chips, leaving 5-inch window for smoke to escape.

Kitchen Technique BUILDING A BETTER TRIFLE

While our **Stars and Stripes Berry Trifle** (inside back cover) looks like it's stuffed with mounds of fresh berries, the center is actually layers of the scraps from the jam sandwiches and loads of vanilla custard. Here's how we assemble the trifle.

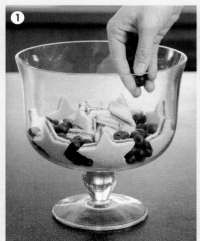

1. After arranging 7 stars around the outside of the trifle bowl, place 2 cups of jam sandwich scraps in a pile in the center of the dish and then arrange 3 cups of blueberries around the stars.

2. For the raspberry layer, spread 2 cups of custard in the trifle dish, place 1 cup of jam sandwich scraps in the center of the custard layer, and then arrange 2 cups of raspberries around the perimeter.

3. Spread the remaining custard in the dish and place 7 stars around the outside. Arrange remaining blueberries around the stars, leaving the center of the custard devoid of blueberries. Top with remaining raspberries.

Shopping with the Test Kitchen

Cutting Your Own Double-Thick Pork Chops

We like juicy blade-end chops that are at least 2 inches thick for our **Smoked Double-Thick Pork Chops** recipe (page 18). If you can't find them prepackaged at your grocery store, just buy a 4½- to 5-pound bone-in blade roast and cut it into 2-inch portions yourself. If cutting your own chops, ask your butcher or meat department manager if the chine bone (a part of the backbone) has been removed from the base of the roast—this thick bone can make carving difficult. If the chine bone has not been removed, ask the butcher to cut the chops for you.

—Diane Unger

When Things Go Wrong in the Kitchen

FLOUR POWER

During my college years, my roommate and I decided to impress our sorority sisters by making peach pies for dessert. I was in charge of the crust and had asked my roommate to get the flour out of the kitchen storage room. Dutifully, she dragged the 50-pound bag of flour to the counter for measuring. After measuring approximately 12 cups of what appeared to be exceptionally fine flour, we began to mix in the shortening and the ice water. As we added the water, the dough became VERY stiff. The more water we added and the more we mixed, the stiffer the dough got. After some time of working on the impossible dough we finally gave up. Imagine our surprise when we turned the bag of flour around to drag it back to the storage room and saw the words "Cement Hardener" on the front of the bag!

Karen Goodwin via e-mail

GARDENING AND COOKING DON'T ALWAYS MIX

One evening I decided to bake a batch of lemon bars to send to my husband's grandmother, who lives in a nursing home out of state. It was late when they finally came out of the oven, so I dusted them with powdered sugar and set them on my kitchen table covered loosely with waxed paper to mail the next day. We'd just had our first frost, and one of my

pots of begonias was just too pretty to leave outside to die, so I brought in the clay pot of bright red blossoms and set it on my kitchen table. When my husband came home from work a few hours later, he lifted the waxed paper to see what I'd been up to that evening and was stunned to see a trail through the powdered sugar that ended in a large garden slug. Evidently, slugs like lemon bars, too!

Carol Ingram Granite City, Ill.

TWO-DAY TURKEY

With my mother-in-law's busy schedule, she often cooks meals ahead of time. One summer day, she decided to slow-roast a turkey on her outdoor gas grill. She got sidetracked, and it wasn't until the next afternoon that she finally remembered about the turkey she started the day before. Rushing to the grill, she found that the tank had run out of gas, and underneath the lid was nothing but a pile of ash and soot in a baking pan.

Min Ryan via e-mail

CREAMIEST CORN MUFFINS

Many years ago, my young daughter was helping me prepare dinner by making corn muffins. After baking for the allotted time, she checked on the muffins, but they had only risen a tiny bit and were very pale. She served them anyway, but when her father bit into one, he couldn't hide the fact that they were awful! I asked her what she had used for ingredients, and she replied that she had used cornmeal from the canister in the cabinet. I immediately knew that something was amiss, since I don't keep my cornmeal in a canister. When I opened the cabinet, I discovered that she had used Coffee-Mate instead!

Susie Stephens Rockford, Ill.

LET THEM EAT CAKE

On my brother's fifth birthday, my mother, a very talented cake decorator, decided to bake a teddy bear–shaped sheet cake for his party. She had just finished decorating the cake when my brother returned from school. She rushed to hide the cake under her bed. When we were ready for the party, I went into my parents' room to retrieve my brother's cake. Although it was still there, most of the bear's legs were missing. While my mom had hidden the cake from my brother's eyes, she had forgotten about our cocker spaniel. He had found the cake and ate as much as the bed's frame would allow. Without batting an eye, Mom cut off another inch from the poor bear's legs and redecorated the cake. No one knew anything had happened!

Gwen MacDonald Chatsworth, Calif.

THE EGGPLANT BLUES

In my younger years, I knew very little about cooking, and the few recipes I made came from my mom's recipe collection. One night, I invited some friends from work over for dinner. I planned to make a side dish of scalloped eggplant. The recipe said to pare and dice a 2-pound eggplant. Unfortunately, I didn't realize that to pare meant to peel. My mother wasn't picking up the phone, so I just decided to ignore that step altogether. I proceeded with the recipe and was shocked when I pulled the casserole out of the oven to see it had turned completely blue from the eggplant skin! My guests were polite and tried some of it, since it tasted fine, but I certainly did have a lot of leftovers that night.

Kate Green Boston, Mass.

LESS ISN'T MORE

In my early 20s, I had my very first apartment with my boyfriend, who was several years older than me. Determined to impress him, I planned a dinner party and invited his brother and sister-in-law. I studied recipes for weeks and finally decided that roasted Cornish game hens would be a dish that would reflect my sophistication. I had never eaten Cornish game hens, but I was delighted that they were so economical, since they came two to every pack at the grocery store. I worked all day on my dinner and followed the recipe to the letter, but when I took the hens out of the oven I was surprised to see they hadn't grown at all. In my naivety, I thought the hens would expand in the oven enough to feed four people—after all, my mother only ever cooked one chicken. We ordered Chinese.

Kathy Houchen Waldorf, Md.

Send us your funniest kitchen disaster stories. E-mail us by visiting **CooksCountry.com/kitchendisasters**. Or write to us at Kitchen Disasters, Cook's Country, P.O. Box 470739, Brookline, MA 02447. If we publish your story, you'll receive a complimentary one-year subscription to *Cook's Country*.

Stars and Stripes Berry Trifle

With creamy custard, tender cake, and fresh fruit, a berry trifle is the perfect summer dessert. The best summer trifles make their appearance right around Independence Day. Along with stripes of red raspberries and blueberries, we've stamped out pound-cake sandwiches in the shape of stars.

To make this cake you'll need:

- **2** store-bought pound cakes (16 ounces each), thawed and edges trimmed
- **3** tablespoons seedless raspberry jam
- **6** cups fresh blueberries
- **1** tablespoon plus 1 teaspoon sugar
- **1** teaspoon water
- **3** cups fresh red raspberries
- **4** cups vanilla custard, refrigerated until firm*
- **1** cup lightly sweetened whipped cream

For the stars: Slice each cake lengthwise into 5 equal pieces. Spread scant 2 teaspoons jam each on 5 cake slices and top with remaining slices to create jam sandwiches. Using 2-inch

star cookie cutter, cut out 3 stars from each sandwich. Chop remaining sandwich scraps into 1/2-inch pieces. Set aside.

For the berries: Toss blueberries, 1 tablespoon sugar, and water in bowl. In separate bowl, toss raspberries with remaining sugar. Let sit until sugar dissolves and berries are glossy, about 5 minutes.

To assemble: Following photos on page 31, arrange 7 star sandwiches upright around bottom of 3-quart trifle dish. Place 2 cups sandwich scraps in center of dish. Arrange 3 cups blueberries around stars, piling up blueberries

so that they surround all edges of stars. Spread 2 cups custard in even layer on top of blueberry and cake layer. Place 1 cup sandwich scraps on center of custard layer. Arrange 2 cups raspberries around perimeter of dish. Spread remaining custard in even layer on top of raspberries. Arrange 7 star sandwiches upright around perimeter of dish. Arrange remaining blueberries around stars and pile remaining raspberries in center of dish. Spoon whipped cream on top of raspberries and top with remaining star.

*Go to **CooksCountry.com** for our custard recipe or use your own.

Recipe Index

RC = Recipe Card

Cook's Country

AUGUST/SEPTEMBER 2007

"Jucy Lucy" Burgers
Cheese-Stuffed and Juicy

Chicago BBQ Ribs
Make Them in Your Backyard!

Skillet Peach Cobbler
Tastier Fruit, Fluffier Topping

GRILLED PORK CUTLETS
With Three Easy Marinades

RATING SLOW COOKERS
Which Features Matter?

GRILLED CORN ON THE COB
Tender Kernels, Smoky Flavor

BBQ BEEF SANDWICHES
Easy Slow-Cooker Recipe

GRILLED CHICKEN TERIYAKI
Big Flavor, Moist Chicken

POTATO CHIP TASTE-OFF
Kettle-Style Takes Top Honors

PEANUT BUTTER COOKIES
Unlikely Ingredient Trims Fat

MEMPHIS COLESLAW
Tangy, Sweet, and Crunchy

EASY FRESH FRUIT TART
Quick and Spectacular!

$4.95 U.S./$6.95 CANADA

Our $1,000 Contest Winner!
Helen Fields of Springtown, Texas, won first place in our summer picnic salad contest with a crisp salad bursting with vibrant Tex-Mex flavors. See page 4 for her **Summer Crunch Salad.**

0 74470 05251 7

09>

Dear Country Cook,

My first "portrait" was as a three-year-old sitting in a canoe with my father; we were headed out for a camping trip on a small island in a lake in northern Maine. The snapshot is in color, but my orange life vest has faded over time. The water is still, the island behind us is dark and out of focus, and my father's paddle is angled, stuck in time. It is the absolute simplicity of the moment that catches the eye as well as the heart.

Other photos have this power, whether it is a group of boys peeling potatoes or another canoe trip, this one with my then eight-year-old Caroline, who is holding a six-pound salmon in both arms on a very cold day in April up on the Miramichi River. The fish was caught in the last hour of the last day of the trip after successive bouts of rain, snow, and sleet. It was the sunniest day of my life.

These simple things—the paddle in the water, the caught fish—are the bread and butter of the good life. But these pleasures aren't limited to faded snapshots. You can walk into the kitchen any day of the week and create these moments by cooking lasagna for supper or brewing coffee for neighbors. It's that simple.

Sure, we pull out the family albums around the holidays and glance at photos on the wall, but memories of peeling potatoes, snapping beans, and cutting biscuits retain their color and focus over generations to come.

Christopher Kimball
Founder and Editor, Cook's Country Magazine

Scouts at Work, August 1960. Three boys peel potatoes for a jamboree that included 700 of their peers.
Photographer: Reg Speller/Fox Photos/Hulton Archive/Getty Images

AUGUST/SEPTEMBER 2007

Cook's Country

Founder and Editor Christopher Kimball
Editorial Director Jack Bishop
Deputy Editor Bridget Lancaster
Senior Editors Scott Kathan
Jeremy Sauer
Test Kitchen Director Erin McMurrer
Test Cooks Kelley Baker
Meredith Butcher
Greg Case
Cali Rich
Diane Unger
Assistant Test Cook Lynn Clark
Web Managing Editor Katherine Bell
Web Editor Kate Mason
Copy Editor Will Gordon
Market Research Manager Melissa Baldino
Editorial Assistant Meredith Smith
Senior Kitchen Assistant Nadia Domeq
Kitchen Assistant David Lentini
Contributing Editor Eva Katz

Design Director Amy Klee
Senior Designer, Magazines Julie Bozzo
Designers Jay Layman
Christine Vo
Staff Photographer Daniel J. van Ackere

Production Director Guy Rochford
Traffic and Projects Manager Alice Cummiskey
Production Assistant Lauren Pettapiece
Color and Imaging Specialist Andrew Mannone

Vice President New Technology Craig Morrow
Systems Administrator S. Paddi McHugh
Web Developer Justin Greenough
Web Designer Lillian Chan

Chief Financial Officer Sharyn Chabot
Human Resources Manager Adele Shapiro
Controller Mandy Shito
Senior Accountant Aaron Goranson
Staff Accountant Connie Forbes
Office Manager Elizabeth Pohm
Receptionist Henrietta Murray

Vice President Marketing David Mack
Circulation Director Bill Tine
Fulfillment Manager Carrie Horan
Circulation Assistant Elizabeth Dayton
Direct Mail Director Adam Perry
Direct Mail Analyst Jenny Leong
Products Director Steven Browall
E-Commerce Marketing Manager Hugh Buchan
Marketing Copywriter David Goldberg
Junior Developer Doug Sisko
Customer Service Manager Jacqueline Valerio
Customer Service Representatives Julie Gardner
Jillian Nannicelli

Vice President Sales Demee Gambulos
Retail Sales & Marketing Manager Emily Logan
Retail Sales Associate Anthony King
Corporate Partnership Manager Allie Brawley
Corporate Marketing Associate Bailey Vatalaro
Publicity Deborah Broide

ON THE COVER: PHOTOGRAPHY: StockFood/Jung. ILLUSTRATION: John Burgoyne.
IN THIS ISSUE: COLOR FOOD PHOTOGRAPHY: Keller + Keller. STYLING: Mary Jane Sawyer, Marie Piraino. ILLUSTRATION: Lisa Perrett.

Cook's Country magazine (ISSN 1552-1990), number 16, is published bimonthly by Boston Common Press Limited Partnership, 17 Station Street, Brookline, MA 02445. Copyright 2007 Boston Common Press Limited Partnership. Periodicals Postage paid at Boston, Mass., and additional mailing offices. Publications Mail Agreement No. 40020778. Return undeliverable Canadian addresses to P.O. Box 875, Station A, Windsor, Ontario N9A 6P2. POSTMASTER: Send address changes to Cook's Country, P.O. Box 8382, Red Oak, IA 51591-1382. For subscription and gift subscription orders, subscription inquiries, or change-of-address notices, call 800-526-8447 in the U.S. or 515-247-7571 from outside the U.S. or write us at Cook's Country, P.O. Box 8382, Red Oak, IA 51591-1382. PRINTED IN THE USA

Visit us at www.CooksCountry.com!
Go online for hundreds of recipes, food tastings, and up-to-date equipment reviews. You can get a behind-the-scenes look at our test kitchen, talk to our cooks and editors, enter recipe contests, and share recipes and cooking tips with the *Cook's Country* community.

Kitchen Shortcuts

READERS SHARE CLEVER TIPS FOR EVERYDAY COOKING CHALLENGES

NEAT TRICK

Dust Buster

Recipes often call for dusting cakes or cookies with sugar, but I'm not fond of having to clean up my countertop. My solution is to place the cake on a small cooling rack over the kitchen sink. Any leftover sugar falls into the sink, so all I have to do to clean up is rinse the sink.

Lucille Yip
Lahaina, Hawaii

Squeeze and Roll

The quickest way to squeeze out excess water from defrosted spinach is with a few clean dish towels and a rolling pin. Place the spinach between the towels and roll over the top of it with a rolling pin. If the towels become too saturated, grab some more and keep on rolling.

Emily W. Easton
Chicago, Ill.

Clean Sweep

I am a very precise baker, and I am always checking the size and thickness of my dough with a ruler. Instead of searching for a pastry scraper to clean off my floured counter, I just use the ruler to scrape any remaining debris into the trash.

Donna Kalevas
Roaring Gap, N.C.

Stick a Fork in It!

NEW WAY TO OIL YOUR GRILL

Instead of wasting paper towels every time I oil the grates on my grill, I came up with a new way. I simply cut an onion in half and stick a fork in the top of the pole end. Then I dip the flat end of the onion into the oil and rub the grates. Once I am done, I cut the onion into rings and grill them up to go along with my steaks.

Justin Fahey Newton, Mass.

SHOO FLY, DON'T BOTHER ME

In the summer, fruit flies can be a problem in my house. To get rid of them, I put a little apple cider vinegar in a bowl and cover it tightly with plastic wrap. I then poke holes in the top. The fruit flies, attracted to the cider vinegar, fly into the holes and can't escape. I discreetly place the bowl in a corner, and I don't have to deal with those pesky fruit flies anymore!

Bob Kennedy
Toronto, Ont.

FRESH COOKIES IN A FLASH

Whenever I bake cookies or brownies, I always save a few and put them in my freezer, wrapped well in plastic wrap and foil. That way, if I have any unexpected company, I can quickly unwrap them, throw them on a baking sheet, and reheat them in the oven. My guests think I just whipped up a batch of cookies.

Amy Gualtieri
Rome, N.Y.

BLENDER GRINDER

I love fresh ground coffee but have never bought a bean grinder. Instead, I place whole beans in my blender and grind away. Within seconds, I have ground coffee ready to percolate.

Dorcas Unger
Wayland, Mass.

RECYCLED SEASONINGS

I save the seasonings that fall off "everything" bagels (sesame and poppy seeds, onion, garlic, and salt) and sprinkle them on scrambled eggs, chicken salad, and tuna salad. It adds a little something extra, and all of my friends have started doing the same thing.

Merel Nissenberg
La Jolla, Calif.

SUGAR IN A PINCH

When there's no powdered sugar on hand, I fill a very clean coffee grinder or food processor halfway with granulated sugar and process for about 15 seconds. The sugar becomes more powder-like and is perfect for sweetening my iced teas and coffee.

Greg Wallingford
Pleasant Hill, Calif.

BUMPING UP THE FLAVOR

I go through a lot of Parmesan cheese in my house, and I always wondered what I could do with the leftover rinds. Now I save them in a small plastic bag, and when I make pasta, I add one or two rinds to the pasta water. You'll be amazed at the flavor! I also add the rinds to flavor soups and stews.

Erin Maness
Hanover, Mass.

KEEP BREAD WARMER LONGER

I often bake biscuits and fresh bread to serve at dinner parties and lunches, but by the time I get the bread into the basket and to the table, it's cold. Now I line my basket with aluminum foil, place a napkin on the foil, and pile the bread on top of the napkin. The foil retains the heat, keeping the bread warmer longer.

Christine LaPlume
Rockland, Mass.

DON'T WASTE YOUR CHIPOTLE

I never use more than one or two chipotle chiles in a recipe, so now I divide the leftovers between little disposable plastic cups with lids and freeze them. When I need one for a recipe, I run the plastic cup under hot water and the chipotle defrosts quickly, ready for use. No more waste!

Teresa McCormack
Hyde Park, Mass.

EASY OPENER

I use an old computer mouse pad as a jar opener. The rubber on the back of the pad is perfect for gripping those stubborn lids.

Deb Johnson
Watertown, Wis.

If you'd like to submit a tip, please e-mail us by visiting **CooksCountry.com/emailus** or send a letter to Kitchen Shortcuts, Cook's Country, P.O. Box 470739, Brookline, MA 02447. Include your name, address, and phone number. If we put your tip, you will receive a free one-year subscription to *Cook's Country*.

PERFECT WAFFLES

Searching for picture-perfect waffles every time, I experimented with measuring cups to find out the right amount of batter to pour on my iron. They look great, and there's no more messy cleanup from excess batter oozing out the sides. So I wouldn't forget, I wrote the amount on a small label and posted it on the handle of my waffle iron, so now I always make perfect waffles.

Jessica Anderson
Galloway, Ohio

OILED PERFECTION

When I set up my grill, I always oil the newspaper before lighting it; the oiled paper burns slowly (the oil coats the paper much like wax coats a candle wick, slowing down the combustion) and fully ignites the coals. But dipping the paper in oil or even brushing the oil on can be messy, so I keep a spray bottle filled with vegetable oil near my grill, and I lightly spray the newspaper before wadding it up and lighting it.

Karl Holtz
Santa Clara, Calif.

NO MORE EYEBALLING

Most cookie recipes call for a specific size dough ball, say 1½ inches. If I try to eyeball it, I end up with fewer or more cookies than the recipe says. But holding up a ruler every time seems even more annoying than having too many or too few cookies. So I take my ruler and pencil and mark the correct size on the parchment paper that the cookies are going to bake on. When I roll my cookie balls, I can just check the size with my reference marks.

Meg Daily
Denver, Colo.

GINGER SNAP

When a recipe calls for grated ginger, I cut a walnut-size piece from a ginger root, peel it, and pop it in my garlic press. With one squeeze I have juice and pulp ready to use.

Max Colgrove
Wickenburg, Ariz.

SMOOTHER EGG SALAD

When making egg salad, I don't want big chunks of egg scattered throughout, so I use my Microplane to grate the eggs. At first my husband didn't believe there was any egg because they were so well blended.

Gretchen Kohl
Alameda, Calif.

MUSTARD VINAIGRETTE

I am never able to get every last drop out of my jars of mustard. Instead of throwing the jars away, I add some oil, vinegar, and seasonings, put the top back on, and shake away. Now I have mustard vinaigrette!

Ramzey Kiyali
Alpharetta, Ga.

EASY RETRIEVAL

Whenever I blanch a bunch of vegetables for my pasta primavera, I keep the asparagus wrapped in the rubber bands from the grocery store. That way, I can easily retrieve it from the hot water once it is cooked and I'm ready to add the next vegetable.

Erica Prussman
Quincy, Mass.

PRESERVE YOUR GARLIC LONGER

If you buy large containers of peeled garlic, stuff the container with paper towels and turn the container upside down in your refrigerator. The excess moisture will drip into the towels instead of rotting the garlic.

Dianne Boate
San Francisco, Calif.

EASY SQUEEZE

I like to use a hand-squeezed juicer to juice my lemons, limes, and oranges, but I was getting frustrated at how awkward and difficult it was to push down on the rounded ends of the fruits (especially pointy lemons). So I started slicing a little bit off of the end of the fruit before juicing —just enough to make a flat surface—and not only is it easier to squeeze the fruit (and easier on your hands), but you get more juice!

Shannon Miehe
Tiburon, Calif.

Don't Crack Up

Sometimes my eggs get stuck to the inside of their cardboard carton, and I used to end up breaking the shells when I tried to pry them out. Now I wet the carton, which makes removing the eggs easy.

Debbie Manning
Wayland, Iowa

Spoonful of Medicine

I keep the small plastic cups that are attached to the tops of cold medicine bottles to measure out my liquid ingredients. Each cap has tablespoon measurements on the side.

Judy Robbins
Knoxville, Tenn.

Clean Joes

Messy sandwiches like Sloppy Joes can be hard to eat, often ending up all over the front of my shirt. Now I cut off the top quarter of a bun that hasn't been presliced, hollow out the bottom portion, spoon the filling into the bottom, and replace the top. No more spills!

Karyn Hickey
Stoneham, Mass.

Whisking Up More Suds

TINY BUBBLES

I like lots of suds when I am doing the dishes. After a few minutes, the suds are practically gone, so to solve this problem, I use my whisk and whip new suds right in the sink without adding any more soap or water.

Todd Hart Bay City, Mich.

DOUBLE DUTY

Better Hull

I use the pointy end of my old-fashioned church key bottle opener to hull my strawberries. Works like a charm.

Kathleen Libbey
Myrtle Beach, S.C.

Top Salad Packs Texas-Sized Crunch

Our $1,000 Grand-Prize Winner!

Helen Fields
Springtown, Texas

Our winning salad recipe features crunchy jicama and bell pepper alongside tender spinach and sweet corn, with a lively Tex-Mex dressing. Toasted pecans add even more crunch to this summer salad. "I grew up with a large pecan tree shading our front yard," says grand-prize winner Helen Fields. "So pecans are one of my favorite ingredients for both sweet and savory dishes." Our runners-up found inspiration for their salads a bit farther afield, in the cuisines of the Mediterranean, Asia, Jamaica, and France.

SUMMER CRUNCH SALAD SERVES 4 TO 6

If making this salad ahead of time, don't dress it until ready to serve.

Salad
- 1 large jicama (see page 31), peeled and cut into matchsticks
- 1 cup frozen corn, thawed
- 1 red bell pepper, seeded and chopped
- 1 pint cherry tomatoes, halved
- 3/4 cup pecans, toasted and chopped
- 1/4 cup chopped fresh cilantro
- 2 cups baby spinach

Dressing
- 2 tablespoons lime juice
- 1 tablespoon honey
- 1 tablespoon Dijon mustard
- 1/2 teaspoon ground cumin
- 1/4 cup olive oil
  Salt and pepper

1. For the salad: Toss jicama, corn, bell pepper, tomatoes, pecans, cilantro, and spinach in large bowl.
2. For the dressing: Combine lime juice, honey, mustard, and cumin in medium bowl. Gradually whisk in oil. Drizzle dressing over salad and toss to combine. Season with salt and pepper. Serve.

Crunchy jicama, red pepper, and toasted pecans give this salad its signature snap.

Upcoming Contest: Pasta Sauces

We want your best summer pasta sauce recipes for an upcoming contest. Please submit entries by September 30, 2007. Send us your recipes by visiting **CooksCountry.com/emailus** or write to us at Recipe Contest, Cook's Country, P.O. Box 470739, Brookline, MA 02447. Include your name, address, and daytime phone number and tell us what makes your recipe special. The grand-prize winner will receive $1,000. All entries become the property of *Cook's Country* and may be edited. For more information on this and other contests, go to **CooksCountry.com**.

Rachel Platter
Nashville, Ind.

Lois Szydlowski
Tampa, Fla.

Mary Louise Lever
Rome, Ga.

Diane Walsh
Waltham, Mass.

ORZO WITH EVERYTHING
SERVES 4 TO 6

Rachel writes: "My husband and I were invited to a dinner party where we discovered the wonderful flavor of orzo in a salad the hostess served. I duplicated the recipe at home, and now I serve orzo with everything for almost every summer get-together we host."

Salad

- 1 tablespoon salt
- 1 pound orzo pasta
- 1/2 cup sun-dried tomatoes, rinsed, patted dry, and minced
- 1/2 cup pitted kalamata olives, halved
- 1 small head radicchio, cored and chopped fine
- 1 cup grated Parmesan cheese
- 1/2 cup pine nuts, toasted
- 1/2 cup chopped fresh basil

Dressing

- 1/4 cup balsamic vinegar
- 2 garlic cloves, minced
- 5 tablespoons extra-virgin olive oil
  Salt and pepper

1. For the salad: Bring 4 quarts water to boil in large pot over high heat. Add salt and orzo to boiling water and cook until just al dente. Drain pasta and let cool to room temperature. Combine cooled orzo, tomatoes, olives, radicchio, Parmesan, pine nuts, and basil in large bowl.

2. For the dressing: Combine vinegar and minced garlic in medium bowl. Gradually whisk in oil. Drizzle dressing over salad and toss to combine. Season with salt and pepper. Serve. (Salad can be refrigerated for up to 2 days.)

SWEET AND SPICY ASIAN SLAW SERVES 4 TO 6

Lois writes: "The versatility and quickness of this slaw make it convenient for my busy lifestyle. I usually bring it to picnics and barbecues. People always love the hint of mint in there." To vary this salad, Lois recommends adding thinly sliced fruit (peaches, mangos, or pineapple), snow peas, or bean sprouts.

Salad

- 1 (16-ounce) bag coleslaw mix
- 1 red bell pepper, seeded and sliced thin
- 1 cucumber, peeled, seeded, and sliced thin
- 4 scallions, sliced thin
- 1/2 cup chopped fresh cilantro
- 1/2 cup chopped fresh mint
- 1/2 cup roasted peanuts, chopped

Dressing

- 5 tablespoons lime juice
- 2 1/2 tablespoons fish sauce
- 3 tablespoons sugar
- 3 tablespoons rice vinegar
- 1 tablespoon grated fresh ginger
- 1/4 teaspoon cayenne pepper
- 4 teaspoons toasted sesame oil
  Salt

1. For the salad: Combine coleslaw mix, bell pepper, cucumber, scallions, cilantro, mint, and peanuts in large bowl.

2. For the dressing: Combine lime juice, fish sauce, sugar, vinegar, ginger, and cayenne in medium bowl. Gradually whisk in oil. Drizzle dressing over salad and toss to combine. Season with salt. Serve. (Salad can be refrigerated for up to 2 days.)

REGGAE RICE AND SWEET POTATO SALAD SERVES 4 TO 6

Mary Louise writes: "On a trip to Jamaica, I discovered a wonderful sweet potato salad. This is my attempt to re-create it."

Salad

- 2 pounds sweet potatoes, peeled and cut into 1/2-inch chunks
- 2 tablespoons salt
- 2 cups cooked long-grain rice
- 1 (15-ounce) can pineapple chunks, drained and chopped, 1/4 cup juice reserved for dressing
- 1 red bell pepper, seeded and chopped
- 3 scallions, sliced thin
- 1/2 cup sliced almonds, toasted

Dressing

- 1 tablespoon Dijon mustard
- 2 teaspoons grated lime zest plus 1 1/2 tablespoons lime juice
- 1 tablespoon poppy seeds
- 1 habanero chile, seeded and minced
- 1 tablespoon grated fresh ginger
- 1/4 cup vegetable oil
  Salt

1. For the salad: Bring sweet potatoes, salt, and water to cover to boil in large saucepan over high heat. Reduce heat and simmer until potatoes are just tender, about 5 minutes. Drain potatoes and cool to room temperature. Toss potatoes with remaining salad ingredients.

2. For the dressing: Combine remaining pineapple juice, mustard, lime zest and juice, poppy seeds, chile, and ginger in bowl. Gradually whisk in oil. Drizzle dressing over salad and toss to combine. Season with salt. Serve. (Salad can be refrigerated for up to 2 days.)

TWO-BEAN SALAD WITH BACON SERVES 4 TO 6

Diane writes: "My friend Lillian, a fan of humble, simple cooking, inspired this recipe. This salad travels well and is picnic-friendly." We prefer the smooth texture and sharp flavor of Dijon mustard here, but any flavorful mustard will work in this recipe.

Salad

- 4 slices bacon, chopped
- 4 ounces green beans, trimmed and cut into 1-inch pieces (about 1 cup)
- 2 (16-ounce) cans white beans, drained and rinsed
- 1 small red onion, chopped fine
- 1/4 cup chopped fresh parsley
- 2 tablespoons chopped fresh mint

Dressing

- 2 tablespoons lemon juice
- 1 tablespoon Dijon mustard
- 1/4 cup olive oil
  Salt and pepper

1. For the salad: Cook bacon in large skillet over medium-high heat until crisp, about 5 minutes. Using slotted spoon, transfer bacon to large bowl. Pour off all but 2 tablespoons bacon fat from skillet and cook green beans in fat until bright green and just tender, about 5 minutes. Add cooked green beans, white beans, onion, parsley, and mint to bowl with bacon.

2. For the dressing: Combine lemon juice and mustard in medium bowl. Gradually whisk in oil. Drizzle dressing over salad and toss to combine. Season with salt and pepper. Serve. (Salad can be refrigerated for up to 2 days.)

Ask Cook's Country

WE'LL ANSWER ANY QUESTION YOU THROW AT US!

CAPER PRIMER

I've been cooking with capers for years, but I have never known where they come from. What are they, exactly?

Dottie Kelsey
Penacook, N.H.

Capers are the unopened flower buds of a shrub that grows in the Mediterranean region. After the dark green buds are picked, they are preserved in one of two ways: brining or salt-curing. Capers are also classified by size, ranging from the smallest nonpareils, which measure less than seven millimeters in diameter (about the size of a corn kernel) to the largest grusas, which are twice the size.

TASTY BUDS
We prefer small brined capers for convenience and flavor.

Curious as to what impact size and preservation method have on flavor, we tried various sizes of brined and salted capers both on their own and in a simple pasta sauce. Smaller capers were favored, as tasters thought larger capers were "too pungent" to eat whole. Salted capers had a "clean," "herby" flavor but required 30 minutes of soaking before they were palatable (rinsing didn't do the trick). On the other hand, brined capers were consistently good both on their own and in the sauce and could simply be drained before use. You may also encounter pickled caperberries in the market, which are capers that were allowed to come to fruit before being picked. They are best used in martinis in place of olives.

CHIPS VERSUS BARS

If a recipe calls for semisweet bar chocolate, is it OK to substitute semisweet chocolate chips instead?

Rachel Fitzgerald
New York, N.Y.

You might think chips are simply miniaturized versions of bar chocolate, but that isn't the case. Chocolate chips have less cocoa butter (i.e., fat) than bar chocolate, to ensure that they maintain their shape when baked. To find out if this would make a difference when the chips were melted, we gathered several of our recipes that call for melted semisweet chocolate, including Chocolate Pudding, Chocolate Ice Cream Sauce, and Devil's Food Cupcakes with Dark Chocolate Icing and made one batch of each with bar chocolate and another with chips. The results were startlingly clear. In the pudding, ice cream sauce, and icing, the chips produced a slightly grainy, overly thick, and viscous texture, while the bar versions were light and silky. However, the crumb of the cupcakes seemed to mask any textural difference between the two versions. Tasters did notice that the

cupcakes made with chips were slightly sweeter. So the next time you're left with only morsels in your pantry, don't hesitate to whip up baked goods, but head to the store if your sights are set on something smooth and creamy.

BRIE RIND, A CUT ABOVE THE REST

Is the white exterior of Brie edible?

Louise Markle
Winston-Salem, N.C.

The soft, pillowy rind of Brie and other bloomed-rind cheeses, such as Camembert, is not only edible, it's the most flavorful part. The ripening process of Brie begins with the application of *Penicillium candidum*, a harmless white mold, on the surface of the immature cheese. Over the next several weeks the mold grows (or "blooms") into a tender white crust around the cheese that provides both textural contrast and concentrated flavor. The mold is also at work internally; as the cheese ages, the mold grows roots that make their way to the center of the Brie, breaking down the protein and softening the cheese as they go. You can tell that the roots have reached the middle and that the Brie is fully ripe when the center feels soft and tender to the touch. If you have an aversion to the rind, it can certainly be trimmed off, but watch where you cut. Brie ripens

GOOD MOLD
The white rind of Brie is actually a harmless—and delicious—mold.

from the outside in, so you might be slicing off the creamiest part of the cheese with the rind.

GRADING BEEF

I've seen different grades of beef available in my grocery store. What's the difference between them?

Joshua Cole
Charleston, S.C.

The U.S. Department of Agriculture classifies beef by eight grades, which denote the amount of marbled fat (fat strands woven throughout the meat that add moisture and flavor, as opposed to tough exterior fat) and the age of the cow. The top three—Prime, Choice, and Select—are generally the only grades you will see at retail. Prime is rich in flavor and tenderness because of the youth of the cow and extensive marbling, but it is typically found only in specialty markets or restaurants. Choice and Select are widely available in grocery stores. Choice has slightly less marbling than Prime but is still very tender and flavorful. Select, the least expensive of the three, is much leaner and lacks juiciness and flavor.

Curious if these labels would track in a taste test,

we seared several strip steaks of each. Although the Prime steaks were favored for their "buttery" texture and "robust beef" flavor, they were also a steep $18 per pound; we'd be happy to settle for our close second, Choice, at $12 per pound. The Select steaks—dry, tough, and not nearly as beefy—weren't worth their $9-per-pound price tag.

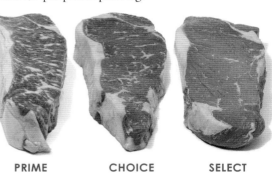

| PRIME | CHOICE | SELECT |

Prime has the best flavor and texture, but Choice is a better value. We don't recommend buying Select steaks.

PAPRIKA PRIMER

I've seen paprika labeled sweet, smoked, and hot. What's the difference, and can they be used interchangeably?

Nathaniel Adams
Hyde Park, Mass.

"Paprika" is a generic term for a spice made from ground dried red peppers. Whether paprika is labeled sweet, smoked, or hot is determined by the variety (or varieties) of pepper used and how the pepper is manipulated. Sweet paprika (sometimes called "Hungarian paprika" or simply "paprika") is the most common. Typically made from a combination of mild red peppers, sweet paprika is prized more for its deep scarlet hue than for its very subtle flavor. Smoked paprika, a Spanish favorite, is produced by drying peppers (either sweet or hot) over smoldering oak embers. Since smoked paprika has a deep, musky flavor all its own, we do not recommend using it for all paprika applications; it is best used to season grilled meats or to add a smoky aroma to boldly flavored dishes. Hot paprika, most often used in chilis, curries, or stews, can be made from any number of hot peppers. It can range from slightly spicy to punishingly assertive, and it shouldn't be substituted for sweet paprika in cooking. On the other hand, sweet paprika can be substituted for hot by simply adding cayenne pepper to boost the burn.

We conducted a taste test of six brands of sweet paprika in our Paprika Chicken recipe. Our favorites are Penzeys Hungarian Sweet, which tasters praised for its "roasty," "bold" bite, and McCormick, which was "incredibly full-flavored."

To ask us a cooking question, visit **CooksCountry.com/emailus.** You can also write to Ask Cook's Country, P.O. Box 470739, Brookline, MA 02447. See if you can stump us!

Recipe Makeover PEANUT BUTTER COOKIES

How do you reduce the fat in a cookie whose main ingredients are butter and peanut butter? The answer will surprise you.

Using less fat actually improves the texture of these cookies, which are crisp and never greasy.

Most cookies get their fat and calories from sugar, eggs, and a whole lot of butter. Peanut butter cookies go a step further by adding at least a cup of the fatty main ingredient to the mix. That's why a single peanut butter cookie weighs in at 200 calories and 12 grams of fat. Could we find a way to lose the fat and keep the peanut flavor?

Many peanut butter cookie recipes contain 2 cups of granulated sugar and a whopping 16 tablespoons of butter. In addition to adding sweetness, sugar also makes cookies pleasantly chewy. When I reduced the amount of sugar, the flavor was fine (peanut butter cookies shouldn't be achingly sweet), but the cookies were too dry. By switching to moister brown

sugar, I was able to get away with using just 1¼ cups. I found recipes that replaced the butter with ingredients like mashed pears, prunes, and applesauce, but the resulting cookies were dry and too fruity. Other recipes cut back on butter by melting it (to make it more easily absorbed into the dough), but too much melted butter made the cookies greasy. A combination of 2 melted tablespoons and 4 softened tablespoons produced good results with much less fat.

I'd saved the big challenge for last: the peanut butter. Simply decreasing the peanut butter left the cookies devoid of flavor. Reduced-fat peanut butter, which replaces some of the peanuts with stabilizers, is wetter and looser than full-fat, and its moisture actually improved the texture of my cookies. The peanut pieces in chunky low-fat peanut butter added an extra layer of flavor.

I searched the supermarket for products to boost the nutty flavor. Sesame oil, tahini (sesame paste), and roasted soy nut butter all lacked peanut punch. Ground peanut butter sand-

wich cookies, peanut brittle, and peanut granola bars all had off-flavors; in desperation, I'd also grabbed a box of Cap'n Crunch's Peanut Butter Crunch cereal. After I ground it down and incorporated it into the flour, the cereal added so much big peanut flavor—with minimal fat—that I had to use only 5 tablespoons of reduced-fat peanut butter. My tasters actually preferred these cookies to the full-fat version. –Meredith Butcher

LOW-FAT PEANUT BUTTER COOKIES MAKES 24 COOKIES
Skippy Reduced Fat Super Chunk is the test kitchen's favorite brand of low-fat peanut butter (see page 30).

- 1½ cups Cap'n Crunch's Peanut Butter Crunch cereal
- ⅓ cup plus 1½ cups all-purpose flour
- ¼ teaspoon baking soda
- ¼ teaspoon salt
- 4 tablespoons unsalted butter, softened; plus 2 tablespoons unsalted butter, melted
- 5 tablespoons reduced-fat crunchy peanut butter (see note)
- 1¼ cups packed light brown sugar
- 2 large egg whites
- 1 teaspoon vanilla extract
- 1 tablespoon water

1. Adjust oven rack to middle position and heat oven to 350 degrees. Line two baking sheets with parchment paper. Pulse cereal and ⅓ cup flour in food processor until finely ground. Add remaining flour, baking soda, and salt and pulse to combine. With electric mixer on medium speed, beat softened butter, peanut butter, and sugar together until fluffy, about 2 minutes. Beat in melted butter, egg whites, and vanilla until combined. Add flour mixture and mix on low until incorporated. Add water and mix until absorbed.

2. Roll 1½ tablespoons dough into 1½-inch balls and space 2 inches apart on baking sheets. Following photos at right, press and crosshatch dough. Bake one sheet of cookies until edges are lightly browned but centers are still soft, 10 to 12 minutes, rotating halfway through baking. Cool on sheet for 5 minutes, then transfer to rack to cool completely. Repeat with remaining cookies. Serve. (Cookies will keep in airtight container for 3 days.)

Better for Baking Than for Breakfast
We found that an unlikely ingredient—Cap'n Crunch's Peanut Butter Crunch cereal—could be ground and used in place of some of the flour to increase peanut butter flavor with a minimum of fat.

And the Numbers. . .
All nutritional information is for one serving (one peanut butter cookie).

TRADITIONAL PEANUT BUTTER COOKIES
CALORIES: **200**
FAT: **12g**
SATURATED FAT: **4.5g**

COOK'S COUNTRY LOW-FAT PEANUT BUTTER COOKIES
CALORIES: **130**
FAT: **4g**
SATURATED FAT: **2.5g**

Kitchen Know-How
SURE SPREADING

Because these cookies contain less fat, they will not spread as easily as full-fat versions. We found that pressing each dough ball into a ½-inch disk gives the cookies a jump-start on spreading in the oven.

1. With the back of a measuring cup or a flat-bottomed glass, press each dough ball into a ½-inch disk.
2. Using a fork, make a crosshatch pattern on top of each cookie.

Could we transform our ordinary slow cooker into a professional BBQ pit?

Kitchen Know-How
THE RIGHT CUT

We found that a large chuck-eye roast retained its moisture better than other cuts, even after 10 hours in a slow cooker. Here's how we prepare the meat before cooking.

1. Select a well-marbled roast and carefully trim and discard any exterior fat.
2. Slicing from the top of the meat, cut the roast in half (as shown) and then cut each piece in half again.

Wake-Up Call

Brewed coffee blends with the other sauce ingredients to add richness without imparting coffee flavor.

SECRET INGREDIENT

Barbecued shredded beef sounds like an ideal recipe for the slow cooker, as both outdoor barbecue and slow cookers use slow-and-low heat to tenderize tough cuts of meat. But most of the slow-cooker recipes I found had me simply dumping a few bottles of barbecue sauce over a piece of brisket, turning on the slow cooker, and calling it a day. Eight hours later, the beef was dry, stringy, and chewy. Even worse, the meat tasted more like sour pot roast than barbecue, as the moist heat of the slow cooker washed away the flavor of the sauce.

With smoky, moist, and tender beef cloaked in a tangy sauce as my goal, I started with the meat. My testing proved brisket to be unreliable—too often it was tough and impossible to shred, even after hours of cooking. Flank steak, round steak, and chuck-eye roast worked better, with tasters preferring the chuck for its big, beefy flavor and silky, pull-apart texture.

Although bottled barbecue sauce can be pretty good, I knew I could do better. To create a smoky flavor base, I rendered bacon and cooked onion, chili powder, and paprika in the drippings. Ketchup, brown sugar, and mustard are a must for any barbecue sauce, but my tasters wanted deeper, more complex flavor. Neither beef nor chicken stock added the necessary richness, but a surprise ingredient—coffee—gave the sauce a depth that tasters appreciated (and couldn't identify as coffee).

I poured this sauce over the beef, and after 10 hours of cooking I had tender meat swimming in a watery sauce; as it cooked, the chuck had exuded juice into the sauce, dulling its flavor and thinning its texture. Using only half the sauce for cooking and reserving half for dressing the cooked meat worked well, especially when I reduced the cooking liquid before adding it back to the beef. Splashes of cider vinegar and hot sauce brightened things up, and a teaspoon of liquid smoke gave the dish nice smoky flavor.

After pulling the tender meat into shreds, tossing it with the sauce, and piling it high on a bun, I knew I'd hit the mark. I'd finally made slow-cooker barbecued beef that looked and tasted like it had come off the grill.

–Diane Unger

SLOW-COOKER BBQ SHREDDED BEEF SANDWICHES SERVES 10
Don't shred the meat too finely in step 3; it will break up more as the meat is combined with the sauce.

1	(5-pound) boneless beef chuck-eye roast, trimmed and cut into 4 pieces
4	slices bacon, chopped fine
1	onion, chopped fine
2	tablespoons chili powder
1	tablespoon paprika
1½	cups brewed coffee
1½	cups ketchup
¼	cup packed dark brown sugar
2	tablespoons brown mustard
1	tablespoon hot sauce
1	tablespoon cider vinegar
1	teaspoon liquid smoke
	Salt and pepper
10	sandwich rolls, split

1. Place beef in slow-cooker insert. Cook bacon in large skillet over medium-high heat until crisp, about 5 minutes. Using slotted spoon, transfer bacon to slow-cooker insert. Pour off all but 2 tablespoons fat from pan and cook onion in remaining bacon fat until softened, about 5 minutes. Add chili powder and paprika and cook until fragrant, about 30 seconds. Stir in coffee, ketchup, sugar, and 1 tablespoon mustard and simmer until reduced slightly, about 10 minutes. Add half of sauce to slow-cooker insert and refrigerate remaining half. Cover and cook on low until meat is tender, 9 to 10 hours (or cook on high for 5 to 6 hours).

2. Using slotted spoon, transfer meat to large bowl and cover with foil. Transfer cooking liquid to large skillet, skim fat, and simmer over medium-high heat until reduced to 1 cup, about 10 minutes. Off heat, stir in reserved sauce, remaining mustard, hot sauce, vinegar, and liquid smoke.

3. Pull meat into large chunks, discarding any excess fat or gristle. Toss meat with 1½ cups sauce and let sit, covered, until meat has absorbed most of sauce, about 10 minutes. Season with salt and pepper. Serve on rolls, passing remaining sauce at table.

A sturdy bulkie roll holds up well under a pile of this rich, smoky barbecue.

Lost Recipes ANGEL BISCUITS

This Southern biscuit gets its characteristic light and fluffy texture from an unexpected source.

Last summer, while vacationing in Charleston, S.C., I pulled into a hole-in-the-wall restaurant for lunch. I grabbed a seat at an empty vinyl-draped table and was immediately greeted by a basket of steaming biscuits. After one bite, I knew that these biscuits were something special. Though modest in height, they were unbelievably light and fluffy and had the hearty yeast flavor of a dinner roll. "Angel biscuits," said the waitress, noticing my delight. These were the best biscuits I'd ever tasted.

Research revealed the reason for the light, cloud-like texture of angel biscuits: They're made with yeast, baking powder, and baking soda, which creates a triple-forced lift. The use of three rising agents also explains why these biscuits are sometimes called "bride's biscuits," as even a novice cook (or a new bride) can make light and fluffy biscuits on the first attempt. The rounds of dough are folded in half before baking, causing the ethereally light biscuits to puff into "angel's wings" in the oven.

Digging deeper into the history of angel biscuits, I learned they were conceived as a use for leftover scraps of sour yeasted bread dough. In her 1846 book *Miss Beecher's Domestic Receipt-Book*, Catherine Beecher instructed cooks to "sweeten" (or neutralize) soured yeast-dough scraps with saleratus (a crude chemical leavener similar to today's baking soda), knead in shortening, and cut the "new" dough into biscuits.

But when I baked a few modern recipes, not one biscuit was as light and fluffy as the ones I had in Charleston. Looking for a bigger and faster rise, I turned to instant yeast. I found that quickly dissolving it in warm buttermilk allowed the yeast to begin working immediately, speeding up the rising time to just 30 minutes and producing the ultra-tender, feathery texture I wanted.

Typically, angel biscuits are made with shortening, rather than butter, to keep the flavor of the fat from competing with the yeast flavor. To minimize oven spread, I reduced the amount of shortening and switched from traditional cake flour to heartier all-purpose flour.

I tore open a hot biscuit and slathered on some butter and jelly. Now this was the heavenly biscuit I had discovered in Charleston. –Cali Rich

ANGEL BISCUITS MAKES 16

You will need a 2½-inch round biscuit cutter for this recipe.

- 1 cup buttermilk, heated to 110 degrees
- 1 envelope (2¼ teaspoons) rapid-rise or instant yeast
- 2½ cups all-purpose flour, plus extra for work surface
- 2 teaspoons baking powder
- ½ teaspoon baking soda
- 2 tablespoons sugar
- 1 teaspoon salt
- 8 tablespoons vegetable shortening, cut into ½-inch pieces and chilled
- 2 tablespoons unsalted butter, melted

1. Adjust oven racks to upper-middle and lower-middle positions and heat oven to 200 degrees. Maintain temperature for 10 minutes, then turn off oven. Line two baking sheets with parchment paper.

2. Stir buttermilk and yeast together until dissolved. In bowl of standing mixer fitted with paddle attachment, mix flour, baking powder, baking soda, sugar, and salt on low speed until combined. Add shortening and mix until just incorporated, about 1 minute. Slowly mix in buttermilk mixture until dough comes together, about 30 seconds. Fit mixer with dough hook and mix on low speed until dough is shiny and smooth, about 2 minutes.

3. On lightly floured surface, knead dough briefly to form smooth ball. Roll dough into 10-inch circle, about ½ inch thick. Using 2½-inch biscuit cutter dipped in flour, cut out rounds and transfer to prepared baking sheets. Gather remaining dough and pat into ½-inch-thick circle. Cut remaining biscuits and transfer to baking sheets.

These wing-shaped Southern biscuits use yeast, baking powder, and baking soda to guarantee a fluffy texture every time.

Shape according to photos at right. Cover dough with kitchen towels and place in warm oven. Let rise until doubled in size, about 30 minutes.

4. Remove baking sheets from oven and heat oven to 350 degrees. Once oven is fully heated, remove kitchen towels and bake until biscuits are golden brown, 12 to 14 minutes, switching and rotating sheets halfway through baking. Remove from oven and brush tops with melted butter. Serve.

Food Processor Method: In step 2, process flour, baking powder, baking soda, sugar, and salt until thoroughly mixed. Add shortening and pulse until only pea-sized pieces of shortening remain, about 6 one-second pulses. Add buttermilk mixture in steady stream and pulse until dough comes together, about 6 more pulses. (Dough will be very sticky.) Turn dough out onto floured work surface and knead until shiny and smooth, about 5 minutes, adding more flour as necessary. Continue recipe with rolling out dough as directed in step 3.

A Brewing Innovation

Until the early 1800s, bread-baking and beer-making were linked by one ingredient, yeast, which home bakers would get from their local brewers. But by the 1830s, brewer's yeast came under scrutiny from the temperance movement, which wanted to ban all alcohol. As a result of the anti-alcohol fervor, bakers started to use alternative leaveners. Pearl ash and saleratus had been used for more than a hundred years to leaven thin batters, but they were undependable for breads and biscuits and produced off-flavors. In 1846, Dr. Austin Church helped create sodium bicarbonate (baking soda), which would later be distinguished by its Arm & Hammer logo. Modern baking powder was first mass-produced in 1898, when August Oetker began marketing his stable leavening combination of baking soda and a powdered acid.

Kitchen Know-How
SHAPED BY AN ANGEL

Here's how we create Angel Biscuits' signature puffed-wing shape.

1. Using a ruler, make an indentation through the center of each round.
2. Lightly brush half of the dough with water.
3. Fold each round of dough in half; press lightly to adhere.

Grilled Bacon-Wrapped Filet Mignon

I like my bacon-wrapped filet mignon to be cooked a perfect medium-rare, but I can never get the bacon fully cooked without overcooking the steak. Fixing that would be great!

–Carey M. Damiani, Winnipeg, Manitoba

Kitchen Know-How
WRAPPING THE STEAKS

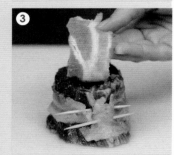

1. Microwaving the bacon between two plates prevents it from curling, making it easier to wrap around the raw filets.

2. After dredging one side of the bacon slices in the sugar mixture, wrap the bacon (sugared-side out) around each filet, overlapping ends, and secure with two toothpicks.

3. For extra bacon flavor, top the bacon-wrapped filet with another slice of raw bacon. As the bacon renders, it will baste and flavor the steak.

When no regular steak or burger will do, I'll splurge and throw a few pieces of filet mignon on the grill. While this expensive cut is very tender, its lean nature means it can be short on flavor. So it's no surprise that wrapping a slice of rich, smoky bacon around the steak to add flavor and moisture became a popular notion. Problem solved, right? Wrong. My initial test showed me that the combination of bacon and high heat (the traditional heat for steaks) is a recipe for disaster: The bacon grease ignited almost immediately, covering my filets in soot. And as well-done as the steak appeared on the outside, the interior was still almost raw, and the bacon was flabby not crisp.

To avoid flare-ups from the bacon drippings, I tried grilling the wrapped filets over low heat; not only did this take a long time, but I had to rotate the steaks frequently to get them to cook evenly, and the bacon was still very flabby. Grilling the filets over medium heat (created by leaving one burner on high but turning the other to low) cooked the steaks evenly in a reasonable amount of time, but the bacon was still undercooked.

Since I couldn't crisp the bacon on the grill, I hoped I could cheat in the kitchen. I cooked bacon for a few minutes in the microwave between paper towels, but when I tried to wrap this bacon around the filets, it wasn't long enough to go around—it had shrunk and curled too much. Microwaving the bacon between two plates kept the bacon from shrinking, making it easy to wrap the filets. To get the bacon more crisp and caramelized, I sprinkled it with a bit of sugar. My tasters were clamoring for even more bacon flavor, so I topped each bacon-wrapped filet with a slice of raw bacon, which basted the meat as it cooked.

Only one thing was missing: the nice char you get from cooking beef over high heat. So to finish the steaks, I removed the extra bacon, moved the steaks to the hottest part of the grill, and quickly seared one side until the meat was a perfect medium-rare. Now I had filet mignon that was tender, flavorful, and worth every penny. **–Diane Unger**

GRILLED BACON-WRAPPED FILET MIGNON SERVES 4

Evenly shaped, center-cut tenderloin steaks work best here.

> ¼ cup sugar
> Salt and pepper
> 8 slices bacon
> 4 tenderloin steaks (6 to 7 ounces each), about 1½ inches thick

1. Combine sugar and ½ teaspoon pepper in pie plate. Lay 4 slices bacon on large plate, weigh down with second plate, and microwave on high power until fat is rendered and bacon is slightly shriveled but still pliable, 1 to 3 minutes. Cool slightly, then dredge one side of rendered bacon in sugar mixture.

2. Pat steaks dry and season with salt and pepper. Following photos at left, wrap each steak with 1 piece sugared bacon and place 1 piece folded raw bacon on top of each steak.

3. Heat all burners on high for 15 minutes, then leave primary burner on high and turn other burner(s) to low. (For charcoal grill, light 100 coals until covered with fine gray ash, then spread two-thirds of coals over half of grill and remaining coals in single layer over other half. Set cooking grate in place and heat covered, with vent lid opened completely, for 5 minutes.) Scrape and oil cooking grate. Grill steaks, covered, over cooler side of grill until internal temperature of meat registers 110 degrees, 7 to 14 minutes. Remove bacon from top of steaks and cook on cooler side until crisp. Flip steaks and grill, covered, over hotter side of grill until steaks register 125 to 130 degrees (for medium-rare), 5 to 10 minutes. Transfer to plate, tent with foil, and let rest 5 minutes. Remove toothpicks. Serve, crumbling bacon over steaks.

Smoky bacon adds much-needed flavor to mild filet mignon.

Grilled Corn on the Cob

I have problems with grilled corn on the cob—the corn is tough and doesn't have a good taste. Making sure the corn is tender is so difficult that I always end up going back to the stove. –Lynn Taylor, Kalamazoo, Mich.

Grilling corn sounds like a simple proposition, so I was amazed at how many techniques my research turned up. I found recipes that suggested grilling the corn husk-on (soaked in water or dry), husk-off, and partially husked; over a hot fire or a medium fire; and even parboiled.

After trying all of these methods, I learned that my tasters wanted corn with a distinctly grilled taste and lightly charred kernels; unfortunately, no single technique was perfect. While grilling the corn husk-on or partially husked helped keep the kernels moist, tasters felt that the husk imparted an unwelcome grassy flavor to the corn. For the best caramelized, smoky flavor, we were going to have to grill the corn shucked.

The husked corn picked up a nice smoky taste from the grill, but the kernels quickly turned tough and dry. Lowering the heat meant longer cooking and mealy, starchy corn—high heat (and fast cooking) was the way to go. I tried basting the corn with oil, butter, and even bacon fat, but all three left the corn greasy. A suggestion from a colleague had me basting the corn with sugar water, and although that corn burned, it got me thinking. A few recipes I tried in earlier tests had called for soaking the corn (still in the husk) in water before grilling. The corn stayed very tender, but it tasted grassy and steamed and lacked grilled flavor. Soaking husked corn might be worth a shot.

For my next test, I soaked the shucked cobs in cold water before they went on the grill.

Although they sputtered and steamed at first, in the end the corn was nicely browned and clearly more tender than it had been in other tests. In the test kitchen, we often presoak lean meats such as chicken and pork in salt water (a process called brining) to add flavor and moisture during cooking. I figured if it works for meat, why not my corn? I whisked some salt into a bowl of water and soaked the corn for an hour; after just a few minutes on the grill, it was apparent I was on the right track. The slightly charred kernels had plumped visibly, and the corn was tender and seasoned throughout due to the salt-water soak.

Ultimately, I found that a 30-minute brine protected corn from drying out on the grill. Brushed with softened butter and sprinkled with salt (or spread with one of our flavored butters below), this was grilled corn that finally lived up to the hype. –Jeremy Sauer

Our easy technique produces smoky, tender, and juicy grilled corn every time.

GRILLED CORN ON THE COB SERVES 4 TO 6

If your corn isn't as sweet as you'd like, stir ½ cup of sugar into the water along with the salt. Avoid soaking the corn for more than 8 hours, or it will become overly salty.

    Salt and pepper
8   ears corn, husks and silks
    removed
8   tablespoons (1 stick) unsalted
    butter, softened, or 1 recipe
    flavored butter (at right)

1. In large pot, stir ½ cup salt into 4 quarts cold water until dissolved. Add corn and let soak for at least 30 minutes or up to 8 hours.

2. Grill corn over hot fire, turning every 2 to 3 minutes, until kernels are lightly charred all over, 10 to 14 minutes. Remove corn from grill, brush with softened butter, and season with salt and pepper. Serve.

CHESAPEAKE BAY BUTTER

Using fork, beat 8 tablespoons (1 stick) softened, unsalted butter with 1 tablespoon hot sauce, 1 teaspoon Old Bay seasoning, and 1 minced garlic clove.

LATIN-SPICED BUTTER

Using fork, beat 8 tablespoons (1 stick) softened, unsalted butter with 1 teaspoon chili powder, ½ teaspoon ground cumin, ½ teaspoon grated lime zest, and 1 minced garlic clove. (Sprinkle cobs with ½ cup grated Parmesan, if desired.)

BASIL PESTO BUTTER

Using fork, beat 8 tablespoons (1 stick) softened, unsalted butter with 1 tablespoon basil pesto and 1 teaspoon lemon juice.

BARBECUE-SCALLION BUTTER

Using fork, beat 8 tablespoons (1 stick) softened, unsalted butter with 2 tablespoons barbecue sauce and 1 minced scallion.

A Good Soak

The grill imparts great flavor but can make corn tough and dry. Soaking the husked corn in salted water keeps the kernels moist and seasons them, too.

Chicago-Style Barbecued Ribs

Hey, *Cook's Country*, you guys always talk up Memphis and Kansas City ribs, but nothing beats our Chicago baby backs! What gives?

–Adam Schaeffer, Chicago, Ill.

In Chicago, baby back ribs are smoky, saucy, and very tender.

Secrets to TENDER RIBS

Adding steam on the grill and in the oven makes these ribs especially moist and tender.

1. To remove the chewy membrane on the bone side of the ribs, loosen it with the tip of a paring knife and, with the aid of a paper towel, pull it off slowly in one big piece.
2. Place a disposable pan on the bottom of the grill and fill it with 2 cups of water. The water creates steam that keeps the ribs from drying out.
3. After smoking, add water to cover the bottom of a rimmed baking sheet. Place wire rack on baking sheet, add ribs, wrap the entire pan in foil, and bake until tender.

They boast about their barbecue pretty loudly in Chicago, where baby back ribs are slow-smoked to fall-apart tenderness and slathered with a spicy sauce. To understand what makes Chicago ribs the source of so much pride, I hopped on a plane to eat my way through a half dozen of the Windy City's finest rib joints.

Aside from discovering that I can eat 65 ribs in two days, I learned that Chicago ribs are typically smoked at about 200 degrees for at least eight hours (and sometimes for up to a day). This slow-and-low cooking method ensures the moist, tender meat that helps define Chicago ribs.

Back home, I hoped to shorten the cooking time by using a slightly hotter fire, but the resulting ribs were tough and chewy. I had better luck starting the ribs on the grill (so they picked up good color and smoke flavor) and finishing them in a 250-degree oven for another two hours or so. Ribs made this way weren't tough, but they weren't really tender or moist, either.

Some recipes suggested precooking the ribs by poaching them in simmering water, but this made them bloated and bland. Other recipes called for mopping or spraying water on the ribs to ensure moistness. The extra humidity helped, but every time I opened the grill lid to apply water, I also allowed heat to escape. Placing a pan of water in the grill during cooking moistened the ribs without lengthening the cooking time. To create really moist ribs, I took this method one step further and steamed the ribs in the oven as well. After just a few hours, these smoky ribs were so tender that I had trouble picking them up.

I smuggled several bottles of Chicago barbecue sauce back to the test kitchen; their labels revealed a few unusual ingredients, namely celery salt and allspice. The other thing that makes this sauce stand out is the heat, which comes from plenty of cayenne. Since Chicago sauce is supposed to be brash and assertive, no simmering was necessary—I just mixed all the sauce ingredients together in a bowl and brushed it on the ribs at the end. These moist, tender, and spicy ribs were just as good as any I had in Chicago.

–**Meredith Butcher**

CHICAGO-STYLE BARBECUED RIBS
SERVES 4 TO 6

The dry spices are used to flavor both the rub and the barbecue sauce. When removing the ribs from the oven, be careful to not spill the hot water in the bottom of the baking sheet.

Ribs

- 1 tablespoon dry mustard
- 1 tablespoon paprika
- 1 tablespoon dark brown sugar
- 1½ teaspoons garlic powder
- 1½ teaspoons onion powder
- 1½ teaspoons celery salt
- 1 teaspoon cayenne pepper
- ½ teaspoon ground allspice
- 2 racks baby back ribs (about 1½ pounds each), membrane removed (see photo 1 at left)
- 1 cup wood chips, soaked for 15 minutes

Sauce

- 1¼ cups ketchup
- ¼ cup molasses
- ¼ cup cider vinegar
- ¼ cup water
- ⅛ teaspoon liquid smoke

1. For the ribs: Combine mustard, paprika, sugar, garlic and onion powders, celery salt, cayenne, and allspice. Reserve 2 tablespoons for sauce. Pat ribs dry with paper towels and massage remaining spice rub into both sides of ribs. (Ribs can be wrapped in plastic and refrigerated for up to 24 hours.)

2. Open bottom vent on grill. Light 100 coals. Arrange 13 by 9-inch disposable aluminum pan filled with 2 cups water on one side of grill. When coals are covered in fine gray ash, arrange in pile on opposite side. Scatter chips over coals and set cooking grate in place. (For gas grill, place chips in small disposable aluminum pan and place directly on primary burner of grill. Place another disposable aluminum pan filled with 2 cups water on secondary burner(s) and set cooking grate in place. Turn all burners to high and heat, covered, until chips are smoking heavily, about 15 minutes. Turn primary burner to medium and shut other burner(s) off.) Position ribs over water-filled pan and cook, covered (open charcoal grill lid vent halfway), rotating and flipping racks once, until ribs are deep red and smoky, about 1½ hours.

3. Adjust oven rack to middle position and heat oven to 250 degrees. Set wire rack inside rimmed baking sheet and add just enough water to cover pan bottom. Arrange ribs on wire rack, cover tightly with aluminum foil, and cook until ribs are completely tender, 1½ to 2 hours. Transfer to serving platter, tent with foil, and let rest 10 minutes.

4. For the sauce: Meanwhile, whisk ketchup, molasses, vinegar, water, liquid smoke, and reserved spice rub in bowl. Brush ribs with 1 cup barbecue sauce. Serve, passing remaining sauce at table.

Regional Favorites: *Memphis Chopped Coleslaw*

I've had a really sweet, tangy, mustard-based coleslaw called "Memphis slaw" at several barbecue joints over the years. Any idea how to make it? –Rick Gasparini, Wethersfield, Conn.

Memphis chopped coleslaw is studded with celery seeds and crunchy green pepper and tossed with an unapologetically sugary mustard dressing that's balanced by a bracing hit of vinegar. With its bold, brash flavors, this bright yellow slaw is a perfect match for even the spiciest and smokiest barbecue.

I started with the cabbage. Due to its high water content, raw cabbage exudes liquid when tossed with a dressing, making the slaw loose and watery. In the test kitchen, we remedy this by salting the chopped cabbage before dressing it; the salt wilts and tenderizes the cabbage, drawing out excess moisture along the way. Prepared in this manner, the cabbage is the base for a sturdy coleslaw that can hold in the fridge for a day without becoming soggy.

When I started researching recipes, I was intrigued that many called for a combination of refrigerator staples (yellow mustard, mayonnaise, sour cream, and ketchup) to give the dressing complex flavor. Tasters told me the complexity was there, but some felt the dressing lacked punch. Switching from ketchup to garlicky chili sauce helped, as did adding shredded onion. Using spicy jalapeño (instead of green bell pepper) and brown sugar (instead of white) gave just the right mix of savory and sweet.

But even though the dressing had the bold tastes I wanted, the flavors still seemed somehow divergent. To help the flavors meld, one recipe I found simmered the sauce before pouring it over the cabbage. While this sounded promising, I feared the heat of the sauce might cook the cabbage and make it soft and soggy. I couldn't have been more wrong. Although the cabbage did absorb some of the hot dressing, it remained crunchy and was seasoned from the inside out. Finally, I had a bold, crisp slaw that was packed with flavor and not waterlogged. Now all I needed was some barbecue.

–Jeremy Sauer

Quickly cooking the spicy dressing helps bring its bold components together and ensures that the cabbage absorbs plenty of flavor.

MEMPHIS CHOPPED COLESLAW
SERVES 8 TO 10

In step 1, the salted, rinsed, and dried cabbage mixture can be refrigerated in a zipper-lock plastic bag for up to 24 hours.

- 1 medium head green cabbage, cored and chopped fine (see page 31)
- 1 jalapeño chile, seeded and minced
- 1 carrot, peeled and shredded on box grater
- 1 small onion, peeled and shredded on box grater
- 2 teaspoons salt
- ¼ cup yellow mustard
- ¼ cup chili sauce
- ¼ cup mayonnaise
- ¼ cup sour cream
- ¼ cup cider vinegar
- 1 teaspoon celery seeds
- ⅔ cup packed light brown sugar

1. Toss cabbage, jalapeño, carrot, onion, and salt in colander set over medium bowl. Let stand until wilted, about 1 hour. Rinse cabbage mixture under cold water, drain, dry well with paper towels, and transfer to large bowl.

2. Bring mustard, chili sauce, mayonnaise, sour cream, vinegar, celery seeds, and sugar to boil in saucepan over medium heat. Pour over cabbage and toss to coat. Cover with plastic and refrigerate 1 hour or up to 1 day. Serve.

How to
FORM A JUCY LUCY

To avoid a burger blowout, it's essential to completely seal in the cheese. Don't worry about overworking the meat—adding milk and bread to the ground beef ensures tender, juicy burgers every time.

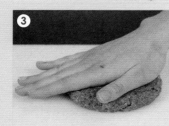

1. Using half of each portion of meat, encase the cheese to form a mini burger patty.
2. Mold remaining half-portion of meat around the mini patty and seal the edges to form a ball.
3. Flatten the ball with the palm of your hand, forming a 3/4-inch-thick patty.

Jucy Lucy Burgers

Here in Minneapolis, we're famous for our Jucy Lucy burgers. It's an American cheese–stuffed burger that most taverns around here serve. Can you create one to rival our local favorite?

–Ed McDonald,
Minneapolis, Minn.

True to its odd name, this burger with the cheese inside is very "juicy," even when well-done.

The signs read "Fear the cheese!" as I stepped into a tavern in South Minneapolis to taste my first Jucy Lucy. The burgers looked typical, but with my first bite, hot American cheese oozed from the center and burned my chin. Locals at neighboring tables nodded knowingly and pointed to the signs. Fear the cheese, indeed. Once cooled for a moment, the burger, despite being well-done, was moist and cheesy. I asked the manager how these burgers were made and was brusquely told to just "stick some cheese inside two burger patties." I'd have to figure out Jucy Lucy on my own.

Although Jucy Lucys are traditionally fried on a tavern griddle, I wanted to grill them. It seemed simple—seal a slice of American cheese between two burger patties and throw it on the grill. But my burgers, cooked until well-done to fully melt the cheese, were dry and tough. Worse still, they had suffered a blowout: The cheese melted through the meat, leaving an empty cavern where the cheese had been (see photo at left). Was there a way to keep this Lucy juicy and hold the cheese inside?

Since a thin slice of American cheese simply disappeared during the long grilling time, I tried sandwiching a chunk of cheese between two patties instead. This improved the odds of keeping the cheese inside, but it was still hit or miss. A coworker suggested sealing the cheese inside a small patty and then molding a second patty around the first one. This created a double-sealed pocket that kept the cheesy center in place every time.

A hot fire scorched the outside of my burgers and left the cheese unmelted. Grilling the burgers over medium heat worked much better, fully cooking the burger and melting the cheese. The burgers were nearly there, but they still weren't as moist as the ones from the tavern. Then I remembered a meatball trick in which a panade—a mixture of bread and milk mashed to a paste—is added to ground beef. This worked, giving me what I had thought was impossible, a tender and juicy well-done burger.

The Jucy Lucys in the Twin Cities are sparsely flavored with salt, pepper, garlic, and Worcestershire sauce. Garlic powder worked better than garlic salt (which was too muted) and minced garlic (too pungent), but I lost the Worcestershire—it made the burgers taste too much like meatloaf. I grilled up a batch of these burgers and, remembering the chin burn, let them cool for a few minutes before diving in. I

was rewarded with a warm, melted center of cheese inside an incredible juicy (but not greasy) Lucy. I fear the cheese no more. –Lynn Clark

GRILLED JUCY LUCY BURGERS SERVES 4

Straight from the grill, the cheesy center of the Jucy Lucy will be molten hot. Be sure to let the burgers rest for at least 5 minutes before serving.

- 2 slices hearty white sandwich bread, torn into rough pieces
- 1/4 cup milk
- 1 teaspoon garlic powder
- 3/4 teaspoon salt
- 1/2 teaspoon pepper
- 1 1/2 pounds 85-percent-lean ground beef
- 1 (1/2-inch-thick) slice deli American cheese, cut into quarters

1. Using potato masher, mash bread, milk, garlic powder, salt, and pepper in large bowl until smooth. Add beef and gently knead until well combined.

2. Divide meat mixture into 4 equal portions. Following photos on page 14, mold each portion of meat around 1 piece of cheese. Transfer patties to plate and refrigerate for 30 minutes or up to 24 hours.

3. Grill burgers over medium fire until well browned and cooked through, 6 to 8 minutes per side. Transfer to plate, tent with foil, and let rest 5 minutes. Serve.

STOVETOP JUCY LUCY BURGERS

Prepare Grilled Jucy Lucy Burgers through step 2. Heat 2 teaspoons vegetable oil in large nonstick skillet over medium heat until just smoking. Add patties and cook until well browned, about 6 minutes. Flip burgers, cover skillet, and continue cooking until well-done, about 6 minutes. Transfer to plate, tent with foil, and let rest 5 minutes. Serve.

24-Hour Picnic Salad

My great-aunt Frances was famous for her 24-hour salad. All the ingredients were layered into a bowl and covered with a thick mayonnaise dressing. The bowl went into the fridge overnight. The next day, the salad was tossed and served. I've tried to re-create her recipe and failed every time—I just get a sloppy mess. Can you help?

–Donna Hunter, Arvada, Colo.

Salt does more than just flavor this salad—it pulls moisture out of the lettuce, which thins the dressing to the perfect consistency.

A t a recent barbecue, I discovered this strange salad myself, sitting alongside the baked beans, chips, and potato salad. It featured layers of iceberg lettuce, peas, hard-cooked egg, shredded cheddar cheese, and bacon, all neatly arranged in a huge glass bowl. On top was a layer of iceberg coated with what looked like mayonnaise spread to the edges, like frosting on a cake. The hostess confirmed that it had been fully assembled a day in advance—what a great idea! After she tossed the salad together, I took the first scoop and was surprised that the lettuce and other vegetables were still crisp after a day in the bowl. The creamy dressing brought all the flavors together.

Determined to re-create this salad, I found a handful of recipes online and prepared them in the test kitchen. All shared the concept of layering the ingredients, but unlike the one I'd had at the barbecue, most of these were overdressed with thick, bland, and sweet dressings (mostly just sugar and mayo) that didn't properly coat the salad. I had a lot of work to do.

I tried using other lettuces, but iceberg retained the most crunch after sitting with the dressing for a day. I found that soft ingredients like mushrooms, spinach, and scal-

lions wilted into mush, while crunchy ones like celery, bell pepper, cucumber, and red onion stayed crisp. My tasters preferred assertive blue cheese over the mild flavor of cheddar, especially when I layered the dressing and blue cheese together, which allowed the flavors to mingle overnight.

For the dressing, my first step was to cut back on the sugar and add tart cider vinegar and hot sauce for brightness and depth. The flavor was great, but the dressing was still too thick to blend into the salad. Thinning it out caused the dressing to run down through the ingredients overnight, resulting in soggy vegetables.

Then I remembered one recipe I had found (and quickly dismissed) that called for salting the layers of lettuce. I dutifully prepared the recipe, and the next day found a pool of water sitting in the bottom of the bowl—I was sure I had made

a mistake. I tossed the salad together anyway and was pleasantly surprised that the thick dressing combined with the water to coat the salad beautifully. I had the perfect make-ahead salad. –Diane Unger

24-HOUR PICNIC SALAD

SERVES 12

Frank's is our favorite brand of hot sauce. If using a hotter brand, such as Tabasco, reduce the amount to 1 tablespoon.

Salad

- 1 medium head iceberg lettuce, cored and chopped rough (about 6 cups)
- 1 teaspoon salt
- 1/2 medium red onion, sliced thin
- 6 hard-cooked eggs, peeled and chopped
- 1 1/2 cups frozen peas

- 4 celery ribs, sliced thin
- 1 red bell pepper, seeded and chopped
- 1 medium cucumber, halved, seeded, and sliced thin
- 1 pound bacon, cooked until crisp and crumbled
- 1 1/2 cups crumbled blue cheese

Dressing

- 1 1/2 cups mayonnaise
- 3 tablespoons cider vinegar
- 2 tablespoons hot sauce (see note)
- 2 teaspoons sugar
- 1 1/2 teaspoons pepper

1. For the salad: Place half of lettuce in large serving bowl and sprinkle with 1/2 teaspoon salt. Rinse sliced onion under cold water; pat dry with paper towels. Layer onion, eggs, peas, celery, bell pepper, and cucumber over lettuce. Add remaining lettuce to bowl, sprinkle with remaining 1/2 teaspoon salt, and top with bacon and cheese.

2. For the dressing: Combine all ingredients and spread dressing evenly over top of salad. Cover with plastic and refrigerate at least 8 hours or up to 24 hours. Remove plastic wrap and toss until salad is evenly coated with dressing. Serve.

A Spinner for All Seasons

To show off the multiple layers of the 24-Hour Salad, we like to serve it in a clear bowl. If you don't have a big glass bowl, you might have a suitable substitute on hand. The bowl from our top-rated OXO Good Grips Salad Spinner works perfectly in this recipe.

A BOWL FOR SPINNING AND SERVING

I'm Looking for a Recipe

READERS HELP READERS FIND RECIPES

We've Got Mail

Several readers sent us recipes in response to the request for Steamed Cherry Pudding in our April/May 2006 issue. We really like the recipe sent by Pat Chandler (right). Go to **CooksCountry.com** and click **Looking for a Recipe** to find hundreds of recipes submitted by readers who responded to other recipe requests in previous issues of *Cook's Country.*

Chocolate Trolley Buns

I am looking for a recipe for chocolate trolley buns. This was one of my aunt's favorite recipes long ago. She lived near a bakery that made the best chocolate trolley buns, and you could smell them baking when you got up in the morning. I would love to reproduce that same aroma for my family.

Blondie Tarentino
Quakertown, Pa.

Graham Cracker Cake

I am looking for a graham cracker cake recipe. We had the Burny Bros. Bakery Graham Cracker Whip Cream Cake (Jewel Food Stores) and loved it—but I've yet to find a good recipe for this light and tasty cake. Thanks!

Nancy Oliver
Via e-mail

Gumdrops

When I was a teenager, there was a recipe for old-fashioned gumdrops on the recipe card that came with the flavored oils you buy to make hard candy. How fun it would be to make them again! I hope someone saved the recipe.

Tammy L. Grant
Cadillac, Mich.

Iced Molasses Cookies

My mother was a great cook, and one of our favorite of her recipes was a molasses or gingerbread cookie with a hard white frosting. When she died, my sister and I looked through everything but couldn't find that recipe. If you or any of your readers happen to have the same recipe, we would certainly appreciate someone sharing it.

Ginny Shirley
Via e-mail

Candlelight Restaurant Popovers

I'm looking for a recipe for a popover-style dinner roll that was served 50 years ago at Patricia Murphy's Candlelight Restaurant in Manhasset, N.Y. I've been looking for these very tasty rolls for some years since the closing of the restaurant and my move to the Midwest. Any assistance you can give would be greatly appreciated.

Thomas Walker
Homewood, Ill.

Double-Boiler Cheese Soufflé

Years ago, I had a foolproof recipe for cheese soufflé that was cooked in a double boiler. Every ingredient was just popped in together in the top pot, the cover was placed on, and in 15 minutes a light, airy, and delicious soufflé was ready to eat. Could you possibly locate the recipe?

Patricia Kresge
San Mateo, Calif.

Salad Monte Carlo

I'm taking a class in classical cuisine and want to find a recipe for salad Monte Carlo. I know that it had diced pineapple and oranges along with pomegranate, hearts of lettuce, and a lemon cream. I can't find the portions I need to create it. Has anyone heard of it?

Adriane Holman
Via e-mail

Tomato Jam

When I was much younger, my mother used to make tomato jam. I think she got the recipe from one of the Sure-Jell boxes. Can you find a recipe for me?

Charles Lawson
Via e-mail

Lithuanian Stuffing

My great-grandmother came to the United States from Lithuania, and she, as well as my grandmother, made a turkey stuffing that contained ground veal. Unfortunately, the recipe was not preserved. I would love to find someone who has the recipe for this stuffing.

Jeff Ray
Morgantown, W.Va.

Ronald Reagan's Mac and Cheese

Do you have Ronald Reagan's recipe for macaroni and cheese? My husband loved it, and the recipe is gone, like our dear, departed president. Thanks!

Sandra Schmidt
Cleveland, Ohio

Indian Corn Pudding

Way back in college, I made an Indian corn pudding. It was such a hit that people argued over who got to lick the pudding bowl to get the last of it. After college, I moved and the recipe was lost. I would love to try this pudding again to see if it really is as good as I remember.

Jean Hansen
Washington, D.C.

Apple Dapple Cake

My mother used to make a deliciously moist apple cake she called "apple dapple cake." It had chunks of apple from our own trees, walnuts, and brown sugar, and sometimes she would make a caramel glaze to drizzle over it. I loved this cake and have searched through many recipe books and haven't been able to find it. Could you help me?

Trisha Kruse
Eagle, Idaho

Chile con Queso Dip

In my hometown of Lake Charles, La., there is a fantastic Mexican restaurant called Casa Mañana. They make, among other wonderful fare, the best chile con queso dip I've ever tasted. The Velveeta variety I make at home just doesn't come close. I miss that dip! I would love a recipe for a chile con queso dip that is creamy, with not too much tomato and a nice hit of spice. Thanks!

Emily Simmons
Detroit, Mich.

Grape Jelly Meatballs

There is a person in my office who makes meatballs in a slow-cooker every potluck, and she won't give out the recipe. She has conceded to my guessing enough to say that it has barbecue sauce, mustard powder, and some grape jelly, but I don't know what else. The end result is a glossy, tangy, sweet sauce that is absolutely delicious. Maybe this is a Midwestern thing?

Neal Hicks
Columbus, Ohio

Celery Seed Meatballs

My Norwegian mother used to make the best meatballs with celery seed gravy. They were especially delicious served over mashed potatoes, but she never wrote down the recipe. Wish I'd asked her for it! Have you ever heard of this recipe?

Colleen Henderson
Escondito, Calif.

Are you looking for a special recipe? Or do you have a recipe a fellow *Cook's Country* reader is seeking? Post your requests and recipes by visiting **CooksCountry.com** and clicking on **Looking for a Recipe.** We'll share recipe requests and found recipes on CooksCountry.com and print as many as we can in the magazine. You may also write to us at Looking for a Recipe, Cook's Country, P.O. Box 470739, Brookline, MA 02447.

STEAMED CHERRY PUDDING Pat Chandler, Vallejo, Calif.

SERVES 8

Pat writes: "My nana Nell used to make this pudding for family get-togethers in the 1940s. I especially like this pudding because it looks impressive—even though it's easy—and unlike heavy-duty steamed puddings, it's quite light." You will need a 6-cup mold for this recipe.

1½	cups all-purpose flour
1	tablespoon baking powder
¼	teaspoon salt
½	cup milk
½	teaspoon almond extract
½	teaspoon vanilla extract
2	tablespoons unsalted butter, softened
½	cup sugar
1	egg
¼	cup light corn syrup
1	(14.5-ounce) can tart cherries, drained, ¾ cup juice reserved
1	teaspoon cornstarch

INSTRUCTIONS: Bring 2 inches water to boil in large Dutch oven. Mix flour, baking powder, and salt in bowl. Mix milk and extracts in measuring cup. Cream butter and ¼ cup sugar. Mix in egg and corn syrup, then flour and milk mixtures. Fold in cherries and spoon batter into greased and floured 6-cup mold. Steam in covered Dutch oven in 350-degree oven until skewer inserted into center of pudding comes out clean, about 2 hours. Meanwhile, mix cornstarch and 1 tablespoon cherry juice in bowl. Boil remaining cherry juice and remaining sugar, whisk in cornstarch mixture, and simmer until slightly thickened, about 1 minute. Invert mold onto serving plate. Serve with sauce.

Find the Rooster!

A tiny version of this rooster has been hidden somewhere in the pages of this issue. If you find it, write to us with its location (plus your name and address) and you will be entered into a random drawing. The first correct entry drawn will receive the All-Clad Stainless Steel Slow Cooker with Ceramic Insert (our test winner—see page 29), and the next five will each receive a complimentary one-year subscription to *Cook's Country.* To enter the contest, e-mail us by visiting **CooksCountry.com/emailus** or write to us at Rooster, Cook's Country, P.O. Box 470739, Brookline, MA 02447. Entries are due by September 30, 2007.

Did you find the rooster in the April/May 2007 issue? It was hidden in the Lemon Asparagus Casserole photo on page 21. Mary T. Livermore of Spencerport, N.Y., spotted it and won a Black & Decker SmartBrew 12-Cup Coffeemaker.

GRILLED STEAKS WITH TOMATO-ONION SALAD

ANGEL HAIR PASTA WITH SHRIMP

BLT SALAD

CRISPY FISH STICKS WITH TARTAR SAUCE

ANGEL HAIR PASTA WITH SHRIMP SERVES 4

Linguine, fettuccine, or spaghetti can also be used here.

- 1 pound large shrimp, peeled and deveined
  Salt and pepper
- 4 tablespoons extra-virgin olive oil
- 2 medium zucchini, diced medium
- 6 garlic cloves, minced
- 1/4 teaspoon red pepper flakes
- 1 pound angel hair pasta
- 3 tablespoons lemon juice
- 1/2 cup chopped fresh parsley

1. Bring 4 quarts water to boil in large pot over high heat. Pat shrimp dry with paper towels and season with salt and pepper. Heat 1 tablespoon oil in large nonstick skillet over medium-high heat until just smoking. Cook shrimp until lightly browned and just cooked through, about 1 minute per side. Transfer to bowl.

2. Heat remaining oil in now-empty skillet until shimmering. Cook zucchini until browned, about 5 minutes. Add garlic and pepper flakes and cook until fragrant, about 30 seconds. Transfer to bowl with shrimp and cover with foil to keep warm.

3. Add 1 tablespoon salt and pasta to boiling water and cook until al dente. Reserve 1/2 cup cooking water. Drain pasta and return to pot. Add shrimp, zucchini, lemon juice, and parsley to pot and toss to combine, adding reserved pasta water as needed. Season with salt and pepper. Serve.

GRILLED STEAKS WITH TOMATO-ONION SALAD SERVES 4

Any ripe summer tomato can be used here.

- 1 red onion, sliced into 1/4-inch rounds
- 3 tablespoons extra-virgin olive oil
- 4 strip steaks, about 1 inch thick
  Salt and pepper
- 6 plum tomatoes, cored and sliced into 1/4-inch rounds
- 2 tablespoons capers, rinsed
- 1/4 cup chopped fresh basil
- 2 tablespoons red wine vinegar

1. Brush onion slices with 1 tablespoon oil and grill over hot fire until lightly charred, about 2 minutes per side. Transfer to large bowl. Season steaks with salt and pepper and grill over hot fire until well browned and cooked to desired doneness, 4 to 8 minutes per side. Transfer to plate, tent with foil, and let rest 5 minutes.

2. Add tomatoes, capers, basil, remaining oil, and vinegar to bowl with grilled onions and toss to combine. Season with salt and pepper. Transfer steaks and tomato salad to individual plates. Serve.

CRISPY FISH STICKS WITH TARTAR SAUCE
SERVES 4

Halibut, haddock, or catfish can be substituted for the cod.

- 4 slices hearty white sandwich bread, torn into large pieces
- 16 saltine crackers
- 1/2 cup all-purpose flour
- 2 large eggs
- 1 cup mayonnaise
- 2 pounds skinless cod, cut into 1-inch-thick strips
  Salt and pepper
- 1/4 cup finely chopped dill pickles, plus 1 tablespoon pickle juice
- 1 tablespoon capers, minced
- 1 cup vegetable oil

1. Adjust oven rack to middle position and heat oven to 200 degrees. Pulse bread and saltines in food processor to fine crumbs; transfer to shallow dish. Place flour in second shallow dish. Beat eggs with 1/4 cup mayonnaise in third shallow dish.

2. Pat fish dry with paper towels and season with salt and pepper. One at a time, coat fish strips lightly with flour, dip in egg mixture, and then dredge in crumbs, pressing on both sides to adhere. Transfer breaded fish to plate. Combine remaining mayonnaise, pickles, pickle juice, and capers in small bowl and set aside.

3. Heat 1/2 cup oil in large nonstick skillet over medium heat until just smoking. Fry half of fish strips until deep golden and crisp, about 2 minutes per side. Drain on paper towel–lined plate and transfer to oven to keep warm. Discard oil, wipe out skillet, and repeat with remaining oil and fish. Serve with tartar sauce.

BLT SALAD SERVES 4

If you can't find thick-cut bacon, use 1 pound of regular bacon.

- 3/4 cup mayonnaise
- 4 (1-inch-thick) slices Italian bread
- 12 slices thick-cut bacon, chopped
- 3 tablespoons red wine vinegar
- 4 cups cherry tomatoes, halved
- 1 (10-ounce) bag chopped romaine lettuce
  Salt and pepper

1. Adjust oven rack to middle position and heat oven to 475 degrees. Spread 1/4 cup mayonnaise over both sides of bread slices and transfer to baking sheet. Bake until golden brown, 8 to 10 minutes. Let cool 5 minutes, then cut into 1-inch croutons.

2. Cook bacon in large skillet over medium heat until crisp, about 8 minutes. Transfer to paper towel–lined plate. Discard drippings.

3. Whisk remaining mayonnaise and vinegar in large bowl. Add bacon, tomatoes, lettuce, and croutons and toss to combine. Season with salt and pepper. Serve.

WEEKNIGHT LASAGNA ROLL-UPS

GRILLED BUFFALO CHICKEN STRIPS

CHICKEN AND ROASTED PEPPER PANINI

PEACH-GLAZED GRILLED PORK CHOPS

GRILLED BUFFALO CHICKEN STRIPS SERVES 4

You can make your own chicken strips by slicing boneless, skinless breasts lengthwise into 3/4-inch strips. Unless you've got a high tolerance for heat, be sure to use a relatively mild hot sauce, such as Frank's Red Hot.

- 1/2 cup crumbled blue cheese
- 6 tablespoons sour cream
- 1/4 cup mayonnaise
- 1 tablespoon cider vinegar
- 1/8 teaspoon celery salt
- 1/2 cup hot sauce (see note)
- 4 tablespoons unsalted butter, melted
- 1 1/2 pounds chicken tenderloins (see note)
  Salt and pepper

1. Combine blue cheese, sour cream, mayonnaise, vinegar, and celery salt in bowl. Whisk hot sauce and butter in large bowl and reserve 1/2 cup. Add chicken strips to bowl with remaining hot sauce mixture and toss to coat.

2. Season chicken with salt and pepper and grill over hot fire until cooked through, about 2 minutes per side. Transfer to platter and brush with reserved hot sauce mixture. Serve with blue cheese sauce.

WEEKNIGHT LASAGNA ROLL-UPS SERVES 4

A 13 by 9-inch Pyrex baking dish can be used in place of the casserole.

- 8 no-boil lasagna noodles
- 1 (15-ounce) container ricotta cheese
- 2 cups shredded mozzarella cheese
- 1 1/2 cups grated Parmesan cheese
- 1 large egg, lightly beaten
- 1/2 cup chopped fresh basil
- 1/2 teaspoon salt
- 1 (28-ounce) can crushed tomatoes
- 3 tablespoons extra-virgin olive oil
- 4 garlic cloves, minced

1. Adjust oven rack to upper-middle position and heat oven to 475 degrees. Place noodles and hot tap water to cover in 2-quart microwave-safe casserole dish. Microwave until noodles are softened, 3 to 6 minutes. Discard water and dry dish. Dry noodles on clean kitchen towel.

2. Meanwhile, combine ricotta, 1 cup mozzarella, 1 cup Parmesan, egg, 1/4 cup basil, and salt in bowl. Combine tomatoes, oil, garlic, and remaining basil in medium bowl. Spread half of tomato mixture in casserole. With short side facing you, dollop 1/4 cup cheese mixture on each noodle, roll, and arrange seam-side down in casserole. Pour remaining tomato mixture over roll-ups.

3. Wrap dish tightly with plastic wrap, poke holes in plastic, and microwave on high until roll-ups are tender and heated through, 6 to 10 minutes. Remove plastic and sprinkle remaining mozzarella and Parmesan over roll-ups. Bake until cheese is melted and lightly browned, about 5 minutes. Let stand 5 minutes. Serve.

PEACH-GLAZED GRILLED PORK CHOPS SERVES 4

Three medium-sized ripe peaches, peeled, pitted, and sliced, can be substituted for the frozen.

- 1 cup peach preserves
- 1/4 cup red wine vinegar
- 1/2 teaspoon minced fresh thyme
- 1/8 teaspoon cayenne pepper
- 1 (16-ounce) bag frozen sliced peaches (see note)
- 1 teaspoon Dijon mustard
- 4 bone-in rib or center-cut pork chops, about 1 inch thick
  Salt and pepper

1. Simmer preserves, vinegar, thyme, and cayenne in saucepan over medium heat until reduced to 1 cup, about 3 minutes. Reserve 1/4 cup glaze. Add peaches to saucepan with remaining glaze and simmer until peaches are soft and glaze is slightly thickened, about 10 minutes. Off heat, stir in mustard. Cover and keep warm.

2. Season pork with salt and pepper and grill over hot fire until well browned and internal temperature reaches 145 degrees, about 6 minutes per side. Brush with reserved glaze and cook 1 minute longer. Transfer to platter and let rest 5 minutes. Pour sliced peach mixture over chops. Serve.

CHICKEN AND ROASTED PEPPER PANINI SERVES 4

If your sub rolls are longer than 6 inches, cook the panini in 2 batches.

- 8 thin-cut boneless, skinless chicken cutlets (about 1 1/2 pounds)
  Salt and pepper
- 4 tablespoons extra-virgin olive oil
- 1/2 cup drained jarred roasted red peppers, chopped
- 1/2 cup pitted kalamata olives
- 1/2 cup chopped fresh basil
- 1 garlic clove, minced
- 4 (6-inch) sub rolls, halved lengthwise
- 8 ounces thinly sliced deli provolone cheese

1. Pat chicken dry with paper towels and season with salt and pepper. Heat 1 tablespoon oil in large nonstick skillet over medium-high heat until just smoking. Cook half of cutlets until lightly browned and cooked through, 1 to 2 minutes per side. Transfer to plate and repeat with additional 1 tablespoon oil and remaining cutlets.

2. Pulse red peppers, olives, basil, garlic, and 1 tablespoon oil in food processor until coarsely chopped. Spread pepper mixture evenly over both sides of rolls. Layer half of cheese and 2 chicken cutlets over each roll bottom. Top with remaining cheese and roll tops.

3. Wipe out skillet. Heat remaining oil over medium-low heat until just shimmering. Arrange panini in skillet and top with large Dutch oven. Cook until bottoms of sandwiches are crisp and cheese is beginning to melt, about 2 minutes. Remove Dutch oven, flip sandwiches, replace Dutch oven, and continue to cook until crisp on second side and heated through, about 2 minutes. Serve.

Coffeecake Muffins

My local coffeehouse sells streusel coffeecake muffins that are so moist and good, but my version tastes like gravel-covered cupcakes. How can I fix this? –Angelique Martin, Reno, Nev.

We use the same base mixture for both the rich cinnamon filling and nutty streusel topping.

With a swirl of cinnamon enriching tender cake and a topping of sweet, nutty streusel, a big slice of coffeecake is pretty hard to beat. Compacting all that goodness into muffin form seems like a great idea, but most of the coffeecake muffins I've tried resemble dry, cottony yellow cupcakes, with little or no cinnamon filling. To hide this misfortune, some recipes simply pack mounds of dry, gritty streusel on top, making it seem like the muffins were dropped at the beach. I wanted to make a coffeecake muffin as good as a regular coffeecake, with the option of taking it to go.

My first objective was to figure out the cake. Most recipes I found were based on cupcake or muffin batters, and the resulting muffins were too fluffy and not as dense and moist as true coffeecake. A few other recipes used rich coffeecake batters that were packed with as much as 1½ sticks of butter, four eggs, and 1 cup of sour cream. These muffins had good flavor but were too dense and flat. To reduce the density while keeping the richness, I cut back to two eggs and 5 tablespoons of butter. But when I tried to cut back on the sour cream, the muffins lost their moist, velvety appeal—the full cup of sour cream would stay.

For the streusel topping, many recipes use a mixture of nuts (pecans were my tasters' favorite), sugar, and cinnamon, but this produced the sandy topping I was trying to avoid. Cutting a little butter and flour into the mixture added moisture and allowed the topping to clump and stay put on top of the muffin. Replacing some of the granulated sugar with brown sugar gave the topping deeper flavor.

Hoping that the streusel topping could double as the cinnamon filling, I filled the muffin cups halfway, sprinkled on some of the topping mixture, and added more batter. Unfortunately, the nuts were steaming inside the muffins and making everything mushy. This was easily fixed—I pulsed the sugars, cinnamon, butter, and flour (without the nuts) in the food processor and pulled some out to use as the filling. I added pecans to the remaining mixture, pulsed again, and used that as the perfect streusel topping to my sweet, rich coffeecake muffins.

–Diane Unger

COFFEECAKE MUFFINS
MAKES 12 MUFFINS

Be sure to use muffin-tin liners for this recipe or the cinnamon filling will stick to the pan.

Streusel
- 8 tablespoons granulated sugar
- ⅓ cup packed light brown sugar
- ⅓ cup all-purpose flour
- 1 tablespoon ground cinnamon
- 4 tablespoons unsalted butter, cut into ½-inch pieces and chilled
- ½ cup pecans

Muffins
- 2 large eggs
- 1 cup sour cream
- 1½ teaspoons vanilla extract
- 1¾ cups all-purpose flour
- ½ cup granulated sugar
- 1 tablespoon baking powder
- ¼ teaspoon salt
- 5 tablespoons unsalted butter, cut into chunks and softened

1. For the streusel: Pulse 5 tablespoons granulated sugar, brown sugar, flour, cinnamon, and butter in food processor until just combined. Reserve ¾ cup sugar mixture for cinnamon filling. Add pecans and remaining granulated sugar to food processor with remaining sugar mixture and pulse until nuts are coarsely ground. Transfer to bowl and set aside for streusel topping. Do not wash food processor.

2. For the muffins: Adjust oven rack to middle position and heat oven to 375 degrees. Grease muffin tin with cooking spray and line with paper liners. Whisk eggs, sour cream, and vanilla in bowl. Pulse flour, sugar, baking powder, salt, and butter in food processor until mixture resembles wet sand. Transfer to large bowl. Using rubber spatula, gradually fold in egg mixture until just combined. Place 1 tablespoon batter in each muffin cup and top with 1 tablespoon cinnamon filling. Using back of spoon, press cinnamon filling lightly into batter, then top with remaining batter. Following photo below, sprinkle streusel topping evenly over batter.

3. Bake until muffins are light golden brown and toothpick inserted into center comes out with a few dry crumbs attached, 22 to 28 minutes. Cool muffins in tin for 30 minutes, then carefully transfer to rack to cool. Serve. (The muffins will keep in airtight container at room temperature for up to 3 days.)

Kitchen Know-How
KEEPING STREUSEL IN PLACE

To make sure the streusel topping ends up on the muffins and not on the muffin tin and countertop, we enlist the help of a 2¾-inch cookie cutter, which fits neatly over a standard muffin-tin cup. Just sprinkle the streusel topping inside the cookie cutter, lift off the cutter, and then gently pat the streusel into the batter with your fingers.

Grilled Pork Cutlets

I'm usually the cook in my house, but my husband is always happy to grill. His "specialty" is grilled pork cutlets tossed with bottled Italian dressing. I don't have the heart to tell him they are bland and dry as a bone. Please help us! –Abbey Wright, Nashville, Tenn.

Kitchen Know-How
TURNING CHOPS INTO CUTLETS

Thin-cut boneless pork chops can be quickly turned into cutlets ready for the grill. Here's how.

Place two chops on the work surface and cover them with plastic wrap. Using a meat pounder, pound the chops into ¼-inch-thick cutlets. Repeat with the remaining chops.

Thin-Cut Chops vs. Cutlets

Prepackaged pork cutlets are often cut from the blade end of the ribs and can be ragged and uneven, which results in uneven cooking. We prefer to make our own cutlets from thin-cut pork chops (see above), which are cut from the loin and generally have a much more uniform shape.

THIN-CUT PORK CHOP POUNDED OUT
Our homemade cutlets have a uniform shape and cook evenly.

RAGGED PREPACKAGED PORK CUTLET
Prepackaged cutlets look sloppy and cook unevenly.

Chicken cutlets are a weeknight standby, but pork cutlets—a relatively new addition to the meat case—are not as well known. Although they are the same size as chicken cutlets, pork cutlets (cut from the blade end of the ribs) are not as tender. My first attempts taught me that pork cutlets become leathery very quickly on the grill, and they cooked so fast that they didn't have time to char or develop much grill flavor. This wasn't going to be an easy fix.

The problems start at the market. Packaged cutlets often have shredded edges and irregular thicknesses that lead to uneven cooking. Returning to the meat case, thin-cut pork chops (cut from the loin) caught my eye—they were almost as thin as the cutlets, and their shape and thickness were much more consistent. I brought the thin-cut chops home and gave them a few quick whacks with my meat pounder to make homemade cutlets. After a few minutes over high heat, they came off the grill evenly cooked, tender, and moist but still a little pale and bland.

Most recipes call for flipping the cutlets halfway through the cooking time, but they cook so quickly that this doesn't give the meat a chance to brown. Since increasing the cooking time would lead to dried-out cutlets, I left them on one side for most of the cooking time (about 2 minutes) to develop a nice char, then finished them for 30 seconds on the other side.

With the cooking method settled, I could focus on infusing the pork with flavor. Pungent spice rubs overwhelmed the thin cutlets, but marinating worked well. While larger cuts are only superficially seasoned by a marinade, these thin cutlets were flavored to the core. Bottled Italian dressing received poor marks for its dull dried-herb flavor, so I used Italian ingredients to make my own vinaigrette. Balsamic vinegar, olive oil, garlic, and thyme formed the base, and a last-minute addition of sugar softened the acidity of the vinegar and helped produce even more caramelization on the cutlets. This simple marinade was easily varied to make pork cutlets an interesting (and easy to prepare) option for the grill. –Cali Rich

GRILLED PORK CUTLETS
SERVES 4 TO 6
Boneless pork chops are typically lean; trim any excess fat as necessary. Marinating for more than 2 hours will make the chops rubbery.

A quick marinade and a simple salsa (see page 19) add big flavor to our homemade pork cutlets.

- ⅓ cup balsamic vinegar
- ⅓ cup olive oil
- 2 garlic cloves, minced
- 1 teaspoon minced fresh thyme
- ¾ teaspoon sugar
- ¾ teaspoon salt
- ¼ teaspoon pepper
- 12 thin-cut boneless pork chops (about 2 pounds), prepared according to photo at left

1. Combine vinegar, oil, garlic, thyme, sugar, salt, and pepper in large zipper-lock plastic bag. Transfer chops to bag and refrigerate for 30 minutes or up to 2 hours.

2. Remove cutlets from bag and discard marinade. Grill cutlets over hot fire until bottom begins to turn opaque around edges, about 2 minutes. Flip cutlets and grill until just cooked through, about 30 seconds. Transfer to platter, tent with foil, and let rest 5 minutes. Serve.

GRILLED PORK CUTLETS WITH ROSEMARY AND RED WINE VINEGAR

Prepare recipe for Grilled Pork Cutlets, substituting ⅓ cup red wine vinegar for balsamic vinegar, 1 teaspoon minced fresh rosemary for thyme, and ¾ teaspoon honey for sugar.

GRILLED PORK CUTLETS WITH CILANTRO AND LIME

Prepare recipe for Grilled Pork Cutlets, adding ½ teaspoon ground cumin to marinade and substituting ⅓ cup lime juice (from 3 limes) for balsamic vinegar, 3 tablespoons minced fresh cilantro for thyme, and ¾ teaspoon brown sugar for granulated sugar.

On the Side: Summer Rice Salad

For a light and easy rice salad, cook the rice like pasta.

Packed with crisp vegetables and bright flavors, a rice salad should be a refreshingly light summer side dish. But most recipes use salty dressings and feature clumps of sticky rice as the main attraction.

Neither steaming nor cooking the rice pilaf-style (by first sautéing it in oil) yielded the separate grains I was looking for. I found that the best way to cook rice for this salad was to boil it in plenty of water, just like pasta, which washes away much of the starch that causes clumping. Letting the rice cool thoroughly on a cookie sheet before dressing it prevented soggy, oversaturated grains.

Tasters loved the sweetness and crunch that both snow and sweet peas offered. Sautéed shiitake mushrooms added a deep, earthy flavor, and instead of including garlic and ginger in the dressing (as many recipes do), I added these ingredients to the sautéing vegetables to bloom their flavor.

Although an Asian-inspired dressing sounded appealing, every recipe I found was too salty. Since soy sauce was the main offender, I tried reducing the amount until tasters agreed that I didn't need it at all—a good shake of salt was all the seasoning this light salad needed. Honey, rice vinegar, and a little toasted sesame oil created the right balance of flavors to complement the rice and vegetables. **–Greg Case**

RICE SALAD WITH PEAS AND MUSHROOMS
SERVES 4 TO 6
Use a fine-mesh strainer to strain the rice.

> Salt
> 1 cup long-grain rice
> 1 tablespoon vegetable oil
> 4 ounces shiitake mushrooms, stemmed and sliced thin
> 1 cup frozen peas
> 3 ounces snow peas (about 1 cup), trimmed and halved
> 2 teaspoons grated fresh ginger
> 1 garlic clove, minced
> 3 tablespoons rice vinegar
> 1 tablespoon toasted sesame oil
> 1 tablespoon honey

1. Bring 4 quarts water to boil in large pot. Add 2½ teaspoons salt and rice to boiling water and cook, uncovered, until tender, 10 to 15 minutes. Drain rice and spread on rimmed baking sheet to cool completely.

2. Heat vegetable oil in large skillet over medium heat until shimmering. Cook mushrooms, covered, until softened, about 2 minutes. Remove lid, add peas, and cook until peas are bright green, about 2 minutes. Add ginger and garlic and cook about 30 seconds. Off heat, stir in vinegar, sesame oil, and honey. Pour mushroom mixture over cooled rice and toss until combined. Season with salt. Serve. (Salad can be refrigerated for 1 day. Bring to room temperature before serving.)

On the Side: Peach and Plum Salsa

What's the key to a spicy-sweet fruit salsa that is never watery or bland?

When I was growing up in California, it seemed that every piece of grilled meat or fish was topped with a fresh salsa—often a fruit salsa. But what should have been a perfect combination of sweet, sour, and spicy flavors was usually nothing more than tired chopped fruit. I wanted to find the right balance of savory flavors to complement the sweet fruit in a lively salsa.

I started with peaches and plums, which needed to be sweetened to draw out their flavor; my tasters preferred the stickiness of honey to dry sugars. The salsa needed acidity, but a squeeze of citrus made it taste like fruit salad. Fruity, tangy cider vinegar brought out the natural flavors of the fruit while keeping the salad savory. Minced jalapeño and shallot offered welcome heat and pungency, and cool basil complemented both the hot and sweet elements.

Whisking the honey and cider vinegar with a little olive oil created a unified dressing that coated the fruit beautifully. But the peaches and plums weren't softening and breaking down (as tomatoes do in a traditional salsa), so my salsa was too much like a relish. To remedy this, I mashed a portion of the fruit with a potato masher before adding it to the rest of the fruit and vinaigrette.
–Meredith Butcher

SWEET AND SPICY FRUIT SALSA
MAKES ABOUT 3 CUPS
The salsa can be made up to 4 hours in advance—if left any longer, the fruit will become mushy. If you like your salsa spicy, don't seed the jalapeño.

> 1 jalapeño chile, seeded and minced (see note)
> 1 shallot, minced
> 2 teaspoons cider vinegar
> 2 teaspoons honey
> 2 tablespoons extra-virgin olive oil
> 2 ripe peaches, pitted and chopped fine
> 2 ripe plums, pitted and chopped fine
> 1 tablespoon finely chopped fresh basil
> Salt

1. Whisk jalapeño, shallot, vinegar, honey, and oil in small bowl. Let sit until flavors combine, about 15 minutes.

2. Combine peaches and plums in large bowl. Add ½ cup of fruit to bowl with jalapeño mixture and mash with potato masher until smooth. Add mashed fruit mixture and basil to bowl with cut fruit and stir until combined. Season with salt and let sit until flavors combine, about 15 minutes. Serve.

Skillet Peach Cobbler

Every summer I take the time to bake a peach cobbler, and every year the whole thing turns out mushy and soupy. What am I doing wrong? –Jennifer Pendarvis, Sumter, S.C.

Anyone who has bitten into an impeccably ripe peach knows just how juicy peaches can be. Unfortunately, so does anyone who's ever made a peach cobbler. The peaches typically shed those juices in the oven, leaving the filling watery and the cobbles soggy. I wanted tender peaches and a crisp, buttery biscuit topping. How was I going to get there?

Most recipes attempt to solve the soupy peach problem by loading them up with starchy thickeners, but this left the fruit as gluey and gummy as canned peach pie filling. Other recipes draw moisture out of the sliced peaches by sprinkling them with sugar and letting them drain in a colander. Although this technique prevented a watery filling, I couldn't help but think that a lot of flavor was draining away with all that peach juice.

Searching for a way to thicken my peach filling without running off any of its flavorful juice, I turned to my skillet. I first sautéed the peaches in butter and sugar to release their juices and then cooked them down until all their liquid had evaporated. The resulting peaches were buttery-sweet, with a concentrated taste, but their texture was reminiscent of baby food. I decided to withhold some of the peaches

from the sautéing process and add them to the skillet just before baking. Prepared in this manner, the filling had a deep, concentrated flavor (from the sautéed peaches) and a tender, but not at all mushy, texture (from the second addition of peaches). To finish, a splash of lemon juice brought out the sweet-tart taste of the fruit, and a dusting of cornstarch brought the filling together.

As for the cobbles, my tasters liked the flavor of buttermilk biscuits, but their texture was too delicate—the biscuits fell apart on top of the juicy peach filling. Buttermilk biscuits get their light and flaky texture from having cold butter cut into the dry ingredients. Using melted butter made my biscuits sturdier, and they held up much better on top of the fruit. These biscuits were also easier to prepare, since they require no gentle handling—in fact, this dough must be briefly kneaded by hand. With a final sprinkling of cinnamon sugar, I finally had a reliable recipe for peach cobbler. –Jeremy Sauer

SKILLET PEACH COBBLER SERVES 6 TO 8

See page 31 for tips on peeling peaches. Four pounds of frozen sliced peaches can be substituted for fresh; there is no need to defrost them. Start step 2 when the peaches are almost done.

Filling
- 4 tablespoons unsalted butter
- 5 pounds peaches, peeled, pitted, and cut into 1/2-inch wedges
- 6 tablespoons sugar
- 1/8 teaspoon salt
- 1 tablespoon lemon juice
- 1 1/2 teaspoons cornstarch

Topping
- 1 1/2 cups all-purpose flour, plus extra for work surface

- 6 tablespoons sugar
- 1 1/2 teaspoons baking powder
- 1/4 teaspoon baking soda
- 1/4 teaspoon salt
- 3/4 cup buttermilk
- 4 tablespoons unsalted butter, melted and cooled
- 1 teaspoon ground cinnamon

1. For the filling: Adjust oven rack to middle position and heat oven to 425 degrees. Melt butter in large oven-safe nonstick skillet over medium-high heat. Add two-thirds of peaches, sugar, and salt and cook, covered, until peaches release their juices, about 5 minutes. Remove lid and simmer until all liquid has evaporated and peaches begin to caramelize, 15 to 20 minutes. Add remaining peaches and cook until heated through, about 5 minutes. Whisk lemon juice and cornstarch in small bowl, then stir into peach mixture. Cover skillet and set aside off heat.

2. For the topping: Meanwhile, whisk flour, 5 tablespoons sugar, baking soda, baking powder, and salt in medium bowl. Stir in buttermilk and butter until dough forms. Turn dough out onto lightly floured work surface and knead briefly until smooth, about 30 seconds.

3. Combine remaining sugar and cinnamon. Break dough into rough 1-inch pieces and space them about 1/2 inch apart on top of hot peach mixture. Sprinkle with cinnamon sugar and bake until topping is golden brown and filling is thickened, 18 to 22 minutes. Let cool on wire rack for 10 minutes. Serve. (Although best eaten the day it is made to maintain the texture of the cobbles, leftovers may be refrigerated for up to 1 day. Individual portions may be removed from skillet and reheated in microwave.)

Using the same skillet to cook the peaches and bake the cobbler saves time and cleanup.

Getting to Know Stone Fruit

With summer in full swing, we hit the farmers market and tasted 12 varieties of stone fruit at the height of their ripeness. Listed below are our tasting notes.

Peach
JUICY GEORGIANS

These fuzzy-skinned fruits are most often associated with Southern states (particularly Georgia), but they're now grown throughout the U.S. Their "tangy" orange flesh is "chin-dribblingly juicy," with a "floral aftertaste" that's "as sweet as candy." Peaches work well in sweet and savory applications alike.

White Peach
PALE IN COMPARISON

White peaches are lighter in color and flavor than their yellow-fleshed cousins, making them less desirable in savory applications with strong flavors. Their flesh is "custardy" and "super-sweet," with a "melon-like" aftertaste and "very low acidity." Eat out of hand or substitute for regular peaches in desserts.

Donut Peach
SAUCER-SHAPED

Also called UFO peaches, these tiny fruits usually measure only two to three inches across. Despite their size, donut peaches have a very high flesh-to-stone ratio. Their flavor is subtle—"like peach for beginners"—with hints of "honey" and "citrus."

Plum
A RAINBOW OF FLAVOR

These diverse fruits display a wide range of colors, from deep purple to green to stark yellow to crimson. Between their "crisp, tannic skin" and "pulpy, jammy" flesh, plums have a "sweet-sour" flavor "not unlike grapes." Eat fresh, bake, or stew into preserves.

Prune Plum
BEST DRIED

These tiny, pear-shaped plums are rarely eaten fresh; they are typically pitted and poached for desserts or dried to make prunes (drying intensifies and sweetens the flavor of the fruit). Their thick, blue-black skin is "leathery and bitter," and the bright yellow flesh is "firm and tart."

Apricot
SMOOTH AS SUEDE

These small fruits, whose smooth skin has a light fuzz, can range in color from light yellow to deep orange. Although apricots are most often found dried, this close relative of the plum is also great eaten out of hand. Both fresh and dried apricots have "dense flesh" with notes of "citrus and almonds."

Pluot
ENGINEERED FOR SWEETNESS

As the name suggests, a pluot is a plum-apricot hybrid that combines the sweetness of a plum with the complex, slightly tart flavor of an apricot. We found their flavor to be "sweet and tropical," like "pineapple minus the acidity." Eat out of hand.

Dinosaur Egg Pluot
FANTASTIC JURASSIC

This brightly colored fruit is often speckled with oranges, purples, and pinks. A relatively large variety of pluot, its "tie-dyed" skin reveals a juicy, "syrupy-sweet" blushing flesh with "tangy, exotic fruit flavor." Eat out of hand.

Nectarine
SMOOTH OPERATOR

Genetically, nectarines are very similar to peaches—the major difference being that nectarines have smooth, thin skin. Their yellow-orange flesh is dense, with a rosy blush toward the stone. The flavor is "tangy and floral," with overtones of "lime and honey." Eat fresh or substitute for peaches in cooked dishes.

White Nectarine
LIGHT AND SWEET

These white-fleshed fruits tend to be lower in acidity than the yellow-fleshed variety and therefore better suited to eating out of hand than cooking. Their texture is "a bit fibrous," and they have a "one-dimensionally sweet" flavor that is similar to "ripe pears."

Honeydew Nectarine
MELON-Y CRISP

With its yellow-green pastel skin, this small variety of nectarine looks like a miniature version of a honeydew melon. Similarly, the pale yellow flesh is also "reminiscent of melon," with a "dense, smooth" texture and a "musky, banana-like" flavor. Best eaten out of hand.

Arctic Rose Nectarine
BLUSHING BEAUTY

This nectarine has scarlet-and-cream-speckled skin and stark ivory flesh. Its flavor is "buttery and sweet," with just a hint of "rose water." In addition to admiring its flavor, farmers love this fruit because it ripens early and its firm flesh makes it ideal for shipping to market. Eat fresh or substitute for peaches in cooked dishes.

Grilled Chicken Teriyaki

Every time I try to make grilled chicken teriyaki, it comes out so salty that it leaves me begging for mercy—and a jug of water. Any way to tame this salty beast?

–Bob Jorgenson, St. Paul, Minn.

Teriyaki sauce may taste complex, but it typically contains only three ingredients: soy sauce, sugar, and mirin (a sweet Japanese rice wine available in the international aisle of most supermarkets). This simple sauce is versatile, too, as it's used as a marinade, basting sauce, and serving sauce. But when I made a handful of recipes, I discovered that grilled chicken teriyaki isn't without problems. Like any sweet sauce, teriyaki can easily burn over the high heat of the grill. If simply brushed on at the end of cooking, it doesn't add much flavor—although that can be a good thing, because most of the recipes I tried were far too sweet and salty. I had two goals: First, to bring the strong flavors into harmony, and second, to make the grilled chicken breasts a worthy ally, with succulent, flavorful meat and thin, crisp (not charred) skin.

Soy sauce is an essential component of teriyaki, but tasters felt battered by its saltiness in every recipe I tried. Diluting the soy sauce with water allowed me to keep its rich flavor while cutting back on the saltiness. My tasters preferred the traditional sweet components of granulated sugar and mirin (brown sugar, honey, and corn syrup all added off-flavors), but they demanded restraint. Instead of the ¾ cup (or more) of sugar

The secret to flavorful, crisp (but not charred) skin is to hold back on the sugar until the last five minutes of cooking.

in some recipes, I cut it back to 6 tablespoons, and I used just ¼ cup of mirin. My tasters loved the flavor boost provided by garlic and ginger.

Using the teriyaki as both a marinade and a basting sauce was my next test. As a marinade, the mixture needed just 30 minutes to thoroughly flavor the meat, but, thanks to the sugar, it burned on the grill. Omitting the sugar from the marinade fixed the burning problem, but when I tried basting with the same mixture (with the sugar added back in), it ran off the chicken as fast as I could brush it on. I tried thickening the

sauce by boiling it down, as suggested by many recipes, but that made the sauce too salty again. Adding a bit of cornstarch turned out to be the key, as it allowed me to just simmer the mixture for a few minutes to get the syrupy texture I wanted—without the salty bite.

My tasters now demanded crisp, rendered skin beneath the glaze. Having grilled plenty of chicken wings (the glory of which is also crisp skin), I knew that long, slow cooking was needed to melt the fat away. I turned the grill burners down and tried cooking the chicken over both direct and indirect

heat. I was pleased to discover that direct cooking with all the burners on medium-low worked best; the meat cooked in a reasonable time, and much of the fat was rendered (without flare-ups). Pricking the skin with the tip of a knife helped render even more fat, leaving the chicken with incredibly crisp skin.

For good measure, I gave the chicken one last slather of teriyaki sauce just as it came off the grill. Finally, this was the chicken teriyaki I was after: crisp, juicy, grill-marked, and powerfully—yet evenly—salty-sweet. **–Adam Ried**

GRILLED CHICKEN TERIYAKI SERVES 8

If you like, reserve 3 chicken breasts and 3 tablespoons of the extra glaze for use in our Teriyaki Chicken Salad (page 23).

- ⅔ **cup soy sauce**
- ⅔ **cup water**
- ¼ **cup mirin (see page 30)**
- 1 **tablespoon grated fresh ginger**
- 2 **garlic cloves, minced**
- 8 **bone-in, skin-on split chicken breasts (about 7 pounds total), trimmed, skin pricked several times with paring knife**
- 6 **tablespoons sugar**
- ¾ **teaspoon cornstarch**

1. Combine soy sauce, water, mirin, ginger, and garlic in saucepan. Toss chicken with ½ cup soy sauce mixture in large bowl and refrigerate for at least 30 minutes or up to 1 day. Meanwhile, whisk sugar and cornstarch into remaining soy sauce mixture in saucepan. Simmer over medium-high heat until thickened and reduced to ¾ cup, about 5 minutes. (Glaze can be refrigerated for up to 1 day.)

2. Heat all burners on high for 15 minutes, then turn all burners to medium-low. (For charcoal grill, light 50 coals; when covered with fine gray ash, spread in even layer. Set cooking grate in place and heat, covered, for 5 minutes.) Scrape and oil cooking grate. Grill chicken skin-side up, covered, until well browned on bottom and internal temperature of meat registers 120 degrees, 15 to 20 minutes. Flip chicken skin-side down and grill, covered, until skin is rendered and deep brown and meat registers 160 degrees, 15 to 20 minutes. Brush chicken with ¼ cup glaze and grill, covered, until glaze is caramelized, about 5 minutes.

3. Transfer chicken to serving platter and brush with ¼ cup glaze. Let rest 10 minutes. Serve, passing remaining glaze at table.

What to Do with Leftovers: Teriyaki Chicken Salad

Crisp vegetables, potent flavors, and some clever use of leftovers make for a simple summer salad.

Extra Grilled Chicken Teriyaki (page 22) is the perfect start for a summery main course salad. Many Asian dressings rely on a balance of salty, sweet, sour, and spicy ingredients. The leftover teriyaki glaze got me rolling with powerful salty and sweet notes. Fresh lime juice added a tart element, and fresh ginger enlivened the dressing with heat. A little vegetable oil rounded things out.

Choosing the right fruit and vegetables for this salad was easy. For texture and kick, my tasters loved the peppery crunch of red radishes. Minced jalapeño and sliced scallions added more spice, and red bell pepper and pineapple chunks lent color and sweetness. Asparagus completed the salad. When tossed with the leftover chicken and my lively dressing,

these ingredients came together in perfect harmony.

–Adam Ried

TERIYAKI CHICKEN SALAD SERVES 4 TO 6

Three split breasts from the Grilled Chicken Teriyaki recipe (page 22) will yield the 3 cups of shredded meat needed for this recipe. You'll also need 3 tablespoons of the teriyaki glaze. If you don't have enough chicken, you can use shredded meat from a rotisserie chicken. A Microplane grater makes quick work of grating ginger.

- 2 tablespoons vegetable oil
- 1 pound asparagus, trimmed and cut into 1-inch pieces
- 1 red bell pepper, seeded and sliced thin
- 3 cups shredded chicken (see note)
- 1 (15-ounce) can pineapple chunks, drained
- 6 radishes, chopped coarse
- 6 scallions, sliced thin
- 1–2 jalapeño chiles, seeded and minced
- 3 tablespoons teriyaki glaze (see note)
- 2 tablespoons lime juice
- 1 teaspoon grated fresh ginger

1. Heat oil in large nonstick skillet over medium-high heat until shimmering. Cook asparagus and red pepper until lightly browned and just tender, about 5 minutes. Transfer to large bowl and let cool 10 minutes. Add chicken, pineapple, radishes, scallions, and jalapeño to bowl and toss to combine.

2. Whisk teriyaki glaze, lime juice, and ginger in small bowl. Drizzle dressing over salad and toss to combine. Serve.

From Your Garden: Cherry Tomato and Onion Salad

The combination of cherry tomatoes and onions makes a perfect summer salad, as long as the tomatoes don't become watery and the onion isn't too harsh.

Sweet, juicy tomatoes and sharp, crisp onions are a perfect pair, whether in a quick salsa, on top of a burger, or in a simple summer salad. But in a summer salad, the tomatoes usually weep too much liquid and the onions can be downright harsh and overpowering.

To rid the tomatoes of excess water, I tried halving and seeding them, but that took too much time and energy. Salting the tomatoes and discarding the liquid they exuded turned out to be the best way to make this salad fresh-tasting and less watery.

Chopped red onion was too harsh when added to the salad raw. Soaking the onion in water didn't temper it enough, and soaking it in

vinegar made the salad taste pickled. I finally tried heating the finely chopped onion briefly in olive oil, which softened the onion in both texture and flavor. Then I dressed the salad with a mild vinaigrette made with the onion-infused olive oil, which allowed the tomatoes to remain the star of the show.

–Lynn Clark

CHERRY TOMATO AND ONION SALAD SERVES 4

Pear or grape tomatoes can also be used here; just halve or quarter them accordingly.

- 2 pints small cherry tomatoes, halved (quartered if large)
  Salt
- 3 tablespoons extra-virgin olive oil
- 1/2 medium red onion, chopped fine
- 2 tablespoons white wine vinegar
- 2 tablespoons minced fresh parsley
  Pinch cayenne pepper

1. Toss tomatoes with 1/2 teaspoon salt in colander set inside bowl. Let drain for 30 minutes.

2. Meanwhile, heat oil and onion in small skillet over medium-low heat until onions are just tender, 5 to 7 minutes. Transfer to large bowl and cool completely, about 20 minutes. Whisk in vinegar, parsley, and cayenne.

3. Toss drained tomatoes with onion mixture and let stand at room temperature for 30 minutes. Season with salt. Serve.

From Your Garden: Tomato Soup

A simple recipe transforms summer tomatoes into a hearty soup.

You think you know tomato soup. It's velvety smooth and creamy—perfect for a cold winter day. But there's another tomato soup—one made without cream, so you can really taste the tomatoes. It's usually flavored with onions, garlic, and basil and is the perfect way to use a surplus of ripe summer tomatoes.

I quickly discovered that soups made with just tomatoes and seasonings were best. Added liquids, such as chicken broth or tomato juice, diluted the tomato flavor. But even without adding any liquid, my soup was watery. To concentrate the tomato flavor and evaporate excess moisture, I switched from the stovetop to the oven. I roasted the tomatoes—tossed with onion, garlic, and olive oil—and then pureed them in my blender to make an intensely flavored roasted tomato soup.

Ninety minutes in the oven had concentrated the flavor of the tomatoes at the expense of freshness. For my next test, I reserved a pound of chopped tomatoes and added them to the finished soup just before serving. Everyone in the test kitchen liked the fresh flavor they added but complained about the firm chunks of tomatoes floating in my smooth soup. When making salsa, I salt tomatoes to soften their structure and break them down; I tossed the reserved tomatoes with a bit of salt and let them sit for 30 minutes. I added the salted tomatoes to a pot with the pureed roasted tomatoes and let everything cook for just five minutes. My soup now boasted complex flavor heightened by tiny bursts of fresh tomato. **–Eva Katz**

FRESH TOMATO SOUP WITH BASIL
SERVES 4 TO 6
Depending on the juiciness of your tomatoes, you may need to thin the soup with a little water.

- 5   pounds ripe beefsteak or plum tomatoes, cored and quartered; plus 1 pound, cored and diced medium
- 2   onions, chopped
- 8   garlic cloves, peeled and left whole; plus 1 clove, minced
- 3   tablespoons extra-virgin olive oil
-     Salt
-     Sugar
- 1   cup chopped fresh basil

1. Adjust oven rack to upper-middle position and heat oven to 450 degrees. Combine quartered tomatoes, onions, whole garlic cloves, oil, 1/2 teaspoon salt, and 1/4 teaspoon sugar in large roasting pan. Roast, stirring once or twice, until tomatoes are brown in spots, about 1 1/2 hours. Let cool 5 minutes. Working in two batches, process roasted tomato mixture in food processor until smooth. (Pureed mixture can be refrigerated for up to 1 day.)

2. When ready to serve, combine diced tomatoes, minced garlic, basil, and 1/4 teaspoon salt in bowl and marinate for 30 minutes. Transfer to large saucepan, add pureed tomato mixture, and simmer over medium heat until diced tomatoes are slightly softened, about 5 minutes. Season with salt and sugar to taste. Serve.

From Your Garden: String Bean Salad

A bright, bold salad starts with fresh beans flavored from the inside out.

String bean salad, made with fresh beans and a light vinaigrette, is a perfect accompaniment to juicy grilled burgers or smoky barbecued chicken. The beans should be tender and deeply flavored by the potent dressing.

Most recipes blanch the beans and then transfer them to a bowl of ice water to stop the cooking, locking in their texture and color. I started out using this technique, but these beans became too waterlogged—the vinaigrette (a working recipe of just olive oil and white wine vinegar) slipped off the beans and into a pool at the bottom of the bowl. I discovered that if I tossed the beans with the dressing immediately after blanching and draining them, the warm beans soaked up some of the vinaigrette and achieved the texture I was looking for— tender and not too crunchy. What I lost in color I more than made up for in flavor.

But although some of the vinaigrette was being absorbed, the remaining dressing was too thin to properly cling to the beans. The classic combination of honey and Dijon mustard thickened the dressing enough for it to coat the beans, with the bite of the mustard intensifying the overall flavor and pairing well with fresh tarragon. These beans tasted best when nicely chilled, which meant I could prepare this salad ahead of time.

–Lynn Clark

TARRAGON-MUSTARD STRING BEAN SALAD
SERVES 6 TO 8
This salad is best served cold but can be served at room temperature for a picnic or barbecue. If you can't find yellow wax beans, use 2 pounds green beans. If you can't find tarragon, fresh dill and parsley also work well.

- 1/4   cup extra-virgin olive oil
- 2   tablespoons white wine vinegar
- 2   tablespoons Dijon mustard
- 1 1/2   tablespoons lemon juice
- 1   tablespoon honey
- 1   tablespoon finely chopped fresh tarragon
- 1/4   teaspoon black pepper
- 1/8   teaspoon cayenne pepper
- 1   tablespoon salt
- 1   pound green beans, stem ends trimmed
- 1   pound yellow wax beans, stem ends trimmed

1. Whisk oil, vinegar, mustard, lemon juice, honey, tarragon, black pepper, and cayenne in large bowl. Set aside.

2. Bring 4 quarts water to boil in Dutch oven. Add salt and beans. Cook, uncovered, until beans are slightly tender but still crisp, about 5 minutes. Drain beans and transfer to bowl with dressing. Toss to combine. Refrigerate for at least 30 minutes or up to 3 days. Serve.

No-Fuss Vegetable Quiche

I always love the sound of zucchini quiche, but it usually comes out waterlogged and bland. I would love to have a foolproof, flavorful recipe! –Shannon Koenig, Simi Valley, Calif.

Everyone has a favorite way to use up late summer's inevitable bumper crop of zucchini, and mine is making a simple quiche. Unfortunately, zucchini's high water content can cause problems; liquid seeps out of the zucchini while the quiche bakes, resulting in diluted flavor, runny custard, and a soggy crust. Some recipes try to address this issue with time- and labor-intensive methods like salting, pressing, and roasting the zucchini, but I wanted to find an easier—and faster—way to make a flavorful zucchini quiche with a firm custard and flaky crust.

To minimize prep work, I started with a store-bought, prerolled pie dough, which I doctored slightly (see "Easy, Cheesy Pie Crust," right). To rid the zucchini of excess water, I sliced it and then sautéed the rounds with a little salt. The resulting quiche was better but still a little wet. Grating the zucchini on the large holes of a box grater was fast, easy, and allowed more of the water to cook out.

The rest of the flavors came together quickly. For richness, I added aromatic onion and garlic to the sautéing zucchini. Tasters liked the creamy texture and robust flavor of fontina cheese. Fresh basil added a summery touch.

Most quiche recipes call for a custard made with eggs and heavy cream; the most common ratio is 3 whole eggs to 1½ cups of heavy cream. But my tasters told me that less was more, so I lost an egg and ½ cup of cream, which produced a lighter quiche with stronger vegetable flavor. But the custard was still a little loose. The solution was to toss the cooled zucchini mixture with a little flour before folding it into the custard.

Now I had a sturdy, perfectly

The key to perfect texture is using a little finesse when preparing moisture-rich zucchini.

sliceable quiche packed with zucchini and cheese flavor—it barely had time to cool off before my fellow test cooks polished it off. –Kelley Baker

ZUCCHINI QUICHE
SERVES 8

If you can't find fontina cheese, Monterey jack makes a good substitute. Grate only the flesh of zucchini and discard the seeds and core. The quiche will keep in the refrigerator for up to 3 days. Bring to room temperature or reheat before serving.

Zucchini Filling
- 2 teaspoons extra-virgin olive oil
- 2 medium zucchini, grated
- 1 small onion, halved and sliced thin
- 1 garlic clove, minced
- ¼ teaspoon salt
- ¼ cup chopped fresh basil
- 1½ teaspoons all-purpose flour

Custard and Pie Crust
- 2 large eggs
- 1 cup heavy cream
- ¼ teaspoon ground nutmeg
- ¼ teaspoon salt
- ¼ teaspoon pepper
- ½ cup shredded fontina cheese
- 1 recipe Easy, Cheesy Pie Crust

1. For the filling: Adjust oven rack to lower-middle position and heat oven to 350 degrees. Heat oil in large skillet over medium-low heat until shimmering. Add zucchini, onion, garlic, and salt and cook, covered, until vegetables are tender and have released their liquid, about 6 minutes. Uncover and cook until bottom of pan is dry, about 3 minutes.

Transfer zucchini mixture to bowl and let cool 5 minutes. Toss with basil and flour until combined.

2. For the custard and crust: Whisk eggs, cream, nutmeg, salt, and pepper in large bowl. Stir in zucchini mixture and cheese and pour into pie crust. Bake until crust is golden brown and center of quiche is just set, 30 to 35 minutes. Cool on wire rack for 15 minutes. Serve.

FRENCH LEEK AND GOAT CHEESE QUICHE

Substitute 1½ pounds thinly sliced leeks (about 5 medium, white and light-green parts only) for zucchini and onion. Substitute 1 tablespoon minced fresh thyme for basil. Substitute ½ cup crumbled goat cheese for fontina.

EASY, CHEESY PIE CRUST
MAKES ONE 9-INCH BAKED PIE SHELL

- 3 tablespoons grated Parmesan cheese
- 1 teaspoon flour
- 1 (9-inch) Pillsbury Ready to Roll Pie Crust

1. Combine Parmesan and flour. Sprinkle half of Parmesan mixture over one side of dough and gently roll mixture into dough with rolling pin. Flip dough and repeat with remaining Parmesan mixture. Roll dough out into 12-inch circle.

2. Move dough to 9-inch pie plate, gently pressing into corners to secure and fluting edges as desired. To prevent shrinkage, refrigerate dough for 20 minutes, then transfer to freezer for 10 minutes.

3. Spray two 12-inch square pieces of foil lightly with cooking spray and arrange, greased-side down, in chilled pie shell. Top with pie weights (see page 30) and fold excess foil over edges of dough. Bake on lower-middle rack at 375 degrees until surface of dough no longer looks wet, about 20 minutes. Carefully remove hot weights and foil and continue to bake (uncovered) until just golden, about 5 minutes. Let cool for 15 minutes before proceeding with recipe.

Tres Leches Cake

When I lived in Texas, I always picked up tres leches cake for special occasions. It's so moist, it melts in your mouth. But when I made it for my birthday this year, it was mushy—not the custardy cake I remember. Can you help? –Evie Ruiz, Oklahoma City, Okla.

Our Tres Leches Cake is made by soaking a sturdy sponge cake in three kinds of milk to produce a rich, moist cake.

To find the secret to great tres leches—a sponge cake soaked with a mixture of "three milks" (heavy cream, evaporated milk, and sweetened condensed milk), then topped with whipped cream—I went to south Texas, where the Mexican-American community has been making this cake for generations. After eating my way through dozens of cakes and talking to several pastry chefs and cooks, I determined that a good tres leches cake should be moist (but not mushy) and not overly sweet.

Most of the cakes I sampled failed in one or both of those regards. I did have a few decent tres leches cakes, but one I had in a San Antonio restaurant stood out for being incredibly moist but not soggy, with the added twist of a caramel topping called dulce de leche. This was a cake worth trying to re-create in the test kitchen.

Although some make tres leches into a layered affair, I preferred the convenience of baking, soaking, and serving the cake all in one 13 by 9-inch baking pan. Everyone in Texas told me that the open crumb of a sponge cake did the best job of absorbing the milk mixture, so I started with the test kitchen's sponge cake recipe, which gets its lift from beaten egg whites. It emerged from the oven puffed and golden but sank in the center when I poured on the milk mixture. In search of a sturdier sponge cake, I tried several other recipes, with no success. A colleague finally suggested

a "hot milk" sponge, made by heating milk and butter and then pouring the mixture into whipped whole eggs (which are sturdier than just whites). This cake baked up tall and sturdy enough to handle the milk mixture.

Most recipes use one can each of evaporated and sweetened condensed milk (12 and 14 ounces, respectively) and an equal amount of cream. Cutting back the cream to just 1 cup produced a thicker mixture that didn't oversaturate the cake. Texans had warned me that the specifics of adding the milk mixture were critical, and they were right. After many tests, I found that pouring room temperature milk over warm cake worked best.

I thought back to the dulce de leche–topped tres leches I'd had in San Antonio. This type of caramel is traditionally made by boiling an unopened can of sweetened condensed milk for about an hour; since I was already using sweetened condensed milk, I wondered if I could cook it down a little to get the dulce de leche flavor inside my cake. Since boiling the can seemed too dangerous, I poured the milk into a bowl and microwaved it until it became slightly thickened and straw-colored. I mixed this with the other milks and poured it over the cake.

With a hint of rich caramel in each custard-laden bite, this was the Tres Leches Cake I had been looking for: one worthy of the Lone Star State. –Cali Rich

TRES LECHES CAKE
SERVES 12

If using a standing mixer to beat the eggs in step 3, be sure to use the whisk attachment. The cake becomes more moist and dense as it sits.

Milk Mixture
- 1 (14-ounce) can sweetened condensed milk
- 1 (12-ounce) can evaporated milk
- 1 cup heavy cream
- 1 teaspoon vanilla extract

Cake
- 2 cups all-purpose flour
- 2 teaspoons baking powder
- 1 teaspoon salt
- 1/2 teaspoon ground cinnamon
- 8 tablespoons (1 stick) unsalted butter
- 1 cup whole milk
- 4 large eggs, room temperature
- 2 cups sugar
- 2 teaspoons vanilla extract

Frosting
- 1 cup heavy cream
- 3 tablespoons corn syrup
- 1 teaspoon vanilla extract

1. For the milk mixture: Pour condensed milk into large microwave-safe bowl and cover tightly with plastic wrap. Microwave on low power, stirring and replacing plastic every 3 to 5 minutes, until slightly darkened and thickened, 9 to 15 minutes. Remove from microwave and slowly whisk in evaporated milk, cream, and vanilla. Let cool to room temperature.

2. For the cake: Adjust oven rack to middle position

and heat oven to 325 degrees. Grease and flour 13 by 9-inch baking pan. Whisk flour, baking powder, salt, and cinnamon in bowl. Heat butter and milk in small saucepan over low heat until butter is melted; set aside off heat.

3. With electric mixer on medium speed, beat eggs in large bowl for about 30 seconds, then slowly add sugar until incorporated. Increase speed to medium-high and beat until egg mixture is very thick and glossy, 5 to 7 minutes. Reduce speed to low and slowly mix in melted butter mixture and vanilla. Add flour mixture in three additions, scraping down bowl as necessary, then mix on medium speed until fully incorporated, about 30 seconds. Using rubber spatula, scrape batter into prepared pan and bake until toothpick inserted into center comes out clean, 30 to 35 minutes. Transfer cake to wire rack and let cool 10 minutes.

4. Using skewer, poke holes at 1/2-inch intervals in top of cake. Slowly pour milk mixture over cake until completely absorbed. Let sit at room temperature 15 minutes, then refrigerate uncovered 3 hours or up to 24 hours.

5. For the frosting: Remove cake from refrigerator 30 minutes before serving. With electric mixer on medium speed, beat heavy cream, corn syrup, and vanilla to soft peaks, 1 to 2 minutes. Frost cake and slice into 3-inch squares. Serve. (The assembled cake can be refrigerated for up to 3 days.)

Easy Fresh Fruit Tart

We kept the puff pastry, "pastry cream," and fresh fruit of a classic French tart—but lost the tedious work.

Sweetened cream cheese (flavored with jelly and vanilla) is a fast and flavorful replacement for fussy pastry cream.

A fresh fruit tart—with glistening, ripe summer fruit nestled atop smooth pastry cream and a buttery pastry crust—seems like the perfect summer dessert, until you try to make one from scratch. First there's making and baking the pastry shell. The pastry cream seems easier by comparison, until it curdles or burns. And having to arrange the berries with the precision of a mosaic artist is nobody's idea of fun. Could I reengineer this classic summer dessert and make it much simpler?

Starting at the bottom, I knew that making homemade pastry would be too much work. Store-bought pie crust was too delicate to hold the filling and berries, but frozen puff pastry was surprisingly strong. I baked the shell unfilled, and it puffed up light and crisp; but when I assembled the tart, the berries rolled off the sides. Folding in the edges of the unbaked puff pastry created a barrier to keep the fruit in place (see photos at right).

I tried replacing homemade pastry cream with instant vanilla pudding, but tasters immediately rejected the artificial flavor. Softened cream cheese (flavored with sugar and vanilla) was a much better approximation of pastry cream, but it was too thick and pasty. To play off the fruit topping, I tried thinning the cream cheese with jams, jellies, and preserves. The jams and preserves were too chunky, but the jelly (strawberry was the tasters' favorite) gave the cheese a silky texture and sweet berry flavor.

Instead of meticulously arranging each piece of fruit on top of the tart and then glazing them all, I put a mixture of blueberries, raspberries, and strawberries into a bowl and poured a little heated strawberry jelly over them. This glazed the fruit before it was assembled on the tart, meaning I could just spoon the berries over the creamy filling. Once piled on the filling, the glazed fruit looked like stained glass.

Unfortunately, after an hour in the refrigerator to set the glaze (which glues the berries in place), the bottom of the pastry shell became soggy. It turned out that a little sugar sprinkled over the pastry before cooking formed a moisture-proof barrier that kept the crust nice and crisp. Now I had all of the great flavor, texture, and stunning appearance of a fancy fruit tart—with almost none of the work. –Diane Unger

EASY FRESH FRUIT TART SERVES 4 TO 6

Turbinado, a coarse raw sugar, works especially well in place of the granulated sugar sprinkled on the pastry. Although we liked a mix of berries, virtually any ripe fruit—alone or in combination—will work here. Smooth jelly (rather than chunky jam or preserves) is a must for this recipe.

- 1 (9½ by 9-inch) sheet puff pastry, thawed overnight in refrigerator
- 2 teaspoons sugar (see note)
- ⅛ teaspoon ground cinnamon
- 4 ounces cream cheese, softened
- ½ cup plus 2 tablespoons strawberry jelly
- 1 teaspoon vanilla extract
- 3 cups fresh berries (see note)

1. Adjust oven rack to upper-middle position and heat oven to 425 degrees. Line baking sheet with parchment paper. Unfold thawed pastry onto baking sheet and, following photos at right, prepare pastry shell.

2. Combine sugar and cinnamon and sprinkle mixture over inside of tart shell. Transfer to oven and bake until pastry and sugar are deep golden brown, 15 to 22 minutes. Transfer to wire rack and let cool at least 1 hour.

3. While crust is baking, stir softened cream cheese, 2 tablespoons jelly, and vanilla in bowl until smooth. Refrigerate until ready to use. (Mixture can be made up to 2 days in advance; stir well before using.)

4. Spread cream cheese mixture over inside of cooled tart shell. Place remaining jelly in large microwave-safe bowl and microwave on high power until jelly melts, about 30 seconds. Add berries to bowl and toss gently until coated with jelly. Spoon berries over cream cheese mixture and refrigerate until jelly is set, at least 1 hour and up to 4 hours. Let sit at room temperature for 30 minutes. Serve.

Kitchen Know-How
TURNING PUFF PASTRY INTO A TART SHELL

1. Brush a ½-inch border along the edges of the pastry with water. Fold the long edges of the pastry over by ½ inch, then fold the short edges over by ½ inch.

2. Working lengthwise, lightly score the outer edge of all folded edges of the tart shell with a paring knife.

3. To prevent the center of the tart from puffing up in the oven, poke the dough repeatedly with a fork.

Easy As 1, 2, 3

You don't need to be a pastry chef to make our Easy Fresh Fruit Tart, which relies on just three key ingredients, plus fresh fruit.

FROZEN PUFF PASTRY   **CREAM CHEESE**   **STRAWBERRY JELLY**

Food Shopping

POTATO CHIPS: Kettle-Style Chips Pack the Most Potato Punch

With annual sales topping $30 billion, potato chips beat out pretzels and tortilla chips as America's favorite snack food. There are endless chip varieties and flavors, but which bag of plain chips should the purist reach for? We grabbed eight national brands and headed into the test kitchen to find out.

Potato chips are made with three basic ingredients—potatoes, oil, and salt. According to our tasters, starchy white russets and Idahos are the only way to go; Terra's "flaky," "vegetal" Yukon Golds left tasters wondering if they were made from real potatoes.

The type of oil used for frying turned out to be very important. Three of the four bottom-ranking chips—Wise, Cape Cod, and Terra—are fried in so-called "neutral" canola oil, which made the chips taste "fishy," with a "stale aftertaste." Why? Canola oil has a very high concentration (11 percent) of unsaturated fatty acids (called linolenic acids), which break down at high temperatures and take on a fishy flavor and odor. The other chips were fried in safflower, sunflower, corn, and cottonseed oils, which have much lower concentrations (3 percent or lower) of these fatty acids.

Kettle-style chips finished first and fourth in our tasting. These thick-cut chips are cooked in small batches and spend more time in the cooking oil. A thicker cut means more potato mass—and thus more potato flavor—and longer cooking times result in crunchier chips. Lay's Kettle Chips were the panel's clear favorite. These crunchy chips were the thickest ones we sampled and just salty enough to keep tasters coming back for seconds. **–Elizabeth Bomze**

① ② ③ ④ ⑤ ⑥ ⑦ ⑧

Highly Recommended

1. LAY'S Kettle Cooked Original $2.89 for 9 ounces
Comments: The classic lunchbox chip, only better—or, as one taster wrote, "thick, salty goodness." Another noted, "These have some body" and "big potato flavor."

Recommended

2. HERR'S Crisp 'N Tasty Potato Chips $2.99 for 11.5 ounces
Comments: These "shatteringly crisp" spuds actually "tasted like potatoes" and were relatively sturdy compared with other thin chips.

3. UTZ Potato Chips $2.99 for 12 ounces
Comments: Though some snackers found these "very light and crisp" chips a bit greasy, most thought the balance of salt and potato flavor was right on.

4. KETTLE CHIPS Lightly Salted $2.69 for 5 ounces
Comments: If you like that "well-done," "earthy" flavor, these are the chips for you. Some tasters found them too dark, while others appreciated their lower salt level and "pure potato flavor."

Recommended with Reservations

5. WISE All Natural Potato Chips $5.39 for 20 ounces
Comments: "Brittle to a fault," one taster noted. These super-salty, super-greasy chips satisfied some tasters' classic chip cravings but came off as "cheap" and "Styrofoamy" to others.

6. LAY'S Classic Potato Chips $2.50 for 13.7 ounces
Comments: Not surprisingly, these archetypal chips from the yellow bag were described as "right down the middle" and "run-of-the-mill: first grease, then salt, minimal potato."

7. CAPE COD Potato Chips $3.19 for 9 ounces
Comments: Despite the pleasing crunch and lack of grease on this classic kettle chip, the "fishy," "off" flavors from canola oil and prevalence of green-tinged potatoes was off-putting.

Not Recommended

8. TERRA Golds Original Potato Chips $2.79 for 5 ounces
Comments: The only sample made from Yukon Gold potatoes also had the lowest fat and salt content. The golden color and crunchy texture of these chips was, as one taster noted, "deceiving," given their "stale" yet "raw potato" flavor.

Taste Test Frozen Vegetables

We use a lot of frozen vegetables in the test kitchen, but not all frozen vegetables are created equal. Vegetables with a lower moisture content generally freeze well, while their high-moisture counterparts turn mushy when frozen. And not all brands of frozen vegetables are created equal. We've had the best luck with the 365 Everyday Value brand from Whole Foods supermarkets, which consistently taste fresh and don't exhibit freezer burn. Here are the frozen vegetables we like best.

Recommended

PEAS: We prefer frozen peas to fresh—they are more convenient (you don't have to shell them) and reliably sweeter. This is because the sugars in peas convert to starch very quickly after they're picked; peas that are to be frozen are blanched almost immediately after picking, which halts the conversion of sugar into starch, keeping frozen peas sweet.

CORN (OUT OF SEASON): During the summer months, freshly picked corn is clearly superior to frozen. But for the rest of the year, we prefer frozen corn kernels (not frozen corn on the cob, which generally has a poor texture) because they are consistently sweet.

PEARL ONIONS: Because pearl onions are generally used in long-cooked recipes, such as beef stew, the compromised texture of the frozen variety doesn't much matter. Frozen pearl onions come peeled and therefore require none of the laborious preparation of fresh.

LIMA BEANS: In the test kitchen, we rarely use fresh lima beans, which are hard to find, and we never use the canned variety, which are too mushy. Frozen lima beans have good texture and flavor, and they hold up well in salads, soups, and side dishes.

SPINACH: While frozen spinach is clearly not suitable for a salad, it is a good option for cooked dishes. Make sure to thaw and thoroughly dry frozen spinach before cooking.

Acceptable

Frozen broccoli, cauliflower, carrots, and green beans are acceptable options for soups, stews, and long-cooked dishes, where their less-than-crisp texture isn't a factor. But we always prefer the crunchy texture of fresh when these vegetables are the main component of the dish.

Don't Bother

High-moisture vegetables like bell peppers, snow peas, snap peas, asparagus, and mushrooms do not freeze well, and you should avoid them both on their own and in frozen vegetable medleys.

–Scott Kathan

Equipment Roundup

SLOW COOKERS: Not All Fancy Features Are Worth Paying For

Part of the appeal of a slow cooker has always been price. But as slow cookers have gained popularity in recent years, manufacturers have added new features—and larger price tags. Does more money buy a better slow cooker? To find out, we rounded up seven models priced between $40 and $150. We chose slow cookers with oval inserts and capacities of 6 quarts or greater—traits we found important when we looked at more basic models back in 2005.

FEATURES NEW AND OLD: The stovetop-safe inserts in the Rival VersaWare and the West Bend Versatility didn't brown meat very well—the recommended medium heat simply doesn't get the job done. A programmable timer was deemed a real asset, especially because all the machines with timers automatically switch to a warming mode when the timed cooking is done. This means that even if you're late coming home from work, your dinner won't be overcooked (or cold). The models without timers were downgraded.

Other features we found beneficial include an "on" light (so you don't accidentally leave it on overnight), insert handles (which make it easy to remove the insert), and a clear lid that allows you to see the food as it cooks.

THE DANGER ZONE: The U.S. Department of Agriculture recommends that meat get out of the "danger zone" (that is, get above 140 degrees) within four hours. We used remote temperature probes to monitor the internal temperature of large chuck roasts, and every machine was able to bring the meat up to temperature in the allotted time—even on "low." And none of the machines had trouble bringing the interior of the roasts up to about 200 degrees, the temperature at which collagen and connective tissue most efficiently melt away to make tough cuts tender.

EVAPORATION: Although excess moisture is often a problem in slow-cooker dishes, most recipes are written assuming there will be little or no evaporation. The All-Clad, Hamilton Beach Stay or Go, Hamilton Beach Probe, Rival, and West Bend machines only allowed about 2 percent of their contents (3 quarts of 42-degree water) to evaporate after three hours of covered cooking on "high." The two cookers that fared worst in this test, the KitchenAid and the Cuisinart, lost about 6 percent and 4 percent of their water, respectively.

SUMMING UP: All the slow cookers we tested did a good job with slow-cooking pot roast on both "high" and "low" and cooking chili and beans on high. But more important than the cooking tests were the features we deemed essential: timers that automatically shift to a "keep warm" setting at the end of cooking; a clear lid; an "on" indicator light; and handles on the insert. The slow cookers are listed in order of preference. **–Scott Kathan**

Highly Recommended

ALL-CLAD Stainless Steel Slow Cooker with Ceramic Insert
Price: $149.95 at Williams-Sonoma.com
Features: 6.5-quart capacity, digital timer, "keep warm" mode.
Comments: This cooker aced the evaporation test and all the cooking tests, and it has every feature we want, including insert handles and a clear lid. Provided a steady, slow heat that is ideal for breaking down the collagen in tough cuts of meat without overcooking them.

Recommended

KITCHENAID Stainless Steel Slow Cooker
Price: $129.95 at Cooking.com
Features: 7-quart capacity, digital timer, "keep warm" mode, "auto" setting starts on high for two hours then shifts to low, "cooking" and "keep warm" indicator lights, capacity markings on inside of insert.
Comments: This model cooked slightly hotter than the other contenders, but none of the finished food suffered as a result. The slightly squared insert shape was praised for being "easy to pour out of."

CUISINART Slow Cooker
Price: $99.95 at Cooking.com
Features: 6.5-quart capacity; analog timer; "keep warm" mode; automatically starts on "high" (even when set to "low") when timer is in use until contents reach 140 degrees, then switches to "low"; cooking rack; "cook" and "warm" indicator lights.
Comments: This machine did very well in all cooking tests. Several testers were surprised that the bulky, boxy exterior of this cooker got very hot during long cooking. "It looks like it should be insulated," said one.

HAMILTON BEACH Programmable Slow Cooker with Temperature Probe
Price: $59.95 at Cooking.com
Features: 6-quart capacity, digital timer, programmable temperature probe, "keep warm" mode.
Comments: While the temperature probe itself wasn't a lure for testers ("slow cooking shouldn't be that temperature-specific"), this model passed the evaporation test and performed well in the cooking tests. This cooker was downgraded for being the only one without handles on the insert, which made removing it difficult—especially when hot.

Recommended with Reservations

HAMILTON BEACH Oval Stay or Go Slow Cooker
Price: $39.95 at Cooking.com
Features: 6-quart capacity, clips that lock lid in place for travel, recipe name tag on front of base, analog dial controls.
Comments: The gimmicky travel clips and recipe name tag were not part of this model's appeal, but testers did appreciate its solid performance in the kitchen and the "straightforward, no frills" ease of operation. This inexpensive cooker does not have a timer, which is a serious drawback.

RIVAL Oval VersaWare Crock Pot
Price: $54.95 at Cooking.com
Features: 6-quart capacity, insert is stovetop-safe to medium heat, detachable cord.
Comments: "No timer?" asked testers. "No 'on' light?" The opaque lid was another strike against this cooker, but it did perform well in the cooking tests. Several testers complained about the "overhanging lip" on the insert, which necessitates complete inversion to pour out contents.

Not Recommended

WEST BEND Oval Versatility Slow Cooker
Price: $64.95 at Cooking.com
Features: 6-quart capacity, insert/pot is stovetop-safe to medium heat, base functions as a griddle, detachable cord.
Comments: Testers complained about the lack of an "on" light, especially since this machine begins heating as soon as it's plugged in—there is no "off" setting. This model was also downgraded for heating faster on "low" than "high" and for having an awkward-fitting lid that "falls into the pot easily."

Should You Buy a $250 Slow Cooker?

We tested the All-Clad Deluxe Slow Cooker ($249.95 at Williams-Sonoma.com) and were impressed. This model is loaded with all the features we like and the insert (basically an aluminum pot) can withstand high heat on the stovetop, so browning meat isn't a problem. Is it worth a small fortune? An insert that goes onto the stovetop sounds great, but, frankly, it's pretty messy. You still have to cook food in batches for big recipes (which means dirtying another bowl), and pouring off excess fat from the insert is a bother. We'd rather buy a cheaper slow cooker and use a separate skillet for stovetop cooking. –S.K.

Notes from Our Test Kitchen

TIPS, TECHNIQUES, AND TOOLS FOR BETTER COOKING

Kitchen Creations
Flavored Hot Fudge

Our **Banana Split Cake** (inside back cover) is topped with hot fudge sauce. When we don't have time to make our own, we doctor store-bought hot fudge sauce. Any leftovers can be refrigerated for up to a week.

PEANUT BUTTER HOT FUDGE SAUCE

Microwave 1 cup jarred hot fudge sauce, covered, in microwave-safe bowl until hot, about 1 minute. Whisk in 2 tablespoons peanut butter, 4 teaspoons water, 1/2 teaspoon vanilla, and pinch of salt.

RASPBERRY-DOUBLE CHOCOLATE SAUCE

Microwave 1 cup jarred hot fudge sauce and 4 tablespoons white chocolate chips, covered, in microwave-safe bowl until chips are melted, about 3 minutes. Whisk in 2 tablespoons seedless raspberry jam and pinch of salt.

DOUBLE ESPRESSO HOT FUDGE SAUCE

Microwave 1 cup jarred hot fudge sauce, covered, in microwave-safe bowl until hot, about 1 minute. Dissolve 1 teaspoon instant coffee and pinch of salt in 2 teaspoons coffee liqueur (such as Kahlúa) and whisk into hot fudge.

All about Mirin

Our **Grilled Chicken Teriyaki** recipe (page 22) calls for mirin, a low-alcohol Japanese wine made from fermented rice. Although mirin is sometimes served as an aperitif in Japan, here it is most commonly used to add a sweet acidity to Asian-inspired sauces, soups, and marinades. Mirin, sometimes labeled "sweetened sake" or "Aji-Mirin," can be found in the international section of most supermarkets. If you cannot find it, sweet sherry makes an acceptable substitute.

Hot and Hotter

Our recipe for **24-Hour Picnic Salad** (page 15) calls for a couple of tablespoons of hot sauce to add a tangy, vinegary kick to the dressing. Over the years, we've found that while most hot sauces share the same core ingredients—chile peppers, vinegar, and salt—their heat levels can vary drastically. To avoid a searingly hot salad, we recommend using the test kitchen's favorite brand of hot sauce, Frank's Red Hot, which has mellow heat and deep flavor. Some brands of hot sauce, such as Tabasco and La Preferida, are nearly twice as hot as Frank's, so we recommend that you start with half the amount and add more to taste.

NOT TOO HOT
Mellow heat and great flavor

Pie Weight Alternatives

The process of weighting pie dough during blind baking (as we do in our recipe for **Easy, Cheesy Pie Crust** on page 25) is an essential step—it helps prevent the bubbling, cracking, and shrinkage that can ruin a pie dough. If you don't have ceramic pie weights, a few common items will work just as well. Our favorite pie-weight substitute, a cup of pennies, proved to be highly effective in conducting heat, making for a crisp, well-browned crust. In a pinch, 3 cups of dried rice or beans can also be used, although they don't conduct heat as well and the crust won't brown as much. Whatever you use, be sure to line the pie shell with aluminum foil to

Inside the Test Kitchen Making the Cake

Our Banana Split Cake (inside back cover) gets its structure and style from an unlikely source: ice cream sandwiches.

1. Cut each sandwich into quarters. arrange the quartered ice cream sandwiches vertically along the inside wall of a chilled 9-inch springform pan. Transfer pan to freezer until sandwiches are very firm.
2. Remove pan from freezer and fill with softened strawberry ice cream. Smooth surface of ice cream so that it is even with top of sandwiches, cover with plastic wrap, and freeze.

maximize heat distribution and prevent off-flavors. The foil also makes it easy to remove the pie weights, so that browning can continue once the pie crust has set.

Blooming Spices

In grilling and barbecuing, a spice rub is key to well-developed flavor. When set over a hot fire, the spices on the exterior of the meat toast and release their essential oils, resulting in deeply complex flavors. For our **Slow-Cooker BBQ Shredded Beef Sandwiches** (page 8), adding spices straight to the slow cooker left the sauce with a harsh raw-spice flavor. Since we didn't have the luxury of grilling a spice-rubbed roast, we made do with what we had—a skillet. Toasting the spices (in this case, chili powder and paprika) in the skillet coaxed every bit of flavor out of them, giving the dish a spicy grilled taste without requiring us to ever leave the

Shopping with the Test Kitchen
Reduced-Fat Peanut Butter

In our recipe makeover for **Peanut Butter Cookies** (page 7), we found that using reduced-fat peanut butter (which replaces 25 percent of regular peanut butter's fat with stabilizers such as corn syrup solids) allowed us to cut down on fat without sacrificing flavor. But which brand is best? To find out, we tasted chunky versions of three of the most popular reduced-fat brands (Skippy, Jif, and Smart Balance Omega) three different ways: straight from the jar, spread on white bread,

OUR FAVORITE REDUCED-FAT PEANUT BUTTER

and baked into peanut butter cookies. Although each brand performed admirably, Skippy Reduced Fat Super Chunk won top honors for its "well-balanced peanut flavor" and "extra-chunky texture." But that doesn't mean we're ready to throw out our full-fat peanut butter. Tasted plain side by side with full-fat Skippy Super Chunk, tasters perceived a "slight graininess" and "unnaturally sweet flavor" in the reduced-fat stuff.

Gadgets & Gear Easy Peach Peeling

The velvety skin of a peach is fine if you're eating the fruit out of hand, but cooked peach skins can turn leathery and unpleasant. Most cookbooks suggest removing the skins by blanching the peaches in hot water and shocking them in an ice bath to help loosen the skins. Although this technique works, there is an easier trick: Pick up a serrated vegetable peeler. The serrated blade removes the skin from peaches, plums, and even tomatoes with very little effort—or expense. Our favorite, the Messermeister Serrated Swivel Peeler, is available at most kitchen supply stores for about $6.

MESSERMEISTER SERRATED SWIVEL PEELER

comfort of the kitchen. We like to toast dry spices in a little fat. In this recipe, we cooked the spices in a bit of the rendered bacon fat for 30 seconds before adding the liquid ingredients.

Shiitake Mushrooms

When we were developing our recipe for **Rice Salad with Peas and Mushrooms** (page 19), tasters loved the addition of shiitake mushrooms, an Asian variety with broad caps and slender, fibrous stems. Available both fresh and dried, shiitakes are prized for their earthy-sweet flavor and pleasantly chewy texture. Look for fresh shiitakes that have smooth, brown caps devoid of any bruising, and be sure to remove the woody stems before cooking. Dried shiitakes, which are darker in color and have a shriveled appearance, should be rehydrated in warm water for 30 minutes before use. Although shiitake mushrooms can be substituted for white mushrooms in most applications, they work particularly well in stir-fries and salads, where their firm texture can be appreciated.

SHIITAKE MUSHROOMS
Big flavor, chewy texture

Preparing Jicama

The cool, crunchy texture of jicama, a bulbous root vegetable that tastes like a combination of apple and water chestnut, is a winning addition to the **Summer Crunch Salad** (page 4). To prepare jicama, peel away the tough skin with a vegetable peeler or paring knife to reveal the milky white flesh. From here, it can be shredded on a box grater, cut into thin rounds, sliced into matchsticks, or cut into chunks. However you slice it, the refreshing texture and flavor of jicama is best enjoyed raw.

Dulce de Leche

The rich, milky-sweet flavor of our **Tres Leches Cake** (page 26) was inspired by the Latin caramel sauce called dulce de leche. Instead of cooking sweetened condensed milk to the pudding-like texture of classic dulce de leche, we microwaved the milk until it was only slightly thickened and honey-colored. This allowed for a fluid texture that was readily absorbed into the cake. But if you don't have a microwave, don't worry. Simply pour the sweetened condensed milk into a 9-inch pie plate, cover the plate with foil, and set it in a roasting pan. Carefully add enough boiling water to the roasting pan to reach halfway up the side of the pie plate and bake in a 425-degree oven. In just 35 to 40 minutes, the milk mixture will be the right texture for our Tres Leches Cake (and after about 80 minutes, you'll have a dark, thick dulce de leche that's perfect for pouring over ice cream).

Celery Seeds

These tiny brown seeds are harvested from a variety of wild celery called lovage. But don't let their diminutive size fool you—their flavor is potent. The seeds pack a strong punch of slightly bitter, warm celery flavor and should be used sparingly. Tasters loved the flavor of celery seeds in our **Memphis Coleslaw** (page 13). They can also be used to add a distinctive kick to potato salads, pickled vegetables, and, our favorite, bloody marys.

Which Ribs Are Right?

One of the hallmarks of **Chicago-Style Barbecued Ribs** (page 12) is that they are made with baby back ribs rather than spareribs. Spareribs come from the fatty belly of the pig and are quite large (upwards of 4 pounds per rack), and baby back ribs come from the loin area near the backbone and are considerably smaller (only 1¼ to 1¾ pounds per rack) and leaner. If baby back ribs are unavailable, loin back ribs make a great substitute. They are cut from the same area as baby back ribs but are slightly larger (up to 2¼ pounds per rack).

A GOOD ALTERNATIVE
Loin back ribs

Grate Gingerly

Although we love the floral pungency of fresh ginger, its fibrous texture can be distracting when coarsely grated or minced. What's the best way to avoid ginger's stringy texture? Although fancy kitchen stores sometimes carry porcelain "ginger graters" designed specifically for the job (at about $15 a pop), we prefer to use our trusty—and versatile—Microplane rasp-style grater. Its fine blades pulverize the ginger, releasing all of its flavorful juices without any stringy segments.

Slow-Cooking Tips

During our testing of slow cookers (page 29), we logged about 200 hours of cooking time and learned a thing or two about slow cooking along the way.

• **Browning:** Searing a flavorful crust onto meat (before it goes into the insert) is not an effective method for slow-cooking, because the long hours of moist cooking wash the crust right off. However, browning meats on the stovetop before they go into the slow cooker can help build a flavorful fond, render fat, and jump-start the cooking.

• **Liquid Assets:** Since slow cookers don't allow for much evaporation, it is important to use less liquid in slow cookers than you would on the stovetop or oven; too much liquid translates into watery, bland sauces. If the recipe you have used yields a watery sauce at the end of cooking, transfer the liquid to a saucepan and reduce it on the stovetop.

• **Timing:** While fatty cuts of beef and pork are hard to overcook in a slow cooker, poultry can become dry and stringy—even when submerged in liquid—if cooked too long. When slow cooking poultry, we recommend using dark meat (legs or thighs), which holds up to the longer cooking better than lean white meat.

How to CHOP CABBAGE

In our recipe for **Chopped Memphis Coleslaw** (page 13), it's important to chop the cabbage by hand. Here's how we do it.

1. Cut the cabbage into quarters, then trim and discard the hard core.
2. Separate the cabbage into small stacks of leaves that flatten when pressed.
3. Cut each stack of cabbage leaves into ¼-inch strips.
4. Cut the strips into ¼-inch pieces.

When Things Go Wrong in the Kitchen

READERS SHARE FUNNY STORIES ABOUT COOKING MISHAPS

BURNT WHEATIES

As a high school student in the 1970s, I needed to get up before the rest of my family to make the school bus on time. One morning I groggily poured a bowl of Wheaties and was annoyed that they were stale and soggy. We had recently gotten a microwave oven, and thinking that the microwave could crisp them, I threw the bowl into the microwave, set the timer for five minutes, and headed back upstairs to get dressed. Fortunately, my mother smelled something burning—the cereal had turned into a charred, tar-like glob in the bottom of the bowl. To this day, I haven't lived down the fact that I am the only person I know who has burned cold breakfast cereal.

Debra Leary St. Louis, Mo.

A FIRST (AND LAST) PIZZA

My husband and I started making our own homemade pizza many years ago. His pizzas were the highlight of every Friday night for our family and sometimes half the neighborhood, as well. One day our next-door neighbor, who never did any cooking, decided to try to outdo my husband by making a pizza of his own. Everything was cut and laid out with great precision. The meat, olives, and cheese were patterned beautifully, and Parmesan cheese was sprinkled on top. I noticed that the Parmesan looked a little green and I asked him where he got it. He replied that it was from a little green can on the counter by the sink. He had accidentally used Comet cleaning powder all over his pizza instead of Parmesan! Although no one was hurt, as far as I know he never cooked again.

Leona Roe Monmouth, Ore.

CROSS YOUR T'S

Many years ago, my father-in-law visited his aunt Liz in Nashville with instructions to bring her carrot cake recipe back to his family in Texas. He dutifully copied down the recipe and brought it home for my mother-in-law to make. The cake was in the oven, smelling just like his aunt's, when a loud noise and billowing smoke came from the oven. Unfortunately, my father-in-law didn't know the difference between a capital T and a lowercase t in a written recipe. So instead of teaspoons, my mother-in-law used several tablespoons of baking powder and soda, resulting in a highly reactive batter. Now he knows the difference!

Jan Blankenship Richardson, Texas

LEAVE IT TO THE PROFESSIONALS

After visiting our local Benihana restaurant, where the chefs flip the food and bottles behind their backs to entertain customers, I started practicing at home with plastic ketchup bottles to entertain my two girls. Their favorite trick was when I flipped the bottle over my back and caught it with one hand in the front. As I did my performance flip before dinner, the bottle slipped from my hand and shattered on the floor, sending ketchup in every direction. Unbeknownst to me, my wife had bought a new glass bottle of ketchup! Needless to say, that was the end of my Benihana routine.

Daniel Hruby Avila Beach, Calif.

NONSTICK CARPET

Not long after my husband and I were married, I decided to make him a nice gourmet dinner with all his favorite dishes. I preheated the oven and was ready to bake the first course when I realized I hadn't moved the oven racks to the appropriate positions. I held the pan in one hand and removed the mispositioned rack with the other, placing the rack on the floor while I put the dish in the oven. When I went to move the rack back into the oven, I realized that I had placed it on the carpet by accident! Instead of smelling like the delicious meal I had prepared, the whole house smelled like burnt carpet. My husband and I spent the rest of our romantic evening cutting the carpet in order to remove the oven rack from the floor.

Lisa Huff Clive, Iowa

UH-OH!

My neighbor came to my house one day requesting a cake recipe that I usually make in my electric skillet. She thanked me and headed home. About 45 minutes later, my phone rang and it was my neighbor asking me, "Should I have left the lid on or taken it off when I put my skillet in the oven to bake the cake?" I screamed, "You put your electric skillet in the oven?!" to which she replied, "Bye!" and I could only imagine her running as fast as she could toward her oven door.

Betty Witte Via e-mail

UPSIDE-DOWN DISASTER

When I was in college, my two best friends and I liked to have friends over for dinner, and dessert was my department. One Sunday I decided I would make pineapple upside-down cake. I hand-grated the nutmeg and cinnamon, carefully arranged the pineapple and cherries, spread the batter evenly, and put my creation in the oven to bake. After the allotted time, I took the cake out and let it cool while we finished dinner. When it came time for dessert, I went into the kitchen to flip the cake, ready for the "oohs" and "aahs" that were sure to follow. However, I forgot to check to see if the cake was completely cooked, and when I flipped it over, the undercooked batter flew all over me, the stove, the counter, and the floor. So much for my beautiful upside-down cake! All was not lost—we ended up sitting around the pan with spoons eating the bits that were fully cooked.

Melissa Schabel Clark, N.J.

GOOD ENOUGH FOR THE DOGS

I have a small dog with several food allergies, so I usually prepare large batches of homemade dog food (stews of chicken, barley, rice, and fish) for him and freeze portions for later use. One day after making a giant pot, I had several friends coming over to hang out for the day. I had to run to the bank, so I left a note on the door for my friends to go ahead and come in and make themselves at home. Much to my surprise, I returned to find my friends eating large bowls of the dog food! And my dog was sitting in the corner whining with amazement. My friends were enjoying the stew and I didn't have the heart to tell them that they were eating my dog's food. I confessed a few years later, and sometimes my friends still jokingly request my special stew.

April Littenecker Melbourne, Fla.

Send us your funniest kitchen disaster stories. E-mail us by visiting CooksCountry.com/kitchendisasters or write to us at Kitchen Disasters, Cook's Country, P.O. Box 470739, Brookline, MA 02447. If we publish your story, you'll receive a complimentary one-year subscription to *Cook's Country*.

The Great American Cake
Banana Split Cake

Festive ice cream cakes are always a summer favorite. Our version duplicates the flavor of a banana split made with strawberry ice cream—with the added twist of ice cream sandwiches. Topped with gooey hot fudge, whipped cream, nuts, and a cherry (if you like), this is a cake you'll go bananas for.

To make this cake you'll need:

- 8 ice cream sandwiches
- 3 pints strawberry ice cream, softened
- 1 cup hot fudge sauce*, warmed
- 1 cup heavy cream, whipped
- 1/3 cup walnuts, chopped
- 1 ripe banana, peeled, halved lengthwise, and sliced
- 1 maraschino cherry for garnish (optional)

For the cake: Chill 9-inch springform pan in freezer. Cut each ice cream sandwich in half lengthwise, then cut in half crosswise to yield 4 pieces. Transfer sandwich pieces to plate and freeze until very firm. Line outer edge of chilled springform pan with sandwich pieces, arranging them lengthwise (see photos on page 30). Fill center of pan with strawberry ice cream and smooth surface. Cover with plastic wrap and freeze until firm, 2 hours or up to 1 week.

To serve: Remove cake from pan and transfer to serving platter. Spoon warmed fudge sauce onto center of cake and spread almost to edge. Dollop with whipped cream and top with nuts and sliced banana. Top with cherry, if desired.

*Visit **CooksCountry.com** for our hot fudge sauce recipe or use your favorite jarred brand.

Recipe Index

RC = Recipe Card

Cook's Country

OCTOBER/NOVEMBER 2007

Herb-Roasted Turkey
Gravy Cooks in Roasting Pan

Scoop-and-Bake Dinner Rolls
60-Minute Muffin Tin Recipe

Apple Slab Pie
Huge Pie Feeds 20 People!

CHICKEN AND DUMPLINGS
Light-As-Feather Dumplings

RATING DISH DETERGENTS
Which Brand Cleans Up?

GARLICKY GREEN BEANS
Roasted Garlic Flavor Fast

PARMESAN MASHED POTATOES
Creamy, Nutty, and Smooth

BANANA BREAD MAKEOVER
The Secret? Roasted Bananas!

CRISPY CHICKEN CUTLETS
Triple Hit of Garlic

SWEET POTATO CASSEROLE
With Bacon and Cheddar

MAKE-AHEAD STUFFED SHELLS
Easy Freeze-and-Bake Recipe

TUNNEL OF FUDGE CAKE
Fudgy Center Guaranteed!

SUNDAY ROAST PORK
Perfect Pepper Crust

$4.95 U.S./$6.95 CANADA

11>

Our $1,000 Contest Winner!
Sharon Phillips of Pembroke, Mass., won first place in our holiday side dish contest with a colorful twist on basic roasted potatoes. See page 4 for her **Winter Squash and Fennel Roast.**

0 74470 05251 7

Cook's Country

Dear Country Cook,

No, I've never harvested cranberries, although I have, on occasion, fly-fished in a cranberry bog not far from Cape Cod. (A small lake on the property is well stocked with trout.) What strikes me there, as does this photograph, is the primitive and time-consuming nature of growing and harvesting the berries. It is one thing to look at a cow and realize that it gives milk. It is something altogether different to get a close look at the sophisticated system of water management necessary to grow the small red berries that end up in your Sea Breeze.

How is it possible that we have grown so far from the land? Just a couple generations ago, there were so many mountain farms in our Vermont town that Floyd Bentley, a neighbor and farmer, used to say that one could look up at Red Mountain on a cold morning and see "40 smokes," each representing a different chimney. In those days, up through my own childhood, most of the food was produced right on the farm, especially the meat, eggs, potatoes, apples, cider, maple syrup, and canned vegetables from the garden. (Even calf's tongue was pickled and preserved. It is an acquired taste.)

Sure, growing even some of your own food takes effort. But as my neighbor Kevin likes to say, he has signed up for the Vermont retirement plan; in flatlander terms, he plans on working until the day he dies. Some things, like good food, are simply worth the effort.

Christopher Kimball
Christopher Kimball
Founder and Editor, Cook's Country Magazine

Woman Harvesting Cranberries, Grayland, Wash., 1960.
Photographer: Josef Scaylea/CORBIS Images

OCTOBER/NOVEMBER 2007

Cook's Country

departments

in every issue

features

Founder and Editor Christopher Kimball
Editorial Director Jack Bishop
Executive Editor Amanda Agee
Deputy Editor Bridget Lancaster
Senior Editors Scott Kathan
Jeremy Sauer
Test Kitchen Director Erin McMurrer
Test Cooks Kelley Baker
Meredith Butcher
Greg Case
Cali Rich
Diane Unger
Assistant Test Cook Lynn Clark
Online Managing Editor Katherine Bell
Web Editor Kate Mason
Copy Editor Will Gordon
Market Research Manager Melissa Baldino
Editorial Assistant Meredith Smith
Senior Kitchen Assistant Nadia Domeq
Kitchen Assistants Maria Elena Delgado
Ena Gudiel
David Lentini
Contributing Editor Eva Katz
Consulting Editor Guy Crosby

Design Director Amy Klee
Senior Designer, Magazines Julie Bozzo
Designers Tiffani Beckwith
Jay Layman
Christine Vo
Staff Photographer Daniel J. van Ackere

Production Director Guy Rochford
Traffic and Projects Manager Alice Cummiskey
Production Assistant Lauren Pettapiece
Color and Imaging Specialist Andrew Mannone

Vice President New Technology Craig Morrow
Systems Administrator S. Paddi McHugh
IT Development Manager Justin Greenough
Web Developer Doug Sisko

Chief Financial Officer Sharyn Chabot
Human Resources Manager Adele Shapiro
Controller Mandy Shito
Senior Accountant Aaron Goranson
Staff Accountant Connie Forbes
Office Manager Elizabeth Pohm
Receptionist Henrietta Murray

Vice President Marketing David Mack
Fulfillment & Circulation Manager Carrie Horan
Circulation Assistant Elizabeth Dayton
Direct Mail Director Adam Perry
Direct Mail Analyst Jenny Leong
Products Director Steven Browall
E-Commerce Marketing Manager Hugh Buchan
Partnership Marketing Manager Pamela Putprush
Marketing Copywriter David Goldberg
Customer Service Manager Jacqueline Valerio
Customer Service Representatives Julie Gardner
Jillian Nannicelli

Vice President Sales Demee Gambulos
Retail Sales & Marketing Manager Emily Logan
Retail Sales Associate Anthony King
Corporate Partnership Manager Allie Brawley
Corporate Marketing Associate Bailey Vatalaro
Publicity Deborah Broide

ON THE COVER: PHOTOGRAPHY: CORBIS/Yarvin. ILLUSTRATION: John Burgoyne.
IN THIS ISSUE: COLOR FOOD PHOTOGRAPHY: Keller + Keller. STYLING: Mary Jane Sawyer, Marie Piraino. ILLUSTRATION: Lisa Perrett.

Cook's Country magazine (ISSN 1552-1990), number 17, is published bimonthly by Boston Common Press Limited Partnership, 17 Station Street, Brookline, MA 02445. Copyright 2007 Boston Common Press Limited Partnership. Periodicals Postage paid at Boston, Mass., and additional mailing offices. Publications Mail Agreement No. 40020778. Return undeliverable Canadian addresses to P.O. Box 875, Station A, Windsor, Ontario N9A 6P2. POSTMASTER: Send address changes to Cook's Country, P.O. Box 8382, Red Oak, IA 51591-1382. For subscription and gift subscription orders, subscription inquiries, or change-of-address notices, call 800-526-8447 in the U.S. or 515-247-7571 from outside the U.S. or write us at Cook's Country, P.O. Box 8382, Red Oak, IA 51591-1382.   PRINTED IN THE USA

Visit us at www.CooksCountry.com!
Go online for hundreds of recipes, food tastings, and up-to-date equipment reviews. You can get a behind-the-scenes look at our test kitchen, talk to our cooks and editors, enter recipe contests, and share recipes and cooking tips with the *Cook's Country* community.

Kitchen Shortcuts

No-Spill Tacos

I love tacos but can't stand when all the ground meat falls out of the shell and onto my plate—or even worse, my lap! Now I mix my seasonings into the meat and form the beef into thin patties. After the patties are cooked through, I cut them in half, making half moons. The cooked meat fits perfectly into the shell, and it doesn't crumble when I take a bite.

Fran Ascencio Flint, Mich.

THE WRITE WAY

Trace Evidence

Far too often, the phone has rung while I was right in the middle of putting ingredients into my mixing bowl. When I would return to the bowl, I had forgotten how many cups of flour I had already added. Now I use a wooden spoon to quickly trace the number in the top of the flour, so I'll never forget how many cups I had added already. Problem solved!

Jenel Looney Georgetown, Texas

Tea Sandwiches

Not owning a sandwich press doesn't stop me from making pressed sandwiches. I fill my teapot full of water, cover the bottom with foil, and place it on top of my sandwiches in a skillet. After a few minutes and a few flips, I have crisp sandwiches without any fancy equipment.

Lisa Kemmerling Denver, Colo.

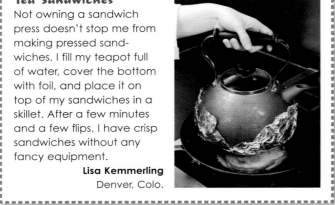

It's a Cinch

BELT YOUR TRASH CAN

I have a standard tall kitchen garbage can, and I hate struggling to keep the bag secured so that it doesn't get pulled in with the trash. I finally came up with something that works: tightening an old belt around the trash bag to keep everything in place.

Theresa Rosekrans Binghamton, N.Y.

PLEASANT SMELL

After I cook something strong-smelling, like broccoli or fish, I put some water, cinnamon sticks, and cloves in a saucepan and simmer it until the house smells wonderful.

Kathy Milano Danville, Calif.

JUICE CATCHER

When cutting tomatoes (or other juicy foods, such as peaches), I place my cutting board on a slightly larger rimmed baking sheet. That way the excess juices fall onto the cookie sheet and my hands and counter do not become a sloppy mess.

Mary Ryan Kutztown, Pa.

MAKING THE LAST COOKIE COUNT

When I make chocolate chip cookies, the last bit of dough in the bowl never has any chips left in it, so I always save a few extra chips to roll into the last scoop. You can never have enough chocolate chips!

Michaela Schlocker Sunnyvale, Calif.

A BETTER VIEW

I have a metal hood over my stove. Whenever I cook something that requires many checks of the recipe, I attach the recipe to the hood with a magnet for easy viewing right where I need it.

Barbara Ravitz Los Angeles, Calif.

FOILED AGAIN

Sometimes it is hard to clean off the stuck-on food on my pots and pans. When sponges just won't do the trick, I crumple up a piece of aluminum foil and use it to scrub. Just like when cleaning my grill grate, the food comes off the pan quickly and effortlessly.

Dabus Koransky Austin, Texas

STICK TO IT

I have found another use for rolls of rug liner. I cut squares of the liner and keep them in each of my cake carriers. When I make a cake to take to a friend, I put the cake on a pretty plate or round, and the liner holds it nicely in the center of the carrier. I don't have to worry that the cake will slide to the edge of the carrier and become smashed and ruined.

Kim Spady Hinton, Okla.

BREAD TERRARIUM

Finding a place in my home for my bread to rise used to be a challenge, but now I just place the bread on the counter and cover it with an inverted glass bowl. It becomes an instant bread "terrarium": warm, clean, and perfect for a slow rise.

DeeDee Edmondson Cambridge, Mass.

GINGER SNAP

When I need ginger juice for a sauce, marinade, or dressing, I cut an acorn-sized piece from a ginger root, peel it, and pop it in my garlic press. With one squeeze, I have juice ready to use.

Max Colgrove Wickenburg, Ariz.

EASY EGG EXTRACTION

I used to have difficulty peeling the shells off hard-cooked eggs when I needed to chop them for egg salad or other recipes. Now I take my knife and cut them in half, then easily scoop the egg out of the shell. It saves a lot of time and frustration!

Robin Barger Forbestown, Calif.

SMART SEPARATING

When prepping vegetables for a stir-fry, instead of putting them in individual bowls, I layer them in one big bowl by separating them with plastic wrap. The vegetables that will be added last to my skillet go into the bowl first. When I am ready to cook, I remove each layer individually before adding it to the skillet. Now there is only one bowl to wash instead of a lot of little ones.

Linda Borders Plano, Texas

If you'd like to submit a tip, please visit us at **CooksCountry.com/kitchenshortcuts** send an e-mail or send a letter to Kitchen Shortcuts, Cook's Country, P.O. Box 4703 Brookline, MA 02447. Include your name, address, and phone number. If we publish your tip, you will receive a free one-year subscription to *Cook's Country*.

DRY IN A FLASH

I know that drying off cooked pasta is the best way to get the dressing to stick to a pasta salad, but I think the tons of paper towels required waste money and trees. Instead, after cooking the pasta, I drain it in my salad spinner insert. I rinse the pasta under cold water right in the insert and then spin it bone-dry. Couldn't be easier.

Kirsten Murphy
Dayton, Ohio

MORE THAN A GRATER

Every now and then, I burn the bottoms of my chocolate chip cookies. I don't have the heart to throw them out, so I use my Microplane grater to scrape off the burned parts. The cookies are saved and no one notices the scuffed bottoms.

Tana Gorglione
West Nyack, N.Y.

GRAVY MASTER

Thanksgiving isn't complete without the gravy, and I make sure to make a lot to feed friends and family. But the gravy on the table always goes cold in minutes, and I get tired of reheating it on the stove. My husband suggested that I use our thermal coffee carafe to house the gravy and keep it hot. It's not a looker on the table, but it sure works wonders.

Camilla Phillips
Beavercreek, Ohio

CORD-SORTING

I have four appliances on the same area in my counter. I got tired of guessing which cord was which when I went to plug something in, so I wrapped a label around each cord's plug and wrote a letter for each appliance: "F" for food processor, "T" for toaster, etc. No more guesswork!

Katherine Havener
San Ramon, Calif.

BETTER BURGER MAKING

I always add special ingredients to the beef when making hamburgers. Instead of dirtying a mixing bowl, I keep the beef in the foam tray it came in, add my seasonings and spices, and mix. Once the patties are formed, I just throw away the container. Easy cleanup!

David Grant
Chicago, Ill.

TRIVET TRIVIA

For my holiday buffet, I used to run out of trivets to put beneath hot serving dishes. Folded towels never looked right, and cork trivets can be expensive. My solution was to purchase an inexpensive roll of cork from an office supply store and cut out trivets myself. One 12 by 24-inch sheet will yield at least 8 trivets, all for less than 10 bucks!

Patricia Blankenship
Plano, Texas

IMPROVISED RACK

During the holiday season, I never have enough drying racks for all of my wine glasses. So I created a makeshift drying rack by lining up wooden chopsticks parallel to each other and setting my glasses on top. The glasses dry quickly, and I don't have to worry about them breaking in my drying rack.

Karel Collins
Sebastopol, Calif.

HOT POTATOES

After scooping my mashed potatoes into the serving bowl, I place a larger overturned mixing bowl over the top until the rest of the food is ready. Right before dinner, I remove the mixing bowl and have still-hot mashed potatoes.

Angela Whitten
Pasadena, Calif.

VARY IT UP

In addition to writing down my appointments on my calendar, I write down what I made for my family for dinner every night. It's a great way to remember when my family likes a new dish I tried or to see what we haven't had for a while. I have saved the calendars over the years, and it is always interesting to see how our tastes have changed.

Donna Quick
Oakland, Md.

Soft in Seconds

BLOW-DRY BUTTER

I bake a lot of cakes and cookies during the holidays. Whenever I need to soften butter quickly, I place it in a bowl and plug in my hair dryer. I turn it on the lowest heat setting, and within a few seconds I have perfectly softened butter.

Carrie Levitt Massapequa, N.Y.

Perfect for a Chef

A quick and easy way to get thin slices of cheese and deli meat for chef's salad is to use my pizza cutter. I stack up several pieces, run a pizza cutter over them, and my salad topping is ready to go.

Machele Christian
Cazenovia, Wis.

Poppin' Packing

TASTY TRICK

When I ship my homemade cookies to relatives for the holidays and I don't want to buy packing peanuts, I wrap the cookies in plastic and pack them in layers of popcorn. Not only does the popcorn prevent breaking, but it's cheap and edible too!

Lauren Ravitz
Los Angeles, Calif.

In a Snap

Whenever I used to break spaghetti for casseroles, little shards would fly all over my kitchen. Now I place the spaghetti in a large zipper-lock bag and break it in half. The spaghetti remains contained, and I don't find little pieces of broken spaghetti in the far corners of my kitchen.

Jennifer Harris
Boston, Mass.

Bottle It Up

I used to always pour too much olive oil on my dishes. Now I use a clean double-spouted soy sauce bottle to drizzle oil on my plates. I have a small, controlled stream of oil, which is really great when I need a very exact drizzle on something.

Bruce Bieber
Seattle, Wash.

Winning Recipe Adds Fruit to Roasted Vegetables

Our $1,000 Grand-Prize Winner!

Sharon Phillips
Pembroke, Mass.

We received hundreds of interesting entries for our holiday side dish recipe contest. The test kitchen's five favorite recipes have their roots in classic holiday dishes, but they all have a twist.

Our grand prize–winning recipe is a fresh take on typical roasted vegetables. Says Sharon, "A few years ago, I began using more vitamin-rich vegetables, such as butternut squash, in my potato recipes. Fennel is a new ingredient for me, and I love the licorice bite and sweetness that it lends to the dish. The dried cranberries add a concentrated tartness."

WINTER SQUASH AND FENNEL ROAST SERVES 8

The feathery green tops (called fronds) of the fennel bulb have a mild licorice flavor. If you can find fennel bulbs with the fronds attached, they can be chopped and added to the roasted vegetables.

- 1 butternut squash (about 2 1/2 pounds), peeled, halved lengthwise, seeded, and chopped
- 2 Granny Smith apples, peeled, cored, and chopped
- 2 fennel bulbs, halved lengthwise, cored, and chopped; plus 2 tablespoons chopped fennel fronds (optional)
- 1/2 cup dried cranberries
- 1/4 cup olive oil
- 1 1/2 teaspoons salt
- 1/2 teaspoon pepper

Adjust oven rack to upper-middle position and heat oven to 400 degrees. Toss squash, apples, fennel (and fronds, if using), cranberries, oil, salt, and pepper in large bowl until well coated. Arrange squash mixture on baking sheet and roast until vegetables are tender and lightly browned, about 1 hour. Serve.

Apples and cranberries make this sweet-and-savory side dish taste as festive as it looks.

Debbie Signor
Broad Brook, Conn.

Trisha McCarty-Luedke
Denver, Colo.

Sheri Wilding-White
Bedford, N.H.

Hildegarde Krumm
Helena, Mont.

AMBROSIA GELATIN MOLD

SERVES 8 TO 10

Debbie writes: "This recipe turns ambrosia fruit salad into a Jell-O mold. I stay true to my mother's tradition of leaving one whole cherry in it. Whoever finds the whole cherry will have good luck in the new year!"

- 4 (3-ounce) boxes pineapple-flavored gelatin
- 2 cups boiling water
- 2 (13.5-ounce) cans coconut milk
- 1 1/2 cups mini-marshmallows
- 1 (15-ounce) can mandarin oranges, drained and halved
- 1 (10-ounce) jar maraschino cherries, drained and halved (reserve one whole cherry, if desired)

1. Dissolve gelatin in boiling water in large bowl. Stir in 1/2 cup cold water and coconut milk. Refrigerate, uncovered, until slightly set (mixture should have consistency of egg whites), about 1 hour.

2. Lightly coat 12-cup mold or nonstick Bundt pan with cooking spray. Whisk slightly set gelatin until well blended, then fold in marshmallows, oranges, and cherries. Pour gelatin mixture into mold and refrigerate, uncovered, until set, about 4 hours. (Can be refrigerated for up to 2 days.) When ready to serve, invert onto large plate.

ARTICHOKE-POTATO GRATIN

SERVES 8 TO 10

Trisha writes: "This dish combines my sister's love for hot artichoke dip and my love for scalloped potatoes. It goes especially well with a holiday ham."

- 2 tablespoons unsalted butter
- 1 onion, halved and sliced thin
- 3 pounds russet potatoes, peeled and sliced 1/8 inch thick
- 2 cups heavy cream
- 1 1/2 teaspoons salt
- 1/2 teaspoon pepper
- 2 (9-ounce) boxes frozen artichokes, thawed and chopped
- 2 cups shredded Gruyère cheese

1. Adjust oven rack to middle position and heat oven to 425 degrees. Melt butter in Dutch oven over medium-high heat. Cook onion until softened, about 5 minutes. Stir in potatoes, cream, salt, and pepper and bring to boil. Reduce heat to medium-low, cover, and simmer until potatoes are almost tender, about 15 minutes. Stir in artichokes and 1 cup cheese and transfer to 13 by 9-inch baking dish.

2. Sprinkle with remaining cheese and bake until golden brown and potatoes are completely tender, about 20 minutes. Let cool 10 minutes. Serve.

STOVETOP BROCCOLI AND CHEESE CASSEROLE SERVES 8

Sheri writes: "This recipe lets me put a crunchy crumb-topped casserole on the holiday table without using my oven."

- 20 Ritz crackers
- 1 cup canned fried onions
- 3 tablespoons unsalted butter
- 1 onion, chopped fine
- 3 garlic cloves, minced
- 1/4 cup all-purpose flour
- 1 cup heavy cream
- 1 cup low-sodium chicken broth
- 1/4 cup brandy
  Salt and pepper
- 2 pounds broccoli, florets cut into 1-inch pieces; stems trimmed and sliced into 1/4-inch rounds
- 1 red bell pepper, seeded and chopped
- 2 cups shredded provolone cheese

1. Crush crackers and fried onions in large zipper-lock bag until coarsely ground. Melt 1 tablespoon butter in Dutch oven over medium heat. Cook cracker mixture until golden brown and crisp, about 6 minutes. Transfer to plate.

2. Add remaining butter and onion to empty pot and cook until softened, about 8 minutes. Stir in garlic and flour and cook until fragrant, about 30 seconds. Whisk in cream, broth, brandy, 1 teaspoon salt, and 1/2 teaspoon pepper and bring to simmer. Add broccoli and bell pepper and cook, covered, stirring occasionally, until broccoli is tender, 7 to 10 minutes.

3. Off heat, stir in cheese until just melted and season with salt and pepper. Transfer to serving dish and sprinkle with toasted cracker crumbs. Serve.

FRUITY HOLIDAY STUFFING

SERVES 8 TO 10

Hildegarde writes: "This recipe comes from my aunt, who always makes this recipe for Thanksgiving dinner. Everyone loves the fruity flavor." Make sure to use whole-berry cranberry sauce for this stuffing.

- 1 (16-ounce) can whole-berry cranberry sauce
- 1 1/2 cups low-sodium chicken broth
- 1 large egg, beaten
- 1/3 cup raisins
- 1 teaspoon grated orange zest
- 1 teaspoon salt
- 1/2 teaspoon pepper
- 6 tablespoons unsalted butter
- 1 onion, chopped fine
- 2 celery ribs, chopped fine
- 1 garlic clove, minced
- 1 teaspoon dried thyme
- 1 teaspoon dried sage
- 1 (20-inch) French baguette, torn into 3/4-inch chunks (about 10 cups)

1. Adjust oven rack to upper-middle position and heat oven to 375 degrees. Grease 13 by 9-inch baking dish. Whisk cranberry sauce, broth, egg, raisins, zest, salt, and pepper in large bowl.

2. Melt butter in large skillet over medium-high heat. Cook onion and celery until softened but not browned, about 5 minutes. Stir in garlic, thyme, and sage and cook until fragrant, about 30 seconds.

3. Toss bread and onion mixture into cranberry mixture, place in baking dish, and bake until lightly browned, about 30 minutes. Serve.

Upcoming Contest: Holiday Pies

We want your best Holiday Pie recipes for an upcoming contest. Please submit entries by November 30, 2007. Send us your recipes by visiting **CooksCountry.com/emailus**, or write to us at Recipe Contest, Cook's Country, P.O. Box 470739, Brookline, MA 02447. Include your name, address, and daytime phone number and tell us what makes your recipe special. The grand-prize winner will receive $1,000. All entries become the property of *Cook's Country* and may be edited. For more information on this and other contests, go to **CooksCountry.com**.

Ask Cook's Country

FREEZING BUTTERMILK

I never seem to use the whole quart of buttermilk before it goes bad. Can it be frozen?

Abby Bielagus Bruceton Mills, W.Va.

We go through buttermilk quickly in the test kitchen, but we realize most home kitchens don't. Wondering if surplus buttermilk could be frozen, we filled ice cube trays with low-fat buttermilk. Once the cubes were frozen solid, we transferred them to plastic bags and returned them to the freezer.

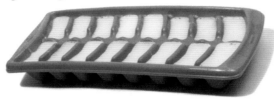

FROZEN BUTTERMILK
A good way to deal with leftover buttermilk is to pour 1 tablespoon portions into ice cube trays and freeze.

Letting the frozen buttermilk defrost in the refrigerator overnight caused the whey and milky solids to separate (they are easily whisked back together with no ill effects). Microwaving the frozen cubes on medium power until melted was a faster, more efficient method of defrosting. We tested the frozen-then-thawed buttermilk versus its fresh counterpart in biscuits, pancakes, and coleslaw. Tasters were hard-pressed to notice any difference between the pancakes and coleslaw made with fresh and previously frozen buttermilk. A few tasters thought the frozen buttermilk made for slightly denser biscuits, but the difference was not significant—the biscuits were perfectly acceptable. Buttermilk can be frozen for up to a month.

PERFECT PIE CRUST

What's the best way to blind bake a pie crust?

Erin Pritchett San Francisco, Calif.

For cream, custard, and chiffon pies, it is necessary to blind bake (or prebake) the empty pie shell. That's because these fillings require little or no baking time, so the crust must be baked separately. But if you simply put the just-rolled pie dough straight into the oven, it will shrink, slump, and toughen. To prevent this, the pie shell first needs to be rested in a cool environment. We've found that a 40-minute rest in the refrigerator followed by a 20-minute rest in the freezer is best; the refrigerator time allows the dough to relax (and thus stay tender), while the trip to the freezer firms the dough up enough so that it will hold its shape in the hot oven.

The second step to ensure a properly blind-baked pie crust is to line the pie crust with foil, then fill it with pie weights for the initial baking; the lining prevents the dough from cooking too quickly (and thus unevenly), and the weights

prevent the dough from puffing and bubbling. After 20 to 25 minutes, the lining and weights need to be removed to allow the dough to dry out and brown for the remaining 10 to 15 minutes of cooking time.

As for the pie weights, while we've used ceramic weights in the test kitchen for years, some recipes call for pennies, dried beans, and uncooked rice as potential substitutes. When put head-to-head, the pie weights worked perfectly, and a cup of heat-conducting pennies produced a comparably brown crust. Rice and dried beans both produced pale and doughy crusts and should be used only as a last resort.

GARLIC SUBSTITUTES

I've seen garlic powder, granulated garlic, dehydrated minced garlic, and garlic salt at my grocery store. What's the difference? Can these be used interchangeably for fresh garlic?

Kristin Griffin New London, Conn.

Garlic powder and granulated garlic are both made from garlic cloves that are dehydrated and then ground (garlic powder has a negligibly finer texture); dehydrated minced garlic is minced while fresh and then dehydrated and packaged; and garlic salt is typically three parts salt to one part garlic powder.

For our testing we compared each product with fresh minced garlic in a Caesar salad (with garlic in both the dressing and the croutons) and garlic bread. We were surprised that the differences were minimal in the Caesar dressing, where the assertive flavor of the anchovies, Dijon mustard, and Worcestershire sauce masked any processed garlic flavor. On the other hand, the results were glaringly different for the crouton and garlic bread tests. Without any other flavors to hide behind, the "sweet and strong" flavor of the fresh garlic stood out among the other "muted," "artificial" contenders. Tasters gave the garlic salt exceptionally low scores, objecting to its "chemical," "super-salty" taste.

When garlic is a predominant flavor in a recipe, nothing comes close to fresh. That said, in recipes where garlic is a background flavor, in a pinch you can use any dried garlic product except garlic salt. We like garlic powder best because of its "natural," "sweet" flavor. Substitute ¼ teaspoon of garlic powder for each clove of fresh garlic.

TOO SALTY TO SUBSTITUTE
Garlic salt is never an acceptable substitute for fresh garlic, even if you attempt to adjust the salt in the recipe.

EGGCELLENT OR UNNECESSARY TOOL?

I've seen egg rings advertised on TV that claim to make perfectly round eggs for sandwiches. Do these really work?

Pam Bellamare Jamaica Plain, Mass.

Egg rings come in nonstick and silicone versions and are marketed specifically for frying perfectly shaped eggs on the stovetop. After purchasing a few, we noted that they resembled round cookie cutters with a vertical handle attached, so we added a metal cookie cutter (coated with cooking spray) to the testing mix for comparison.

As soon as we cracked an egg into it, the lightweight nonstick ring leaked. In contrast, the silicone version and the cookie cutter held their seal with the pan bottom throughout cooking. When the egg whites were set, we removed each mold (using tongs for the cookie cutter, which didn't have a handle) and flipped the eggs as usual. Since the results were the same, we wouldn't waste our money or drawer space on these rings, but if your heart is set on perfectly shaped fried eggs, grab a 3½-inch cookie cutter, coat it with cooking spray, and be sure the cutter is lying flat in the pan during cooking.

PICTURE-PERFECT EGGS
If you have a 3½-inch cookie cutter (left), there is no need to buy an egg ring (right).

HIGH-ALTITUDE BAKING 101

I've just moved to Colorado and wonder if there are any basic adjustments I will need to make for baking at a high altitude. I especially want to make sure I can still make my famous oatmeal cookies.

Marilyn L. Winicott Denver, Colo.

Most people know that water boils faster at higher altitudes, but what does that mean for baking? Problems with baking recipes developed at sea level typically arise around 3,500 feet and intensify as altitude increases. The reduced air pressure at higher elevations means water will evaporate more quickly in the oven and that chemical leaveners will react with more strength.

Since every recipe is different, we recommend first baking your recipe without adjustments and then troubleshooting for corrections when necessary. Many recipes will benefit from shorter baking times in a slightly hotter oven, as well as from additional liquid or eggs. For a more extensive list of common high-altitude baking problems and solutions, visit CooksCountry.com/highaltitude.asp.

To ask us a cooking question, visit CooksCountry.com/emailus. You can also write to Ask Cook's Country, P.O. Box 470739, Brookline, MA 02447. See if you can stump us!

Slow Cooking BEEF BARLEY SOUP

Most beef barley soups from the slow cooker are thin, bland, and vegetal. We set out to create a soup in which the star ingredients—beef and barley—shine through.

Browning the beef and vegetables on the stovetop ensures the deepest, richest flavor.

A good bowl of beef barley soup takes time to make, but the results are well worth it. The beef, usually stew meat, needs hours of slow, steady cooking to become tender and flavorful. The beef shares the pot with carrots, onions, tomatoes, and plenty of barley to thicken the rich broth, which is simmered away until the soup becomes hearty and almost stew-like.

I wanted this soup on a weeknight, so I thought the stew meat and my slow cooker would be a perfect match. Following a standard slow-cooker beef barley soup recipe, I simply added all the ingredients to the insert, turned the slow cooker on, and walked away. Nine hours later, I cracked open the lid to find a sad medley of bland meat, soggy vegetables, and sparse barley floating in a watery, tasteless broth. I would have to find a way to pump up the flavor.

I tested several cuts before concluding that rich, flavorful chuck was the best choice for the slow cooker. To build flavor from the onset, I browned the beef and vegetables before adding them to the slow cooker. Canned diced tomatoes added brightness to the soup, but tasters wanted a deeper flavor. I found

several recipes that called for tomato sauce, but it made the soup taste canned and watery. Instead, a few tablespoons of thick, rich tomato paste (which I sautéed with the vegetables to bring out its flavor) gave the soup a sweeter flavor and more satiny texture.

The broth for this soup needs to be hearty and full of beef flavor. Most recipes use water, with predictable results. It was no surprise that beef broth worked much better. Looking for even more beef flavor, I stole an idea from my grandmother's homemade beef broth recipe and added a couple of beef bones, which are easily found at the supermarket. Now the soup had the intense beef flavor that it had been lacking.

The final component was the barley, and while most slow-cooker recipes use ½ cup, I found that I needed a full cup of barley to add the proper substance and heft to the soup. After nine hours in the slow cooker, this beef barley soup was full of rich beef flavor, tender vegetables, and just the right amount of nutty barley. I had the soup I had been trying to make all along—and it was **waiting for me** when I got home from work. **–Lynn Clark**

BEEF BARLEY SOUP SERVES 6 TO 8

Beef shin bones or oxtails will work in place of the marrow bones. Since the barley will absorb liquid as it sits, leftovers should be thinned with water when reheated.

- 3 pounds boneless beef chuck stew meat, trimmed and cut into 1-inch pieces
  Salt and pepper
- 2 tablespoons vegetable oil
- 2 onions, chopped
- 2 carrots, peeled and chopped
- 6 garlic cloves, minced
- 1 tablespoon minced fresh thyme or 1 teaspoon dried thyme
- 3 tablespoons tomato paste
- ½ cup red wine
- 8 cups low-sodium beef broth
- 1 (28-ounce) can diced tomatoes
- 1 cup pearl barley
- 2 beef marrow bones (see note)
- 1 tablespoon cider vinegar

1. Pat beef dry with paper towels and season with salt and pepper. Heat 2 teaspoons oil in large skillet over medium-high heat until just smoking. Brown half of beef, about 8 minutes. Transfer to slow cooker and repeat with additional 2 teaspoons oil and remaining beef.

2. Add remaining oil, onions, and carrots to skillet and cook until vegetables are softened, about 5 minutes. Cook garlic, thyme, and tomato paste until fragrant, about 30 seconds. Stir in wine, using wooden spoon to scrape up browned bits. Transfer to slow cooker.

3. Add broth, tomatoes, barley, and bones to slow cooker. Cover and cook on low until meat is tender, 7 to 9 hours (or cook on high 4 to 5 hours). Skim fat from surface and discard bones. Stir in vinegar and season with salt and pepper. Serve.

Make Ahead: You can prepare the recipe through step 2 the night before the ingredients go into the slow cooker. Refrigerate the browned beef and the vegetable mixture in separate containers. In the morning, transfer the beef and vegetable mixture to the slow cooker and proceed with step 3. Cooking time will be on the high end of the ranges given.

Best Beef Broth

Commercial beef broth can be overly salty, tinny, and lacking in beef flavor. After tasting eight supermarket brands, we prefer Pacific for its rich, toasty beefiness. It also has less sodium than most of the competition.

RICH, BEEFY, AND NOT TOO SALTY

Throw Me a Bone

Adding beef marrow bones to the slow cooker greatly intensified the meaty flavors in the soup.

BEEF BONES = BIG FLAVOR

The original recipe relied on a now-defunct ingredient. Is this historic cake out of production, too?

BUNDT BOOM
Tunnel of Fudge Cake was a 1960s craze th transformed the Bund pan from curiosity to kitchen essential.

In 1966, Ella Helfrich of Houston, Texas, won second place—and $5,000—in the annual Pillsbury Bake-Off for her Tunnel of Fudge Cake recipe. Ella's glazed, nutty, and brownie-like cake was baked in a Bundt pan, but its most distinguishing feature was the ring (or "tunnel") of creamy fudge that formed inside the cake as it baked. More important, it was my birthday cake from the time I was eight years old.

Wanting to bake this cake for my son on his birthday, I dusted off my mother's old Pillsbury recipe, in which three sticks of butter were creamed with 1½ cups of white sugar, and then eggs, flour, and nuts were mixed in along with a secret ingredient: a package of powdered Pillsbury Two Layer Double-Dutch Fudge Buttercream Frosting mix. This mix was the key to the cake, as it contained large amounts of cocoa powder and confectioners' sugar, which separated out during baking—this cake was always slightly underbaked—and came together to help form the fudgy center. Pillsbury no longer sells this frosting mix, but they do offer an updated recipe (which includes lots of cocoa powder and confectioners' sugar) on their website.

I had high hopes as I pulled the new Pillsbury recipe out of the oven—it looked just like the Tunnel of Fudge Cake I remembered from my youth. Sadly, it was lacking in chocolate flavor, and even worse, it had no fudgy center. Other modern recipes attempt to replace the frosting mix with ingredients like instant chocolate pudding and homemade chocolate ganache (melted chocolate and heavy cream) hardened into a ring and set in the middle of the batter, but they also failed to create the signature tunnel. Some recipes plant chunks of chocolate inside the batter, but they baked up with a liquid interior that gushed when the cake was sliced. A proper Tunnel of Fudge Cake has a creamy, frosting-like filling that holds its shape when the cake is cut. I decided to return to the updated Pillsbury recipe and see if I could fix it.

To add more chocolate flavor, I switched from natural cocoa powder (which can be sour) to less-acidic Dutch-processed cocoa. Adding melted chocolate to the batter made the cake more moist and contributed big chocolate punch. As for the tunnel, I knew that slightly underbaking the cake was a big part of it. But even when underbaked, the interior of my cake was still too dry and decidedly nonfudgy.

To add moisture (and flavor), I swapped out almost half of the granulated sugar with brown sugar. But the big key was adjusting the amounts of two base ingredients: flour and butter. Cutting back on the flour made the cake much more moist, and using less butter helped the cakey exterior set more quickly; together these changes created the perfect environment for the fudgy interior to form. Finally, after two dozen failed cakes, the "tunnel" was back. And so was my birthday cake.

–Bridget Lancaster

TUNNEL OF FUDGE CAKE
SERVES 12 TO 14

Do not use a cake tester, toothpick, or skewer to test the cake—the fudgy interior won't give an accurate reading. Instead, remove the cake from the oven when the sides just begin to pull away from the pan and the surface of the cake springs back when pressed gently with your finger.

Cake
- ³/4 cup Dutch-processed cocoa powder, plus extra for dusting pan
- ¹/2 cup boiling water
- 2 ounces bittersweet chocolate, chopped
- 2 cups all-purpose flour
- 2 cups pecans or walnuts, chopped fine
- 2 cups confectioners' sugar
- 1 teaspoon salt
- 5 large eggs, room temperature
- 1 tablespoon vanilla extract
- 1 cup granulated sugar
- ³/4 cup packed light brown sugar
- 2 ¹/2 sticks unsalted butter, softened

Chocolate Glaze
- ³/4 cup heavy cream
- ¹/4 cup light corn syrup
- 8 ounces bittersweet chocolate, chopped
- ¹/2 teaspoon vanilla extract

1. For the cake: Adjust oven rack to lower-middle position and heat oven to 350 degrees. Grease 12-cup Bundt pan and dust with cocoa powder. Pour boiling water over chocolate in medium bowl and whisk until smooth. Cool to room temperature. Whisk cocoa, flour, nuts, confectioners' sugar, and salt in large bowl. Beat eggs and vanilla in large measuring cup.

2. With electric mixer on medium-high speed, beat granulated sugar, brown sugar, and butter until light and fluffy, about 2 minutes. On low speed, add egg mixture until combined, about 30 seconds. Add chocolate mixture and beat until incorporated, about 30 seconds. Beat in flour mixture until just combined, about 30 seconds.

3. Scrape batter into prepared pan, smooth batter, and bake until edges are beginning to pull away from pan, about 45 minutes. Cool upright in pan on wire rack for 1½ hours, then invert onto serving plate and cool completely, at least 2 hours.

4. For the glaze: Cook cream, corn syrup, and chocolate in small saucepan over medium heat, stirring constantly, until smooth. Stir in vanilla and set aside until slightly thickened, about 30 minutes. Drizzle glaze over cake and let set for at least 10 minutes. Serve. (Cake can be stored at room temperature for up to 2 days.)

The American Table:
Birth of the Bundt Pan

Metallurgical engineer H. David Dalqui invented the Bundt pan in 1950 at the request of bakers in Minneapolis who were using old-fashioned ceramic par of the same design. Dalquist turned to cast aluminum to produce a pan that was much lighter and easier to use. Sales of his Bundt pan (a name he trad marked) were underwhelming until Ello Helfrich's Tunnel of Fudge Cake made its debut in 1966. The Pillsbury Compan quickly received over 200,000 requests for the pan, and to meet demand Dalquist's company, NordicWare, wen into 24-hour production. Over 50 millio Bundt pans have been sold worldwide

The "tunnel" in this cake is a soft, fudgy layer that separates from the rest of the batter during baking.

Recipe Makeover BANANA BREAD

Could we find a way to make a low-fat banana bread with the rich flavor and texture of the best full-fat versions?

Even though our banana bread has very little fat, it bakes up moist and tender.

Most home cooks are familiar with the traditional recipe for banana bread: mashed over-ripe bananas, vegetable oil, and eggs are combined in one bowl and mixed with flour, sugar, and leavener; the batter is then poured into a loaf pan and baked. But with ½ cup (or more) of oil and as much as a cup of sugar in every loaf, a single slice can pack almost 300 calories and 10 grams of fat. I wanted to find a leaner way to make moist, full-flavored banana bread.

I found low-fat recipes that called for using baby food, applesauce, and even avocados to replace some of the sugar and oil. All of these breads had dry or gummy textures and baked up with weak and/or strange flavors. I was going to have to start from scratch and find another way to replace the sweetness, richness, and moisture of the sugar and oil.

I started by upping the amount of bananas, which boosted the flavor and sweetness of the bread, but the center baked up wet and gummy. I found one recipe that called for roasting unpeeled bananas, and I wondered if that might help the flavor. I roasted the bananas in

the oven until their skins were totally black and their flesh was caramelized, which took about 20 minutes. Once the bananas cooled, I peeled and mashed them. The roasted bananas were sweeter and more intense than raw bananas, meaning I could now use less sugar.

Like carrot cake, banana bread is normally made with vegetable oil. My tasters liked the flavor of a loaf made with butter, but my plan to get more richness from less fat didn't work out, as recipes made with just a modicum of butter baked up spongy and dry. Looking for another ingredient to add moisture and structure, I tried buttermilk, reduced-fat sour cream, and reduced-fat cream cheese. Butter-milk was distractingly tangy, and the reduced-fat sour cream made the bread too spongy. But the reduced-fat cream cheese (combined with just a tablespoon of oil) gave the bread good moisture and texture. Since my tasters couldn't identify my secret ingredient as cream cheese, I made a batch with a product the test kitchen usually doesn't like, fat-free cream cheese. My tasters couldn't tell the difference between the breads made with the reduced-fat and fat-free

cream cheeses, so the fat-free was in.

Now I had a moist, rich banana bread that was loaded with banana flavor—and my tasters couldn't even tell that I'd dramatically reduced the fat and calories.

–Meredith Butcher

LOW-FAT BANANA BREAD
MAKES ONE 9 BY 5-INCH LOAF
Adding more than 1½ cups of the roasted bananas to the batter will result in a dense, gummy loaf.

- 4 large ripe bananas
- 2 large eggs
- 2 teaspoons vanilla extract
- 1¾ cups all-purpose flour
- ½ cup sugar
- 2 teaspoons baking powder
- ¾ teaspoon baking soda
- ¼ teaspoon salt
- 1 tablespoon vegetable oil
- 2 ounces fat-free cream cheese, cut into 4 pieces and chilled

1. Adjust oven rack to middle position and heat oven to 325 degrees. Bake bananas on rimmed baking sheet until skins are completely black, about 20 minutes. (Do not turn off oven.) Cool bananas completely, peel, and mash with potato masher until smooth. Measure 1½ cups mashed bananas and discard any excess.

2. Grease a 9 by 5-inch loaf pan. Whisk eggs and vanilla in small bowl. With electric mixer on medium-low speed, mix flour, sugar, baking powder, baking soda, and salt in large bowl until combined. Add oil and cream cheese, 1 piece at a time, and mix until only pea-sized pieces of cream cheese remain, about 1 minute. Slowly mix in egg mixture, then add mashed bananas and beat until incorporated, about 30 seconds.

3. Scrape batter into prepared pan and bake until golden brown and toothpick inserted into center comes out with a few crumbs attached, 50 to 60 minutes. Cool for 10 minutes, then turn out onto wire rack and let cool at least 1 hour. Serve. (Bread can be stored at room temperature for up to 3 days.)

Trimming Tricks
While trying to trim every last calorie from our Low-Fat Banana Bread, we found that roasted bananas gave the bread a more pronounced banana flavor, and their extra sweetness allowed us to cut sugar (and calories) from the recipe. Swapping fat-free cream cheese for some of the oil was just the ticket to reduced fat.

ROASTED BANANAS
Allowed us to use less sugar

FAT-FREE CREAM CHEESE
Allowed us to use less oil

Herb Butter-Roasted Turkey and Gravy

I've tried making herb-butter turkey a few times, and although it looks incredible, the herb flavor never really comes through. What am I doing wrong? –Randy Morrison, Bakersville, Calif.

Simmering vegetables in stock and the turkey drippings while the bird cooks helps to build a flavorful base for the gravy.

Kitchen Know-How
GETTING UNDER THE SKIN

To deeply season the bird with the best herb flavor, you need to place the herb butter under the skin.

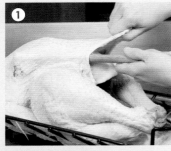

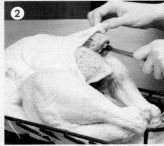

1. Loosen the turkey skin by inserting the handle of a wooden spoon between the skin and the breast meat.
2. Spoon half of the herb butter under the skin, then rub the remaining butter all over the turkey and inside the cavity.

Rubbing the holiday bird with herb butter sounds like a promising way to add flavor. Unfortunately, every recipe I tried proved that while the butter does help to season and color the bird, the flavor of the fresh herbs withers to nothing in the heat of the oven. I'd have to start from scratch.

Following the test kitchen's standard technique, I set my oven to 400 degrees and got out my roasting pan and V-rack. While we typically flip the turkey one or more times to promote even cooking, in this case flipping caused the melted butter to drain out of the turkey. What's more, the relatively high roasting temperature caused the butter to burn rather than brown, leaving the turkey

nearly blackened. Fortunately, roasting the turkey at a lower temperature solved both issues. The perfect temperature turned out to be 325 degrees: The gentler heat helped the turkey cook more evenly without flipping and allowed the butter to brown without scorching.

Turning my attention to the herb flavor, I started by folding different combinations of fresh minced herbs into a stick of softened butter. I rubbed the butter under the skin, in the cavity, and over the exterior of the turkey before roasting. I quickly realized that leafy herbs, like parsley and basil, weren't going to work; their flavor dissipated over the course of cooking. Sturdier woody herbs, like thyme and rosemary, are drier and held their flavor

better—too well, in fact, as they were too strong. Although it felt odd to try dried herbs in a recipe so defined by its herb flavor, the dried herbs retained their flavor without any of the unpleasant pungency. I didn't need to purchase multiple dried herbs to get complex flavor, because herbes de Provence, a French herb blend containing rosemary, marjoram, thyme, lavender, and fennel (among others), did the job.

To brighten up the herb-butter mixture even more, I added grated lemon zest. But even after adding good pinches of salt and pepper, something was still missing. Common additions like Worcestershire sauce, soy sauce, and Marsala wine overwhelmed the herb flavor. I finally hit upon the

solution when I replaced the salt with packaged chicken bouillon, which enhanced the poultry and herb flavors.

With all the buttery, herbed turkey drippings in the bottom of the roasting pan, it was time to start making the gravy. To build flavor, I added chicken broth, white wine, and aromatic vegetables to the roasting pan; as the bird cooked, the drippings fell into the broth mixture and infused it with intense flavor.

After thickening the gravy with flour, I finally found a place for fresh herbs. Added just before the gravy came off the stove, fresh parsley, thyme, and rosemary packed a vibrant, floral punch that perfectly complemented the deep herbal taste of the turkey. –Jeremy Sauer

HERB BUTTER-ROASTED TURKEY AND GRAVY
SERVES 10 TO 12

We recommend using a frozen Butterball turkey—they are injected with a salt solution that helps them stay moist—but kosher or brined "natural" turkeys also work well (for information on brining, see page 31). Any chicken bouillon will work here, but Better Than Bouillon, a concentrated paste, is our favorite. To read the results of our bouillon tasting, see page 30.

Turkey
- 1 (12- to 14-pound) frozen Butterball turkey (see note), thawed
- 8 tablespoons (1 stick) unsalted butter, softened
- 2 tablespoons dried herbes de Provence (see "Many Herbs, One Bottle" below)
- 4 garlic cloves, minced
- 1 tablespoon grated lemon zest
- 1½ teaspoons chicken bouillon (see note)
- 1 teaspoon pepper
- 2 onions, chopped
- 1 carrot, peeled and chopped
- 1 celery rib, chopped
- 4 cups low-sodium chicken broth
- 1 cup white wine

Herb Gravy
- 4 tablespoons unsalted butter
- 5 tablespoons all-purpose flour
- 2 tablespoons finely chopped fresh parsley
- 1 teaspoon minced fresh thyme
- ½ teaspoon minced fresh rosemary
  Salt and pepper

1. For the turkey: Adjust oven rack to lowest position and heat oven to 325 degrees. Pat turkey dry inside and out with paper towels. Using fork, beat butter, herbs, garlic, zest, bouillon, and pepper until combined.

2. Following photos on page 10, spoon half of butter mixture under skin of turkey. Rub remaining butter mixture over outside of turkey and inside of cavity.

3. Scatter vegetables in bottom of large roasting pan, then add broth and wine. Tuck wings behind back and arrange turkey on V-rack set inside roasting pan. Roast until internal temperature of breast registers 165 degrees and thigh registers 170 to 175 degrees, 2½ to 3 hours. Transfer turkey to cutting board and let rest 30 minutes.

4. For the gravy: Carefully strain contents of pan into large measuring cup. Let liquid settle so that fat separates, then skim (if necessary, add enough water to measure 4 cups). Melt butter in saucepan over medium heat. Add flour and whisk constantly until honey-colored, about 2 minutes. Gradually whisk in strained juices. Bring to boil, then reduce heat to low and simmer until slightly thickened, about 5 minutes. Off heat, stir in herbs and season with salt and pepper. Carve turkey and serve with herb gravy.

Many Herbs, One Bottle

In an effort to boost the herb flavor in our turkey, we took to the spice aisle of our supermarket. After trying jars of poultry seasoning, lemon pepper, and even Mrs. Dash, we found a perfect solution, herbes de Provence. This French-inspired mix of dried herbs commonly includes rosemary, marjoram, thyme, lavender, and fennel; it lent a balanced, herby flavor to the turkey without a laundry list of ingredients. If you can't find herbes de Provence, substitute the following: 2 teaspoons dried marjoram, 2 teaspoons dried thyme, 1 teaspoon dried basil, 1 teaspoon dried rosemary (crumbled), 1 teaspoon dried sage, and ⅛ teaspoon ground fennel.

HERBES DE PROVENCE

What to Do with Leftovers:
Creamy Turkey and Wild Rice Soup

Leftover turkey can add rich flavor to a pot of soup—if you know how to handle it.

With its silky broth, pleasantly chewy wild rice, and chunks of tender turkey, creamy turkey and wild rice soup is a great way to make use of leftover Thanksgiving turkey. Unfortunately, most of the recipes we found tasted of weak broth studded with undercooked rice and rubbery turkey.

Though many turkey soup recipes are content to simply stir leftover turkey into chicken broth, more traditional (and thriftier) recipes make use of the turkey carcass by simmering it for hours to make a deeply flavorful broth. To coax every ounce of flavor out of the carcass as quickly as possible, we chopped it into pieces and sautéed it with onion and celery until it was lightly browned. We then simmered the carcass and vegetables in a combination of chicken broth (for rich poultry flavor) and white wine (for brightness) for an hour; this method produced a rich, savory broth that was definitely worth the time.

Since wild rice can take well over an hour to cook, some recipes call for toasting the grains in a dry pan to break down the tough exterior of the rice prior to cooking. This cut a few minutes off the cooking time, but we were eager to lop off even more time. In the test kitchen, we often add baking soda to cooking beans to help them soften, as baking soda breaks down the beans' tough fibers. Hoping that this might work for the rice, we stirred ¼ teaspoon of baking soda into the soup. Sure enough, this reduced the rice's cooking time by about 15 minutes.

The cream tasted best when it was added toward the end of cooking. we thickened the soup by simply whisking some flour into the cream before it went into the pot. Adding the leftover turkey at the very end of cooking ensured that it stayed tender.

–Jeremy Sauer and Greg Case

CREAMY TURKEY AND WILD RICE SOUP SERVES 6 TO 8
Leftover turkey wings, thighs, or drumsticks can be used in place of the carcass.

Turkey Broth
- 2 tablespoons unsalted butter
- 2 onions, chopped
- 1 celery rib, chopped
- 1 leftover turkey carcass, chopped into 4 pieces (see note)
- 3 cups white wine
- 6 cups low-sodium chicken broth

Soup
- 1 cup wild rice
- 2 carrots, peeled and chopped
- ½ teaspoon dried thyme
- ¼ teaspoon baking soda
- ¼ cup all-purpose flour
- 1 cup heavy cream
- 3 cups chopped cooked turkey
  Salt and pepper

1. For the turkey broth: Melt butter in large Dutch oven over medium-high heat. Cook onions, celery, and turkey carcass until lightly browned, about 5 minutes. Add wine and chicken broth and simmer over medium-low heat for 1 hour. Strain broth, discarding solids.

2. For the soup: Wipe out Dutch oven and toast rice over medium heat until rice begins to pop, 5 to 7 minutes. Stir in turkey broth, carrots, thyme, and baking soda and bring to boil. Reduce heat to low and simmer, covered, until rice is tender, about 1 hour.

3. Whisk flour and cream in bowl until smooth. Slowly whisk flour mixture into soup. Add turkey and simmer until soup is slightly thickened, about 10 minutes. Season with salt and pepper. Serve.

On the Side: Savory Sweet Potato Casserole

Hold the marshmallows! Sugar and spice may be nice for dessert, but we wanted a savory sweet potato casserole for our holiday table.

As a native southerner, it took me a long time to realize that sweet potatoes don't have to be candied. My epiphany came when I was served a decidedly savory sweet potato casserole that resembled jazzed-up scalloped potatoes. This casserole featured creamy, cheesy sweet potatoes accented with smoky bacon and a subtly spicy bite, all under a coating of crunchy bread crumbs. I had to re-create this dish for myself.

Baking a casserole of raw sweet potatoes created an unevenly cooked disaster, so I turned to precooking the sweet potatoes and then baking them. I tried boiling, baking, and microwaving, but I found that gently simmering the sweet potatoes in a combination of heavy cream and buttermilk (similar to the method we use in the test kitchen for traditional scalloped potatoes) was the most successful option. The sweet potatoes were soft (not mealy) and absorbed the flavors of the dairy mixture. Unlike regular potatoes, sweet potatoes don't soak up moisture, so they required only half as much dairy as regular potatoes.

Now that the sweet potato mixture was precooked, it was easy to assemble my casserole. I mixed in bacon for salt and smoke, cayenne for kick, cheddar cheese for richness, and chopped scallions for a fresh bite. I topped the seasoned sweet potatoes with coarse bread crumbs, melted butter, and more cheddar, then popped the casserole into the oven. After just 15 minutes, it emerged golden and bubbly, with rich, savory flavor that was even better than I remembered. **–Cali Rich**

SPICY SWEET POTATO AND BACON CASSEROLE SERVES 10

For a milder heat, reduce cayenne to 1/4 teaspoon.

- 4 slices hearty white sandwich bread, torn into large pieces
- 2 tablespoons unsalted butter, melted
- 2 1/2 cups shredded sharp cheddar cheese
- 8 slices bacon, chopped
- 1 onion, chopped fine
- 4 garlic cloves, minced
- 1/2 teaspoon cayenne pepper (see note)
- 5 pounds sweet potatoes (about 8 medium), peeled, halved lengthwise, and sliced thin
- 3/4 cup heavy cream
- 3/4 cup buttermilk
- 2 1/2 teaspoons salt
- 5 scallions, sliced thin

1. Adjust oven rack to middle position and heat oven to 425 degrees. Pulse bread, butter, and 1/2 cup cheese in food processor until coarsely ground.

2. Cook bacon in Dutch oven over medium heat until crisp, about 8 minutes. Transfer bacon to paper towel–lined plate and pour off all but 1 tablespoon fat. Cook onion until softened, about 5 minutes. Add garlic and cayenne and cook until fragrant, about 30 seconds. Stir in sweet potatoes, cream, buttermilk, and salt. Reduce heat to medium-low and cook, covered, until potatoes are

just tender, about 30 minutes. Off heat, stir in remaining cheese, cooked bacon, and 4 scallions.

3. Transfer mixture to 13 by 9-inch baking dish and top with bread crumbs. Bake until crumbs are golden brown, about 15 minutes. Cool 10 minutes, then sprinkle with remaining scallion. Serve.

Make Ahead: The casserole can be prepared through step 2 and refrigerated for up to 1 day. The bread crumb mixture should be refrigerated separately and will keep for up to 2 days. When ready to bake, cover with foil and bake until hot and bubbly, about 40 minutes. Uncover, sprinkle with bread crumbs, and bake until topping is golden brown, about 15 minutes.

Dressing Up: Cranberry Sauce

Why just sweeten cranberries when you can add flavor, too?

Tired of watching the traditional back-of-the-bag cranberry sauce go untouched every Thanksgiving, this year I decided to give this side dish a kick in the pants. I came across an intriguing recipe that added apricot preserves and powdered ginger to the cooked cranberries, so I headed into the test kitchen to give it a try. While the flavors were promising (if a little subdued), the texture of this sauce was a runny, sugary mess.

To correct the loose texture, I added the preserves to the berries, sugar, and water and cooked the mixture down until it thickened. Since the preserves contain a lot of sugar, I was able to cut back on the amount of granulated sugar I used. Chopped dried apricots improved both the flavor and the texture.

But the powdered ginger in my recipe tasted bland. Cooking fresh ginger with the cranberry mixture didn't help, as the flavor was still surprisingly muted. Stirring the freshly grated ginger into the sauce at the end of cooking preserved its clean and spicy bite. A tiny hit of cayenne pepper rounded out the heat. This cranberry sauce is destined to become a holiday staple. **–Meredith Butcher**

APRICOT-GINGER CRANBERRY SAUCE
MAKES 3 CUPS

Frozen cranberries may be used instead of fresh.

- 1/2 cup water
- 1/4 cup dried apricots, chopped fine
- 1/4 cup sugar
- 1/4 teaspoon salt
- 1/8 teaspoon cayenne pepper
- 1 1/2 cups apricot preserves
- 1 (12-ounce) bag cranberries, picked through (see note)
- 1 teaspoon grated fresh ginger

Bring water, apricots, sugar, salt, cayenne, and apricot preserves to boil in large saucepan over medium heat. Add cranberries and simmer until slightly thickened and two-thirds of berries have popped open, about 5 minutes. Stir in ginger, transfer to serving bowl, and cool completely. Serve. (Sauce can be refrigerated for up to 1 week.)

Scoop-and-Bake Dinner Rolls

With all my time and effort spent on the Thanksgiving turkey and pies, I have little energy left for dealing with homemade dinner rolls. Is there a recipe that's truly easy, or will I have to settle for popping open a can of rolls again? –Erin Lockwood, Brewster, N.Y.

After the mixing, kneading, rising, shaping, rising again, and baking, homemade dinner rolls can make the turkey seem like the simple part of a holiday meal. But there is one glimmer of hope: batter-style dinner rolls.

The ingredients for batter-style rolls (flour, yeast, milk, eggs, shortening, salt, and sugar) are simply stirred together into a pancake-batter consistency, briefly risen in the same bowl, and scooped into a muffin tin to bake without ever touching the counter or your hands. I had never made these rolls but was intrigued.

The recipes I uncovered promised rich rolls with a soft, moist texture that comes from the large amount of liquid in the batter, which steams in the oven and creates a puffy, popover-like effect.

After testing a handful of recipes, I learned that batter-style rolls really are a snap to put together—I was able to turn them out in minutes, not hours. However, these rolls have a pungent yeast flavor, as the quick rise doesn't give the yeast time to mellow. Just as worrisome, the recipes I tried baked up squat and heavy.

Fixing the flavor was my first challenge. Shortening was the fat of choice in most recipes, but my tasters wanted butter, and they weren't happy until the amount stood at 6 tablespoons. The richness of the butter also helped temper the strong yeast flavor, but it made the batter heavier and the rolls flatter. Most recipes call for two eggs, but cutting back to one and switching from milk to water helped to lighten the batter and give the rolls more lift. But it still wasn't enough.

I turned my attention to the mixing method. Standard yeast doughs are kneaded to develop gluten in the flour, which builds structure and height in the rolls. Kneading my thin batter was out of the question, but what about beating? My hand mixer did the job—and then some—leaving me with rolls that were tall but too tough (from too much gluten). Looking for a more gentle approach that would work—but not over-work—the batter, I beat the batter mixture with a whisk for a few minutes. It worked like a charm, producing the extra lift needed to make these rolls tall but without a trace of toughness.

With their rich flavor, fluffy texture, and quick, easy preparation, homemade rolls never sounded—or tasted—so good.

–Cali Rich

SCOOP-AND-BAKE DINNER ROLLS MAKES 12

In step 3, use an ice cream scoop to transfer the sticky batter to the muffin tin.

- 2¼ cups all-purpose flour
- ¼ cup sugar
- 1 teaspoon salt
- 1 envelope (2¼ teaspoons) rapid-rise or instant yeast
- 1 cup water, heated to 110 degrees
- 6 tablespoons unsalted butter, softened
- 1 large egg

1. Adjust oven rack to middle position and heat oven to 200 degrees. Maintain temperature for 10 minutes, then turn off oven. Grease muffin tin.

2. Whisk 1¼ cups flour, sugar, salt, and yeast in large bowl. Whisk in water, butter, and egg until very smooth, about 2 minutes. Add remaining flour and mix with rubber spatula until just combined. Cover bowl with greased plastic wrap and place in warm oven until batter has doubled in size, about 30 minutes.

3. Remove batter from oven and heat oven to 375 degrees. Punch dough down. Scoop batter evenly into muffin tin. Cover with greased plastic wrap and let rise at room temperature until batter nearly reaches rims of muffin cups, about 15 minutes. Remove plastic and bake until rolls are golden, 14 to 18 minutes. Serve. (Rolls can be stored in an airtight container at room temperature for 3 days.)

Make Ahead: After being covered with greased plastic wrap in step 3, the batter can be refrigerated in the muffin tin for up to 24 hours. When ready to bake, let the batter sit at room temperature for 30 minutes before proceeding with the recipe.

Kitchen Know-How
MIX, REST, AND SCOOP

Follow these simple steps for quick batter-style rolls.

1. Whisk the batter until smooth to develop structure and then stir in the last cup of flour until just combined.
2. Once the batter has risen for 30 minutes, scoop it into a greased muffin tin (the batter will fill the cups halfway) and let it continue to rise for 15 minutes at room temperature before baking. The batter will rise almost to the rim of the cups.

A Roll That Bakes Like a Muffin

Our fast dinner rolls start with a muffin-like batter—and from the outside, they look like muffins. But the yeasty interior reveals their true nature as fluffy dinner rolls.

LIKE A MUFFIN

LIKE A ROLL

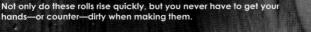
Not only do these rolls rise quickly, but you never have to get your hands—or counter—dirty when making them.

Pepper-Crusted Pork Loin

When I make pepper-crusted pork loin, I have problems getting the pepper flavor to penetrate into the meat, and the crust is always too harsh. Is there any way to deeply season this dish without it burning my mouth? –Karla Ginevan, Tucson, Ariz.

Kitchen Know-How
THE RIGHT GRIND

A crunchy, fiery crust of cracked peppercorns may work well with an assertively flavored cut of beef, but when it comes to pork, moderation is essential. To give a nice spicy kick without overwhelming the mild taste of the pork, we found that we had to grind the pepper just right—and not use too much of it.

CRACKED PEPPER
Packs a scorching heat

COARSELY GROUND PEPPER
Lends welcome heat, spice, and texture

The Right Rack

A V-rack helps keep roasts and poultry out of the drippings, where they can steam and become mushy. We prefer nonstick V-racks with easily accessible handles.

KITCHEN ESSENTIAL
Keeps meat high and dry

Cutting the pepper rub with brown sugar, fresh rosemary, and salt helped to deeply season the meat and temper the pepper burn.

A spicy, savory crust of crushed peppercorns is the perfect adornment for a relatively bland pork loin, but balancing the two elements isn't as easy as it might seem. Pepper-crusted beef works so well because beef has enough richness to offset some of the pepper's sharp heat, but lean pork doesn't have enough flavor to stand up to the same peppery bite. I wanted to find a way to deeply infuse a pork loin with spicy pepper flavor while eliminating the harsh burn.

To get a substantial crust on the entire surface of the pork loin, I started by rubbing 5 tablespoons of cracked peppercorns over the roast. After browning the pork on the stovetop and finishing it in the oven (the test kitchen's technique for most roasts), the jolt of pepper was way too harsh. Cutting back on the amount of peppercorns resulted in a speckled, uneven crust. I hoped the test kitchen trick of gently heating the peppercorns in oil to bloom their flavor and mellow their heat would work, but the resulting roast still had too much pepper burn.

Since the bite of the cracked pepper was proving to be too strong no matter how I handled it, I wondered if I could temper the pepper's heat, while keeping most of its flavor, by using a finer grind. After testing several grinds from barely cracked to finely ground, my tasters and I settled on a middle ground (see "The Right Grind," left) that allowed for a thinner, milder crust with plenty of pepper flavor. Two tablespoons of coarsely ground pepper gave me the right amount of spice, but it didn't yield enough rub to fully coat the roast.

To stretch the rub, I tried supplementing the pepper with other ingredients; strong spices like mustard, coriander, and cumin overwhelmed the mellow pork, but my tasters appreciated the piney tang of fresh rosemary as a complement to the pepper. Adding brown sugar and salt worked to further extend the rub; the sugar tamed the heat even more, and the salt helped carry all the flavors into the meat, especially when I let the rubbed roast sit for an hour. The peppery flavor was definitely still present, but now it brought lively spice and complexity—and no harsh burn—to the mild pork.

There was still one problem: The pepper crust was burning during the initial sear on the stovetop. Simply switching the searing from the stovetop to a hot oven solved the problem. Finishing the roast at a more moderate temperature ensured juicy pork with bold flavor both inside and out. I'd finally made a Pepper-Crusted Pork Loin to be proud of. –**Diane Unger**

PEPPER-CRUSTED PORK LOIN SERVES 6

Serve plain or with fruit chutney, applesauce, or our Cherry-Brandy Sauce (below).

- 3 tablespoons light brown sugar
- 2 tablespoons coarsely ground black pepper
- 2 tablespoons minced fresh rosemary
- 1½ teaspoons salt
- 1 (3-pound) boneless center-cut pork loin

1. Combine sugar, pepper, rosemary, and salt and rub all over pork. Let roast stand at room temperature for 1 hour or refrigerate for up to 24 hours.

2. Adjust oven rack to upper-middle position and heat oven to 450 degrees. Arrange pork on V-rack set in roasting pan. Roast for 15 minutes, then lower oven temperature to 375 degrees and cook until meat registers 140 degrees, about 50 minutes longer. Transfer pork to cutting board and tent with foil. Let rest 20 minutes. Slice pork and serve.

CHERRY-BRANDY SAUCE
MAKES ABOUT 2 CUPS

If you can't find frozen cherries, substitute one 14.5-ounce can of pitted tart red cherries in water, drained.

- 4 tablespoons unsalted butter
- 2 onions, chopped
- 3 cups low-sodium chicken broth
- ½ cup brandy
- 1 (8-oz) bag frozen pitted sweet cherries, thawed (see note)
- 1 cup dried cherries
- 2 tablespoons balsamic vinegar
  Salt

Melt 2 tablespoons butter in large saucepan over medium heat. Cook onions until golden, about 8 minutes. Stir in broth, brandy, and cherries and simmer until thick and syrupy, about 15 minutes. Off heat, stir in vinegar and remaining butter. Season with salt. Serve. (Sauce can be refrigerated for up to 2 days.)

On the Side: Parmesan Mashed Potatoes

Can we get big Parmesan flavor without sacrificing creamy texture?

Most recipes for Parmesan mashed potatoes simply stir grated cheese into the potatoes either before or after mashing. But when I put those methods to the test, the potatoes became thick and stodgy, with an unpleasant grit from the grainy Parmesan. Adding insult to injury, none of the recipes I tried had noticeable cheese flavor. I'd have to start from scratch.

Since I was using the test kitchen's technique of heating the butter and cream (which was preferred over buttermilk, half-and-half, and sour cream for its sweetness and luxurious texture) before adding it to the potatoes, I tried adding grated Parmesan to the hot dairy; the resulting mash was suitably smooth and creamy but still lacking in cheese flavor. Upping the amount of cheese (I made my way up to 3 cups of Parmesan for 4 pounds of potatoes) only made the potatoes thick and gluey, and cutting back on the butter and cream made the mash taste and feel too lean.

I tried simmering a Parmesan rind in the cream and butter mixture, but this did little to improve the flavor. Nearing the end of my rope, it occurred to me that adding a small amount of a stronger cheese might help accentuate the nutty Parmesan flavor in my potatoes. I

made batches substituting pecorino and Asiago (both hard Italian cheeses) for a portion of the Parmesan. The pecorino had sour undertones that my tasters disliked, but the Asiago added subtle cheese flavor without overly asserting itself. Who knew that the secret to perfect Parmesan mashed potatoes was adding another cheese? **–Cali Rich**

PARMESAN MASHED POTATOES SERVES 8 TO 10

For the best flavor, buy wedges of Parmesan and Asiago and grate the cheeses yourself.

- 4 pounds Yukon Gold potatoes, peeled and cut into 1-inch chunks
- 1 1/2 cups heavy cream
- 6 tablespoons unsalted butter, cut into pieces
- 2 cups grated Parmesan cheese
- 1/2 cup grated Asiago cheese
- 2 teaspoons salt

1. Bring potatoes and enough water to cover by 1 inch to boil in large pot over high heat. Reduce heat to medium and simmer until potatoes are tender, about 20 minutes.

2. Heat cream, butter, cheeses, and salt in saucepan over medium heat, whisking until smooth, about 5 minutes. Keep warm.

3. Drain potatoes and return to pot. Stir over low heat until potatoes are thoroughly dried, 1 to 2 minutes. Pour cream mixture over potatoes and mash with potato masher until evenly incorporated and creamy. Serve.

On the Side: Roasted-Garlic Green Beans

Green beans and roasted garlic can be a great side dish—but there's nothing great about waiting an hour for the garlic to roast.

Roasting garlic tames its bite and intensifies its sweet flavor; unfortunately, it also takes about an hour. For a simple green-bean side dish, we wanted to find a faster way to achieve the nutty flavor and buttery texture of roasted garlic.

Slowly heating peeled garlic cloves in a skillet filmed with oil took too much time and stirring, and the garlic browned unevenly before it was softened on the inside. The microwave proved to be a better tool to quickly and evenly cook the garlic through to its center. I cut a dozen cloves in half, placed them in a small bowl with oil to cover and a little sugar (to promote caramelization), and microwaved the mixture on high for one minute. The garlic now had that creamy texture I was looking for, and I was doubly rewarded with an intensely flavored garlic oil I could use when preparing the green beans.

I started cooking the beans by steaming them in a covered skillet with a little water and a tablespoon of the garlic oil. After a few minutes I added the softened garlic and the rest of the garlic oil, and when the beans were almost done I took the lid off to allow the beans and garlic to brown. After finishing the dish with a splash of vinegar, I had perfectly cooked beans studded with soft, nutty "roasted" garlic—all in about 10 minutes. **–Diane Unger**

ROASTED-GARLIC GREEN BEANS SERVES 6

Microwave temperatures vary—be sure to check the garlic after 45 seconds to see if it has softened. Both red and white wine vinegar work well here.

- 12 garlic cloves, peeled and halved lengthwise
- 2 tablespoons extra-virgin olive oil
- 1/4 teaspoon sugar
- 1 1/2 pounds green beans, trimmed
- 3 tablespoons water
- 4 teaspoons wine vinegar (see note)
  Salt and pepper

1. Microwave garlic, oil, and sugar, uncovered, in small microwave-safe bowl until garlic is softened and fragrant, about 1 minute. Carefully transfer 1 tablespoon oil from garlic mixture to large nonstick skillet. Reserve remaining garlic mixture.

2. Heat skillet over medium-high heat until oil is shimmering. Add green beans and water and cook, covered, until bright green, about 3 minutes. Add reserved garlic mixture to pan; do not stir. Continue to cook, covered, until beans are almost tender, about 3 minutes. Remove lid and cook, stirring occasionally, until beans are browned in spots and garlic is golden, 2 to 3 minutes. Off heat, stir in vinegar and season with salt and pepper. Serve.

I'm Looking for a Recipe

READERS HELP READERS FIND RECIPES

We've Got Mail

Scores of readers sent us recipes in response to the request for Potato Candy in our April/May 2006 issue. We really liked the recipe sent by Pat Nagle (right). Go to **CooksCountry.com** and click **Looking for a Recipe** to find hundreds of recipes submitted by readers who responded to recipe requests in previous issues of *Cook's Country*.

PEANUT BUTTER PINWHEELS Pat Nagle Danbury, Conn.

MAKES 40 PIECES

"Every Christmas when I was a little girl, I made a potato candy called Peanut Butter Pinwheels with my mother. We would offer the candy to family and friends who dropped by. I haven't made it in years, but I can still remember the delight and pride I found in the tradition." Use a bench scraper to free the slightly sticky dough from the work surface while rolling it into a cylinder. For the mashed potato, peel and boil 1 small russet potato, mash until smooth, and cool (do not add butter or milk).

Ingredients	Instructions
1/2 cup mashed potato (see note), room temperature 1/2 teaspoon vanilla extract 1/8 teaspoon salt 4 cups confectioners' sugar, sifted, plus extra for dusting work surface 1 cup peanut butter	**1.** Combine potato, vanilla, and salt in large bowl. Slowly mix in sugar to form dough. **2.** Divide dough into 2 even pieces. Dust work surface with confectioners' sugar and roll 1 piece dough into 7-inch square, about 1/4 inch thick. Spread 1/2 cup peanut butter over dough, leaving 1/2-inch border around edges. Use both hands to roll dough into even cylinder. Wrap dough tightly in plastic wrap and refrigerate for at least 3 hours or up to 3 days. Repeat with remaining dough and peanut butter. Cut into 1/2-inch rounds and serve.

Cottage Pudding

My grandmother from Connecticut used to make a wonderful dessert called cottage pudding. It was a rich loaf cake with a warm, light lemon sauce. I would appreciate finding a comparable "receipt," as she called them.

Patricia Sullivan
Livingston, N.J.

Forty Carrots Fried Zucchini

I've been searching for a recipe from a restaurant called Forty Carrots, which was in the Lakeforest Mall in Gaithersburg, Md. They served the best fried zucchini I've ever eaten. The zucchini was cut into rounds, dipped into a tempura-like batter seasoned with dill and cayenne pepper (I think), and fried. The wonderfully crisp rounds were served with a sour cream dipping sauce that also had dill in it. I've been searching for this recipe for years and would be forever grateful to find it. Thank you!

Patricia Flynn
Via e-mail

Rockwood Chocolate Cookies

In the late 1940s, my mom made a recipe that came inside a box of Rockwood Chocolate disks. First she made a cookie dough that was rolled into 1-inch balls, then she pushed a chocolate disk into each dough ball and topped it with a smaller ball. The chocolate disk remained soft for days after baking. The recipe was lost. I've tried making these cookies with Hershey's Kisses, but they're not the same. I'd love to have these cookies again!

Dot Maley
Milpitas, Calif.

Apple Pancakes

One of my grandmothers was of Swiss descent. She's been gone for 22 years, but I still remember the apple pancakes she made when we were kids. She used McIntosh apples from the tree in the backyard. She would drop the thin batter into an oiled skillet, and they'd cook up puffy—not spongy like regular pancakes. The ingredients were simple—flour, beaten eggs, a splash of milk, and maybe some salt—but I have no idea how much of each to use. Any help would be appreciated.

Paula Thomas
Omaha, Neb.

Kentucky-Style Corn Casserole

My father was from a little town in southeastern Kentucky. He was a great cook who made dishes like homemade biscuits, fried chicken, and pinto beans with corn bread. I especially miss his sweet corn casserole. I never saw him assemble the ingredients, but I think it was made with canned corn and crackers. Our dad passed away from cancer in 1980, and I'd love to re-create this dish for my mom and siblings. Thanks!

Nancy Walton
Minneapolis, Minn.

Angel Pie

I made angel pie years ago when I was first married, but I can no longer find the recipe. The pie has a meringue base and is topped with whipped cream and frozen strawberries. Many thanks.

Lois Ulreich
Via e-mail

Key Lime Cake

I have a friend in Atlanta who makes the most delicious Key lime cake. The tangy lime flavor of the cake is perfectly complemented by a rich cream cheese frosting. I've searched everywhere and can't find a successful recipe that doesn't rely on a boxed mix—and, of course, my friend won't share her secret recipe. I've tried making it from scratch, but either the cake's texture was destroyed from using too much lime juice, or it wasn't flavorful enough from using too little juice.

Wambui Maina
Alpharetta, Ga.

Baker's Dozen Coffeecakes

I'm looking for a recipe for overnight refrigerator yeast dough that was published in either *Woman's Day* or *Family Circle* in the late 1980s. The dough was made with sour cream and orange juice, and the recipe gave 13 different ways to use it. I made it many times but have since lost the recipe. I've tried the magazine websites with no luck.

Kitty Walloch
Wauwatosa, Wis.

Apricot and Cream Cheese Fold-Overs

When I was 5, some 55 years ago, my parents baked fresh cookies that had a cream cheese–and–pie dough base and were filled with a sweetened apricot mixture. They were formed by pressing two opposite corners of the dough together, which allowed the filling to show on either end. I've looked for years and years but have never found a recipe that looks or tastes the same. I hope someone can help.

Sandi Herebia
Houston, Texas

Barbecued Bananas

My grandmother used to make something called barbecued bananas, although they were actually baked in the oven. I don't know the specific ingredients, but I remember her wrapping a banana, orange juice, and spices in foil. They were wonderful, and I'd love to have a recipe so I can enjoy them again!

Lynn Bisset
Whittier, Calif.

Eccles

I'm interested in finding a recipe for a pastry called Eccles. I used to buy them at my local supermarket in New Hampshire about 20 years ago. They were round, sugar-crusted, flaky pastries filled with seedless red jam and raisins. I used to eat them at least three times a week; I thought they were the best thing I'd ever tasted. I miss them like crazy!

Amy Dumit
Montrose, Colo.

Cherry Chews

I'm looking for a recipe for bar cookies called cherry chews. They contain maraschino cherries and nuts and are coated with powdered sugar. I've tried many recipes and haven't found the right one yet. If any of your readers can help me, I would be most appreciative.

Diana Steed
Hamilton, Texas

Are you looking for a special recipe? Or do you have a recipe a fellow *Cook's Country* reader is seeking? Post your requests and recipes by visiting **CooksCountry.com** and clicking on **Looking for a Recipe**. We'll share recipe requests and found recipes on CooksCountry.com and print as many as we can in the magazine. You may also write to us at Looking for a Recipe, Cook's Country, P.O. Box 470739, Brookline, MA 02447.

Find the Rooster!

A tiny version of this rooster has been hidden somewhere in the pages of this issue. If you find it, write to us with its location (plus your name and address) and you will be entered into a random drawing. The first correct entry drawn will receive an All-Clad Stainless Steel Slow Cooker, and the next five will each receive a complimentary one-year subscription to *Cook's Country*. To enter the contest, visit **CooksCountry. com/emailus** or write to us at Rooster, Cook's Country, P.O. Box 470739, Brookline, MA 02447. Entries are due by November 30, 2007.

Did you find the rooster in the June/July 2007 issue? It was hidden in the Blueberry Streusel Muffin photo on page 22. Nick Hiller of Columbia, S.C., spotted it and won an All-Clad Stainless Steel 4-Quart Sauce Pan.

30-Minute Supper

KUNG PAO SHRIMP

30-Minute Supper

GARLIC-ROSEMARY PORK CHOPS

30-Minute Supper

STEAK FIORENTINA

30-Minute Supper

FRENCH BREAD PIZZA

GARLIC-ROSEMARY PORK CHOPS SERVES 4

To prevent the chops from curling while they cook, cut 2 slits about 2 inches apart through the fat and connective tissue on 1 side of each chop.

- 4 bone-in rib or center-cut pork chops, 3/4 to 1 inch thick (see note)
  Salt and pepper
- 1 tablespoon vegetable oil
- 6 garlic cloves, sliced thin
- 1 cup low-sodium chicken broth
- 1 sprig fresh rosemary plus 1/2 teaspoon minced
- 1 teaspoon red wine vinegar
- 2 tablespoons unsalted butter

1. Pat chops dry with paper towels and season with salt and pepper. Heat oil in large skillet over medium-high heat until just smoking. Cook chops until well browned and meat registers 145 degrees, about 5 minutes per side. Transfer to platter and tent with foil.

2. Add garlic to empty skillet and cook until fragrant, about 30 seconds. Add broth and rosemary sprig and simmer, scraping up any browned bits with wooden spoon, until reduced by half, about 5 minutes. Discard rosemary sprig. Add any accumulated pork juices back to pan and whisk in minced rosemary, vinegar, and butter. Pour sauce over chops. Serve.

KUNG PAO SHRIMP SERVES 4

Serve over steamed rice or lo mein noodles. Oyster sauce can be found in the international section of most grocery stores.

- 1 cup low-sodium chicken broth
- 3 tablespoons oyster sauce (see note)
- 2 teaspoons hot sauce
- 2 teaspoons cornstarch
- 2 tablespoons vegetable oil
- 1 pound extra-large shrimp, peeled and deveined
- 1/2 cup dry-roasted peanuts
- 1 red bell pepper, seeded and chopped
- 3 garlic cloves, minced
- 1 tablespoon grated fresh ginger

1. Whisk broth, oyster sauce, hot sauce, and cornstarch in bowl.

2. Heat 1 tablespoon oil in large skillet over medium-high heat until just smoking. Add shrimp and peanuts and cook until shrimp are spotty brown, about 2 minutes; transfer to plate. Add remaining oil and bell pepper to empty skillet and cook until lightly browned, about 3 minutes. Stir in garlic and ginger and cook until fragrant, about 30 seconds. Stir in broth mixture and bring to boil. Add shrimp and peanuts and simmer until sauce has thickened and shrimp are cooked through, about 1 minute. Serve.

FRENCH BREAD PIZZA SERVES 4 TO 6

Contadina brand pizza sauce is the test kitchen's favorite. For crisp (but not tough) crust, use soft supermarket French bread rather than a baguette.

- 6 tablespoons extra-virgin olive oil
- 4 garlic cloves, minced
- 4 tablespoons finely chopped fresh basil
- 1/8 teaspoon red pepper flakes
- 1 (24-inch) loaf French bread, halved lengthwise and cut crosswise into 8 even pieces
- 1/2 cup grated Parmesan cheese
- 1 cup pizza sauce (see note)
- 2 cups shredded mozzarella cheese

1. Adjust oven rack to upper-middle position and heat oven to 475 degrees. Microwave oil, garlic, 2 tablespoons basil, and pepper flakes on high power in small microwave-safe bowl until fragrant, 30 to 60 seconds.

2. Brush half of oil mixture over crust and edges of bread and arrange cut-side up on foil-lined baking sheet. Sprinkle Parmesan evenly over bread and bake until cheese begins to brown, about 3 minutes.

3. Whisk pizza sauce, remaining basil, and remaining oil mixture in bowl. Spread sauce evenly over bread, then top with mozzarella. Bake until cheese is melted and spotty brown, 5 to 7 minutes. Serve.

STEAK FIORENTINA SERVES 4

Baby spinach can be substituted for the arugula. A 4- to 5-ounce bag of arugula will yield 6 cups. To round out the meal, serve with a loaf of crusty Italian bread.

- 3 strip steaks (10 to 12 ounces each), about 1 inch thick
  Salt and pepper
- 5 tablespoons extra-virgin olive oil
- 1 garlic clove, minced
- 1 tablespoon lemon juice
- 6 cups arugula (see note)
- 1/2 cup shredded Parmesan cheese
  Lemon wedges for serving

1. Pat steaks dry with paper towels and season with salt and pepper. Heat 1 tablespoon oil in large skillet over medium-high heat until just smoking. Cook steaks until well browned, 3 to 5 minutes per side. Transfer to cutting board and tent with foil.

2. Whisk garlic, lemon juice, and 2 tablespoons oil in large bowl. Toss arugula and Parmesan with garlic mixture and season with salt and pepper. Slice steaks and drizzle with remaining oil. Serve with arugula and lemon wedges on side.

CREAMY PASTA WITH ASPARAGUS, PARMESAN, AND CRISPY PROSCIUTTO

CRISPY DIJON CHICKEN BREASTS

BEEF TACO BAKE

TURKEY POT PIE WITH STUFFING CRUST

CRISPY DIJON CHICKEN BREASTS SERVES 4

To make fresh bread crumbs, process 2 slices of hearty white sandwich bread in a food processor until coarsely ground.

- 1 cup bread crumbs, preferably fresh (see note)
- 2 tablespoons extra-virgin olive oil
  Salt and pepper
- 1/2 cup Dijon mustard
- 1/2 cup mayonnaise
- 4 tablespoons minced fresh chives
- 2 tablespoons sour cream
- 2 teaspoons white wine vinegar
- 4 boneless, skinless chicken breasts (about 1 1/2 pounds), trimmed

1. Adjust oven rack to upper-middle position and heat oven to 425 degrees. Combine bread crumbs, oil, 1/2 teaspoon salt, and 1/2 teaspoon pepper in bowl. Combine mustard and mayonnaise in small bowl; reserve 1/4 cup mustard-mayonnaise mixture for chicken, then stir in 1 tablespoon chives, sour cream, and vinegar to make sauce for serving.

2. Pat chicken dry with paper towels, season with salt and pepper, and transfer to 13 by 9-inch baking dish. Spread reserved mustard-mayonnaise mixture evenly over chicken. Sprinkle with bread crumb mixture, pressing lightly to adhere.

3. Bake until crumbs are golden brown and chicken registers 160 degrees, 18 to 22 minutes. Sprinkle remaining chives over chicken. Serve with mustard sauce.

CREAMY PASTA WITH ASPARAGUS, PARMESAN, AND CRISPY PROSCIUTTO SERVES 4

Four finely chopped strips of bacon can be substituted for the prosciutto.

- 1 tablespoon olive oil
- 4 ounces thinly sliced prosciutto, cut into 1/4-inch strips (see note)
- 1 garlic clove, minced
- 1 cup heavy cream
- 2 tablespoons lemon juice
  Salt and pepper
- 1 pound fusilli or penne
- 1 pound asparagus, trimmed and cut into 1-inch pieces
- 1 1/2 cups grated Parmesan cheese
- 3/4 cup chopped fresh basil

1. Bring 4 quarts water to boil in large pot. Heat oil in large nonstick skillet over medium heat until just smoking. Cook prosciutto until lightly browned and crisp, about 5 minutes. Transfer to paper towel–lined plate. Add garlic to pan and cook until fragrant, about 30 seconds. Stir in cream and lemon juice and simmer until slightly thickened, 3 to 5 minutes.

2. Add 1 tablespoon salt and pasta to boiling water and cook until just beginning to soften, about 8 minutes. Add asparagus to pot and cook until bright green and tender and pasta is al dente, about 4 minutes. Reserve 1 cup cooking water, drain pasta and asparagus, and return to pot. Add sauce, 1/2 cup reserved cooking water, cheese, and basil to pot and toss to combine, adding remaining cooking water as needed. Season with salt and pepper. Sprinkle portions with crispy prosciutto. Serve.

TURKEY POT PIE WITH STUFFING CRUST
SERVES 6 TO 8

Although leftover homemade stuffing works best here, one 6-ounce box of stuffing mix, prepared according to package instructions and chilled, will suffice. You will need a 12-inch oven-safe skillet for this recipe.

- 3 tablespoons unsalted butter
- 1 onion, chopped
- 1 celery rib, chopped
- 2 tablespoons all-purpose flour
- 2 cups low-sodium chicken broth
- 1/2 cup heavy cream
- 1 cup frozen peas and carrots mix, thawed
- 4 cups cooked turkey meat, shredded
- 3 cups prepared stuffing (see note)
- 1 large egg, lightly beaten

1. Adjust oven rack to upper-middle position and heat oven to 475 degrees. Melt butter in large oven-safe skillet over medium-high heat. Cook onion and celery until soft, about 4 minutes. Stir in flour and cook until lightly browned, about 1 minute. Slowly whisk in broth and cream and simmer until thickened, 5 to 7 minutes. Add peas and carrots mix and turkey and cook until heated through, about 2 minutes.

2. Meanwhile, combine stuffing and egg in large bowl. Place stuffing mixture between pieces of parchment paper and roll into 11-inch circle. Remove top layer of parchment and cut into 6 wedges. Arrange wedges evenly over filling and bake until stuffing is golden brown and crisp, about 12 minutes. Serve.

BEEF TACO BAKE SERVES 4 TO 6

If you can't find Ro-Tel tomatoes, substitute one 14.5-ounce can diced tomatoes and one 4-ounce can chopped green chiles.

- 2 (10-ounce) cans Ro-Tel tomatoes (see note), drained, 1/2 cup juice reserved
- 1 (16-ounce) can refried beans
- 1 tablespoon hot sauce
- 1/4 cup chopped fresh cilantro
- 3 cups shredded Mexican cheese blend
- 1 1/2 pounds 90-percent-lean ground beef
- 1 (1.25-ounce) package low-sodium taco seasoning mix
- 12 taco shells
- 3 scallions, sliced thin

1. Adjust oven rack to upper-middle position and heat oven to 475 degrees. Combine half of tomatoes, beans, hot sauce, and cilantro in bowl. Spread evenly in 13 by 9-inch baking dish. Sprinkle with 1 cup cheese.

2. Cook beef in large nonstick skillet over medium-high heat until no longer pink, about 5 minutes. Pour off fat, then stir in taco seasoning, remaining tomatoes, and reserved tomato juice. Simmer over medium-low heat until thickened and nearly dry, 5 to 7 minutes.

3. Spoon 1 tablespoon cheese into each taco shell and top with beef mixture. Arrange tacos upright in bean mixture, cover with foil, and bake until bubbling, about 10 minutes. Remove foil, top with remaining cheese, and bake until cheese is melted, about 6 minutes. Sprinkle with scallions. Serve.

Cranberry Upside-Down Cake

Last year I made a cranberry upside-down cake for my mother-in-law's Thanksgiving buffet. What an embarrassment! Everyone discreetly scraped off the inedibly tart topping and meekly picked at the soggy cake. I need help redeeming myself this year! –Vance Smith, Harrodsburg, Ky.

You'd be hard-pressed to find someone who isn't familiar with pineapple upside-down cake, but its cranberry counterpart is far less famous. And that's a shame. This ruby-crowned cake is a visual stunner, and the delicate balance of sweet-tart cranberry topping and tender butter cake makes it every bit as appealing as the pineapple version. But as with all upside-down cakes, the inverted preparation (with the berries baked on the bottom, then turned out to the top) can easily spell disaster. The fruit topping is often thin and runny or, worse, a super-sticky candied mess that won't leave the pan at all. As for the cake itself, though a sturdy texture is a must to support the fruit, most recipes overcompensate and bake up dry and dense.

I baked a lineup of cakes that ranged from fluffy to leaden in texture, with one coarse-crumbed cake standing out as my tasters' favorite. This cake featured ground almonds, which lent a moist richness and hearty texture to the crumb. The cake was a little heavy, so rather than beating whole eggs into the batter, I added the yolks and then whipped the egg whites separately. Folding the fluffy beaten whites into the finished batter produced a beautiful cake—light and tender but still sturdy enough to support the heavy fruit topping.

Recipes that called for lining the cake pan with berries tossed with sugar produced watery, runny toppings. Precooking the cranberries and sugar on the stovetop to evaporate some of the fruit's moisture proved to be a better option. It was important to cook the berries for just a few minutes—otherwise they broke down into mush. To make the topping more cohesive, I strained out the berries after four minutes and continued to reduce the juices into a thick syrup.

The topping now had the right consistency, but it was a little too tart. Increasing the sugar made the topping taste like candy, and after trying sweeteners like honey, maple syrup, and corn syrup, my tasters settled on raspberry jam, which perfectly rounded out the tartness of the cranberries and enhanced the fruit flavor of the topping. I now had a Cranberry Upside-Down Cake that wowed both the eyes and the palate. –Cali Rich

CRANBERRY UPSIDE-DOWN CAKE SERVES 8

To prevent this cake from sticking, do not let it cool in the pan for more than 10 minutes before turning it out (see page 30 for more details).

Topping
- 6 tablespoons unsalted butter
- 3 cups fresh or defrosted frozen cranberries
- 3/4 cup sugar
- 2 tablespoons seedless raspberry jam
- 1/2 teaspoon vanilla extract

Cake
- 1/4 cup blanched slivered almonds
- 1 cup all-purpose flour
- 1 teaspoon baking powder
- 1/4 teaspoon salt
- 1/2 cup milk
- 1/2 teaspoon vanilla extract
- 1/2 teaspoon almond extract
- 6 tablespoons unsalted butter, softened
- 3/4 cup sugar
- 3 large eggs, separated

1. For the topping: Adjust oven rack to middle position and heat oven to 350 degrees. Grease and flour 9-inch round cake pan, line with parchment paper round, and spray with cooking spray. Melt butter in large nonstick skillet over medium heat. Add cranberries, sugar, and jam and cook until cranberries are just softened, about 4 minutes. Strain cranberry mixture over bowl, reserving juices.

2. Add strained juices to empty skillet and simmer over medium heat until syrupy and reduced to 1 cup, about 4 minutes. Off heat, stir in vanilla. Arrange strained berries in single layer in prepared pan. Pour juice mixture over berries and refrigerate for 30 minutes.

3. For the cake: Process almonds and 1/4 cup flour in food processor until finely ground. Add remaining flour, baking powder, and salt and pulse to combine. Whisk milk and extracts in measuring cup. With electric mixer on medium speed, beat butter and sugar until fluffy, about 2 minutes. Beat in egg yolks, one at a time, until combined. Reduce speed to low and add flour mixture in 3 additions, alternating with 2 additions of milk mixture.

4. Using clean bowl and beaters, beat egg whites on medium-high speed until they hold soft peaks, about 2 minutes. Whisk one-third of whites into batter, then fold in remaining whites. Pour batter over chilled cranberry mixture and bake until toothpick inserted in center comes out clean, 35 to 40 minutes. Cool on wire rack 10 minutes, then run paring knife around cake and invert onto serving plate. Serve.

Top slices of this cake with a dollop of sweetened whipped cream or vanilla ice cream.

Kitchen Know-How
GETTING THE CRANBERRY TOPPING RIGHT

We encountered two recurring problems with this recipe. Cranberries shed a surprising amount of liquid, which can make the cake quite soggy (top). Precooking the cranberries causes them to release liquid, which can then be reduced to a thick syrup. We also had trouble with the topping sticking to the pan (bottom). Keeping the sugar to a minimum and removing the cake from the pan before it fully cools solves this problem.

RUNNY MESS

STUCK-ON TOPPING

Crispy Garlic Chicken Cutlets

My family loves breaded chicken cutlets, so I make them a lot. I'm getting a little bored, so I've tried to add some punch with garlic. But whenever I add it, I'm left with a garlic hangover. –Trish Maduger, Alexandria, Va.

Over the years, the test kitchen has perfected a method for making crispy chicken cutlets: We coat the cutlets in flour, dip them in egg wash, then coat them with fresh bread crumbs before pan-frying. But when you add fresh garlic to the mix for more flavor, you also get more problems. Overcooked garlic tastes harsh and bitter, and too much garlic can give you breath that will peel paint. I wanted crispy cutlets with an intensely sweet, sharp—but not overpowering—garlic bite.

My first test was to try a minced garlic–and-oil marinade for the cutlets. Determined to keep the marinating time to under 30 minutes, I kept upping the garlic until I got to four minced cloves, which provided good garlic punch to the breaded and fried chicken (better than when I tried adding fresh garlic to the egg wash). This thick paste of minced garlic, safely tucked under the flour, egg, and bread crumbs, cooked gently and lent a caramelized (rather than burnt) garlic flavor.

The whole eggs I was using in my egg wash helped the bread crumbs stick to the chicken, but they made for soggy crumbs when combined with the oil paste. I tried replacing the eggs with mayonnaise and mustard, but both imparted too much flavor. Egg whites, whisked until foamy to increase their sticking power, made the perfect glue, getting the coating to adhere to the chicken without adding competing flavor or grease.

As for the breading, the test kitchen prefers toasted homemade bread crumbs to supermarket crumbs, which can be stale-tasting and gritty. Looking to add another layer of garlic flavor, I tried making my crumbs from garlic-flavored croutons and pita chips and supermarket garlic bread. Unfortunately, every product either tasted artificial or made the coating soggy. Returning to white bread, I tried infusing the crumbs with fresh garlic, garlic salt, and garlic powder. The fresh garlic burned on the outside of the cutlets, and the garlic salt didn't provide enough kick; the garlic powder, however, added a welcome and distinct flavor.

Tasters wanted even more garlic flavor, but where else could I add it? The chicken was marinated in garlic, and the bread crumbs were garlic-flavored. The only thing left to flavor was the cooking oil. Throwing whole garlic cloves into hot oil while cooking the chicken brought back the burnt flavor. So rather than cooking the garlic with the chicken, I simply added cloves (smashed to release more flavor) to the cold oil and heated them up together. When it was time to add the chicken, I removed the garlic cloves from the hot oil.

We like to serve these garlicky cutlets with pasta, over rice, or even in sandwiches

This batch had it all—mellow, caramelized garlic flavor from the chicken on the inside and a crispy, garlicky crust on the outside. –Lynn Clark

CRISPY GARLIC CHICKEN CUTLETS
SERVES 3 TO 4

Look for cutlets that are between 1/4 inch and 1/2 inch thick or make your own by slicing 3 boneless, skinless chicken breasts in half horizontally.

- 1 cup plus 3 tablespoons vegetable oil
- 4 garlic cloves, minced, plus 6 cloves peeled and smashed
- 6 thin-cut boneless, skinless chicken cutlets (about 1 1/4 pounds), trimmed
- 3 slices hearty white sandwich bread, torn into large pieces
- 1 cup all-purpose flour
- 3 large egg whites
- 1 tablespoon garlic powder
- 4 teaspoons cornstarch
  Salt and pepper

1. Adjust oven rack to middle position and heat oven to 200 degrees. Combine 3 tablespoons oil, minced garlic, and cutlets in zipper-lock bag and refrigerate while preparing remaining ingredients. Pulse bread in food processor until coarsely ground. Bake bread crumbs on baking sheet until dry, about 20 minutes.

2. Spread flour in shallow dish. In another shallow dish, whisk egg whites until foamy. Combine bread crumbs, garlic powder, and cornstarch in third shallow dish. Remove cutlets from bag and season with salt and pepper. One at a time, coat cutlets lightly with flour, dip in egg whites, and dredge in crumbs, pressing to adhere. Place cutlets on wire rack set over baking sheet and let dry 5 minutes.

3. Heat 1/2 cup oil and 3 smashed garlic cloves in large nonstick skillet over medium heat until garlic is lightly browned, about 4 minutes. Discard garlic and fry 3 cutlets until crisp and deep golden, about 2 minutes per side. Transfer to paper towel–lined plate and place in warm oven. Discard oil, wipe out skillet, and repeat with remaining oil, garlic cloves, and cutlets. Serve.

Grilled Brats and Beer

I could use some help with beer-braised bratwurst, as mine are always mushy and tasteless. My boyfriend is from Wisconsin, where they know their sausages, so you could really make me look like a hero if I turned out a tasty brat. –Gina Osterkorn, via e-mail

Burgers and dogs may be the tailgating staples in the rest of the country, but in the Midwest the pregame ritual is not complete without grilled bratwurst and beer. A disposable aluminum pan filled with cheap lager and sliced onions is placed on one half of the grill, with the sausages on the other half. Some people cook the sausages in the beer first before finishing them on the grill, while others grill and then simmer. The idea is that the beer and onions flavor the bratwurst, which is then nestled into a bun, smothered with the beer-soaked onions, and doused with plenty of mustard. It sounds foolproof, but my first attempts resulted in gray, soggy sausages and bland onions floating in hot beer.

I began by setting all the burners to high and placing a pan full of beer and onions on one side. I discovered that first braising the bratwurst in the beer and onions resulted in that unappealing gray color, which persisted even after grilling. I had better luck by first browning the sausages over medium-high heat (they burned over high heat) to give them good seared flavor and color before finishing them in the beer and onion mixture. Brats prepared this way picked up nice flavor, but they also became soggy. The solution to perfect texture was simple: throw the grilled-then-braised brats back over the flames for a final crisping.

The bratwurst tasted great, but the pale onions didn't. While most recipes simply add raw onions to the beer, I saw the hot grill as a tool to add serious flavor. I sliced the onions into rounds and threw them on the grill to acquire a nice char before adding them to their beer bath; the seared flavor of the onions enhanced the beer and, by extension, the sausages. Looking to add even more flavor, I tried dark ales and expensive lagers, but I quickly discovered that their big flavors become overly harsh and bitter when reduced. Cheap, mild lagers remained mellow when simmered for half an hour (see box below).

Once the bratwurst and onions have been cooked, the braising liquid is normally dumped on the ground. But because the grilled onions and brats had infused the beer with so much flavor, I couldn't bear to see it go to waste. I tried adding the mustard to this liquid instead of saving it for the bun. When reduced in the beer and onion mixture, the mustard lent brightness and body to the liquid, which was now more like a sauce. A little bit of sugar, black pepper, and some caraway seeds added richness and complexity.

Now my recipe has it all: crisp, charred, and flavorful bratwurst nestled onto a bun and slathered with my beer-onion-mustard sauce. All I need now are tickets to the big game.
–Meredith Butcher

The Best Beer for Brats

We tested eight lagers in our recipe for Grilled Brats and Beer, and tasters overwhelmingly preferred the mellow sweetness of Budweiser. Miller Genuine Draft was our second choice, with tasters praising its mild, malty flavor. Expensive imported beers, such as Heineken and Spaten, were bitter when reduced in the sauce, so keep those beers for drinking.

SWEET AND MELLOW

Our grill-simmer-grill method for cooking the bratwurst delivers big flavor and perfect texture every time.

GRILLED BRATS AND BEER SERVES 10

Light-bodied lagers work best here; see box at left for our tasting results. Depending on the size of your grill, you may need to cook the onions in 2 batches in step 2. Standard hot dog buns will be too small for the bulky brats.

- 4 onions, sliced into ¹/₂-inch rounds
- 3 tablespoons vegetable oil Pepper
- 2 (12-ounce) beers (see box at left)
- ²/₃ cup Dijon mustard
- 1 teaspoon sugar
- 1 teaspoon caraway seeds
- 10 bratwurst sausages
- 10 (6-inch) sub rolls

1. Turn all burners to medium-high and heat, covered, for 15 minutes. (For charcoal grill, arrange 50 coals over bottom of grill. Light 100 coals; when covered with fine gray ash, pour evenly over cold coals. Set cooking grate in place and let heat, covered, with lid vent open completely, for 5 minutes.) Scrape and oil cooking grate. Brush onions with oil and season with pepper. Whisk beer, mustard, sugar, caraway, and 1 teaspoon pepper in 13 by 9-inch disposable aluminum pan.

2. Following photos at right, arrange disposable pan on one side of grill and grill onions on other side of grill until lightly charred, 6 to 10 minutes. Transfer onions to pan and grill sausages until browned, 6 to 10 minutes. Transfer sausages to pan, cover grill, and simmer until sausages are cooked through, about 15 minutes. Remove cooked sausages from pan and grill until lightly charred, about 4 minutes. Transfer sausages to platter and tent with foil.

3. Continue to simmer beer mixture, with grill covered, until onions are tender and sauce is slightly thickened, about 5 minutes. Place bratwurst in rolls and spoon on sauce and onions. Serve.

Make-Ahead Stuffed Shells

How do you make stuffed shells ahead of time without letting the freezer burn you?

How to
FILL WITH NO MESS

To make quick work of stuffing the shells, spoon the ricotta mixture into a plastic storage bag, snip off the end with scissors, and pipe the filling into the shells.

Freeze with Ease

To help keep the shells saucy and to prevent the cheese topping from becoming rubbery, freeze (and defrost) some of the sauce and cheese separately from the shells, then add them to the baking dish 10 minutes before the shells are done.

Cheese-stuffed pasta shells are simple weeknight family fare. But because it takes so long to cook the pasta, make the filling, prepare the sauce, and stuff the shells, the work is usually done on weekends and the unbaked shells are frozen. Freezing and thawing is tough on most foods, and this dish really suffers. When I tried to freeze a handful of classic recipes, the results were especially bad—gummy pasta, grainy filling, pasty sauce, and rubbery mozzarella. It was clear that a make-ahead recipe would have to account for the moisture loss that occurs during the freezing, thawing, and heating process.

I started with the shells. Most recipes call for cooking the pasta just short of completely soft, figuring it will finish cooking in the oven. But when I froze al dente pasta, it baked up gummy. For this dish, I needed to cook the pasta until it was tender.

Traditional recipes stuff the shells with a mixture of ricotta, mozzarella, Parmesan, eggs, and seasonings. Ricotta is great for straight-to-the-oven recipes, but it loses moisture when frozen and reheated, making for a separated, grainy texture. The solution turned out to be adding two more egg yolks to the two whole eggs I was using as a binder; the fat and emulsifiers in the

yolks helped the ricotta filling stay creamy. Increasing the salt and pepper and using plenty of Parmesan, garlic, and fresh basil ramped up the flavor of the filling enough that it could withstand a trip to the freezer.

I tried topping the shells with the test kitchen's marinara sauce, but the freezer washed out its flavor and dried it to a thick, pasty texture. To boost the flavor, I upped the garlic and added red pepper flakes. Fresh basil blackened and lost its flavor in the marinara, so I turned to durable dried basil. To bring more moisture to the sauce, I added a cup of savory chicken broth, which tasters preferred over vegetal tomato juice or plain water. I also reserved some of the sauce and froze it separately, so I could add it back to the baking dish to guarantee a saucy finished product.

The mozzarella topping on the shells was still becoming

rubbery during baking. To remedy this, I froze the cheese separately and added it at the very end of baking, so it melted into a bubbling, golden crust. I'd finally produced great stuffed shells ready to be pulled from the freezer whenever a craving hits.

–Kelley Baker

Two secrets to perfect make-ahead shells are to aggressively season the filling and add extra liquid to the sauce; both tactics compensate for the effects of freezing.

Shells in a Hurry
To guarantee even cooking, the shells must be thawed before they are baked. This will take eight hours in the refrigerator. For quicker microwave defrosting, assemble the shells in Pyrex or ceramic baking dishes and defrost until the sauce has thawed and the shells have slightly softened. Bake as directed, reducing the initial baking time to 40 minutes.

MAKE-AHEAD STUFFED SHELLS SERVES 8
Assembled shells may be frozen for up to 2 months. You need two 8-inch-square baking dishes (preferably microwave-safe) for this recipe. If you want to pull the baking dishes from the freezer individually, divide the tomato sauce and cheese into smaller containers (see photo at left).

Marinara Sauce
- 2 tablespoons extra-virgin olive oil
- 3 garlic cloves, minced
- 1/4 teaspoon red pepper flakes
- 1/4 cup red wine
- 2 tablespoons balsamic vinegar
- 2 (28-ounce) cans crushed tomatoes
- 1 cup low-sodium chicken broth
- 2 tablespoons dried basil
- 2 teaspoons sugar
- 1/2 teaspoon salt

Stuffed Shells

Salt
1 (12-ounce) box jumbo pasta shells
3 cups ricotta cheese
1 cup grated Parmesan cheese
3 cups shredded mozzarella cheese
2 garlic cloves, minced
1/4 cup finely chopped fresh basil
2 large eggs plus 2 yolks, lightly beaten

1. For the sauce: Heat oil, garlic, and pepper flakes in large saucepan over medium heat until fragrant, about 1 minute. Add wine and vinegar and simmer until reduced by half, about 2 minutes. Stir in tomatoes, broth, basil, sugar, and salt and simmer until slightly thickened, about 15 minutes. Set aside to cool.

2. For the shells: Bring 4 quarts water to boil in large pot. Add 1 tablespoon salt and shells and cook until tender, 12 to 14 minutes. Drain and cool shells. Reserve 30 shells, discarding any that have broken.

3. Combine ricotta, Parmesan, 1½ cups mozzarella, garlic, basil, eggs, and ½ teaspoon salt in bowl. Following photo on page 20, fill each shell with 2 tablespoons filling.

4. To assemble: Divide 2 cups cooled marinara between two 8-inch-square baking dishes. Arrange half of filled shells, seam-side up, in each dish, then top each dish with 1½ cups marinara. Wrap dishes with plastic and cover with foil. Transfer remaining sauce to airtight container and remaining mozzarella to zipper-lock freezer bag. Freeze shells, sauce, and cheese.

5. When ready to serve: Defrost shells, sauce, and cheese in refrigerator for 8 hours (or see "Shells in a Hurry," page 20). Adjust oven rack to middle position and heat oven to 400 degrees. Remove plastic from shells and replace foil. Bake until sauce is bubbling and shells are heated through, about 50 minutes. Remove foil and top shells with reserved sauce and cheese. Bake until cheese is spotty brown, about 10 minutes. Cool 15 minutes. Serve.

Taming Caesar Salad

We tamed the strong flavors in this classic dressing to create a lighter, brighter, and more balanced salad.

Dumping a potent mixture of anchovies, garlic, and Worcestershire sauce over romaine lettuce doesn't sound appealing, but those ingredients (along with raw egg, olive oil, lemon juice, mustard, croutons, and Parmesan cheese) are the foundation of Caesar salad. In most Caesar recipes, the forceful flavors run out of control, resulting in a dressing that tastes fishy, too garlicky, or just plain sour. Good Caesar dressing demands a delicate balance of these strongly flavored ingredients.

Traditional Caesars are thickened with an emulsion of raw egg and oil; for food safety reasons, I wanted to find a replacement for the egg. Mayonnaise, which is made from eggs and oil and comes already emulsified, was the obvious choice, and it worked perfectly when thinned with olive oil. Extra-virgin olive oil was too strong; my tasters preferred the milder flavor of regular olive oil.

To keep the flavors in balance, I decreased the lemon juice from the ¼ cup called for in most recipes to 1 tablespoon. When fortified with 1 tablespoon each of white wine vinegar, Worcestershire sauce, and Dijon mustard, the dressing had the right balance of acidity and pungency. A mere two anchovies (some recipes use up to five) provided a welcome depth and complexity. And mixing everything together in a blender ensured a stable dressing that didn't separate.

I had one last ingredient to deal with: garlic. Most Caesar recipes go way overboard. I used just one raw garlic clove in the dressing to keep its sharpness at bay, but added another layer of mellow garlic flavor by tossing cubes of fresh bread with garlic oil and baking them to make croutons. Parmesan cheese in both the dressing and the finished salad provided a classic touch. Tasters agreed that this was a Caesar truly worth hailing.

–Kelley Baker

Cool, creamy mayonnaise tempers the sharpness of the anchovy, lemon, and garlic in this updated classic.

CAESAR SALAD

SERVES 6 TO 8

Two 10-ounce bags of chopped romaine lettuce can be substituted for the hearts.

1/2 cup olive oil
2 garlic cloves, minced
1 (12-inch) piece French baguette, cut into 1/2-inch cubes (about 4 cups)
   Salt and pepper
1/2 cup mayonnaise
1/4 cup finely grated Parmesan cheese, plus 1 cup shredded
2 anchovy fillets, rinsed and patted dry
1 tablespoon lemon juice
1 tablespoon white wine vinegar
1 tablespoon Worcestershire sauce
1 tablespoon Dijon mustard
3 romaine hearts, torn into bite-sized pieces (about 12 cups; see note)

1. Adjust oven rack to middle position and heat oven to 350 degrees. Whisk oil and garlic in large bowl. Reserve half of oil mixture. Toss bread cubes with remaining oil mixture and season with salt and pepper. Bake croutons on rimmed baking sheet until golden, about 20 minutes. Cool completely.

2. Process mayonnaise, grated Parmesan, anchovies, lemon juice, vinegar, Worcestershire, mustard, ½ teaspoon salt, and ½ teaspoon pepper in blender until smooth. With blender running, slowly add reserved oil mixture until incorporated.

3. Toss romaine, shredded Parmesan, and dressing in large bowl. Toss in croutons and serve.

Make Ahead: The croutons and dressing can be made up to 2 days in advance. Store the croutons at room temperature and refrigerate the dressing.

Better Braised Short Ribs

The marbling in short ribs gives them great flavor, but it can also make the sauce greasy. Here's how we cut the fat.

1. Trim any visible fat from the exterior of the ribs before cooking.
2. Roast the ribs in a foil-covered pan to render fat from the interior of the meat.
3. Pour off the fat and drippings (there should be at least 1 cup), reserving just 2 tablespoons for building the sauce. The browned ribs will need about 2 hours of braising in the sauce to become tender.

Braised short ribs can be fatty and chewy. We set out to create a reliable recipe that produces tender ribs and flavorful—but not greasy—sauce.

In the cooler months, I like to make comfort food like beef short ribs braised until tender in a flavorful wine sauce. Short ribs can make for a very special meal, but they take a long time to prepare. First the ribs are browned in batches to build flavor and render exterior fat, then the vegetables are sautéed, and then everything is braised for hours (to break down the tough connective tissue in the meat) in broth flavored with wine and herbs. Unfortunately, when the fat and collagen melt out of the meat, they end up in the sauce. Some recipes go so far as to require refrigerating the cooked ribs in their sauce overnight to make it easier to remove the rendered fat. I wanted to create fork-tender, silky (but not fatty) short ribs with a bold, clean sauce—and I wanted to serve it on the same day I made it.

Starting with a recipe that employed classic braising technique, I browned a batch of short ribs in my Dutch oven and found about three tablespoons of fat left behind in the pot. Not bad, but I knew there was still fat from the ribs' interior to be lost, and I didn't want it to end up in my sauce. Some recipes forgo stovetop browning in favor of roasting the ribs in the oven before braising. I tried this method, and after an hour the ribs had lost plenty of fat—but valuable moisture, too; they looked like beef jerky. For my next test, I covered the ribs with foil to prevent them from drying

out while they roasted. After about two hours, I discovered my nicely browned ribs had rendered a whopping cup of fat. It was time for the sauce.

I built a braising sauce on the stovetop using traditional ingredients: onion, carrot, celery, garlic, tomato paste, red wine, and beef broth. I added the roasted ribs, covered the pot, and transferred it to the oven. Moist, tender meat emerged (the defatted ribs had soaked up the braising liquid), but I wanted bolder flavor. I tried replacing the red wine with port, and my tasters loved the rich sweetness it imparted. (See "Ports of Call," page 30.) A little balsamic vinegar added a nice acidity that complemented the meatiness of the ribs, and a sprig of rosemary lent a welcome herbal flavor. This was the bold sauce I sought; the only problem was its thin consistency.

It was tricky to turn the large quantity of liquid required to cover the ribs into a glossy sauce. Simply reducing it left me with an overly sticky sauce (the sweet port reduces to syrup) and not nearly enough for serving—only ½ cup. Instead, I decided to add a thickener to the braising liquid at the outset, hoping that by the time the ribs were done the sauce would have the right consistency. Flour and cornstarch seemed like the logical choices, but they made the braising liquid too thick and gravy-like. I had better luck with instant tapioca, which

imparted no flavor of its own and gave the sauce a smoother, more refined consistency. With a quick skimming and straining of the sauce, I now had short ribs that were perfect every time. –Kelley Baker

PORT-BRAISED SHORT RIBS SERVES 4 TO 6

Short ribs come in two styles. English-style ribs contain a single rib bone and a thick piece of meat. Flanken-style ribs are cut thinner and have several smaller bones. While either will work here, we prefer the less expensive and more readily available English-style ribs.

5	pounds beef short ribs (6 to 8 English-style ribs), trimmed of excess fat (see note)
	Salt and pepper
1	onion, chopped
1	carrot, peeled and chopped
1	celery rib, chopped
4	garlic cloves, minced
1	tablespoon tomato paste
3	cups low-sodium beef broth
1½	cups ruby port
¼	cup balsamic vinegar
¼	cup Minute tapioca
1	sprig fresh rosemary

1. Adjust oven rack to middle position and heat oven to 375 degrees. Season ribs with salt and pepper and arrange bone-side up in roasting pan. Cover tightly with aluminum foil and roast until fat has rendered and ribs are browned, 1½ to 2 hours. Transfer ribs to paper towel–lined plate. Reserve 2 tablespoons rendered beef fat and discard remaining drippings.

2. Reduce oven temperature to 300 degrees. Heat reserved fat in large Dutch oven over medium-high heat until shimmering. Cook onion, carrot, and celery until lightly browned, about 5 minutes. Add garlic and tomato paste and cook until fragrant, about 1 minute. Add broth, port, vinegar, tapioca, rosemary, and ribs to pot and bring to simmer.

3. Cover pot and transfer to oven. Cook until sauce is slightly thickened and ribs are completely tender, about 2 hours. Transfer ribs to serving platter. Strain and skim sauce. Serve, passing sauce at table.

Make Ahead: Ribs and sauce can be refrigerated separately for up to 3 days. When ready to serve, heat sauce and ribs together over medium heat until ribs are warmed through.

We roast our short ribs before braising them and then thicken the braising liquid with an unlikely ingredient to guarantee great results every time.

Getting to Know Root Vegetables

A trip to the market reveals that root vegetables are no longer just wintertime fare. Listed below are 16 varieties, some common and some obscure, as well as our tasting notes.

Carrot
CULINARY CORNERSTONE

Before Dutch farmers bred orange carrots to honor the House of Orange in the 17th century, this member of the parsley family was white, yellow, green, red, and even black. Most bagged "baby" carrots sold in supermarkets are actually mature carrots that are cut down to size.

Celeriac
UGLY BEAUTY

Also known as celery root, this gnarled bulb is a variety of celery grown specifically for the root. The flavor is a cross between "celery and parsley," with a "lemony tinge" and a soft but "slightly fibrous" texture. Peel, finely chop, and eat raw or steam, boil, or roast.

Parsnip
WHITE CARROT

Parsnips are "sugary and floral," like a "carrot doused in perfume." Since older, larger parsnips can be tough and fibrous, look for parsnips that are no more than 1 inch in diameter. Peel and steam, boil, sauté, or use our favorite method, roasting.

Sweet Potato
TENDER TUBER

Sweet potatoes can have light-yellow to deep-orange flesh; as a rule, the orange-fleshed tubers are sweeter and more tender. They do not store as well as potatoes and should be eaten within a week or two of purchase.

Yam
BIG AND BLAND

Yams are not a variety of sweet potato but rather wooly-skinned tubers from the tropics; true yams are uncommon in American home cooking. Yams have an "over-the-top-starchy" texture and a "bland, cardboard" taste. Steam or boil.

Purple Carrot
TWO-TONED

Purple carrots hold their striking color when cooked. Their flavor is "floral and winey" but "less sweet" than orange carrots. Be aware that, once peeled, the flesh of this carrot has a staining effect similar to beets.

Turnip
SMALLER IS BETTER

Turnips are recognizable by their off-white skin capped with a purple halo. When young, turnips are tender and sweet, but as they age they become increasingly "sulphurous," with a "tough, woody texture" and "bitter aftertaste." Peeled turnips can be steamed, boiled, or roasted.

Rutabaga
TURNIP COUSIN

A close relative of the turnip, this large root has thin skin and sweet, golden flesh. Its flavor is reminiscent of "broccoli and mustard," with a "horseradish aftertaste" and "dense, crunchy" texture. Steam, boil, or roast.

Jicama
CRISP AND CRUNCHY

Jicama's thin skin is easily peeled to reveal cream-colored, "crisp-textured" flesh that tastes like a mix of "apple, potato, and watermelon." It is often cut into matchsticks and added to salads, but it can also be steamed, boiled, fried, or even pickled.

Cassava
SUPER STARCHY

Also called yuca or manioc, cassava has a "dry, super-starchy" texture and a "boring" flavor that "is vaguely reminiscent of popcorn." Although raw cassava can be poisonous, thorough cooking eliminates any danger. Steam, boil, or fry.

Crosne
SCARY BUT TASTY

Though sometimes called Japanese or Chinese artichokes, these tiny, segmented tubers are native to France. The skin is edible and the flesh pleasantly crunchy, with a "water chestnut–like" texture and a "slight artichoke flavor." Steam, boil, sauté, or roast.

Jerusalem Artichoke
CRUNCHY AND SMOKY

Also called sunchokes, these tubers are the roots of a variety of sunflower. Although they resemble gingerroot, their thin skin covers a "crunchy" white flesh that is "distinctly nutty," with a slight "smoky" taste. Slice thinly and eat raw or steam, boil, or roast.

Red Beet
SWEET STUFF

Sometimes called "garden beets," red beets have a "smooth, dense" flesh with a "sweet, earthy" flavor. Peel, shred, and eat raw; roast, boil, or steam until tender; or sauté the flavorful greens.

Golden Beet
GOLDEN GLOW

Golden beets have brilliant yellow flesh that is "sweet and mild." Although they taste similar to red beets, their juices do not stain in the same way, making them ideal for tossing into salads or combining with other vegetables.

Salsify
OYSTER ROOT

This elongated root vegetable comes in two varieties, black and white. They can be used interchangeably, and both exhibit a "briny, oyster-like" taste and a "firm, artichokey" quality. Steam, boil, or roast.

Lotus Root
WATER WORLD

Lotus root is the subaquatic stem of a variety of water lily. Its smooth skin hides tunneled, flower-patterned flesh with a "slippery but crisp" texture and "subtle mushroom" flavor. Store lotus root submerged in water. Peel and steam or boil.

Recipe Revival: Salisbury Steak

Two unlikely ingredients—one from the pantry, the other from the liquor cabinet—rescue this recipe from the supermarket freezer section.

Our Salisbury steak features tender beef and a rich, flavorful sauce—and no aluminum tray.

It's hard to imagine that chopped steak could be considered health food, but that's just what Dr. James Henry Salisbury had in mind when he invented his eponymous dish as a "meat cure" for wounded and ill Civil War soldiers (who were instructed to eat it three times a day—with no vegetables allowed). Some 60 years later, during the period of World War I food rations, restaurateurs ground up their lean beef scraps, shaped them into patties, dressed the cooked patties with a rich mushroom cream sauce, and called it Salisbury steak. I knew Salisbury steak only from

the cafeteria lunch line and the frozen food section, and I wanted to make a version worthy of its storied past.

I gathered up several modern recipes and headed to the test kitchen. Most of them featured fatty ground beef drowning in a weak, gray mushroom sauce—my tasters felt these versions were more ailment than cure. I decided to use 90-percent-lean ground beef. But because Salisbury steak is cooked to well-done, the lean meat needed special handling to keep the patties from becoming dry and tough. The patties are typically sautéed until well-done, removed from the pan while the sauce is

made, and then submerged in the simmering sauce to absorb flavor. This technique made the beef tough; quickly browning the patties on both sides (rather than cooking them through) worked much better. I slid the

browned patties back into the skillet to gently simmer and finish cooking in the sauce.

My "steaks" were more tender now, but not tender enough. I tried adding a panade (bread and milk mixed together) to the meat; this did help keep the patties tender, but it also made them taste too much like meat loaf. On a lark, I tried adding the mashed potatoes I had seen in one recipe, and I was surprised when the spuds gave the meat a silky texture without imparting potato flavor. Wondering if dehydrated potato flakes (instant mashed potatoes) might save me a little time (since you couldn't really taste them anyway), I mixed some flakes and milk into the raw meat. These patties were tender and moist, and they held together well.

Most modern recipes call for a bland sauce made of mushrooms, onions, and beef broth, and I wanted to bring richness back to this dish. After sautéing the mushrooms and onions, I added tomato paste for deeper flavor and body. To further enrich the sauce, I tried adding sherry, red wine, white wine, and port: The first three were fine, but port provided the best depth of color and flavor.

Now I had tender and perfectly cooked patties that were infused with great mushroom flavor. With this recipe, you can forget the freezer and

remember what Salisbury steak was meant to be. **–Diane Unger**

SALISBURY STEAK

SERVES 4

When shaping the patties in step 1, be sure to wet your hands to prevent sticking. Tawny port or dry sherry can be substituted for the ruby port (see "Ports of Call," page 30). Do not use potato granules, which add an off-flavor.

- 1/2 cup milk
- 7 tablespoons instant potato flakes (see page 30)
- 1 pound 90-percent-lean ground beef
  Salt and pepper
- 4 tablespoons unsalted butter
- 1 onion, halved and sliced thin
- 1 pound white mushrooms, sliced thin
- 1 tablespoon tomato paste
- 2 tablespoons all-purpose flour
- 1 3/4 cups low-sodium beef broth
- 1/4 cup ruby port (see note)

1. Whisk milk and potato flakes in large bowl. Add beef, 1/2 teaspoon salt, and 1/2 teaspoon pepper and knead until combined. Shape into four 1/2-inch-thick oval patties and transfer to parchment-lined plate. Refrigerate for 30 minutes or up to 4 hours.

2. Melt 1 tablespoon butter in large nonstick skillet over medium-high heat. Cook patties until well browned, about 5 minutes per side. Transfer to plate.

3. Add onion and remaining butter to empty skillet and cook until onion is softened, about 5 minutes. Add mushrooms and 1/2 teaspoon salt and cook until liquid has evaporated, 5 to 7 minutes. Stir in tomato paste and flour and cook until browned, about 2 minutes. Slowly stir in broth and port and bring to simmer. Return patties to skillet, cover, and simmer over medium-low heat until cooked through, 12 to 15 minutes. Season sauce with salt and pepper. Serve.

DR. SALISBURY

The Original Dr. Atkins

Dr. James Henry Salisbury (1823–1905) was one of America's earliest proponents of a high-protein, low-carbohydrate diet. His notion that diet could greatly affect overall wellness was revolutionary at the time. In addition to advocating a diet of lean ground beef and coffee for Civil War soldiers, Dr. Salisbury also believed that vegetables and starches were unhealthy and caused disease.

Easier Chicken and Dumplings

A one-hour version puts this classic recipe back on the dinner table.

Chicken and dumplings may be a cornerstone of American comfort food, but who has time to cut up a chicken, clean and chop the vegetables, make a stock, let the stew simmer on the stove for hours, and then finish it off with from-scratch dumplings? I wanted to resurrect this old-fashioned recipe by making it quicker and easier.

My first move was to replace the stock with canned broth and the chicken parts with boneless, skinless breasts. The canned broth proved a good substitute for homemade, especially after adding all the vegetables and seasonings, but the lean chicken breasts were much trickier. I wanted to end up with large chunks of roughly shredded chicken, but cooking the breasts in the stew from the outset (then shredding the meat) left me with dry, stringy bits of chicken. I eventually had success by poaching the chicken in the broth first and then removing it while I made the stew.

With the basic technique down, I could focus on the vegetables and seasonings. Tasters liked a mix of carrot and onion, and welcomed the fresh pop of peas stirred in at the end. Dry sherry, garlic, thyme, and bay leaves added flavor. The best way to give my stew the rich, thick texture it needed was to cook flour in the butter and vegetables early in the process, before adding the broth and cream.

Depending on the recipe origins, dumplings can resemble either noodles or biscuits. Rolled, noodle-style dumplings were too labor-intensive for my streamlined stew. Dropped biscuit-style dumplings (with flour, baking powder, salt, and melted butter and/or dairy) were easier, but I had to get the ingredients right. Milk was too lean and made the dumplings too tough. Melted butter made delicate dumplings that disintegrated into the stew. Cream produced nice, soft dumplings, but they were flat and heavy. Bumping the baking powder up to a full tablespoon (twice as much as most recipes use) gave me perfect—and easy—dumplings that were just as good as Grandma's.

–Stephanie Alleyne

EASIER CHICKEN AND DUMPLINGS

SERVES 6 TO 8

For tender dumplings, the dough should be gently mixed right before the dumplings are dropped onto the stew.

Stew

- 5 cups low-sodium chicken broth
- 2 pounds boneless, skinless chicken breasts, trimmed
- 5 tablespoons unsalted butter
- 4 carrots, peeled and sliced ¼ inch thick
- 1 large onion, chopped fine
- 1 teaspoon salt
- 3 garlic cloves, minced
- 6 tablespoons all-purpose flour
- ¾ cup dry sherry
- ⅓ cup heavy cream
- ½ teaspoon dried thyme
- 2 bay leaves
- ½ teaspoon pepper
- 1½ cups frozen peas
- 4 tablespoons minced fresh parsley

Dumplings

- 2 cups all-purpose flour
- 1 tablespoon baking powder
- ½ teaspoon salt
- 1⅓ cups heavy cream

1. For the stew: Bring broth to simmer in Dutch oven over high heat. Add chicken and return to simmer. Cover, reduce heat to medium-low, and simmer until chicken is just cooked through, about 10 minutes. Transfer chicken to plate and tent loosely with aluminum foil. Transfer broth to large bowl.

2. Return empty Dutch oven to medium-high heat and melt butter. Add carrots, onion, and salt and cook until softened, about 7 minutes. Stir in garlic and cook until fragrant, about 30 seconds. Stir in flour and cook, stirring frequently, for 1 minute. Stir in sherry, scraping up browned bits. Stir in reserved broth, cream, thyme, bay leaves, and pepper and bring to boil. Cover, reduce heat to low, and simmer until stew thickens, about 20 minutes.

3. For the dumplings: Stir flour, baking powder, and salt in large bowl. Stir in cream until incorporated (dough will be very thick and shaggy).

4. To finish: Discard bay leaves and return stew to rapid simmer. Shred reserved chicken and add to stew along with any accumulated juices, peas, and 3 tablespoons parsley. Using 2 large soup spoons or small ice cream scoop, drop golf ball–sized dumplings onto stew about ¼ inch apart (you should have 16 to 18 dumplings). Reduce heat to low, cover, and cook until dumplings have doubled in size, 15 to 18 minutes. Garnish with remaining parsley. Serve.

Make Ahead: Follow recipe through step 2, refrigerating stew and chicken in separate airtight containers up to 24 hours ahead. When ready to proceed, warm stew in Dutch oven and proceed with step 3.

Kitchen Know-How
MAKING THE DUMPLINGS

Here's how we shape and cook our easy, stir-together dumplings.

1. A small ice cream scoop (1 ounce is ideal) makes quick work of shaping the dumplings.
2. Turn the heat to low and cover the pot to gently cook the dumplings.
3. The dumplings will puff and double in size after about 15 minutes in the pot.

We save lots of time and kitchen work by using boneless chicken breasts and store-bought broth for this hearty stew.

Apple Slab Pie

A neighbor recently brought a glazed apple pie made in a sheet pan to our annual block party. She called it "slab pie," and it was a great way to feed a big crowd. Do you know how to make it?

–Audrey Shaw, Hingham, Mass.

How to MAKE APPLE SLAB PIE

1. Use water to "glue" together two pie crusts.

2. Add flavor to the store-bought crust by rolling it out in a mixture of crushed cookie crumbs and sugar.

3. Brush dough with melted butter for extra richness.

4. Top filled pie with second "double" crust.

5. Use a fork to tightly seal edges of crust.

Traditional apple pie and apple slab pie are both two-crusted affairs filled with spiced apples—but that's where the similarities end. Unlike a traditional pie, slab pie is made in a baking sheet and can feed 20 people. It is short in stature, its filling is thickened to ensure neat slicing, and it's topped with a sugary glaze. I was excited to give this pie a try.

I have no problem making homemade pie dough for a regular pie, but I wasn't thrilled to learn I needed to make a quadruple batch to cover the bottom and top of this mammoth pie. Rolling the dough out to such a big size was very difficult; all the required stretching, rolling, and flipping was ripping my delicate home-made pie dough beyond repair.

It was easier to start with sturdier store-bought pie dough rounds. By gluing two of them together with water and then rolling the double-dough out into a large rectangle, I was able to get the crust into the pan without a tear. Now that I had the shaping down, I needed to find a way to improve the bland flavor of the store-bought dough. Using an old test kitchen trick, I tried rolling the dough in crushed cookie crumbs. Gingersnaps lent too much spice, but crushed animal crackers contributed a welcome sweet and buttery flavor. Brushing the rolled dough with melted butter added even more richness.

The test kitchen likes to use two kinds of apples in pies: a firm variety that will hold its shape and a softer one that will cook down to create a saucy filling. Using firm Granny Smiths and softer Golden Delicious, I needed eight of each to adequately fill my pie. I added cinnamon, sugar, lemon juice, and a little flour (to help thicken the filling) to the sliced apples, filled and covered the pie, and baked it. The flavor was great, but the filling was too soupy to cut into neat squares. I tried adding more flour, but because a slab pie filling needs to be more cohesive than regular apple pie filling, it took a lot of flour, and the result was too pasty. Cornstarch made the filling slimy, but tapioca thickened the filling without making it starchy.

But even with this thickened filling, the bottom crust was getting soggy—especially in the middle. I'd been making the filling right before assembling the pie, but for one test I got pulled away from the kitchen and left a batch of apples sitting for about 30 minutes. When I returned, I noticed a pool of juice in the bottom of the bowl, so I drained away the juice and baked the pie as usual. This time the filling was much firmer, and the crust wasn't soggy at all.

As for the glaze, the traditional combination of confectioners' sugar and milk tasted a little flat. Remembering the pool of apple juice that had drained from the filling, I reduced it in a saucepan to concentrate its flavor, then mixed the reduced juice with confectioners' sugar and lemon juice. Spread over the cooled top crust, this glaze offered just the right finish for my crisp and buttery giant of a pie.

–Diane Unger

Sugaring and then draining the apples makes the filling more cohesive and provides a flavorful liquid with which to build the glaze.

APPLE SLAB PIE

SERVES 18 TO 20

We prefer an 18 by 13-inch nonstick baking sheet for this pie. If using a conventional baking sheet, coat it lightly with cooking spray. You will need 4 ounces of animal crackers.

Pie

- 8 Granny Smith apples (about 3½ pounds), peeled, cored, and sliced thin
- 8 Golden Delicious apples (about 3½ pounds), peeled, cored, and sliced thin
- 1½ cups granulated sugar
- ½ teaspoon salt
- 1½ cups animal crackers (see note)
- 2 (15-ounce) boxes Pillsbury Ready to Roll Pie Crust
- 4 tablespoons unsalted butter, melted and cooled
- 6 tablespoons Minute tapioca
- 2 teaspoons ground cinnamon
- 3 tablespoons lemon juice

Glaze

- ¾ cup reserved apple juice (from filling)
- 2 tablespoons lemon juice
- 1 tablespoon unsalted butter, softened
- 1¼ cups confectioners' sugar

1. For the pie: Combine apples, 1 cup sugar, and salt in colander set over large bowl. Let sit, tossing occasionally, until apples release their juices, about 30 minutes. Press gently on apples to extract liquid and reserve ¾ cup juice.

2. Adjust oven rack to lower-middle position and heat oven to 350 degrees.

Pulse crackers and remaining sugar in food processor until finely ground. Dust work surface with cracker mixture, brush half of one pie round with water, overlap with second pie round, and dust top with cracker mixture. Roll out dough to 19 by 14 inches and transfer to rimmed baking sheet. Brush dough with butter and refrigerate; roll out top crust in the same way.

3. Toss drained apples with tapioca, cinnamon, and lemon juice and arrange evenly over bottom crust, pressing lightly to flatten. Brush edges of bottom crust with water, and arrange top crust on pie. Press crusts together and use a paring knife to trim any excess dough. Use fork to crimp and seal outside edge of pie, then to pierce top of pie at 2-inch intervals. Bake until pie is golden brown and juices are bubbling, about 1 hour. Transfer to wire rack and let cool 1 hour.

4. For the glaze: While pie is cooling, simmer reserved apple juice in saucepan over medium heat until syrupy and reduced to ¼ cup, about 6 minutes. Stir in lemon juice and butter and let cool to room temperature. Whisk in confectioners' sugar and brush glaze evenly over warm pie. Let pie cool completely, at least 1 hour longer. Serve.

Make Ahead: The pie can be made up to 24 hours in advance and refrigerated. Bring to room temperature before serving.

A New Use for an Old Favorite

We grind animal crackers (and sugar) to a powder in the food processor and then use this mixture—instead of flour— to facilitate rolling out the dough. The animal cracker–sugar mixture lends much-needed flavor to bland store-bought pie dough.

BETTER THAN FLOUR

Bake-Sale Favorites: Pumpkin Cake with Cream Cheese Frosting

Balancing flavor and texture is a formidable challenge that most recipes for this snack cake get all wrong.

Pumpkin cake is an easy recipe: Just stir together canned pumpkin, flour, sugar, eggs, oil, and spices; pour the batter into a pan; bake it; and top the cake with cream cheese frosting. The cake should be moist and velvety, with just the right balance of pumpkin and spice, but the recipes I tried made damp cakes with a harsh burn of spice. And the cream cheese frosting was way too sweet and rich in my recipe tests.

Canned pumpkin pie filling proved to be too watery and spicy. Instead I reached for the other canned pumpkin product at the supermarket, 100-percent packed pumpkin puree, which has just pumpkin and no spices. The cake made with the puree actually tasted pumpkiny. Using the puree also meant I could control the amount of spice; I used 2 teaspoons of cinnamon and ¼ teaspoon each of ground ginger and allspice to add a subtle spiciness to the cake.

The texture of my cake was still too wet. My working recipe had 1½ cups of oil; I tried reducing the amount. Anything less than a cup resulted in dry cakes with no structure, but the lone cup of oil was still making cakes that were too heavy and wet. I finally found the solution in one recipe that beat the oil, eggs, and sugar together until they were creamy and emulsified (which took just a few minutes). Because the oil was suspended in the other ingredients, it didn't have a chance to saturate the cake, which was now soft, moist, and velvety.

The solutions to heavy and cloyingly sweet cream cheese frosting were simple: Pull back on the butter and confectioners' sugar and increase the amount of cream cheese. These changes resulted in a tangy frosting that perfectly complemented the spiced cake.

–Greg Case

We hold back on the spice to let the pumpkin flavor shine through.

PUMPKIN CAKE WITH CREAM CHEESE FROSTING SERVES 16

Cake

- 2 cups all-purpose flour
- 2 teaspoons baking powder
- 1 teaspoon baking soda
- 1 teaspoon salt
- 2 teaspoons ground cinnamon
- ¼ teaspoon ground allspice
- ¼ teaspoon ground ginger
- 4 large eggs
- 1 cup vegetable oil
- 1⅔ cups granulated sugar
- 1 (15-ounce) can plain pumpkin puree

Frosting

- 6 tablespoons unsalted butter, softened
- 1½ cups confectioners' sugar
- 1 (8-ounce) package cream cheese, cut into 8 pieces and softened
- 1 teaspoon vanilla extract

1. For the cake: Adjust oven rack to middle position and heat oven to 350 degrees. Grease and flour 13 by 9-inch baking pan. Whisk flour, baking powder, baking soda, salt, and spices in bowl. With electric mixer on medium-high speed, beat eggs, oil, and granulated sugar until thick and fluffy, about 5 minutes. Reduce speed to low, add pumpkin, and mix until incorporated. Slowly add flour mixture and mix until only a few small lumps of flour remain, about 1 minute. Scrape batter into prepared pan and bake until toothpick inserted in center comes out clean, 30 to 35 minutes. Transfer pan to wire rack and cool completely.

2. For the frosting: With electric mixer on medium-high speed, beat butter and confectioners' sugar until fluffy, about 2 minutes. Add cream cheese 1 piece at a time, beating thoroughly after each addition. Add vanilla and mix until smooth. Turn cooled cake out onto wire rack, then invert onto serving platter. Frost cake and serve. (Cake can be refrigerated for up to 3 days. Bring to room temperature before serving.)

Visit us online!

For Butter-Pecan and Rum-Raisin frosting variations, visit CooksCountry.com and look for **Cook's Country Extras**.

Food Shopping

WHOLE WHEAT BREAD: Tasters Want Wheat, Not Sweetness

Every major commercial producer of bread now sells at least one type of wheat bread. To determine which brand is best, we rounded up nine types of 100-percent whole wheat bread (breads made with only whole wheat—and not refined white—flour) and headed into the tasting lab to sample them plain and toasted with butter.

Overall, our tasters had a preference for breads with a distinct, clean, and nutty wheat flavor that was balanced by just a hint of sweetness. How is this achieved? A look at the ingredients lists reveals two very important factors: the presence (or absence) of high-fructose corn syrup and chemical preservatives.

Many manufacturers add chemical preservatives that inhibit the growth of microbes and mold. The six lowest-rated brands all contain preservatives; the three winners do not—instead they rely on vinegar to perform this function. According to our science editor, the preservatives can lend a slight off-flavor to the breads, which our tasters detected in several of the low-rated brands.

To mask those off-flavors, most of these low-rated breads use high-fructose corn syrup as their primary sweetener; the corn syrup is powerfully sweet and can make off-flavors—as well as desirable wheat flavor—less apparent. Our top three brands do not contain high-fructose corn syrup (instead they rely on white and brown sugars, raisin juice, honey, and molasses), and tasters praised them for stronger wheat flavor.

As for texture, our tasters liked breads that were heartier, chewier, and more dense than white bread. The breads are listed below, with tasters' comments, in order of preference. **–Scott Kathan**

Highly Recommended

1. PEPPERIDGE FARM 100% Natural Whole Wheat Bread $3.39 for 24 ounces
Comments: This bread, which had a low level of sugars and no corn syrup, was praised for its "whole-grain, earthy flavor" and "nuttiness." The "dense, chewy" texture was lauded as being "grainy but moist."

Recommended

2. RUDI'S ORGANIC BAKERY Honey Sweet Whole Wheat Bread $3.79 for 22 ounces
Comments: This bread earned high marks for its "dense and wholesome" texture. It also had the lowest total sugars of any brand in the lineup. "Closest to traditional wheat bread in taste and texture," said one taster.

3. ARNOLD Natural 100% Whole Wheat Bread $2.50 for 20 ounces
Comments: "Nutty and wheaty," said tasters, who appreciated this bread's "complex" and "strong, healthy" flavor. Its texture was praised as "hearty." A few panelists complained about a "bitter" aftertaste.

Recommended with Reservations

4. FREIHOFER'S Stoneground 100% Whole Wheat Bread $2.99 for 24 ounces
Comments: This "middle-of-the-road" bread had a "soft and gummy" texture. Its very "sweet" flavor (courtesy of high-fructose corn syrup) led a few tasters to comment that it "doesn't taste like real wheat bread."

5. J.J. NISSEN Canadian 100% Whole Wheat Premium Bread $2.99 for 24 ounces
Comments: This bread was deemed "halfway between white and wheat" and "less wholesome-tasting" than most. It had a "very soft," "gummy" texture.

6. ARNOLD Whole Grains 100% Whole Wheat Bread $3.19 for 24 ounces
Comments: This bread had "nutty" wheat flavor, but several tasters complained about "rancid" or "sour" notes. Texture was deemed "chewy."

7. OROWEAT Whole Grains 100% Whole Wheat Bread $3.49 for 24 ounces
Comments: This bread contains high-fructose corn syrup and a relatively high amount of total sugars, and our tasters noticed, saying it was "sweet and almost fruity."

Don't Bother

8. WONDER Stoneground 100% Whole Wheat Bread $2.99 for 24 ounces
Comments: With "sour" and "bitter" flavors and "no wheat flavor," this bread scored lowest in the plain tasting. "Soft" and "springy" texture didn't win fans, either.

9. OROWEAT Country 100% Whole Wheat Bread $3.49 for 24 ounces
Comments: "Very sweet, with little wheat flavor" was a common complaint about this bread, which had the most total sugars of any bread in the tasting.

Taste Test Sugars

Sugar has uses other than just sweetening. In the test kitchen, we use it to accelerate the browning of meats, vegetables, and baked goods; to tenderize doughs; for textural contrast; and to stabilize meringues. Because different types of sugar taste and behave differently in cooking applications, we stock several kinds in the test kitchen. Here are the sugars we always have on hand, with notes on usage.

White Granulated Sugar

This common "table" sugar is (like all sugar) refined from sugar cane or beets; in taste tests, cane and beet sugars were indistinguishable from each other. The relatively fine crystals and neutral flavor make this sugar the most versatile sweetening agent. When processed to a smaller size, white sugar is known as superfine sugar.

Brown Sugar

Brown sugar, whether light or dark, is simply white sugar with molasses added. Dark brown sugar has more molasses and thus a stronger flavor than light brown. If brown sugar is exposed to air, moisture in the molasses can evaporate, causing the brown sugar to dry out. To revive hard brown sugar, spread the sugar on a pie plate (or square of aluminum foil) and place in a 250-degree oven for 3 to 7 minutes, checking often. Cool the softened sugar before using.
* To approximate 1 cup of dark brown sugar, add 2 tablespoons of molasses to 1 cup of granulated sugar and pulse three or four times in a food processor; to approximate light brown sugar, add 1 tablespoon of molasses to 1 cup of granulated sugar and pulse.

Confectioners' (Powdered) Sugar

This sugar is ground to a fine powder and mixed with a small amount of cornstarch to prevent clumping. This sugar is preferred for icings and candy because it dissolves very easily; it is also used as a decorative dusting for baked goods.
* To approximate 1 cup of confectioners' sugar, grind 1 cup of granulated sugar and 1 teaspoon of cornstarch together in a blender (a food processor will not work) for about 3 minutes.

Turbinado Sugar

Turbinado is a type of raw cane sugar: It's made from the residue remaining after sugar cane has been processed into granulated sugar. We don't use turbinado sugar in batters or doughs, because its large crystals do not readily dissolve in those applications. We prefer this sugar for topping muffins or other baked goods where its crunchy texture is desirable.**–S.K.**

Equipment Roundup

LIQUID DISH DETERGENTS: Two Unlikely Brands Clean Up

Liquid dish detergent is one of those household staples that most of us don't put a lot of thought into. After all, how different can dish detergents be? They all work, right? Most of us buy what's on sale or whichever product smells or looks the best. In recent years, "natural," more ecologically friendly, dye- and perfume-free detergents (like Seventh Generation and Method, which swap out all or most of the petroleum-based cleaning agents for vegetable-based ones) have hit the market. Curious about how they stacked up against traditional brands, we rounded up seven detergents (in each brand's original or most basic formulation), rolled up our sleeves, and headed into the test kitchen to put them through their paces.

COMING CLEAN: To test each detergent, we systematically burned carefully measured portions of several classic hard-to-clean foods—beef and bean chili, béchamel sauce, and skin-on chicken thighs marinated in teriyaki sauce—onto stainless-steel skillets. We measured out equal ratios of each dish detergent and temperature-controlled water, submerged the dirty pans, and started scrubbing, counting our strokes for each pan; the scrub strokes for each heavily soiled pan are averaged in the chart at right. (The sugar and fat in the chicken teriyaki made those pans especially difficult to clean: It took us between 56 and 83 scrub strokes to remove the gunk.) At the end of the testing, every pan was clean: Yes, all dish detergents work. But a few detergents stood out above the others for being able to clean the pans as much as 25 percent more quickly. We were very surprised to find that the two most effective dish detergents were the "natural" ones, Method Go Naked and Seventh Generation Free & Clear; our assumption had always been that the more expensive eco-friendly detergents didn't clean as well as the mass-market products.

WETTER IS BETTER: To help us better understand our kitchen results, we turned to our science editor, who explained that the active ingredients in dish detergents are chemical compounds called surfactants. Surfactants help oil and water (which normally repel each other) mix; when made "wet" by the surfactants, the oil-based food grease is surrounded by

water droplets and carried away, resulting in clean dishes. The amount and type of surfactants will determine how effective a dish detergent is at attacking grease.

LAB WORK: To measure the "wetting" ability of each detergent, we carefully mixed equal proportions of each liquid detergent and water and suspended a strip of paper from a grocery bag (paper, like oil, repels water) over the liquid, with its bottom edge just touching the surface of the detergent-and-water solution (see box below). In this test, the hydrophobic paper stands in for water-fearing grease. The dish detergents with the most effective surfactants (Method, Seventh Generation, Dawn, and Ajax) defied gravity and aggressively climbed the paper in the same way they attack the grease on dirty dishes.

IS NATURAL BETTER? Since Method uses primarily vegetable-based surfactants, Seventh Generation uses all vegetable surfactants, and the other detergents in our lineup use considerably more petroleum-based surfactants, one could assume that vegetable-based cleaning agents are more effective. Not so fast, says Marj Besemer, an independent consultant on detergent formulation and performance with over 40 years of experience in the field. "Vegetable-based surfactants are not inherently more effective than petroleum-based surfactants; in fact, many of the mass-market brands contain surfactants of both origins," Besemer says. So why did Method and Seventh Generation outperform the other detergents?

YOU GET WHAT YOU PAY FOR: It may come down to cost. Nick Mahan, Director of Formulations at Method, says that their detergent works so well because they are willing to pay for the right ingredients. Martin Wolf, Director of Product and Environmental Technology at Seventh Generation, echoed the comment: "We put a lot of surfactants, all vegetable-based, into our products to make sure they're effective." Quite simply, these companies say they spend the money to load their products with high concentrations of effective surfactants, which ensures a high-performing detergent. We'd have to say this approach works. The detergents are listed at right in order of preference. **–Scott Kathan**

Science Desk: Measuring Wetting Ability

The best dish detergents are the ones that encourage the most mixing of oil and water. To measure how well each dish detergent could do this—and thus how effective each detergent is—we devised a test in which a carefully controlled ratio of a detergent-and-water solution was measured into a separate cup for each brand. We suspended a strip of paper cut from a brown grocery bag (paper, which is also hydrophobic, stands in for the oil/grease in this test) from a wooden skewer at the top of the cup, with the bottom of the paper just touching the surface of the liquid. After one hour, we removed the paper and measured how far the detergent-and-water solutions had traveled up the paper. We repeated this test three times with each brand of detergent. The winning detergent, Method Go Naked, climbed 53 millimeters, while the least aggressive detergent, Joy, climbed only 39 millimeters. Plain water traveled only 10 millimeters. We used this data to calculate the "times more effective than plain water" in the chart at right. **–S.K.**

WETTING TEST
Effective detergents helped the water to "climb" up the paper.

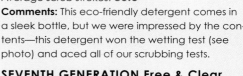

BEST BUY

Notes from Our Test Kitchen

Kitchen Creations
Flavored Dipping Oils

Don't be tempted to buy the expensive bottles of infused olive oils at fancy stores: These flavorful oils are easy (and cheap) to make at home. Just start with extra-virgin olive oil and add ingredients you probably already have on hand. Serve these oils in a shallow dish for dipping crusty bread. All the oils can be refrigerated for up to 3 days (let them come to room temperature before serving).

ROSEMARY-OLIVE OIL

Heat 1/2 cup extra-virgin olive oil, 2 smashed garlic cloves, 1 tablespoon finely chopped pitted kalamata olives, and 1 sprig fresh rosemary in skillet over medium heat until bubbling and fragrant, about 3 minutes. Cool to room temperature before serving.

LEMON-THYME OIL

Heat 1/2 cup extra-virgin olive oil, 2 smashed garlic cloves, 1 tablespoon finely chopped capers, 1/2 teaspoon grated lemon zest, and 1 sprig fresh thyme in skillet over medium heat until bubbling and fragrant, about 3 minutes. Cool to room temperature before serving.

SPICY RED PEPPER AND GARLIC OIL

Heat 1/2 cup extra-virgin olive oil, 4 smashed garlic cloves, 3/4 teaspoon red pepper flakes, and 1/2 teaspoon dried oregano in skillet over medium heat until bubbling and fragrant, about 3 minutes. Cool to room temperature before serving.

Instant Potatoes

For our **Salisbury Steak** recipe (page 24), we found that instant potato flakes gave the ground beef patties a tender, silky texture. Instant potatoes are real potatoes that have been cooked, mashed, and dried before being further processed into flakes, buds, or granules. While both potato flakes and buds will work well in our Salisbury Steak, we prefer the airy texture of flakes, which dissolve more thoroughly than the coarser buds. Avoid the granules at all cost here—they made the steaks heavy and gummy.

POTATO FLAKES
Instant potato flakes have a smoother texture than either potato granules or buds and are our top choice.

Ports of Call

Our recipes for **Port-Braised Short Ribs** (page 22) and **Salisbury Steak** (page 24) call for port, a sweet fortified wine that originated in the city of Oporto in northern Portugal. Port is now produced around the world, and there are a wide variety of ports on the market. For cooking, we prefer to use ruby port—an inexpensive, garnet-colored wine with a decidedly sweet, fruity flavor. Two other varieties of port, tawny and vintage, are typically aged for years before bottling, yielding a more complex—and much more expensive—spirit. While both tawny and vintage port certainly could be used in either of our recipes, their higher price tags and subtle, nuanced flavors make them better suited for sipping than simmering.

Tapioca Primer

While doing research for **Getting to Know Root Vegetables** (page 23), we learned that one of our favorite thickeners, tapioca, is a derivative of the cassava root, a staple of Latin American and African cooking. To make tapioca, starch is extracted from the root and processed into flakes. The flakes can then be ground into tapioca flour, extruded into tapioca pearls, or further processed into instant, or Minute, tapioca granules. While tapioca flour is most often used in commercial applications, pearl tapioca and Minute tapioca are available in most supermarkets. While both have their merits, we prefer the small granules of Minute tapioca, which do not require soaking and dissolve easily in liquids.

Better Bratwurst

A recipe for **Grilled Brats and Beer** (page 19) isn't authentic unless it uses true bratwurst sausages. German in origin, bratwurst are made from ground pork and veal that is gently seasoned with caraway, coriander, ginger, and nutmeg. Brats are sold partially cooked or fresh, but we vastly prefer the uncooked fresh variety (such as the widely available Johnsonville brand). In our experience, partially cooked brats have a tendency to split on the grill and have a dry, almost chalky texture.

① ②

Inside the Test Kitchen A Clean Turn-Out

Our Cranberry Upside-Down Cake (page 17) is a real showstopper—if it comes out of the pan cleanly. To ensure this happens, allow the cake to cool for 10 minutes and gently run the tip of a paring knife around the outside of the cooled cake. Test cook Cali Rich shows how to flip the cake onto a plate.

1. Cover the cake with a clean serving plate and invert.
2. Using a straight upward motion, carefully remove the cake pan, shaking gently as needed to get a clean release of the cake and topping.

Shopping with the Test Kitchen
Chicken Bouillon

While the assertive saltiness of bouillon can overpower a dish, it proved to be a successful addition to our **Herb Butter–Roasted Turkey** (page 10). Used in lieu of salt, the bouillon lent a distinctly meaty flavor and slightly herbal, salty component to the turkey. But not all bouillons are created equal. While any bouillon will work in this recipe, after tasting four of the major leading brands of bouillon cubes, bouillon granules, and bouillon pastes, we found Superior Touch Better Than Bouillon paste had the most balanced poultry flavor.

BEST BOUILLON
Honest chicken flavor

Pumpkin Purity

When it came time to add the pumpkin to our **Pumpkin Cake with Cream Cheese Frosting** (page 27), we learned that selecting the type of pumpkin filling is very important. Canned pumpkin pie mix already has the sugar and spices added; we found its spice flavor overwhelming and its pumpkin flavor stale and muted. A better option is canned pumpkin puree, which consists of 100-percent pure pumpkin with no salt, sugar, artificial flavorings, or color added.

PICK THE BEST PUMPKIN
Plain pumpkin puree (without spices or sugar) packs the best flavor.

Grating Parmesan

Although past tastings have confirmed the superiority of freshly grated Parmesan to the pregrated variety, after grating through 8 pounds of cheese while testing our **Parmesan**

MICROPLANE-GRATED PARMESAN
Fluffy texture means less cheese in every cup you measure.

PREGRATED PARMESAN
Pulverized texture means more cheese in every cup you measure.

Mashed Potatoes (page 15), we figured pregrated cheese might be worth revisiting. When tasted side by side in the potatoes, it wasn't surprising that the "bold, nutty" flavor of the freshly grated Parmesan was preferred, but we were surprised at the "strong, pungent" taste in the potatoes containing the pregrated cheese. Further investigation showed that this had less to do with the quality of the cheese than it did with the weight of the cheese.

In the test kitchen, unless otherwise specified, we prefer a rasp-style grater, such as a Microplane, which grates cheese into thin, fluffy wisps. Pregrated Parmesan, on the other hand, is typically pulverized into a dense (and heavy) powder. Thus, an equal volume of the powdery pregrated cheese weighed in at nearly twice as much as the fluffy, Microplane-grated cheese. So what does that mean to the home cook? If you choose to use pregrated Parmesan, start by adding half the amount of cheese the recipe calls for, and then add more to taste if desired.

Barley: Not Just for Beer

Barley, a whole grain most widely used for animal feed and beer production, has been grown for thousands of years—it is even mentioned in the Bible. There are two types of whole barley: hulled (or whole grain) and pearl. Hulled barley is difficult to digest and is typically steamed and polished to remove some of the tough outer layer of bran. The result of this polishing process is pearl barley, which has a nutty, malty flavor. Although pearl barley needs to be boiled for about 40 minutes to soften, it is hard to overcook, making it an excellent choice for soups (such as our **Beef Barley Soup**, page 7), stews, and slow cookers.

Turkey Types

While developing our recipe for **Herb Butter–Roasted Turkey** (page 10), we found that there are more turkey options than you might think. Turkeys can be fresh, frozen, organic, kosher, even "heritage" (as heirloom breeds of turkey are known). So what's the best choice? We recommend using frozen Butterball turkeys, as they are enhanced with a salty broth that keeps the meat moist and juicy during cooking. Our second choice, kosher turkeys, are prepared according to Jewish dietary laws. They are first soaked in water, then heavily salted and left to sit for an hour, and finally rinsed with cold water. The salt and water combine to tenderize the meat while adding moisture and flavor. As for the fresh, organic, and heritage turkeys, although they all taste great, we find that they have a tendency to roast up dry as a bone. If you choose to purchase one of these untreated turkeys, we highly recommend that you brine it before cooking. Here are a few rules for brining:

- **Make the Right Brine:** Our overnight brine (12 to 14 hours) uses ½ cup of table salt per gallon of cold water. For a hurry-up brine (that will have the turkey ready to roast in just four to six hours), use 1 cup of table salt per gallon of cold water. For most birds, you'll need 2 gallons of cold water.
- **Keep It Cold:** The refrigerator is the best place to brine, because the cold temperature ensures food safety. If your bird won't fit in the fridge, use a big cooler and ice packs.
- **Rinse and Dry:** Don't let the turkey brine beyond the recommended time or it will be overly salty. When the turkey is ready to come out of the brine, be sure to rinse away the salty water and then pat the turkey dry with paper towels.

Wild Thing

Firm, chewy, and nutty wild rice isn't actually rice; rather, it is the seed of a marsh grass native to the Great Lakes region. Until recently, wild rice was harvested only in this area by American Indians operating under strict cultural guidelines; now it is also grown as far away as California and Texas. Because of its price (four to five times that of white rice), it is often sold in a "wild rice mix," a combination of wild rice, white rice, and any number of inexpensive grains. Avoid the aforementioned mixes, which lack the character of the real thing, and stick with pure wild rice. Since wild rice can take upward of an hour to cook, we recommend boiling the rice (as you would pasta) or adding the raw grains to long-simmered stews or soups (such as our **Creamy Turkey and Wild Rice Soup**, page 11).

Gadgets & Gear Sheet Pans

Our **Apple Slab Pie** (page 26) is baked in an 18 x 13 x 1-inch pan, which is more commonly called a half sheet pan or rimmed baking sheet. We have over 100 of these pans in the test kitchen, and they see a lot of use. Half sheet pans are great for cookies, large batches of brownies, sheet cakes, roasting vegetables, and baking bread and biscuits. With a rack set in them, half sheet pans are great for poultry and roasts. These sturdy pans heat up quickly and won't warp at high heat, as some cookie sheets are prone to do, and their rimmed edge makes them easy to handle with an oven mitt.

KITCHEN WORKHORSE
We use half sheet pans for cookies, roasts, and even pies.

Shopping with the Test Kitchen Anchovy Paste

Anchovies are often used to contribute a rich, savory background flavor to salad dressings, pasta sauces, and even roasts and beef stews. But since just a single fillet is all you need for most recipes, we wondered whether a tube of anchovy paste might be a more convenient option than whole anchovies. Made from pulverized anchovies, vinegar, salt, and water, anchovy paste promises all the flavor of oil-packed anchovies without the mess of draining, drying, and chopping the whole fillets. After a head-to-head tasting of our **Caesar Salad** (page 21) recipe prepared with equal amounts of anchovy paste and anchovy fillets, we found little difference. Though a few astute tasters felt that the paste had a "saltier" and "slightly more fishy" flavor, in such small quantities it was deemed an acceptable substitute. For dishes that use just a touch of anchovy, the squeeze-and-go convenience of the tube can't be beat.

ANCHOVY PASTE
Salty but acceptable

OIL-PACKED ANCHOVIES
Great flavor but messy

When Things Go Wrong in the Kitchen

FROG SALAD

Several years ago, my very large family (I have six siblings, who bring their spouses and children) gathered at my parents' home for our traditional Thanksgiving dinner. While my sister was washing the grapes for the fruit salad, a small—and very quick—frog jumped out of the bunch and landed on the kitchen counter. Chaos ensued until my nephew picked up the frog, deposited it in an empty jar, and brought it outside. We did not have any grapes in our fruit salad that year, but "Frog Salad" is a family Thanksgiving Day story that has been retold many times since.

Deborah Dorsey Munster, Ind.

EVERLASTING QUICHE

In the mid-1970s, I volunteered to bring a ham-and-cheese quiche to a neighbor's party. I pulled out what I thought was pie dough from my freezer. The dough rolled out beautifully, and the finished quiche looked spectacular, with not a crack in it. I proudly brought this masterpiece to my neighbor's house, but when I went to cut the quiche into slices, it was like trying to cut through cement. I then realized I had used the salt dough that my children and I were going to use to make Christmas decorations. I tried to salvage the filling, but needless to say, it was very salty!

Bonnie Stephenson New Smyrna Beach, Fla.

TURKEY FAKE-OUT

Years ago, a friend of mine (who was an inexperienced cook) took the turkey out of the freezer to defrost on Thanksgiving morning. After realizing this was going too slowly, she somehow thought she could fry the turkey instead of waiting for it to thaw. Since the turkey was large enough that only a part of the leg fit in her largest frying pan, she tried frying it little by little, turning it constantly. With spattered oil all over the kitchen, she turned to her husband's saw in desperation. The turkey was quickly mutilated, but time was running out. She tossed the turkey in the dumpster, ran to the nearest restaurant, brought home a complete meal, set the table, and planned her story. Soon her dining companion arrived, sat down to the wonderful "homemade" meal, and said, "You should have seen the dumpster when I arrived—there must have been 20 cats in there!"

Pat Ash Lancaster, Calif.

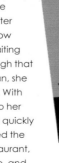

TUPPERWARE PORK

Several years ago, my entire family got together for Christmas at my in-laws' place. One night my mother-in-law spent hours preparing a dish of oven-baked boneless pork ribs, which were delicious. When the meal was almost finished, we noticed a layer of what looked like caramelized sauce on the bottom of the casserole pan. My sister leaned over for a closer inspection and announced, "That's the top to a piece of Tupperware!" Sure enough, a plastic Tupperware lid had fallen into the casserole pan, and my mother-in-law hadn't noticed before baking. Since that day, we've referred to this dish as "Tupperware Pork."

Elizabeth Kowalski Gainesville, Fla.

JAILED BIRD

It was Thanksgiving morning, and I had spent several hours preparing the turkey and all the vegetables. I placed the bird in the oven, but when I closed the oven door it wouldn't shut tight, so I decided to pull the lock mechanism to keep the door closed. Little did I know that this automatically started the self-cleaning cycle! Twenty frantic minutes went by as I tried and tried, without luck, to open the oven and save the turkey from incinerating. I called my family around to try to figure out how to free the trapped bird! I called the oven's manufacturer, but because of the holiday, no one was on duty to answer. Finally, much to my astonishment, my son somehow managed to dismantle the locking mechanism without burning or breaking anything, and the turkey was saved. The turkey had earned a "get out of jail free" card, and we all had a great Thanksgiving!

Charlotte Mirman Rockville, Md.

CITY GIRL COOKS ON THE CAMPFIRE

When my husband and I were younger, we would take our three sons camping every hunting season. One cold winter night, my husband built a fire and I decided to cook a large can of pork and beans. Not wanting to wash any pans (and as a born and bred city girl), I thought it would be a great idea to cook the beans directly in their can. I set the can next to the fire and walked away. A few minutes later the can exploded with a bang, sending hot beans everywhere! Beans covered the tent, the car, the trees, and us. My husband looked at me in complete shock and broke the silence by asking, "Didn't you know you were supposed to open the can first?" I replied, "I do now!"

Lisa Dover Cleveland, Texas

MYSTERY STOPPER

One Thanksgiving years ago, we had extra guests, and I wanted everything perfect for them. After scrubbing and sanitizing the sink, I placed the huge turkey in the sink to fill it with stuffing. After hours and hours of preparations and cooking, my guests were seated and anxiously awaiting the turkey. The dinner—and especially the turkey—was delicious. After dinner, I went to fill the sink with soap and water, but I could not find the metal sink stopper. For the life of me, I could not figure out what happened to it. After finishing slicing the turkey, my son found the metal stopper embedded in the bottom of the bird. It must have gotten stuck on the underside of the turkey when I stuffed it!

Josie Brockbank via e-mail

Send us your funniest kitchen disaster stories. E-mail us by visiting **CooksCountry.com/kitchendisasters** or write to us at Kitchen Disasters, Cook's Country, P.O. Box 470739, Brookline, MA 02447. If we publish your story, you'll receive a complimentary one-year subscription to Cook's Country.

Minnehaha Cake

Minnehaha cake was named after the fictional princess in Henry Wadsworth Longfellow's famous 1855 poem *Song of Hiawatha*. By the late 1800s, newspapers and cookbooks all across the country were publishing recipes for this popular special-occasion dessert. The cake is traditionally a three-layered affair filled with raisins and almonds and topped with a burnt-sugar frosting.

To make this cake, you will need:

- 2¹/₂ **cups packed dark brown sugar**
- 16 **tablespoons (2 sticks) unsalted butter,** softened
- ²/₃ **cup heavy cream**
- 1¹/₄ **cups sliced almonds**
- ²/₃ **cup raisins**
- 3 **(8-inch) baked white cake rounds***

For the frosting: Combine sugar, 10 tablespoons butter, and cream in saucepan set over medium heat. Boil, stirring occasionally, until mixture is slightly thickened and registers 240 degrees on candy thermometer. Carefully transfer to bowl of standing mixer fitted with paddle attachment and beat on medium speed until cooled to room temperature, about 15 minutes. Beat in remaining butter, 1 tablespoon at a time, until well incorporated.

For the filling: Pulse ³/₄ cup almonds, raisins, and 1 cup frosting in food processor until coarsely ground.

To assemble: Spread half of filling on bottom cake layer. Top with second cake layer and remaining filling. Top with final cake layer and frost top and sides with plain frosting. Decorate with remaining almonds.

* Go to **CooksCountry.com** for our white cake recipe or use your own.

Recipe Index

RC = Recipe Card

Cook's Country

DECEMBER/JANUARY 2008

Easy Holiday Menu
Starts with Herbed Prime Rib

Mashed Potato Casserole
Light, Fluffy, and Make-Ahead

Caramel Bread Pudding
We Double the Caramel Flavor

SKILLET SPAGHETTI SUPPER
One Pan, 30 Minutes

RATING STANDING MIXERS
Best Buy for Budget Shoppers

CHICKEN PARMESAN
Cheesy, Crisp, and Low-Fat

JUICY BROILED STEAKS
Foolproof No-Smoke Method

EXTRA-SHARP CHEDDAR
Does Age Really Matter?

SWEDISH MEATBALLS
Slow-Cooker Make & Serve

HOMEMADE PARTY SNACKS
Fresher and Crunchier

MILE-HIGH OMELETS
Secrets to Fluffiest-Ever Eggs

BLACK-BOTTOM PIE
Rum Chiffon Meets Chocolate

$4.95 U.S./$6.95 CANADA

Our $1,000 Contest Winner!
Lori Mahaney of Hillsborough, N.C., won first place in our Christmas cookie contest with peppermint-flavored cookies. See page 4 for her **Candy Cane Pinwheels.**

Cook's Country

Dear Country Cook,

Before my wife and I had our four kids, I used to provide plenty of child-rearing advice to our friends who were already parents. As the saying goes, I had a dozen theories about raising children before I got married, and now I have a dozen kids and no theories.

What has always struck me about the country is that children grow up fast. Sure, the kids in the photo below are playing grown-up, the young girl looking especially mature and about to utter, I would guess, words of "advice" about the proper kitchen techniques. All spouses know that look. But kids in the country quickly shoulder the mantle of responsibility, and they are not just playing at it, either. As a young kid in Vermont, I remember pounding 16-penny nails into floor joists, creosoting fence posts, watering horses, shoveling barns, and taking charge of the "burn barrel."

But the real McCoys, those kids who have grown up on authentic working farms, walk differently, with a slow, rolling gait and a steady hundred-yard stare. I've known one such kid, Nate, since he was 3 or 4. At the age of 7, he would hunker down all day in a cold March drizzle and boil maple sap in a large cast-iron pot over an open fire or just swing a hammer next to his dad. And that is what he did for fun.

We are told that growing up is all about figuring out who we are, yet country kids seem to have that sorted out by the time they get their hunting license. So when I hear experts telling me to "find my inner child," I am inclined to take a page out of Nate's book. I'll just grab a hammer or boil some sap. By all indications, his inner child was left on a shelf long ago, just where it belongs.

Christopher Kimball
Founder and Editor, Cook's Country Magazine

Two Young Cooks Help Out in the Kitchen, 1941
Photographer: Felix Man/Hulton Archive

DECEMBER/JANUARY 2008

Cook's Country

departments

in every issue

features

Founder and Editor Christopher Kimball
Editorial Director Jack Bishop
Executive Editor Amanda Agee
Deputy Editor Bridget Lancaster
Senior Editors Scott Kathan
Jeremy Sauer
Test Kitchen Director Erin McMurrer
Test Cooks Kelley Baker
Meredith Butcher
Greg Case
Cali Rich
Diane Unger
Assistant Test Cook Lynn Clark
Online Managing Editor Katherine Bell
Web Editor Kate Mason
Copy Editor Will Gordon
Market Research Manager Melissa Baldino
Editorial Assistant Meredith Smith
Senior Kitchen Assistant Nadia Domeq
Kitchen Assistants Maria Elena Delgado
Ena Gudiel
David Lentini
Contributing Editor Eva Katz
Consulting Editor Guy Crosby

Design Director Amy Klee
Senior Designer, Magazines Julie Bozzo
Designers Tiffani Beckwith
Jay Layman
Christine Vo
Staff Photographer Daniel J. van Ackere

Production Director Guy Rochford
Traffic and Projects Manager Alice Cummiskey
Production & Imaging Specialist Lauren Pettapiece
Color and Imaging Specialist Andrew Mannone

Vice President New Technology Craig Morrow
Systems Administrator S. Paddi McHugh
IT Development Manager Justin Greenough
Web Developer Doug Sisko

Chief Financial Officer Sharyn Chabot
Human Resources Manager Adele Shapiro
Controller Mandy Shito
Senior Accountant Aaron Goranson
Staff Accountant Connie Forbes
Office Manager Elizabeth Pohm
Receptionist Henrietta Murray

Vice President Marketing David Mack
Fulfillment & Circulation Manager Carrie Horan
Circulation Assistant Elizabeth Dayton
Direct Mail Director Adam Perry
Direct Mail Analyst Jenny Leong
Products Director Steven Browall
E-Commerce Marketing Manager Hugh Buchan
Partnership Marketing Manager Pamela Putprush
Marketing Copywriter David Goldberg
Customer Service Manager Jacqueline Valerio
Customer Service Representatives Julie Gardner
Jillian Nannicelli

Vice President Sales Demee Gambulos
Retail Sales & Marketing Manager Emily Logan
Retail Sales Associate Anthony King
Corporate Partnership Manager Allie Brawley
Corporate Marketing Associate Bailey Vatalaro
Publicity Deborah Broide

ON THE COVER: PHOTOGRAPHY: Keller + Keller. ILLUSTRATION: John Burgoyne.
IN THIS ISSUE: COLOR FOOD PHOTOGRAPHY: Keller + Keller. STYLING: Mary Jane Sawyer, Marie Piraino. ILLUSTRATION: Lisa Perrett.

Cook's Country magazine (ISSN 1552-1990), number 18, is published bimonthly by Boston Common Press Limited Partnership, 17 Station Street, Brookline, MA 02445. Copyright 2007 Boston Common Press Limited Partnership. Periodicals Postage paid at Boston, Mass., and additional mailing offices. Publications Mail Agreement No. 40020778. Return undeliverable Canadian addresses to P.O. Box 875, Station A, Windsor, Ontario N9A 6P2. POSTMASTER: Send address changes to Cook's Country, P.O. Box 8382, Red Oak, IA 51591-1382. For subscription and gift subscription orders, subscription inquiries, or change-of-address notices, call 800-526-8447 in the U.S. or 515-247-7571 from outside the U.S. or write us at Cook's Country, P.O. Box 8382, Red Oak, IA 51591-1382.   PRINTED IN THE USA

Visit us at www.CooksCountry.com!
Go online for hundreds of recipes, food tastings, and up-to-date equipment reviews. You can get a behind-the-scenes look at our test kitchen, talk to our cooks and editors, enter recipe contests, and share recipes and cooking tips with the Cook's Country community.

Kitchen Shortcuts

New Use for Floss
Instead of using a spatula to loosen baked-on cookies from a baking sheet, I use unflavored, unwaxed dental floss. With a long strand held safely away from the hot surface of the pan, I can loosen all the cookies with one swipe!

Elizabeth Roberts
Cambridge, Mass.

Freezing Cake Slices
When I bake a cake, my husband and I eat a few pieces, and then I freeze the rest. Instead of having to defrost the whole cake every time we want just a piece or two, I cut the entire cake into slices and wrap a piece of wax paper around each before freezing. This way, I can take out slices whenever I want.

Lois Lindquist
La Mesa, Calif.

QUICK DIP
Burnt Cookie Quick Fix
Sometimes I get distracted and my cookies get a little burnt on the bottom, but I don't throw them away. Instead, I dip the bottom of the cookies in melted chocolate. The cookies look fancy, and there's no burnt taste!

Theresa Lawler
Blackstone, Mass.

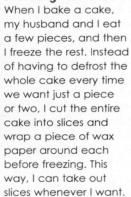

No-Mess Mixing!
SPLATTER-FREE
I used to splatter food all over my kitchen every time I used my electric mixer. To avoid the mess, I now stick a paper plate through the beaters: The paper plate stops any food that splatters up. No more mess!

Kathy Parker Hoge Houston, Texas

PLUMBER'S TAPE
When using my decorative oil and vinegar shakers, the caps used to leak and make a mess. Wrapping a little bit of white plumbing tape around the top of the bottles before screwing on the lids made them leakproof.

Susan Massare
Webster, Texas

STUFF IT
I find the best way to prepare stuffed peppers is to prop them upright in a muffin pan. The peppers are easy to fill, and since the pan holds them in place without falling over, I don't lose any filling.

Deb Minchhoff
Tamaqua, Pa.

MELON BALLER STRAINER
I use my melon baller (the one with a small hole in the middle of it) to remove olives from the jar when I want just a few. The brine drains back into the jar through the hole with no mess.

Tricia Vogel
Mooresville, Ind.

SEED REMOVAL
I make a lot of salsa, and instead of using a paring knife to take the seeds out of a jalapeño, I use an old metal baby spoon. The spoon is just the right size to take the seeds out in one quick swoop.

Didi Orr
Shelley, Idaho

RICE-COOKER OATMEAL
In addition to our evening rice dish, we have always used our rice cooker to cook our morning oatmeal. It cooks the oatmeal slowly, so you don't have to worry about it burning while you're in the shower.

Emily Taylor
Tacoma, Wash.

TIMESAVER
Whenever I make dough, whether it is for cookies, pies, or pastries, I make a copy of the recipe and put it in a small sandwich bag to freeze along with the dough. When it's time to bake, I don't have to search for the recipe.

Bernadette Hines
Ashburnham, Mass.

SPIN CYCLE
A salad spinner is not just for drying lettuce; it can be used to remove the moisture from other foods. When making dishes like hash-browned potatoes or potato pancakes, I put the grated potatoes (and onions, too) in the salad spinner and give them a good whirl. The juices are easily extracted, and I am left with thoroughly dry ingredients.

Bart Gordon
Via e-mail

NO MORE RUNAWAY MUSHROOMS
When preparing stuffed mushrooms, slice a very small amount off the top of the rounded part of the mushroom. When you place the mushroom cap-side down, it won't roll around in the baking dish and can be easily stuffed and baked.

Darren Krafczek
Guelph, Ontario

COOL DOWN
When I make beef and vegetable soup, I always want to eat it right away, but it's too hot. A quick way to cool the soup is to add the frozen peas and corn at the very end of cooking, just before serving—the vegetables cool the soup as they defrost. No more waiting!

Sue Johnson
East Weymouth, Mass.

GRATING JALAPEÑOS
We grow a large crop of jalapeños every year. I slice them in half and remove the seeds before packing them into plastic bags to freeze. When a recipe calls for jalapeños, I take the desired amount and grate them frozen, which I find easier than chopping.

Rosemarie Carneal
Excelsior Springs, Mo.

If you'd like to submit a tip, please visit us at CooksCountry.com/ kitchenshortcuts or send a letter to Kitchen Shortcuts, Cook's Country, P.O. Box 470739, Brookline, MA 02447. Include your name, address, and phone number. If we publish your tip, you will receive a free one-year subscription to Cook's Country.

EASIER WAY TO FILL SHELLS

I was making stuffed shells this week and found an easy way to stuff them instead of making a mess with a spoon. I used a small ice-cream scoop (the spring-loaded kind that ejects the contents) and scooped the filling into the shells much more quickly and neatly.

Evan Allen
Via e-mail

PEPPER CHECKER

These days it seems like most jalapeños are bred to be as bland as bell peppers, so I never automatically seed them, because the seeds and ribs contain most of the heat. But occasionally I encounter a really fiery specimen. To test the heat, I halve a pepper and run my thumb along the flesh. I then stick my thumb in my mouth: If there is a mild sting, I leave in the seeds; if I leap up screaming, I seed the pepper.

Anne Jolles
Hanover, Mass.

LOOSEN UP

If the blade in your blender seizes up and you don't want to use a chemical lubricant like WD-40 near your food, try a shot or two of cooking spray (not baking spray) on the top and underside of the blade assembly. Carefully work it by hand until the blade rotates freely, then wipe off the excess cooking spray with a towel.

Rich Sanders
Brooklyn, N.Y.

SPICE BALL

When I cook corned beef, I don't like having to fish out all the whole spices I use to season the broth, so I put all of my spices in a tea infuser ball and place it in the pot with the corned beef. It seasons the dish without the mess of having spices stuck to the cooked meat.

Candy Barnhart
Makawao, Hawaii

BRINGING BROWNIES UPTOWN

I volunteered to bring a nice dessert for a community fundraiser but couldn't decide what to bring. I love my brownie recipe, but regular brownies aren't exactly fancy. So I took my biscuit cutter and stamped out rounded brownies to fit inside colorful, festive cupcake papers. They were a big hit!

Elizabeth Ruhl
Cody, Wyo.

STACK THEM UP

I keep a lot of ground meat in my freezer for meatloaf, tacos, hamburgers, and chili. But the package the ground meat comes in is cumbersome, so as soon as I get home from the store, I take the meat out of the package and flatten it into a thin disk that I place in a zipper-lock bag. I remove all of the air and pile the disks of meat high in my freezer, where they take up much less room than they would have in the original packaging.

Marie Sullivan
Tuckahoe, N.Y.

QUICK GARLIC PEELING

Peeling garlic can be very time consuming, especially when I need several cloves. Instead of taking the time to peel the cloves individually, I throw a bunch in the food processor and pulse them just enough to loosen the skins. The food processor gets the job started for me, making my life much easier.

Derek Surabian
Schenectady, N.Y.

CLIP YOUR CRUST

I like to make thin-crust pizza, but I have trouble getting the finished pie off the pizza stone and onto the cutting board, so I came up with this idea. I use chip clips to grab the edge of the hot crust and gently pull the pizza off the stone and onto my cutting board.

Mark Colb
West Roxbury, Mass.

IN A PINCH

I began using saffron in a couple of dishes about a month ago, but I had trouble getting small pinches out of the jar: The strands would get stuck on my fingers or would fall on the counter or floor, and I didn't want to waste a single strand of this expensive spice. My solution? I use tweezers to gently pick out what I need. It takes just a little bit longer, but now I don't waste anything.

Barbara Soldano
Ridgefield, Conn.

Double Duty!
GET TO THE BOTTOM OF IT

A few years ago I decided to make punch for a party, but I didn't have a ladle to go with my punch bowl. But I did have a brand-new turkey baster! My guests thought it was a hysterical idea, but I had the last laugh when I got every last drop of punch out of the bowl.

Theresa Sparano Via e-mail

Decorate with Ease
When I serve ice-cream cones to my kids, I put sprinkles in a muffin tin. They can dip their cones into the sprinkles without all the mess!
Tracey Witham
Braintree, Mass.

TIDY TIP

Ruler of the Dough
I love to bake cookies for family and friends during the holidays, and I came up with an easy way to measure dough size. I keep a ruler on top of the mixing bowl, and when I am ready to roll the dough into balls, I can easily see if they are the right size. This way, I always get the right number of cookies with every batch.
Pat Bowler
San Diego, Calif.

Not Just for Honey
Instead of throwing away empty honey containers, I wash them out and make my own salad dressings in the container. With a few shakes, the dressing is ready to go, and the convenient spout keeps me from pouring too much at a time. It never spills, and I can easily transport it when I bring a salad to a party.
Fenna Beverly
Framingham, Mass.

Weights and Measures
To make sure your kitchen scale is accurate, place 10 pennies on the scale. It should add up to one ounce.
Karen Bland
Gove, Kan.

New Twists on Holiday Favorites Win Cookie Contest

Our $1,000 Grand-Prize Winner!

Lori Mahaney
Hillsborough, N.C.

Our winning Christmas cookie recipe features the flavors of a candy cane in a pretty cookie. Lori says that she found a chocolate version of this recipe some years ago, but her daughter doesn't like chocolate, so she adapted it to use a sugar cookie base. Lori tells us, "It's been a family hit every year," and we can see why.

CANDY CANE PINWHEELS

MAKES ABOUT 4½ DOZEN

Grind the peppermint candies in a food processor until they are pulverized.

- 3 cups all-purpose flour
- ¾ teaspoon baking powder
- ¼ teaspoon salt
- 16 tablespoons (2 sticks) unsalted butter, softened
- 1 cup sugar
- 1 large egg
- 1 teaspoon vanilla extract
- 1 teaspoon peppermint extract
- ½ cup finely ground peppermint candies (about 20)
- 6 drops red food coloring

1. Whisk flour, baking powder, and salt in bowl. With electric mixer on medium-high speed, beat butter and sugar until light and fluffy, about 2 minutes. Beat in egg until incorporated. Reduce speed to low, add flour mixture, and mix until dough forms, about 1 minute. Remove half of dough from bowl and reserve. Add extracts, candy, and food coloring to remaining dough and mix until combined.

2. Place reserved dough between 2 sheets of parchment paper and roll into 14 by 8-inch rectangle. Repeat with peppermint dough, then place on top of plain dough and press gently to adhere. With long side facing you, roll dough into log. Wrap dough in plastic wrap and refrigerate until firm, at least 2 hours or up to 3 days.

3. Adjust oven racks to upper-middle and lower-middle positions and heat oven to 375 degrees. Line 2 baking sheets with parchment paper. Slice chilled dough into ¼-inch rounds and place 1 inch apart on prepared baking sheets. Bake until edges are just golden, 12 to 14 minutes, switching and rotating sheets halfway through baking. Let cool 10 minutes on sheet, then transfer to wire rack and cool completely. Repeat with remaining dough. (Cookies can be stored in airtight container at room temperature for up to 1 week.)

Our winner features a sugar cookie base enlivened by a swirl of crushed peppermint candies.

Johanna Johnson
Scottsdale, Ariz.

Diane Nemitz
Ludington, Mich.

Lorraine Fina Stevenski
Clearwater, Fla.

CHOCOLATE-COVERED CHERRY COOKIES
MAKES ABOUT 2½ DOZEN

Johanna says: "When our daughter was in school in the 1970s, a friend made these for a class party. I've made them almost every year during the holidays ever since!" Don't overbake these cookies; they should be chewy.

Cookies
- 1½ cups all-purpose flour
- ½ cup Dutch-processed cocoa
- ¼ teaspoon baking powder
- ¼ teaspoon baking soda
- ¼ teaspoon salt
- 8 tablespoons (1 stick) unsalted butter, softened
- 1 cup sugar
- 1 large egg
- 1½ teaspoons vanilla extract

Chocolate-Cherry Topping
- 1 cup semisweet chocolate chips
- ½ cup sweetened condensed milk
- 2 (12-ounce) jars maraschino cherries, drained and stemmed, 2 tablespoons juice reserved

1. For the cookies: Whisk flour, cocoa, baking powder, baking soda, and salt in bowl; set aside. With electric mixer on medium-high speed, beat butter and sugar until light and fluffy, about 2 minutes. Beat in egg and vanilla until incorporated. Reduce speed to low, add flour mixture, and mix until dough forms, about 1 minute.

2. For the chocolate-cherry topping: Heat chocolate and milk in saucepan over low heat until chocolate is melted, about 5 minutes (mixture should have consistency of mayonnaise). Off heat, stir in reserved cherry juice. Cover and keep warm.

3. To finish: Adjust oven racks to upper-middle and lower-middle positions and heat oven to 350 degrees. Roll dough into 1-inch balls and place 2 inches apart on 2 rimmed baking sheets. Using thumb, make indentation in center of each cookie. Place 1 cherry in center of each cookie, then top with 1 teaspoon warm chocolate mixture. Bake until cookies are just set, 10 to 12 minutes, switching and rotating sheets halfway through baking. Transfer cookies to wire rack and cool completely. Repeat with remaining dough. (Cookies can be stored in airtight container at room temperature for up to 4 days.)

COCONUT SNOWDROPS
MAKES ABOUT 4 DOZEN

Diane says: "These cookies contain snowy mounds of coconut with an almond accent. They are perfect for a wintry afternoon in front of the fire with a nice, hot cup of tea." These buttery cookies will spread and fall during baking if the dough gets too warm. For the best texture, chill the dough well before forming the cookies and roll only half the dough at a time, keeping the other half in the refrigerator.

Cookies
- 16 tablespoons (2 sticks) unsalted butter, softened
- 1 cup granulated sugar
- ¼ cup packed light brown sugar
- 1 large egg plus 1 egg yolk
- 1 teaspoon vanilla extract
- 1 teaspoon coconut extract
- 2 cups all-purpose flour
- 2 cups sweetened, shredded coconut
- ½ cup finely chopped blanched almonds

Chocolate Filling
- ½ cup semisweet chocolate chips
- 2 tablespoons unsalted butter

1. For the cookies: With electric mixer on medium-high speed, beat butter and sugars until fluffy, about 2 minutes. Beat in egg, yolk, and extracts until incorporated, about 1 minute. Reduce speed to low; add flour, coconut, and almonds; mix until dough forms, about 1 minute. Cover bowl with plastic wrap and refrigerate until firm, at least 1 hour or up to 3 days.

2. Adjust oven racks to upper-middle and lower-middle positions and heat oven to 350 degrees. Line 2 baking sheets with parchment paper. Roll dough into ¾-inch balls and place 1 inch apart on prepared baking sheets. Bake until edges are just golden, 12 to 14 minutes, switching and rotating sheets halfway through baking. Let cool 10 minutes on sheets, then transfer to wire rack and cool completely. Repeat with remaining dough.

3. For the chocolate filling: Melt chocolate and butter in saucepan over low heat until smooth, about 5 minutes. Spread chocolate mixture on bottom of 1 cookie, then press bottom of second cookie onto chocolate to form sandwich. Repeat with remaining cookies and chocolate mixture. (Cookies can be stored in airtight container at room temperature for up to 4 days.)

PECAN TOFFEE SHORTBREAD STARS
MAKES ABOUT 2 DOZEN

Lorraine says: "I often dip my cookie cutters in red or green sugar so the edges look picture-perfect for the holidays. I wrap my cookies in cellophane bags and tie them with ribbons. I print a recipe card and attach it to each cookie bag."

- 1½ cups all-purpose flour
- ¼ cup cornstarch
- ¼ teaspoon salt
- 12 tablespoons (1½ sticks) unsalted butter, softened
- ¼ cup granulated sugar
- ¼ cup packed light brown sugar
- 2 teaspoons vanilla extract
- ½ cup mini semisweet chocolate chips
- 1 cup finely chopped pecans
- ½ cup Heath Toffee Bits (without chocolate)
  Confectioners' sugar for serving

1. Whisk flour, cornstarch, and salt in bowl; set aside. With electric mixer on medium-high speed, beat butter, sugars, and vanilla until smooth, about 1 minute. Reduce speed to low; add flour mixture, chocolate, pecans, and toffee; mix until dough forms, about 1 minute. Gather dough, wrap in plastic, and refrigerate until firm, at least 1 hour or up to 3 days.

2. Adjust oven racks to upper-middle and lower-middle positions and heat oven to 350 degrees. Line 2 baking sheets with parchment paper. On lightly floured work surface, roll half of dough into 11-inch circle, about ¼ inch thick. Using 3-inch star-shaped cookie cutter, cut out cookies, gathering and rerolling dough as necessary. Place cookies 1 inch apart on prepared baking sheets and bake until edges are golden brown, 12 to 14 minutes, switching and rotating sheets halfway through baking. Let cool 10 minutes on baking sheets, then transfer to wire rack and cool completely. Repeat with remaining dough. (Cookies can be stored in airtight container at room temperature for up to 1 week.)

Ask Cook's Country

WE'LL ANSWER ANY QUESTION YOU THROW AT US!

PREMELTED CHOCOLATE

I have seen packets of premelted unsweetened chocolate in the grocery store. Can this product be used interchangeably with melted and cooled chocolate?

Valerie Gardner
Chubbuck, Idaho

Nestlé's Choco Bake Pre-Melted Unsweetened Chocolate Flavor ($3.49 for 8 ounces) looks like melted chocolate, but it's actually an emulsion of cocoa powder and vegetable oils. Each box contains eight 1-ounce packets of liquid chocolate product that can be directly substituted for each ounce of bar chocolate; each packet can also be substituted for 3 tablespoons of cocoa powder plus 1 tablespoon of shortening or oil.

To see how the product stacked up to real melted chocolate and cocoa powder, we made melted chocolate–based brownies and a cocoa-based chocolate cake. For the brownies, the bar chocolate produced "true chocolate flavor," while the Choco Bake was "a little sweet," with marginally less chocolate flavor. Tasters liked the "super-fudgy" texture of the Choco Bake brownies, a result of the extra oil in the product. The cake yielded similar results. The cocoa version had deeper chocolate flavor, but the cake made with Choco Bake was praised for being "very moist." Our conclusion: Nestlé's Choco Bake is an acceptable substitute for melted chocolate, especially if you're willing to trade some flavor intensity for added moistness and convenience.

JUST SQUEEZE AND BAKE
Nestlé's premelted chocolate product is an acceptable option when you're short on time.

ORANGE PEELER

I recently saw an orange-peeling gadget in a home goods store. It had what looked like a knife on one end and a slightly curved hook on the other. Does this tool really work?

Prim Sawyer
Winchester, Mass.

Although peeling an orange by hand is simple enough, we're always looking for gadgets, like the Wingknife Orange Peeler you saw, that promise to make everyday jobs easier. As you mentioned, there's a plastic serrated blade at one end that's used for scoring or slicing through the rind. The opposite end is curved and used for removing the scored segments of the rind.

Working with room-temperature oranges (which are easier to peel than chilled fruit), feedback from testers was varied. The gadget didn't increase the peeling speed for anyone, and one left-handed tester found it especially difficult to maneuver. However, most testers were impressed with how neatly the Wingknife was able to do the job at hand. In our testing, hand-peeled fruit was often left a bit mangled, but the plastic guard underneath the blade of the Wingknife prevents it from cutting the orange's flesh, thus resulting in perfectly peeled fruit. While this certainly isn't an essential kitchen tool, the Wingknife peeler does work, and costs only about three dollars.

EASY PEELING
It may not be any quicker, but the Wingknife Orange Peeler does the job without mangling the fruit.

HAM PRIMER

How do city hams differ from fresh and country varieties?

Laura Ladd
Ahoskie, N.C.

There are three basic kinds of ham, all of which come from the hind leg of a pig: fresh ham, which is the leg in its raw state, and country and city hams, which are both cured. Country hams are dry-cured (salted, spiced, smoked, and aged for up to a year), and city hams are wet-cured by brining or injection with a saltwater solution that typically includes sugar and other seasonings, such as liquid smoke.

City hams are usually sold fully cooked and are categorized by the amount of water added to their original weight during curing. We prefer those labeled "ham" or "ham with natural juices," which contain little added water and therefore have a less spongy texture.

City hams are sold either spiral-sliced or uncut and with or without the bone. Spiral-sliced hams are easy to carve, but it's easier to put a thick glaze or crust on an uncut ham. And while boneless hams are also easy to carve, they are compressed to a solid mass after the bone is removed, which can result in a "processed" texture. We recommend buying a bone-in ham.

NONREACTIVE COOKWARE

Your recipe for lemon curd calls for using a nonreactive saucepan and bowl. What type of pans and bowls are nonreactive?

Jon Turner
Via e-mail

The reactivity of cookware refers to the potential chemical interaction between food and metal. Aluminum, copper, and iron are the most reactive metals; they commonly react with acidic ingredients such as lemon juice, tomatoes, vinegar, and wine. The acid in these ingredients causes the release of metal molecules from the pan's surface into the food, causing the food to taste metallic and become discolored. Aluminum also reacts with highly alkaline foods like dried beans, corn, and egg whites. Nonreactive materials include stainless steel, glass, and ceramics. Because aluminum is prized for its efficiency in conducting heat, manufacturers produce nonreactive anodized aluminum pans by altering the aluminum's molecular structure. The surface of these harder, denser, and less porous pans has been sealed, which prevents the release of aluminum molecules during cooking. Another good nonreactive option is a pan with an aluminum core that is "clad" (or bonded) with nonreactive (and very durable) stainless steel on the outside.

SKINNING HAZELNUTS

What's the best way to remove the skin of a hazelnut?

Jeanne Berry
Via e-mail

Over the years, we've read several tips that promise the quick and easy removal of the bitter dark brown skins on hazelnuts. Most methods fall into one of two camps: roasting the nuts to dehydrate their skins before rubbing them off (with anything from a dish towel to a mesh onion bag to a wire rack) or blanching the nuts in a water-and–baking soda solution to similarly loosen the skins for easy removal.

We found that roasting removed only half the skins, no matter what was used to rub them off. Blanching the nuts in the baking soda solution worked much better. We put 1 cup of nuts in a large saucepan with 3 cups of water and ¼ cup of baking soda and brought the mixture to a boil for four minutes. The nuts were then drained, rinsed, brushed with a towel to free the skins, and browned for 15 minutes in a 350-degree oven to remove excess moisture.

Wondering if the baking soda played an essential role, we tried the same method but omitted the baking soda. Sure enough, the skins were almost impossible to remove. The reason? The alkaline nature of baking soda extracts acidic tannins from the skins, weakening and softening them for easy removal.

ROASTED
Roasting hazelnuts in the oven loosens some of the skin, but patches will remain.

BLANCHED
Blanching the hazelnuts in water and baking soda loosens their skins for easy removal.

To ask us a cooking question, visit **CooksCountry.com/ emailus.** You can also write to Ask Cook's Country, P.O. Box 470739, Brookline, MA 02447. See if you can stump us!

Lost Recipes MORAVIAN SUGAR CAKE

A crunchy caramelized brown sugar topping and tender potato-based dough make this North Carolina coffee cake unique.

Using a Pyrex baking pan (instead of metal) helps prevent the bottom of the coffee cake from overbrowning.

One of the best things about growing up in Winston-Salem, N.C., was enjoying a big piece of Moravian sugar cake from Winkler Bakery every Christmas morning. Sugar cake, also known locally as sugar bread, is a coffee cake made by enriching a bread dough (made with yeast, mashed potatoes, milk, eggs, flour, and butter) with bursts of buttery brown sugar through a unique shaping method: The unbaked dough is indented by hand to form small craters for a topping of light brown sugar, butter, and cinnamon to nestle into during baking.

In 1766, a group of Moravians (Protestants with roots in the present-day Czech Republic) left Bethlehem, Pa., and established Salem, N.C. Many religious communities of the era were centered around farming, but the Moravians in Salem focused on producing consumer goods like furniture and candles, as well as food. The Moravians have a long history as bakers, and in 1808 Brother Christian Winkler took over the bakery that now bears his name and still uses the original wood-fired beehive oven. Today, employees at Winkler Bakery wear period costumes and bake an array of cookies, cakes, and breads using traditional Moravian recipes and techniques.

Now that I live in Boston, I wanted to develop a recipe that rivaled the sugar cake I still eat back home every Christmas. I found a few basic recipes and got to work. Curious as to what the potato was adding to the dough, I prepared

cakes with and without it. The potato-free cake was dry, tough, and overwhelmingly yeasty, whereas the cake made with potato was moist, tender, and rich. The potato adds moisture to a fairly lean dough (my working recipe contained just one egg and 4 tablespoons of butter), creating a slightly chewy, breadlike texture. But I disliked having to make mashed potatoes before I made my coffee cake. Instant potatoes were a logical substitution, and they provided a comparably light texture and round flavor without the work of making a mash.

As for the topping, most recipes call for brown sugar to be sprinkled over the dough before a stream of melted butter is poured on top, but toppings prepared this way baked up greasy in some areas and lean in others. Striving for a more homogenous topping, I melted the butter and brown sugar together, but this time the topping baked up tough and candied. I had better luck by combining cold butter, brown sugar, and cinnamon into a streusel-like mixture to sprinkle over the dimpled dough. After 20 minutes in the oven, the cake emerged golden and bubbly, but the top was smooth, devoid of the signature sugary craters. I was disappointed when I left the kitchen to do more research, but when I returned 30 minutes later, the cake had transformed itself! The hot sugar mixture had cooled and sunk into the cake, creating the characteristic pocketed appearance.

This rich and chewy Moravian Sugar Cake is my new go-to coffee cake all year long. –**Cali Rich**

MORAVIAN SUGAR CAKE
SERVES 12
While potato flakes or potato buds both work well here, avoid potato granules, which can have off-flavors.

- 3/4 cup milk, heated to 110 degrees
- 1 1/2 teaspoons rapid-rise or instant yeast
- 1/3 cup granulated sugar
- 1/4 cup instant potato flakes
- 1/2 teaspoon salt
- 4 tablespoons unsalted butter, softened; plus 6 tablespoons unsalted butter, cut into 1/2-inch pieces and chilled
- 1 large egg
- 2 cups all-purpose flour
- 1 1/2 cups packed light brown sugar
- 1 tablespoon ground cinnamon

1. Adjust oven rack to middle position and heat oven to 200 degrees. Maintain temperature for 10 minutes, then turn off oven. Grease medium bowl and 13 by 9-inch Pyrex baking pan.

2. Stir milk and yeast together until yeast is dissolved. In bowl of standing mixer fitted with paddle attachment, mix yeast mixture, granulated sugar, potato flakes, salt, softened butter, egg, and flour on medium speed until smooth and shiny, about 2 minutes. Transfer dough to prepared bowl, cover with plastic, and place in warm oven. Let rise until doubled in size, about 30 minutes.

3. Press dough into prepared pan according to photo 1 at right. Cover pan with plastic and place in warm oven. Let rise until doubled in size, about 30 minutes. Meanwhile, combine chilled butter, brown sugar, and cinnamon according to photo 2.

4. Remove pan from oven and heat oven to 375 degrees. Following photos 3 and 4, indent surface of dough and sprinkle with brown sugar mixture. Once oven is fully heated, bake until topping is bubbling and deep brown, 18 to 22 minutes. Let cool 30 minutes. Serve. (Cooled cake can be wrapped with plastic and stored at room temperature for up to 2 days.)

Make Ahead: After pressing dough into baking pan and covering, dough can be refrigerated for up to 24 hours. When ready to bake, let sit at room temperature for 30 minutes before proceeding with step 4.

Kitchen Know-How
HOW TO SHAPE SUGAR CAKE

Creating the signature sugary craters of Moravian Sugar Cake requires a little technique. Here's how we do it.

1. Press the dough into an even layer in a greased 13 by 9-inch baking pan and let rise.
2. Using your fingers, work the chilled butter into the brown sugar and cinnamon until the mixture resembles coarse meal.
3. Using floured fingertips, make shallow indentations over the entire surface of the risen dough.
4. Evenly sprinkle the brown sugar mixture over the indented dough.

We take this cocktail party favorite from the stovetop to the slow cooker—and try to keep it tender.

These rich meatballs are browned in the oven to cook off most of the grease before they're added to the slow cooker. The sauce is enriched with sour cream and fresh dill.

Swedish meatballs have long been standard cocktail party fare, and for good reason: They're easy to eat off a toothpick in a crowd, and they look appetizing set out in a chafing dish. These meatballs are typically made with ground beef and pork; bound with egg; seasoned with allspice, nutmeg, and dill; and served in a thick sauce enriched with sour cream. The problem with Swedish meatballs is in making them. Rolling and browning dozens of little meatballs and then building a sauce leaves little time to get everything (including the host) ready before company arrives.

Enter the slow cooker. My research turned up several slow-cooker Swedish meatball recipes that promise perfectly cooked meatballs made in and served right out of the slow cooker—all the cook has to do is form the meatballs, drop them raw into the cooker with some broth and flour, and walk away while everything cooks together. I tried a few of these recipes, and the results were horrible. The meatballs were gray and hard as marbles, and the sauce was bland, watery, and greasy.

Determined to make this dish work in the slow cooker, I took another look at the meatballs themselves. I started by mixing the ground beef and pork with egg, spices, and sautéed onion. Since greasy sauce was a big problem in my early tests, I knew I needed to precook the meatballs to render some of their fat before they went into the slow cooker. Browning 60 little meatballs in my skillet was messy and time-consuming, so I decided to shift gears. I arranged the raw meatballs on a rack set over a rimmed baking sheet and popped them into a hot oven. After about 15 minutes, the meatballs were nicely browned and had left most of their fat on the bottom of the pan. But they were still tough.

Many Italian meatball recipes incorporate a panade (bread or bread crumbs soaked in milk) to help keep the meatballs tender. Since these were Swedish meatballs, I saw this as an opportunity to add more Swedish flavors by using rye bread flavored with caraway, a spice popular throughout Scandinavia. My tasters loved how the rye panade made the meatballs both tender and more Swedish in flavor.

The sauce came together quickly. I started with a base of a flour-and-butter roux (for thickening) and beef broth, which cooked down to the perfect consistency to coat the meatballs. For a meatier flavor, I turned to an ingredient the test kitchen often uses to enrich soups, stews, and sauces: soy sauce. Just 2 tablespoons gave the sauce much more backbone without overpowering the other flavors. After mixing in the sour cream at the end of cooking—any earlier and it separated and became clumpy—I had tender, full-flavored meatballs in a rich, well-seasoned sauce, all prepared in the convenience of my slow cooker.

–Diane Unger

SWEDISH COCKTAIL MEATBALLS SERVES 10 TO 12

A 1¼-inch ice-cream scoop makes it easy to form these cocktail-sized meatballs. If you are keeping the meatballs warm in step 4, do not fully cover the slow cooker or the sauce will break.

- 6 tablespoons unsalted butter
- 2 onions, minced
- 4 slices caraway-rye bread, crusts removed, torn into pieces
- 3½ cups low-sodium beef broth
- 1 cup sour cream
- 2 large egg yolks
- ½ teaspoon ground allspice
- ¼ teaspoon ground nutmeg
- ½ teaspoon salt
- ½ teaspoon pepper
- 1 pound 90 percent lean ground beef
- 1 pound ground pork
- ½ cup all-purpose flour
- 2 tablespoons soy sauce
- 2 teaspoons minced fresh dill

1. Adjust oven rack to middle position and heat oven to 475 degrees. Melt 1 tablespoon butter in large skillet over medium-high heat. Cook onions until softened, about 8 minutes; transfer to large bowl. Add bread, ¼ cup broth, ¼ cup sour cream, yolks, allspice, nutmeg, salt, and pepper to bowl with onions and mash with fork until smooth. Add beef and pork and knead with hands until well combined.

2. Form mixture into 1¼-inch meatballs (you should have about 60 meatballs) and arrange on wire rack set inside rimmed baking sheet. Bake until lightly browned, about 15 minutes. Transfer to slow cooker.

3. Melt remaining butter in large skillet over medium heat. Whisk in flour and cook until beginning to brown, about 3 minutes. Slowly whisk in remaining broth, bring to boil, and transfer to slow cooker. Cover and cook on low until meatballs are tender and sauce is slightly thickened, 4 to 5 hours.

4. Transfer ½ cup sauce from slow cooker to small bowl. Whisk in remaining sour cream, soy sauce, and dill; gently stir into slow cooker. Serve. (If desired, meatballs can be held in slow cooker on low, partially covered, for 1 to 2 hours. Stir meatballs occasionally, adding up to 2 tablespoons water as needed to thin sauce.)

Make Ahead: Meatballs and sauce can be prepared and refrigerated separately for up to 3 days. To finish, transfer meatballs to slow cooker. Microwave sauce on high power, stirring every 30 seconds, until heated through, about 3 minutes. Pour sauce over meatballs and heat with slow cooker on low until heated through.

Building Better Flavor

We use a milk-and-bread panade to help keep our Swedish Meatballs tender. Rye bread flavored with caraway seeds gives these meatballs a Swedish-inspired flavor.

SECRET INGREDIENT

Make It a Meal

These tiny meatballs can also be served as a main course. To turn the Swedish Meatballs into a main course, in step 2 simply roll the meat mixture into 2-inch meatballs (you should have about 35 meatballs) and proceed with the recipe as directed. When spooned over hot buttered egg noodles or steamed white rice, these larger meatballs will serve 6 to 8.

Recipe Makeover CHICKEN PARMESAN

An unlikely ingredient (mayonnaise) and doubtful technique (partial breading) deliver a surprisingly good rendition of this high-fat Italian classic.

With its fried exterior and blanket of melted cheese, chicken Parmesan seems a perfect candidate for slimming down. But when I tried several lower-fat recipes, I wasn't pleased with what I found. Most offered a tiny portion size. All were scantily clad in a crust of store-bought bread crumbs or cracker crumbs that either fell away from the meat or turned to mush at first contact with tomato sauce. And the coating of melted cheese was either plasticky (nonfat cheese doesn't melt well) or skimpy. I had a lot of work to do.

Classic chicken Parmesan begins with dredging chicken cutlets in flour, eggs, and bread crumbs before frying them in oil. My first task was to use a full-sized 5-ounce cutlet and replace the flour-and-egg binding with something sticky that had less fat and calories. Plain egg whites didn't adhere without the flour, and neither buttermilk, low-fat milk, nor reduced-fat sour cream was a strong enough glue for the bread crumbs. A small amount of fat-free mayonnaise worked much better as a binder.

The test kitchen's oven-frying method (which involves lightly misting the breaded cutlets with cooking spray) allowed me to cut out most of the oil, but the cutlets weren't crispy. Fresh bread crumbs tasted better than stale crumbs from the supermarket, but they weren't crunchy enough. Dry-toasting the bread crumbs in the oven made the coating sandy, but toasting them in a skillet with just 1 tablespoon of oil made the exterior very crisp, and elevating the breaded cutlets on a wire rack in the oven helped it stay that way.

Since jarred tomato sauce contains a lot of sugar and oil, it was healthier to make a quick, full-flavored homemade version. But pouring the sauce on top of my "fried" cutlets made the coating soggy. Adding all the sauce to the plate before placing the cutlet on top kept the top nice and crispy but didn't feel right. Instead, I spooned half of the sauce on top of each cutlet during the last few minutes of baking and saved the other half for the plate. The coating remained crunchy, and the cutlets now looked like real chicken Parmesan.

As for the cheese, I wasn't going to follow other low-fat recipes and skimp: Chicken Parm needs plenty of melted cheese. One ounce of part-skim mozza-

rella per cutlet was the right amount, but a sprinkling of shredded cheese looked too sparse. Thinly sliced mozzarella from the deli nicely blanketed each cutlet.

Could I trim more calories and fat? With a nice amount of sauce on the plate, I wondered if tasters would miss the bottom breading. To my surprise, no one did. In fact, tasters thought my breading-on-the-top cutlets were even crisper. –Meredith Butcher

LOW-FAT CHICKEN PARMESAN
SERVES 4

If part-skim mozzarella isn't available at the deli counter, buy a 16-ounce block and cut it into 1-ounce slices. You will need cooking spray for this recipe.

Marinara
- 1 teaspoon olive oil
- 3 garlic cloves, minced
- 1/2 teaspoon dried oregano
- 1 tablespoon tomato paste
- 1/4 cup red wine
- 1 (14.5-ounce) can diced tomatoes
- 1 (8-ounce) can tomato sauce
- 1 tablespoon chopped fresh basil
  Salt and pepper

Chicken
- 2 slices hearty white sandwich bread, torn into large pieces
- 1 tablespoon olive oil
- 2 tablespoons grated Parmesan cheese
- 1/2 teaspoon salt
- 4 teaspoons fat-free mayonnaise
- 4 boneless, skinless chicken breasts (5 ounces each), trimmed and pounded 1/2 inch thick
- 4 (1-ounce) slices deli part-skim mozzarella cheese

1. For the marinara: Heat oil in large saucepan over medium heat until shimmering. Cook garlic, oregano, and tomato paste until fragrant, about 1 minute. Stir in wine and simmer until nearly evaporated, about 1 minute. Add tomatoes and tomato sauce and cook until slightly thickened and reduced to 2½ cups, about 10 minutes. Off heat, stir in basil and season with salt and pepper. Keep warm.

2. For the chicken: Adjust oven rack to middle position and heat oven to 475 degrees. Pulse bread in food processor until coarsely ground. Heat oil in large nonstick skillet over medium heat until shimmering. Add bread crumbs and cook, stirring often, until golden brown, about 6 minutes. Off heat, stir in Parmesan and salt; transfer to shallow dish and let cool.

3. Spray wire rack with cooking spray and set inside rimmed baking sheet. Following photos 1 and 2 at right, spread mayonnaise over top of cutlets and dip into crumb mixture. Arrange crumb-side up on prepared rack and mist with cooking spray. Bake until crumbs are dark golden brown, about 8 minutes.

4. Top each cutlet with ¼ cup marinara and 1 slice mozzarella. Bake until cheese has melted and chicken is cooked through, about 5 minutes. Spoon ¼ cup marinara evenly over each plate and top with chicken. Serve, passing remaining sauce at table.

Kitchen Know-How
BREADING CHICKEN CUTLETS

Coating just one side of the cutlet with fat-free mayonnaise and bread crumbs helped keep the chicken crisp.

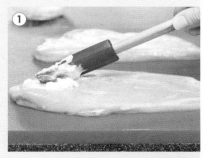

1. Spread 1 teaspoon of fat-free mayonnaise over the top of each chicken cutlet.
2. Press the chicken cutlet, mayonnaise-side down, into the toasted bread crumb mixture until the crumbs adhere.

Unlike most reduced-fat recipes for chicken Parmesan, ours doesn't compromise on the portion size—or the amount of cheese.

Ham and Bean Soup

Served with bread and a salad, this hearty soup makes a satisfying main course.

Two Hams Are Better Than One

For an intensely flavorful soup with meaty chunks of ham, we use a combination of smoked ham hocks and ham steak.

SMOKED HAM HOCK

HAM STEAK

What's the best way to add more heft (and more ham) to this old-fashioned soup?

Ham and bean soup had very humble beginnings. The simplest recipes are nothing more than dried beans and ham hocks simmered in water until the beans are tender and the ham has transformed the water into a smoky broth. A stray carrot or onion provides a bit more flavor, but that's about it. This recipe is the perfect example of making something from almost nothing.

While I admire the thrift behind this approach, my pantry at home is rarely so bare. And I do have one serious complaint about this make-do recipe: The soup is not terribly meaty. I wanted a heartier version with serious chunks of ham—something I could serve as a main course for dinner.

Thinking I could get both smoke and meat into this soup from one source, I replaced the ham hocks (which are mostly bone and gristle) with a ham steak. While it provided nice chunks of meat, the ham steak wasn't nearly as smoky as the hocks, so the broth was pretty bland. I decided to try a combination of the ham hocks for smoke flavor and ham steak for meaty chunks. I simmered the soup for an hour with both the hocks and diced ham steak. I had smoky flavor and lots of ham—but the ham tasted bland and the soup was overly salty.

To improve the flavor of the ham, I tried first sautéing it and then simmering it in the soup, which gave it a caramelized flavor that tasters enjoyed. With the ham problem fixed, I turned my attention to the saltiness issue. I had been following the lead of most modern recipes and using chicken broth for added flavor, but even low-sodium store-bought broth comes with added salt. In an effort to tame the salt, I tried switching to water, but the soup tasted flat. Ultimately, a blend of water and broth was just right.

Dried navy beans are the classic choice for ham and bean soup. When I tried to fully cook them right in the soup pot, the vegetables and meat turned to mush by the time the beans had softened. The texture of the beans also suffered—some beans burst open while others remained undercooked. For this recipe, I found it best to soak the dried beans overnight. This shortened their cooking time by at least 30 minutes. Once cooked, the texture of the soaked beans was firm but creamy.

For vegetables, I sautéed onion, carrots, celery, and garlic with the ham, which gave them the same deep, caramelized flavor. Fresh thyme added a welcome herbal note. Tasters thought the soup needed something to brighten up and balance the robust flavors. A few tablespoons of red wine vinegar, preferred by tasters over cider and white wine vinegars, provided the acidity my soup needed. **–Kelley Baker**

HAM AND BEAN SOUP
SERVES 6 TO 8

To speed up their cooking time, soak the beans in cold water for at least 8 hours (or up to 24 hours) before cooking. (See box below for a quick soaking method.)

- 2 tablespoons vegetable oil
- 1 pound ham steak, patted dry and diced
- 1 onion, chopped
- 3 carrots, peeled and chopped
- 2 celery ribs, chopped
- 6 garlic cloves, minced
- 4 cups low-sodium chicken broth
- 6 cups water
- 2 smoked ham hocks
- 1 pound dried navy beans, soaked overnight (see note)
- 2 teaspoons minced fresh thyme
- 1/2 teaspoon pepper
- 3 tablespoons red wine vinegar

1. Heat oil in Dutch oven over medium heat until just smoking. Add diced ham and cook until browned, about 3 minutes. Add onion, carrots, and celery and cook until softened, about 8 minutes. Stir in garlic and cook until fragrant, about 30 seconds. Stir in broth, water, hocks, and beans. Bring to boil, then reduce heat to medium-low and simmer until beans are completely tender and soup is slightly thickened, 1¼ to 1½ hours.

2. Remove hocks from pot. (If desired, let cool 5 minutes, then shred meat and add to soup.) Stir in thyme, pepper, and vinegar. Serve.

Make Ahead: This soup can be refrigerated for several days, but the beans will continue to soak up liquid. If the soup becomes too thick, stir in ¼ cup water at a time until the consistency is to your liking. Simmer the soup over medium-low heat until it's hot. Serve.

Soaking in a Hurry

When we need to soften beans in a hurry (or forget to start soaking them the night before), we use this shortcut method. Cover the beans with 3 inches of cold water in a medium saucepan. Bring to a boil, cover, and remove the pot from the heat. Let the beans stand for an hour, then drain them and cook as directed.

Beer-Batter Cheese Bread

I always have a hard time with beer-batter cheese bread. The loaves taste more like leftover beer than cheese and are so greasy I feel like scrubbing down after eating just one slice. –Kathy Griffin, Natick, Mass.

Nothing warms up the house like the smell of baking bread—but making a yeasted loaf from scratch can take half the day. Luckily, there are quick breads, like beer-batter cheese bread, that can be on the table in less than an hour. The basic recipe for this bread is simple: Just stir together flour, sugar, cheese, salt, beer, and baking powder; scrape the batter into a loaf pan; pour melted butter on top (to create a rich and craggy crust); and bake. There are no long rises, kneading, or hassle. Best of all, the beer gives this bread a hearty flavor.

Unfortunately, there were a lot of problems with the recipes I found. Many loaves tasted sour, like stale beer, while others had negligible cheese flavor. And some breads were so greasy that I had to pass out extra napkins at each tasting. I wanted a lighter loaf of bread enhanced with the yeasty flavor of beer and a big hit of cheese. And I wanted it to be as easy as advertised.

To test beer flavor, I made two loaves, using an inexpensive American lager in one and a dark ale in the other. The dark ale tasted great in a glass, but its strong flavor turned bitter when baked in the bread. The mild domestic lager (Budweiser and Miller Genuine Draft were our favorites in a later tasting) provided a clean, subtle grainy flavor without any sourness at all. And while a few recipes specifically called for room-temperature beer, I found no discernible difference between breads baked with warm or cold beer.

Mild cheddar is typically the cheese of choice in this recipe, but no matter how much I used—up to 3 cups for a single loaf—the flavor was, well, mild. I turned to more assertive cheeses like Gruyère, smoked Gouda, and extra-sharp cheddar. The bolder cheeses let me get away with using less (about two cups per loaf), so the bread was less greasy. Since my tasters professed a preference for biting into pockets of cheese in the bread, I shredded half the cheese and diced the rest for added texture.

While some of the greasiness was gone, the loaves still felt too stodgy and heavy. Increasing the amount of baking powder helped lighten the crumb a little, but I knew that pouring melted butter over the batter before baking—which creates the beautiful crust—was part of the problem. Cutting back the butter from a full stick to half a stick made the loaf considerably lighter while still producing that craggy crust. I finally had a Beer-Batter Cheese Bread that was as easy to eat as it was to make.

–Diane Unger

Pouring melted butter over the batter creates the crunchy, craggy top crust of this bread.

BEER-BATTER CHEESE BREAD

MAKES ONE 9-INCH LOAF
Insert the toothpick in a few spots when testing for doneness; it may hit a pocket of cheese, which resembles uncooked batter on the toothpick. Strongly flavored beers make the bread bitter, so mild American lagers like Budweiser work best here.

- 8 ounces Gruyère cheese, 4 ounces shredded and 4 ounces cut into 1/4-inch cubes
- 3 cups all-purpose flour
- 3 tablespoons sugar
- 4 teaspoons baking powder
- 1 1/2 teaspoons salt
- 1/2 teaspoon pepper
- 1 (12-ounce) light-bodied beer, such as Budweiser (see note)
- 4 tablespoons unsalted butter, melted

1. Adjust oven rack to middle position and heat oven to 375 degrees. Grease 9 by 5-inch loaf pan.

2. Combine shredded and cubed cheese, flour, sugar, baking powder, salt, and pepper in large bowl. Stir in beer and mix until well combined. Pour into loaf pan, spreading batter to corners. Drizzle melted butter evenly over top of batter.

3. Bake until deep golden brown and toothpick inserted into center of loaf comes out clean, 45 to 50 minutes. Cool bread in pan for 5 minutes, then turn out onto rack. Cool completely and slice as desired. (Although this bread can be kept in an airtight container at room temperature for up to 3 days, after the second day the bread is best toasted.)

BEER-BATTER BREAD WITH SMOKED GOUDA AND BACON

Follow recipe for Beer-Batter Cheese Bread, substituting 8 ounces smoked Gouda for Gruyère. Stir 8 slices bacon, cooked until crisp and crumbled, into bowl with cheese.

BEER-BATTER BREAD WITH CHEDDAR AND JALAPEÑO

Follow recipe for Beer-Batter Cheese Bread, substituting 8 ounces extra-sharp cheddar for Gruyère. Stir 2 seeded and minced jalapeño chiles into bowl with cheese.

Visit us online!
For a free Everything-Bagel Beer-Batter Cheese Bread recipe, visit **CooksCountry.com** and click on **Cook's Country Extra.**

Cider-Baked Ham

I recently prepared a recipe for cider-baked ham, and although it looked stunning, it didn't have any cider flavor. Is there a way to make a ham that tastes as good as it looks?

–Peggy Ann Hoke, Thurmont, Md.

1. Soaking the ham in spice-infused cider lends a concentrated flavor to the ham.
2. Baking the ham with a cup of cider in the oven bag keeps the meat moist and lends even more cider flavor.
3. Brushing the ham with a sticky cider reduction provides big apple flavor and a base for the crust.
4. Pressing a mixture of brown sugar and pepper onto the ham gives the exterior a spicy-sweet, crackly crust.

A big, smoky ham glazed with sweet apple cider and studded with cloves certainly sounds great. But the reality, as Peggy Ann found out, is that most cider-baked hams are lacking in apple flavor. And most recipes call for frequent basting, which is a lot of work for a ham with little cider character. Could I develop a relatively hands-off technique that would infuse my ham with big apple flavor?

I quickly discovered that I preferred an uncut cured ham (as opposed to a spiral-cut ham) for this recipe, as uncut ham has a fat layer that can be trimmed and scored to give the glaze something to hang on to. The test kitchen's method for cooking cured ham is to enclose it in an oven bag to help retain moisture and then bake it in a relatively cool oven until the interior reaches 100 degrees. Then we take off the bag, crank up the heat, and repeatedly baste the ham until a thick, glossy coating forms. This gave me a nice-looking ham with almost no apple flavor. Adding cider to the oven bag helped keep the ham moist, but it didn't contribute much in the way of apple flavor. Looking for more cider punch, I tried marinating the ham in cider overnight. After several tests, I determined that just four hours in the cider was enough time to add significant apple flavor.

But I still needed to work on the glaze. The cider rolled right off the ham and required constant reapplication. Thicker apple jelly and apple butter coated the ham better than the cider, but they didn't provide the same fresh apple flavor. Reducing the cider to a syrupy state on the stovetop proved to be a much better solution; the reduced cider was sticky enough to cling to the ham in just one application, meaning that I didn't have to continually baste my ham, and it provided superior apple flavor. A little mustard added to the glaze provided a spicy contrast to the sweet cider. As a final touch, I concocted a simple brown sugar and pepper mixture to pat on the ham after the glaze was applied; this mixture caramelized into a crunchy, flavorful crust that provided a nice contrast to the tender meat.

Cider-baked hams are traditionally studded with cloves—one of the most potent spices in the world. But both powdered and whole cloves proved to be too harsh. Wondering if I could take the edge off of whole cloves by adding them to the cider marinade, I tossed a handful of cloves and a cinnamon stick (which always pairs well with apple) into the mix. This worked great, especially when I first dry-toasted the cloves and cinnamon in a skillet to release their flavor before adding the cider. Now this ham not only looked amazing but had deep cider flavor and a spicy crust.

–Cali Rich

CIDER-BAKED HAM
SERVES 16 TO 20

We prefer a bone-in, uncut, cured ham for this recipe, because the exterior layer of fat can be scored and helps create a nice crust. A spiral-sliced ham can be used instead, but there won't be much exterior fat, so skip the trimming and scoring in step 2. This recipe requires nearly a gallon of cider and a large oven bag. In step 4, be sure to stir the reduced cider mixture frequently to prevent scorching.

This ham's caramelized cider glaze and brown sugar and pepper crust make for an appealing contrast of textures.

1 cinnamon stick, broken into rough pieces
1/4 teaspoon whole cloves
13 cups apple cider
8 cups ice cubes
1 cured bone-in half ham (7 to 10 pounds), preferably shank end
2 tablespoons Dijon mustard
1 cup packed dark brown sugar
1 teaspoon pepper

1. Toast cinnamon and cloves in large saucepan over medium heat until fragrant, about 3 minutes. Add 4 cups cider and bring to boil. Pour spiced cider into large stockpot or clean bucket, add 4 more cups cider and ice, and stir until melted.

2. Meanwhile, remove skin from exterior of ham and trim fat to ¼-inch thickness. Score remaining fat at 1-inch intervals in crosshatch pattern. Transfer ham to container with chilled cider mixture (liquid should nearly cover ham) and refrigerate for at least 4 hours or up to 12 hours.

3. Discard cider mixture and transfer ham to large oven bag.

Add 1 cup fresh cider to bag, tie securely, and cut 4 slits in top of bag. Transfer to large roasting pan and let stand at room temperature for 1½ hours.

4. Adjust oven rack to lowest position and heat oven to 300 degrees. Bake ham until internal temperature registers 100 degrees, 1½ to 2½ hours. Meanwhile, bring remaining cider and mustard to boil in saucepan. Reduce heat to medium-low and simmer, stirring often, until mixture is very thick and reduced to ⅓ cup, about 1 hour.

5. Combine sugar and pepper in bowl. Remove ham from oven and let rest for 5 minutes. Increase oven temperature to 400 degrees. Roll back oven bag and brush ham with reduced cider mixture. Using hands, carefully press sugar mixture onto exterior of ham. Return to oven and bake until dark brown and caramelized, about 20 minutes. Transfer ham to cutting board, loosely tent with foil, and let rest 15 minutes. Carve and serve.

Mashed Potato Casserole

The last thing I want to do right before everyone sits down for my holiday meal is worry about mashing pounds of potatoes. Is there a way to avoid the last-minute fuss? –Joan Garner, Falmouth, Mass.

The appeal of mashed potato casserole is considerable, with the promise of fluffy, buttery, creamy potatoes nestled under a savory golden crust. And with all the mashing and mixing done beforehand, it's the perfect convenience dish during the holiday season—you can prepare this casserole a day in advance and just pop it in the oven before mealtime. But upon making several existing recipes, I found that most simply threw mashed potatoes into a casserole dish and baked them in the oven. The results were bland, gluey, dense potatoes that were definitely not worth the convenience.

To fix this recipe, I focused first on the choice of potato. I prepared casseroles with russet, Yukon Gold, and all-purpose potatoes and determined that russets were the least heavy of the lot. Heavy cream was much too rich for this dish, but whole milk tasted too lean. I split the difference with half-and-half, which helped to lighten the dish, but tasters weren't happy until I cut the half-and-half with chicken broth, which kept the potatoes moist and provided an even lighter texture.

Taking a cue from shepherd's pie (another recipe where mashed potatoes are baked), I tried beating eggs into the potato mixture. An egg or two helped a little, but it wasn't until I added four that I achieved the fluffy, airy texture I wanted. And since the potatoes were rising in the dish, the top crust was browning even better than before.

We usually like to mash potatoes with a potato ricer to guarantee a uniform, lump-free consistency, but since I had broken out my hand-held mixer to beat the eggs into the potatoes, I wondered if I could simplify things by using it to mash the potatoes. In the past, the test kitchen has found that hand-held mixers make mashed potatoes gluey, but that wasn't an issue here, because the eggs gave the casserole an airy lift.

Some recipes season the mashed potatoes with ingredients like dried mustard and thyme, but we preferred the sharpness of Dijon mustard and fresh garlic. Not only was this dish easy to make ahead of time, but my tasters agreed that these potatoes—with their creamy, light interior and crisp, brown crust—were now the star of the holiday table.

–Meredith Butcher

MASHED POTATO CASSEROLE SERVES 6 TO 8

The casserole may also be baked in a 13 by 9-inch pan.

- 4 pounds russet potatoes, peeled and cut into 1-inch chunks
- 1/2 cup half-and-half
- 1/2 cup low-sodium chicken broth
- 12 tablespoons (1 1/2 sticks) unsalted butter, cut into pieces
- 1 garlic clove, minced
- 2 teaspoons Dijon mustard
- 2 teaspoons salt
- 4 large eggs
- 1/4 cup finely chopped fresh chives

1. Adjust oven rack to upper-middle position and heat oven to 375 degrees. Bring potatoes and water to cover by 1 inch to boil in large pot over high heat. Reduce heat to medium and simmer until potatoes are tender, about 20 minutes.

2. Heat half-and-half, broth, butter, garlic, mustard, and salt in saucepan over medium-low heat until smooth, about 5 minutes. Keep warm.

3. Drain potatoes and transfer to large bowl. With electric mixer on medium-low speed, beat potatoes, slowly adding half-and-half mixture, until smooth and creamy, about 1 minute. Scrape down bowl; beat in eggs 1 at a time until incorporated, about 1 minute. Fold in chives.

4. Following photos 1 and 2 at right, transfer potato mixture to greased 2-quart baking dish. Bake until potatoes rise and begin to brown, about 35 minutes. Let cool 10 minutes. Serve.

Make Ahead: The baking dish with the potatoes can be covered with plastic and refrigerated for up to 24 hours. When ready to bake, let the casserole sit at room temperature for 1 hour. Increase baking time by 10 minutes.

Secrets to PERFECT MASHED POTATO CASSEROLE

1. The mashed potatoes will look very soupy when they are poured into the casserole dish. They will firm up and rise in the oven.
2. For better browning and an impressive presentation, use a fork to make a peaked design on top of the potato casserole.

Using a hand-held mixer to beat eggs into the mashed potatoes ensures that the casserole will rise to the occasion every time.

Perfecting Broiled Steaks

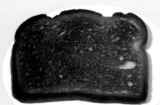

After one minute under a hot broiler, this bread is toast.

After one minute under a cold broiler, this bread isn't brown yet.

Every time I broil steaks, the results are disastrous. All I end up with are gray, steamed steaks and a kitchen full of smoke. What am I doing wrong? –Leslie Siggins, Framingham, Mass.

I usually rely on a red-hot skillet or my grill for putting a crusty sear on steaks, but I wondered if my oven broiler—which throws out a ton of heat—could do the job just as well. The promise of a perfectly cooked steak without a greasy stovetop or a trip outside to the grill was very attractive.

I adjusted my oven rack to the top position, preheated the broiler on "high," and threw a couple of strip steaks on the broiler pan. The results weren't pretty. Though some of the moisture and fat from the steaks drained through the broiler pan slits, much of it sat around the steaks, which caused the meat to steam and turn gray, with absolutely no char or crust. And if that wasn't bad enough, the drippings that made their way through the pan burned, filling the test kitchen with smoke.

Getting some color on the steaks was my first order of business. I quickly discovered that the broiler pan—not the broiler itself—was causing most of the problems. Because broiler pans are only about an inch tall, they don't bring steaks close enough to the broiler element to get a proper sear, even on the top oven rack. To remedy this, I brought in a 3-inch-deep disposable aluminum roasting pan, moved the oven rack down a notch, and set the steaks on a cooling rack placed over the pan. This brought the meat closer to the heat, where it could acquire a good sear. The cooling rack (which is more porous than the broiler-pan rack) also allowed surface moisture to immediately drain away.

Cooking the steaks evenly was another problem. Steaks that went directly from the refrigerator to the broiler had charred exteriors before the centers were done, no matter how many times I flipped them. Letting the steaks sit at room temperature for an hour before cooking helped, but it took too long. Instead, I started the steaks in a moderate oven to take the chill off. I removed them after 6 to 10 minutes, let them rest while the broiler heated, then cooked them as before. This method produced evenly cooked meat every time.

Only one problem remained: the smoke. The fat that was cooking out of the steaks was still burning on the bottom of the pan. To put a stop to the smoke, I tried adding water to the pan, but the steam it produced softened the crust I had worked so hard to create. I tried putting bread in the pan to absorb the grease before it had a chance to burn, but that idea (and bread) went up in smoke. I had much better results by covering the bottom of the pan with salt, which soaked up the grease and greatly minimized the smoke. Finally, I had crusty, charred steaks—and a good reason to use my broiler a lot more often. **–Diane Unger**

Our novel method produces broiled steaks that rival the best grilled steaks.

Perfectly Broiled Steaks

The first step to perfectly broiled steaks is knowing exactly how thick your steaks are. Using a ruler, measure each steak and then follow the guidelines below.

STEAK THICKNESS	PREBAKE	BROIL
1 inch	6 minutes	Turn steaks every 2 minutes
1½ inches	8 minutes	Turn steaks every 3 minutes
2 inches	10 minutes	Turn steaks every 4 minutes

Broiler Prep

Since oven-rack positioning varies greatly from model to model, we suggest you ensure correct positioning with a dry run before turning on your oven.

COLD SETUP: Before preheating your oven and with your oven racks adjusted to the upper-middle and lower-middle positions, place a wire rack on top of a 3-inch-deep disposable aluminum pan and place it on the upper-middle rack. Place the steaks on top of the rack and use a ruler to measure the distance between the top of the steaks and the heating element of the broiler. For optimal searing, there should be ½ inch to 1 inch of space.

MEASURE AND ADJUST: If there is more than 1 inch of space, here's how to close the gap: Elevate the aluminum pan by placing it on an inverted rimmed baking sheet; use a deeper-sided disposable aluminum pan; or stack multiple aluminum pans inside one another. If there's less than ½ inch of space, adjust the oven rack or use a shallower pan.

BROILED STEAKS

SERVES 4

To minimize smoking, be sure to trim as much exterior fat and gristle as possible from the steaks before cooking. Try to purchase steaks of a similar size and shape for this recipe. If you like your steaks well-done, continue cooking and flipping as directed in step 3 until the steaks reach the desired internal temperature.

- **4** tablespoons unsalted butter, softened
- **1** teaspoon minced fresh thyme
- **1** teaspoon Dijon mustard
  Salt and pepper
- **4** strip steaks, rib-eye steaks, or tenderloin steaks, 1 to 2 inches thick, trimmed (see note)

1. Adjust oven racks to upper-middle and lower-middle positions and heat oven to 375 degrees. Beat butter, thyme, mustard, ¼ teaspoon salt, and ¼ teaspoon pepper in bowl and refrigerate.

2. Spread 2 cups salt over bottom of 3-inch-deep disposable aluminum pan. Pat steaks dry with paper towels, season with salt and pepper, and transfer to wire rack. Set rack over aluminum pan and transfer to lower-middle oven rack. Cook 6 to 10 minutes (see "Perfectly Broiled Steaks" chart, "Prebake" column, page 14), then remove pan from oven. Flip steaks, pat dry with paper towels, and let rest 10 minutes.

3. Heat broiler. Transfer pan to upper-middle oven rack and broil steaks, flipping every 2 to 4 minutes (see "Perfectly Broiled Steaks" chart, "Broil" column, page 14), until meat registers 125 to 130 degrees (for medium-rare), 6 to 16 minutes. Transfer steaks to platter, top with reserved butter mixture, and tent with foil. Let rest 5 minutes. Serve.

The Rack Is Right

We prefer a roasting pan covered with a cooling rack to a standard broiler pan for this recipe. Here's why.

1. The narrow slits in the broiler-pan insert don't allow adequate drainage, leaving the steak to steam in its own juices and hindering crust development.

2. A rack set over a deep disposable aluminum pan allows the drippings to fall away from the steak, resulting in a well-developed crust. Salt in the pan absorbs grease and prevents smoking.

On the Side:
Green Beans Amandine

A bland lemon-butter sauce and soggy almonds are no way to treat green beans. We set out to revive this classic side dish.

When French cuisine first became popular in this country in the early 1960s, green beans amandine (also called "almondine") was one of the signature recipes. A simple dish of tender green beans tossed with crisp, toasted almonds and a light lemon-butter sauce, it was refined yet not intimidating. Unfortunately, the recipes I tried yielded limp beans swimming in pools of numbingly acidic sauce, with soft, pale almonds thrown on as an afterthought.

To build my own version of this iconic recipe, I saw no reason to deviate from the test kitchen's method for steaming the green beans with a little water in a covered skillet: Beans cooked this way were consistently crisp-tender. Most recipes pour 4 tablespoons of melted butter over 2 pounds of beans, but I had better results—and more

nutty flavor—using just 3 tablespoons of butter cooked until it was light brown. I tried toasting the almonds in the rich browned butter to enhance their flavor, but the butter burned by the time the almonds were toasted. Instead, I dry-toasted the almonds in the skillet before browning the butter. This produced a flavorful mixture of golden brown nuts and browned butter, which I could pour into a bowl while the beans cooked in the same skillet.

When I added the butter-and-almond mixture and 2 teaspoons of lemon juice to the cooked beans, the sharp lemon flavor overwhelmed the entire dish. Instead of simply reducing the amount of juice (I really wasn't using all that much), I wondered if I could temper its bite. I tried adding the lemon juice to the hot butter-and-almond mixture while the beans cooked, and

sure enough, the heat took the edge off the lemon juice, leaving behind a more subtle, balanced flavor. **–Cali Rich**

GREEN BEANS AMANDINE **SERVES 8**

Use a light-colored traditional skillet instead of a darker non-stick skillet for this recipe to easily monitor the butter's browning.

- **⅓** cup sliced almonds
- **3** tablespoons unsalted butter, cut into pieces
- **2** teaspoons lemon juice
- **2** pounds green beans, stem ends trimmed
- **½** cup water
  Salt

1. Toast almonds in large skillet over medium-low heat, stirring often, until just golden, about 6 minutes. Add butter and cook, stirring constantly, until butter is golden brown and has nutty

aroma, about 3 minutes. Transfer almond mixture to bowl and stir in lemon juice.

2. Add beans, water, and ½ teaspoon salt to empty skillet. Cover and cook, stirring occasionally, until beans are nearly tender, 8 to 10 minutes. Remove lid and cook over medium-high heat until liquid evaporates, 3 to 5 minutes. Off heat, add reserved almond mixture to skillet and toss to combine. Season with salt. Serve.

I'm Looking for a Recipe

READERS HELP READERS FIND RECIPES

We've Got Mail

Scores of readers sent us recipes in response to the request for Chocolate Cottage Cheese Drop Cookies in our February/March 2007 issue. We really liked the recipe sent by Sarah Vaughan (right). Go to CooksCountry.com and click **Looking for a Recipe** to find hundreds of recipes submitted by readers who responded to this and other recipe requests in previous issues of *Cook's Country*.

CHOCOLATE COTTAGE CHEESE DROP COOKIES Sarah Vaughan Waterville, Maine

MAKES ABOUT 5½ DOZEN

"I found the recipe for these moist and cakey cookies in a *Farm Journal* cookie cookbook. I love to bake, and every time I make these cookies I get rave reviews. Not only are they delicious, they are perfect for church luncheons or even the holidays, because the recipe produces such a big batch." Use small-curd, whole milk cottage cheese for this recipe.

2³/₄	cups all-purpose flour, sifted
¹/₂	cup cocoa powder
1	teaspoon baking powder
1	teaspoon baking soda
¹/₂	teaspoon salt
16	tablespoons (2 sticks) unsalted butter, softened
1³/₄	cups sugar
1	cup small-curd, whole milk cottage cheese
2	large eggs
1	teaspoon vanilla extract

INSTRUCTIONS:

1. Mix together flour, cocoa, baking powder, baking soda, and salt.

2. Cream butter and sugar on medium speed until light and fluffy. Add cottage cheese, eggs, and vanilla and blend well. Reduce speed to low and gradually add flour mixture to creamed mixture in 3 additions, beating well after each addition.

3. Drop level tablespoons of dough onto greased baking sheets. Bake in 350-degree oven for 12 to 14 minutes, or until no imprint remains when pressed lightly with finger. Cool on wire rack.

French Chew Candy

Years ago, my mother-in-law used to make French chew candy that would melt in your mouth. It was an off-white taffy that was pulled after cooking and then tightly covered and frozen in 4- to 6-inch-long coils. When you wanted a piece, you just whacked off the end of a frozen coil with the handle of a knife. (The coil would need to be in a small plastic bag, or the broken piece would fly across the kitchen!)

Stephanie Thompson
Parker City, Ind.

Texas Weiner Sauce

I grew up in Newburgh, N.Y., home of a hot dog called the Texas weiner, which comes with a special meat sauce. I've looked for a recipe for years without any luck. Does anybody know of one?

Jack Corwin
Villa Hills, Ky.

Ladrillos

I've seen rectangular bar cookies called *ladrillos* in several Mexican bakeries in Texas. They taste a little like graham crackers and look like gingerbread. I've tried to find a recipe online, but all I get are recipes for adobe bricks, not bar cookies. Can you help?

J.R. LeClerc
Via e-mail

Bienenstichkuchen

I've always wanted to find a recipe for a German dessert cake called *Bienenstichkuchen*. I remember it from my travels as being a delicious, light cake with mild honey flavor. In fact, I believe the name means "bee sting cake."

Andrew Kleeger
Norfolk, Va.

Date Bars

One of the few boxed mixes we had in our house was for Betty Crocker Date Bars. This was a comfort of my childhood that my mother used to crank out on especially cold winter days. After moving to the East Coast, I had great difficulty finding it in grocery stores and therefore ordered cases at a time directly from Betty Crocker for about a decade—until the time I went to reorder only to find they had discontinued the product altogether. I would love to find a recipe to fill this void from my childhood.

Val Giddings
Silver Spring, Md.

Today's Catch Baked Fish

There used to be a frozen fish product on the market called Today's Catch. It came with a recipe booklet that included a baked fish dish with tomatoes and white wine. I've searched high and low for this recipe. If you can find it, you'll be my hero for life. Thanks.

Lourdes Marquez
Tucson, Ariz.

Malted Wagon Wheels

My mother passed away three years ago, and we've been unable to locate our favorite childhood cookie recipe since. The dough was flavored with malt powder and cut out with the top of a 1-pound coffee can. The cookies were decorated to look like wagon wheels: After applying a layer of malt frosting, we put a chocolate chip in the center to serve as the hub and surrounded it with whole roasted almonds to look like spokes. I would greatly appreciate any help in locating this recipe.

Barbara Anderson
Maitland, Fla.

Vita Bread

During the late 1970s and early 1980s, I attended the University of Arizona. The cafeteria sold a dark, sweet wheat bread called vita bread, which could be purchased in a sandwich or alone with a side of butter and jam. I would love to have the recipe to make this bread that got me through my finals. Thank you.

Liz Finn
Via e-mail

Brahm's Black Pot

I was vacationing in Jackson Hole, Wyo., with a friend about 10 years ago and our search for sustenance one day led us to a little restaurant (I think it was named Anthony's) that looked like a log cabin and had only six or eight tables. I ordered a dish called Brahm's (or Brom's) black pot, which was a thick sirloin steak and a chicken breast served in a delicate brown gravy, with a side of pesto. I haven't seen it on a menu since, and I couldn't find the restaurant again when I later honeymooned in Jackson Hole. Have you ever heard of such a dish? Many thanks to the person who can satisfy my 10-year craving.

Brian Zupko
Marysville, Ohio

Aggression Cookies

Years ago I had a recipe for aggression cookies. The dough was mixed by hand, and the more you pounded, the better the cookies became—thus the name. I know brown sugar, butter, and oatmeal were used, but I can't remember the amounts of each or the remaining ingredients. My daughter loved making these, and now I want to teach my granddaughter. Thank you!

Janice Wing
Via e-mail

Caramel Popcorn

I used to make a recipe for easy caramel popcorn that I got from the Osseo, Minn., newspaper years ago. It was made with marshmallows that were melted in the microwave. I've had such a sweet tooth lately and would love to find this recipe!

Linda Dewall
Maple Grove, Minn.

Hoosier Corn Pone

About 60 years ago, my grandmother used to make a prize-winning cornmeal and flour cake. It was sweet-tasting, with a rather dense texture (instead of being light and crumbly). She baked it in a large glazed earthenware crock that gave it a thick, well-browned crust. The recipe has long been lost, but I still savor the taste of the pone in my mind! None of the conventional corn pone recipes I've made bear any resemblance to my grandmother's. Please help!

Warren Mauzy
Florham Park, N.J.

Mallow Bars

Back in the 1970s, I was given a recipe for mallow bars from an old edition of a King Arthur cookbook. They had a shortbread crust and a gelatin-based filling, but I can't remember what other ingredients were used. My grandchildren loved them, but I've been unable to make them since losing the recipe. Thank you for your help.

S.E. Azzara
Via e-mail

Are you looking for a special recipe? Or do you have a recipe a fellow *Cook's Country* reader is seeking? Post your requests and recipes by visiting **CooksCountry.com** and clicking on **Looking for a Recipe**. We'll share recipe requests and found recipes on CooksCountry.com and print as many as we can in the magazine. You may also write to us at Looking for a Recipe, Cook's Country, P.O. Box 470739, Brookline, MA 02447.

Find the Rooster!

A tiny version of this rooster has been hidden somewhere in the pages of this issue. If you find it, write to us with its location (plus your name and address) and you will be entered into a random drawing. The first correct entry drawn will receive the KitchenAid Classic Plus Stand Mixer (our test winner—see page 29), and the next five will each receive a complimentary one-year subscription to *Cook's Country*. To enter the contest, visit **CooksCountry.com/emailus** or write to us at Rooster, Cook's Country, P.O. Box 470739, Brookline, MA 02447. Entries are due by January 31, 2008.

Did you find the rooster in the October/November 2007 issue? It was hidden in the animal cracker photo on page 27. Beth Redman of Wellsburg, N.Y., spotted it and won an All-Clad Stainless Steel Slow Cooker.

EASY CHICKEN CACCIATORE

PASTA WITH TOMATO, BACON, AND ONION

**PORK TENDERLOIN MEDALLIONS
WITH BROWN RICE, SAGE, AND WALNUTS**

MAPLE-GINGER GLAZED CHICKEN

PASTA WITH TOMATO, BACON, AND ONION SERVES 4

Top with grated Romano or Parmesan cheese if desired.

- 6 slices bacon, chopped
- 1 onion, chopped fine
- 1 garlic clove, minced
- 1/2 teaspoon red pepper flakes
- 2 (14.5-ounce) cans diced tomatoes
  Salt
- 1 pound spaghetti or linguine
- 1/4 cup chopped fresh parsley

1. Bring 4 quarts water to boil in large pot. Cook bacon in large nonstick skillet over medium-high heat until crisp, about 5 minutes. Transfer bacon to paper towel–lined plate and pour off all but 2 tablespoons fat. Add onion to skillet and cook until softened, about 5 minutes. Add garlic and pepper flakes and cook until fragrant, about 30 seconds. Add tomatoes and simmer until slightly thickened, about 10 minutes.

2. Add 1 tablespoon salt and pasta to boiling water and cook until al dente. Reserve 1/2 cup cooking water, drain pasta, and return to pot. Add tomato sauce, parsley, and cooked bacon to pot and toss to combine, adding reserved pasta water as needed. Season with salt. Serve.

EASY CHICKEN CACCIATORE SERVES 4

White mushrooms can be substituted for cremini. For a hearty dinner, serve with pasta, rice, or polenta.

- 4 boneless, skinless chicken breasts (about 1 1/2 pounds)
  Salt and pepper
- 2 tablespoons olive oil
- 1 onion, chopped fine
- 1 red bell pepper, seeded and chopped
- 8 ounces cremini mushrooms (see note), quartered
- 2 garlic cloves, minced
- 1 (14.5-ounce) can diced tomatoes
- 1/4 cup red wine
- 1/4 cup chopped fresh basil

1. Pat chicken dry with paper towels and season with salt and pepper. Heat oil in large skillet over medium-high heat until just smoking. Cook chicken until golden brown, about 5 minutes per side. Transfer to plate.

2. Add onion, bell pepper, and mushrooms to skillet and cook until lightly browned, about 8 minutes. Stir in garlic and cook until fragrant, about 30 seconds. Add tomatoes, wine, and browned chicken along with any accumulated juices and bring to boil. Reduce heat to medium and simmer, covered, until chicken is cooked through, 2 to 4 minutes.

3. Transfer chicken to serving platter and tent with foil. Simmer sauce, uncovered, until slightly thickened, about 5 minutes. Off heat, stir in basil and season with salt and pepper. Pour sauce over chicken. Serve.

MAPLE-GINGER GLAZED CHICKEN SERVES 4

Be sure to use 100 percent pure maple syrup rather than "pancake syrup."

- 1/4 cup maple syrup
- 1 tablespoon soy sauce
- 1 teaspoon grated fresh ginger
- 1/8 teaspoon cayenne pepper
- 4 boneless, skinless chicken breasts (about 1 1/2 pounds)
  Salt and pepper
- 1 tablespoon vegetable oil

1. Combine syrup, soy sauce, ginger, and cayenne in small bowl and set aside. Pat chicken dry with paper towels and season with salt and pepper. Heat oil in large nonstick skillet over medium-high heat until just smoking. Cook chicken until golden brown, about 5 minutes per side.

2. Reduce heat to medium-low and add syrup mixture to skillet. Simmer, turning chicken once or twice to coat, until glaze is slightly thickened and chicken is cooked through, 2 to 4 minutes. Serve.

PORK TENDERLOIN MEDALLIONS WITH BROWN RICE, SAGE, AND WALNUTS SERVES 4

For this recipe, two pork tenderloins are cut crosswise into thick medallions that can be sautéed. There is no need to heat the rice before adding it to the skillet, but do squeeze the package to break up any large pieces.

- 2 pork tenderloins (1 1/2 to 2 pounds total), cut crosswise into 1 1/2-inch pieces
  Salt and pepper
- 3 tablespoons vegetable oil
- 1 onion, chopped fine
- 1/2 cup chopped walnuts
- 2 tablespoons finely chopped fresh sage
- 3/4 cup dried cranberries
- 2 (8.8-ounce) packages Uncle Ben's Whole Grain Brown Ready Rice
- 3/4 cup orange juice

1. Pat pork dry with paper towels and season with salt and pepper. Heat 2 tablespoons oil in large nonstick skillet over medium-high heat until just smoking. Add pork and cook until well browned, about 4 minutes per side. Reduce heat to medium and, using tongs, stand each piece of pork on its side, turning as necessary, until sides are well browned and internal temperature registers 145 degrees, 6 to 10 minutes. Transfer to plate and tent with foil.

2. Add remaining oil, onion, and walnuts to empty skillet and cook until onion is softened, about 5 minutes. Add sage and cook until fragrant, about 30 seconds. Stir in cranberries, rice, and orange juice and cook until liquid has evaporated, about 3 minutes. Season with salt and pepper. Spoon rice onto individual plates and top with pork. Serve.

30-Minute Supper

ROSEMARY CHICKEN WITH BALSAMIC VEGETABLES

30-Minute Supper

**CRISPY PORK CUTLETS
WITH BUTTERED NOODLES**

30-Minute Supper

SWEET, HOT, AND SOUR PORK CHOPS

30-Minute Supper

SKILLET SMOTHERED STEAK TIPS

CRISPY PORK CUTLETS WITH BUTTERED NOODLES
SERVES 4

- 5 slices hearty white sandwich bread, torn into pieces
- 1/2 cup all-purpose flour
- 2 large eggs
- 2 tablespoons Dijon mustard
- 8 boneless pork cutlets (3–4 ounces each), about 1/4 inch thick
  Salt and pepper
- 1/2 cup vegetable oil
- 6 ounces egg noodles (about 4 cups)
- 4 tablespoons unsalted butter, cut into pieces
- 1/2 cup chopped fresh parsley

1. Bring 4 quarts water to boil in large pot. Adjust oven rack to middle position and heat oven to 200 degrees. Pulse bread in food processor until coarsely ground; transfer to shallow dish. Place flour in second shallow dish. Beat eggs with mustard in third shallow dish. Pat pork dry and season with salt and pepper. One at a time, coat cutlets lightly with flour, dip in egg mixture, and then dredge in bread crumbs, pressing to adhere.

2. Heat 1/4 cup oil in large nonstick skillet over medium-high heat until just smoking. Fry half of cutlets until deep golden and crisp, about 3 minutes per side. Drain on paper towel–lined plate and transfer to oven to keep warm. Wipe out skillet and repeat with remaining oil and cutlets.

3. Meanwhile, add 1 tablespoon salt and noodles to boiling water and cook until al dente. Reserve 1/4 cup cooking water, drain pasta, and return to pot. Add butter, parsley, and reserved pasta water to pot and toss until butter is melted. Transfer noodles to serving platter and top with cutlets. Serve.

ROSEMARY CHICKEN WITH BALSAMIC VEGETABLES
SERVES 4

If you do not have an ovenproof skillet, in step 3 transfer the microwaved vegetables to an 8-inch baking dish, top with the browned chicken, and bake as directed.

- 1/2 head cauliflower, cut into 1-inch florets
- 2 carrots, peeled and sliced thin
- 1 red bell pepper, seeded and chopped
- 1 red onion, sliced into 1/4-inch rings
- 3 garlic cloves, minced
- 2 tablespoons balsamic vinegar
- 2 tablespoons olive oil
- 4 bone-in, skin-on chicken breasts (about 3 pounds), halved crosswise
  Salt and pepper
- 1 1/2 teaspoons minced fresh rosemary

1. Adjust oven rack to upper-middle position and heat oven to 475 degrees. Toss cauliflower, carrots, bell pepper, onion, garlic, vinegar, and 1 tablespoon oil in large microwave-safe bowl. Cover with plastic wrap and microwave on high power until vegetables are slightly softened, 2 to 5 minutes.

2. Meanwhile, pat chicken dry with paper towels, season with salt and pepper, and sprinkle with rosemary. Heat remaining oil in large oven-safe skillet over medium-high heat until just smoking. Cook chicken until well browned, about 5 minutes per side.

3. Remove chicken from pan and add vegetable mixture to skillet. Arrange chicken, skin-side up, over vegetables and transfer to oven. Roast until chicken is cooked through and vegetables are tender, about 15 minutes. Serve.

SKILLET SMOTHERED STEAK TIPS SERVES 4

Steak tips can be sold as whole steaks, cubes, or strips. For this recipe, use strips and cut them into 6- to 8-inch-long pieces, if necessary. Bull's-Eye brand barbecue sauce is the test kitchen's favorite.

- 2 tablespoons vegetable oil
- 1 large red onion, halved and sliced thin
  Salt and pepper
- 1 1/2 pounds steak tips (see note)
- 1 cup low-sodium chicken broth
- 2 tablespoons barbecue sauce
- 2 tablespoons unsalted butter

1. Heat 1 tablespoon oil in large nonstick skillet over medium-high heat until shimmering. Cook onion and 1/4 teaspoon salt, covered, until softened and lightly browned, about 5 minutes. Transfer to plate.

2. Pat steak dry with paper towels and season with salt and pepper. Heat remaining oil in empty skillet until just smoking. Cook steak until browned all over and cooked to desired doneness, 6 to 10 minutes. Transfer to platter and tent with foil.

3. Add browned onions, broth, and barbecue sauce to empty skillet and simmer over medium-low heat until slightly thickened, about 5 minutes. Whisk in butter and season with salt and pepper. Spoon onion mixture over steak tips. Serve.

SWEET, HOT, AND SOUR PORK CHOPS SERVES 4

Serve these chops with egg noodles or rice.

- 1/4 cup cider vinegar
- 1/4 cup sugar
- 2 tablespoons pineapple juice
- 1 tablespoon tomato paste
- 1/2 teaspoon red pepper flakes
- 4 bone-in rib or center-cut pork chops, 3/4 to 1 inch thick
  Salt and pepper
- 1 tablespoon vegetable oil

1. Whisk vinegar, sugar, pineapple juice, tomato paste, and pepper flakes in bowl until sugar dissolves.

2. Pat chops dry with paper towels and season with salt and pepper. Heat oil in large skillet over medium-high heat until just smoking. Add chops and cook until golden brown, about 3 minutes per side. Add vinegar mixture to pan and simmer, turning chops once or twice to coat, until meat registers 145 degrees and sauce is very thick, about 5 minutes. Serve.

Getting to Know Beef Steaks

With the wide variety of steaks at the supermarket these days (see page 31 for our primer on beef), it's tough to know which cut of meat to purchase. Here are 12 of our favorite beef steaks, rated on a scale from 1 to 4 stars for both tenderness and flavor.

Top Blade Steak ALL-PURPOSE STEAK

Top blade (or simply blade) steak is a small shoulder cut. While it is very tender and richly flavored, a line of gristle that runs through the center of the meat makes it a poor option for serving whole. Remove the gristle and slice the meat thinly for stir-fries or cut into cubes for kebabs or stews.

Tenderness: ★★★ **Flavor:** ★★★

Flat-Iron Steak BEEFY BUT ELUSIVE

This cut is named for its flat, tapered shape, which is reminiscent of the business end of a clothes iron. Cut from the same area as the top blade, but in a manner that eliminates the gristle, the flat-iron is inexpensive, flavorful, and tender. Unfortunately, most are sold to restaurants, making this cut scarce in supermarket meat cases. Grill, pan-sear, or slice thinly and stir-fry.

Tenderness: ★★★ **Flavor:** ★★★

Shoulder Steak CHEAP AND TASTY

Sometimes labeled London broil or chuck steak, this 1½- to 2-pound boneless steak is a great value for cost-conscious cooks. Although cut from the shoulder, it is relatively lean, with a moderately beefy flavor. Since this steak can be a bit tough, it should be sliced thinly on the bias after cooking. Grill or pan-roast.

Tenderness: ★★ **Flavor:** ★★

Strip Steak GREAT FOR GRILLING

Available both boneless and bone-in, this moderately expensive steak is also called top loin, shell, sirloin strip, Kansas City strip, or New York strip. Cut from the middle of the steer's back, strip steaks are well-marbled, with a tight grain, pleasantly chewy texture, and big beefy flavor. Grill, pan-sear, or broil.

Tenderness: ★★★ **Flavor:** ★★★★

Rib-Eye Steak FATTY AND FLAVORFUL

Cut from the rib area just behind the shoulder, a rib-eye steak is essentially a boneless slice of prime rib. This pricey, fat-streaked steak is tender and juicy, with a pronounced beefiness. In the West, rib-eyes are sometimes labeled Spencer steaks; in the East, they may be called Delmonico steaks. Grill, pan-sear, or broil.

Tenderness: ★★★ **Flavor:** ★★★★

Tenderloin Steak TENDER BUT EXPENSIVE

Cut from the center of the back, the tenderloin is the most tender (and most expensive) cut on the cow. Depending on their thickness, tenderloin steaks may be labeled (from thickest to thinnest) Châteaubriand, filet mignon, or tournedos. Tenderloin steaks are buttery-smooth and very tender, but have little flavor. Grill, pan-sear, or broil.

Tenderness: ★★★★ **Flavor:** ★

T-Bone Steak THE BEST OF BOTH WORLDS

A classic grilling steak, this cut is named for the T-shaped bone that runs through the meat. This bone separates two muscles, the flavorful strip (or shell, top of photo) and the buttery tenderloin (bottom of photo). Because the tenderloin is small and will cook more quickly than the strip, it should be positioned over the cooler side of the fire when grilling. Grill or pan-sear.

Tenderness: ★★★ **Flavor:** ★★★★

Porterhouse Steak STEAK FOR TWO

The porterhouse is really just a huge T-bone steak with a larger tenderloin section, which accounts for its higher price. It is cut farther back on the animal than the T-bone. Like the T-bone, the porterhouse, with both strip and tenderloin sections, has well-balanced flavor and texture. Most porterhouse steaks are big enough to serve two. Grill or pan-sear.

Tenderness: ★★★ **Flavor:** ★★★★

Top Sirloin Steak ECONOMY CUT

Cut from the hip, this steak (along with its bone-in version, round-bone steak) is sometimes called New York sirloin or sirloin butt. Top sirloin is a large, inexpensive steak with decent tenderness and flavor, but do not confuse it with the superior strip steak. Slice thinly against the grain after cooking. Grill or pan-sear.

Tenderness: ★★ **Flavor:** ★★

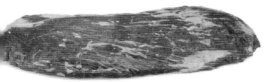

Flank Steak COOKS IN A JIFFY

Flank steak, aka jiffy steak, is a large, flat cut from the underside of the cow, with a distinct longitudinal grain. Flank steak is thin and cooks quickly, making it ideal for the grill. Although very flavorful, flank is slightly chewy. It should not be cooked past medium and should always be sliced thinly across the grain. Grill, pan-sear, or slice thinly and stir-fry.

Tenderness: ★★ **Flavor:** ★★★

Skirt Steak FAJITAS AND MORE

This long, thin steak is cut from the underside (or "plate") of the animal. Also known as fajita or Philadelphia steak, it has a distinct grain and an especially beefy taste. As its alias implies, sliced skirt is a good option for fajitas, but it can also be cooked as a whole steak. Grill, pan-sear, or slice thinly and stir-fry.

Tenderness: ★★ **Flavor:** ★★★

Flap Meat Sirloin Steak Tip BUY IT WHOLE

Cut from the area just before the hip, this large (upward of 2½ pounds) rectangular steak is most often sold in strips or cubes. To ensure that you are buying the real thing, buy the whole steak and cut it yourself. Though not particularly tender, flap meat has a distinct grain and a robust beefiness. Slice thinly against the grain after cooking. Grill, pan-roast (whole), or pan-sear (strips).

Tenderness: ★★ **Flavor:** ★★★

The Best Homemade Party Snack Mixes

Get great flavor and big crunch without the seasoned salt and margarine.

Crunchy, salty, and borderline addictive, homemade party snack mix is guaranteed to disappear quickly at any gathering. But after making a back-of-the-box recipe recently, I felt there was room for improvement. The cereal and other snacks (which included pretzels, Melba toast, and nuts) were tossed with melted margarine and a splash of Worcestershire before being sprinkled with seasoned salt. It's not that I'm complaining—I had more than a few handfuls—but I knew it could be so much better.

In head-to-head tests, the nutty sweetness of melted butter was preferred to margarine and olive oil, both of which left a greasy finish. Though Worcestershire sauce certainly added flavor to the mix, some tasters found it too domineering. Substitutes such as soy sauce, hot sauce, barbecue sauce, and even maple syrup were more successful, lending inspired flavors without steamrolling the other ingredients.

As for the seasonings, a few carefully chosen dried spices gave well-rounded flavors without the staleness of seasoned salt. Bold seasonings such as chili powder, garlic powder, cayenne pepper, and ground ginger held their flavor

With ingredients like soy sauce, lemon juice, and hot sauce—not to mention an inspired selection of unusual snacks—these party mixes are anything but ordinary.

through baking (unlike more subtle spices like paprika and onion powder, whose flavor faded). When it came to the baking, the original recipe was pretty much spot-on: Forty-five minutes in a 250-degree oven was sufficient to bloom the spices and crisp the snacks.

I found that no one combination of snacks was best. Along with the usual Chex cereal, Melba toasts, and nuts, I punctuated the mixes with unexpected ingredients such as oyster crackers, smoked almonds, and wasabi peas. Tossed with a dash of creativity, these mixes are sure to be winners at your next get-together. –Jeremy Sauer

BBQ PARTY MIX
MAKES ABOUT 10 CUPS
Fritos corn chips work well here.

- 5 **cups Corn Chex cereal**
- 2 **cups corn chips**
- 1 **cup Melba toast rounds**
- 1 **cup pretzel sticks**
- 1 **cup smoked almonds**
- 6 **tablespoons unsalted butter, melted**
- 1/4 **cup barbecue sauce**
- 1 **teaspoon chili powder**
- 1/2 **teaspoon dried oregano**
- 1/4 **teaspoon cayenne pepper**

1. Adjust oven rack to middle position and heat oven to 250 degrees. Combine cereal, corn chips, Melba toast, pretzels, and almonds in large bowl. Whisk butter and barbecue sauce in small bowl, then drizzle over cereal mixture. Sprinkle evenly with chili powder, oregano, and cayenne and toss until well combined.

2. Spread mixture over rimmed baking sheet and bake, stirring every 15 minutes, until golden and crisp, about 45 minutes. Cool to room temperature. Serve. (Mix can be stored in airtight container at room temperature for up to 1 week.)

FISHERMAN'S FRIEND PARTY MIX
MAKES ABOUT 10 CUPS
The test kitchen prefers Frank's Red Hot hot sauce. If using a spicier brand, you may not need as much.

- 5 **cups Corn Chex or Rice Chex cereal**
- 2 **cups oyster crackers**
- 1 **cup Pepperidge Farm Cheddar Goldfish**
- 1 **cup Pepperidge Farm Pretzel Goldfish**
- 1 **cup Melba toast rounds**
- 6 **tablespoons unsalted butter, melted**
- 2 **tablespoons hot sauce (see note)**
- 1 **tablespoon lemon juice**
- 1 **tablespoon Old Bay seasoning**

1. Adjust oven rack to middle position and heat oven to 250 degrees. Combine cereal, oyster crackers, Goldfish, and Melba toast in large bowl. Whisk butter, hot sauce, and lemon juice in small bowl, then drizzle over cereal mixture. Sprinkle evenly with Old Bay and toss until well combined.

2. Spread mixture over rimmed baking sheet and bake, stirring every 15 minutes, until golden and crisp, about 45 minutes. Cool to room temperature. Serve. (Mix can be stored in airtight container at room temperature for up to 1 week.)

ASIAN FIRECRACKER PARTY MIX
MAKES ABOUT 10 CUPS
Wasabi peas can be found in the international aisle of most grocery stores.

- 5 **cups Rice Chex cereal**
- 2 **cups sesame sticks**
- 1 **cup wasabi peas**
- 1 **cup chow mein noodles**
- 1 **cup honey-roasted peanuts**
- 6 **tablespoons unsalted butter, melted**
- 2 **tablespoons soy sauce**
- 1 **teaspoon ground ginger**
- 3/4 **teaspoon garlic powder**
- 1/4 **teaspoon cayenne pepper**

1. Adjust oven rack to middle position and heat oven to 250 degrees. Combine cereal, sesame sticks, wasabi peas, chow mein noodles, and peanuts in large bowl. Whisk butter and soy sauce in small bowl, then drizzle over cereal mixture. Sprinkle evenly with ginger, garlic powder, and cayenne and toss until well combined.

2. Spread mixture over rimmed baking sheet and bake, stirring every 15 minutes, until golden and crisp, about 45 minutes. Cool to room temperature. Serve. (Mix can be stored in airtight container at room temperature for up to 1 week.)

Visit us online!
For a free Sweet and Salty Kettle Corn Party Mix recipe, visit CooksCountry.com and click on **Cook's Country Extra.**

The American Table:
The History of Breakfast Cereal
Breakfast cereal is a relatively new addition to the American culinary landscape. About 100 years ago, a number of health-conscious entrepreneurs, most notably Will Keith (W.K.) Kellogg, began to market grain-based cereals as a healthy, filling, and affordable alternative to the traditional meat-and-eggs breakfast. While these first cereals were little more than primitive granola—some even needed to be soaked in water overnight to make them edible—consumers slowly began to warm to them. The breakfast cereal industry truly boomed in the 1920s, when milk pasteurization made fresh milk more readily available. –J.S.

Easier Than You Think: Cheddar Cheese Rounds

How do you make these savory shortbread-like crackers flaky and cheesy rather than floury and bland?

Homemade cheddar cheese rounds are as easy as hors d'oeuvres get. Just mix shredded cheddar cheese, flour, and softened butter to form the dough; refrigerate until firm; slice; and bake. But while the best versions are flaky-crisp and pleasantly sandy—like tiny rounds of savory shortbread—many that I tried were tough and floury, with little cheddar flavor.

Some recipes called for three times as much flour as cheese (these baked up too crackery), and others used half as much flour as cheese (and were greasy and chewy). Tasters preferred a middle ground of 1 1/2 cups of flour and 2 cups of cheese mixed with a stick of softened butter. Sharp cheddar (rather than mild) and cayenne bumped up the flavor. Still, the rounds were plagued by a slight raw-flour taste.

Could nuts mask the floury taste? I discovered that by finely grinding pecans in the food processor, I could use them in place of some of the flour. The moisture from the pecans made the rounds slightly softer, so I added a tablespoon of cornstarch to the dough, which left the rounds with a crisp, pleasantly shortbread-like texture to go along with their nutty, cheddary flavor. –Jeremy Sauer

CHEDDAR CHEESE ROUNDS
MAKES ABOUT 5 DOZEN

Orange-colored sharp cheddar will give the rounds a deep golden hue. To make this dough with a hand-held mixer, chop the nuts finely and then mix all the ingredients until combined, about 3 minutes.

- 1/4 cup pecans
- 1 1/4 cups all-purpose flour
- 1 tablespoon cornstarch
- 2 cups shredded sharp cheddar cheese (see note)
- 8 tablespoons (1 stick) unsalted butter, cut into pieces and softened
- 1/4 teaspoon cayenne pepper
- 1/2 teaspoon salt

1. Process pecans, flour, and cornstarch in food processor until finely ground. Add remaining ingredients and pulse until dough forms. Turn dough out onto lightly floured surface and roll into two 8-inch logs. Wrap tightly with plastic wrap and refrigerate until firm, at least 1 hour or up to 3 days.

2. Adjust oven racks to upper-middle and lower-middle positions and heat oven to 400 degrees. Line 2 baking sheets with parchment paper. Slice logs into 1/4-inch rounds and place 3/4 inch apart on prepared

baking sheets. Bake until golden, about 15 minutes, switching and rotating baking sheets halfway through baking. Let cool 3 minutes on sheets, then transfer to wire rack and cool completely. Serve. (Rounds can be kept in airtight container at room temperature for up to 3 days.)

Make Ahead: At the end of step 1, logs can be wrapped in plastic, then foil, and frozen for up to 1 month. Defrost in refrigerator before proceeding with step 2.

Party Favorites: Hot Spinach and Artichoke Dip

This classic dip is often greasy and bland. We set out to make it creamy and flavorful.

Hot spinach and artichoke dip is a chain restaurant staple. Served bubbling-hot from the broiler, this creamy, cheesy dip is studded with chunks of artichokes and earthy spinach.

Most of the recipes I found called for folding frozen spinach, artichokes, and seasonings into a mixture of softened cream cheese (thinned with mayonnaise or sour cream) and cheddar. But these recipes came out of the oven greasy, pasty, and bland. I found a few recipes that replaced the cream cheese and mayo or sour cream with a flour-thickened cream sauce. The flour stabilized the dip, so the cheese didn't separate and make things greasy. Tasters preferred the assertive nuttiness of Parmesan to the more traditional cheddar or Monterey Jack. And because the cream sauce was much thinner than cream cheese, the dip was creamy, not pasty or stiff.

As for the headliners, sautéed fresh spinach had an unappealing, slimy texture. Frozen chopped spinach was a better (and easier) option, provided it was squeezed dry to prevent a watery dip. Since fresh artichokes would take too much work, I tested canned, bottled, and frozen artichoke hearts. Tasters dismissed the "tinny" taste of canned artichokes and the greasy, briny flavor of bottled artichokes, but the frozen ones showed promise. To help develop their flavor, I browned them in butter (along with some onion and garlic) before building the sauce. After a quick bake in the oven, I had a fresh-tasting, creamy dip better than any I could order in a restaurant. –Jeremy Sauer

HOT SPINACH AND ARTICHOKE DIP
MAKES ABOUT 3 CUPS

Be sure to squeeze as much liquid as possible from the spinach and artichoke hearts. Serve with crackers, Melba toast, or tortilla chips.

- 4 tablespoons unsalted butter
- 1 onion, chopped fine
- 2 (9-ounce) boxes frozen artichoke hearts, thawed, squeezed dry, and chopped
- 2 garlic cloves, minced
- 1/4 cup all-purpose flour
- 2 cups half-and-half
- 1 1/2 cups grated Parmesan cheese
- 1 tablespoon lemon juice
- 1 tablespoon hot sauce
- 1 teaspoon salt
- 1 (10-ounce) box frozen chopped spinach, thawed and squeezed dry

1. Adjust oven rack to middle position and heat oven to 450 degrees. Melt 2 tablespoons butter in large saucepan over medium-high heat. Cook onion until softened, about 5 minutes. Add artichokes and cook until lightly browned, about 5 minutes. Stir in garlic and cook until fragrant, about 30 seconds. Transfer artichoke mixture to plate and reserve.

2. Melt remaining butter in empty pan. Stir in flour and cook until just golden, about 1 minute. Slowly stir in half-and-half, 1 1/4 cups Parmesan, lemon juice, hot sauce, and salt. Reduce heat to medium-low and simmer until thickened, about 3 minutes. Off heat, stir in spinach and reserved artichoke mixture.

3. Transfer to 1-quart soufflé or baking dish and sprinkle with remaining cheese. Bake until golden brown and bubbling, about 15 minutes. Cool 5 minutes. Serve.

Make Ahead: Dip can be prepared through step 2 and refrigerated in an airtight container for up to 24 hours. To heat, let dip sit at room temperature for 1 hour, then sprinkle with cheese and bake, covered with foil, in a 450-degree oven for 10 minutes. Remove foil and bake until golden brown and heated through, about 15 minutes longer.

Test Kitchen's Holiday Menu

We simplify classic recipes to create an elegant menu that's easy on the cook.

SHRIMP BISQUE

SERVES 8 TO 10

The shrimp shells are cooked with vegetables and bottled clam juice to create a potent base for this creamy soup. If desired, stir 1 tablespoon of brandy into the bisque just before serving.

- 4 tablespoons unsalted butter
- 2 pounds medium shrimp, peeled, deveined, and chopped; shells reserved
- 2 onions, chopped
- 2 celery ribs, chopped
- 2 carrots, peeled and chopped
- 2 garlic cloves, minced
- 6 tablespoons all-purpose flour
- 6 tablespoons tomato paste
- 6 (8-ounce) bottles clam juice
- 2 cups white wine
- 2 sprigs fresh thyme
- 2 cups heavy cream
  Salt and pepper

1. Melt butter in large Dutch oven over medium heat. Add reserved shrimp shells and cook until spotty brown, about 5 minutes. Stir in onions, celery, and carrots and cook until beginning to soften, about 8 minutes. Add garlic and cook until fragrant, about 30 seconds. Stir in flour and cook, stirring constantly, until lightly browned, about 2 minutes. Stir in tomato paste and cook for 1 minute. Add clam juice, wine, and thyme and bring to boil. Reduce heat to medium-low and simmer until slightly thickened, about 30 minutes.

2. Pour broth through fine-mesh strainer into large saucepan, pressing on solids to extract juices. Discard solids in strainer.

3. Bring broth to simmer over medium heat. Stir in shrimp and cream and simmer until shrimp are cooked through, about 5 minutes. Season with salt and pepper. Serve.

Make Ahead: The broth can be prepared through step 2 and refrigerated in an airtight container for up to 24 hours.

HERB-ROASTED PRIME RIB AND POTATOES

SERVES 8 TO 10

Look for the first cut of rib roast (which is also labeled as the loin end) from ribs 10 through 12—it's much less fatty than the second cut (also labeled as the chuck end). If the roast is tied with butcher's twine, remove the twine prior to beginning the recipe.

- 1 (7-pound) beef standing rib roast, 3 to 4 ribs
- 2 1/2 teaspoons salt
- 1 1/4 teaspoons pepper
- 3 tablespoons minced fresh thyme
- 3 tablespoons minced fresh rosemary
- 2 tablespoons Dijon mustard
- 2 tablespoons olive oil
- 1 tablespoon all-purpose flour
- 1 teaspoon sugar
- 3 pounds small red potatoes, scrubbed and halved

1. Adjust oven rack to lowest position and heat oven to 450 degrees. Season roast with 2 teaspoons salt and 1 teaspoon pepper and arrange on V-rack set inside roasting pan. Roast until well browned, about 1 hour.

2. Combine herbs, mustard, oil, flour, and sugar in small bowl. Remove roast from oven and reduce heat to 250 degrees. Spread herb mixture evenly over top of roast. Return to oven and roast until center of meat registers 125 degrees (for medium-rare), about 1 1/2 hours. Transfer to cutting board and let rest, uncovered, for 30 minutes.

3. Meanwhile, increase oven temperature to 450 degrees. Pour off all but 3 tablespoons fat from roasting pan. Toss potatoes, remaining salt, and remaining pepper in large bowl. Arrange potatoes, cut-side down, in roasting pan. Roast until golden brown and tender, about 30 minutes.

4. Transfer potatoes to serving bowl. Following photos on page 31, carve meat off bones and slice to desired thickness. Serve.

Make Ahead: The herb paste in step 2 can be prepared 24 hours in advance and refrigerated in an airtight container.

CRANBERRY-GLAZED CARROTS

SERVES 8 TO 10

Two tablespoons of chopped fresh parsley can be substituted for the tarragon. If using frozen cranberries, defrost them before starting this recipe.

- 2 tablespoons unsalted butter
- 2 (16-ounce) bags baby carrots
- 1 teaspoon salt
- 1/2 teaspoon pepper
- 3 garlic cloves, minced
- 1/2 cup sugar
- 8 ounces fresh or frozen cranberries (see note)
- 2 teaspoons chopped fresh tarragon

1. Melt butter in large Dutch oven over medium heat. Cook carrots, salt, and pepper until lightly browned, about 8 minutes. Stir in garlic and cook until fragrant, about 30 seconds. Add sugar and cook, covered, stirring occasionally, until carrots are glazed and nearly tender, about 15 minutes.

2. Stir in cranberries and tarragon and cook, uncovered, until carrots are completely tender and cranberries have softened, about 5 minutes. Serve.

CREAMY PEAS WITH BACON AND GOAT CHEESE
SERVES 8 TO 10

Because the cream is reduced to a thick consistency before the peas are added to the pan, the peas should be cooked with the cover on to limit further reduction.

- 6 slices bacon, chopped
- 1 cup heavy cream
- 2 pounds frozen peas, not thawed
- 6 scallions, sliced thin
- 4 ounces goat cheese, cut into 4 pieces
  Salt and pepper

1. Cook bacon in large nonstick skillet over medium-high heat until crisp, about 5 minutes. Transfer to paper towel–lined plate and discard drippings.

2. Add cream to empty skillet and simmer until thickened, about 5 minutes. Stir in peas and scallions, cover, and cook until heated through, about 8 minutes. Off heat, stir in goat cheese until smooth. Season with salt and pepper and sprinkle with bacon. Serve.

Diner-Style Omelet at Home

When I try to make omelets at home, the eggs cooks up flat. How can I make huge, fluffy omelets like the ones they serve in diners? –Josie McGuffy, San Diego, Calif.

While a typical omelet can make a fine breakfast or light dinner, the omelets at my local diner can satisfy the biggest of appetites. They're impossibly tall and fluffy and loaded with cheese and other fillings. But the recipes I've tried for these huge omelets have left me with flat and flabby eggs. How do those short-order cooks do it?

Most omelet recipes call for the eggs to be quickly beaten with a fork or whisk, but a peek behind the counter at the diner revealed a drastically different mixing method: using a milkshake blender. Many diners use these blenders (or a similar tool) to incorporate air into the eggs until they've tripled in volume, which results in tall and fluffy cooked omelets. Using five eggs (for a hearty omelet that would serve two), I got the eggs to triple in volume in just a few minutes with my mixer, and the resulting omelet cooked up huge and light—but lacking in richness.

Many omelet recipes add milk or cream to the whipped eggs for richness and stability. My tasters liked the flavor of cream, but when I added it to the whipped eggs, the cooked omelet lost its fluffiness and height. Combining the cream and eggs before whipping didn't work, either—the mixture refused to increase in volume, as the fat in the

cream was making it impossible to whip air into the eggs. I had much better results when I whipped the cream to soft peaks and then folded the whipped cream into the whipped eggs. The resulting omelet had rich flavor, creamy texture, and that tall and fluffy diner-style height.

My final task was to find the perfect cooking technique. Since I was using such a large volume of eggs, the bottom of the omelet was overcooking by the time the top was set. Flipping the big mass of egg was messy and dangerous, so I turned to a method we often use when pan-searing meats: Start cooking on the stove and finish in the oven. After letting the bottom of the omelet set on the stovetop, I popped the skillet into a preheated oven, and six minutes later the omelet came out puffy, fluffy, and cooked to perfection. All I had to do was fold it in half and I had a diner-style omelet as thick as any I'd ever seen.

–Meredith Butcher

To ensure the tallest, fluffiest omelets possible, we lost the whisk and plugged in the mixer.

Double Your Pleasure

To make two omelets, double this recipe and cook the omelets simultaneously in two skillets. If you have only one skillet, prepare a double batch of ingredients and set half aside for the second omelet. Be sure to wipe out the skillet in between omelets.

FLUFFY DINER-STYLE CHEESE OMELET
SERVES 2

Although this recipe will work with any electric mixer, a handheld mixer makes quick work of whipping such a small amount of cream. If using a standing mixer in step 1, transfer the whipped cream to a separate bowl, wipe out the mixing bowl, and then beat the eggs in the clean bowl.

- 3 tablespoons heavy cream, chilled
- 5 large eggs, room temperature
- ¼ teaspoon salt
- 2 tablespoons unsalted butter
- ½ cup shredded sharp cheddar cheese
- 1 recipe omelet filling (see box above right), optional

1. Adjust oven rack to middle position and heat oven to 400 degrees. With electric mixer on medium-high speed, beat cream to soft peaks, about 2 minutes. Set whipped cream aside. Beat eggs and salt in clean bowl on

Filling Station

Here are two of the test kitchen's favorite fillings for Fluffy Diner-Style Cheese Omelets. To help some of the filling integrate into the eggs, add half of the cooked filling to the omelet right before it goes into the oven and add the other half right when it comes out, prior to folding.

SAUSAGE AND PEPPER FILLING

- 4 ounces bulk sausage meat
- 1 tablespoon unsalted butter
- 1 small onion, chopped
- ½ red bell pepper, seeded and chopped
- Salt and pepper

Cook sausage in nonstick skillet over medium heat, breaking up clumps with wooden spoon, until browned, about 6 minutes. Transfer to paper towel–lined plate. Add butter, onion, and bell pepper to

empty skillet and cook until softened, about 10 minutes. Stir in sausage and season with salt and pepper.

LOADED BAKED POTATO FILLING

- 1 large Yukon Gold potato, peeled and cut into ½-inch pieces
- 4 slices bacon, chopped
- 2 scallions, sliced thin
- Salt and pepper

Microwave potatoes on high power, covered, in large bowl until just tender, 2 to 5 minutes. Cook bacon in nonstick skillet over medium heat until crisp, about 8 minutes. Transfer bacon to paper towel–lined plate and pour off all but 1 tablespoon bacon fat. Cook potatoes in bacon fat until golden brown, about 6 minutes. Transfer potatoes to bowl, add cooked bacon, and stir in scallions. Season with salt and pepper.

high speed until frothy and eggs have tripled in size, about 2 minutes. Gently fold whipped cream into eggs.

2. Melt butter in 10-inch ovensafe nonstick skillet over medium-low heat, swirling pan to completely coat bottom and sides with melted butter. Add egg mixture and cook until edges are nearly set, 2 to 3 minutes. Sprinkle with ¼ cup cheese (and half of filling, if using) and transfer to oven. Bake until eggs are set and

edges are beginning to brown, 6 to 8 minutes.

3. Carefully remove pan from oven (handle will be very hot). Sprinkle with remaining cheese (and remaining filling, if using) and let sit, covered, until cheese begins to melt, about 1 minute. Tilt pan and, using rubber spatula, push half of omelet onto cutting board. Tilt skillet so that omelet folds over itself to form half-moon. Cut omelet in half. Serve.

It's in the Mix

Most recipes call for using a whisk to gently beat the eggs and dairy; we found this produced a flat omelet. We use an electric mixer to incorporate air into the eggs and cream, which results in a tall, fluffy omelet.

FLAT OMELET
Whisked eggs and cream yield a flat omelet.

Sunday Brunch French Toast

Cooking French toast two pieces at a time is no way to feed a table full of hungry diners. Could we find a way to cook eight slices at once?

I always look forward to the French toast my dad makes for holiday brunch. He soaks sandwich bread in a creamy egg custard and fries eight pieces at a time to a crisp golden brown on a griddle he inherited from Grandma. We all sit down together to toast that is light and fluffy, with a crunchy exterior. But I don't own a griddle, so cooking French toast for brunch guests is tricky: Since my skillet holds only two pieces at a time, I have to either try to keep the toast warm in the oven (which makes it soggy and limp) or feed everyone in stages. If I was going to make eight slices of French toast without Grandma's griddle, I was going to have to try to cook them in the oven.

I soaked eight slices of hearty white sandwich bread in a mixture of milk and eggs until the bread was wet and heavy, put them on a buttered baking sheet, and popped them into the oven. The results of this

first test were discouraging, as the French toast came out of the oven mushy and falling apart. Drying the bread in the oven before the soak gave it enough structure to withstand a long, deep bath in the custard (to ensure a custardy center) without falling apart. To ensure the best possible texture, I found that it was necessary to soak the bread for 30 seconds on each side and then let the slices rest briefly on an elevated rack so that any excess surface custard could drain away, thus preventing a soggy exterior. As I fine-tuned the flavor, my tasters let me know they preferred the richness of half-and-half to milk, especially when I added a little lemon juice to mimic the tang of buttermilk—a familiar flavor in many breakfast dishes, such as pancakes and waffles.

The French toast was now custardy and holding together well, but it wasn't browning or getting crisp. In the test kitchen, we oven-fry potato

wedges by coating a baking sheet with vegetable oil and preheating it in a hot oven. Using this technique, I placed the soaked bread slices on the sizzling, oiled sheet and flipped them halfway through cooking. After about 15 minutes, the toast came out crisp and golden on the outside and creamy and custardy inside. Now that I wasn't slaving over the stovetop for several skillet batches, I had some time to think about how I could dress up this French toast for guests.

Since I serve my French toast with powdered sugar and maple syrup, I wondered if I could incorporate these flavors as a topping in the oven. I made a paste of powdered sugar and maple syrup and brushed it on the toast after I flipped it. While the powdered sugar became gummy, the maple syrup brought welcome moisture, flavor, and sweetness (and allowed me to eliminate the sugar in the custard). Swapping out the powdered sugar

for brown sugar helped the maple topping caramelize into a delectable candied crust that my tasters loved. –**Lynn Clark**

SUNDAY BRUNCH FRENCH TOAST SERVES 4

Be sure to use a firm-textured bread such as Arnold Country Classic White or Pepperidge Farm Farmhouse Hearty White here.

- 8 **slices hearty white sandwich bread**
- 6 **large eggs**
- 3/4 **cup half-and-half**
- 1 **tablespoon vanilla extract**
- 2 **teaspoons lemon juice**
- 1/4 **teaspoon salt**
- 1/4 **cup vegetable oil**
- 6 **tablespoons light brown sugar**
- 1 **tablespoon maple syrup**
- 1/2 **teaspoon ground cinnamon**

1. Adjust oven rack to lower-middle position and heat oven to 300 degrees. Bake bread on rimmed baking sheet until dry, about 8 minutes per side. Let bread cool 5 minutes. Increase oven temperature to 475 degrees.

2. Whisk eggs, half-and-half, vanilla, lemon juice, and salt in 13 by 9-inch pan. Soak 4 slices bread in egg mixture until just saturated, about 30 seconds per side. Transfer to wire rack and repeat with remaining bread.

3. Pour oil onto rimmed baking sheet, turning sheet to coat. Transfer to oven and heat until just smoking, about 4 minutes. Using fork, stir brown sugar, maple syrup, and cinnamon in small bowl until mixture resembles wet sand.

4. Arrange soaked bread on hot baking sheet and bake until golden brown on first side, about 10 minutes. Flip bread and sprinkle evenly with sugar mixture. Cook until sugar is deep brown and bubbling, about 6 minutes. Cool toast on wire rack for 2 minutes. Serve.

Our dressed-up French toast features a caramelized brown sugar and maple crust.

Kitchen Know-How
OVEN-FRIED FRENCH TOAST

Follow these steps for French toast that is light and crispy, with a maple and brown sugar crust.

①

②

③

1. After a dip in the custard, resting the bread on a wire rack gives the custard time to penetrate the interior while preventing the exterior from becoming oversaturated.

2. Placing the bread on a preheated sheet tray coated with oil creates a crisp coating on the exterior of the bread.

3. Sprinkling the toast with a mixture of brown sugar, cinnamon, and maple syrup gives it a caramelized, golden exterior.

Skillet-Baked Spaghetti with Meat Sauce

Can fresh ingredients and a few test kitchen tricks transform this casserole into a quick and flavorful one-pot meal?

We make the meat sauce, cook the pasta right in it, and broil the topping to a golden brown—all in one skillet.

Kitchen Know-How
SPAGHETTI BREAKDOWN

Here's how we break spaghetti into 2-inch pieces without noodles flying all over the test kitchen.

1. Place spaghetti in large zipper-lock bag and, grasping both ends of pasta, press spaghetti firmly against edge of countertop.

2. Continue pressing smaller pieces of pasta against edge of countertop until it has been broken down into rough 2-inch pieces.

tial cheesy crust. And best of all, cleanup consisted of only one pan. **–Lynn Clark**

SKILLET-BAKED SPAGHETTI SERVES 4 TO 6

You will need either 1 large or 2 small links of Italian sausage for this recipe. If using hot Italian sausage, use just 1/8 teaspoon of red pepper flakes.

- 12 ounces 90 percent lean ground beef
- 4 ounces hot or sweet Italian sausage (see note), casings removed
- 4 garlic cloves, minced
- 1/4 teaspoon red pepper flakes
- 1/4 teaspoon dried oregano
- 1 (28-ounce) can crushed tomatoes
- 8 ounces spaghetti, broken int rough 2-inch pieces
- 2 cups water
- 1 1/2 teaspoons salt
- 1/4 cup heavy cream
- 6 tablespoons finely chopped fresh basil
- 1 cup shredded Italian cheese blend

Baked spaghetti with meat sauce is as simple as it sounds: Spaghetti and meat sauce are topped with mozzarella and baked into a melted, cheese-crusted casserole. The reality of this dish, however, is that boiling pasta, making a meat sauce, transferring it to a casserole dish, and baking it requires too many pots and too much time for a weeknight meal. More important, most versions that I tried were bland and boring. I set out to make a skillet spaghetti casserole that was quick and flavorful, and required as little cleanup as possible.

I decided to employ the test kitchen's technique of cooking the pasta in the skillet along with the sauce. When using this method, we add a few cups of water to the mixture to help the pasta cook more evenly and to

keep the sauce from drying out. This works well with smaller pasta shapes, but my skillet was filled to the rim with sauce and water, and the spaghetti was floating on the top. Breaking the spaghetti into 2-inch pieces helped the pasta cook more evenly, and I could fit more of it (a full half-pound) in the skillet.

I made a quick meat sauce using ground beef, crushed tomatoes, garlic, and spices. But the flavors became diluted when I added water. Using less water meant the pasta didn't cook evenly in the thick sauce, and adding more beef didn't provide enough flavor. I had better results by swapping out some of the beef for Italian sausage, which gave the sauce extra seasoning and a long-simmered complexity. To add even deeper, richer flavor (and to make the pasta mixture more cohesive), I mixed a small amount of

heavy cream and some of the mozzarella into the pasta before tackling the cheese topping.

Since I didn't want to dirty a baking dish for the cheesy baked crust, I decided to melt the mozzarella right in the skillet. I topped the pasta and sauce with mozzarella and covered the skillet to try to melt the cheese on the stovetop, but it became rubbery. Baking the spaghetti mixture in the skillet melted the cheese and created a decent crust, but it wasn't as fast—and it didn't create as nice a crust—as running it under a hot broiler. Replacing the straight mozzarella with a packaged blend that contained sharper cheeses like Parmesan and asiago as well as mozzarella provided a welcome contrast of flavors and textures.

With a finishing hit of fresh basil, I had a flavorful skillet pasta casserole with a substan-

1. Adjust oven rack to upper-middle position and heat broiler. Cook beef and sausage in large ovensafe nonstick skillet over medium heat, breaking up meat with wooden spoon, until no longer pink, about 5 minutes. Drain meat on paper towel–lined plate and pour off fat from skillet. Return meat to skillet. Add garlic, pepper flakes, and oregano and cook until fragrant, about 1 minute.

2. Stir in tomatoes, spaghetti, water, and salt. Cover and cook, stirring often, until spaghetti begins to soften, about 7 minutes. Reduce heat to medium-low and continue to simmer, covered, until spaghetti is al dente, about 7 minutes.

3. Stir in cream, basil, and 1/3 cup cheese. Sprinkle with remaining cheese and broil until surface is spotty brown, about 3 minutes. Let cool 5 minutes. Serve.

Easier Than You Think: *Herbed Breadsticks*

Which frozen dough is the best choice for soft, restaurant-style breadsticks?

At my favorite Italian restaurant, the baskets of warm, pull-apart breadsticks seasoned with olive oil and herbs are so good that I'm almost tempted to forgo the rest of the meal. Looking for an easy way to make these bread-sticks at home, I turned to refrigerator-case breadstick dough; I popped open the can and baked off a batch, but they were greasy and tasted processed. Premade supermarket pizza dough tasted better, but it was very lean, and the breadsticks were too tough and chewy. Frozen sandwich-bread dough fared much better—it contained more fat and sugar, which translated into tender breadsticks. After rolling the dough out into a rectangle, I used a knife (a bench scraper also works well) to perforate it into 1-inch sticks that baked up pillowy soft and pulled apart perfectly at the seams.

A brush of extra-virgin olive oil before baking lent additional flavor, but the dried herbs on top of the oil became tired and stale in the oven. I opted instead for a sprinkle of fresh rosemary, which bloomed in the oven to perfume the kitchen—and the breadsticks—with deep herb flavor. –**Kelley Baker**

HERBED BREADSTICKS MAKES 12

Most frozen bread dough comes in packages of 3 loaves; our favorite brand is Rhodes. These breadsticks can be served with additional extra-virgin olive oil for dip-ping. In step 3, be careful to not cut all the way through the dough. See photos on page 31.

- ¼   **cup extra-virgin olive oil**
-      **Flour for dusting work surface**
- 1   **(16-ounce) loaf frozen bread dough, thawed**
- ¼   **teaspoon salt**
- ¼   **teaspoon pepper**
- 1   **teaspoon minced fresh rosemary**

1. Adjust oven rack to middle position and heat oven to 350 degrees. Brush rimmed baking sheet with 1 table-spoon oil.

2. On lightly floured surface, roll dough into 12 by 6-inch rectangle about ¼ inch thick. Transfer dough to prepared baking sheet. Brush dough with remaining oil and sprinkle with salt, pepper, and rosemary.

3. With long side of dough facing you, use a bench scraper or sharp knife to cut halfway through dough at 1-inch intervals. Bake until golden brown, rotating pan halfway through baking, 20 to 25 minutes. Let cool 5 minutes. Pull apart and serve.

Make-Ahead: *Italian Dressing Mix*

Why use the store-bought stuff when you can make a better, equally convenient version at home?

There is something to be said for the convenience of shelf-stable dried salad-dressing mixes: Just add oil, vinegar, and water; shake; and serve. But most mixes are sugary-sweet and taste of stale dried herbs. I wanted to create a dressing mix that had fresher herb flavor, a bright balance of sweet and tart, and enough thickness to cling to my salad.

I found several recipes that attempted to re-create supermarket dressing mixes using similar ingredients: sugar, dehydrated onion and garlic, and myriad dried herbs. After assembling my own variations on this theme, I quickly realized that I didn't have to empty the spice rack to achieve big flavor. In addition to the onion and garlic, all I needed were a little dried oregano and dried basil, plus red pepper flakes for heat and color. Rehydrating the onion, garlic, and herbs in water and vinegar in the microwave bloomed their flavors and also enhanced the vinegar, which made for a richer dressing.

Lemon juice added sparkle to the dressing, and a bit of sugar balanced the acidity. But I don't always have a fresh lemon on hand. A colleague suggested replac-ing the sugar and lemon with powdered lemonade mix—and to my surprise, it added just the right amount of sweetness and acidity.

The last problem was textural: I wanted the dressing to be thick and emulsified. Common emulsifiers like mustard powder and cornstarch didn't work here, but pectin (a fruit-based thickener commonly used in jams and jellies)

bulked the dressing up perfectly. I finally had a conve-nient salad-dressing mix with a lively herb flavor that was ready at a moment's notice. –**Greg Case**

ITALIAN DRESSING MIX

MAKES 1 CUP OF MIX,
ENOUGH FOR ABOUT 10 BATCHES OF DRESSING
Each batch of dressing makes about ½ cup, enough to dress 16 cups of greens and serve 6 to 8 people. Leftover dressing can be refrigerated for up to 3 days.

- ¼   **cup powdered lemonade mix**
- 3   **tablespoons dehydrated minced onion**
- 3   **tablespoons dehydrated minced garlic**
- 3   **tablespoons pectin (Sure-Jell)**
- 1   **tablespoon dried oregano**
- 2   **teaspoons dried basil**
- 1   **teaspoon red pepper flakes**
- 1   **tablespoon salt**

Whisk all ingredients in bowl until well combined. Store in airtight container for up to 3 months. To make salad dressing, whisk 1½ tablespoons mix, 2 tablespoons red wine vinegar, and 1 tablespoon water in bowl. Cover with plastic wrap and microwave until garlic and onion are just softened, about 15 seconds. Cool to room temperature, then slowly whisk in 6 tablespoons olive oil.

Black-Bottom Pie

Secrets to
SILKY CHIFFON

Traditional whipped egg whites and sugar aren't sturdy enough to support the whipped cream topping. Using those ingredients to make a sturdy seven-minute frosting is essential.

1. Using electric mixer on medium-high speed, beat egg white mixture over pot of barely simmering water to soft peaks, about two minutes.
2. Remove bowl from heat and beat until egg white mixture becomes very thick and glossy and cools to room temperature, about three minutes.

My mom has been looking for just the right recipe for her favorite childhood dessert, black-bottom pie, for years. I'd love to surprise her with a great pie for her birthday. –Lindy Jefferson, Atlanta, Ga.

This dressed-up chocolate cream pie (it has a layer of silky rum chiffon and a chocolate cookie crust) has been an American favorite for generations.

The American Table:
Duncan Hines, Restaurant Critic

Duncan Hines crisscrossed the country as a traveling salesman for a Chicago printing company during the early decades of the 20th century. Displeased by the food, service, and cleanliness of many of the restaurants he visited, Hines began compiling a list of acceptable establishments. In 1935, his list of 167 recommended restaurants went out as a Christmas greeting to friends and family, and soon complete strangers were contacting Hines for copies. Hines began critiquing restaurants full time, leaving "Recommended by Duncan Hines" plaques along the way. His first book, *Adventures in Good Eating,* was a state-by-state catalog of favored dining destinations. Several more books and cookbooks followed, though it was Hines's decision to license his name for packaged foods, including boxed cake mixes, that guaranteed his fame for generations to come.

Black-bottom pie is a chocolate cream pie—chocolate custard and sweetened whipped cream—with two added bonuses: an airy rum chiffon layer between the chocolate and whipped cream layers and a chocolate cookie crust. Recipes for this pie first appeared in the early 20th century, but its popularity didn't take off until the late 1930s, when restaurant reviewer Duncan Hines (yes, *that* Duncan Hines; see sidebar at left) wrote about experiencing the pie's "unbelievably light texture" at the Dolores Restaurant and Drive-In in Oklahoma City, Okla.

But after preparing a handful of recipes, I realized why black-bottom pie is so rarely made. Between making the cookie crumb crust, chocolate custard,

rum layer (which must be stabilized with gelatin, chilled over an ice bath to set, and lightened with beaten raw egg whites to create a chiffon texture), and whipped cream, I dirtied three saucepans, seven bowls, and four whisks during three hours in the kitchen. But I had to admit, the contrast in texture and flavor between the chocolate custard, fluffy rum chiffon, and whipped cream was worth the mess.

I started my kitchen work at the bottom, with the crust. Although the pie was originally made with a gingersnap crust, by the 1940s, recipes began to shift to pastry or chocolate cookie crusts. We compared all three, and tasters agreed that the chocolate crust provided superior flavor—and actually lived up to the name black-bottom. I crushed chocolate cookies, bound them with melted butter,

pressed the mixture into a pie plate, and then baked the crust for 10 minutes to assure a crisp foundation for my pie.

A few recipes saved time by making one large batch of custard, which is used as a base for both the chocolate and rum layers. This sounded promising, so I made a basic custard with sugar, half-and-half, egg yolks, and cornstarch. I removed half of the custard and stirred in chopped chocolate until it was melted, and then I poured this portion into the crust to chill and set.

For the rum chiffon layer, my plan was to flavor the remaining custard with rum, stabilize it with a little gelatin, and then add whipped raw egg whites for the signature light and airy texture. I was disappointed to find that the whipped whites weren't quite sturdy enough to support the sweetened whipped cream on top. One way to make egg whites sturdier is to cook them, so I tried making a seven-minute frosting (made by beating egg whites, sugar, water, and cream of tartar over a double-boiler) and adding it to the rum-enhanced custard. This worked like a charm, producing a voluminous, sturdy, and flavorful chiffon that was well worth the effort. With a piping of whipped cream on top, it was easy to see why Duncan Hines was so impressed with black-bottom pie all those years ago.

–Cali Rich

BLACK-BOTTOM PIE
SERVES 8 TO 10

Nabisco Famous Chocolate Wafers are the test kitchen's favorite brand for making the crust. This recipe makes a generous amount of filling; to prevent the filling from overflowing the pie crust, add the final ½ cup of the rum layer after the filling has set for 20 minutes.

Crust
32 chocolate cookies (see note) broken into rough pieces (about 2½ cups)
4 tablespoons unsalted butter, melted

Pie

2/3 cup sugar

4 teaspoons cornstarch

2 cups half-and-half

4 large egg yolks
   plus 1 egg white

6 ounces semisweet chocolate,
   chopped fine

3 tablespoons golden or
   light rum (see page 31)

2 tablespoons water

1 teaspoon unflavored gelatin

1/4 teaspoon cream of tartar

3 cups sweetened whipped
   cream

1. For the crust: Adjust oven rack to middle position and heat oven to 350 degrees. Grind cookies in food processor to fine crumbs. Add butter and pulse until combined. Press crumbs into bottom and sides of 9-inch pie plate and refrigerate until firm, about 20 minutes. Bake until set, about 10 minutes. Cool completely.

2. For the pie: Whisk 1/3 cup sugar, cornstarch, half-and-half, and egg yolks in saucepan. Cook over medium heat, stirring constantly, until mixture comes to boil, about 8 minutes.

3. Divide hot custard evenly between two bowls. Whisk chocolate into one bowl until smooth, then pour into cooled pie crust; refrigerate. Whisk rum, 1 tablespoon water, and gelatin into third bowl and let sit 5 minutes; stir into bowl with plain custard and refrigerate, stirring occasionally, until mixture is wobbly but not set, about 20 minutes.

4. Combine remaining sugar, egg white, remaining water, and cream of tartar in large heatproof bowl set over medium saucepan filled with 1/2 inch of barely simmering water (don't let bowl touch water). With electric mixer on medium-high, beat egg white mixture to soft peaks, about 2 minutes; remove bowl from heat and beat egg white mixture until very thick and glossy and cooled to room temperature, about 3 minutes.

5. Whisk cooled egg white mixture into chilled rum custard until smooth. Pour all but 1/2 cup of rum custard into chocolate custard–filled pie crust. Refrigerate 20 minutes, then top with remaining rum custard. Refrigerate until completely set, 3 hours or up to 24 hours. Top with whipped cream. Serve.

Caramel Bread Pudding

I love bread pudding. The best I've ever tasted was a caramel bread pudding drenched with the flavors of caramelized sugar, but I can't find a recipe that comes close. –Rachel Cooney, Portland, Maine

The test kitchen's recipe for basic bread pudding starts with soaking stale or oven-dried bread in a rich custard of egg yolks, heavy cream, and sugar before baking the pudding at a low temperature. This rustic dessert emerges from the oven with a soft, creamy interior and a slightly crunchy crust. I hoped that I could introduce caramel flavor by simply adding store-bought caramel sauce to the egg custard, but that made the custard too heavy. Worse, the custard was so sweet that the caramel flavor was barely detectable. I wanted the whole package—silky interior, crispy top, and deep caramel flavor throughout—and I had a long way to go to get there.

I started with the bread. Tasters thought French bread was too chewy for this pudding, and challah and brioche were too rich. White sandwich bread (dried in the oven so it absorbed more custard) was preferred for its light texture and mild flavor. As for the custard, taking the sugar out of the recipe and relying on the caramel sauce to sweeten the pudding was a step in the right direction, but the heavy cream and egg yolks were muting the flavor of the caramel sauce. I switched to half-and-half and whole eggs, which lightened the custard up enough to allow more of the caramel flavor to come through.

I was making progress, but the flavor of the jarred caramel sauce was still too weak. For my next test, I made a traditional, from-scratch caramel by carefully boiling sugar and water to 350 degrees (measured on a candy thermometer) and adding cream; although better, the caramel flavor was too subtle and the overall dish was too sweet. Because brown sugar is more flavorful than white, my next test was to make a quick caramel (technically more of a butterscotch sauce) with brown sugar, butter, cream, and corn syrup, and it worked much better: The caramel flavor was more prominent in the pudding, and the method was much less fussy than making a true caramel sauce.

I was almost there, but tasters wanted still more caramel pop. Topping the baked pudding with extra caramel was a nice touch, but starting with an additional layer of caramel sauce under the bread pudding as it baked elevated the caramel flavor to new heights. Finally, my tasters were treated to Caramel Bread Pudding that truly lived up to its name.

–Lynn Clark

CARAMEL BREAD PUDDING SERVES 8

Firm-textured breads such as Arnold Country Classic White or Pepperidge Farm Farmhouse Hearty White work best here.

15 slices hearty white sandwich bread, cut into 1-inch pieces (about 16 cups)

12 tablespoons (1 1/2 sticks) unsalted butter

2 cups packed light brown sugar

1 cup heavy cream

1/4 cup light corn syrup

5 teaspoons vanilla extract

3 cups half-and-half

5 large eggs

1/4 teaspoon salt

1. Adjust oven racks to upper-middle and lower-middle positions and heat oven to 450 degrees. Arrange bread in single layer on 2 baking sheets. Bake until golden and crisp, flipping bread and switching and rotating sheets halfway through baking, about 12 minutes. Let cool. Reduce oven temperature to 325 degrees.

2. Grease 13 by 9-inch baking pan. Melt butter and sugar in large saucepan over medium-high heat, stirring often, until bubbling and straw-colored, about 4 minutes. Off heat, whisk in cream, corn syrup, and 2 teaspoons vanilla. Pour 1 cup caramel over bottom of prepared pan; set aside. Reserve additional 1 cup caramel for serving, then whisk half-and-half into remaining caramel.

3. Whisk eggs and salt in large bowl. Whisk in half-and-half mixture, a little at a time, until incorporated, then stir in remaining vanilla. Fold in toasted bread and let sit, stirring occasionally, until bread is saturated, about 20 minutes.

4. Transfer bread mixture to caramel-coated pan and bake on lower-middle rack until top is crisp and custard is just set, about 45 minutes. Let cool 30 minutes. Drizzle with 1/2 cup reserved caramel sauce and serve, passing remaining sauce at table.

We add caramel to the soaking liquid, the bottom of the baking pan, and the top of the bread pudding to ensure ultimate caramel flavor.

Food Shopping

EXTRA-SHARP CHEDDAR CHEESE: Is Older Better?

So what is extra-sharp cheddar? It depends on whom you ask. The USDA's only requirement regarding cheddar is that the final product contain at least 50 percent milk-fat solids and no more than 39 percent moisture by weight. As for what distinguishes different varieties of cheddar—mild, medium, sharp, extra-sharp, and beyond—that is left in the hands of the cheese makers. Our research revealed that most extra-sharp cheddars are aged from nine to 18 months. This much we do know for sure: As cheddar ages, new flavor compounds are created, and the cheese gets firmer in texture and more concentrated in flavor—and it gets sharper.

But is more sharpness desirable? Does it make for better cheddar? To find out which supermarket extra-sharp cheddar cheese our tasters liked best, we purchased eight varieties (plus Cabot Sharp Cheddar, the winner of our previous tasting of regular sharp cheddars) and headed into the tasting lab to sample them plain (at room temperature to fully appreciate their nuances) and melted into grilled cheese sandwiches.

Our tasters generally liked the older, sharper cheeses best. Our three top-rated cheeses—Cabot Private Stock, Cabot Extra Sharp, and Grafton Village—are all aged for at least 12 months, and tasters rated them the three sharpest. Tasters praised the Cabot Private Stock's considerable but well-rounded sharpness and depth of flavor; it was not, however, as sharp as the Grafton Village, whose sharpness was described by some tasters as "overwhelming."

As for texture, tasters preferred the older cheeses for their denser, more crumbly bite. Younger cheeses like Heluva Good, Land O'Lakes, and presumably Cracker Barrel (Kraft Foods, which owns Cracker Barrel, declined to tell us how long their cheeses are aged) had more moisture and a springier, more rubbery texture—fine in a young cheese, but not what we wanted in extra-sharp cheddar. As for melting ability, tasters didn't mind a little greasiness (older cheddars separate when melted, because they contain less water and thus have less insulation against some of their fat melting out) as long as there was big flavor to back it up. The cheeses are listed below in order of preference. **–Scott Kathan**

Highly Recommended

1. CABOT Private Stock Cheddar Cheese
$3.99 for 8 ounces ($7.98 per pound) AGED: 16 to 18 months
"One great cheese," commented one taster. "The flavor is balanced—salty, pleasantly bitter, creamy, sweet. This is what I expect from an extra-sharp cheddar," said another. Tasters rated this cheese second-sharpest overall.

2. CABOT Extra Sharp Cheddar Cheese
$3.29 for 8 ounces ($6.58 per pound) AGED: 12 to 18 months
"This is a substantial cheese," stated one impressed taster; the panel agreed, as it rated a close second overall. "Supersharp" was a common refrain, while "sharp and smelly, like I like it" was a more unique perspective.

Recommended

3. GRAFTON VILLAGE Cheese Company Premium Cheddar
$4.99 for 8 ounces ($9.98 per pound) AGED: 12 months
Our panel rated this cheese the sharpest. "It explodes with tanginess," wrote one taster. "Really nice crumbly texture; complex flavor, with an aftertaste that is sharp and tangy—yum," said another taster. "Very funky and delicious."

4. CABOT Sharp Cheddar Cheese
$3.29 for 8 ounces ($6.58 per pound) AGED: 8 to 12 months
Winner of our prior tasting of sharp cheddars, this sample was judged as the sharpest cheese outside of our top three.

5. TILLAMOOK Special Reserve Extra Sharp Cheddar Cheese
$4.99 for 8 ounces ($9.98 per pound) AGED: at least 15 months
"Decent sharpness and good flavor" was the general opinion about this orange cheddar (tinted with annatto; see page 31); a few tasters found it "a little sour."

6. CRACKER BARREL Extra Sharp White Cheddar Cheese
$3.49 for 8 ounces ($6.98 per pound) AGE NOT DISCLOSED BY MANUFACTURER
Tasters appreciated the "soft and creamy texture" of this Kraft product but complained about "pedestrian" flavor that "lacked complexity."

7. LAND O'LAKES Extra Sharp Cheddar Cheese
$2.99 for 8 ounces ($5.98 per pound) AGED: at least 9 months
"Pleasant but unremarkable" was our tasters' consensus on this "mild," "not very sharp" cheddar from Wisconsin.

8. HELUVA GOOD New York State Extra-Sharp Cheddar
$3.29 for 8 ounces ($6.58 per pound) AGED: at least 9 months
"Lacking in complexity, but decent flavor" summarizes our tasters' opinions of this cheese. Some complaints about "gummy" texture, but cheese did melt nicely.

Recommended with Reservations

9. CRACKER BARREL Natural Extra Sharp Cheddar 2% Milk Reduced Fat
$3.49 for 8 ounces ($6.98 per pound) AGE NOT DISCLOSED BY MANUFACTURER
"Texture is rubbery and not cheddarlike," said one displeased taster. "Are you sure this is cheddar?" asked another. The flavor was best described as "sour, not sharp."

Taste Test Flour

Here are the four types of wheat flour we regularly stock in the test kitchen and how we use them. **–S.K.**

All-Purpose

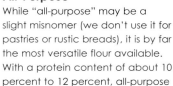

While "all-purpose" may be a slight misnomer (we don't use it for pastries or rustic breads), it is by far the most versatile flour available. With a protein content of about 10 percent to 12 percent, all-purpose flour provides enough structure to make good sandwich bread, yet it's light enough to use for cakes of a medium-to-coarse crumb. We prefer unbleached all-purpose flour, as bleached versions can impart off-flavors to baked goods that don't have enough fat or sugar to mask the flavor of the flour.

Cake

Cake flour has a low protein content—about 6 percent to 8 percent—and thus yields cakes and pastries with less gluten, which translates to a finer, more delicate crumb. We use cake flour for light cakes, such as pound cake, angel food cake, and yellow layer cake.

Bread

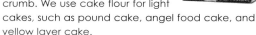

This flour has a protein content of about 12 percent to 14 percent, meaning it develops a lot of gluten to provide strong, chewy structure for rustic breads, especially those made with little or no fat. For sandwich breads (recipes made with butter and/or milk and baked in loaf pans) we prefer using all-purpose flour, which creates a softer crumb. Bread flour is often labeled "made for bread machines."

Whole Wheat

In the test kitchen, we generally don't like breads and baked goods made with 100 percent whole wheat flour; they are too heavy and sour-tasting. Instead, we usually replace 25 percent to 35 percent of a recipe's all-purpose flour with whole wheat flour for a lighter texture and milder flavor.

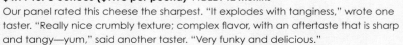

Equipment Roundup

INEXPENSIVE STANDING MIXERS: Can You Buy a Solid Mixer for Under $200?

The $500 standing mixers in our test kitchen are powerful enough to work all day. Can the home cook who needs less muscle buy a good standing mixer for less money? To find out, we rounded up eight models priced under $200.

THE WORKOUT: We whipped cream, creamed butter and sugar, made chunky cookie dough (with chocolate chunks, pecans, oatmeal, and dried cherries), and kneaded pizza dough in each machine. These are tasks that larger, pricier mixers (including the KitchenAid Professional 600, which won our prior testing of high-end mixers) can do effortlessly.

SIZING UP THE COMPETITION: Expensive mixers come with 5- or 6-quart bowls, big enough to knead a double batch of bread dough. Bowl size in the models we tested ranged from 3.5 to 4.6 quarts—large enough to mix and knead the dough for one large loaf of bread or three medium pizzas. Among the eight models tested, variances in bowl size and shape did not impact our results.

TEST DRIVING: A standing mixer should be easy to operate, and some in our lineup weren't. Both Sunbeam mixers required substantial strength to engage the head-tilt and beater-eject buttons. The EuroPro mixer has two sets of controls to manage. In contrast, all testers found the KitchenAid and Hamilton Beach Eclectrics mixers intuitive and easy to operate. Most mixers handled the whipped cream and cookie dough tasks with aplomb. The pizza dough, however, was another story.

DO OR DYE: To measure the power and efficiency of each mixer, we mixed 35 ounces of pizza dough in each bowl, then added 10 drops of blue food coloring to one side of the dough and 10 drops of yellow to the other. We then set the mixers to medium-low and timed how long it took them to turn the dough a uniform green. The KitchenAid and the Bosch made relatively quick work of this task, producing an evenly colored dough in about 6 minutes. Half of the mixers, however, failed this test because they didn't complete the task in 10 minutes. Some struggled and bucked because they weren't powerful enough for such prolonged kneading jobs.

THE ONE BIG THING: Our three winning mixers—the KitchenAid, Bosch, and Hamilton Beach Eclectrics—passed the pizza test. They all have one beater arm instead of two. So why is one beater better? One-beater mixers utilize "planetary action," meaning the beater rotates on its axis while spinning around the bowl, thus ensuring the mixing attachment interacts with the entire contents of the bowl. Dual stationary beaters, on the other hand, rely on a rotating bowl, and the attachments never touch the entire contents of the mixing bowl—they carve through a single trough. In the pizza dough tests, dual dough hooks bored holes into the dough and never kneaded it into a cohesive mass.

A SURPRISINGLY GOOD VALUE: Our test cooks aren't ready to trade in their $500 mixers, but the top three models tested offer good value and performance for the average home cook. The mixers are listed at right in order of preference. –Scott Kathan

Highly Recommended
KITCHENAID Classic Plus Stand Mixer
Price: $199 at target.com
Pizza Dough: ★★★
Cookie Dough: ★★★
Whipped Cream: ★★★
Features: 4.5-quart bowl, enameled metal dough hook and paddle, metal whisk
Comments: This mixer aced every test. Testers praised the "intuitive" controls and "solid" feel. While not as powerful as more expensive KitchenAid models, this mixer is a great value.

Recommended
BOSCH Compact Kitchen Machine
Price: $129 at theconsumerlink.com
Pizza Dough: ★★★
Cookie Dough: ★★
Whipped Cream: ★★★
Features: 4-quart bowl; metal dough hook, paddle/whisk hybrid, and whisk; plastic splatter guard
Comments: Despite a few mechanical quirks (the beater hits the bowl when you raise the arm, and the bowl doesn't feel securely locked in), this mixer performed at a high level. It was even faster than the KitchenAid in the tough pizza dough test.

HAMILTON BEACH Eclectrics Stand Mixer
Price: $179.95 at cooking.com
Pizza Dough: ★★
Cookie Dough: ★★★
Whipped Cream: ★★★
Features: 4.5-quart bowl, enameled metal dough hook and paddle, metal whisk, plastic splatter guard
Comments: Testers praised the design of this mixer, especially the head-tilt button, which was "easy to engage by feel, without looking." It creamed butter and sugar "effortlessly" and whipped cream with "impressive efficiency."

Recommended with Reservations
EUROPRO Convertible Hand/Stand Mixer
Price: $59.99 at target.com
Pizza Dough: ★★
Cookie Dough: ★
Whipped Cream: ★★
Features: 3.5-quart bowl, 2 metal beaters, 2 metal dough hooks, spatula, plastic bowl with cover, motorized bowl
Comments: This mixer allows you to select speeds for both the beaters and the bowl. While some users found this confusing, it helped keep the pizza dough moving around the bowl. This model struggled with the cookie dough, "really fighting" the heavy mix-ins.

Recommended with Reservations (continued)
SUNBEAM Heritage Mixmaster, Legacy Edition
Price: $159.99 at cooking.com
Pizza Dough: ★
Cookie Dough: ★★★
Whipped Cream: ★★
Features: 4.5-quart and 2.2-quart bowls, 2 metal beaters, 2 metal beater/whisk hybrids, 2 metal dough hooks, motorized bowl
Comments: This mixer (and the three that follow) had a damning flaw: It couldn't effectively knead the pizza dough. This "sturdy" mixer had no trouble working the heavy mix-ins into the cookie dough, and testers liked the "simple" dial control.

FARBERWARE Select Series Electronic Stand Mixer
Price: $99.99 at esalton.com
Pizza Dough: N/A
Cookie Dough: ★★
Whipped Cream: ★★
Features: 4-quart bowl, 2 metal beaters, 2 metal dough hooks, 1 metal whisk
Comments: This machine whipped cream acceptably, but labored to produce good cookie dough. Manual warns against kneading more than 8 ounces of dough (a ridiculously small amount), so we skipped this test. A few testers disliked the "involved" 3-step sequence of turning the mixer on, but others liked how each speed automatically ramped up to minimize spillage.

SUNBEAM Heritage Mixmaster
Price: $129 at buysunbeam.com
Pizza Dough: ★
Cookie Dough: ★★
Whipped Cream: ★★
Features: 4.6-quart and 2.2-quart bowls, 2 metal beaters, 2 metal dough hooks
Comments: This mixer "felt less powerful" than the Legacy Edition. Also, its bowl is not motorized, which contributed to its poorer (but still acceptable) showing with the cookie dough.

Don't Bother
HAMILTON BEACH Power Delux Stand Mixer
Price: $44.99 at hamiltonbeach.com
Pizza Dough: ★
Cookie Dough: ★
Whipped Cream: ★
Features: 4-quart bowl, 2 metal beaters, 2 metal dough hooks
Comments: This hybrid hand/standing mixer finished last or nearly last in every test. Impressions like "feels flimsy" were reinforced by performance observations such as "contents don't circulate" and "wouldn't cream butter and sugar."

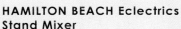

Notes from Our Test Kitchen

TIPS, TECHNIQUES, AND TOOLS FOR BETTER COOKING

Kitchen Creations
Flavored Mustards

Whether spread on sandwiches, used as a dip for pretzels, or served as a simple condiment for our **Cider-Baked Ham** (page 12), these creative flavored mustards are easy to make at home. Each mustard yields about ½ cup and can be refrigerated, covered, for up to 1 week.

SPICY HORSERADISH-CAYENNE MUSTARD
Whisk ¹/₂ cup Dijon mustard, 1 tablespoon prepared horseradish, and ¹/₄ teaspoon cayenne pepper in small bowl.

SESAME-SOY MUSTARD
Whisk ¹/₂ cup Dijon mustard, 1 tablespoon soy sauce, and 2 teaspoons toasted sesame oil in small bowl.

BOURBON BBQ MUSTARD
Whisk ¹/₂ cup Dijon mustard, 1 tablespoon bottled barbecue sauce, and 1 tablespoon bourbon or whiskey in small bowl.

DIRTY MARTINI MUSTARD
Whisk ¹/₂ cup Dijon mustard, 2 tablespoons minced pimento-stuffed green olives, and 1 tablespoon dry vermouth in small bowl.

Inside the Test Kitchen
Oven Bag Alternative

When preparing a whole or spiral-sliced ham, such as our Cider-Baked Ham (page 12), we prefer cooking it in an oven bag—the bag helps reduce cooking time and prevents the ham from drying out. But if you don't have an oven bag on hand, aluminum foil makes an acceptable substitute. Keep in mind that foil doesn't trap heat or moisture as well as oven bags, so the cooking time may need to be slightly increased, and the meat may be marginally drier.

1. Line a roasting pan with two 30-inch-long sheets of foil. Place the flat end of the ham on the foil, add liquid or seasonings if desired, and wrap the foil tightly around the ham.
2. When you're ready to apply the glaze or crust, simply roll the foil out of the way (being mindful of the hot pan and juices).

Thicken with Pectin

To give our **Italian Dressing Mix** (page 25) just the right viscosity to cling to the lettuce, we used a small amount of fruit pectin. Pectin is a natural carbohydrate found in the peels of lemons, oranges, and apples. The peels are washed, ground, and then processed to extract the pectin. Pectin is most widely used to thicken jams and jellies; it allows them to set quickly without long boiling. Once sold in only liquid form, pectin is now more widely available as a dried powder, making it perfect for our pantry dressing mix.

A QUICK THICKENER

Smoked Ham Hocks

Ham hocks added a deep meaty flavor to our **Ham and Bean Soup** (page 10). Cut from the ankle joint of the hog's leg, hocks contain a great deal of bone, fat, and connective tissue, which lend complex flavor and a rich, satiny texture to soups. Though ham hocks can contain quite a bit of meat, they must be braised or slow-cooked for long periods of time to break down the connective tissue. Once tender, the meat can be picked off the bone, shredded, and added to soups, stews, or chilis.

Caraway Seeds

Our recipe for **Swedish Cocktail Meatballs** (page 8) uses rye bread, which is flavored with caraway seeds. Caraway seeds, which come from a plant in the parsley family, have a nutty, mild, licorice flavor that is prized in the cuisines of Scandinavia, Germany, Austria, and Hungary. In this country, caraway seeds are a common addition to coleslaws, sausages, pickles, and spice rubs for meat.

Warm Eggs = Fluffy Omelets

Baking recipes commonly call for room-temperature eggs because the warmer the egg, the more relaxed its proteins become, allowing for more air bubbles to be incorporated when whipped. We also found that egg temperature was very important for our **Fluffy Diner-Style Cheese Omelet** (page 22). Taking the chill off the eggs allowed them to whip up to a larger volume and made the omelet lighter and fluffier than one made with cold eggs.

Almond Primer

Almonds are sold in a dizzying array of varieties: raw, roasted, blanched, slivered, sliced, and smoked. So which almonds do we prefer? It all depends on the recipe. When it comes to decorating cookies, we usually prefer the clean presentation of whole skinless blanched almonds. For cakes, other baked goods, leafy salads, and light side dishes like our **Green Beans Amandine** (page 15), we find that thinly sliced raw almonds (with or without their skins) deliver a nice, light flavor and texture. On the other hand, we love the substantial crunch of thick-cut slivered almonds in stir-fries and rice pilafs. Roasted almonds are best for eating out of hand. As for smoked almonds, we found their bold flavor and crunch were welcome additions to our **BBQ Party Mix** (page 18). Like all nuts, almonds are highly perishable (the oils in the nuts go rancid quickly) and best stored in the freezer to prevent spoilage.

SUBTLE CRUNCH
Sliced almonds are best used in lighter dishes or as a garnish for baked goods.

BIG CRUNCH
Slivered almonds are best in more substantial dishes.

Gadgets & Gear Offsetting the Competition

When preparing **Chocolate Candy Cane Cake** (inside back cover), we used an offset spatula to make sure the icing was applied in an even layer. Unlike a regular spatula, the blade of an offset spatula dips down at the handle, keeping your fingers and knuckles out of the way. Though they come in many sizes, we prefer the 8¹/₂-inch Ateco model (about $5) because it's also perfect for spreading cake and brownie batter—and can even be used to flip burgers in a pinch.

OFFSET SPATULA
Indispensable for even spreading.

How to MAKE BREADSTICKS

In developing our recipe for **Herbed Breadsticks** (page 25), we found that frozen bread dough produced perfectly tender breadsticks (unlike tough pizza dough and greasy canned refrigerator dough). When ready to prepare the dough, thaw it according to package instructions, roll it out, and top it with desired seasonings. We portion the dough into sticks by perforating it with a knife or bench scraper, which creates seams that allow for easy separation of the breadsticks after baking.

1. Using a bench scraper or knife, slice halfway through the dough at 1-inch intervals to make 12 breadsticks.

2. Separate baked breadsticks just before serving.

Powdered Lemonade Mix

To lend a tangy-sweet flavor to our **Italian Dressing Mix** (page 25), we found powdered lemonade mix was a good pantry substitute for sugar and lemon juice. But since our recipe only calls for ¼ cup of the lemonade mix, we wanted to make sure the rest of the stuff would be worth keeping around. After gathering and tasting four major brands of powdered lemonade, our tasters preferred Kool-Aid and Country Time for their balance of natural lemon flavor and mild sweetness.

GOOD BALANCE OF SWEET AND TART

Cheddar: Orange or White?

Although our tasters generally prefer white cheddars (page 28), bright orange varieties make especially attractive **Cheddar Cheese Rounds** (page 19). Most cheddar is naturally white, and the orange varieties are colored with ground annatto seed. Also known as achiote, these small, hard seeds are prized in Indian and Latin cooking for their mild earthy taste and brilliant yellow-orange hue. Since just a small amount of annatto is needed to dye the cheese, the flavor differences between orange and white cheddar are imperceptible. So why do cheese makers dye the cheese? It all goes back to the old world, specifically the village of Cheddar, England.

Centuries ago, this village produced a cheese that was characterized by its dry, tangy flavor and slight orange tint, which was a byproduct of the local dairy cows' diet, one that was particularly high in beta carotene. Since this cheese from Cheddar was reputed to be of such high quality, cheese makers in surrounding areas began dyeing their cheese various shades of orange and yellow in order to dupe consumers into purchasing inferior cheese. The process stuck and even to this day, cheddar cheese can be found in colors ranging from stark white to pumpkin orange.

Types of Rum

Wondering how the type of rum in the chiffon layer would affect the flavor of the finished pie, we whipped up **Black-Bottom Pie** (page 26) using light, golden, dark, and spiced rums. Golden rum narrowly edged out light rum for its balanced flavor, but we recommend using either in this pie. The dark variety, however, was compared to "taking a shot," and tasters picked up very little rum flavor in the spiced rum version. You can substitute 1½ teaspoons of rum extract for the 3 tablespoons of rum, with the water used in the gelatin mixture in step 3 increased to ¼ cup.

GOLDEN RUM   LIGHT RUM

ILLUSTRATION: JAY LAYMAN

Primal Cuts: Location Is Everything

In our **Getting to Know Beef Steaks** (page 17) feature, we explain the merits and uses of each cut in detail. But where on the animal do those steaks come from? Steers are divided into eight primal (or large) cuts, each of which is later broken down by a butcher into the smaller, more familiar retail cuts. The primal cuts are as follows.

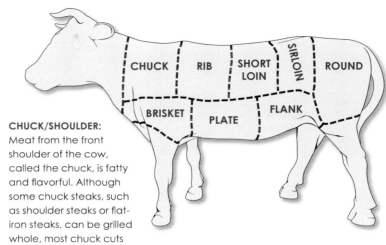

CHUCK/SHOULDER: Meat from the front shoulder of the cow, called the chuck, is fatty and flavorful. Although some chuck steaks, such as shoulder steaks or flat-iron steaks, can be grilled whole, most chuck cuts are sold as roasts, ground, or cut into stew meat.

RIB: Behind the chuck is the rib. The meat here is well marbled and tender, with an excellent beefy flavor. Rib steaks are expensive and best roasted, grilled, or seared.

SHORT LOIN: Another premium cut, the short loin contains both the tenderloin and the shell or strip. Because the short loin is in the center of the cow's back (where the muscles are rarely used), the meat is very tender. Short loin cuts are best roasted, grilled, or pan-seared.

SIRLOIN: Situated just in front of the rear legs of the cow, the sirloin contains inexpensive cuts that are sold as both steaks and roasts. Though flavorful, sirloin cuts tend to be lean and fairly tough. If these cuts are roasted or grilled, be sure to slice them thinly across the grain.

ROUND: The back of the cow is called the round. Many economical roasts, such as top round, bottom round, eye round, and rump roast, come from this primal cut. Though flavorful, they can be tough, particularly when over-cooked. Round is also ground or cut into stew meat.

BRISKET, PLATE, AND FLANK: The underside of the animal is divided into these three sections. The brisket is flavorful but very tough and therefore best suited to slow cooking techniques, such as barbecuing or braising. From the plate and flank come skirt steak and flank steak, respectively. These steaks are best grilled, but don't cook them past medium and be sure to slice the meat thinly against the grain to ensure maximum tenderness.

Inside the Test Kitchen PRIME RIB CARVING

Carving a bone-in roast as large (and expensive) as a prime rib can be a bit intimidating, but when developing our recipe for **Herb-Roasted Prime Rib** for our Holiday Menu (page 20), we got plenty of practice. Here's the best way to remove the bone and carve this centerpiece roast into perfect rosy slices.

1. Holding the roast in place with a carving fork, remove the meat from the bone by cutting parallel to the rib bones.

2. Place the now-boneless roast cut-side down and carve the meat across the grain to the desired thickness.

When Things Go Wrong in the Kitchen

READERS SHARE FUNNY STORIES ABOUT COOKING MISHAPS

TOO MUCH OF A GOOD THING

When I was a little girl, my grandma and I decided to make her famous peanut butter cookies together. After the dough was made, she started rolling it into little balls and handing them to me. I didn't know that I was supposed to be placing the dough balls on the cookie sheet to be flattened down and marked with her special crisscross pattern. Instead, I thought she was giving me a little ball of dough to taste, then another and another and another. I was eating them as fast as she was giving them to me. I remember thinking to myself, "Wow, my mom would never let me eat this many!" When my grandmother turned around to see if we had enough to fill the cookie sheet, much to her surprise, the cookie sheet was empty. When she looked at my packed cheeks, she saw what had happened and began to laugh. Now every time I make her cookies, I think fondly of the day she taught me to bake.

Linda Schaftenaar Holland, Mich.

MY FIRST ROAST BEEF

As a young newlywed, I was so excited when we finally had enough money to buy our first beef roast. I removed the plastic wrap and the tray the meat had been packed in and was delighted to find the roast encased in another sealed plastic bag. I thought it was so thoughtful of the market to have the roast already in a cooking bag. After cooking the roast, I was surprised to find it had not browned and was an unappealing shade of gray. The cooking bag, instead of puffing up so I could remove it, had melted into the meat. I called my mother, who told me that it wasn't a cooking bag but another layer of plastic wrap put on by the butcher. To this day, we laugh about my plastic-crusted roast beef.

Lynda Breeze Bayview, Texas

FOR LEMON LOVERS ONLY

One day in the 1980s, my mother made our family a lemon Bundt cake with a lemon pudding center and a delicious lemon glaze. She made it in the afternoon, and we all had to wait until dessert that evening before we could eat it. Until then, we could only enjoy the sweet lemony smell. When the moment finally arrived, we cut the cake and served everyone a piece. My mother took the first bite, spat it out, and said, "Don't eat the cake!" Apparently my 3-year-old brother had enjoyed watching her put the lemon glaze on the cake and decided later on to try to glaze it again himself—using lemon-scented dish soap.

David Jackman Cedar Hills, Utah

IMPRESSING THE BOSS'S WIFE

I was a young bride with no cooking skills whatsoever, and my young husband wanted to invite his supervisor and his wife to our home for dinner. I immediately panicked, since I barely knew how to boil hot dogs! What could I possibly fix that would be fancy enough for company? We decided on meatloaf, and I found my mother-in-law's recipe. After several hours of cooking, everything was ready and everyone was seated, so I began bringing the platters and bowls of food to the table. As I was bringing the meatloaf to the table, the toe of my sandal caught on the corner of the rug and I watched in horror as the meatloaf flew off the platter and landed directly on top of the boss's wife's patent leather pump. She nonchalantly picked the whole thing up, brushed off one corner, and set it back on the platter. She then licked her fingers and asked for two pieces because it tasted delicious.

Betty Chaney Felton, Calif.

CHECK IT OUT

I was very nervous about cooking my first Thanksgiving turkey, so I asked my mother-in-law for advice. She told me to soak a clean rag in melted butter and drape it over the breast. Unfortunately, she did not tell me to use a white rag, so when I took the bird out of the oven, lo and behold, the skin was red and white checked! After the laughter subsided, we took off the skin and enjoyed our meal, but I still get requests from my husband for my infamous plaid turkey.

Shirley Sampson Cocoa, Fla.

Send us your funniest kitchen disaster stories. E-mail us by visiting CooksCountry.com/kitchendisasters. Or write to us at Kitchen Disasters, Cook's Country, P.O. Box 470739, Brookline, MA 02447. If we publish your story, you'll receive a complimentary one-year subscription to Cook's Country.

UNITED STATES POSTAL SERVICE. Statement of Ownership, Management, and Circulation (All Periodicals Publications Except Requester Publications)

1. Publication Title: Cook's Country
2. Publication Number: 1552-1990
3. Filing Date: 9-28-07
4. Issue Frequency: Bi-Monthly
5. Number of Issues Published Annually: 6 Issues
6. Annual Subscription Price: $29.70
7. Complete Mailing Address of Known Office of Publication: 17 Station Street, Brookline, MA 02445
   Contact Person
   Telephone: 617-232-1000
8. Complete Mailing Address of Headquarters or General Business Office of Publisher: Same as Publisher
9. Full Names and Complete Mailing Addresses of Publisher, Editor, and Managing Editor
   Publisher: Christopher P. Kimball, Boston Common Press, 17 Station Street, Brookline, MA 02445
   Editor: Same as Publisher
   Managing Editor: Jack Bishop, Boston Common Press, 17 Station Street, Brookline, MA 02445
10. Owner: Boston Common Press Limited Partnership — 17 Station Street, Brookline, MA 02445
    (Christopher P. Kimball)
11. Known Bondholders, Mortgagees, and Other Security Holders: N/A

13. Publication Title: Cook's Country
14. Issue Date for Circulation Data Below: October/November 2007
15. Extent and Nature of Circulation

		Average No. Copies Each Issue During Preceding 12 Months	No. Copies of Single Issue Published Nearest to Filing Date
a.	Total Number of Copies (Net press run)	342,277	350,820
b. Paid Circulation	(1) Mailed Outside-County Paid Subscriptions Stated on PS Form 3541	245,758	265,919
	(2) Mailed In-County Paid Subscriptions Stated on PS Form 3541	0	0
	(3) Paid Distribution Outside the Mails Including Sales Through Dealers and Carriers, Street Vendors, Counter Sales, and Other Paid Distribution Outside USPS®	29,200	28,736
	(4) Paid Distribution by Other Classes of Mail Through the USPS	0	0
c.	Total Paid Distribution	274,958	294,655
d. Free or Nominal Rate Distribution	(1) Free or Nominal Rate Outside-County Copies included on PS Form 3541	819	729
	(2) Free or Nominal Rate In-County Copies Included on PS Form 3541	0	0
	(3) Free or Nominal Rate Copies Mailed at Other Classes Through the USPS	0	0
	(4) Free or Nominal Rate Distribution Outside the Mail	275	100
e.	Total Free or Nominal Rate Distribution	1,094	829
f.	Total Distribution (Sum of 15c and 15e)	276,052	295,484
g.	Copies not Distributed	66,225	55,336
h.	Total (Sum of 15f and g)	342,277	350,820
i.	Percent Paid	99.60%	99.72%

16. Publication of Statement of Ownership. If the publication is a general publication, publication of this statement is required. Will be printed in the Dec/Jan 2008 issue of this publication.

17. Signature and Title of Editor, Publisher, Business Manager, or Owner. Date 9/19/07

I certify that all information furnished on this form is true and complete.

PS Form 3526, September 2006 (Page 2 of 3)

The Great American Cake
Chocolate Candy Cane Cake

The shimmering sparkle of the ground peppermint candy coating gives this chocolate layer cake the feel of a classic Christmas tree decoration.

To make this cake, you will need:

- 1 **pound (4 sticks) unsalted butter, softened**
- 1 **cup confectioners' sugar**
- 1/8 **teaspoon salt**
- 2 **teaspoons vanilla extract**
- 4 **tablespoons heavy cream**
- 8 **ounces white chocolate, melted and cooled**
- 1 3/4 **cups finely ground peppermint candies (about 70), plus 6 whole candies for garnish**
- 3 **(8-inch) chocolate cake rounds***

** Go to **CooksCountry.com** for our chocolate cake recipe or use your own.*

For the frosting: With electric mixer, beat butter at medium-high speed until smooth, about 30 seconds. Add confectioners' sugar and salt; beat at medium-low speed, scraping bowl once, until smooth, about 1 minute. Add vanilla and cream and beat at medium speed until incorporated, about 10 seconds. Increase speed to medium-high and beat until light and fluffy, about 4 minutes, scraping down bowl once or twice. Transfer half of frosting to clean bowl and stir in white chocolate. Add 3/4 cup ground peppermint candies to remaining frosting.

To assemble: Place one cake layer on serving platter. Spread half of peppermint frosting over cake. Repeat with second cake layer and remaining peppermint frosting. Top with final cake layer and frost top and sides with white chocolate frosting, reserving 3/4 cup for final garnish. Press remaining ground peppermint candies into sides of cake and sprinkle evenly over top of cake. Use remaining white chocolate frosting to pipe ring of dots around base of cake and pipe 6 rosettes on top of cake. Place 1 whole peppermint candy on each rosette.

Recipe Index

RC = Recipe Card